BIBLICAL AND THEOLOGICAL
STUDIES

Dr. Alexander's.   Chapel.

THEOLOGICAL SEMINARY OF THE PRESBYTERIAN CHURCH, PRINCETON, N. J.

Dr. Hodge's.

BIBLICAL AND THEOLOGICAL STUDIES

BY

THE MEMBERS OF THE FACULTY OF PRINCETON THEOLOGICAL SEMINARY

PUBLISHED IN COMMEMORATION
OF THE ONE HUNDREDTH ANNIVERSARY
OF THE FOUNDING OF THE SEMINARY

Solid Ground Christian Books
Birmingham, Alabama

SOLID GROUND CHRISTIAN BOOKS
PO Box 660132, Vestavia Hills, AL 35266
205-443-0311
sgcb@charter.net
http://www.solid-ground-books.com

Biblical and Theological Studies

by The Faculty of Princeton Theological Seminary

Taken from the 1912 edition by Charles Scribner's Sons, New York, NY

Published by Solid Ground Christian Books

Classic Reprints Series

First printing November 2003

ISBN: 1-932474-18-8 (paperback)
ISBN: 1-932474-17-X (hardcover)

SPECIAL THANKS to Dr. David B. Calhoun of Covenant Theological Seminary in St. Louis, MO for his Introduction and Biographical Summaries, and to the Special Collections, Princeton Theological Seminary Libraries for assisting us in providing the right photos for this project.

Faculty Photo on the Cover from 1910

Row 1 - Jesse Lee Cotton, Wm. Benton Greene, Gerhardus Vos, F.S. Schenck

Row 2 - Robert Dick Wilson, B.B. Warfield, F.L. Patton, John Davis, W. Armstrong

Row 3 - Henry W. Smith, John De Witt, Charles Erdman, James Oscar Boyd

Row 4 - Paul Martin, J. Gresham Machen, Dulles, K.D. Macmillan, C.W. Hodge, Jr.

Manufactured in the United States of America

THE FIRST SESSION OF PRINCETON THEO-
LOGICAL SEMINARY COMMENCED ON THE
TWELFTH DAY OF AUGUST 1812. ON THE
SEVENTH DAY OF MAY 1912, ITS ONE-HUN-
DREDTH SESSION CLOSES.

THIS VOLUME OF ESSAYS HAS BEEN PRE-
PARED BY THE MEMBERS OF THE FACULTY
OF THE SEMINARY IN COMMEMORATION OF
THE COMPLETION OF THE SEMINARY'S
FIRST CENTURY OF SERVICE TO THE CHURCH.

INTRODUCTION

In 1912, to commemorate the first hundred years of its history, the Princeton Theological Seminary faculty published a hefty volume of *Biblical and Theological Studies*. It was the faculty's fitting tribute to a school founded to study and teach the Word of God and to set forth and defend the faith "once delivered to the saints." All but one of the fifteen professors had at one time also been students at the seminary.

The first chapter of the book, "Theological Encyclopaedia" by the seminary's president, Francis Landey Patton, asserts the necessity of a thorough theological education for preachers of the Gospel. It is as relevant today as it was almost a hundred years ago. B. B. Warfield is at his best (and that is very, very good) in writing on "The Emotional Life of Our Lord." Here we worship as we learn. Church historian John De Witt sets forth his and Princeton Seminary's appreciation of Jonathan Edwards (He gave this address originally in the Meeting House of the Parish Church of Stockbridge, Massachusetts, at the 1903 celebration of the two hundredth anniversary of Jonathan Edwards' birth). Chapters by Geerhardus Vos and Gresham Machen anticipate their great contributions to come in biblical theology and New Testament studies. "Sin and Grace in the Biblical Narratives Rehearsed in the Koran" by James Oscar Boyd demonstrates the breadth of interest and expertise of the 1912 Princeton faculty, perhaps the strongest in its history, as do the chapters by Robert Dick Wilson ("The Aramaic of Daniel") and Kerr Duncan Macmillan ("The Interpretation of the Shepherd of Hermas"). Practical theology is represented by Frederick William Loetscher's "Homiletics as a Theological Discipline" and Charles Erdman's "Modern Spiritual Movements."

In his essay, "Theological Encyclopaedia," Francis Patton writes:

> And so I say to my younger brethren in the ministry, and especially to the young men who have not yet entered it: get powers of expression, get knowledge, get thought-power, get rich Christian experience, get a knowledge of homiletical technique, and then let the sermon be yours— nay, rather, let it be you. Let it be an arrow shot from the tense bow-string of conviction and it will hit the mark every time.

It could be said of the fifteen chapters of this book that they are fifteen arrows "shot from the tense bow-string of conviction." And they "hit the mark every time."

David B. Calhoun
Covenant Theological Seminary
Saint Louis, Missouri

Biographical Summaries of the Authors Found in *BIBLICAL AND THEOLOGICAL STUDIES* (adapted from the *Biographical Catalogue of the Princeton Theological Seminary, 1815-1932* by David B. Calhoun)

FRANCIS LANDEY PATTON—*"Theological Encyclopaedia"*

Born, Warwick, Bermuda, January 22, 1843; Knox College, Toronto; University of Toronto; Princeton Theological Seminary, 1863-65; ordained, New York Presbytery, June 1, 1865; pastor, Eighty-fourth Street Church, New York City, 1865-67; pastor, Nyack, New York, 1867-70; pastor, South Church, Brooklyn, 1871; pastor, Jefferson Park Church, Chicago, Illinois, 1874-81; professor, Theology, Theological Seminary of the Northwest, 1871-81; professor, Relations of Philosophy and Science to Christian Religion, Princeton Theological Seminary, 1881-88; president, Princeton University, 1888-1902, professor, Ethics, 1886-1913; president, Princeton Theological Seminary, 1902-13, lecturer, Theism, 1888-1903, professor, Philosophy of Religion, 1903-13, president emeritus, 1913-32; residence, Warwick, Bermuda, 1913-32; died, Warwick, November 25, 1932. DD, Hanover College, 1872, Yale University, 1888; LLD, Wooster College, 1878, Harvard University, 1889, University of Toronto, 1894, Yale University, 1901, Johns Hopkins University, 1902, University of Maryland, 1807, Princeton University, 1813; honorary MA, Princeton University, 1896; Moderator, General Assembly, 1878.

BENJAMIN BRECKINRIDGE WARFIELD—*"On the Emotional Life of Our Lord"*

Born, Lexington, Kentucky, November 5, 1851; College of New Jersey, 1871; Europe; editor; Princeton Theological Seminary, 1873-76; University of Leipzig, 1876-77; stated supply, Concord Church, Kentucky, 1875; stated supply, First Church, Dayton, Ohio, 1876; stated supply, First Church, Baltimore, Maryland, 1877-78; ordained evangelist, Ebenezer Presbytery, April 26, 1879; instructor, New Testament Literature and Exegesis, Western Theological Seminary, 1878, professor, 1879-87; professor, Didactic and Polemic Theology, Princeton Theological Seminary, 1887-1921; died, Princeton, New Jersey, February 16, 1921. DD, College of New Jersey, 1880; LLD, College of New Jersey and Davidson College, 1892; LittD, Lafayette College, 1911; STD, University of Utrecht, 1913.

JOHN D. DAVIS—*"The Child Whose Name is Wonderful"*

Born, Pittsburgh, Pennsylvania, March 5, 1854; College of New Jersey, 1879; University of Bonn, 1879-80; Europe, 1880-81; Princeton Theological Seminary, 1881-83; instructor, Hebrew, Princeton

Theological Seminary, 1883-84; Hebrew Fellowship, University of Leipzig, 1884-86; instructor, Hebrew, Princeton Theological Seminary,1886-88; ordained, Pittsburgh Presbytery, April 26, 1887; professor, Hebrew and Cognate Languages, Princeton Theological Seminary, 1888-92, Semitic Philology and Old Testament History, 1892-1900, Oriental and Old Testament Literature, 1900-26; died, Philadelphia, Pennsylvania, June 21, 1926. PhD, College of New Jersey, 1886; DD, Princeton University, 1898; LLD, Washington and Jefferson College, 1902.

JOHN De WITT—*"Jonathan Edwards: A Study"*

Born, Harrisburg, Pennsylvania, October 10, 1842; College of New Jersey, 1861; law student; Princeton Theological Seminary, 1861-63; Union Theological Seminary (New York); ordained, New York Presbytery, June 9, 1865; pastor, Irvington, New York, 1865-69; pastor, Centennial Congregational Church, Boston, Massachusetts, 1869-76; pastor, Tenth Presbyterian Church, Philadelphia, 1876-82; professor, Ecclesiastical History, Lane Theological Seminary, 1882-88; professor, Apologetics, McCormick Theological Seminary, 1888-92; professor, Church History, Princeton Theological Seminary, 1892-1912, professor emeritus; died, Princeton, New Jersey, November 19, 1923. DD, College of New Jersey, 1877; LLD, Hanover College, 1888.

WILLIAM BRENTON GREENE, JR.—*"The Supernatural"*

Born, Providence, Rhode Island, August 16, 1854; College of New Jersey, 1876; teacher; Princeton Theological Seminary, 1877-80; ordained, Boston Presbytery, June 3, 1880; pastor, First Church, Boston, Massachusetts, 1880-83; pastor, Tenth Church, Philadelphia, Pennsylvania, 1883-92; Stuart professor, Relation of Philosophy and Science to the Christian Religion, Princeton Theological Seminary, 1892-1903, Apologetics and Christian Ethics, 1903-28; died, Princeton, New Jersey, November 16, 1928. DD, College of New Jersey, 1891.

GEERHARDUS VOS—*"The Eschatological Aspect of the Pauline Conception of the Spirit"*

Born, Heerenveen, Netherlands, March 14, 1862; Amsterdam Gymnasium, 1881; Calvin Theological Seminary, 1881-83; Princeton Theological Seminary, 1883-85; Fellowship, Hebrew, University of Berlin, 1885-86; University of Strasbourg, 1886-88, PhD; professor, Theology, Calvin Theological Seminary, 1888-93; ordained evangelist, New Brunswick Presbytery, April 24, 1894; professor, Biblical Theology, Princeton Theological Seminary, 1893-1932, professor emeritus, 1932-49; residence, Roaring Branch, Pennsylvania, 1932-33; Santa Ana, California, 1933-41; and Grand Rapids, Michigan, 1941-49; died, Grand Rapids, August 13, 1949. DD, Lafayette College, 1893.

ROBERT DICK WILSON—*"The Aramaic of Daniel"*

Born, Indiana, Pennsylvania, February 4, 1856; College of New Jersey, 1876, 1879, MA, 1886, PhD; Western Theological Seminary, 1880-81; University of Berlin, 1881-83; instructor, Old Testament, Western Theological Seminary, 1883-85, professor, 1885-1900; professor, Semitic Philology and Old Testament Introduction, Princeton Theological Seminary, 1900-29; professor, Semitic Philology and Old Testament Criticism, Westminster Theological Seminary, 1929-30; died, Philadelphia, Pennsylvania, October 11, 1930. DD, Lafayette College, 1894; LLD, Wooster College, 1921.

WILLIAM PARK ARMSTRONG—*"The Place of the Resurrection Appearances of Jesus"*

Born, Selma, Alabama, January 10, 1874; College of New Jersey, 1894, 1896, MA; Princeton Theological Seminary, 1894-97, 1899; University of Marburg, 1897; University of Berlin, 1897-98; University of Erlangen, 1898; ordained, New Brunswick Presbytery, July 2, 1900; instructor, New Testament Literature, Princeton Theological Seminary, 1899-1903, professor, New Testament Literature and Exegesis, 1903-40, graduate professor, New Testament Exegesis, 1940-44; died, Princeton, March 25, 1944. DD, Temple University, 1915.

CHARLES ROSENBURY ERDMAN—*"Modern Spiritual Movements"*

Born, Fayetteville, New York, July 20, 1866; College of New Jersey, 1886; teacher; Princeton Theological Seminary, 1887-89, 1890-91; ordained, Philadelphia North Presbytery, May 8, 1891; stated supply, Overbrook Church, Philadelphia, Pennsylvania, 1890-91, pastor, 1891-97; pastor, First Church, Germantown, 1897-1906; professor, Practical Theology, Princeton Theological Seminary, 1905-36, professor emeritus, 1936-60; pastor, First Church, Princeton, New Jersey, 1924-34; died, 1960. DD, Wooster College, 1912, Princeton Uni-versity, 1925; LLD, Davidson College, 1924; Moderator, General Assembly, 1925.

FREDERICK WILLIAM LOETSCHER—*"Homiletics as a Theological Discipline"*

Born, Dubuque, Iowa, May 15, 1875; Princeton University, 1896, 1901, MA, 1906, PhD; teacher, Lawrenceville School, New Jersey; Princeton Theological Seminary, 1897-1901; Newberry Scholar; University of Berlin, 1901-1902; University of Strasbourg, 1902-1903; ordained, New Brunswick Presbytery, December 19, 1903; instructor, Church History, Princeton Theological Seminary, 1903-1907; pastor, Oxford Church, Philadelphia, Pennsylvania, 1907-10; professor, Homiletics, Princeton Theological Seminary, 1910-13, Church History, 1913-45; professor,

Church History, Temple University, 1945-51; died, Princeton, July 31, 1966. DD, Lafayette College, 1914; LLD, University of Dubuque, 1918.

JAMES OSCAR BOYD—*"Sin & Grace in the Biblical Narratives Rehearsed in the Koran"*

Born, Rahway, New Jersey, October 17, 1874; New York University, 1895; Butler Fellow, New York University, University of Erlangen, 1895-96; Princeton Theological Seminary, 1896-99, BD, GS Green Fellow, 1899-1900; Princeton University, 1905, PhD; ordained, New York Presbytery, June 3, 1900; instructor, Old Testament Literature, Princeton Theological Seminary, 1900-1907, assistant professor, Oriental and Old Testament Literature, 1907-15; pastor, Church of the Redeemer, Paterson, New Jersey, 1915-21; YMCA, war service, 1918-19; secretary, Arabic-Levant Agency, American Bible Society, 1921-26; secretary, Levant Agency, 1926-44; died, Oneida, New York, August 14, 1947. DD, NY University, 1915.

CASPAR WISTAR HODGE, Jr.—*"The Finality of the Christian Religion"*

Born, Princeton, New Jersey, September 22, 1870; College of New Jersey, 1892, 1894, PhD; Heidelberg University; University of Berlin; instructor, Philosophy, Princeton University, 1895-97; associate professor, Ethics, Lafayette College, 1897-98; Princeton Theological Seminary, 1898-1901; ordained, New Brunswick Presbytery, September 18, 1902; instructor, New Testament, Princeton Theological Seminary, 1901-1902, assistant, Dogmatic Theology, 1901-1907, assistant professor, Didactic and Polemic Theology, 1907-15, professor, Dogmatic Theology, 1915-21, professor, Systematic Theology, 1921-37; died, Princeton, February 26, 1937. DD, Grove City College, 1935.

KERR DUNCAN MACMILLAN—*"The Interpretation of the Shepherd of Hermas"*

Born, Mount Forest, Ontario, Canada, March 17, 1871; University of Toronto, 1894; Princeton Theological Seminary, 1894-97, BD; instructor, Old Testament, Princeton Theological Seminary, 1897-1900; licensed, Presbytery Lindsay, July 11, 1899; University of Berlin, 1900-03; instructor, Semitic Philology, Princeton Theological Seminary, 1903-07, Church History, 1907-13; president, Wells College, Aurora, New York, 1913-36; died, Clifton Springs, New York, March 13, 1938. STD, Hobart College, 1914.

JOHN GRESHAM MACHEN—*"Jesus and Paul"*

Born, Baltimore, Maryland, July 28, 1881; Johns Hopkins University, 1901, graduate study, 1901-1902; Princeton Theological Seminary,

1902-1905, BD; Princeton University, 1904, MA; New Testament Fellow, University of Marburg and University of Göttingen, 1905-1906; instructor, New Testament, Princeton Theological Seminary, 1906-14, assistant professor, New Testament Literature and Exegesis, 1914-29; ordained, New Brunswick Presbytery, June 23, 1914; YMCA, war service, 1918-19; professor, New Testament, Westminster Theological Seminary, 1929-37; died, Bismark, North Dakota, January 1, 1937. DD, Hampden-Sydney College, 1921; LittD, Wheaton College (Illinois), 1928.

OSWALD THOMPSON ALLIS—*"The Transcendence of Jehovah, God of Israel"*

Born, Wallingford, Pennsylvania, September 9, 1880; University of Pennsylvania, 1901; Princeton Theological Seminary, 1902-1905, BD; GS Green Fellow, Hebrew, 1905-1907; Princeton University, 1907, MA; University of Berlin, 1907-10, 1913, PhD; ordained, Philadelphia Presbytery, May 31, 1914; instructor, Semitic Philology, Princeton Theological Seminary, 1910-22, assistant professor, 1922-29; professor, Old Testament History and Exegesis, Westminster Theological Seminary, 1929-30, Old Testament 1930-49; died, Wayne, Pennsylvania, January 12, 1973. DD, Hampden-Sydney College, 1927.

CONTENTS

THEOLOGICAL ENCYCLOPAEDIA

Francis Landey Patton

The practical aim of the Theological Seminary does not justify disparagement of thorough theological education. Outline of the history of theological encyclopaedia. Sources of Theology: Reason, Scripture, the Church.

Thesis: 1. Rational Theology: Science of Religion, Philosophy of Religion.

2. Scriptural Theology: the Higher Criticism, the Lower Criticism, Exegesis, Biblical Theology.

3. Ecclesiastical Theology: History of the Church, Organization of the Church, Work and Worship of the Church.

Antithesis: The content of Christian Theology is antithetically related to the opposing views of those within and those without the pale of Christian faith. Hence the place in Theological Encyclopaedia for Polemic Theology and Apologetic Theology.

Synthesis: Systematic Theology is the synthesis of all the foregoing theological disciplines: Christian Ethics, Dogmatics.

THEOLOGICAL ENCYCLOPAEDIA

A Theological Seminary is, first of all, a school for the training of men to preach the Gospel. The claims of theological learning should never supersede or relegate to a subordinate position the practical aims which were contemplated by those who founded this Seminary; and if we magnify these claims, it is only because we believe that the minister who would most effectively discharge the duties of his high calling is he who, other things being equal, is best equipped in his knowledge of the Disciplines that enter into the theological *curriculum*. It is not necessary now to call attention to those elementary studies which underlie a minister's theological education. For we have made a complete separation between the disciplinary studies which enter into what is called a liberal education, and the more distinctively technical and specialized studies which constitute the *curriculum* of the professional school. Every student of the theological seminary is supposed to have graduated in Arts, or to have had an education equivalent to that required for the Bachelor of Arts degree. With that maturity of mind which such an education betokens, and with that seriousness of purpose which may be fairly presupposed on the part of men who have all attained their majority, and who besides are looking forward to a professional career in the sacred calling of the ministry, as conditions precedent of the successful prosecution of theological study, it should not be difficult for us to secure from those who enter the Seminary an intelligent interest in the problem of the theological *curriculum*, and a hearty coöperation with us in carrying it out in the details of class-room instruction.

I venture to hope, therefore, that however dry and uninteresting much that I have to say may be to many, I may have the interested attention of my brethren in the

ministry and of theological students. The practical value
of much that is taught in a theological seminary is sometimes challenged, I doubt not, even by very good students;
and their skepticism on this head arises generally out of
the fact, so I at least believe, that they do not see the relations which the several parts of theological instruction sustain to each other. Have these various additions to the *curriculum* been accidental accretions, or do they maintain an
organic relation to each other? Are chairs of theology to
be multiplied indefinitely in obedience to the varying demands of the times, or as increased endowments make it
possible for us to increase the professorial staff, or is there
a logical limit to this sort of expansion, which can be indicated and rationally defended? It may seem to some that
what I say may serve, in a measure at least, as an answer
to these questions. My theme embraces the entire circle
of theological learning. But I have not set myself so am-
bitious a task as these words may lead you to suppose; for I
desire only to ask your attention to some thoughts of mine on
what is technically known as Theological Encyclopædia.

This word " encyclopædia " was probably first used by Galen.
As denoting the circle of the sciences it was used by Martinius,
1606. In the popular sense familiar to us all it was used by
Alsted, 1620, and as indicating the totality of materials germane to a special science it was used in the eighteenth century
by several writers, and applied to Jurisprudence by Pütter, to
Medicine by Boerhaave, and to Theology by Mursinna.

Theological Encyclopædia undertakes to classify and reduce
to system the different Disciplines or departments of theological science. It seeks to show the organic relations between
these Disciplines, and it may even go so far as to lay down
the methods that should be followed, and to state and compare
the methods that have been followed in the different Disciplines.

It would be interesting to trace the history of Theological
Encyclopædia from its crude beginnings in Chrysostom's six
books *De Sacerdotio* in the fourth century, in the advice of
Cassiodorus to the monks of Vivarium in the sixth century,

and later in the *Institutio clericorum* of Rabanus Maurus and the *Didascalia* of Hugo of St. Victor, down to the days of Scholasticism when, by the union of theology and philosophy, as Räbiger says, theology became a learned Discipline with the primacy, we may add, vested in philosophy. Such a history would tell the story of the subsequent protest against over-intellectualism in theology made by Roger Bacon and then by Erasmus, the modifying influence of Pietism after the Reformation as represented in such a work as the *Isagoge* of Buddaeus, and then the waning interest in theological study which led men like Bertholdt, Planck, Thym and Tittmann (1796, 1798, 1813) to write their Theological Encyclopædias as manuals for those entering upon the study of theology and for the purpose of awakening a new interest in it. There is nothing in these systems of encyclopædia that need claim our attention, and I venture to say that none of us would think of adopting the divisions of theological science set forth in these manuals. The next writer worthy of notice is the Reformed theologian of Holland, Clarisse, who divides theology according to the familiar and simple plan into four parts—*exegetica, historica, systematica* and *pastoralis*. This also is the division adopted by Hagenbach, one of the later encyclopædists, and is the one most generally accepted among theologians to-day.

But in Schleiermacher we have an illustration of the way in which one's fundamental conception of theology will inevitably determine his distribution of theological material. All theology is divided, according to him, into three parts—Philosophical, Historical and Practical. Under the head of Historical Theology he includes Dogmatics and Exegetics. From the point of view which makes the Bible the rule of faith, it is, of course, an error to put Dogmatic Theology under the historical rubric. But from Schleiermacher's point of view it was most natural to do it. For we have only to conceive of the Church as an organism possessed of a corporate life and undivided corporate consciousness, and it will at once appear that in the Bible you have the record of the religious consciousness of the Church for a certain period, and that in

Church History you have the record of the religious life of the Christian society through the subsequent centuries. Now part of that religious life or thought takes the form of dogma. Dogmatic Theology, therefore, is not the systematic exhibition of the truths of Scripture, but is rather a crystallization of the religious consciousness in the form of religious belief, and may vary in different periods. Dogmatic Theology is thus a part of history. The affinity of this view promulgated by Schleiermacher with that of the later Roman Catholic doctrine of development, and also the more recent Protestant doctrine of the Christian consciousness, is apparent. It is not difficult to see, moreover, how Schleiermacher has furnished the philosophy which enables Roman Catholic theologians to give a systematic and philosophic explication of their dogmatic system; and it is not surprising, therefore, to find that in the hands of Dobmeyer and Staudenmaier Schleiermacher's principle becomes the basis of a Roman Catholic encyclopædia.

The serious objection to Schleiermacher's encyclopædia is that it proceeds upon a basis that antagonizes the Protestant principle that the Bible is the rule of faith and practice. Other objections may be urged against the mode of distributing the theological Disciplines in the encyclopædias of Dantz, Pelt, Lange, Tholuck, Hagenbach and Kuyper.

Take Hagenbach's for example. The four parts of theology according to him, are Historical, Exegetical, Systematic and Practical. But what is Historical Theology? And if the development of doctrine in the post-Biblical period is put down under Historical Theology, why is the development of doctrine within the Biblical period cut off from the domain of Historical Theology and erected into a separate department called Exegetical Theology? And why is Practical Theology not logically a part of Christian Ethics, except that the practical duties enjoined in it pertain not so much to the private Christian as to the Church in its organic life, or to the individual in his official relations to the Church? These are only illustrations of the difficulties we meet in attempting a logical distribution of the Theological Disciplines. Apologetics again—to take another illustration—is a subject that the encyclopædists have difficulty with; some treating it as belonging to the Prolegomena of Theology, and others as part of Systematic Theology. But it is much easier to see defects than to remedy them, and it is quite likely that the scheme which I propose will reveal weaknesses to the eyes of others which I do not see.

In organizing the Theological Disciplines I proceed upon this postulate: that man knows God through his reason, that God has superadded to the light of nature the Revelation of himself in the Bible, and that this enlarged and corrected knowledge is embodied in the Church.

The materials for all our theological knowledge are to be found, therefore, in these three sources: the Reason, the Bible, the Church. We shall accordingly have Rational Theology, Scriptural Theology and Ecclesiastical Theology. Assuming now that our point of view is that of the Reformed Theology, it is obvious that the body of belief involved in these Disciplines just mentioned stands antithetically related to opposing views, and that it will be necessary to carry on a systematic defense of that theology, first, against those who assail our Reformed position from within the Church, and, secondly, against those who assail Christianity from without. Accordingly we shall have Polemic Theology and Apologetic Theology.

And yet again the need will be felt of gathering into one compact system the results of all these Disciplines in a body of divinity which will represent the sum total of theological inquiry. This will be Systematic Theology. I do not claim any minute acquaintance with the Hegelian philosophy, and I do not profess any great regard for it; but it is evident that in the scheme which I propose the dominant words are those which have such large place in Hegelian literature—Thesis, Antithesis and Synthesis.

I.

THESIS.

Man derives some knowledge of God through his reason. This I know is disputed, and the Ritschlians are particularly fond of disparaging Natural Theology. But apart from the question of the possibility of a Natural Theology, the fact remains that the religious phenomena of the world call for consideration. We cannot very well avoid, therefore, giving a place in our Theological Encyclopædia to Rational or Philosophical Theology.

1. *Rational Theology.*—Under this head I should include the Science of Religion and the Philosophy of Religion.

It is a matter of very considerable importance to study the various religions of the world and to systematize the knowledge thus obtained in regard to the beliefs men have actually entertained regarding God. I hardly think it necessary to go, as Ebrard does, into the history of religions simply for the little apologetic material to be derived from it, and I would not make comparative religion therefore a branch of Apologetics. We shall learn many things from the Science of Religion: we shall learn the solidarity of religious life throughout the world, and that will quicken our sympathies with others of our kind; we shall be made cognizant of the common elements held in solution by all religions, and shall know the deep foundation already laid on which the superstructure of the Gospel can be built; we shall see the insufficiency of heathen religions, and in the contrast between them and Christianity find an argument for the exclusive character of Christianity; and we shall be able to account for the analogies between Christianity and other religions without resorting to the hypothesis that our religion has been a wholesale plagiarism from the start. Still our object should be to find out what men have actually believed regarding God as the result of the light of nature. Our inquiries under this broad statement of aim may be made as detailed and independent as we choose, and should not be conditioned by the practical use in Missions or Apologetics which we may wish to make of our results.

Then, again, we have the old subject of Natural Theology, and more particularly of Theism, which, of course, belongs to the department of Philosophical Theology. With those who in our day would make our theology more distinctively Christian by making it appear that our only knowledge of God comes to us through Christ, I have no sympathy. For it seems to me that Christ can teach Theism to an Atheist to-day only by an inferential passage from the phenomena of his earthly life to belief in the Divine existence. But if the phenomena of the universe are powerless to produce this result, it is vain to suppose that the phenomena of a single human life can produce it. It is a disservice to revealed religion to disparage Natural Theology in the hope of thereby exalting Christ. Natural Theology is the basis of Revealed Theology, and the true order of thought is found in the Saviour's words: " Ye believe in God: believe also in me." But be the didactic scope of Natural Theology more or less, it is a fact that the phenomena of religious experience are receiving a great deal of attention at the hands of philosophers, and Christian theologians cannot afford to ignore the work of the psychologists and metaphysicians in this field. We are having our religious life interpreted for us in the terms of empirical psychology. We are having our Christian doctrine explained according to the Hegelian metaphysics. Religion is being looked upon as a pathological condition, or as a mystical emotionalism that needs nothing for its content beyond a spirit of submission to the inevitable.

How the profound problems of metaphysics bear upon the philosophy of religion we can see in the Gifford lectures of Ward and Royce. How the distinctive features of Christianity disappear under the touch of the Hegelian dialectic we can see in the writings of the Cairds. We may be thankful, perhaps, that something of supernaturalism is saved from the wreck when we read the brilliant pages of James's *Varieties of Religious Experience;* but then how little it is! And when in despair of a rational basis for religious belief we are left by

Höffding and Mallock to console ourselves with value-judg-ments, we are tempted to ask: Has it come to this? And does our philosophy of religion say for its last word that we keep our religious beliefs simply because we cannot and will not give them up? The Christian theologian must come into this field as a defender of the faith. He must strengthen the outposts if he would save the citadel.

But I go farther than this. I believe that there is need just now of a philosophy of the Christian religion which will work on the basis of contemporary philosophy and the apolo-getic *minimum,* and give us such a synthesis of natural and revealed religion as shall satisfy the intellectual needs of those who turn away from the pages of Starbuck and Caird, on the one hand, and who are not ready to accept a complete Systematic Theology, on the other, but are nevertheless crav-ing for a *rationale* of Christianity.

2. *Scriptural Theology.*—This department, commonly called Exegetical Theology, includes all those studies which terminate directly upon the Bible. Among these we have the studies ancillary to the study of the Scriptures, such as Archaeology, Biblical Geography and, of course, the original languages of the Scripture. The encyclopædists have a dis-heartening way of writing on this subject, for they not only tell us to read Greek and Hebrew, but they would have us un-derstand that in order to know Hebrew one must know the cognate languages, and we begin to think of the Aramaic, Syriac, Arabic and Assyrian. Hagenbach's Encyclopædia is pretty dry reading, but our heart warms toward it when, after reading dreary pages of what the author calls Exegetische Hülfswissenschaften, he condescendingly tells us that a com-prehensive knowledge of all the Semitic languages cannot be demanded of every Christian theologian. And it was very kind in him to put in a footnote the following from Luther, which we lay aside for our comfort along with other choice bits of cheap erudition: " One is not a truly wise Christian *quia Græcus sit et Hebræus,*—because he is a Greek or He-brew scholar—*quando beatus Hieronymus quinque linguis monoglosson Augustinum non adæquavit,*—since Jerome of

blessed memory, with all his learning, could not come within gunshot of the monoglot Augustine." It is wonderful indeed what an amount of good thinking one may do in one language!

But beside these ancillary studies there is the vexed question of the Canon, which may be regarded perhaps as belonging to the Prolegomena of Scriptural Study. Coming, then, more closely to the study of the Bible we have—

(1) The Higher Criticism. Were there no questions regarding the date and authorship of the books of the Bible which affect historical results, most of the material of this department might be handed over to the department of history; or if results were considered without placing the emphasis upon the critical investigations which precede them, the subject might still be considered as historical. But it is usual to rubricise this department under the head of criticism; and however rubricised there is no escape from the necessity of entering upon the work of the Higher Criticism. A Church may say that for a minister to reach certain conclusions in his critical exegesis is to put in jeopardy his ministerial standing; but a Church which should forbid inquiry would stultify herself. This business of the Higher Criticism on its ecclesiastical side does not seem to be so difficult after all. We do not believe in an infallible Church; and we cannot very well assume the infallibility of the Bible in order to prove its infallibility. We are therefore, in a sense in the hands of the specialists. I do not see how it can be helped. If our attorney is not managing our case right, my advice is to dismiss him and get another. But the advice of many seems to be: let the case go by default: the attorneys are a bad lot.

Then we have (2) the Lower Criticism, or that which is concerned with the task of securing a correct text. The theological student needs no explanation of the meaning of this Discipline, but if the intelligent layman wishes to know what is involved in inquiries under this head, let him read the admirable treatise on the Textual Criticism of the New Testament by my friend and colleague, Dr. Warfield. Suffice it to say that this is the sphere of the labors of such men as Tregelles and Tischendorf and Drs. Westcott and Hort.

Then we have (3) Exegesis: Interpretation. And it is here that Calvin and Hodge and Addison Alexander and Eadie and Alford and Ellicott and Lightfoot and Meyer have made the world of Christian students their debtors. It is to be regretted that this department of theology is receiving less attention than it once did, for it is the minister who feeds his mind and heart by close contact with the mind of God as revealed in the very words of Scripture whose ministry will be rich in spiritual power. Time was when the intellectual life of scholarly ministers centred in exegetical studies. Time was when every religious controversy was fought out on exegetical grounds. But ministers have shared in the intellectual unrest of the day. Doubt in regard to the inspiration of the Scriptures and the convergence of literary criticism and the evolutionary philosophy upon the sacred books has tended to paralyze all theological effort or has transferred it to another *locus.*

And finally we have (4) Biblical Theology. I sympathize with Räbiger in the regret that this designation has been given to this department. It would have been better if the term could have been kept to indicate (and Pelt so uses it in his Encyclopædia) all the studies that terminate on the Bible. My friend and colleague, Dr. Vos, following Nösgen, makes the happy suggestion that this department be called the History of Revelation. But the term has a pretty fixed meaning and is generally well understood, though now and then we find a man who still gives vent to his dislike of Dogmatic Theology by professing great devotion to Biblical Theology, as though the latter were a protest against the former, and were a little more loyal to the authority of the Bible. It is true that Biblical Theology takes little or no account of ecclesiastical controversies and is silent about the decisions of Councils. Still it must be remembered that Biblical Theology does not consist in grouping the teaching of the Scriptures under certain *loci communes,* such as sin and redemption. That would be a Biblical Dogmatic. The Biblical Theologian seeks to trace the development of doctrine as revealed truth. His subject is the crowning Discipline of Exegesis, but it is an historical Discipline too. It is the task of the Dogmatic Theologian to exhibit the logical unfolding of the Covenant of Grace, but it is the task of the Biblical Theologian to exhibit its chronological unfolding.

In that fine fragment on the History of Redemption, by the great theologian in connection with whose bicentenary celebrated a few years ago in this Seminary, there was delivered an address by Dr. DeWitt which the readers of this volume will have the pleasure of reading, we have the true conception of this department; and I think I do not err in saying that, at least so far as we in America are concerned, Jonathan Edwards is the father of Biblical Theology. I do not think that Biblical Theology can ever supersede Systematic Theology, but it is a most important part of theological learning; and besides serving to systematize our exegetical studies, it will render great service to us in the construction of Systematic Theology. We shall gain an insight into the genetic relations of the great concepts of Redemption as we watch their gradual unfolding. We shall acquire an historical habit in the study of Scripture. Texts whose doctrinal significance we have overlooked will be seen in a new light; and proof-texts that have been quoted by generations of dogmaticians in support of doctrines which they do not prove will, so far as the purposes of Dogmatic Theology are concerned, be sent into honorable retirement.

3. *Ecclesiastical Theology.*—Under this head we are to group all those studies that are involved in our conception of the Church. And of course there is—

(1) The History of the Church, which may be considered as general and special. Now the historian's method will be determined largely by his conception of the Church. If organization is of the essence of the Church, the liberal-minded historian will be embarrassed by the varieties of ecclesiastical organization. If, on the other hand, organization is not of the essence of the Church (which is, I think, the better view), he is relieved at once of a very serious difficulty. The Roman

Catholic historian has his own way of disposing of Presbyterians, and the Presbyterian historian has his way (I think a better way) of disposing of Roman Catholics. He treats them as constituent members of the Church—meaning by it that great body of men throughout the world who profess the true religion. With the problem of coexistence in space satisfactorily disposed of, the historian has on his hands the less important, but still important problem of succession in time. We have been told so much of late that history is not a matter of dates that I am afraid that some people are losing all sense of historical perspective. I should think a good deal, it seems to me, if I were writing Church history, on how I should periodize. Ideally speaking, one would think that the divisions of history should be those of time; that epochs should be indicated by events marking the *terminus a quo* and the *terminus ad quem;* and that all minor divisions should be absorbed in the even and uninterrupted flow of narrative. This is Gibbon's plan, and Milman's. But it would not have suited a work like Neander's. The detailed treatment he was to give his subject under each category required him to make his categories clear, distinct and comprehensive. And so under each of his periods he deals with the Church in the history of her spread abroad, of her life and discipline, and of her doctrine. If, as we cannot very well avoid, we keep the familiar rubrics of ancient, mediæval and modern history, we should naturally expect that temporal divisions after that would be subdivisions of these three, and should feel it would not be exactly logical to absorb them in another scheme which gives nine periods of history coördinate with one another. Yet this is what Dr. Schaff does in his most learned history of the Church.

It would be impossible to deal with or even to mention here all the subjects of special Church history that may properly fall under the *curriculum* of theological study; but I must mention two, Symbolics and the History of Doctrine. It may strike some as an anachronism for me to attach any importance to the study of Creeds and Confessions, and yet I think that they ought to be considered as to their origin,

the men who made them, the circumstances which gave rise
to them, and the controversies that called for their preparation. We should know our own Confession of Faith in its
relation to the great family of Reformed Confessions, of
which it is the last and the best; we should see how the
Reformed Confessions differ from the Lutheran—the Augs-
burg and the Formula of Concord; we should know the beginnings of Arminianism, and be ready to say whether we
divide the Protestant world into three great families, Lutheran, Arminian and Reformed, or whether we make Armin-
ians and Calvinists two species under the *genus* Reformed.
We should have clearly in our minds the points that separate
all Protestant confessions from the Greek and Roman
Churches; and we should know—by no means an unimportant
thing to know—how much our Protestantism holds in common with the Greek Catholic and the Roman Catholic communions. Turning now to the History of Doctrine, two methods are open to us. We may divide the history into short
periods, and treat all the doctrines under every period; or we
may divide by making doctrine the basis and tracing each
doctrine through the centuries. Think now of Baur's great
work on the history of the doctrine of the Trinity, Müller on
Sin, Dorner on the Person of Christ, Ritschl on Justification—
marvels of learning, every one; then look through the histories
of Doctrine, such as Shedd's and Hagenbach's and Harnack's,
and imagine the literature that is to be studied before one is
master of this field. Consider what it means to study the
history of doctrine. It means not only that we watch the
changes from the indefinite to the definite that a doctrine has
undergone, not only that we know what the great Doctors
and Fathers have said regarding it; but that we understand,
too, the influences that led to these opinions, and particularly
the coloring of current philosophy, whether it be Platonic or
Aristotelian; whether it be Manichean or Scholastic, whether it
be Kantian or Hegelian. And think of the work that this involves! If I were having an historian of dogma made to order
I would require him to have great acquisitive powers, and I
would have him at home in the languages of the Bible. I would

have him secure a mastery of Church History in general. I would make him as thorough in his mastery of the history of Philosophy. I would have him become a systematic dogmatician of the highest logical powers; and when I had done all, I would put him early at the task of studying the history of doctrine. Then we might get what at present we do not have—a satisfactory treatment of the subject.

The second topic under the head of Ecclesiastical Theology is (2) the Organization of the Church. There are wide differences of opinion in regard to the way in which the Church should be organized, officered and governed. The theologian who wishes to discuss the question of the primitive *ecclesia* without being dependent upon second-hand sources must be able to handle patristic literature for himself, as Hatch and Lightfoot do. He should be familiar with the great systems of Church and State relationships—the Byzantine, the Roman, the Erastian—as well as that which proceeds upon the theory of the entire separation of the one from the other. Because a man is a Presbyterian minister he is not cut off from interest in other communions, and if his specialty is Church government he ought to know and be familiar with the great administrative problems in other communions. The decisions of the Court of Arches and of the Judicial Committee of the Privy Council in regard to points of doctrine and ritual in the Church of England ought to interest him. The great struggle for spiritual independence which culminated in the Scottish disruption of 1843 should be known by him as he knows the history of his own Church; and the law of his Church, as laid down in the Book of Discipline, and the judicial decisions of the General Assembly should be read in the light of Pardovan's Collections and, for that matter, in the light of the Canon law. What would be said if I should recommend theological students to take a course in Roman Law? And yet I am sure that such a course would be useful to them. And then there is the whole question of the Church in relation to the law of the land—the law of the land regarding Church property, regarding the conclusive character of ecclesiastical sentences, as laid down in the decision of the Supreme Court of the United States in the Walnut Street Church case, and the laws of the several States regarding marriage and divorce. These are all matters which are within the legitmate province of the minister.

The last subject which claims consideration under the head of Ecclesiastical Theology is (3) the Work and Worship of the Church. Two questions present themselves in this connection: the question of extending the Church's influence and that of promoting the spiritual well-being of her members. Missions, Pastoral Theology, Liturgics, Homiletics— these and topics like these should be dealt with under this department. A course of lectures on Missions, such as those delivered here by Dr. Dennis and others, is a great addition to the Seminary's *curriculum*. Lectures on the history of missions, the missionary problems, the bearing of missions on the statesmanship of the world, and the bearing of diplomacy on the future of Christianity—these are great subjects and fitted to awaken the highest enthusiasm of any man who will approach them with interest and sufficient breadth of vision.

I do not dwell on the subject of Pastoral Theology, but I will take the liberty to say to my younger brethren that we ministers need all the good advice we can get respecting the exercise of tact and good sense, respecting the care of our life and the avoidance of those things that mar our influence. A Professor in this Seminary once thought it not beneath his dignity to write a book on Clerical Manners and I have sometimes thought that a new edition of that book, brought down to date, with some additional suggestions as to the amenities of social life, is greatly needed.

I have very little to say regarding Homiletics, though if, as with most of us it is the case, our productive activity is to spend itself in making sermons, I do not see how we can fail to attach great importance to the subject. The minister who does not know what Shedd and Phelps have said on sermonizing shows great indifference, it seems to me, to the attainment of excellence in his profession. A man who makes a serious study of this subject and brings to it a well-furnished mind, will need none of the popular homiletical helps and can afford to throw his Dictionary of Illustrations out of the window. I do not feel the difficulty which some experience in settling the boundary lines of plagiarism. A full man, with a fresh mind, after sufficient brooding on his text, will get down to the roots of the text, will see what nobody else will see in the same light; for the thing seen, to use a Kantianism, is not the text-in-itself, but the text-in-itself in relation to the man-in-himself; and this being the case, if the man-in-himself be a man—that is, if he has grown out of his babyhood and rounded into a separate mind—the possibilities are infinite respecting the sermons that may be preached from any text. And so I say to my younger brethren in the ministry, and especially to the young men who have not yet entered it: get powers of expression, get knowledge, get thought-power, get rich Christian experience, get a knowledge of homiletical *technique,* and then let the sermon be yours—nay, rather, let it be you. Let it be an arrow shot from the tense bow-string of conviction and it will hit the mark every time.

But the sermon is not the only thing in the worship of the Church, and in some Churches it is not the most important thing. We belong to the non-liturgical family of Churches, and music does not hold the place in our Church that it occupies in some other branches of Christendom. But that is no reason why we should fail to provide proper instruction in our Seminaries in Church music of the better sort or ignore the great devotional formulas which have fed the spiritual life of generations of Christians. I should say that it is the minister of the non-liturgical Church, since he is expected to be ready at a moment's notice to express himself in apt, elevated, rhythmical, devotional language, who is likely to be most profited by familiar acquaintance with the liturgical formulas of the Christian Church. For the nurture of his own spiritual life, and for his greater efficiency as a minister of the Word, I commend to every theological student the duty of having an intimate acquaintance with the Word of God in the English tongue; but I would also commend to him the duty of familiarizing himself with the Church's best literature of devotion, and whether it be the *Imitation of Christ,* or *The Christian*

Year, or *The Book of Common Prayer* that claims his attention; whether it be the hymns of Watts or Doddridge or Wesley, or Faber or Newman, or Bonar or Heber in which his religious feelings find expression, let him remember that the meditations, the prayers, the hymns of Christian men of all ages are the common heritage of the Christian world.

II.

ANTITHESIS.

We are now to deal with that part of Theology which regards the Christian system as antithetically related to opposing forms of thought. In the early days of the Reformed Theology all defenses of revealed truths were included under the name Polemic Theology. Thus Stapfer, in the second and third volumes of his Polemic Theology, deals in succession with Atheism, Deism, Epicureanism, Ethnicism, Naturalism, Judaism, Mohammedanism, Socinianism, Romanism, Fanaticism, Pelagianism, and reaches his climax in his chapter against the Remonstrants and the Anabaptists. The classification exhibits all the faults that are conceivable in a discussion of this kind. I shall not call attention to them further than to say that there is a great difference between those controversies whose area is within the Christian communions and those which are carried on against men who deny the supernaturalism of Christianity. Polemic Theology pertains to the first, Apologetic Theology to the second.

1. *Polemic Theology.*—The phrase does not have a very amiable sound, and on that account some would like to have it superseded by a less warlike form of expression. But I do not know that we should quarrel with the adjective, if that for which it stands is an accepted fact. If the rupture with Rome was justifiable a Protestant polemic becomes a necessity— that is to say, we must defend our position. It is a pity that Protestantism has undergone the process of division into sects, but it is the inevitable logic of its postulates. When the doctrine of the one visible corporate Church is parted with, as Protestantism necessarily parts with it, there is no

logical stopping-place, and we may multiply sects indefinitely. For when the basis of the organization is not the Creed which shall include the largest number of Christians, but that which shall embrace the largest number of doctrines, and which shall express them in the best and most Scriptural manner, you of course see what will be the result. Creeds will multiply, and sects will multiply. The greater the extension the less the intension; the greater the intension the less the extension.

Suppose, now, that you belong to one of these Churches and accept its creed-statements. Suppose that men outside of your communion revile your doctrines, ridicule your faith and misrepresent your most cherished convictions. Are you not to be allowed to defend yourself? Suppose that when there is peace within your walls and prosperity within your palaces, there arise those within your communion who flaunt their ridicule of the creed to which they have subscribed in the faces of the congregations which they serve. Are you to do nothing? Have you no right to stand up in defense of what you believe to be precious truth? Now these are precisely the occasions that develop the controversial element in the Church's life. I do not see, therefore, how we can help having a place for Polemic Theology in the Theological Encyclopædia. I do not understand Polemic Theology to mean a bitter spirit. It is simply the intellectual outcome of a condition of things in which a witness-bearing Church, prompted by zeal for the truth and a holy instinct of self-preservation, girds itself to do battle against what it believes to be error.

2. *Apologetic Theology.*—Polemic Theology, as I have said, at one time included all that we now designate as Apologetics; and Apologetics is in the nature of the case polemic, only its warfare is carried on between those who believe and those who deny a Supernatural Revelation. And yet the irenic character of Apologetics is very decided also. It must needs soften the tone of controversy for us to remember that, differ as we may, in some points, from our brethren in other communions, we stand shoulder to shoulder with them in defense of more important truth. Says Delitzsch in his *Apologetik*: "When we are carried along by Tertullian's Apologetics and

wonder at his depth and wealth of thought, we thank God
that the Church has had a man who with such power was
able to wield the sword of the Spirit, and we forget his Montanism. And when we read the learned and elegant book *de
veritate religionis Christianæ* which Grotius wrote as a pastime
during a sea voyage for those who traveled in heathen lands,
we take our Christian brother by the hand without feeling sore
at his Arminianism. So, too, we recognize Paley, the author
of the *Evidences of Christianity*, and Butler, the author of the
Analogy, and all the great English and American defenders
of Christian truth, without asking questions respecting their
ecclesiastical connections. And when among the later apologetes we recognize in Drey, Dreisinger, Staudenmeier, and
lastly Hettinger four distinguished Catholic investigators,
without, in so doing, making any treaty with the Roman
Catholic Church, we greet them with a hearty *pax vobiscum*."

The encyclopædists are fond of distinguishing between
Apology and Apologetics—and the distinction is a sound one.
Apologies are as old as Christianity; systems of Apologetics
do not go back of the nineteenth century. Tertullian wrote
an Apology, and when the early Christian Fathers defended
themselves and their religion against the particular allegations
made against them they wrote Apologies; so when the eighteenth century deists called out the great apologetic literature
of that period, the greatest in the annals of the Church of
any period, they wrote Apologies. That is to say, they wrote
special defenses of Christianity from particular points of view
and covering the particular questions then in issue. But when,
instead of dealing with a particular controversy, we consider
how the Christian religion shall justify its claims to be a
supernaturally revealed religion, we are dealing with a much
broader and more abstract question. When Lightfoot defends
the historical trustworthiness of the books of the New Testament against the author of *Supernatural Religion,* he is writing an Apology. But when Ebrard or Sack or Baumstark
writes a systematic defense of Christianity as a supernatural
religion, he writes an Apologetic. It is because Apologetic
has this character of systematic or organic completeness, I

suppose, that some encyclopædists regard it as a branch of Systematic Theology. But there is a great difference, I think, between our conception of Apologetic and that of Systematic Theology. The motive in Systematic Theology is didactic; that in Apologetic Theology is polemic. Let it be understood, then, that Apologetics is a systematic exhibition of the defenses of Christianity. The apologete is not seeking to defend Calvinism or Arminianism or Lutheranism or Romanism as such. He is seeking to defend that core of truth which these systems hold in common. We are in a different attitude altogether when we speak as dogmaticians and when we speak as apologetes. As dogmaticians we ask: What do we know concerning God? It is the truth and the whole truth we are in quest of. It will be the *maximum quid* of belief, therefore, that will be our object. But as apologetes we ask: How can the truth which differentiates Christianity from all other religions, and which the various sects of Christians hold in common, be defended? It is the *minimum quid* which we are seeking. What is that truth which, if a man believe, he shall be saved? What is the truth which represents the essence of Christianity—understanding by essence, to use Spinoza's words, " that without which the thing, and which itself without the thing, can neither be nor be conceived "? On the one hand the man who reduces Christianity to morality, who gives up miracles and makes no numerical distinction between God and the finite spirits whom he has created, minimizes too much. Therefore, when men like Matthew Arnold play the part of apologetes and wish to be regarded as defenders of the faith, we reject their kind offers at once—*non tali auxilio nec defensoribus istis*. And yet is it not just as true that there are good Christian men whose views on the Trinity, the Person of Christ, the Atonement, the nature of Sin, the question of Retribution, and the doctrine of Inspiration are erroneous?

Clearly, therefore, when we undertake the work of Apologetics we must take as our starting-point what we regard as essential Christianity. Where shall we find it? Is it not here—to wit, "that God was in Christ reconciling the world unto himself, not imputing unto men their trespasses "?

III.

SYNTHESIS

The cathedral, some one has said, is the synthesis of all the forms of art. Its beauty and the impressiveness of its services are largely in the fact that it is the blending of architecture, sculpture, painting and music. What the cathedral is to the arts, Systematic Theology is to the several Disciplines that enter into theological study. The Systematic Theologian is an architect. Less accomplished, perhaps, than others in the knowledge of any one specialty, he must be more accomplished than any in the knowledge of all specialties. His specialty is the knowledge of the results in all specialties. Like the professed Biblical Theologian he gets his doctrines out of the Bible, but his work does not stop with exegesis. He sees the doctrines not only as separately deducible from Scripture, but as progressively unfolded in Scripture. He sees them as the subjects of varying fortunes in the course of history, as defended here and antagonized there. He sees them as the subjects of controversy and as the constituent elements in ecclesiastical symbols. He knows, moreover, that while some truths regarding God are taught in the Bible and nowhere else, other truths may be seen in the light of nature. But these truths of natural religion stand polemically related to those forms of philosophic thought which deny them. And the truths of Revealed Religion have felt the warping, blighting, compromising influence of a false philosophy. The Systematic Theologian in the very act of being a Systematic Theologian must be an Apologetic Theologian, must be a Polemic Theologian, must be a student of philosophy, must be a Biblical Theologian, must be familiar with ecclesiastical history, must know the ins and outs of ecclesiastical life. All this goes to justify me in saying that Systematic Theology is not a department that is coördinate with Exegetical Theology, with Historical Theology, with Practical Theology. Rather is it the synthesis of all these Disciplines which we have been considering. This, at least, is the place that I feel bound to give it in the outline of Theological Encyclopædia which I am presenting here.

The grandeur of Systematic Theology thus conceived will hardly be denied. The legitimacy of the Systematic Theologian's undertaking cannot be called in question. Even when men have given form to systems foreign to our mode of thought and far away from what we believe to be true it is impossible not to admire and to wonder at the vast constructive power their systems manifest. The first question is, of course, whether or no God has spoken. For if he has spoken, it is certain that he has not said one thing or two. He has said a great many things. And these parts of the Divine message sustain relations to one another. What are these relations? It is said that God has not given us a Systematic Theology in the Bible. Neither has he given us a ready-made Astronomy nor a ready-made Biology. Linnæus had to work for his classification. God has not planted nature like a park with studied reference to orders, genera and species. It is said that logic is a snare, and I have heard ministers in the pulpit grow eloquent over the ensnaring power of logic when it was quite evident that, however much other people were suffering by it, they were entirely safe themselves. I am not ready to say *credo quia impossibile,* or *credo quia absurdum est.* I do not think we can save our faith by discarding our intellects. The world will not long continue to value a religion which it believes to be irrational, no matter who it is that commends it to our consideration. And whether it be Tertullian or Ritschl, or Herrmann or Coleridge, or Isaac Taylor or Balfour, or Kidd or Mallock, or the modern high-potency dilutionists of the Ritschlian School, who in this country are giving us an ethico-sentimental naturalism as the new Gospel for the twentieth century, I make bold to tell them all alike that Christianity will be denied a hearing in the court of feeling once she has been non-suited at the bar of reason.

The theme of Systematic Theology is the sum of our knowledge regarding God. This includes of course, human conduct; and it is quite possible to include both faith and practice under one set of categories. Thus Turretine discusses morality under the Law; so does Dr. Charles Hodge. But it is not common to do this. In the Roman Catholic Church the distinction is clearly marked between Dogmatic and Moral Theology—the latter being largely occupied with the solution of difficult questions of casuistry. And in the Protestant Churches the distinction between dogmatics and ethics has been recognized since the seventeenth century. It was first made for the Reformed Church by Danæus, and for the Lutheran Church by Calixtus.

1. *Christian Ethics.*—A theologian, of course, can limit himself to the discussion of those practical questions of conduct which represent the difference between rational ethics and revealed ethics. He may say that his field of conduct is conditioned by Christianity. But, perplexing as some of the questions will be that fall within this area, I am inclined to think that he cannot limit himself to this area. He will feel, I am confident, that the entire territory of morals is his. Fundamental questions regarding Moral Obligation, the Good and the Right, will confront him and he will find it impossible to ignore what is being said or what has been said by men like Sidgwick and Green, and Spencer and Martineau, and Taylor and Shadworth Hodgson and Paulsen.

Again, the Professor of Christian Ethics must not only consider the law of Christianity conditioning conduct; he must also, or, rather, he may also, consider the Christian's ethical state in relation to this law; for Christian ethics not only sees the Christian in the light of the new obligations imposed by the law of Christ, it also sees him in the light of his new ethical state produced by the Holy Spirit. So that the whole question of Regeneration and Sanctification may properly come under Christian Ethics, and this is a very large part of Dogmatic Theology. In fact, to such an extent do Dogmatics and Ethics overlap that in some writers, as in Nitzsch and Rothe, the whole or nearly the whole dogmatic area is covered by the department of Christian Ethics.

But it is distinctly to the department of Christian Ethics, and not to that of Practical Theology, that the discussion of the great social problems of the day belongs. That these problems should be discussed, that the Church should have something to say in regard to the poverty, disease and crime that seem to be the inevitable result of the congested life of our large cities, and that there is moreover a great and practical work to be done in reference to the pathological conditions of society through organized philanthropic agency, there can be no doubt; but it is a mistake to call this Sociology, and it is worse than a mistake when under the name of Christian Sociology work of this sort is made a substitute for the preaching of the Gospel. For Sociology in its proper sense I have great respect; but for that shallow compound of sociology and sentimentality which is just now the largest output of the new Christianity, I have none, for it satisfies neither my intellect nor my feelings.

The man who would deal adequately with the social problem must know, to begin with, what men like Baldwin and Giddings have to say regarding the psychology of social life; he must know, whether he agrees with them or not, what men like Mackenzie and Bosanquet have to say regarding the metaphysics of society and its final cause. He must have more than a superficial knowledge of the evolution of our institutional life which has given us in their present forms the Family, the Church and the State; he must understand the principles of the great normative sciences of ethics and jurisprudence which deal respectively with the life of the individual and the organism; he must know something of the economic laws that underlie the growth of industrialism; and then, perhaps, he may hope to address himself to the great pathological problems and make an intelligent application to them of the ethical principles of Christianity. But, then, who is sufficient for these things?

2. *Dogmatics.*—I cannot undertake to name and criticise the various definitions that have been given of Dogmatic Theology; but I prefer to say that Dogmatic Theology is a systematic exhibition of our knowledge regarding God. Its content, then, is knowledge. It is what we know and have good reason for knowing, whatever that reason may be. It is knowledge regarding God. It may, and does, include the

knowledge of a great many things besides God; but it is the knowledge of those things in their Godward relationships. God is the great category under which all the knowledge which Dogmatic has for content is subsumed. It is systematic knowledge. It is not simply the knowledge of separate dogmas. It is articulated knowledge. It is knowledge that has been brought together under great dominant generalizations. You see, then, at once what a broad field the dogmatic theologian has before him. What a splendid history Dogmatic Theology has had! I can hardly imagine a more interesting study than that of going through the dogmatic writers from the Reformation down to our own day, for the purpose of comparing their methods and of watching the influence of prevailing philosophies upon their forms of statement. With the help of writers on dogmatic history like Gass and Ebrard, and Schweizer and Heppe, this ought not to be a difficult thing, and it certainly would be an interesting thing to do.

As the result of such a study we should find that the Systematic Theology which had been developed so fully under philosophical domination from Albert the Great to Aquinas, and which in the declining days of Scholasticism went through a waning process, was developed under the polemic conditions of the Reformation into new activity. The Reformation principle of the Bible as the rule of faith gave us a period of dogmatic supernaturalism. First we have the three great dogmaticians of the Reformation—Melanchthon in his *Loci communes,* Zwingli in his *de vera et falsa Religione,* and Calvin in his *Institutio Christianæ religionis.* Then came the separation of the Lutheran and Reformed Theologies, the latter proceeding until differences found expression in the antithesis of Gomarus and Arminius, when we had the Synod of Dort and the extrusion of the Arminian party. Reformed Theology still developed, ending in rival, antagonistic and mediating schools. There were the Scholastics, building deductively and taking the eternal purpose as their starting-point. Then there were the Federalists—Cocceius and Witsius—presenting theology as the progressive exhibition of the covenants. There were the Cartesians, representing the influence of philosophy and particularly of natural science—men like Voetius and Maresius, who distinguished between natural and revealed religion, and saw that supernatural revelation presupposed the light of nature and the use of reason. Then came the period when the differences were reconciled and under the influence of the Leibnitzo-Wolfian philosophy a theological Scholasticism was presented which served as a mould by means of which these varying elements could be pressed into shape and symmetry. The federal idea was retained; the decrees were given a conspicuous place; philosophy was recognized as having some function and the great systems of the seventeenth century came forth, notably that of Turretine—the Thomas Aquinas of Protestantism.

Lutheranism, too, went through its period of development, as Ebrard shows; but I have time only to refer to this fact which Ebrard brings out, that while the Reformed Theology was systematic first and dogmatic afterward, the Lutheran Theology was dogmatic first and systematic afterward. The genius of Calvinism was to schematize. Lutheranism dwelt first upon particular dogmas, and reached its schematizing stage later. This is worthy of notice, inasmuch as in later years Lutheranism has distanced all competitors in regard to constructive Dogmatics.

The age of Supernaturalism was followed by that of Rationalism, in which the attempt was made to reduce the doctrines of Christianity to the level of human reason and reject those which resisted the attempt. Following this period of Rationalism or, rather, when Rationalism and Supernaturalism were the contending foes, when it was a duel between infallible Bible and infallible reason, came Schleiermacher, a sort of Platonic Methodist, to protest against the deification of the intellect and plead for the place of the feelings in religion. But his very subjectivism of the feelings, though protesting against the subjectivism of the intellect, was in close alliance with the subjectivism of the intellect. Hence, when Hegel arose, though he was the antithesis of Schleiermacher and ridiculed his definition of religion, he was yet so related to him that mediation was not impossible, so that subsequent writers have given evidence of both influences; and Rothe, when he wrote his *Ethics,* was now a mystic and now a speculative theologian, having one foot, as Lange expresses it, in Schleiermacher's slipper and the other in Hegel's boot. Hence arose the mediating school, the school that seeks to keep the good in both systems and preserve the historic continuity of Church doctrine. To this school belonged Nitzsch and Ullmann, and Dorner and Martensen. And now the last movement is in progress, and the note of the Ritschlian revolt from the reign of Hegel is the banishment of metaphysics from theology. The good side of the movement is its return to the historic basis and its impatience of a theology which resolves the historic faith of Christianity into the glittering generalities of the Hegelian dialectic. The bad side of it is the inevitable schism which it introduces into the life of the individual Christian, between the theology of the intellect and the theology of the feelings. Say what its leaders may respecting the continued hold which these doctrines have as value-judgments, the system must be judged by its net result of fact and rational conviction. No system can stand the strain of an inner contradiction which is implied in holding for true what is believed to be false; of believing with the heart what is discredited by the head. And sooner or later Ritschlianism must give up its see-saw of Intellect and Feeling between Socinianism and Evangelical Christianity and settle down to one or the other.

Assuming now that the Systematic Theologian has his materials ready for organization into system, what method shall he adopt? This, of course, is an important question as a matter of logic; but the impression seems to prevail in some quarters that it is a vital question as a matter of theological content. This, however, I fail to see. There is the strictly local or topical method of the early theologians of Reformation times; there is the federal method of Witsius; there is the method which makes the Trinity the basis of division, which Calvin adopts in his *Institutes;* there is the method which starts from the anthropological standpoint and discusses Sin and its Remedy, as Chalmers does; there is the strictly theological method where everything is discussed under the concept of

God; and then there is the Christocentric method, of which
so much has been said in recent years by way of disparaging
other methods. But, after all, how can a Christocentric method
of schematizing the doctrines affect the doctrines themselves?
Here are your separate blocks of dogma, and each has its own
significance. You can build these blocks into any shape you
please: you may build castles or cathedrals; but however much
you change the relations of these blocks to each other, you
do not on that account change the individuality of each. Well,
then, put your dogmatic blocks together as symmetry, logic and
the suggestions of your own intellect may dictate; you do not
thereby change the doctrines themselves. Your schematism
may not be the same as mine, but neither of us by mere schematism can modify a single doctrinal unit. No, depend upon it, no
new light is going to break forth from the Word of God as
the result of a new schematization of the doctrines. The question as to whether a system of doctrine is true is to be tested
first of all by the inquiry whether the doctrines of the system
are true. If they are true, then the building of them into systems is not only the natural but the necessary outcome of that
type of intellect that seeks order and symmetry, and sees related truths in the light of great generalizations.

I know that Systematic Theology is discredited in some
quarters; some seem to think that it stands as a barrier to
religious fervor and practical piety; some tell us that we
must get ready for a theological reconstruction and that the
time for that reconstruction is at hand. But the only consistent despisers of Systematic Theology are those who in
their hearts believe, however slow they may be to confess
it, that in the light of history as it is now read, and of
philosophy as it is now studied, and of science as it is now
proclaimed, there is little or no rational content for Systematic Theology. If the Church's Dogmatic is the result
of a Hellenizing process; if the body of Catholic doctrines is
a parasitic growth which has fastened itself upon the original
simple cult of Jesus, and if, as Harnack believes, the Reformation is only an imperfect attempt to restore this simple undog-
matic faith, then I grant you that a Systematic Theology of

very modest proportions is all we need. We need talk no more of cathedrals as symbols of our dogmatic system. The humblest two-room hut, without paint or decoration, without even a common wayside flower in the window to tell the presence within of a heart that is touched with feeling or an eye that kindles in the warming presence of beauty, will be a sufficient exponent of the poverty and desolation that must inevitably come as the result of this conception of the origin and growth of the Christian Church. But if the Bible is true, and the Church is built upon the foundation of the apostles and prophets, Jesus Christ himself being the chief cornerstone, then the labors of the Fathers, and the decisions of Councils, and the controversies of theologians have been inspired by the efforts of earnest men to do honor to the Word of God. And the great systems of divinity which stretch like mountain peaks before the field of our vision are monumental tributes which the Church of God, through the writings of her gifted men, has had the unspeakable honor of paying to her exalted and incarnate Head.

I do not look for an immediate revival of interest in Systematic Theology, and yet I know that the greatest achievement of the American Church is in this sphere. The Church of England has done magnificent work in Biblical literature, in Apologetics and in Dogmatic discussion. But nearly half a century ago Bishop Ellicott deplored her lack of interest in Systematic Theology. The American Churches—I refer particularly to the Presbyterian and Congregational Churches—have won the conspicuous place they hold in theological literature through the labors of their systematic theologians. Think of the names in the great roster of American theologians which come instantly to your lips without effort or need of reference to the books that stand on your shelves—Edwards, Hopkins, Emmons, Taylor, Park, Hodge, Breckinridge, Thornwell, Dabney, Finney, Shedd, Henry B. Smith—systematic theologians every one. Shall we turn this page in the history of American theology and look upon it as the record of a vast mistake? Has the new Christianity taught us only to believe that these were visionary and misguided men?

I agree with Harnack and the Ritschlians generally in giving the primacy to our instinctive judgments of worth; but I do not believe that there is a schism between faith and knowledge, between our value-judgments and scientific truth. And what is more, I believe that unless these value-judgments are rooted in a sound metaphysic, they will lose their controlling influence on life. I admit that it is religion, as Harnack says, that gives life its meaning. Rob life of its faith in God, its hope of immortality and the ethical ideals we owe to the teachings of Jesus, and life shrivels into a meaningless medley of hope and fear, of pain and struggle, of unsatisfied desire, of sated appetite, of selfish ambition and the tender memories of cherished love. But who shall say that Nature has anything better for us than bitter disappointments? Jesus, you tell me, has revealed God and told me that God is my Father. But how do we know that Jesus speaks with authority? How, without the Divinity which we claim for him and the miraculous evidence that accredits that Divinity, do we feel sure of his authority? Because his message wakes echoes in our souls, you say, and his words find responses in our nature. Then his authority is no higher than our higher impulses. But when we are told that these higher impulses have come by way of natural development, and that even Jesus is only an event in the great cosmic process, what shall our answer be? When these finer feelings, these ethical ideals, these tender instincts are nipped by the frost of a pitiless naturalism, what shall we say? Say that we will not give up? Say that we will set the world of value-judgments against the world of cosmic fact and by sheer assertion win the victory for faith and love? Very well; but then your minimized Christianity is no help in the fight against a naturalistic philosophy. It is only a theistic ethic taught by Jesus, and instead of banishing metaphysics from its realm it is itself a philosophy, and stands or falls with a theistic metaphysic.

Let us understand the issue in the great battle of to-day for fundamental Christianity. We had thought that Christianity was more than philosophy and spoke with Divine authority; but in the minimized version of Christianity there is nothing but philosophy left. We had thought it necessary to defend a theistic metaphysic and a theistic ethic as the necessary philosophic basis of a gospel which presented a way of salvation through an incarnate Christ. But we have little heart even for this struggle if Christianity itself turns out, after all, to be only a theistic ethic. If our great Leader is slain and the citadel has capitulated, why need we longer make a fruitless struggle?

Give us the Incarnation and Resurrection of Christ, then Sin, the Atonement and Justification follow; and you have a Dogmatic and Systematic Theology. But eliminate the Incarnation, and then your religion is an emotional morality connected with the name of Jesus, of whom you still speak in the language made sacred by long use and early association; but in its last analysis it is a moral philosophy in competition with other moral philosophies, and defended by a theistic metaphysic that has to cope with another metaphysic which denies God, or makes no distinction between him and the works of his hand.

I am pronouncing no judgment on men. I am dealing only with the relationships of thought. I know that men are often better than their creeds; and that deep in the core of a man's being there is often a better faith than that which he can formulate in words. I am far from saying that apart from Dogmatic Christianity there is no valid ground for a theistic ethic. But the motive that will make a man fight as for his hearthstone and his home in support of that theistic ethic is his abiding belief in the incarnate Christ; and the historic evidence for the incarnate Christ is one of the great bulwarks of theistic belief. Theism is the logical *prius* of the Incarnation, it is true, but theism and the Incarnation are reciprocally influential on each other. This is what I mean when I say that in the defense of supernatural Christianity everything is at stake. And this is the reason that in the crisis of to-day we are witnessing the greatest war of intellect that has ever been waged since the birthday of the Nazarene.

Sooner or later I am sure the eyes of men will be opened and they will see—would to God they might see it now!—that the great battle of the twentieth century is in its final issue a struggle between a Dogmatic Christianity on the one hand and an out-and-out naturalistic philosophy on the other.

ON THE EMOTIONAL LIFE OF OUR LORD

Benjamin Breckinridge Warfield

ON THE EMOTIONAL LIFE OF OUR LORD

It belongs to the truth of our Lord's humanity, that he was subject to all sinless human emotions.[1] In the accounts which the Evangelists give us of the crowded activities which filled the few years of his ministry, the play of a great variety of emotions is depicted. It has nevertheless not proved easy to form a universally acceptable conception of our Lord's emotional life. Not only has the mystery of the Incarnation entered in as a disturbing factor, the effect of the divine nature on the movements of the human soul brought into personal union with it being variously estimated. Differences have arisen also as to how far there may be attributed to a perfect human nature movements known to us only as passions of sinful beings.

Two opposite tendencies early showed themselves in the Church. One, derived ultimately from the ethical ideal of the Stoa, which conceived moral perfection under the form of ἀπάθεια, naturally wished to attribute this ideal ἀπάθεια to Jesus, as the perfect man. The other, under the influence of the conviction that, in order to deliver men from their weak-

[1] "Certainly", remarks Calvin (*Commentarius in Harmoniam Evangelicarum*, Mt. xxvi. 37), "those who imagine that the Son of God was exempt from human passions, do not truly and seriously acknowledge him to be a man." "But Christ having a human nature the same for substance that ours is, consisting both of soul and body," argues Thomas Goodwin (*Works*, Edinburgh ed., 1862, iv. p. 140), "therefore he must needs have affections,—even affections proper to man's nature and truly human. And these he should have had, although this human nature had, from the very first assumption of it, been as glorious as it now is in heaven." "In what sense the soul is capable of suffering", says John Pearson (*An Exposition of the Creed*, New York ed., 1843, p. 288), "in that he was subject to animal passion. Evil apprehended to come tormented his soul with fear, which was as truly in him in respect of what he was to suffer, as hope in reference to the recompense of a reward to come after and from his sufferings."

nesses, the Redeemer must assume and sanctify in his own person all human πάθη, as naturally was eager to attribute to him in its fulness every human πάθος. Though in far less clearly defined forms, and with a complete shifting of their bases, both tendencies are still operative in men's thought of Jesus. There is a tendency in the interest of the dignity of his person to minimize, and there is a tendency in the interest of the completeness of his humanity to magnify, his affectional movements. The one tendency may run some risk of giving us a somewhat cold and remote Jesus, whom we can scarcely believe to be able to sympathize with us in all our infirmities. The other may possibly be in danger of offering us a Jesus so crassly human as scarcely to command our highest reverence. Between the two, the figure of Jesus is liable to take on a certain vagueness of outline, and come to lack definiteness in our thought. It may not be without its uses, therefore, to seek a starting point for our conception of his emotional life in the comparatively few[2] affectional movements which are directly assigned to him in the Gospel narratives. Proceeding outward from these, we may be able to form a more distinctly conceived and firmly grounded idea of his emotional life in general.

It cannot be assumed beforehand, indeed, that all the emotions attributed to Jesus in the Evangelical narratives are intended to be ascribed distinctively to his human soul.[3] Such is

[2] There is some exaggeration in the remark: "The notices in the Gospels of the impressions made on his feelings by different situations in which he was placed, are extraordinarily numerous" (James Stalker, Imago Christi, 1890, p. 302). The Gospel narratives are very objective, and it is only occasionally (most frequently in Mark) that they expressly notify the subjective movements of the actors in the drama which they unfold.

[3] Direct mention of our Lord's human 'soul', under that term (ψυχή), is not frequent in the Gospels: cf. Swete on Mk. xiv. 34, "Though the Gospels yield abundant evidence of the presence of human emotions in our Lord, (e. g. iii. 5, vi. 6, x. 14, Jno. vi. 33), this direct mention of his 'soul' has no parallel in them if we except Jno. vii. 27; for in such passages as x. 45, Jno. x. 11 ψυχή is the individual life (see Cremer s. v.) rather than the seat of the emotions." J. A. Alexander on Mk. xiv. 34 remarks that "my soul" there "is not a mere periphrasis for the pronoun,

no doubt the common view. And it is not an unnatural view to take as we currently read narratives, which, whatever else they contain, certainly present some dramatization of the human experiences of our Lord.[4] No doubt the naturalness of this view is its sufficient general justification. Only, it will be well to bear in mind that Jesus was definitely conceived by the Evangelists as a two-natured person, and that they made no difficulties with his duplex consciousness. In almost the same breath they represent him as declaring that he knows the Father through and through and, of course, also all that is in man, and the world which is the theatre of his activities, and that he is ignorant of the time of the occurrence of a simple earthly event which concerns his own work very closely; that he is meek and lowly in heart and yet at the same time the Lord of men by their relations to whom their destinies are determined, —" no man cometh unto the Father but by me." In the case of a Being whose subjective life is depicted as focusing in two centers of consciousness, we may properly maintain some reserve in ascribing distinctively to one or the other of them mental activities which, so far as their nature is concerned,

(1), but refers his strange sensations more directly to the inward seat of feeling and emotion." Cf., however, the Greek text of Ps. xlii. 6, 12, xlv. 5; but also Winer, *Grammar*, etc., Thayer's tr., 1872, p. 156. The term πνεῦμα occurs rather more frequently than ψυχή, to designate the seat of our Lord's emotions: Mk. viii. 12; Jno. xi. 33, xiii. 21; cf. Mk. ii. 8; Mt. xxvii. 50; Jno. xix. 30.

  [4] Such an attempt as that made by W. B. Smith (*Ecce Deus*, 1911, p. 101), to explain away the implication of our Lord's humanity in the earliest Gospel transmission, is, of course, only a " curiosity of literature." " Mark ", says he, " nowhere uses of Jesus an expression which suggests an impressive or even amiable human personality; or, indeed, any kind of human personality whatever." What Mark says of Jesus, is what is commonly said of God—of Jehovah. The seeming exceptions are merely specious. He ascribes " compassion " to Jesus: it is the very core of the oriental conception of God that he is merciful. He speaks of Jesus "rebuking" (ἐπιτιμάω) or "snorting at" (ἐμβριμάομαι) men: these are expressions suitable to God and employed in the Old Testament of Jehovah. He tells us that Jesus " loved " the rich young man—the *only* ascription of love to Jesus, by the way, in the Synoptics: but the rich young man is just a symbol, the symbol of Israel, whom Jehovah loves. And so on.

might properly belong to either. The embarrassment in studying the emotional life of Jesus arising from this cause, however, is more theoretical than practical. Some of the emotions
attributed to him in the Evangelical narrative are, in one way
or another, expressly assigned to his human soul. Some of
them by their very nature assign themselves to his human
soul. With reference to the remainder, just because they
might equally well be assigned to the one nature or the other, it
may be taken for granted that they belong to the human
soul, if not exclusively, yet along with the divine Spirit; and
they may therefore very properly be used to fill out the picture.
We may thus, without serious danger of confusion, go simply
to the Evangelical narrative, and, passing in review the definite
ascriptions of specific emotions to Jesus in its records, found
on them a conception of his emotional life which may serve
as a starting-point for a study of this aspect of our Lord's
human manifestation.

The establishment of this starting-point is the single task of
this essay. No attempt will be made in it to round out our view
of our Lord's emotional life. It will content itself with an
attempt to ascertain the exact emotions which are expressly assigned to him in the Evangelical narrative, and will leave
their mere collocation to convey its own lesson. We deceive
ourselves, however, if their mere collocation does not suffice
solidly to ground certain very clear convictions as to our Lord's
humanity, and to determine the lines on which our conception
of the quality of his human nature must be filled out.

I.

The emotion which we should naturally expect to find most
frequently attributed to that Jesus whose whole life was a mission of mercy, and whose ministry was so marked by deeds of
beneficence that it was summed up in the memory of his followers as a going through the land " doing good " (Acts xi. 38),
is no doubt "compassion". In point of fact, this is the emotion
which is most frequently attributed to him.[5] The term em-

[5] Mt. xx. 34; Mk. i. 41; Lk. vii. 13; Mt. ix. 36, xiv. 14, xv. 32; Mk.
vi. 34, viii. 2. Cf. Mk. ix. 22. Not at all in John.

ployed to express it[6] was unknown to the Greek classics, and was perhaps a coinage of the Jewish dispersion.[7] It first appears in common use in this sense, indeed, in the Synoptic Gospels,[8] where it takes the place of the most inward classical word of this connotation.[9] The Divine mercy has been defined as that essential perfection in God " whereby he pities and relieves the miseries of his creatures": it includes, that is to say, the two parts of an internal movement of pity and an external act of beneficence. It is the internal movement of pity which is emphasized when our Lord is said to be "moved with compassion" as the term is sometimes excellently rendered in the English versions.[10]   In the appeals made to his mercy, a more external word[11] is used; but it is this more internal word that is employed to express our Lord's response to these appeals: the petitioners besought him to take pity on them; his heart responded with a profound feeling of pity for them.   His

---

[6] Σπλαγχνίζομαι: see Bleek, *An Introduction to the New Testament*, § 33, (vol. i, p. 75)'; J. A. Alexander on Mk. i. 41; Plummer on Mt. ix. 36. Buttig's monograph, *De Emphasi* σπλαγχνίζομαι, we have not seen.

[7] So Lightfoot, on Phil. i. 8.

[8] It is found in the LXX in this metaphorical sense apparently only at Prov. xvii. 5. Cf. Swete on Mk. i. 41.

[9] Οἰκτείρω, which does not occur in the Synoptic Gospels, and indeed only once (Rom. ix. 15) in the N. T. The adjective, οἰκτίρμων occurs at Lk. ix. 36 (also Jas. v. 11 only in N. T.); the noun οἰκτιρμός, occurs in Paul (Rom. xii. 1; 2 Cor. i. 3; Phil. ii. 1; Col. iii. 12; also Heb. x. 28 only).

[10] A. V. Mk. i. 41, vi. 34; Mt. ix. 36, xiv. 14; R. V. Mk. i. 41; Mt. ix, 36, xx. 34.

[11] Ἐλεέω (sometimes, ἐλεάω), Mt. ix. 27, xv. 22, xvii. 15, xx. 30-31; Mk. x. 47-48; Lk. xvii. 13, xviii. 38-39; cf. Mk. v. 19; Mt. xviii. 33. This word also is not found in John. In Mk. ix. 22 only is σπλαγχνίζομαι used in an appeal, and even there its more subjective sense is apparent. On ἔλεος and its synonymy see J. H. Heinrich Schmidt, *Synonymik der griechischen Sprache* iii., 1879, § 143, pp. 572sq.; and the excellent summary statement by Thayer in Thayer-Grimm, *Lexicon etc., sub voc.* ἐλεέω. G. Heine, *Synonymik des N. T.-lichen Griechisch*, 898, p. 82, states it thus: "ἔλεος (חֶסֶד, חֵן) is the inclination to succor the miserable, οἰκτιρμός the feeling of pain arising from the miseries of others . . . οἰκτιρμός is the feeling of sympathy dwelling in the heart; ἔλεος is sympathy expressing itself in act." Σπλαγχνίζομαι is a term of feeling, taking the place of οἰκτείρω.

compassion fulfilled itself in the outward act;[12] but what is
emphasized by the term employed to express our Lord's response is, in accordance with its very derivation, the profound internal movement of his emotional nature.

This emotional movement was aroused in our Lord as well
by the sight of individual distress (Mk. i. 41; Mt. xx. 34;
Lk. vii. 13) as by the spectacle of man's universal misery
(Mk. vi. 34, viii. 2; Mt. ix. 36, xiv. 14, xv. 32). The appeal
of two blind men that their eyes might be opened (Mt. xx.
34), the appeal of a leper for cleansing (Mk. i. 41),—though
there may have been circumstances in his case which called
out Jesus' reprobation (verse 43),—set our Lord's heart throb-
bing with pity, as did also the mere sight of a bereaved widow,
wailing by the bier of her only son as they bore him forth
to burial,[13] though no appeal was made for relief (Lk.
vii. 13). The ready spontaneity of Jesus' pity is even more
plainly shown when he intervenes by a great miracle to relieve
temporary pangs of hunger: "I have compassion on "—or
better, "I feel pity for"—" the multitude, because they continue
with me now three days, and have nothing to eat: and if I

[12] W. Lütgert, *Die Liebe im Neuen Testament*, 1905, thinks it important to lay stress on this side of our Lord's love. "In the Synoptic
portrait of Christ the trait which stands out most clearly is the love of
Jesus. He not only commanded love, but first himself practiced it.
It is not merely his thought but his will, and not merely his will but above
all his deed. He therefore not only required it but aroused it. It
expresses itself accordingly not merely in his word, but in the first
instance in his act. Jesus' significance to the Synoptists does not
consist in his having discovered the command of love, but in his having
fulfilled it. For them Jesus is not a 'sage' who teaches old truths or
new, but a doer, who brings the truth true, that is, acts it out " (p. 53).
"His love never remains a powerless wish, that is, an unsuccessful
willing, but it always succeeds. The working of Jesus is described
in the Gospels as almighty love " (p. 54). "Since his acts are really love,
they have primarily no other purpose but to help. Their motive is
nothing but the compassion of Jesus" (p. 56). Accordingly, Lütgert
insists, no cry to Jesus for help was ever made in vain: "Jesus acts
precisely according to his own command, Give to him that asketh thee "
(p. 55).

[13] Render, not "he had ", but "he felt compassion ", to bring out the
emphasis on the " feeling ".

send them away fasting to their home, they will faint in the way; *and some of them are come from far*" (Mk. viii. 2; Mt. xv. 32),—the only occasion on which Jesus is recorded as testifying to his own feeling of pity. It was not merely the physical ills of life, however,—want and disease and death,— which called out our Lord's compassion. These ills were rather looked upon by him as themselves rooted in spiritual destitution. And it was this spiritual destitution which most deeply moved his pity. The cause and the effects are indeed very closely linked together in the narrative, and it is not always easy to separate them. Thus we read in Mark vi. 34: "And he came forth and saw a great multitude, and he had compassion on them"—better, "he felt pity for them",—"because they were as sheep not having a shepherd, and he taught them many things." But in the parallel passage in Mt. xiv. 14, we read: "And he came forth and saw a great multitude, and he had compassion on" ("felt pity for") "them, and he healed their sick." We must put the two passages together to get a complete account: their fatal ignorance of spiritual things, their evil case under the dominion of Satan in all the effects of his terrible tyranny, are alike the object of our Lord's compassion.[14] In another passage (Mt. ix. 36) the emphasis is thrown very distinctly on the spiritual destitution of the people as the cause of his compassionate regard: "But when he saw the multitude, he was moved with compassion for them, because they were distressed and scattered, as sheep not having a shepherd." This description of the spiritual destitution of the people is cast in very strong language. They are compared to sheep which have been worn out and torn by running hither and thither through the thorns with none to direct them, and have now fallen helpless and hopeless to the

[14] J. A. Alexander's note (on Mk. vi. 34, repeated verbally at Mt. ix. 36 and xiv. 14) is therefore too exclusive: "What excited his divine and human sympathy was not, of course, their numbers or their physical condition, but their spiritual destitution." It was both. Cf. Lütgert, as above, p. 68: "It is a characteristic trait of Jesus that he feels pity not merely for the religious, but also for the external, need of the people and that he acts out of this pity. The perfection of his love stands precisely in this—that it is independent of gratitude. He helps to help."

ground.[15]   The sight of their desperate plight awakens our
Lord's pity and moves him to provide the remedy.

No other term is employed by the New Testament writers
directly to express our Lord's compassion.[16]   But we read
elsewhere of its manifestation in tears and sighs.[17]   The tears
which wet his cheeks[18] when, looking upon the uncontrolled
grief of Mary and her companions, he advanced, with heart
swelling with indignation at the outrage of death, to the conquest of the destroyer (Jno. xi. 35), were distinctly tears of
sympathy.   Even more clearly, his own unrestrained wailing
over Jerusalem and its stubborn unbelief was the expression
of the most poignant pity: "O that thou hadst known in this
day, even thou, the things which belong unto peace" (Lk.
xix. 41)![19]   The sight of suffering drew tears from his
eyes; obstinate unbelief convulsed him with uncontrollable
grief.   Similarly when a man afflicted with dumbness and deaf-
ness was brought to him for healing we are only told that he
"sighed"[20] (Mk. vii. 34); but when the malignant unbelief of

[15] Cf. Plummer *in loc.*: "A strong word (ἐσκυλμένοι) is used to express their distress. . . Originally it meant 'flayed' or 'mangled', but
became equivalent to 'harassed' or 'vexed' with weariness or worry. . .
'Scattered' seems to suit shepherdless sheep, but it may be doubted if
this is the exact meaning of ἐρριμένοι. . . . 'Prostrated' seems to be
the meaning here."

[16] According to some commentators, συλλυπούμενος at Mk. iii. 5 expresses
sympathetic compassion (so e. g. Meyer, Weiss, Morrison, J. B. Bristow,
art. "Pity" in *DCG*); see note 36.   Some commentators also read
ἀγαθός, Mk. x. 18, of 'benevolence'; cf. κάλος, Jno. x. 11, 14.

[17] Cf. James Stalker, *Imago Christi,* 1890, p. 303.   "He not only gave
the required help in such cases, but gave it with an amount of sympathy
which doubled its value.   Thus, he not only raised Lazarus, but wept
with his sisters.   In curing a man who was deaf, he sighed as he said
'Ephphatha'.   All his healing work cost him feeling."

[18] Δακρύω, silent weeping: see Schmidt, *Synonymik der griechischen
Sprache,* I .1876, § 26, p. 470sq.

[19] Κλαίω, audible wailing: see Schmidt, as above.   Cf. Hahn *in loc.*:
"ἔκλαυσεν of the loud and violent wailing called out by an inner feeling
of pain. . . The contrast should be observed between the joyful out-
cry of his disciples, and the inner feeling of Jesus whose spirit saw the
true situation of things, undeceived by appearances."

[20] Στενάζω, "pitying as I think", comments Fritzsche, "the calamities
of the human race" and so Euth. Zig., Grotius, Meyer.   On the other

the Pharisees was brought home to him he " sighed from the bottom of his heart " (Mk. viii. 12).[21] " Obstinate sin ", comments Swete appropriately, " drew from Christ a deeper sigh than the sight of suffering (Lk. vii. 34 and cf. Jno. xiii. 20), a sigh in which anger and sorrow both had a part (iii. 4 note)." [22] We may, at any rate, place the loud wailing over the stubborn unbelief of Jerusalem and the deep sighing over the Pharisees' determined opposition side by side as exhibitions of the profound pain given to our Lord's sympathetic heart, by those whose persistent rejection of him required at his hands his sternest reprobation. He " sighed from the bottom of his heart " when he declared, " There shall no sign be given this generation "; he wailed aloud when he announced, " The days shall come upon thee when thine enemies shall dash thee to the ground." It hurt Jesus to hand over even hardened sinners to their doom.

It hurt Jesus,—because Jesus' prime characteristic was love, and love is the foundation of compassion. How close to one another the two emotions of love and compassion lie, may be taught us by the only instance in which the emotion of love is attributed to Jesus in the Synoptics (Mk. x. 21). Here we are told that Jesus, looking upon the rich young ruler, "loved"[23] him, and said to him, " One thing thou lackest." It is not the " love of complacency " which is intended, but the " love of benevolence "; that is to say, it is the love, not so much that finds good, as that intends good,—though we may no doubt allow that " love of compassion is never "—let us rather say, " seldom "—" absolutely separated from love of approbation ";[24] that is to say, there is ordinarily some good to be found

hand, DeWette, Weiss, Lagrange think the sigh, a sigh not of sympathy but of prayer (Rom. viii. 23, 26).

[21] 'Ἀναστενάζω, intensive form, here only in the N. T., but found in LXX. " The Lord's human spirit ", comments Swete, " was stirred to its depths."

[22] " In both cases ", Swete (on Mk. vii. 34) suggests, " perhaps the vast difficulty and long delays of the remedial work were borne in upon our Lord's human spirit in an especial manner."

[23] Ἠγάπησε. On the words for " love " see Schmidt, *Synonymik*, etc. III. 1879; § 136, pp. 474sq; ἀγαπάω, pp. 482sq.

[24] Morrison *in loc.* Cf. Lütgert, as cited, p. 59: " According to the Gospels, therefore, Jesus loves the needy. When Wernle maintains that

already in those upon whom we fix our benevolent regard. The heart of our Saviour turned yearningly to the rich young man and longed to do him good; and this is an emotion, we say, which, especially in the circumstances depicted, is not far from simple compassion.[25]

It is characteristic of John's Gospel that it goes with simple directness always to the bottom of things. Love lies at the bottom of compassion. And love is attributed to Jesus only once in the Synoptics, but compassion often; while with John the contrary is true—compassion is attributed to Jesus not even once, but love often. This love is commonly the love of compassion, or, rather, let us broaden it now and say, the love of

the Evangelists have shown us a Christ who leads his life 'in joy over nature and good men' (p. 63), this conception of Christ contradicts the earnestness of the Gospels through and through: it is precisely the characteristic of the Gospels that the motive of Jesus' love according to them, so far as it lies in men, is in the first instance negative. The people called out his compassion (Mt. ix. 36). Jesus' love does not have the character of admiration, but simply of *compassion*. It is not delight, but deed, gift, help. It required therefore a needy recipient. But the love of Jesus to the people has also a positive motive, which is, however, nowhere expressed,—that is, pleasure in their good." Cf. what Lütgert says, pp. 92sq., of the coexistence with Jesus' love of hate, directed to all that is evil in men.

[25] The negative side of the exposition is stated very well by Wohlenberg *in loc.*: "It would contradict fundamental elements of Jesus' preaching if those were right who hold that Jesus was inwardly of the young man's mind, and, looking upon him, conceived an affection for him, precisely because he had already made so much progress in keeping the divine commandments, and showed himself burning with enthusiasm for undertaking more. And how would this harmonize with what is afterwards said in verses 23 and 24sq. " . . . The positive side is given excellently by J. A. Alexander *in loc.*: " Most probably, love, as in many other places, here denotes not moral approbation, nor affection founded upon anything belonging to the object, but a sovereign and gratuitous compassion, such as leads to every act of mercy on God's part (compare Jno. iii. 16; Gal. ii. 20; Eph. ii. 4; 1 Jno. iv. 10, 19). The sense will then be, not that Jesus loved him on account of what he said, or what he was, or what he did, but that, having purposes of mercy towards him, he proceeded to unmask him to himself, and to show him how entirely groundless, although probably sincere, was his claim to have habitually kept the law. The Saviour's love is then mentioned, not as the effect of what precedes, but as the ground or motive of what follows."

benevolence; but sometimes it is the love of sheer delight in its object. Love to God is, of course, the love of pure complacency. We are surprised to note that Jesus' love to God is only once explicitly mentioned (Jno. xiv. 31); but in this single mention it is set before us as the motive of his entire saving work and particularly of his offering of himself up. The time of his offering is at hand, and Jesus explains: " I will no more speak much with you, for the prince of this world cometh; and he hath nothing in me; but [I yield myself to him] that the world may know that I love the Father, and as the Father gave me commandment, even so I do." [26] The motive of Jesus' earthly life and death is more commonly presented as love for sinful men; here it is presented as loving obedience to God. He had come to do the will of the Father; and because he loved the Father, his will he will do, up to the bitter end. He declares his purpose to be, under the impulse of love, " obedience up to death, yea, the death of the cross."

The love for man which moved Jesus to come to his succor in his sin and misery was, of course, the love of benevolence. It finds its culminating expression in the great words of Jno. xv. 13: " Greater love hath no man than this, that a man lay down his life for his friends: ye are my friends, if ye do the things which I command you "[27]—rather an illuminating definition of ' friends ', by the way, especially when it is followed by: " Ye did not choose me but I chose you and appointed you that ye should go and bear fruit." " Friends ", it is clear, in this definition, are rather those who are loved than those who love. This culminating expression of his love for his own, by which he was sustained in his great mission of humiliation for them, is supported, however, by repeated declarations of it in the immediate and wider context. In the immediately preceding verses, for example, it is urged as the motive and norm of the love—spring of obedience—which he seeks from his disciples: " Herein in my Father glorified, that ye bear much fruit; and so shall ye be my disciples. Even as my Father hath loved me,

---

[26] For the construction, see Westcott *in loc.* The term is, of course, ἀγαπάω.

[27] The term is ἀγάπη—although its correlative is οἱ φίλοι.

I also have loved you: abide ye in my love. If ye keep my commandments ye shall abide in my love; even as I have kept my Father's commandments, and abide in his love. These things have I spoken unto you, that my joy may be in you and that your joy may be fulfilled. This is my commandment, that ye love one another, even as I have loved you " (Jno. xv. 8-12). As his love to the Father was the source of his obedience to the Father, and the living spring of his faithfulness to the work which had been committed to him, so he declares that the love of his followers to him, imitating and reproducing his love to them, is to be the source of their obedience to him, and through that, of all the good that can come to human beings, including, as the highest reach of social perfection, their love for one another. Self-sacrificing love is thus made the essence of the Christian life, and is referred for its incentive to the self-sacrificing love of Christ himself: Christ's followers are to "have the same mind in them which was also in Christ Jesus." The possessive pronouns throughout this passage—" abide in *my* love ", " in *my* love ", " in *his* (the Father's) love "—are all subjective:[28] so that throughout the whole, it is the love which Christ bears his people which is kept in prominent view as the impulse and standard of the love he asks from his people. This love had already been adverted to more than once in the wider context (xiii. 1, 1, 34, xiv. 21) in the same spirit in which it is here spoken of. Its greatness is celebrated: he not only " loved his own which were in the world ", but " loved them utterly " (xiii. 1).[29] It is presented as the model for the

[28] Cf. Meyer *in loc.*: " The ἀγάπη ἡ ἐμή is not love *to me*, but: *my* love *to you*, as is clear from ἠγάπησα ὑμᾶς and from the analogy of ἡ χαρὰ ἡ ἐμή verse 11, cf. verses 12, 13." This instance carries the others with it. Westcott, if we understand him, wishes to take this phrase undifferentiatedly as including both the subjective and objective senses: " The meaning of the words cannot be limited to the idea of Christ's love for men, or to that of man's love for Christ: they describe the absolute love which is manifested in these two ways, the love which perfectly corresponds with Christ's being." " His love ", he apparently takes objectively, of love to God.

[29] Westcott: "to the uttermost": so Godet, etc. Lütgert, as cited, p. 154 note: "εἰς τέλος means, not ' until the end ' but ' to the utmost ', abso-

imitation of those who would live a Christian life on earth:
" even as I have loved you " (xiii. 34). It is propounded as
the Christian's greatest reward: " and I will love him and manifest myself unto him " (xiv. 21).

The emotion of love as attributed to Jesus in the narrative
of John is not confined, however, to these great movements—
his love to his Father which impelled him to fulfil all his
Father's will in the great work of redemption and his love
for those whom, in fulfilment of his Father's will, he had
chosen to be the recipients of his saving mercy, laying down
his life for them. There are attributed to him also those
common movements of affection which bind man to man in the
ties of friendship. We hear of particular individuals whom
"Jesus loved ", the meaning obviously being that his heart
knit itself to theirs in a simple human fondness. The term
employed to express this friendship is prevailingly that high
term which designates a love that is grounded in admiration
and fulfils itself in esteem;[30] but the term which carries with it
only the notion of personal inclination and delight is not
shunned.[31] We are given to understand that there was a particular one of our Lord's most intimate circle of disciples on
whom he especially poured out his personal affection. This
disciple came to be known, as, by way of eminence, " the disciple whom Jesus loved," though there are subtle suggestions

lutely; cf. 1 Thess. ii. 16; Lk. xviii. 5, and besides the parallels from
Hermas adduced by Jülicher, *Gleichnisreden Jesu*, II. p. 282, also Barnabas
iv. 6, εἰς τέλος ἀπώλεσαν αὐτήν and xix. 11, εἰς τέλος μισήσεις τὸν πονηρόν.
Therefore John too has the conception of complete, purified love."
In the text he had written: " The word xiii. 1 is a parallel to xii. 28.
According to the one word the life of Jesus hitherto is described as a
glorification of God, according to the other as love to his people. The
love which he practiced in his death, the Apostle places by the side
of the love which he had hitherto practiced: on the other hand it is distinguished from his love hitherto as an especial, new manifestation of
love. By the love which he practiced in his death, he loved them to the
uttermost. Now his love is become an absolute, purified love, for his
love first becomes absolute when he gives his soul. The death of Jesus
serves therefore for John not only as the last and highest proof of his
love, but as its perfecting."

[30] Ἀγαπάω: xi. 5, xiii. 23, xix. 26, xxi. 7, 20. Cf. Mk. x. 21.

[31] Φιλέω : xi. 3, 36, xx. 2.

that the phrase must not be taken in too exclusive a sense.[82]
Both terms, the more elevated and the more intimate, are
employed to express Jesus' love for him.[83] The love of Jesus
for the household at Bethany and especially for Lazarus, is
also expressly intimated to us, and it also by both terms,—
though the more intimate one is tactfully confined to his affection for Lazarus himself. The message which the sisters
sent Jesus is couched in the language of the warmest personal
attachment: " Behold, he whom thou lovest is sick "; and
the sight of Jesus' tears calls from the witnessing Jews an ex-
clamation which recognizes in him the tenderest personal feeling: " Behold, how he loved him! " But when the Evangelist
widens Jesus' affection to embrace the sisters also, he instinc-
tively lifts the term employed to the more deferential expression of friendship: " Now Jesus loved Martha, and her sister,
and Lazarus." Jesus' affection for Mary and Martha, while
deep and close, had nothing in it of an amatory nature, and
the change in the term avoids all possibility of such a misconception.[84] Meanwhile, we perceive our Lord the subject of those
natural movements of affection which bind the members of
society together in bonds of close fellowship. He was as far
as possible from insensibility to the pleasures of social intercourse (cf. Mt. xi. 19) and the charms of personal attractiveness. He had his mission to perform, and he chose his servants with a view to the performance of his mission. The relations of the flesh gave way in his heart to the relations of the
spirit: " whosoever shall do the will of my Father which is in
heaven, he is my brother, and sister, and mother" (Mt. xii.

---

[82] Jno. xx. 2, not " the disciple whom Jesus loved ", but " the *other* disciple
whom Jesus loved." Jesus loved both Peter and John. Cf. Westcott *in
loc.* Hence Westcott says (on xiii. 23) that the phrase " the disciple
whom Jesus loved ", " marks an acknowledgment of love and not an
exclusive enjoyment of love."

[83] Ἀγαπάω: xiii. 23, xix. 26, xxi. 7, 20; φιλέω: xx. 2.

[84] Cf. Meyer on Jno. xi. 5: " ἠγάπα : an expression chosen with delicate tenderness (the more sensuous φιλεῖν is not again used as in verse
4), because the *sisters* are mentioned ": and Westcott: " The Evangelist
describes the Lord's affection for this family as that of moral choice
(ἠγάπα . .)."

50) and it is "those who do the things which he commands them" whom he calls his "friends" (Jno. xv. 14). But he had also the companions of his human heart: those to whom his affections turned in a purely human attachment. His heart was open and readily responded to the delights of human association, and bound itself to others in a happy fellowship.[35]

II.

The moral sense is not a mere faculty of discrimination between the qualities which we call right and wrong, which exhausts itself in their perception as different. The judgments it passes are not merely intellectual, but what we call moral judgments; that is to say, they involve approval and disapproval according to the qualities perceived. It would be impossible, therefore, for a moral being to stand in the presence of perceived wrong indifferent and unmoved. Precisely what we mean by a moral being is a being perceptive of the difference between right and wrong and reacting appropriately to right and wrong perceived as such. The emotions of indignation and anger belong therefore to the very self-expression of a moral being as such and cannot be lacking to him in the presence of wrong. We should know, accordingly, without instruction that Jesus, living in the conditions of this earthly life under the curse of sin, could not fail to be the subject of the whole series of angry emotions, and we are not surprised that even in the brief and broken narratives of his life-experiences which have been given to us, there have been preserved records of the manifestation in word and act of not a few of them. It is interesting to note in passing that it is especially in the Gospel of Mark, which rapid and objective as it is in its narrative, is the channel through which has been preserved to us a large part of the most intimate of the details concerning our Lord's demeanor and traits which have come down to us, that we find these records.

It is Mark, for instance, who tells us explicitly (iii. 5) that the insensibility of the Jews to human suffering exhibited in

[35] Cf. Mt. xi. 19, Lk. vii. 34 (xii. 4), Jno. xi. 11 (xv. 14, 15).

a tendency to put ritual integrity above humanity, filled Jesus with indignant anger. A man whose hand had withered, met with in the synagogue one Sabbath, afforded a sort of test-case. The Jews treated it as such and " watched Jesus whether he would heal him on the Sabbath day, that they might accuse him." Jesus accepted the challenge. Commanding the man to " rise in the midst " of the assemblage, he put to them the searching question, generalizing the whole case: " Is it lawful to do good or to do evil on the Sabbath, to save life or to kill ? " " But ", says the narrative, " they kept silent." Then Jesus' anger rose: " he looked around at them with anger, being grieved at the hardness of their heart." What is meant is, not that his anger was modified by grief, his reprobation of the hardness of their hearts was mingled with a sort of sympathy for men sunk in such a miserable condition. What is meant is simply that the spectacle of their hardness of heart produced in him the deepest dissatisfaction, which passed into angry resentment.[36] Thus the fundamental psychology of anger is curiously illustrated by this account; for anger always has pain at its root, and is a reaction of the soul against what gives it discomfort.[37] The hardness of the Jews' heart, vividly realized, hurt Jesus; and his anger rose in repulsion of the cause of his pain. There are thus two movements of feeling brought before us here. There is the pain which the gross manifestation of the hardness of heart of the Jews inflicted on Jesus. And there is the strong reaction of indignation which sprang out of this pain. The term by which the former feeling is expressed has at its basis the simple idea of pain, and is

[36] The preposition in the participle συλλυπούμενος merely emphasizes the inwardness of the emotion (Thayer-Grimm, *Lexicon, etc. sub voc.* σύν, ii. 4). Cf. Fritsche *in loc.*: "Beza and Rosenmüller have properly seen that the preposition σύν is not without force. But their interpretation: *'when he had looked indignantly about him at the same time grieving,* etc.' would require ἅμα λυπούμενος and does not render the force of συλλυπούμενος. We have no doubt, therefore, that the preposition σύν, should be referred to the mind of Jesus, i. e., *'when he had looked about him with anger, grieving in his mind . . . he said'*"

[37] " It is " says James Denney (*DCG.,* I. p. 60) justly, "the vehement repulsion of that which hurts."

used in the broadest way of every kind of pain, whether physical or mental, emphasizing, however, the sensation itself,
rather than its expression.[38] It is employed here appropriately,
in a form which throws an emphasis on the inwardness of the
feeling, of the discomfort of heart produced in Jesus by the
sight of man's inhumanity to man. The expression of this
discomfort was in the angry look which he swept over the
unsympathetic assemblage. It is not intimated that the pain
was abiding, the anger evanescent. The glance in which the
anger was manifested is represented as fleeting in contrast
with the pain of which the anger was the expression. But the
term used for this anger is just the term for abiding resentment, set on vengeance.[39] Precisely what is ascribed to Jesus,
then, in this passage is that indignation at wrong, perceived as
such, wishing and intending punishment to the wrong-doer,
which forms the core of what we call vindicatory justice.[40]

[38] See Schmidt, *Synonymik* etc. II, 1878, § 83.14, pp. 588sq. Trench,
*Synonyms of the New Testament*⁷ 1871, p. 224: "This λύπη, unlike the
grief which the three following words [πενθέω, φρηνέω, κόπτω] express,
a man may so entertain in the deep of his heart, that there shall be no
outward manifestation of it, unless he himself be pleased to reveal it
(Rom. ix. 2)."

[39] See Schmidt, as above III, 1879, § 142: ὀργή is "wrath (*Zorn*) as
it is directed to punishment or vengeance" (p. 512); "ὀργή stands in
closer relation to the vengeance which is to be inflicted than θυμός " (p.
553); " it accordingly can be nothing else than the violently outbreaking
natural impulse, uncontrolled by the reason, which we call by the word
'wrath' (*Zorn*); and the idea that such an impulse seeks its end, and
therefore the thought of vengeance or punishment which this impulse seeks
to wreak on the guilty one, lies close " (p. 555). Cf. Trench, p. 124. Lütgert, as cited, pp. 96, 99, is careful to point out that Jesus' anger is never
personal, and never passes into revengeful feelings on his own behalf.

[40] Cf. "the wrath of the Lamb" Rev. vi. 16. Thomas Goodwin (*Works*,
IV. p. 144) wishes us to understand that when such emotional movements
are attributed to the Exalted Christ, they have their full quality as human
emotions, affecting the whole Christ body as well as spirit. "Therefore,
whenas we read of the 'wrath of the Lamb', as Rev. vi. 16, namely,
against his enemies, as here of his pity and compassion towards his
friends and members, why should this be attributed only to his deity, which
is not capable of wrath, or to his soul and spirit only? And why may it
not be thought he is truly angry as a man, in the whole man, and so with
such a wrath as his body is afflicted with, as well as that he is wrathful in

This is a necessary reaction of every moral being against perceived wrong.

On another occasion Mark (x. 14) pictures Jesus to us as moved by a much lighter form of the emotion of anger. His disciples,—doubtless with a view to protecting him from needless drafts upon his time and strength,—interfered with certain parents, who were bringing to him their babies (Lk. xviii. 15) " that he should touch them ". Jesus saw their action, and, we are told, " was moved with indignation." The term employed here[41] expresses, originally, physical (such, for example, as is felt by a teething child), and then mental (Mt. xx. 24, xxi. 15, xxvi. 8; Mk. x. 41, xiv. 4; Lk. xiii. 14, cf. 2 Cor. vii. 11) " irritation ". Jesus was " irritated ", or perhaps we may better render, was " annoyed ", " vexed ", at his disciples. And (so the term also suggests) he showed his annoyance,—whether by gesture or tone or the mere shortness of his speech: " Let the children come to me; forbid them not !" [42] Thus we see Jesus as he reacts with anger at the spectacle of inhumanity, so reacting with irritation at the spectacle of blundering misunderstanding, however well-meant.

Yet another phase of angry emotion is ascribed to Jesus by Mark, but in this case not by Mark alone. Mark (xiv. 3) tells us that on healing a leper, Matthew (ix. 30) that on healing two blind men, Jesus " straitly ", " strictly ", " sternly ", " charged " them,—as our English versions struggle with the term, in an attempt to make it describe merely the tone and manner of his injunction to the beneficiaries of his healing power, not to tell of the cures wrought upon them. This term,[43]

his soul only, seeing he hath taken up our whole nature, on purpose to subserve his divine nature in all the executions of it? "

[41] 'Αγανακτέω: see Schmidt, *Synonymik* etc. III, 1879, pp. 360-562: 'Αγανακτεῖν and ἀγανάκτησις designate, to wit, the *displeasure* (*Unwillen*) which we feel at an act in which we see a wrong (*Unrecht*) or which outrages our human sentiment and feeling" (p. 561). " Jesus " comments Lagrange *in loc.* " was irritated by their hardness."

[42] Swete *in loc.:* " We hear the Lord's indignant call, as it startles the disciples in the act of dismissing the party."

[43] 'Εμβριμάομαι : see especially the detailed discussion of this word by Fr. Gumlich in the *Theologische Studien und Kritiken*, 1862, pp. 260-269. " It is, now, exegetically certain that Jesus here (Jno. xi. 33) was

however, does not seem to mean, in its ordinary usage, to
"charge", to "enjoin", however straitly or strictly, but
simply to "be angry at", or, since it commonly implies
that the anger is great, to "be enraged with", or, perhaps
better still, since it usually intimates that the anger is
expressed by audible signs, to "rage against". If we are
to take it in its customary sense, therefore, what we are
really told in these passages is that Jesus, "when he had raged
against the leper, sent him away"; that "he raged against
the blind men, saying, 'See that no one know it!'" If
this rage is to be supposed (with our English versions) to
have expressed itself only in the words recorded, the meaning
would not be far removed from that of the English word
"bluster" in its somewhat rare transitive use, as, for example,
when an old author writes: "He meant to bluster all princes
into perfect obedience." [44] The implication of boisterousness,
and indeed of empty noise, which attends the English word,
however, is quite lacking from the Greek, the rage expressed by
which is always thought of as very real. What it has in common with "bluster" is thus merely its strong minatory import.
The Vulgate Latin accordingly cuts the knot by rendering it
simply "threatened", and is naturally followed in this by

angry. Only this, *open and vehement anger,* and no other meaning belongs philologically to ἐμβριμᾶσθαι''(p. 260, opening the discussion). "From
what has been said, it is sufficiently clear that, 1) βρέμω, just like *fremo*
always expresses, transferred to man, nothing but the active affection of
anger, never 'a general [mental movement]', least of all 'sorrow'; 2) that
moreover βρίμη and its frequentatively heightened and yet at the same
time interiorizing (ἐν) intensive ἐμβριμᾶσθαι, expresses only a strong,
or *the strongest degree* of wrath, which, precisely on account of this
strength being incapable of being held in, breaks out externally, but still
gives vent to itself rather in uncontrollable sound than words" (pp. 265-6,
closing the discussion). Cf. p. 209: "'Εμβριμᾶσθαι designates primarily
a *single* emotion, and this one is a vehement ebullition of his anger, a
real *infremere.*" Cf. Meyer on Jno. xi. 33: "The words βριμάομαι
and ἐμβριμάομαι are never used otherwise than of hot *anger* in the
Classics, the Septuagint, and the New Testament (Mt. ix. 30; Mk. i. 43,
xiv. 5), save when they denote snorting or growling proper (Aeschyl,
Sept. 461, Lucean, *Necyom.* 20."

[44] Fuller (Webster), about 1601, cited in *The Oxford Dictionary of the
English Language,* I. 951, where other citations also are given.

those English versions (Wycliffe, Rheims) which depend on
it.[45] Certainly Jesus is represented here as taking up a menacing attitude, and threatening words are placed on his lips:
" See that thou say nothing to any man," " See that no one
know it "—a form of speech which always conveys a threat.[46]
But "threaten" can scarcely be accepted as an adequate rendering of the term whether in itself or in these contexts.   When
Matthew tells us "And he was enraged at them, saying . . ."
the rage may no doubt be thought to find its outlet in the threatening words which follow :[47] but the implication of Mark is
different: " And raging at him ", or " having raged at him "
—" he straightway sent him forth."   When it is added: " And
saith to him, ' See that thou say nothing to any one ' " a subsequent moment in the transaction is indicated.[48]   How our Lord's
rage was manifested, we are not told.   And this is really just
as true in the case of Matthew as in that of Mark.   To say,
" he was enraged at them, saying (threatening words)," is
not to say merely, " he threatened them ": it is to say that a
threat was uttered and that this threat was the suitable accompaniment of his rage.

The cause of our Lord's anger does not lie on the surface
in either case.   The commentators seem generally inclined to
account for it by supposing that Jesus foresaw that his injunc-

[45] Certain late grammarians (see Stephens' *Thesaurus* sub. voc. ἐμβριμᾶσθαι and βριμόομαι) define βριμόομαι " to threaten "; and some of the
lexicographers do the like: Hesychius for example defines βρίμη as
"threat", and Suidas ἐμβριμᾶσθαι itself as " to speak with anger and
to blame with harshness ", the latter part of which is repeated in the
Etym. Mag.   A scholiast on Aristophanes, *Eq.* 855 defines βριμᾶσθαι as
" to be angry and to threaten ".

[46] Mt. viii. 4, ix. 30, xviii. 10, xxiv. 6; Mk. i. 44; 1 Thess. v. 15; Rev.
xix. 10, xxii. 9 only.

[47] So that Zahn (on Mt. ix. 30, p. 385) is misled into explaining: " He
admonished them in a menacing tone."   Something more than this is said.

[48] Meyer on Mk. i. 43 quite accurately connects the ἐμβριμησάμενος αὐτῷ
with ἐξέβαλεν only, translating: " after he had been angry at him,"
though he supposes the ἐξέβαλεν to have been accompanied by " a vehement
begone now! away hence! " and accordingly arbitrarily paraphrases the ἐμβριμησάμενος " wrathfully addressed him."   On Mt. ix. 30 he accurately
translates: "He was displeased with them, and said."

tion of silence would be disregarded.[49] But this explanation, little natural in itself, seems quite unsuitable to the narrative in Mark where we are told, not that Jesus angrily enjoined the leper to silence, but that he angrily sent him away. Others accordingly seek the ground of his anger in something displeasing to him in the demeanor of the applicants for his help, in their mode of approaching or addressing him, in erroneous conceptions with which they were animated, and the like. Klostermann imagines that our Lord did not feel that miraculous healings lay in the direct line of his vocation, and was irritated because he had been betrayed by his compassion into undertaking them. Volkmar goes the length of supposing that Jesus resented the over-reverential form of the address of the leper to him, on the principle laid down in Rev. xix. 10, " See thou do it not : I am a fellow-servant with thee." Even Keil suggests that Jesus was angry with the blind men because they addressed him openly as " Son of David ", not wishing " this untimely proclamation of him as Messiah on the part of those who held him as such only on account of his miracles." It is more common to point out some shortcoming in the applicants : they did not approach him with sufficient reverence or with sufficient knowledge of the true nature of his mission ; they demanded their cure too much as a matter of course, or too much as if from a mere marvel-monger ; and in the case of the leper at least, with too little regard to their own obligations. A leper should not approach a stranger ; certainly he should not ask or permit a stranger to put his hand upon him ; especially should he not approach a stranger in the streets

[49] J. A. Alexander, in Mt. ix. 30, puts this view in its most attractive form : " It can only mean a threatening in case of disobedience, charging them on pain of his serious displeasure and disapprobation." It comes to the same thing when Westcott (on Jno. xi. 33) says : " There is the notion of coercion springing out of displeasure." Cf. Morrison : " Peremptorily charged them " (Mk. i. 43) ; Zahn : " He enjoined them in a menacing tone " (Mt. ix. 30). Others, of course, transfer the matter from Christ to the Evangelists ; thus even Weiss can write (on Mt. ix. 39) : " Perhaps the Evangelist is thinking with respect to this ebullition of the resultlessness of such prohibitions, which is so strongly emphasized by Mark (cf. vii. 36)."

of a city (Lk. v. 12) and very particularly not in a house (Mk.
i. 43: "He put him *out*"), above all if it were, as it might
well be here, a private house. That Jesus was indignant at such
gross disregard of law was natural and fully explains his
vehemence in driving the leper out and sternly admonishing
him to go and fulfil the legal requirements.[50] This variety of
explanation is the index of the slightness of the guidance given
in the passages themselves to the cause of our Lord's anger;
but it can throw no doubt upon the fact of that anger, which is
directly asserted in both instances and must not be obscured by
attributing to the term by which it is expressed.some lighter
significance.[51] The term employed declares that Jesus exhibited vehement anger, which was audibly manifested.[52] This

[50] Three or four such comments on Mk. i. 43 as the following, when
read consecutively, are instructive. Weiss: "But obviously Mark thinks
of the healing as taking place in a house (ἐξέβαλεν), perhaps, according
to the connection with verse 39, in a synagogue. Entrance into the house
of another was, no doubt, forbidden to lepers, according to Lev. xiii. 46
cf. Num. v. 2 (see Ewald on the passages, and *Alterth.* p. 180), but
not altogether access to the synagogues: in any case the resort of the
people to Jesus and his healing of the sick broke through the restrictions
of the law, and from this also is explicable Jesus' demeanor of haste
and vehemence." Wohlenberg: "After or with the manifestation of
vehement anger, Jesus sends the man forthwith away (ἐξέβαλεν) from
his presence . . . and nothing indicates that Mark conceived the
occurrence to have taken place in a house. An intensely angry emotion
was exhibited by Jesus towards the healed man, because he observed
in him a false and perverse idea of the transaction." Keil: "The
occasion, however, of the angry expulsion of the healed man, we certainly are not to seek in the leper's breach of the law through entering
the house of another (Lev. xiii. 46 cf.. Num. v. 2) but chiefly in his
state of mind" . . . Edersheim (*Life and Times*, etc., I. 496): "This
['cast him out'], however, as Godet has shown (*Comm. on St. Luke*,
German trans. p. 137), does not imply that the event took place either in
a house or in a town, as most commentators suppose. It is, to say
the least, strange that the Speaker's Commentary, following Weiss,
should have located it in a synagogue! It could not possibly have occurred there, unless all Jewish ordinances and customs had been reversed."

[51] As e. g. Lagrange on Mk. i. 43: "'Εμβριμάομαι (again xiv. 5; Mt.
ix. 30; Jno. xi. 33, 38) cannot mean anger here, but only a certain
severity. Jesus speaks in a tone which does not admit of reply."

[52] Zahn on Mt. ix. 30 (p. 385) reminds us that the word suggests "the

anger did not inhibit, however, the operation of his compassion (Mk. i. 41; Mt. ix. 27) but appears in full manifestation as its accompaniment. This may indicate that its cause lay outside the objects of his compassion, in some general fact the nature of which we may possibly learn from other instances.

The same term occurs again in John's narrative of our Lord's demeanor at the grave of his beloved friend Lazarus (Jno. xi. 33, 38). When Jesus saw Mary weeping—or rather "wailing", for the term is a strong one and implies the vocal expression of the grief[53]—and the Jews which accompanied her also "wailing", we are told, as our English version puts it, that "he *groaned* in the spirit and was troubled"; and again, when some of the Jews, remarking on his own manifestation of grief in tears, expressed their wonder that he who had opened the eyes of the blind man could not have preserved Lazarus from death, we are told that Jesus "again *groaned* in himself." The natural suggestion of the word "groan" is, however, that of pain or sorrow, not disapprobation; and this rendering of the term in question is therefore misleading. It is better rendered in the only remaining passage in which it occurs in the New Testament, Mk. xiv. 5, by "murmured", though this is much too weak a word to reproduce its implications. In that passage it is brought into close connection with a kindred term[54] which determines its meaning. We read: "But there were some that had indignation among themselves . . . and they murmured against her." Their feeling of irritated displeasure expressed itself in an outburst of temper. The margin of our Revised Version at Jno. xi. 33, 38, therefore, very properly proposes that we should for "groaned" in these passages, substitute "moved with indignation", although that phrase too is scarcely strong enough. What John tells us, in point of fact, is that Jesus approached

audible expression of wrath". Cf. Mk. xiv. 4-5 where we are told that "there were some that had indignation (ἀγανακτοῦντες), among themselves—and they murmured (ἐνεβριμῶντο) against her". The inward emotion is expressed by ἀγανακτέω, its manifestation in audible form by ἐμβριμάομαι.

[53] See above, note 19; and cf. Gumlich, *TSK*, 1862, p. 258.

[54] Ἀγανακτέω : see above, notes 41 and 52.

the grave of Lazarus, in a state, not of uncontrollable grief,
but of irrepressible anger. He did respond to the spectacle
of human sorrow abandoning itself to its unrestrained expression, with quiet, sympathetic tears: "Jesus wept" (verse
36).[55] But the emotion which tore his breast and clamored
for utterance was just rage. The expression even of this rage,
however, was strongly curbed. The term which John employs
to describe it is, as we have seen, a definitely external term.[56]
"He raged." But John modifies its external sense by annexed qualifications: "He raged *in spirit*," "raging *in himself*." He thus interiorizes the term and gives us to understand that the ebullition of Jesus' anger expended itself within
him. Not that there was no manifestation of it: it must have
been observable to be observed and recorded;[57] it formed a
marked feature of the occurrence as seen and heard.[58] But
John gives us to understand that the external expression of our
Lord's fury was markedly restrained: its manifestation fell
far short of its real intensity. He even traces for us the movements of his inward struggle: "Jesus, therefore, when he
saw her wailing, and the Jews that had come with her wailing, was enraged in spirit and troubled himself"[59] . . . and
wept. His inwardly restrained fury produced a profound agitation of his whole being, one of the manifestations of which
was tears.

, Why did the sight of the wailing of Mary and her companions enrage Jesus? Certainly not because of the extreme
violence of its expression; and even more certainly not because
it argued unbelief—unwillingness to submit to God's providen-

---

[55] Δακρύω (not κλαίω as in verse 33): see above, note 18.

[56] See above: note 43.

[57] So Hengstenberg, in particular, and many after him.

[58] John Hutchison, *The Monthly Interpreter*, 1885, II. p. 286: "A
storm of wrath was seen to sweep over him."

[59] Καὶ ἐτάραξεν ἑαυτόν. Many commentators insist on the voluntari-
ness of Jesus' emotion, expressed by this phrase. Thus John Hutchison,
as above, p. 288: "It was an act of his own free will, not a passion
hurrying him on, but a voluntarily assumed state of feeling which
remained under his direction and control. . . In a word there was no
ἀταξία in it." For the necessary limitations of this view see Calvin
on this passage. Cf. Lütgert as cited, p. 145.

tial ordering or distrust of Jesus' power to save. He himself wept, if with less violence yet in true sympathy with the grief of which he was witness. The intensity of his exasperation, moreover, would be disproportionate to such a cause; and the importance attached to it in the account bids us seek its ground in something less incidental to the main drift of the narrative. It is mentioned twice, and is obviously emphasized as an indispensable element in the development of the story, on which, in its due place and degree, the lesson of the incident hangs. The spectacle of the distress of Mary and her companions enraged Jesus because it brought poignantly home to his consciousness the evil of death, its unnaturalness, its " violent tyranny " as Calvin (on verse 38) phrases it. In Mary's grief, he " contemplates "—still to adopt Calvin's words (on verse 33),—" the general misery of the whole human race " and burns with rage against the oppressor of men. Inextinguishable fury seizes upon him; his whole being is discomposed and perturbed; and his heart, if not his lips, cries out,—

> " For the innumerable dead
> Is my soul disquieted." [60]

It is death that is the object of his wrath, and behind death him who has the power of death, and whom he has come into the world to destroy. Tears of sympathy may fill his eyes, but this is incidental. His soul is held by rage: and he advances to the tomb, in Calvin's words again, " as a champion who prepares for conflict." The raising of Lazarus thus becomes, not an isolated marvel, but—as indeed it is presented throughout the whole narrative (compare especially, verses 24-26)—a decisive instance and open symbol of Jesus' conquest of death and hell. What John does for us in this particular statement is to uncover to us the heart of Jesus, as he wins for us our salvation. Not in cold unconcern, but in flam-

---

[60] Cf. John Hutchison, as above, p. 375: " He was gazing into ' the skeleton face of the world ', and tracing everywhere the reign of death. The whole earth to him was but ' the valley of the shadow of death ', and in these tears which were shed in his presence, he saw that

> ' Ocean of Time, whose waters of deep woe,
> Are brackish with the salt of human tears '."

ing wrath against the foe, Jesus smites in our behalf. He has
not only saved us from the evils which oppress us; he has
felt for and with us in our oppression, and under the impulse
of these feelings has wrought out our redemption.[61]

There is another term which the Synoptic Gospels employ
to describe our Lord's dealing with those he healed (Mt. xii.
16), which is sometimes rendered by our English versions—as
the term we have just been considering is rendered in similar
connections (Mk. i. 43; Mt. ix. 30)—by "charged" (Mt. xii.
16, xvi. 20; Mk. iii. 12, viii. 30, ix. 21); but more frequently
with more regard to its connotation of censure, implying displeasure, "by rebuked" (Mt. xvii. 18; Mk. ix. 21; Lk. iv. 35-
41, xix. 42; Mk. viii. 30; Lk. ix. 55; Mt. viii. 20; Mk. iv. 39;
Lk. iv. 39, viii. 24).[62] This term, the fundamental meaning of
which is "to mete out due measure", with that melancholy
necessity which carries all terms which express doing justice
to sinful men downwards in their connotation, is used in the
New Testament only *in malam partem,* and we may be quite
sure is never employed without its implication of censure.[63]
What is implied by its employment is that our Lord in work-

---

[61] The classical exposition of the whole passage is F. Gumlich's, *Die
Räthsel der Erweckung Lazari,* in the *Theologische Studien und Kritiken,*
1862, pp. 65-110, and 248-336. See also John Hutchison, in *The Monthly
Interpreter,* 1885, II. pp. 281-296 and 374-386.

[62] Ἐπιτιμάω: See Schmidt, *Synonymik* etc. I. 1876, § 4, 11, p. 147:
"ἐπιτιμᾶν is properly to impute something to one (as a fault) . . .
And indeed it denotes harsh and in general vehement reproaches with
reference to unworthy deeds or customs, construed ordinarily with the
dative of the person: to condemn with harsh words, to heap reproaches
on." Cf. also Trench, § 4 (p. 12).

[63] Swete, on Mk. i. 25: "ἐπιτιμᾶν, Vg. comminari, Wycliffe and Rheims
'threaten', other English Versions, 'rebuke': the strict meaning of
the word is 'to mete-out due measure', but in the N. T. it is used only
of censure". Plummer on Lk. iv. 35: "In N. T. ἐπιτιμάω has no other
meaning than 'rebuke'; but in classical Greek it means—1. 'lay a value
on, *rate*'; 2. 'lay a penalty on, sentence'; 3. 'chide, *rate, rebuke*'."
"The verb is often used of rebuking *violence* (verse 41, viii. 24, ix. 42;
Mt. viii. 26, xviii. 18; Mk. iv. 39; Jud. ix); yet must not on that account
be rendered 'restrain' (Fritzsche on Mt. viii. 26, p. 325)." Morrison
accordingly thinks that "rated" might give the essential meaning of the
word. Lagrange (on Mk. i. 28) unduly weakens the term.

ing certain cures, and, indeed, in performing others of his miracles—as well as in laying charges on his followers—spoke, not merely " strongly and peremptorily ",[64] but chidingly, that is to say, with expressed displeasure.[65] There is in these instances perhaps not so strong but just as clear an ascription of the emotion of anger to our Lord as in those we have already noted, and this suggests that not merely in the case of the raising of Lazarus but in many other instances in which he put forth his almighty power to rescue men from the evils which burdened them, our Lord was moved by an ebullition of indignant anger at the destructive powers exhibited in disease or even in the convulsions of nature.[66] In instances like Mt. xii. 16; Mk. iii. 12; Mt. xvi. 20; Mk. viii. 30; Lk. ix. 21, the censure inherent in the term may almost seem to become something akin to menace or threat: " he chided them to the end that they should not make him known;" he made a show of anger or displeasure directed to this end. In the cases where, however, Jesus chided the unclean spirits which he cast out it seems to lie in the nature of things that it was the tyrannous evil which they were working upon their victims that was the occasion of his displeasure.[67] When he is said to have " rebuked " a fever which was tormenting a human being (Lk. iv. 39) or the natural elements—the wind and sea—menacing human lives (Mt. viii. 26; Mk. iv. 39; Lk. viii. 24), there is no reason to suppose that he looked upon these natural powers as themselves personal, and as little that the personification is only figurative; we may not

[64] Morrison on Mk. iii. 12.

[65] Hahn on Lk. iv. 35: "ἐπιτίμησεν αὐτῷ, that is, he vehemently commanded him, charged him with strong, chiding words (cf. verses· 39, 41, viii. 24, ix. 21, 42, 55), an expression by which Luke would say that Jesus spoke the following words in a tone of highest displeasure:" cf. on verse 39.

[66] Cf. Gumlich, TSK, 1862 p. 287: " Similar movements of anger, ἐπιτιμᾶν instead of ἐμβριμᾶσθαι directly before or after a miracle, we find also elsewhere in him: threats (Bedrohen) to the wind and the sea (Mt. viii. 26), most frequently in the case of healings of possessed people of a difficult kind (Mt. viii. 26, vii. 18; Mk. ix. 21, i. 25, iii. 12; Lk. iv. 41)."

[67] In Mk. viii. 33; Lk. ix. 55 the objects of his displeasure were his followers.

improperly suppose that the displeasure he exhibited in his up-braiding them was directed against the power behind these manifestations of a nature out of joint, the same malignant in-fluence which he advanced to the conquest of when he drew near to the tomb of Lazarus.[68]   In any event the series of pas-sages in which this term is employed to ascribe to Jesus acts inferring displeasure, greatly enlarges the view we have of the play of Jesus' emotions of anger.   We see him chiding his disciples, the demons that were tormenting men, and the natural powers which were menacing their lives or safety, and speak-ing in tones of rebuke to the multitudes who were the recipients of his healing grace (Mt. xii. 16).   And that we are not to suppose that this chiding was always mild we are advised by

[68] Cf. Zahn, *Das Evangelium des Johannes,* 1908, p. 480, note 82: " Since Jesus, without prejudice to his faith in the all-embracing providence and universal government of God, looked upon all disease, and not merely possession, as the work of Satan (Lk. xiii. 16, x. 19, cf. Acts xvi. 38; 2 Cor. xii. 7), and held him to be the author not only of isolated miseries, but of the death of man in general (Jno. viii. 44) ; Heb. ii. 14 does not go beyond Jesus' circle of ideas."—Also Henry Norris Bernard, *The Mental Characteristics of the Lord Jesus Christ,* 1888, pp. 90-91 : " The miracles of Christ formed part of that warfare which was ever waging between the Son of God and the power of evil which he was manifested to destroy.   The rage of the elements, the roaring wind, and the surging waves ever seeking to engulf the fishers' boat; the fell sickness racking with pain man's body; the paralysis of the mental powers destroying man's intellect, and leaving him a prey to unreasoning violence, or to unclean desires; the death which shrouded him in the unknown darkness of the tomb—these things were to the Saviour's vision but objective forms of the curse of sin which it was his mission to remove.   The Kingdom of God and the Kingdom of Satan were brought together in opposition. The battle between the Lord's Christ and the great adversary was ever going on.   Man's infirmities and his sicknesses, in the eyes of Christ, were the outward symbols of the sin which was their cause.   So the inspired writer, in the healing of the sick, and in the casting out of devils, sees direct blows given, which, in the end, shall cause Satan's empire to totter to its fall.   Every leper cleansed, every blind man restored to sight, every helpless paralytic made to walk, every distracted man brought back to the sweetness of life and light of reason, above all the dead recalled to life—each, in the salvation accorded them, furnished a proof that a greater than Satan was here, and that the Kingdom of God was being manifested upon earth."

the express declaration that it was in one instance at least, " vehement " (Mk. iii. 12).[69]

Perhaps in no incidents recorded in the Gospels is the action of our Lord's indignation more vividly displayed than in the accounts of the cleansings of the Temple. In closing the account which he gives of the earlier of these, John tells us that " his disciples remembered that it was written, The zeal of thine house shall eat me up " (Jno. ii. 17). The word here employed—" zeal "—may mean nothing more than " ardor "; but this ardor may burn with hot indignation,—we read of a " zeal of fire which shall devour the adversaries " (Heb. x. 27). And it seems to be this hot indignation at the pollution of the house of God—this " burning jealousy for the holiness of the house of God " [70]—which it connotes in our present passage. In this act, Jesus in effect gave vent " to a righteous anger ",[71] and perceiving his wrathful zeal[72] his followers recognized in it the Messianic fulfilment of the words in which the Psalmist represents himself as filled with a zeal for the house of Jehovah, and the honor of him who sits in it, that " consumes him like a fire burning in his bones, which incessantly breaks through and rages all through him." [73] The form in which it here breaks forth is that of indignant anger towards those who defile God's house with traficking, and it thus presents us with one of the most striking manifestations of the anger of Jesus in act.

It is far, however, from being the only instance in which the action of Jesus' anger is recorded for us. And the severity of his language equals the decisiveness of his action. He does

[69] Cf. Swete *in loc.;* also Lagrange: "πολλά, taken adverbially, does not mean in Mk. 'often', nor even 'in a prolonged fashion', but 'earnestly', 'strongly', 'greatly' (except perhaps in i. 45); cf. v. 10, 23, 43, vi. 20, ix. 26; the Vulgate has, therefore, well rendered it *vehementer* (here and xvi. 43)."

[70] Westcott *in loc.*

[71] Zahn *in loc.:* p. 168.

[72] Meyer *in loc.:* " In this wrathful zeal which they saw had taken hold of Jesus, they thought they saw the Messianic fulfilment of that word of the psalm. . . . "

[73] Delitzsch *in loc.*

not scruple to assault his opponents with the most vigorous denunciation. Herod he calls " that fox " (Lk. xiii. 32) ; the unreceptive, he designates briefly " swine " (Mt. vii. 6) ; those that tempt him he visits with the extreme term of ignominy— Satan (Mk. viii. 33). The opprobrious epithet of " hypo- crites " is repeatedly on his lips (Mt. xv. 7, xxiii. passim; Lk. xiii. 15), and he added force to this reprobation by clothing it in violent figures,—they were " blind guides ", " whited sepul- chres ", and, less tropically, " a faithless and perverse genera- tion ", a " wicked and adulterous generation ". He does not shrink even from vituperatively designating them ravening wolves (Mt. vii. 15), serpents, brood of vipers (Mt. xii. 34), even children of the evil one : " Ye are ", he declares plainly, " of your father, the Devil " (Jno. viii. 44). The long arraign- ment of the Pharisees in the twenty-third chapter of Matthew with its iterant, " Woe unto you, Scribes and Pharisees, hypo- crites ! " and its uncompromising denunciation, fairly throbs with indignation, and brings Jesus before us in his sternest mood, the mood of the nobleman in the parable (Lk. xix. 27), whom he represents as commanding: "And as for these my enemies, bring them hither and slay them before me." [74]

The holy resentment of Jesus has been made the subject of a famous chapter in *Ecco Homo*.[75] The contention of this chap- ter is that he who loves men must needs hate with a burning hatred all that does wrong to human beings, and that, in point of fact, Jesus never wavered in his consistent resentment of the special wrong-doing which he was called upon to witness. The chapter announces as its thesis, indeed, the paradox that true mercy is no less the product of anger than of pity: that what differentiates the divine virtue of mercy from " the vice

[74] Cf. James Denney, article " Anger ", and E. Daplyn, article " Fierce- ness ", in Hastings' *DCG*. Also Lütgert, as cited, p. 97 where instances of our Lord's expressions of anger, " which occupy a large place in the Synoptics " are gathered together, and p. 99 where it is pointed out that " Jesus grounds his declarations of woe, not on what his opponents had done to him, but purely on their sins against the law and the prophets . . . Jesus' anger remains therefore pure because it burns against what is done against God, and not against what has happened to himself ".

[75] Chapter xxi. " The Law of Resentment."

of insensibility " which is called " tolerance ", is just the underlying presence of indignation. Thus—so the reasoning runs,—
" the man who cannot be angry cannot be merciful," and it
was therefore precisely the anger of Christ which proved that
the unbounded compassion he manifested to sinners " was
really mercy and not mere tolerance." The analysis is doubtless incomplete; but the suggestion, so far as it goes, is fruitful. Jesus' anger is not merely the seamy side of his pity; it
is the righteous reaction of his moral sense in the presence of
evil. But Jesus burned with anger against the wrongs he met
with in his journey through human life as truly as he melted
with pity at the sight of the world's misery : and it was out of
these two emotions that his actual mercy proceeded.

III.

We call our Lord " the Man of Sorrows ", and the designation is obviously appropriate for one who came into the world
to bear the sins of men and to give his life a ransom for many.
It is, however, not a designation which is applied to Christ in
the New Testament, and even in the Prophet (Is. liii. 3) it
may very well refer rather to the objective afflictions of the
righteous servant than to his subjective distresses.[76] In any
event we must bear in mind that our Lord did not come into the
world to be broken by the power of sin and death, but to break
it. He came as a conqueror with the gladness of the imminent
victory in his heart; for the joy set before him he was able
to endure the cross, despising shame (Heb. xii. 2). And as
he did not prosecute his work in doubt of the issue, neither
did he prosecute it hesitantly as to its methods. He rather
(so we are told, Lk. x. 21) " exulted in the Holy Spirit " as
he contemplated the ways of God in bringing many sons to
glory. The word is a strong one and conveys the idea of exuberant gladness, a gladness which fills the heart;[77] and it is

[76] So e. g. Cheyne, G. A. Smith, Skinner, Workman.

[77] Ἀγαλλιάομαι : see G. Heine, *Synonymik des N.T.-lichen Griechisch*
1898, p. 147 : " χαίρω in general, *gaudeo, laetor* (χαρά, שָׂמַח), ἀγαλλιάω, -ομαι
(גִּיל) *exsulto, vehementer gaudeo*, Mt. v. 12; Lk. x. 21 (ἀγαλλίασις)
Lk i. 14, 44, *summum gaudium* (frequently in LXX; not classical) ".

intimated that, on this occasion at least, this exultation was a product in Christ—and therefore in his human nature—of the operations of the Holy Spirit,[78] whom we must suppose to have been always working in the human soul of Christ, sustaining and strengthening it.   It cannot be supposed that, this particular occasion alone being excepted, Jesus prosecuted his work on earth in a state of mental depression.   His advent into the world was announced as "good tidings of great joy" (Lk. ii. 10), and the tidings which he himself proclaimed were " the good tidings " by way of eminence.   Is it conceivable that he went about proclaiming them with a " sad countenance " (Mt. vi. 16) ?   It is misleading then to say merely, with Jeremy Taylor, " We never read that Jesus laughed and but once that he rejoiced in spirit."[79]   We do read that, in con-

There is a good brief account of the word given by C. F. Gelpe, in the *Theologische Studien und Kritiken*, 1849, pp. 645-646: " the profoundest and highest transport ".   Cf. Godet *in   loc.* " Ἀγαλλιᾶσθαι, to *exult*, denotes an inner transport, which takes place in the same deep regions of the soul of Jesus as the opposite emotion expressed by the ἐμβριμᾶσθαι, to *groan* (Jno. xi. 33).   This powerful influence of external events on the inner being of Jesus proves how thoroughly in earnest the Gospels take his humanity."

[78] Plummer *in loc.*:   " This joy is a divine inspiration.   The fact is analogous to his being ' led by the Spirit in the wilderness ', (iv. 1)."

[79] *The Whole Works of Jeremy Taylor.*   Ed. Heber, London 1828. II. p. lxvii.   Jeremy Taylor's object is to show that Christ is not imitable by us in everything; hence he proceeds at once: " But the declensions of our natures cannot bear the weight of a perpetual grave deportment, without the intervals of refreshment and free alacrity."   This whole view of our Lord's deportment lacks justification: but it has been widely held from the earliest times.   Basil the Great, for instance, in condemning immoderate mirth, appeals to our Lord's example,—although he accounts for his deportment on a theory which bears traces of the " apathetic " ideal of virtue so wide-spread in his day.   " And the Lord appears to have sustained " says he (*Regulae fusius Tractatae,* 17: Migne, *PG.* xxxi. p. 961), " the passions which are necessary to the flesh and whatever of them bear testimony to virtue, such as weariness, and pity to the afflicted: but never to have used laughter, so far as may be learned from the narrative of the Evangelists, but to have pronounced a woe upon those who are held by it (Lk. vi. 25)."   Chrysostom (*Hom. vi in Matth.:* Migne, *PG.* lvii, p. 69) in commending a grave life by the example of Christ, exaggerates the matter: " If thou also weep thus, thou hast become an imitator of thy Lord.   For he also himself wept, both over Lazarus

trast with John the Baptist, he came " eating and drinking ", and accordingly was malignantly called " a gluttonous man and a wine-bibber, a friend of publicans and sinners" (Mt. xi. 19; Lk. vii. 34); and this certainly does not encourage us to think of his demeanor at least as habitually sorrowful.

It is pure perversion, to be sure, when Renan, after the debasing fashion of his sentimentalizing frivolity, transmutes Jesus' joy in his redemptive work (Jno. xv. 11, xvii. 13) into mere pagan lightness of heart and delight in living, as if his fundamental disposition were a kind of " sweet gaiety " which " was incessantly expressing itself in lively reflections, and kindly pleasantries." He assures us that Jesus travelled about Palestine almost as if he was some lord of revelry, bringing a festival wherever he came, and greeted at every doorstep " as a joy and a benediction ": " the women and children adored him." The infancy of the world had come back with him " with its divine spontaneity and its naïve dizzinesses of joy." At his touch the hard conditions of life vanished from sight, and there took possession of men, the dream of an imminent paradise, of " a delightful garden in which should continue forever the charming life they now were living." " How long ", asks Renan, " did this intoxication last? ", and answers: " We do not know. During the continuance of this magical apparition, time was not measured. Duration was suspended; a week was a century. But whether it filled years or months, the dream was so beautiful that humanity has lived on it ever since, and our consolation still is to catch its fading fragrance. Never did so much joy stir the heart of man. For a moment in this most vigorous attempt it has ever made to lift itself above its planet, humanity forgot the leaden weight which holds it to the earth and the sorrows of the life here below. Happy he who could see with his own eyes this divine effloresence and share, if even for a day, this unparalleled illusion!" [80]

The perversion is equally great, however, when there is

and over the city; and touching Judas he was greatly troubled. And this, indeed, he is often to be seen doing, but never laughing (γελῶντα), and not even smiling even a little; at least no one of the Evangelists has mentioned it."

[80] *Vie de Jésus*, ch. xi. *ad fin.*; ed. 2. 1863, pp. 188-194.

attributed to our Lord, as it is now very much the fashion to
do, "before the black shadow of the cross fell athwart his
pathway," the exuberant joy of a great hope never to be fulfilled: the hope of winning his people to his side and of inau-
gurating the Kingdom of God upon this sinful earth by the
mere force of its proclamation.[81] Jesus was never the victim
of any such illusion: he came into the world on a mission
of ministering mercy to the lost, giving his life as a ransom
for many (Lk. xix. 10; Mk. x. 4; Mt. xx. 28); and from the
beginning he set his feet steadfastly in the path of suffering
(Mt. iv. 3 f.; Lk. iv. 3 f.) which he knew led straight onward
to death (Jno. ii. 19, iii. 14; Mt. xii. 40; Lk. xii. 49-50; Mt.
ix. 15; Mk. ii. 1-9; Lk. v. 34, etc.). Joy he had: but it was
not the shallow joy of mere pagan delight in living, nor the de-
lusive joy of a hope destined to failure; but the deep exultation
of a conqueror setting captives free. This joy underlay all
his sufferings and shed its light along the whole thorn-beset
path which was trodden by his torn feet. We hear but little
of it, however, as we hear but little of his sorrows: the narratives are not given to descriptions of the mental states of the
great actor whose work they illustrate. We hear just enough
of it to assure us of its presence underlying and giving its color
to all his life (Lk. iv. 21;[82] Jno. v. 11, xvii. 13[83]). If our
Lord was "the Man of Sorrows", he was more profoundly
still "the Man of Joy".[84]

[81] Cf. the article "Foresight" in Hastings' *DCG*. See for example, A.
Jülicher, *Die Gleichnisreden Jesu,* I. p. 144; Paul Wernle, *Die Anfänge
unserer Religion,* p. 65: "There was a time in Jesus' life, when a wholly
extraordinary hope filled his soul. . . Then, Jesus knew himself to be
in harmony with all the good forces of his people . . . that was the
happiest time of his life. . . . We only need to ask whether Jesus
retained this enthusiastic faith to the end. To that period of joyful hope
there succeeded a deep depression."

[82] Ἀγαλλιάομαι ; see note 77 above.

[83] Χαρά: consult also the use in parables of both χαρά, Mt. xxv. 21, 23;
Lk. xv. 10, and χαίρω, Mt. xviii. 13; Lk. xv. 5, 32.

[84] A. B. Bruce, *The Humiliation of Christ,*[2] 1881, p. 334: "Hence,
though a man of sorrow, he was even on earth anointed with the oil
of gladness above his fellows. . . . Shall we wonder that there was
divine gladness in the heart of him who came into the world, not by
constraint, but willingly; not with a burning sense of wrong, but with a

Of the lighter pleasurable emotions that flit across the mind in response to appropriate incitements arising occasionally in the course of social intercourse, we also hear little in the case of Jesus. It is not once recorded that he laughed; we do not ever hear even that he smiled; only once are we told that he was glad, and then it is rather sober gratification than exuberant delight which is spoken of in connection with him (Jno. xi. 15). But, then, we hear little also of his passing sorrows. The sight of Mary and her companions wailing at the tomb of Lazarus, agitated his soul and caused him tears (Jno. xi. 35); the stubborn unbelief of Jerusalem drew from him loud wailing (Lk. xix. 41). He sighed at the sight of human suffering (Mk. vii. 34) and " sighed deeply " over men's hardened unbelief (viii. 12): man's inhumanity to man smote his heart with pain (iii. 5). But it is only with reference to his supreme sacrifice that his mental sufferings are emphasized. This supreme sacrifice cast, it is true, its shadows before it. It was in the height of his ministry that our Lord exclaimed, " I have a baptism to be baptized with; and how am I straitened till it be accomplished " (Lk. xii. 50).[85] Floods lie before him

grateful sense of high privilege; and that he had a blessed consciousness of fellowship with his Father who sent him, during the whole of his pilgrimage through this vale of tears?" A. E. Garvie, *Studies in the Inner Life of Jesus,* 1907, p. 318: " Although in his emotions, varying notes of joy or grief were struck by the changeful experiences of his life among men, yet the undertone was the sense of a great good to be gained by the endurance of a great sorrow." G. Matheson, *Studies in the Portrait of Christ,*[10] 1909, I. pp. 274 sq.: " We speak of the 'Man of Sorrows', yet I think the deepest note in the soul of Jesus was not sorrow but joy." C. W. Emmet, *DCG.* ii. p. 607 b: Christ " is the Man of Sorrows, yet we cannot think of him for a moment as an unhappy man. He rather gives us the picture of serene and unclouded happiness. Beneath not merely the outward suffering, but the profound sorrow of heart, there is deeper still a continual joy, derived from the realized presence of his Father and the consciousness that he is doing his work. Unless this is remembered, the idea of the Man of Sorrows is sentimentalized and exaggerated." F. W. Farrar, *The Life of Christ,* 1874, i. p. 318; ii. p. 103.

[85] Hahn *in loc.:* " We see from this verse that Jesus had a distinct foreknowledge of his passion, as indeed he bears witness already in ix. 22, 44. There meets us here, however, the first intimation that he

under which he is to be submerged,[86] and the thought of passing beneath their waters "straitens" his soul. The term rendered "straitened"[87] imports oppression and affliction, and bears witness to the burden of anticipated anguish which our Lord bore throughout life. The prospect of his sufferings, it has been justly said, was a perpetual[88] Gethsemane; and how complete this foretaste was we may learn from the incident recorded in Jno. xii. 27,[89] although this antedated Gethsemane, by only a few days. "Now is my soul[90] troubled," he cries and adds a remarkable confession of shrinking at the prospect of death, with, however, an immediate revulsion to his habitual attitude of submission to, or rather of hearty embracing of, his Father's will.—"And what shall I say? Father, save me from this hour![91] But for this cause, came I to this hour!

looked forward to it with inner dread (*Angst*), though there are repeated testimonies to this later (Cf. xxii. 42; Jno. xii. 2; Mt. xxvi. 37)." Cf. Mt. xx. 22: "Are you able to drink the cup that I am about to drink?"; Mk. x. 38: "Are you able to drink the cup that I drink? or to be baptized with the baptism that I am baptized with?"

[86] Cf. Meyer on Mk. x. 38: "The *cup* and *baptism* of Jesus represent *martyrdom*. In the case of the figure of baptism . . . the point of the similitude lies in the being *submerged* . . . Cf. the classical use of καταδύειν and βαπτίζειν, to *plunge* (immerge) into sufferings, sorrows, and the like."

[87] Συνέχω : see G. Heine, *Synonymik* etc., 1898. p. 149: "συνέχομαι, *affligor, laboro*". Cf. Plummer *in loc.*: "How am I oppressed, afflicted, until it be accomplished! Comp. viii. 37; Jno. v. 24. The prospect of his sufferings was a perpetual Gethsemane: cf. Jno. xii. 27." Weiss *in loc.*: "And how I am afflicted (*bedrängt*) until it be accomplished! Expression of human anxiety in prospect of the sufferings which were to come, as in Gethsemane and Jno. xii. 27."

[88] The ἕως ὅτου emphasizes the whole intervening time: "I am straitened through all the time up to its accomplishment."

[89] Zahn *in loc.*, (p. 509): "The essential content of this incident, narrated by John alone, is the same that the Synoptics record in the prayer-conflict in Gethsemane, which John passes over in silence when his narrative brings him to Gethsemane (xviii. 1-11)".

[90] See note 3.

[91] This prayer is frequently taken as a continuation of the question. So, e. g. Zahn. (p. 507): "To the question τί εἴπω, the words which follow: πάτερ, σῶσόν με ἐκ τῆς ὥρας ταύτης cannot bring the response; for the prayer is at once corrected and withdrawn (ἀλλὰ κτλ), and replaced by an absolutely different one (verse 28). The first prayer shares

Father, glorify Thy name!" He had come into the world to die; but as he vividly realizes what the death is which he is to die, there rises in his soul a yearning for deliverance, only however, to be at once repressed.[92] The state of mind in which this sharp conflict went on is described by a term the fundamental implication of which is agitation, disquietude, perplexity.[93] This perturbation of soul is three times attributed by John to Jesus (xi. 33, xii. 27, xiii. 21), and always as expressing the emotions which conflict with death stirred in him. The anger roused in him by the sight of the distress into which death had plunged Mary and her companions (xi. 33); the anticipation of his own betrayal to death (xiii. 21); the clearly realized approach of his death (xii. 27); threw him inwardly into profound agitation. It was not always the prospect of his own death (xii. 27, xiii. 21), but equally the poignant realization of what death meant for others (xi. 33) which had the power thus to disquiet him. His deep agitation was clearly, therefore, not due to mere recoil from the physical experience of death,[94] though even such a recoil might be the expression

therefore in the interrogatory inflection of τί εἴπω and is to be filled out by an ἄρα (or ἤ) εἴπω derived thence, with the new question, 'Am I to say, perhaps: Father save me from this hour?'" Against this, however, Wescott forcibly urges "that it does not fall in with the parallel clause, which follows: 'Father glorify Thy Name'; nor with the intensity of the passage, nor yet with the kindred passages in the Synoptics (Mt. xxvi. 39 and parallels)."

[92] Zahn (p. 509): "Into the world of Jesus' conceptions the possibility of going another way than that indicated by God could intrude; that was his temptation; but his will repelled it."

[93] Ταράσσω: see Schmidt, Synonymik etc., iii. 1879. § 739. 6. p. 516: Heine, Synonymik etc., 1898. p. 149.

[94] Cf. Calvin Com. in Harm. Evang., on Mt. xxvi. 37: "And whence came to him both sorrow and anxiety and fear, except because he felt in death something sadder and more horrible than the separation of the soul and body? And certainly he underwent death, not merely that he might move from earth to heaven, but rather that he might take on himself the curse to which we were liable, and deliver us from it. His horror was not, then, at death simpliciter, as a passage out of the world, but because he had before his eyes the dreadful tribunal of God, and the Judge Himself armed with inconceivable vengeance; it was our sins, the burden of which he had assumed, that pressed him down with

not so much of a terror of dying as of a repugnance to the idea of death.[95]   Behind death, he saw him who has the power of death, and that sin which constitutes the sting of death.   His whole being revolted from that final and deepest humiliation, in which the powers of evil were to inflict upon him the precise penalty of human sin.   To bow his head beneath this stroke was the last indignity, the hardest act of that obedience which it was his to render in his servant-form, and which we are told with significant emphasis, extended " up to death " (Phil. ii. 8).

So profound a repugnance to death and all that death meant, manifesting itself during his life, could not fail to seize upon him with peculiar intensity at the end.   If the distant prospect of his sufferings was a perpetual Gethsemane to him, the immediate imminence of them in the actual Gethsemane could not fail to bring with it that " awful and dreadful torture " which Calvin does not scruple to call the " exordium " of the pains of hell themselves.[96]   Matthew and Mark almost exhaust the resources of language to convey to us some conception of

their enormous mass.   It is, then, not at all strange if the dreadful abyss of destruction tormented him grievously with fear and anguish."

[95] Thus Mrs. Humphrey Ward reports a conversation with Mr. Gladstone ("Notes of Conversation with Mr. Gladstone," appended to the second volume of *Robert Elsmere,* Westmoreland ed. 1911) : "He said that though he had seen many deaths, he had never seen any really peaceful.   In all there had been much struggle.   So much so that 'I myself have conceived what I will not call a terror of death, but a repugnance from the idea of death.   It is the rending asunder of body and soul, the tearing apart of the two elements of our nature,—for I hold the body to be an essential element as well as the soul, not a mere sheath or envelope.' "

[96] *Institutes.* II. xvi. 12: "If anyone now ask, whether Christ was already descending into hell when he prayed to be delivered from death, I reply that this was the *exordium,* and we may learn from it what *diros et horribiles cruciatus* he sustained when he was conscious of standing at the tribunal of God, arraigned on our account."   "It is our wisdom," Calvin remarks in the context, "to have a fit sense of how much our salvation cost the Son of God."   Cf. the discussion in the same spirit of Thomas Goodwin, *Works.* v. pp. 278-288 : "For it is God's wrath that is hell, as it is his favor that is heaven" (p. 281).

our Lord's "agony" [97] as an early interpolator of Luke (Lk. xxii. 44) calls it, in this dreadful experience.[98] The anguish of reluctance which constituted this "agony" is in part described by them both—they alone of the Evangelists enter into our Lord's feelings here—by a term the primary idea of which is loathing, aversion, perhaps not unmixed with despondency.[99] This term is adjoined in Matthew's account to the common word for sorrow, in which, however, here the fundamental element of pain, distress, is prominent,[100] so that we may perhaps render Matthew's account: "He began to be distressed and despondent" (Mt. xxvi. 37). Instead of this wide word for distress of mind, Mark employs a term which more narrowly defines the distress as consternation,—if not exactly dread, yet alarmed dismay:[101] "He began to be appalled and despond-

[97] Ἀγωνία: see G. Heine, *Synonymik* etc., 1898, p. 189: "Contest, quaking, agitation (and anxiety of the issue?) Lk. xxii. 44; Luther, 'he grappled with death', Weizsäcker, 'he struggled', Bengel; 'supreme grief and anguish. It properly denotes the anguish and passion of the mind, when it enters upon a conflict and arduous labor, even when there is no doubt of a good issue'." Plummer *in loc.*: "Field contends that *fear* is the radical notion of the word. The passages in which it occurs in LXX confirm this view. . . . It is therefore an agony of fear that is apparently to be understood." It would be better to say consternation, appalled reluctance.

[98] The discussion of the language employed, by John Pearson, *An Exposition of the Creed*, (New York, 1843), p. 288, note †, is very penetrating.

[99] Ἀδημονέω: see Heine, *Synonymik* etc., 1898, p. 148: "*pavesco, angor.*" Cf. Lightfoot, on Phil. ii. 26: "The primary idea of the word will be loathing and discontent." "It describes the confused, restless, half-distracted state, which is produced by physical discouragement, or by mental distress, or grief, shame, disappointment, etc." Lagrange on Mk. xviii. 33: "seized with despondency". Thomas Goodwin (*Works.* v. 276): "so that we see Christ's soul was sick and fainted," "his heart failed him."

[100] Λυπέομαι: see note 38.

[101] Ἐκθαμβέομαι: see Hastings' *DCG.* i. p. 48, article "Amazement"; G. Heine, *Synonymik* etc., p. 149: It "is used of those whose minds are horror-struck by the sight or thought of something great or atrocious, not merely because it injects fear, but because the mind scarcely takes in its magnitude." Weiss *in loc.*: "ἐκθαμβεῖσθαι cannot designate the dread (*Angst*) but only the horror (*Erschrecken*) which attacks Jesus at the thought of the sufferings which stand before him." Thomas Goodwin (*Works*, v. p. 275): "It signifies 'to be in horror'."

ent " (Mk. xiv. 33). Both accounts add our Lord's own
pathetic declaration: " My soul[102] is exceeding sorrowful even
unto death ", the central term[103] in which expresses a sorrow,
or perhaps we would better say, a mental pain, a distress, which
hems in on every side, from which there is therefore no escape; or rather (for the qualification imports that this hem-
ming-in distress is mortally acute, is an anguish of a sort that
no issue but death can be thought of[104]) which presses in and
besets from every side and therefore leaves no place for defence. The extremity of this agony may have been revealed,
as the interpolator of Luke tells us, by sweat dropping like
clots of blood on the ground, as our Lord ever more impor-
tunately urged that wonderful prayer, in which as Bengel
strikingly says,[105] the horror of death and the ardor of obedience met (Lk. xxii. 44). This interpolator tells us (Lk. xxii.
43) also that he was strengthened for the conflict by an angelic
visitor, and we may well suppose that had it not been for some
supernatural strengthening mercifully vouchsafed (cf. Jno.
xii. 27f.), the end would then have come.[106]   But the cup
must needs be drained to its dregs, and the final drop was not
drunk until that cry of desertion and desolation was uttered,
" My God, my God, why hast Thou forsaken me?" (Mt. xxvii.

[102] See note 3.

[103] Περίλυπος. J. A. Alexander: "Grieved all round, encompassed,
shut in by distress on every side." Morrison: "The idea is, My soul is
sorrowful all round and round."

[104] Swete's "a sorrow which well-nigh kills" is too weak: the meaning
is, it is a sorrow that kills. Thomas Goodwin (Works. v. p. 272) distinguishes thus: "A heaviness unto death, not extensive, so as to die,
but intensive, that if he had died, he could not have suffered more."

[105] On Jno. xii. 27. The evidence derived from the conflict of wills in
this prayer that these emotions had their seat in our Lord's human nature
is often adverted to,—e. g. by J. R. Willis, Hasting's DCG. i. p. 17a:—
"The thrice-repeated prayer of Jesus in which he speaks of his own will
as distinct from but distinctly subordinate to his Father's adds to the impression already gained, of the purely human feelings exhibited by him in
this struggle."

[106] Cf. the description of this "agony" in Heb. v. 7: "Who, in the
days of his flesh, having offered up, with strong crying and tears, prayers
and supplications unto him that was able to save him from death".

46; Mk. xv. 34).[107] This culminating sorrow was actually unto death.

In these supreme moments our Lord sounded the ultimate depths of human anguish, and vindicated on the score of the intensity of his mental sufferings the right to the title of Man of Sorrows. The scope of these sufferings was also very broad, embracing that whole series of painful emotions which runs from a consternation that is appalled dismay, through a despondency which is almost despair, to a sense of well-nigh complete desolation. In the presence of this mental anguish the physical tortures of the crucifixion retire into the background, and we may well believe that our Lord, though he died on the cross, yet died not of the cross, but, as we commonly say, of a broken heart, that is to say, of the strain of his

[107] Calvin, *Commentarius in Harmoniam Evangelicarum*, on Mt. xxvii. 46: "And certainly this was his chief conflict, and harder than all his other torments, because he was so far from being supported in his straits by his Father's help or favor, that he felt himself in some measure estranged. For he did not offer his body only in payment for our reconciliation with God, but in his soul also he bore the punishments due to us; and thus became in very fact the man of sorrows, as Isaiah says (liii. 3). . . For that Christ should make satisfaction for us, it was necessary that he be sisted as guilty before the tribunal of God. But nothing is more horrible than to incur the judgment of God, whose wrath is worse than all deaths. When, then, there was presented to Christ a kind of temptation as if he were already devoted to destruction, God being his enemy, he was seized with a horror in which a hundred times all the mortals in existence would have been overwhelmed; but he came out of it victor, by the amazing power of the Spirit". . . Also *Institutes* II. xvi. 11: "And certainly it is not possible to imagine a more terrible abyss than to feel yourself forsaken and abandoned (*derelictum et alienatum*) by God, and, when you call upon him, not to be heard as though he had conspired for your destruction. Christ we see to have been so dejected (*dejectum*) as to be constrained in the urgency of his distress (*urgente angusta*) to cry out, 'My God, My God, why hast Thou forsaken me?'" Calvin adds with clear insight that though it is evident that this cry was *ex intimi animi angore deductam*, yet this does not carry with it the admission that "God was ever either hostile or angry with him." "For how could he be angry with his beloved son, in whom his soul delighted, or how could Christ appear in his intercession for others before a Father who was incensed with him?" All that is affirmed is that "he sustained the weight of the Divine severity; since, smitten and afflicted by the hand of God, he experienced all the signs of an angry and punishing God."

mental suffering.[108]   The sensitiveness of his soul to affectional movements, and the depths of the currents of feeling which flowed through his being, are thus thrown up into a very clear light.   And yet it is noticeable that while they tore his heart and perhaps, in the end, broke the bonds which bound his fluttering spirit to its tenement of clay, they never took the helm of life or overthrew either the judgment of his calm understanding or the completeness of his perfect trust in his Father.   If he cried out in his agony for deliverance, it was always the cry of a child to a Father whom he trusts with all and always, and with the explicit condition, Howbeit, not what I will but what Thou wilt.   If the sense of desolation invades his soul, he yet confidingly commends his departing spirit into his Father's hands (Lk. xxiii. 46).[109]   And through all

[108] That his death was due to psychical rather than physical causes may be the reason why it took place so soon. Jacobus Baumann in a most distressing book (*Die Gemütsart Jesu*, 1908, p. 10) appeals to the rapidity with which Jesus succumbed to death as evidence of a certain general lack of healthful vigor which he finds in Jesus: "With this liability to easy exhaustion, his quick death on the cross agrees—a thing which was unusual."

[109] Calvin, *Institutes* ii. xv. 12 does not fail to remind us that even in our Lord's cry of desolation, he still addresses God as "*My* God": "although he suffered agony beyond measure, yet he does not cease to call God *his* God, even when he cries out that he is forsaken by him." Then at large in the *Comm. in Harm. Evang.*, on Mt. xxvii. 46: "We have already pointed out the difference between natural feeling and the knowledge of faith.   There was nothing to prevent Christ from mentally conceiving that God had deserted him, according to the dictation of his natural feeling, and at the same time retaining his faith that God was well-disposed to him.   And this appears with sufficient clearness from the two clauses of the complaint.   For before he gives expression to his trial, he begins by saying that he flees to God as his God and so he bravely repels by this shield of faith that appearance of dereliction which presented itself in opposition.   In short, in this dire anguish his faith was unimpaired, so that in act of deploring that he was forsaken, he still trusted in the present help of God."   Similarly Thomas Goodwin (*Works*. v. p. 283): "And both these differing apprehensions of his did Christ accordingly express in that one sentence, 'My God, My God, why hast Thou forsaken me?'   He speaks it as apprehending himself a son still united to God and beloved by him, and yet forsaken by him as a surety accursed."

his agony his demeanor to his disciples, his enemies, his judges, his executioners is instinct with calm self-mastery. The cup which was put to his lips was bitter: none of its bitterness was lost to him as he drank it: but he drank it; and he drank it as his own cup which it was his own will (because it was his Father's will) to drink. " The cup which the Father hath given me, shall I not drink it? " (Jno. xviii. 11),—it was in this spirit, not of unwilling subjection to unavoidable evil, but of voluntary endurance of unutterable anguish for adequate ends, that he passed into and through all his sufferings. His very passion was his own action. He had power to lay down his life; and it was by his own power that he laid down his life, and by his own power that he trod the whole pathway of suffering which led up to the formal act of his laying down his life. Nowhere is he the victim of circumstances or the helpless sufferer. Everywhere and always, it is he who possesses the mastery both of circumstances and of himself.[110]

The completeness of Jesus' trust in God which is manifested in the unconditional, " Nevertheless, not as I will but as Thou wilt " of the " agony ", and is echoed in the " Father, into Thy hands I commend my spirit " of the cross, finds endless illustration in the narratives of the Evangelists. Trust is never, however, explicitly attributed to him in so many words.[111] Except in the scoffing language with which he was assailed as he hung on the cross: " He trusteth in God; let him deliver him now if he desireth him " (Mt. xxvii. 43), the term " trust " is never so much as mentioned in connection with his relations

[110] Cf. the remarks of H. N. Bernard, *The Mental Characteristics of our Lord Jesus Christ*, 1888, pp. 257sq.

[111] Cf. Heb. ii. 13. In Jno. ii. 24 we are told that Jesus "did not trust himself (ἐπίστευσεν)" to those in Jerusalem who believed on him when they saw the signs which he did. Cf. Lütgert, as cited, p. 63: "From this the relation of Jesus to God receives a two-fold form: on the one side it is absolute trust, a certainty of receiving everything, a wish and prayer directed to God, which leads to a complete exaltation above nature; but this side of his faith Jesus makes use of only for men. By virtue of this his confidence he fulfils the wish of all who ask him. In this use of his faith he expresses his love for men. The faith of Jesus has however also another side; it is bowing, renunciation and subordination to God. This side of his faith Jesus employs only for himself. The story of the tempta-

with God. Nor is the term " faith ".[112] Nor indeed are
many of what we may call the fundamental religious affections
directly attributed to him, although he is depicted as literally
living, moving and having his being in God. His profound
feeling of dependence on God, for example, is illustrated in
every conceivable way, not least strikingly in the constant
habit of prayer which the Evangelists ascribe to him.[113] But
we are never directly told that he felt this dependence on God
or "feared God" or felt the emotions of reverence and awe
in the divine presence.[114] We are repeatedly told that he re-

tion shows that Jesus uses this renunciation in order to glorify God."
(Further, p. 89).

[112] Cf. A. Schlatter, *Die Theologie des Neuen Testaments*, 1909, p. 317:
" Perfect love involves perfect trust, and is not thinkable without it.
Yet though the disciples have declared that Jesus empowered them for
faith and demanded faith of them, they have said nothing of Jesus' own
faith. Even John has said nothing of it although he has rich formulas
for the piety of Jesus and speaks of faith as the act by which Jesus unites
his disciples with himself. The notion of faith is introduced by him only
with respect to Jesus' relations to men, ' He trusted himself not to them ';
while, of Jesus' relation to God, he says ' He heard him, loved him, knew
him, saw him,' but not, ' He believed on him ' (Jno. ii. 24, viii. 26, 40,
xi. 10, xiv. 31, x. 15, xvii. 25, iii. 11, vi. 46, viii. 35). As a rule for the
conduct of the disciples toward Jesus is expressly drawn from Jesus'
conduct towards the Father, the formula ' Believe in me as I believe in the
Father ' might have been expected. But it does not occur."

[113] Mk. i. 35, vi. 46, xiv. 32, 35; Mt. xiv. 23, xix. 13, xxvi. 36-39, 42-44;
Lk. iii. 21, v. 16, vi. 12, ix. 18-28, xi. 1, xxii. 41, 44. Cf. Lütgert, as cited,
p. 90: " Also in the expression of his love to God, Jesus fulfilled, according to the Evangelists, his own commandment, not to exhibit his piety
openly, but to practice it in secret. The Evangelists therefore designedly
lay stress on Jesus' seeking solitude for prayer. The communion of Jesus
with God, the ' inner life ' of Jesus, falls accordingly outside their narrative. The relation of Jesus with God is not discussed, his communion with God remains a secret." This is spoken of the Synoptics who
alone tells us of Jesus' habit of prayer (προσεύχομαι, προσευχή do not occur
in John).

[114] Cf. Heb. v. 7: " having been heard for his godly fear (εὐλάβεια)",
i. e. for his reverent and submissive awe, " that religious fear of God and
anxiety not to offend him which manifests itself in voluntary and humble
submission to his will" (Delitzsch *in loc.*). Davidson *in loc.*: " The
clause throws emphasis on the Son's reverent submission." Humanitarian
writers debate whether " fear " of God is to be attributed to Jesus. Well-

turned thanks to God,[115] but we are never told in so many words that he experienced the emotion of gratitude. The narrative brings Jesus before us as acting under the impulse of all the religious emotions; but it does not stop to comment upon the emotions themselves.

The same is true of the more common emotions of human

hausen (*Israel. und jüd. Geschichte*[5], p. 383, expanded in *Skizzen und Vorarbeiten*, i. 1884, p. 98) represents him as passing his life in fear of the judge of all: "He feels the reality of God dominating life, he breathes in the fear of the Judge who demands account of every idle word and has power to destroy body and soul in hell." Similarly Bousset (*Jesus*, 1904, pp. 54, 99, E. T. pp. 112, 203) speaks of him as learning by his own experience "that God is terrible (*furchtbar*) and that an awful darkness and dread encircles him even for those who stand nearest to him," and as "sharing to the bottom of his soul" "the fear of that almighty God who has power to damn body and soul together," which he "has stamped upon the hearts of his disciples with such marvellous energy." Karl Thieme, however, from the same humanitarian standpoint (*Die christliche Demut*, i. 1906, pp. 109 sq.) repels such representations as without historical ground: we may historically ascribe reverential awe (*Ehrfurcht*) to Jesus but not fear (*Furcht*). "Of course he comprehended God in the whole overtowering majesty of his being, and adored his immeasurable exaltation in the deepest reverence (*Ehrfurcht*)." But "we may maintain in Jesus' case an altogether fearless (*furchtlos*) assurance of God and self." "We cannot speak of a 'fear of the Judge' in Jesus' case, because it does not well harmonize with his faith in his own judgeship of the world. But we can no doubt call the intensity of his obedience, the living sense of responsibility in which he made it his end, his whole life through, to walk, in all his motions, with the utmost exactness according to the will of God as the almighty majestic Lord, his fear of God." Lütgert (*Die Liebe im Neuen Testament*, 1895, pp. 88, 89) points to Jesus' turning to the Father in Gethsemane and on the cross, not as something terrible (*furchtbar*) but with loving confidence, as decisive in the case. On the place of 'the fear of God' in Christian piety, see Lütgert's article *Die Furcht Gottes*, published in the *Theologische Studien*, presented to Martin Kähler on 6 January 1905 (Leipzig, 1905, pp. 163 sq.).

[115] Ἐυχαριστέω , Jno. xi. 41; Mt. xv. 36; Mk. viii. 6; Jno. vi. 11, 23; xxvi. 27; Mk. xiv. 23; Lk. xxii. 17, 19; 1 Cor. xi. 24. On the word, see Lobeck, *Phrynicus*, p. 18; Rutherford, *The New Phrynicus*, p. 69. Ἐξομο λογέομαι, Mt. xi. 25; Lk. x. 21; R. V. mg. 'praise': so Meyer, Hahn, Zahn, also Kennedy, *Sources of N. T. Greek*, p. 118. Fritzsche: "*Gratias tibi ago, quod*". Better, Plummer: "acknowledge openly to thine honour, give thee praise." Similarly J. A. Alexander.

life. The narrative is objective throughout in its method. On two occasions we are told that Jesus felt that occurrences which he witnessed were extraordinary and experienced the appropriate emotion of "wonder" regarding them (Mt. viii. 10; Lk. vii 9; Mk. vi. 6).[116] Once "desire" is attributed to him (Lk. xxii. 15),—he had "set his heart", as we should say, upon eating the final passover with his disciples—the term used emphasizing the affectional movement.[117] And once our Lord speaks of himself as being conceivably the subject of "shame", the reference being, however, rather to a mode of action consonant with the emotion, than to the feeling itself (Mk. viii. 38; Lk. iv. 26).[118] Besides these few chance suggestions, there are none of the numerous emotions that rise and fall in the human soul, which happen to be explicitly attributed to our Lord.[119] The reader sees them all in play in his vividly narrated life-experiences, but he is not told of them.

We have now passed in review the whole series of explicit attributions to our Lord in the Gospels of specific emotional movements. It belongs to the occasional manner in which these emotional movements find record in the narrative, that it is only our Lord's most noticeable displays of emotion which are noted. One of the effects of this is to give to his emotions

[116] Θαυμάζω: see Schmidt, *Synonymik* etc., iv. § 165, pp. 184sq.: "it is perfectly generally 'to wonder' or 'to admire', and is distinguished from θαμβεῖν precisely as the German *sich wundern*, or *bewundern* is from *staunen*: that is, what has seized on us in the case of θαυμάζειν is the extraordinary nature of the thing while in the case of θαμβεῖν it is the unexpectedness and suddenness of the occurrence." Cf. Art. "Amazement" in Hasting's *DCG*. I, pp. 47, 48.

[117] 'Επιθυμία: see Schmidt, *Synonymik*, III, § 145, 3, 5; 146, 8; and cf. J. C. Lambert, art. "Desire" in Hastings' *DCG*, I, 453.

[118] 'Επαισχύνομαι : see Schmidt, *Synonymik*, III, § 140; Trench *Synonyms*, §§ 19, 20. On Shame in our Lord's life cf. James Stalker, *Imago Christi*, p. 190, and Thieme, as above, p. 111.

[119] When Wellhausen (*Geschichte Israels,*[2] p. 346) says, "There broke out with him from time to time manifestations of enthusiasm, but to these elevations of mood there corresponded also depressions,"—he is going beyond the warrant of the narrative, which pictures Jesus rather as singularly equable in his demeanor. Cf. Lütgert, as cited, p. 103.

as noted the appearance of peculiar strength, vividness and completeness. This serves to refute the notion which has been sometimes advanced under the influence of the " apathetic " conception of virtue, that emotional movements never ran their full course in him as we experience them, but stopped short at some point in their action deemed the point of dignity.[120] In doing so, it serves equally, however, to carry home to us a very vivid impression of the truth and reality of our Lord's human nature. What we are given is, no doubt, only the high lights. But it is easy to fill in the picture mentally with the multitude of emotional movements which have not found record just because they were in no way exceptional. Here obviously is a being who reacts as we react to the incitements which arise in daily intercourse with men, and whose reactions bear all the characteristics of the corresponding emotions we are familiar with in our experience.

Perhaps it may be well explicitly to note that our Lord's emotions fulfilled themselves, as ours do, in physical reactions. He who hungered (Mt. iv. 2), thirsted (Jno. xix. 20), was weary (Jno. iv. 6), who knew both physical pain and pleasure, expressed also in bodily affections the emotions that stirred his soul. That he did so is sufficiently evinced by the simple circumstance that these emotions were observed and recorded. But the bodily expression of the emotions is also frequently expressly attested. Not only do we read that he wept (Jno. xi. 35) and wailed (Lk. xix. 41), sighed (Mk. vii. 34) and groaned (Mk. viii. 12); but we read also of his angry glare (Mk. iii. 5), his annoyed speech (Mk. x. 14), his chiding words (e. g. Mk. iii. 12), the outbreaking ebullition of his rage (e. g. Jno. xi. 33, 38); of the agitation of his bearing when under strong feeling (Jno. xi. 35), the open exultation

---

[120] Origen, for example, in his comment on Mt. xxvi. 37 lays great weight on the words: "He began to be", in the sense that the implication is that he never completed the act. Jesus only *entered* upon these emotions, but did not suffer them in their fulness. He was subject to προπάθεια but not to the πάθη themselves. Similarly Cornelius a Lapide wishes us to believe that Christ instead of "passions" had only "*propassiones libere assumptae*". For a modern writer approaching this position, see John Hutchison, *The Monthly Interpreter*, 1885, II, p. 288.

of his joy (Lk. x. 21), the unrest of his movements in the
face of anticipated evils (Mt. xxvii. 37), the loud cry which
was wrung from him in his moment of desolation (Mt. xxvii.
46). Nothing is lacking to make the impression strong that
we have before us in Jesus a human being like ourselves.

It is part of the content of this impression, that Jesus appears before us in the light of the play of his emotions as a
distinct human being, with his own individuality and—shall
we not say it?—even temperament. It is, indeed, sometimes
suggested that the Son of God assumed at the incarnation not
a human nature but human nature, that is to say, not human
nature as manifesting itself in an individual, but human nature
in general, "generic" or "universal" human nature. The
idea which it is meant to express, is not a very clear one,[121] and
is apparently only a relic of the discountenanced fiction of the
"real" existence of universals. In any case the idea receives

[121] It is not clear, for example, precisely what is meant by A. J. Mason
(*The Conditions of our Lord's Life on Earth*, 1896, p. 46), when he
says: "When Christ is called 'a Man' it sounds as if he were considered only an incidental specimen of the race, like one of ourselves, and not,
as he is in fact, the universal Man, in whom the whole of human nature is
gathered up,—the representative and head of the entire species." What
is a "universal man"? And how could "the whole of human nature"
be "gathered up" in Jesus, except representatively,—which is not what
is meant—unless universal human nature is an entity with "real existence"? And if even Mason is unintelligible, what shall we say of a writer
like J. P. Lange (*Christliche Dogmatik; Zweiter Theil; Positive Dogmatik*, 1881, pp. 770-771): "The man in the God-man is not an individual man of itself, but the man which takes mankind up into itself, as
mankind has taken nature up into itself. And so it coalesces with the
divine self-limitation, as the Son of God unites with the human limitation.
The man in the God-man embraces the eternal Becoming of the whole
world as it goes forth from God according to the energy of his nature.
So it is also radically the real passage of the Becoming through the perfected Becoming into the absolute Being, and therefore the proper organ
of the Son of God according to his ideal entrance into the absolute Becoming. It is the limited unlimitation which coalesces with the unlimited
limitation of the divine man, who takes up into itself the human God." It
is only fair to bear in mind, however, that this statement is partly relieved
of its unintelligibility when it is read in connection with Lange's exposition of the ideas of man and the God-man in his *Philosophical Dogmatics*, which, in his system, precedes his *Positive Dogmatics*.

no support from a survey of the emotional life of our Lord as it is presented to us in the Evangelical narratives. The impression of a distinct individuality acting in accordance with its specific character as such, which is left on the mind by these narratives is very strong. Whether our Lord's human nature is " generic " or " individual ", it certainly—the Evangelists being witness—functioned in the days of his flesh as if it were individual; and we have the same reason for pronouncing it an individual human-nature that we have for pronouncing such any human nature of whose functioning we have knowledge.[122]

This general conclusion is quite independent of the precise determination of the peculiarity of the individuality which our Lord exhibits. He himself, on a great occasion, sums up his individual character (in express contrast with other individuals) in the declaration, " I am meek and lowly of heart." And no impression was left by his life-manifestation more deeply imprinted upon the consciousness of his followers than that of the noble humility of his bearing. It was by the " meekness and gentleness of Christ " that they encouraged one another to a life becoming a Christian man's profession (2 Cor. x. 1); for " the patience of Christ " that they prayed in behalf of one another as a blessing worthy to be set in their aspirations by the side of the " love of God " (2 Thess. iii. 5); to the imitation of Christ's meek acceptance of undeserved outrages that they exhorted one another in persecution—" because Christ also suffered for sin, leaving you an example, that ye should follow in his steps; who did no sin, neither was guile found in his mouth; who, when he was reviled, reviled not again; when he suffered, threatened not; but committed himself to him that judgeth righteously " (1 Pet. ii.

[122] Cf. A. B. Bruce, *The Humiliation of Christ*,[2] 1881, pp. 262, and pp. 427-428: " I see in him traces of strongly marked, though not one-sided individuality . . . Generally speaking, the reality, not ideality, of the humanity is the thing that lies on the surface; although the latter is not to be denied, nor the many-sidedness which is adduced in proof of it by Martensen and others." Cf. Martensen, *Christian Dogmatics*, ET, pp. 280sq.

21-23). Nevertheless we cannot fix upon humility as in such a sense our Lord's "quality" as to obscure in him other qualities which might seem to stand in conflict with it; much less as carrying with it those "defects" which are apt to accompany it when it appears as the "quality" of others. Meekness in our Lord was not a weak bearing of evils, but a strong forbearance in the presence of evil. It was not so much a fundamental characteristic of a nature constitutionally averse to asserting itself, as a voluntary submission of a strong person bent on an end. It did not, therefore, so much give way before indignation when the tension became too great for it to bear up against it, as coëxist with a burning indignation at all that was evil, in a perfect equipoise which knew no wavering to this side or that. It was, in a word, only the manifestation in him of the mind which looks not on its own things but the things of others (Phil. ii. 5), and therefore spells "mission", not "temperament". We cannot in any case define his temperament, as we define other men's temperaments, by pointing to his dominant characteristics or the prevailing direction of his emotional discharges.[123]   In this sense he had no particular temperament, and it might with truth be said that his human nature was generic, not individual. The mark of his individuality was harmonious completeness: of him alone of men, it may be truly said that nothing that is human was alien to him, and that all that is human manifested itself in him in perfect proportion and balance.

[123] E. P. Boys-Smith, Hastings' *DCG*, II, p. 163a: "The fulness, balance, and unity of the Master's nature make it impracticable to use in his case what is the commonest and readiest way of portraying a person. This is to throw into the fore-ground of the picture those features in which the character is exceptionally strong, or those deficiencies which mark it off from others, and to leave as an unelaborated back-ground the common stuff of human nature. Thus, by sketching the idiosyncracies, and casting a few high lights, the man is set forth sufficiently. But what traits are there in the Lord Jesus which stand out because more highly developed than other features? Nothing truly human was wanting to him, nothing was exaggerated. The fact which distinguished him from all others was his completeness at all points. . ."

The series of emotions attributed to our Lord in the Evangelical narrative, in their variety and their complex but harmonious interaction, illustrate, though, of course, they cannot of themselves demonstrate, this balanced comprehensiveness of his individuality. Various as they are, they do not inhibit one another; compassion and indignation rise together in his soul; joy and sorrow meet in his heart and kiss each other. Strong as they are—not mere joy but exultation, not mere irritated annoyance but raging indignation, not mere passing pity but the deepest movements of compassion and love, not mere surface distress but an exceeding sorrow even unto death, —they never overmaster him. He remains ever in control.[124] Calvin is, therefore, not without justification, when, telling us[125] that in taking human affections our Lord did not take inordinate affections, but kept himself even in his passions in subjection to the will of the Father, he adds: "In short, if you compare his passions with ours, they will differ not less than the clear and pure water, flowing in a gentle course, differs from dirty and muddy foam."[126] The figure which is here

[124] T. B. Kilpatrick, Hastings' *DCG*, I. pp. 294b-295a: "Yet we are not to impute to him any unemotional callousness. He never lost his calmness; but he was not always calm. He repelled temptation with deep indignation (Mk. viii. 33). Hypocrisy aroused him to a flame of judgment (Mk. iii 5, xi. 15-17; Mt. xxiii. 1-36). Treachery shook him to the center of his being (Jno. xiii. 21). The waves of human sorrow broke over him with a greater grief than wrung the bereaved sisters (Jno. xi. 33-35). There were times when he bore an unknown agony . . . Yet whatever his soul's discipline might be, he never lost his self-control, was never distracted or afraid, but remained true to his mission and to his faith. He feels anger, or sorrow, or trouble, but these emotions are under the control of a will that is one with the divine will, and therefore are comprehended within the perfect peace of a mind stayed on God." There is a good deal of rhetorical exaggeration in the language in which the phenomena are here described; but for the essence of the matter the representation is sound: our Lord is always master of himself.

[125] Com. on Jno. xi. 35.

[126] Fr. Gumlich. *TSK*, 1862, p. 285 note b, calls on us to "guard ourselves from" Calvin's statement that "his feelings differ from ours as a *pure*, untroubled, *powerful* but onflowing stream from restless, foaming, muddy waves." But do not his sinless emotions differ precisely so from our sinful passions?

employed may, no doubt, be unduly pressed:[127] but Calvin has no intention of suggesting doubt of either the reality or the strength of our Lord's emotional reactions. He expressly turns away from the tendency from which even an Augustine is not free, to reduce the affectional life of our Lord to a mere show, and commends to us rather, as Scriptural, the simplicity which affirms that "the Son of God having clothed himself with our flesh, of his own accord clothed himself also with human feelings, so that he did not differ at all from his brethren, sin only excepted." He is only solicitous that, as Christ did not disdain to stoop to the feeling of our infirmities, we should be eager, not indeed to eradicate our affections, "seeking after that inhuman ἀπάθεια commended by the Stoics," but "to correct and subdue that obstinacy which pervades them, on account of the sin of Adam," and to imitate Christ our Leader,—who is himself the rule of supreme perfection—in subduing all their excesses. For Christ, he adds for our encouragement, had this very thing in view, when he took our affections upon himself—"that through his power we might subdue everything in them that is sinful." Thus, Calvin, with his wonted eagerness for religious impression, points to the emotional life of Jesus, not merely as a proof of his humanity, but as an incitement to his followers to a holy life accordant with the will of God. We are not to be content to gaze upon him or to admire him: we must become imitators of him, until we are metamorphosed into the same image.

Even this is, of course, not quite the highest note. The highest note—Calvin does not neglect it—is struck by the Epistle to the Hebrews, when it declares that "it behooved him in all things to be made like unto his brethren, that he

---

[127] Piscator enlarges upon it and applies it thus: "Just as pure and limpid water when mixed with a pure dye if agitated, foams indeed but is not made turbid; but when mixed with an impure and dirty dye, if agitated, not only forms foam but is made turbid and dirty; so the heart of Christ pure from all imperfection, was indeed agitated by the affections implanted in human nature, but was soiled by no sin; but our hearts are so agitated by affections that they are soiled by the sin which inheres in us."

might be a merciful and faithful High-priest in things pertaining to God, to make propitiation for the sins of the people " (Heb. ii. 17). " Surely ", says the Prophet (Is. liii. 4), " he hath borne our griefs and carried our sorrows "—a general statement to which an Evangelist (Mt. viii. 1) has given a special application (as a case in point) when he adduces it in the form, " himself took our infirmities and bore our diseases." He subjected himself to the conditions of our human life that he might save us from the evil that curses human life in its sinful manifestation.   When we observe him exhibiting the movements of his human emotions, we are gazing on the very process of our salvation: every manifestation of the truth of our Lord's humanity is an exhibition of the reality of our redemption.   In his sorrows he was bearing our sorrows, and having passed through a human life like ours, he remains forever able to be touched with a feeling of our infirmities. Such a High Priest, in the language of the Epistle to the Hebrews, " became " us.   We needed such an one.[128]   When we note the marks of humanity in Jesus Christ, we are observing his fitness to serve our needs.   We behold him made a little lower than the angels for the suffering of death, and our hearts add our witness that it became him for whom are all things and through whom are all things, in bringing many sons unto glory to make the author of their salvation perfect through suffering.

It is not germane to the present inquiry to enter into the debate as to whether, in assuming flesh, our Lord assumed the flesh of fallen or of unfallen man.   The right answer, beyond doubt, is that he assumed the flesh of unfallen man: it is not for nothing that Paul tells us that he came, not in sinful flesh, but in " the likeness of sinful flesh " (Ro. viii. 3).   But this does not mean that the flesh he assumed was not under a curse: it means that the curse under which his flesh rested was not the curse of Adam's first sin but the curse of the sins of his people: " him who knew no sin, he made sin in our behalf "; he who

---

[128] Westcott *in loc.:* " Even our human sense of fitness is able to recognize the complete correspondence between the characteristics of Christ as High Priest and the believers' wants."   Davidson, *in loc.:* " He suited our necessities and condition."

was not, even as man, under a curse, " became a curse for us ".
He was accursed, not because he became man, but because he
bore the sins of his people; he suffered and died not because
of the flesh he took but because of the sins he took. He was,
no doubt, born of a woman, born under the law (Gal. iv. 4), in
one concrete act; he issued from the Virgin's womb already our
sin-bearer.   But he was not sin-bearer because made of a
woman; he was made of a woman that he might become sin-
bearer; it was because of the suffering of death that he
was made a little lower than the angels (Heb. ii. 9).   It is
germane to our inquiry, therefore, to take note of the fact that
among the emotions which are attested as having found place
in our Lord's life-experiences, there are those which belong to
him not as man but as sin-bearer, which never would have
invaded his soul in the purity of his humanity save as he stood
under the curse incurred for his people's sins. The whole series
of his emotions are, no doubt, affected by his position under the
curse.   Even his compassion receives from this a special quality: is this not included in the great declaration of Heb. iv. 15?
Can we doubt that his anger against the powers of evil which
afflict man, borrowed particular force from his own experience
of their baneful working?   And the sorrows and dreads which
constricted his heart in the prospect of death, culminating in
the extreme anguish of the dereliction,—do not these constitute the very substance of his atoning sufferings?   As we survey the emotional life of our Lord as depicted by the Evangelists, therefore, let us not permit it to slip out of sight, that
we are not only observing the proofs of the truth of his humanity, and not merely regarding the most perfect example of a
human life which is afforded by history, but are contemplating
the atoning work of the Saviour in its fundamental elements.
The cup which he drank to its bitter dregs was not his cup but
our cup; and he needed to drink it only because he was set
upon our salvation.

THE CHILD WHOSE NAME IS WONDERFUL

An Address on Isaiah ix. 5 and 6 (English Version 6 and 7)

John D. Davis

The Messianic element in the Book of the Prophet Isaiah, Chapters vii-xii.
The child of chapter ix. Three constructions given to the words
of the name. The expectation awakened by the title Wonderful.
The title that is translated Mighty God. The title that is ren-
dered Everlasting Father. The upholding of the kingdom. The
attributes of the Messiah in the light of similar phenomena in
Scripture, particularly identification with, yet distinctness from,
Jehovah.

THE CHILD WHOSE NAME IS WONDERFUL[1]

Unto us a child is born, unto us a son is given; and the government shall be upon his shoulder: and his name shall be called Wonderful, Counsellor, Mighty God, Everlasting Father, Prince of Peace. Of the increase of his government and of peace there shall be no end, upon the throne of David, and upon his kingdom, to establish it, and to uphold it with justice and with righteousness from henceforth even for ever. The zeal of Jehovah of hosts will perform this (Isaiah ix. 5, 6: English version 6, 7; American revision.)

These words of the prophet are apt to send the music of Händel's Messiah surging through the mind. We hear again the burst and volume of sound and the crash of instruments as these names are repeated one after the other and emphasized by the beat of the loud kettledrum. One cannot do better, when meditating on these verses, than allow the strains of the oratorio to form an accompaniment to the thought and exalt the spirit; for Händel made no mistake in giving this prophetic utterance a place in an oratorio of the Messiah. The verses are found in that section of the prophecies of Isaiah, extending from chapter vii. to chapter xii., which has received the title The Book of Immanuel or The Consolation of Immanuel[2]

[1] An address.

[2] Immanuel (Is. vii. 14), however, is not understood by all students of prophecy to be the Messianic king. The main counter-theories are two:

1. Immanuel is not an individual; but is the representative of a new generation, the regenerate Judah. So von Hofmann, Budde (*New World*, 1895, p. 739), Kuenen (*Einleitung*, II. S. 41). Dillmann guardedly says that Immanuel, "if not the future Messiah himself, is at least the beginning and representative of the new generation, out of which finally one occupies the throne (*Commentar*, 5te Aufl., S. 74). Smend, too, once held this view (*Lehrbuch der alttestamentlichen Religionsgeschichte*, S 215), but he has retracted it in favor of Immanuel's identity with the Messiah (2te Aufl., S. 229).

2. Any boy, born within a year, may be properly called Immanuel by his mother as a memorial that God's active presence has been manifested

(Delitzsch). In these six chapters prophecies regarding the promised deliverer of Israel follow each other in rapid succession. The whole section is aglow with the Messianic glory. Judgment, indeed, is predicted; but it is transfigured and glorified by the hope centered in the remnant of Judah and in the ideal son of David (Giesebrecht, *Beiträge zur Jesaiakritik*, S. 87). And this particular passage in the ninth chapter of Isaiah has its own distinguishing Messianic marks. There are those, it is true, who question its authorship and the date when it was uttered; but questions of date and authorship do not obscure

in Judah; and the lad's increasing years will serve conveniently to measure the time of predicted events. Such substantially is the interpretation given by Roorda (*Orientalia*, 1840 I. 130-135), W. Robertson Smith (*The Prophets of Israel*, new ed., p. 272), Giesebrecht (*Studien und Kritiken*, 1888, S. 218 and Anm. 1), Hackmann (*Zukunftserwartung des Jesaia*, S. 63, 161), Volz (*Vorexilische Jahweprophetie und der Messias*, S. 41), Marti (*Kurzer Hand-commentar: Jesaja*, S. 76), and Schultz (*Alttestamentliche Theologie*, 5te Aufl., S. 615, 616), who, however, prefers to regard Immanuel as the prophet's son, and the bestowal of the name as a pledge that God will not forsake his people. Compare Kirkpatrick (*The Doctrine of the Prophets*, p. 189-191), who explains that a mother "may with confidence give him a name significant of the Presence of God with His people. That Presence will be manifested in deliverance and in judgement. . . . He is the pledge for his generation of the truth expressed in his name." Duhm's curious modification may be included in this class. He believes that superstitious meaning was attributed to the first words spoken by a woman after the birth of her child. The utterance was regarded as an oracle, and was used as a name for the new-born child. In the moment that the Syrians are obliged to withdraw God will prompt some woman, who has just borne a son, to call out Immanuel, God with us (*Handkommentar zum Alten Testament: Jesaia*, S. 53 f.).

In the judgment of Duhm, Hackmann, Volz, Marti, the genuineness of vii. 15 and 17 must be denied and the verses exscinded. It is significant that according to Duhm (S. 54), Volz (S. 41), Marti (S. 77, 85), Nowack (*Die kleinen Propheten*, on Mic. v. 2 [3]), and Wellhausen (*Die kleinen Propheten*, Mic. v. 2), the existence of passages like Is. vii. 15 and Mic. v. 2 [3], and Immanuel in Is. viii. 8, 10, prove that even in Old Testament times Immanuel in Is. vii. 14 was understood to be the Messiah.

Umbreit "cannot with entire confidence explain vii. 14 as Messianic;" and Nowack is unable to convince himself of the correctness of the Messianic interpretation of it (*Theologische Abhandlungen . . . für Heinrich Julius Holtzmann dargebracht*, S. 58).

the identity of the person upon whom the prophet's gaze is fixed. The child is the Messiah. Noted Jewish commentators, indeed, have explained him to be Hezekiah. This explanation was given by Solomon Jarchi, Abenezra, and David Kimchi during the Middle Ages, by Luzzatto in the middle of the nineteenth century, and yet more recently in Jewish circles by the Orientalist James Darmesteter (*Les Prophètes d'Israël,* 1892, p. 60), the historian David Cassel (*Geschichte der jüdischen Literatur,* 1873, 1ste Abth., 2ter Abschnitt S. 182, Anm. 4), and by Professor Barth (*Beiträge zur Erklärung des Jesaias,* 1885, S. 15 ff.); and it lives among the rabbis (J. H. Schwarz, *Geschichtliche Entstehung der messianischen Idee des Judenthums,* S. 39; Hirsch, *Das Buch Jesaia*). The same interpretation was offered by Grotius, Hensler, Paulus, Gesenius, Hendewerk; but was rejected by their contemporaries Cocceius, Vitringa, Eichhorn, Rosenmüller; and its general rejection by the more recent exegetes has made clear that it cannot be held (Hackmann, S. 130). The main reasons for dismissing it are sufficiently stated in the words of Dillmann: 1. "All the tenses from viii. 23^b, onward relate either to the past or to the future; the impossibility of referring viii. 23^b, ix. 3, 4 to actual events of history is clear." There is a look forward into the future. (Cf. also Alexander.) 2. The titles given to the child "can be understood of Hezekiah only in greatly weakened manner" (so already Vitringa; and cp. Rosenmüller). 3. "From viii. 9, 10, 16-18 it follows with certainty that Isaiah is treating of hopes belonging to the ideal future. And if the Messianic hope is certain in chapter xi., what interest has one to remove it from this passage [in the ninth chapter] by unnatural interpretations?" Modern exegesis and criticism have given their verdict: Without doubt the child is the great king of the future, of the house and lineage of David.[3]

The composer of the oratorio was right, too, in calling to

[3] "The child of chap. 9 . . . is admitted, on all hands, to be the Messiah of the house of David" (A. B. Davidson, *Old Testament Prophecy,* p. 357); e. g., within the last quarter of a century by Briggs, Cheyne, Driver, G. A. Smith, Kirkpatrick, Skinner, Davidson, Dillmann,

his aid all the resources of the orchestra for a burst of triumphant music at the mention of each name in the manifold title
of the Messiah. For the prophet is bringing to the people of
God tidings of greatest joy. He tells them, as they sit in
darkness and despair, that the night is passing and the dawn
is drawing nigh. Sorrow is vanquished forever, conflict ended,
peace at last. The prophet proclaims to the oppressed people
of God the advent of their deliverer, enumerates one by one
his superb qualities, discloses his sufficiency for the task imposed upon him, and describes the peace without end under
his beneficent reign.

Three principal interpretations have been proposed for the
name. 1. The child's name is merely Prince of Peace (Solomon Jarchi, David Kimchi, and recently Rabbi Hirsch). The
other exalted epithets are titles of God. The translation should
be: The Wonderful, the Counsellor, the mighty God calls his
name Prince of Peace. There is, however, a fatal objection
to this translation; namely, the order of the words. In Hebrew the word ' name ' cannot be separated by the subject of
the sentence from the name itself. There is no exception to
this rule. Cocceius demonstrated the fact (*Consideratio respon-
sionis Judaicae,* cap. vi. 14) ;[4] and since his day, the middle of
the seventeenth century, this interpretation of the name has
had no standing before a court of scholars.

2. It has been proposed to take all the titles, given to the
child, together and read them as a sentence. Names that consist of a sentence are the rule rather than the exception in the
Hebrew literature that is preserved in the Old Testament. To
be sure there are names like Terah, ' wild goat ', Deborah, ' a
bee ', Barak, ' lightning ', Hannah, ' grace ', Saul, ' asked ',
Amos, ' a burden ', Jonah, ' a dove ', Nahum, ' compassionate '.
But the majority of proper names are sentences, as Ishmael,

Kuenen, Guthe (*Zukunftsbild des Jesaia*), Giesebrecht, Duhm, Cornill
(*Der israelitische Prophetismus*[6], S. 60), Hackmann, Volz, Marti, Smend,
Nowack).

[4] Calvin had already stated that the order of words makes it impossible
to construe all the titles, from Wonderful to Prince of Peace inclusive, as
the subject of the verb call and thus obtain the meaning that God names
the child.

Israel, Isaiah, Jeremiah, Ezekiel, Daniel; and not a few are
comparatively long sentences, and sometimes contain a direct
object.   Such are the names of Isaiah's two sons, Shear-ja-
shub, ' a remnant shall return ', and Maher-shalal-hash-baz,
that is, ' spoil speedeth, prey hasteth '; also Micaiah, ' who is
like Jehovah? ', and Elihoenai, ' my eyes are toward Jehovah ',
and Romamti-ezer, ' I have exalted him who is a help ', and
Tob-adonijah, ' good is my Lord Jehovah '.   Even Immanuel
is a sentence: ' God is with us '.   Following such analogies it
has been proposed to read all the words in the name given to
the child as a sentence.   A verb is needed.   Now the word
rendered ' counsellor ' is in fact a participle, ' the counseling
one '.   Instead of treating it as a noun denoting the agent, it
is taken as the verb of the sentence.   Then the first word,
' wonderful ', is construed as the direct object, and is understood to have been placed at the beginning of the sentence for
the sake of emphasis.   All the words that follow ' counsellor '
are regarded as titles of God and are construed as the subject.
The sentence then reads: The mighty God, the everlasting
Father, the Prince of Peace is counseling a wonderful thing.
The prophet announces the birth of a child whose name being
interpreted shall be, A wonderful thing does God the strong,
the eternal father, the prince of peace, resolve.   Luzzatto
advanced this interpretation.   It has caused merriment among
solemn commentators.   Dillmann calls it an unparalleled mon-
strosity, and Delitzsch speaks of it as a sesquipedalian name.
The jest is dropped and objections are formally stated.   " If
the intention is to emphasize the Divine wisdom, why accum-
ulate epithets of God which do not contribute to that object? "
(Cheyne).   " Why employ the participle instead of the usual
verbal form, viz., the imperfect or perfect? " (Cheyne, Duhm).
Finally the title of ' Prince of Peace ' belongs to the child and
not to God according to the unmistakable context.

   3.   The several words or word-groups are so many titles
descriptive of the child.   He is wonderful, he is a counselor,
he is the mighty God, he is the everlasting father, he is the
prince of peace.   There are a number of familiar analogues
to this composite name.   Thus in the New Testament our

blessed Master is frequently entitled Lord Jesus Christ. He is our Lord; he is Jesus, for he saves his people from their sins; he is the Christ, the long expected Messiah (see also Is. lviii. 12, lxii. 12; Amos iv. 13; Rev. xvii. 5, xix. 16). In the name of the child the number of titles is counted variously: six, as in the Vulgate and in Luther's Bible; five, as in the English version; or four, as on the margin of the revised version, each title being a pair of words. The very first of these titles, on any enumeration, introduces the child to us as an extraordinary person. A noun, great enough in meaning to denote the wonders wrought by the God of Israel (Ex. xv. 11; Ps. lxxvii. 14, lxxviii. 12; Is. xxv. 1; cf. Judg. xiii. 18), describes the character of the child. Undue importance is not attached to this fact; still the word does betoken the peculiar greatness of the child, and prepares the mind for the exalted predicates that follow; and when combined with its next neighbor so as to yield the meaning "A very wonder of a counselor," the title associates the child in a measure with "Jehovah, who is wonderful in counsel" (Is. xxviii. 29).

Of these titles two, in the familiar translation Mighty God, Everlasting Father, at once attract attention. Marvelous attributes for a son of David! What explanation is possible?

Regarding the title which is rendered Mighty God, one may be tempted to see a formal similarity between 'el gibbor, mighty God, and 'eley gibborim in Ezek. xxxii. 21, and in this latter verse seek the meaning of the title. The words of Ezekiel are rendered in the English version by " the strong among the mighty " (so also by Delitzsch, *Messianische Weissagungen*, S. 101). They may be translated literally, " the strong of the mighty, where ' strong ' is not a class among the mighty, but identical with them—the strong mighty ones, genitive of apposition (A. B. Davidson in *Cambridge Bible; Ezekiel*). Thus regarded, the phrase on its face might appear to be merely the plural of the Messianic title 'el gibbor (G. A. Smith, *Expositor's Bible: The Book of Isaiah*, p. 137). The title accordingly would mean, not ' a very god of a hero ', but ' the strong mighty one '. This construction is outwardly the same as that of the three other Messianic titles (when the number is thought

of as four), since in each case a noun stands in the construct
relation before another noun; but it yields a meaning that is
not symmetrical with their meaning. The epithet strong mighty
one is a form of words unlike that seen in ' wonder of a counselor ', ' father of eternity ', and ' prince of peace '. A different interpretation is offered by Gesenius. He includes
' hero ' among the meanings which he assigns to the word *'el*
(also Brown, Hebrew and English Lexicon), and renders the
title in Is. ix. 5 by ' mighty hero ' (*Thesaurus*). On this interpretation symmetry of construction does not exist among the
titles. Dillmann denies that *'el* is attested as meaning ' hero '
by Ezek. xxxii. 21, xxxi. 11, since in those passages *'ayil*, ' ram ',
' leader ', may be at the basis of the forms *(Commentar*[5] S. 94;
Alttestamentliche Theologie, S. 210; *Commentar zu Exodus*
xv. 15; so also Buhl's edition of Gesenius' *Handwörterbuch,*
and Siegfried-Stade, *Hebräisches Wörterbuch); and he retains the meaning God in the Messianic title. But Dillmann
does not adopt the rendering " a mighty God ". Following
Roorda (*Orientalia,* i. 173) he prefers the translation " a god
of a hero ", because the three other names are formed by
means of the construct state. There is attractiveness in this
argument from symmetry. Then, too, each of the four titles
consists of three syllables in Hebrew (if the word for ' wonder ', being a segholate, is pronounced as one syllable). And
the theory receives some confirmation from the symmetrical
form of the name given to Isaiah's son Maher-shalal-hash-baz,
' Spoil speedeth, prey hasteth '. In the name of the prophet's
son the symmetry is both external and internal, both in form
and meaning. But in the name of the Messianic king, if the
second title is rendered ' a god of a hero ', the symmetry of the
four titles is external only. It extends to the use of the construct relation, and perhaps to the trisyllabic form, but ends
there; for even on the translation ' wonder of a counselor ',
' god of a hero ', ' father of booty ', or ' father of perpetuity ',
' prince of peace ', while the first and second titles would be
similar in construction and force, they would not be similar
in force with either the third or the fourth. Assuming, however, the correctness of the attractive theory that symmetry of

construction does belong to each of the four titles so that in each case the first word of the pair is in the construct state before the second word, the second title may still be properly rendered ' mighty God '; for a noun not infrequently stands in the construct state before its adjective or, as the matter is sometimes stated, before an adjective treated as an abstract noun (Is. xvii. 10, xxii. 24, xxviii. 4, xxxvi. 2; Ps. lxxiii. 10, lxxiv. 15; Prov. vi. 24). On this construction ' mighty God ' is the correct rendering of the title.

Two arguments in particular have had weight with exegetes against any other rendering than ' mighty God '.

1. The Hebrew word *'el* is always used by the prophet Isaiah in the high sense of God (Delitzsch), always "in an absolute sense . . . . never hyperbolically or metaphorically " (Cheyne). 2. In the very next chapter exactly the same phrase means ' the mighty God ' (x. 21).[5] The phrase was traditional among the Hebrews as a title of God (Deut. x. 17; Jer. xxxii. 18; Neh. ix. 32). The consideration of such facts as these drove Luzzatto to the expedient of combining the titles into a sentence, in order that he might retain the sense of ' mighty God ' without admitting it to be descriptive of the Davidic king. And Gressmann, whose premises allow him a free hand in exegesis, remarks: " Whatever the explanation be, the fact itself stands fast: a divine attribute is here assigned to the Messiah " (S. 282).

[5] The attribution of x. 21 to a different author than the writer of ix. 5 does not destroy the force of these facts, for the usage of the phrase as an exalted title of God is still attested by x. 21. Nor is escape to be had by referring the title in both passages to the messianic king (Marti; Mitchell, *Isaiah*, p. 212); for even assuming that it does denote the king in the two passages, it must still be translated mighty God or given an equivalent rendering (Delitzsch; von Orelli), in accordance with the uniform usage of the word *'el*, God, in the book of Isaiah and with the traditional meaning of the title. The reference of x. 21, moreover, is to Jehovah rather than to his Anointed (Gesenius; Ewald; Riehm, 116; Dillmann; Schultz, 611; Cheyne; Driver, 71; Kirkpatrick[2], 193; Smend[2], 232; Skinner; Volz, 41; Gressmann, 281), for " it is Jehovah who acts alone throughout this part of the prophecy" (Cheyne, *Prophecies of Isaiah*[3], 73), in the paragraphs comprised in verses 16-34 (Ewald, *Propheten*[2], ii. 461).

What does this great title 'mighty God' signify when bestowed upon the Messianic king? 1. Ilgen lightly dismisses it
as the flattery of a court poet (Paulus' *Memorabilia,* vii. 152).
But in times of dire distress (Is. viii. 22, 23), flattery is
seldom heard. The hope of deliverance held out to the oppressed people of God by the prophet would be a mockery of
their plight were it based on empty or extravagant term's in
which he spoke to them of the promised deliverer. The remark may be made at this point that the titles given by the
prophet to the Messianic king are often compared by commentators with the epithets found in addresses to the ancient rulers
who held sway in the valleys of the Nile and the Tigris. The
comparison is sometimes made in order to discount the value of
the titles given to the Messiah. But the epithets bestowed by
the Babylonians, Assyrians, and Egyptians upon their kings
were not always words of flattery. They often deserve respect,
notably in ancient Egypt; for very frequently they express
deep conviction and reveal genuine faith.

2. The title 'mighty God' is explained as given to the
Messianic king by popular hyperbole (Hitzig, Duhm). But
even in extravagance of speech the Hebrews did not employ a
form of words that might suggest even superficially identification with God. They make plain that comparison only is intended, and are careful to introduce a term that expresses
comparison (Gen. xxxiii. 10; Ex. iv. 16, Zech. xii. 8; also
1 Sam. xxix. 9; 2 Sam. xiv. 17, xix. 27); and they use
the word *'elohim,* not *'el* (Cheyne, *Prophecies of Isaiah,*[3]
p. 62). Quite different is Ex. vii. 1, 2. There Jehovah
speaks, and not man. Jehovah makes Moses a god to Pharaoh; puts Moses in the place of God to Pharaoh, makes him
the authoritative representative of God at the Egyptian court,
to speak the words that God himself commands and do the
deeds that God bids and empowers him to do. The passage
demands and illustrates a far higher interpretation of Messiah's
title than the explanation which sees nothing in it but hyperbole.

3. The Messiah is called God, not in a metaphysical sense,
but as equipped of God with power that exceeds the human
measure, by reason of the Spirit of God that rests upon him;

Is. xi. 2; Mic. v. 3 [4]; Zech. xii. 8 (Dillmann, *Isaiah*[5] S. 94; *Alttestamentliche Theologie*, S. 530 f; Marti on ix. 5 and xi. 2). The Messianic king is thus a glorified Samson. He is a purely human figure, but one whom the Spirit of God fills with might. He will not be a fitful deliverer of the people like Samson, upon whom the Spirit of God came occasionally; but he will be a king permanently armed with might by the abiding presence of the Spirit. This explanation contains a precious truth (xi. 2; cp. Mat. xii. 28), but it does not set forth all the facts.

4. Perhaps, then, the prophet, when he uses the title 'mighty God', thinks of "the Messiah, somewhat as the Egyptians, Assyrians, and Babylonians regarded their king, as an earthly representative of Divinity" (Cheyne, *Prophecies of Isaiah*,[3] p. 61, referring to Is. xiv. 13).[6] If by this is meant "the Oriental belief in kings as incarnations of the Divine" (Cheyne on Is. xiv. 13; Rosenmüller on Is. ix. 5, *deum natura humana indutum*), a term, 'incarnation', is used to which a vague signification must be given, and not its technical theological sense. The ancient Hebrews believed, indeed, that Jehovah might manifest himself in human form, and had occasionally so manifested himself on earth (Gen. xviii. 1, 33); but that is quite different from an incarnation of himself in a son of man. And it is not the idea in Is. ix. 5, where a descendant of David is called mighty God; nor is it the Egyptian belief regarding the king, who was a son of man, and yet somehow a manifestation of the deity. In Egypt the king was addressed as god, regarded as the presence of the god, and approached with prayer and offerings (Wiedemann, *Religion der alten Aegypter*, S. 92; Brugsch, *Aegyptologie*, S. 203; Maspero, *Dawn of Civilization*, pp. 262-265). A certain

---

[6] It is proper to remark that in his more recent work, *The Book of the Prophet Isaiah: A new English Translation*, 1898, p. 145, Professor Cheyne, speaking of the title *'el gibbor* in ix. 5, refers to x. 21, "which shows", he says, "that we are not to render *divine hero* [but Mighty Divinity (p. 15)]: the king seems to Isaiah, in his lofty enthusiasm, like one of those *angels* (as we moderns call them), who in old time were said to mix with men, and even contend with them, and who, as superhuman beings, were called by the name of *'el* (Gen. xxxii. 22-32).

vagueness remains about this Egyptian belief, even after the matter has been stated. Perhaps the conception was vague in the Egyptian mind; but at least these three features appear in their attitude toward the king. Professor Cheyne suggests that the prophet conceived of the Messiah, " somewhat as the Egyptians . . . regarded their king, as an earthly representative of divinity." If so, it was evidently a profound conception which the prophet entertained concerning the nature of the Messiah, and corresponded more closely with the revelation of himself made by the Christ than some exegetes have been willing to believe.

A just appreciation of the greatness of the idea which the Messianic title ' mighty God' conveyed to the Israelites may be formed by a consideration of the following facts. The Hebrews could readily think of a human being as a representative of God, and speak of the representative as God (*'elohim*). Judges, as the representatives of God and invested with his authority, are called gods (Ps. lxxxii. 1, 6; cp. Ex. xxii. 8, 9, 28). The conception becomes larger as the authority and power of God's representative increase. When Jehovah sent Moses as his agent and representative to the court of Pharaoh, made him superior to the Egyptian monarch, appointed him to lay commands upon Pharaoh, and empowered him to enforce obedience, he made Moses a god to Pharaoh (Ex. vii. 1). All this and more is true of the Messiah. A son of man, heir to the throne of Judah, he is declared to be the representative of Jehovah, in the place of God on the throne; he is clothed with power unceasingly by the divine Spirit, and rules in the strength and majesty of Jehovah (Is. xi. 2, Mic. v. 4); and he is hailed by the prophet, or at least named, ' Mighty God'. No other human representative of God, equipped though this representative be by the Spirit, no judge, no prophet, no king, not even Moses, is ever called ' Mighty God'. That title is given to Jehovah alone and the Messiah. Let no one say to himself that " the Prince is only called by " this name. " It is not said that *he is,* but that *he shall be called* " the mighty God (Geo. A. Smith, *The Book of Isaiah,* p. 140). To argue thus is to deceive oneself. The meaning of the prophet is clear. It is written in the fourth chapter of Isaiah that, when the judgment has passed and Zion has been purified of dross, " he that remaineth in Jerusalem shall be called holy ". The prophet does not mean that in the new Jerusalem the inhabitants shall be nominally holy. He means that they shall in truth be holy. Again it is recorded that the angel said unto Mary: " The Holy Ghost shall come upon thee, and the power of the Highest shall overshadow thee: therefore also that holy thing which shall be born of thee shall be called the Son of God." He shall not be nominally divine, but actually. Even so the king whose advent the prophet announces is called ' Prince of Peace ' and ' Mighty God ', because he is such.

Leaving this title for the present, we turn to that one which is rendered ' Everlasting Father '. This name of the Messiah, '^a bi 'ad, has been interpreted as meaning ' possessor of eternity ' (Dathe, Hengstenberg, Guthe), in accordance with the well-known Arabic idiom. The employment of the word ' father ' in construction with a noun for the purpose of paraphrasing an adjective is not attested with certainty in Hebrew. Perhaps it is so used in proper names, like Absalom; but in every case a different interpretation is possible. The title has also been rendered ' Booty-father ', and sometimes explained as meaning a distributor of booty. The word 'ad in the sense of booty is very rare, but this meaning is fully attested for it by Gen. xlix. 27. A stubborn fact lies against the translation ' Booty-father '. " The meaning is, owner, possessor, or distributor of booty " (Briggs, Messianic Prophecy, p. 200). The word ' father ' is thus given an interpretation that " verges on the unprovable sense of possessor " (Marti). And in particular the word father is never used in the sense of distributor. Nor does the title mean ' Producer or provider of booty ' (Siegfried-Stade, Wörterbuch, art. 'ad; cp. art. 'ab); for although 'ab is used tropically for the creator, who calls a thing into existence, and can be employed figuratively to denote a kindly provider, the assigned meaning, unless most carefully restricted, makes plunder an end sought in the conflict, and not the mere result of victory, and introduces into the description the spirit of selfish gloating over the rich spoil, whereas the salvation of the people and the reign of peace are the absorbing hope. Finally, the general objection to every interpretation which employs the word booty in the title is that the thought yielded thereby is incongruous among these designations of the Messianic king, and is too meager in content, when the preceding title is rendered mighty God; and for this rendering of the preceding title substantial reasons exist. It is exegetically needful, therefore, to give to the word 'ad in the Messianic title its customary sense of endurance, continuance, and render the title 'father of endurance' and understand the designation to denote a continual father, one who enduringly acts as a father to his people (Gesenius, Delitzsch, Dillmann, Riehm, Cheyne, Skinner, Marti). Is any limitation to be placed on the word continuance? None that appears. The Hebrew word may denote eternity, and not a few representative exegetes understand it in that sense in this Messianic title (e. g. Hengstenberg, Alexander, Delitzsch, Cheyne, Gressmann). But it does not necessarily signify endless time. A prepositional phrase formed with it is rendered forever, and has a latitude of meaning similar to that of the English word 'always' (Ps. xix. 9 [10]; xxii. 26 [27]; lxxxix. 29 [30]; cxii. 3; Prov. xxix. 14; Amos i. 11, "perpetually"; Mic. vii. 18; cp. "of old", Job. xx. 4). In the five cases where it is used in combination with a noun, as in the Messianic title, it certainly means very long time, unbounded time. Babylon fondly expected to be "a lady forever" (Is. xlvii. 7, see Hitzig, Cheyne, Duhm, Marti; literally, a mistress of duration). No limit is set or even thought of by the proud city of the Chaldeans, no time when she shall cease to be. The 'mountains of duration' (Gen. xlix. 26; Hab. iii. 6) are well spoken of as everlasting hills, eternal mountains. 'Ages of duration' (Is. xlv. 17) mean world without end, all eternity. And Is. lvii. 15 must be translated " the high and lofty One that inhabiteth eternity ". In the title of the Messianic king the word bears in it a like fulness of meaning; for nowhere in prophecy is it intimated that the Messiah shall cease to reign. No limit of time is set to his administration. In fact, this particular title is explicit. It contains a

word for the express purpose of withholding bounds of time
from the Messiah's activity. He shall enduringly act as a
father to his people.

The Messianic king comes with the qualifications signified
by the titles for a definite beneficent purpose, which the prophet proceeds to state: namely, for the expansion of the rule,
and for welfare without end over David's throne and kingdom,
in order to establish the kingdom and to uphold it by means of
justice and righteousness which he exercises from henceforth
even forever. As one maintains his bodily strength by a mor-
sel of bread (Judg. xix. 5), as God's right hand supports one,
and his mercy holds one up, when one's foot slippeth (Ps. xviii.
35 [36], xciv. 18), as a king upholdeth his throne by mercy
(Prov. xx. 28); so the Messianic king upholds the throne of
David forever by justice which he administers and by righteousness which he exercises (s^e dakah, not sedek). If the upholding hand is withdrawn, the faint and feeble fall; if the bread
is withheld, the strength fails; if justice and righteousness are
not exercised, the throne totters. This prophecy is a distinct
advance over the promise made to David by the prophet Nathan. The promise is that God will make David a house and
establish the throne of David and of David's son forever (2
Sam. vii. 16, 19). But the prophet Isaiah declares that the
Messianic king himself shall uphold the kingdom forever. To
deny that a perpetual reign is promised the child (Marti), and
to assert that the reference is "to the rule of David's descend-
ants" (Duhm), is arbitrary and not drawn from the words
of the prophet. Professor Cheyne, commenting on the words
"from henceforth even forever", states the matter thus:
"Two meanings are exegetically possible: 1. That the Messiah
shall live an immortal life on earth, and, 2. That there shall be
an uninterrupted succession of princes of his house. The latter is favored by 2 Sam. vii. 12-16; comp. Ps. xxi. 4, lxi. 6, 7;
but the former seems to me more in accordance with the general
tenor of the description." Certainly it is; for, 1. The prophecy
marks a distinct advance over the promise of 2 Sam. vii. 16
and 19. 2. Unto us a child is born. It is a solitary figure in
whom the hope of the nation rests. 3. To the prophet the final

stage of history has been reached, and he beholds the prince upholding the kingdom. 4. No prophet ever contemplates an end of Messiah's reign or speaks of Messiah's successors. " Were the Messiah to cease to be, how could the Lord's people maintain their ground " (Cheyne). Whether the Messiah lives an immortal life on earth or on earth and in heaven, need not be discussed (Mt. xxviii. 20).

The results of this study so far are: 1. The title ' Mighty God ' indicates a personage of peculiar exaltation. No one save this king and Jehovah is called ' Mighty God '. 2. The title ' Father of duration ' not only describes him as the father of his people, but assigns to his fatherly activity duration from which bounds of time are expressly withheld. 3. The prediction that the Messiah shall uphold the kingdom of David forever demands in accordance with the usage of the word, the tenor of the passage, and the drift of other prophecies of the pre-exilic period the perpetuity of his reign. These three declarations are complementary and mutually explanatory. He is mighty God; a father to his people during long, unbounded time; and upholds the kingdom forever. At the same time the Messianic king is a man, a descendant of David (xi. 1). A problem is here; yet it cannot be solved by the attempt to tone down the declarations concerning this child until they sound applicable to a human being. For not only have the titles shown inherent power to maintain themselves in full strength and value in biblical interpretation; but nothing would be gained by the method, if successful, for the fundamental question does not concern the Messianic king alone. The underlying conception of identity with Jehovah and possession of his attributes, yet distinctness from him, comes to the front elsewhere in the Hebrew Scriptures. It is met in connection with the angel of the Lord and also with the suffering servant of the Lord, on any interpretation of the fifty-third chapter of Isaiah which does not neglect the doctrine taught in Israel in the prophet's day concerning sin and atonement (Davis, *Dictionary of the Bible*,[3] art. Servant of the Lord). The illustration afforded by the angel of the Lord must suffice for the present discussion, although the important particular of human

descent is not involved in it as in the case of the Messiah.
Mention is made of an angel, and under the circumstances
it is proper always to think of the same angel, who is distinguished from Jehovah, and yet is identified with him (Gen.
xvi. 10, 13, xviii. 2, 33, xxii. 11-16, xxxi. 11, 13; Ex. iii. 2, 4;
Josh. v. 13-15, vi. 2; Zech. i. 10-13, iii. 1, 2), who revealed the
face of God (Gen. xxxii. 30), in whom was Jehovah's name
(Ex. xxiii. 21), and whose presence was equivalent to Jehovah's presence (Ex. xxxii. 34, xxxiii. 14; Is. lxiii. 9).
The angel of the Lord thus appears as a manifestation of Jehovah himself, one with Jehovah and yet distinguishable from
him. How these things could be is not explained; but the idea
was familiar. The objection has been raised that neither the
prophet nor his hearers " conceived of the Messiah, with the
conceiving of Christian theology, as a separate Divine personality " (Geo. A. Smith, *The Book of Isaiah,* p. 137). Well,
what if they did not? The conception of distinct persons in
the Godhead may have been formed in the minds of men later,
and be quite true. Likewise the formulated doctrine of the
incarnation; it came later because important facts on which it
rests came to man's knowledge later. The Messiah, a descendant of David, is simply given a unique divine name and spoken
of as the possessor of divine attributes. No explanation is offered, no theory advanced. It is enough to know that in the
days of the prophets the conception of identity with, yet dis-
tinguishableness from, Jehovah was present in Hebrew thought
and was consistent with the pure monotheism which was taught
in Israel.

JONATHAN EDWARDS: A STUDY

John DeWitt

Introduction. Relations between New England and Princeton. Edwards' self-consistent career. His dominating and unifying quality. Edwards and Emerson. Likenesses and contrasts. Spirituality the characteristic of each.

I. *Edwards' Spirituality.* In what sense a racial trait intensified by Puritanism. Its manifestations, in his vision of the spiritual universe, his self-interpretation, his style, his emotional life, the work he did, his habits, his limitations.

II. *His intellect and work.* Calvin and Luther greater than Edwards. Edwards' subtlety of intellect. His likeness to Anselm of Canterbury. Lack of historical culture and spirit. His three capital gifts. His distinct and complete world-view. His purpose to embody it in the *History of Redemption* frustrated by death. His portrayal and analysis of the religious life. His contributions to theological science. The impetus he gave to theological speculation and construction. The polemic against his *Freedom of the Will*. The attack on him as the author of the sermons on the punishment of the wicked. Edwards' sermons and Dante's *Inferno.* Conclusion.

JONATHAN EDWARDS: A STUDY[1]

I am deeply indebted to your Committee for the honor they
have done me in inviting me to take part in this celebration. My
hesitation in accepting their invitation was due solely to the
feeling I had that a son of New England could more appropriately than a stranger ask your attention to an appreciation of
this great New Englander. This hesitation was overcome,
partly by the cordiality with which the invitation was extended,
and partly by the consideration that Princeton, where Edwards
did his last work and where his body lies to-day, might well
be represented on the occasion by which we have been assembled. Moreover, Princeton College, when Edwards was called
to its presidency, was largely a New England institution of
learning. Both of his predecessors in that office, Jonathan
Dickinson and Aaron Burr, were natives of New England,
graduates of the College at New Haven and Congregational
ministers. Associated with Dickinson and Burr in the plant-
ing of the College were not only other Yale men, but Harvard
men also: Ebenezer Pemberton and David Cowell and Jacob

[1] Address delivered in the Meeting House of the Parish Church of
Stockbridge, Mass., October 5, 1903, at the celebration, by the Berkshire
Conferences of Congregational Churches, of the two hundredth anniversary of the birth of Jonathan Edwards; and repeated in Miller Chapel,
Princeton Theological Seminary, October 16, 1903. It is reproduced
here, because it seems peculiarly appropriate that, in a volume celebrating
the Century of Princeton Theological Seminary, Jonathan Edwards should
be commemorated. He was the earliest of the great theologians who have
lived in Princeton. When he accepted the call to Princeton College he
expressed his willingness "to do the whole work of a professor of divinity". He lived in Princeton only eight weeks. He came in January and
died in March 1758. During the interval his only teaching was "in
divinity," and from the chair which may be said to have been transferred
from the College to the Theological Seminary when the Seminary was
opened in 1812.

Green and, above all, Jonathan Belcher, sometime Royal Governor of the Colony of Massachusetts and *ex-officio* Overseer of Harvard, his *alma mater;* who, when afterward he was commissioned Royal Governor of the Province of New Jersey, to repeat his own words, " adopted as his own this infant College," gave to it a new and more liberal charter, and so largely aided it by private gifts and official influence that its Trustees called him its " founder, patron and benefactor ". I am glad as a Princeton man to find in the anniversary of the birth of one of its Presidents an opportunity to acknowledge the University's great debt to New England. And, if you will permit a personal remark, I cannot forget that in coming to these services I am returning to the Commonwealth of which I am proud to have been a citizen, and to the Massachusetts Association of Congregational Ministers whose list of pastors for six successive years contained my name.[2] I should have to efface the memory of a pastorate exceptionally happy, and of unnumbered acts of kindness from the living and the dead, in order not to feel grateful and at home to-day.

But, after all, the highest justification of this commemoration of a man born two centuries ago is not that his genius and character and career reflect glory on the people and the class from whom he sprang, but that they contain notable elements of universal interest and value. The great man is great because in some great way he adequately addresses, not what is exceptional, not what is distinctive of any class or people, but what is human and common to the race; to whose message, therefore, men respond as men; whose eulogists and interpreters are not necessarily dwellers in his district or people of his blood; who is the common property of all to study, to enjoy, to revere and to celebrate. It is, above all, because Jonathan Edwards belongs to this small and elect class that we are gathered to honor his memory by recalling his story and reflecting on the elements of his greatness.

It would be inappropriate, certainly in this place and before this audience, for a stranger to repeat the well-known story of his life. I shall better meet your expectations if I shall

---

[2] Pastor of the Central Church, Boston, from Dec. 1869 to Jany. 1876.

reproduce the impressions of the man made on me by a renewed study of his collected writings and his life.

We shall agree that the inward career of Edwards was singularly self-consistent; that from its beginning to its close it is exceptionally free from incongruities and contradictions; that in him Wordsworth's line, " The child is father to the man," finds a signal illustration. When we are brought into contact with a life so unified, whose development along its own lines has not been hindered or distorted by external disturbances as violent even as that suffered by Edwards at Northampton, we naturally look for its principle of unity, the dominating quality which subordinated to itself all the others, or, if you like, which so interpenetrated all his other traits as to become his distinctive note. We are confident that such a quality there must have been, and that if we are happy enough at once to find it, we shall have in our possession the master key which, so far as may be to human view, will open to us the departments of his thought and feeling and activity.

A century later than Edwards there was born another great New Englander—Ralph Waldo Emerson—between whom and Edwards there is a strong likeness as well as a sharp contrast. Because this is his centennial year, Emerson like Edwards is just now especially present to our minds, and one is tempted to compare and contrast the two. To this temptation I shall not yield. But in order that we may properly approach and seize for ourselves a fine formula of Edward's dominant quality, permit me to recall to you a study of Emerson by a *litterateur* of great charm and wide acceptance. Mr. Matthew Arnold in his well-known lecture, says that Emerson is " not a great poet ", he " is not a great man of letters ", he " is not a great philosopher ". Mr. Arnold, I think, does great injustice to Emerson in two of these negations. If I did not think so I should not associate him with so great a man as Edwards. I am not, indeed, concerned to defend the claims of Emerson to "a place among the great philosophers ". His treatment of particular subjects was marked by discontinuity; and his tendency to gnomic, sententious forms of speech betrayed him not seldom into overstatement or exaggeration. Now, than discontinuity and overstatement there can scarcely be conceived more deadly foes to system-building, to the construction of a world-theory; and the construction of a world-theory is the end of all philosophizing. It may be questioned whether Emerson ever permitted himself to rest in any fixed theory of the universe. I have the impression that for a fixed view of the universe he never felt the need, and that from all actual views of the universe which have been fixed in formulas he revolted. And, therefore, when Mr. Arnold says, " Emerson cannot be called with justice a great philosophical writer—he cannot build, he does not construct a philosophy," I do not know on what grounds we can dissent from his statement.

But when he goes further and, with the same positiveness, says, " We have not in Emerson a great writer or a great poet," Mr. Arnold passes from the region of opinion based on considerations whose force all estimate alike, into the region of opinion which has its source and ground in mere individual temperament and taste. Moreover, greatness is a word so vague as scarcely to raise a definite issue; and this fact might well have prevented so careful and acute a critic from employing it to deny to Emerson a quality which Mr. Arnold would have found difficult to define. Certainly this much can be said. If Emerson is not "a great writer, a great man of letters," yet, in his unfolding of ideas and in his portrayal and criticism of nature and of life, he has nobly fulfilled and is still fulfilling the function of a great man of letters to thousands of disciplined minds; interpreting for them and teaching them to interpret nature and man, educating their judgments, cultivating their taste, introducing them to " the best that has been thought and written," and stimulating and ennobling their whole intellectual life. And if he is not, as Mr. Arnold says he is not, " senuous and impassioned " in his poetry, we must not forget that reflective poetry is Emerson's best and most characteristic poetic achievement; that reflective poetry cannot possibly be " sensuous and impassioned "; and that Mr. Arnold is prejudiced against all reflective poetry, and, indeed, does not think it poetry, whether it be Emerson's or Wordsworth's.

But though Mr. Arnold does Emerson injustice in these two

negative propositions; I think that, in his positive statement, he has firmly seized and happily formulated Emerson's dominating quality. He has given us the real clue to the significance of Emerson's literary product, regarded as a whole, when he says of him: "Emerson is the friend and aider of those who would live in the spirit." The friendship of Emerson for "those who would live in the spirit" is, indeed, his characteristic trait. He is also their "aider", as Mr. Arnold says. But the aid he offers them is conditioned precisely by the fact that he is a man of letters and a poetic interpreter of nature and of life, and that he does not bring to them a philosophy. I say, the aid he offers is conditioned by this lack of a philosophy; and by conditioned I mean limited. For because of it the realm of nature and spirit, as he presents it, is vast indeed, but vague and undefined and, so far forth, unrevealed. And therefore, as Mr. Arnold himself points out, his aid is confined to the sphere of the moral sentiments and action. Mr. Arnold does, indeed, express the opinion that "as Wordsworth's poetry is the most important work done in verse in our language in the nineteenth century, so Emerson's essays are the most important work done in prose." But this is the language of purely personal judgment. Far more important for us in estimating Emerson, with Mr. Arnold's help, as "an aider of those who would live in the spirit," is the sentence in which he formulates the precise content of the aid which Emerson extends. And this is the sentence: "Happiness in labor, righteousness and veracity; in all the life of the spirit; happiness and eternal hope—that was Emerson's gospel." A fair and felicitous description it is. And how clearly it reveals the limit of the aid which Emerson's gospel offers! How clearly it reveals that the aid extended is not the aid of a great thinker in the sphere of ultimate knowing and absolute being, but is aid confined to the sphere of the moral sentiments and action!

Thus, by a route somewhat circuitous indeed, but I trust not wholly without interest or propriety, we reach, in Mr. Arnold's characterization of Emerson, the formula of which I spoke as finely expressing Edward's dominating and unifying quality.

Edwards like Emerson is, above all else and by eminence, " the friend and aider of those who would live in the spirit." Who that knows him at all will deny to him a right equal to that of Emerson to this high title? Of course, they differ widely both in the aid they offer and in their methods of offering it. Emerson's aid is conditioned and limited, as I have already said, by his want of a firm and self-consistent doctrine of the universe, by his want of a philosophy. And we must be just as ready to acknowledge that Edwards' aid is as clearly conditioned and limited by his unfortunate poverty in the humanities, by his notable lack of feeling for poetry and letters. On the other hand and positively I think we may say, that it would be hard to name a man of letters who, having separated himself from all formulated philosophical and religious beliefs, has more nearly than Emerson exhausted the resources of letters and poetry in the service of " those who would live in the spirit." And among the great doctors of the Christian Church, it would be as hard to name one more distinctively spiritual in character and aim than Edwards, or one who, in cultivating the spiritual life in himself and promoting it in others, has more consistently or more ably drawn on the resources of his philosophy, his world-view, his Christian doctrine of the universe.

I am quite sure that this obvious likeness and difference between Edwards and Emerson is the right point of departure for any large study of their affinity and opposition. Such a study the day invites us to mention, but does not permit us to undertake. The day belongs, not to the great Puritan who gave up the Puritan conception of the universe for its interpretation by poetry and letters, but to the great Puritan who denied himself the high satisfactions of literature, that through his distinctively Christian doctrine of God and man he might be " the friend and aider of those who would live in the spirit." It is to his spirituality, and to his intellectual gifts and work, that I ask your attention.

I.

How many writers have portrayed what one of them calls the " spirituality of mind " of the Northern and Teutonic peoples! One of the most striking passages in Taine's *English Literature* contrasts in this particular the Latin and Teutonic races. And a New England theologian and man of letters, in unfolding the truth that the Northern nations of Europe, unlike the Southern, were " spiritual in their modes of thought ", calls attention to the fact that " the Northern heathen had fewer gods than the Southern, and could believe in their reality without the aid of visible form. He hewed no idol, and he erected no temple; he worshipped his divinity in spirit, beneath the open sky, in the free air." How far this spiritual temper can be attributed to climate, to "the influences which rained down from the cold Northern sky," we cannot say. Racial character would best be accepted as an ultimate fact. The fact itself is certain, that among the European peoples, the race to which Edwards belonged was most strongly marked by this spiritual quality. Moreover, it was precisely by the greater strength and intensity of this racial quality that the Puritan class was separated as a class from their own people. Spirituality is what the logicians call the specific difference of Puritanism. The unshaken belief in the reality of the spiritual universe, the ability to realize its elements without the aid of material symbols, the strong impulse to find motives to action in the unseen and eternal, to feed the intellect and the heart on spiritual objects, and in distinctively spiritual experiences or exercises to discern the highest joys and the deepest sorrows and the great crises of life—these were the traits of the Puritans. And these traits were exhibited, not by a few cloistered souls who obeyed the " counsels of perfection " and were secluded from their fellows by special vows of poverty, celibacy and obedience, but by the mass of the population in Puritan New England; by countrymen and villagers and citizens and statesmen. This spirituality organized the governments and determined the politics of vigorous commonwealths. Theocratic republics, as spiritual as that which, under Savonarola, had so short a life in Florence, flourished for generations on American soil. It was in this Puritan society that Jonathan Edwards' American ancestors lived. They were typical Puritans, justly esteemed and influential in the communities in which they dwelt. The convictions, traditions and spirit of the class were theirs. This was especially true of both his father and his mother. The simplicity, the sincerity, the spirituality of Puritanism at its best were incarnate in them; and it was the Puritan ideal of life which, before his birth, they prayed might be actualized in their unborn child.

Belonging to this spiritual race, sprung from this spiritual class, descended from such an ancestry and born of such a parentage, we have the right to anticipate that his dominant quality will be this spirituality of which I have spoken. We have the right to look for what Dr. Egbert Smyth calls, " Edwards' transcendent spiritual personality," and concerning which he says, that " the spiritual element " in Edwards " is not a mere factor in a great career, a strain in a noble character. It is his calmest mood as well as his most impassioned warning or pleading, his profoundest reasoning, his clearest insight, his widest outlook. It is the solid earth on which he treads." Dr. Smyth has thus stated in suggestive phrase the supreme truth concerning Edwards; the truth that his dominating quality, his differentiating trait, his prevailing habit of mind, is spirituality. The time at my disposal does not permit the illustration of this great quality in any adequate way. I can only touch on a few particulars which may help us better to appreciate it.

The careful student of Edwards is deeply impressed, first of all, by his immediate vision of the spiritual universe as the reality of realities. When I speak of the spiritual universe, I am giving a name to no indefinite object of thought. I mean God in his supernatural attributes of righteousness and love, the moral beings created in his image, the relations between them and the thoughts and feelings and activities which emerge out of these relations. This was the universe in which Edwards lived and moved and had his being. As he apprehended it, it was no mere subjective experience, no mere plexus of sensations and thoughts and volitions. It was the one fundamental substance and the one real existence. It was the one objective certainty which stands over against the shadowy and illusory phenomena that we group under the title matter. And his vision of it was vivid and in a sense complete. He knew it not only in its several parts, but as a whole; as an ordered universe; as the macrocosm which he, the microcosm, reflected and to which he responded.

All this is true in a measure, to be sure, of all the other saints and, indeed, of the sinners also. It is in what I have called the immediacy of his spiritual apprehension that his distinction lies. There is, of course, a sense in which the spiritual world is immediately discerned by all of us. It is of spirit rather than of matter that our knowledge is direct. That consciousness of a self which cannot be construed in terms of matter, or that idea of self which is a necessary postulate of all our thinking brings us at once into the universe of spirit. But in order to the vivid realization of this spiritual universe, there is necessary for the most of us a special activity or experience. And by this activity or experience our realization of the spiritual world is mediated. Edwards, in this respect, is a remarkable exception in his own class. Consider some great and notable men of the spiritual type. Consider St. Augustine. How true it is that the great elements of the spiritual world became vivid to Augustine through the mediation of his experience of sin! And that these spiritual elements were always interpreted by the aid of that experience his *Confessions* abundantly testify. Or think of Dante. As Augustine reveals in his *Confessions* the instrumental relation to his deepening spirituality of the long period of sinful storm and stress. Dante makes perfectly clear to us in *The New Life* that it was the love of Beatrice which so mediated for him the spiritual world and so brought him under its sway, that in order to repeat and interpret the vision of it he laid under contribution his total gifts and learning. Or take John Calvin. That fruitful conception—more fruitful in church and state than any other conception which has held the English-speaking world—of the absolute and universal sovereignty of the Holy God as a revolt from the conception then prevailing of the sovereignty of the human head of an earthly church, was historically the mediator of his spiritual career.

Now Edwards is distinguished from Augustine, Dante and Calvin by the fact that his intuition of the spiritual universe was, in the sense which I have used the word, immediate. To a degree I should be unwilling to affirm of any other man I have studied, except one, his spirituality was natural. That he was a sinner, needing regeneration and atonement, he knew. That these were his blessed experience he was gratefully assured. But except the apostle called by eminence " the Theologian ", St. John the Divine, I know no other great character in Church History of whom it can so emphatically be said, that when he " breathed the pure serene " of the spiritual world and gazed upon its outstanding features, or explored its recesses, or studied the inter-relations of its essential elements, he did so as " native and to the manner born ". To quote again the words of Dr. Smyth: " It is the solid earth on which he treads, its sleeping rocks and firm-set hills."

The spiritual universe, thus vividly and immediately apprehended as the reality of realities, of course, became, in turn, the interpreter to himself of all he did and felt. It became even the regnant principle of his association of ideas, so that the unpurposed movements of his mind in reverie were determined by it. How influential in his earliest thinking it was, you will see if you study his *Notes* on mind and ultimate being ; and how persistent it was, you will see in his latest observations on *The End of God in Creation*. It governed his æsthetics also. The line between æsthetic emotion and spiritual feeling is sharp, and wide, and deep. Often as the two are confounded by those whose sensibilities are strongly stirred by beauty in nature or in fine art, it is still true that they are as distinct as spirit and matter. The æsthetic emotion is ultimate and never can be made over into spiritual affection. No one knew this better than Edwards. But through both reflection and experience he reached and formulated the conclusion, that the highest and most enduring æsthetic emotion is that which is called out not by material beauty but by holiness. And he may be said to have unfolded the great mediæval phrase, " The beatific vision of God ", into the doctrine of the highest beauty, in his epoch-making treatise—epoch-making in America certainly the treatise was—on *The Nature of Virtue.* This seems to me a striking instance of the way in which his spirituality permeated and irradiated his thinking.

I think that even the traits of Edwards' style are best explained by this same quality. It has often been said of him that style is precisely what Edwards lacked. We are told that, after reading *Clarissa Harlowe,* he expressed regret that in his earlier years he did not pay more attention to style. We may be thankful certainly that he did not form his style on that of the affluent Richardson. I am unable to share the regret he expressed; unless, indeed, it was a regret that he did not always take pains to make his literary product eminent in the qualities of style which always marked it. Edwards was above all things sincere; and his style is the man. Its qualities are clearness, severe simplicity, movement and force. In these he is eminent, almost as eminent as John Locke; and he is more eminent in his later than in his earlier compositions. They finely fit his theme and his spirit. His theme in substance is one. It is the spiritual universe, in some aspect of it. And his spirit is that of a man dominated by those spiritual affections which he teaches us are a lively action of the will. It was appropriate that his style should be calm and severe, and that even in his sermons it should lack the dilation and rhythm of a rapt prophet's emotional utterance. Edwards was no Montanist. He was a seer, indeed, but a seer with a clear vision; and the spirit of the prophet was subject to the prophet. No man of his day was, so far as I know, the subject of stronger or deeper spiritual affections. But no one knew better just what spiritual affections are. He knew especially how different they are from mere sensibility; and he was always calm under their sway. No other style than his could have so well reflected and expressed this spiritual, unhysterical man. And I must believe that his is the direct fruit of his spiritual quality. Certainly, it was spiritually effective. Never did any one's discourse

make a more powerful and at the same time a more distinctively and exclusively spiritual impression on audience or readers.
One of the most charming modern poems is that in which
Tennyson portrays the Lady Godiva, that she might take the
tax from off her people, riding at high noon through Coventry
" naked, but clothed on with chastity." So seem to me the
bare and unadorned sermons and discussions of Edwards.
Straight through his subject to his goal this master moves;
unadorned yet not unclothed, but clothed upon with spirituality.

Or consider Edwards' emotional life. Dr. Allen, of Cambridge, in his paper on *The Place of Edwards in History* has
dwelt fondly on what he calls the spiritual affinity between
Dante and Edwards. He makes the remark, that " the deepest
affinity of Edwards was not that with Calvin or with Augustine, but with the Florentine poet." Now, I am sure, that of
his affinity with Augustine and with Calvin Edwards was distinctly conscious. But nowhere, so far as I know, is there the
slightest intimation that he had any interest in Dante's *New
Life* or *The Divine Comedy*. He was no idealizing poet, no
literary artist, no allegorizer; and he seems to have taken little
or no pleasure in this kind of literature. Had there been a fundamental sympathy between Dante and Edwards, it would have
expressed itself in Edwards' works with Edwards' characteristic distinctness. But not only is Dante not mentioned, but,
what is more striking, there is not an allusion, I think, in Edwards' works to the poems of the Puritan John Milton or the
allegories of the Puritan John Bunyan. This seems inexplicable on Dr. Allen's theory of a strong affinity between the New
England theologian and the Florentine poet. Most unhappy,
however, is the palmary instance of this alleged affinity selected
by Dr. Allen for remark. It is what he calls the striking spiritual likeness between Dante's words touching his first sight
of Beatrice and Edwards' description of Sarah Pierpont. I
refer to them, not to criticise Dr. Allen, but because the striking contrast between them helps us the better to appreciate the
regnancy of Edwards' spiritual quality, even when he was
under the spell of earthly love.

And the contrast is striking. Dante in noble and beautiful

words describes the dress that Beatrice wore. " Her dress on that day was a most noble color, a subdued and goodly crimson, girded and adorned in such sort as best suited with her tender age." He exalts her in a way which Edwards would have severely reproved, in the words, " Behold the deity which is stronger than I, who coming to me will rule within me." And he confesses in powerful and poetic phrases the violent effect upon his body which his strong emotion produced. The whole picture is charming, poetic, ideal, and was written in a book for the public years after the boy had seen a girl. The greatest poet of his time, if not of all time, in maturer life looks back upon the meeting and, with consummate art, I do not say with insincerity, transfigures it.

How different is Edwards' well-known description of Sarah Pierpont! It was written in Edwards' youth, four years before his marriage; not in a book for the public, but on a blank leaf for his own eye. In its own way it is as engaging as Dante's. But its way is not artistic or imaginative at all. It is distinctively and exclusively spiritual. There is no idealization, no translation of the object of his love into a symbol, no physical transport, no agitation, no " shaking of the pulses of the body." We learn nothing of Sarah Pierpont's dress or appearance or temperament. All he tells us about her is about her spiritual qualities and her relations to the spiritual universe. And at the last, on his deathbed, he sends to his absent wife, this Sarah Pierpont, his love; and again speaks of the uncommon union between them as, he trusts, spiritual and therefore immortal. Read in connection with the brief references to his household life to be found in his biography, these passages bring before us a man whose closest and tenderest earthly love was transfigured not by artistic genius but by what I have called his dominating spirituality. And both passages issue naturally out of that spiritual conception of beauty which he has so finely unfolded in the great essay on Virtue.

This same quality manifests itself in the impartiality and impersonality of his feelings under conditions well calculated to awaken strong partial and personal feelings. Go through the whole history of the unfortunate Northampton controversy.

Read the correspondence of Edwards, his speeches before the several Councils and the *Farewell Sermon*. Or mark his behavior under the trying conditions of a recrudescence in Stockbridge of the enmity shown at Northampton. And you will see what I mean, when I say that his spirituality is exhibited in the impartiality of his feelings and the impersonality of their objects. You will agree with me that in all of it he was true to his thesis; that private feelings must be subordinated to that benevolence, that spiritual love of being in general, which is the essence of virtue. Indeed, I recall no other instance of a severe and protracted trial, in which the chief figure appears so unconcerned about everything except its spiritual significance.

But it is in the work to which he gave himself, in the subjects on which he labored, in his method of treatment, in the conclusions he reached, that Edwards' spirituality is most impressively revealed. He was interested apparently in nothing but the spiritual universe and the spiritual life. Of course, the whole of Edwards is not known to us. We rarely, if ever, catch sight of him in his avocations, so strong was his sense of vocation. I discover in him no interest in politics, in literature, in the plastic or even the intellectual arts. In distinctively intellectual pursuits other than religious he did at times engage. But he engaged in them, certainly in his maturer years, only in order to the thorough concentration of his powers on spiritual work. Thus, when his mind was strained by excessive study and would not hold itself to a severely spiritual train of thought, or when his imagination rose in rebellion and tempted him, he whipped each into subjection by setting his powers to the solution of a difficult mathematical problem; and so he regained possession of himself solely for high spiritual purposes. And how spiritual his purposes were let the titles of his works testify, from the first published sermon to the great treatises on Sin, Virtue and the Will, and finally the great Body of Divinity in historical form, which in his letter to the Trustees of Princeton he describes as his coming work, and in describing which his soul expands and his style, almost for the first time, becomes rhythmical.

We are therefore entitled to say with emphasis that the dominant quality of Edwards is spirituality—spirituality of mind, of feeling, of aim and action. The spiritual universe was for him not only the most certain and substantial of realities, but the exclusive object of contemplation. Purely spiritual feeling seems to have filled in his life the great spaces which in the lives of most men are occupied by passionate sensibilities and æsthetic pleasures. Or we may better say, that his exceptional personality was the alembic in which these sensibilities and pleasures were transmuted into the pure distillate of spiritual feeling; until all his outgoing and active affections rested on spiritual qualities and objects, and all his reactions of emotion were the blessednesses of the spirit. When his will energized and called the great powers of his intellect into action, it was on the most spiritual themes that his mind was wrought with the greatest ease and geniality. Distant in manner and reserved on most subjects, whenever he conversed about heavenly and divine things of which his heart was so full, " his tongue ", says Dr. Samuel Hopkins, " was as the pen of a ready writer." The spiritual world so completely possessed him that its contemplation and exposition seems never to have tired him. After receiving the invitation to Princeton, he told his eldest son that for many years he had spent fourteen hours a day in his study. Spiritual thinking and feeling were thus both his labor and his recreation.

This exclusive spirituality of Edwards explains his lack of charm and interest. For obviously he is lacking here. Compare with the lack of interest in Edwards the interest the world has always taken in Luther, in the stormy career of Knox, in the incessant and varied activity of Calvin, and earlier than these in the dramatic life of Augustine. Shall we say that he charms us less because he was a more spiritual man, or only because he was more exclusively spiritual; because he was less wealthily endowed with humane sympathies? Is it because of his delicate organization and feeble vitality? Or is it because, under the domination of the spiritual universe, and knowing well his own powers and limitations, he determined to know this one thing only? Or is it, after all, only the defect of his biographers? I do not know. Certainly he presents a striking contrast to the other great spiritual men whom I have named. And I think we are bound to acknowledge that his remarkable separation in spirit from the feelings and tastes and occupations of the people seriously limited his usefulness, and seriously limits it to-day. But when all is said, his spirituality is his strength. And in a world where social charm and sympathy is abundant, and where high and exclusive spirituality is in the greatest men as rare as radium; we ought to rejoice that of one of the greatest it is true that he was bondslave to the spiritual world.

The clue to Edwards then, his dominating and irradiating quality, the trait which gave unity to his career, is his spirituality. His was indeed, to repeat the fine word of Dr. Egbert Smyth, " a transcendent spiritual personality."

II.

I have detained you so long on this subject that I must treat briefly and inadequately Edwards' intellect and work.

It was as a bond-slave then to the spiritual universe that all his work was done. Now his work was not that of a philanthropist or a missionary. It was the work of a thinker. The instrument with which he wrought was his intellect; and the word which describes the quality as distinguished from the subject of his writings is the word, intellect. This is as true of his sermons as it is of his elaborate treatises. And, as a whole, his works constitute an intellectual system of the spiritual universe.

Eminently intellectual in his activity, Edwards, so far as I can see, had no intellectual pride. His intellect he regarded simply as an instrument to be employed in the service of the spiritual world. And as such an instrument, if we would do him justice, we must regard it. We must seize and estimate its outstanding traits, as they reveal themselves in this characteristic activity which he solemnly accepted as his vocation. What, then, were the distinctive traits of Edwards' intellect, and what position must we assign to him among intellectual men, especially among theologians?

The genius of Luther and that of Calvin have often been

contrasted. There is a general agreement that while Luther saw single truths with the greater clearness and the sooner recognized their capital value, to Calvin must be attributed in greater measure the gift of construction; the great gift by which he organized in a system the principles of the Protestant Reformation. Now though Edwards nowhere shows the boldness and originality of either of these men; though he never inaugurated a new mode of Christianity like Luther or organized its theology like Calvin, and, therefore, holds no place beside them in history; he had both a gift of penetration like Luther's and a gift of construction like Calvin's. It is also true, I think, that in the subtlety of his intellect he was greater than either. The man of all men whom he seems to me most like intellectually and, indeed, every way—in the character of his religious experience, in his genial acceptance of the theological system he inherited, in his philosophical insight, in his power in the exposition of abstract truth, in his fruitfulness, in his constructive ability and in his failure nevertheless to leave behind him a completed system, in his fundamental philosophical and theological views, in his idealism and Platonism—is Anselm of Canterbury. And, having regard to the works they have left behind them—the one, the *Monologium* and *Proslogium*, the *Tract on Predestination*, the *Prayers and Meditations*, the *Essay on Free Will* and the *Cur Deus Homo*, and the other, the great sermons, the treatises on *The Nature of Virtue*, *The End of God in Creation*, *Original Sin*, *Justification by Faith*, *The Religious Affections* and *The Nature of the Freedom of the Will*—I think that Edwards stands fully abreast of the mediæval philosopher and theologian. Had Dante known Edwards as we know him, he would have given him a place beside Anselm in the Heaven of the Sun.

In saying that Edwards is like Anselm, I have also in mind the fact that there are two great classes of theologians. All Christian theology rests on Holy Scripture. But theologians strikingly differ among themselves in the importance they respectively assign to the history of doctrine and the Church's symbols on the one hand; and to the concord between the Word of God and the reason on the other. In the mediæval

Church there were school divines who rested solely on history and authority; who had no confidence in the argument from the reason; who did not believe that there is a *theologia naturalis.* This tendency was strongest, perhaps, in the Franciscan, Duns Scotus. In modern Protestant Churches, the tendency is, perhaps, strongest in the high Anglican writers. Now while Edwards was in harmony with the Reformed Confessions; the absence of the Confessional or historical spirit is noticeable in all his theological treatises. The lack of it is explained partly by his training. In the curriculum of the American Colonial College historical studies were slight and elementary, while studies which discipline the powers were pursued with a vigor and sincerity which the modern University would do well to promote. We must regret, I think, the lack in this great American theologian of large historical culture and, by consequence, of the historical spirit. Because of it there is, in the positiveness of his assertions, in his strong confidence in logical analysis and dialectic in themselves, and in his historical generalizations in *The History of Redemption,* a quality which it is right to call provincial.

But if he is defective at this point, it is not too much to say, that he is one of the greatest Doctors of the Universal Church by reason of his singular eminence in three capital qualities. In the first place, he is far more powerful than most theologians in his appeal to the reason in man. I mean the reason in its largest sense and as distinguished from the understanding. The reason itself, he held, as if he were a Cambridge Platonist, has a large spiritual content. If I understand him, he went beyond the Westminster Divines in the value he put upon the Light of Nature. Of his actual appeal to the reason, including under that term the conscience and the religious nature, I have time only to say that it permeates and gives distinction to his entire theological product. He addresses it with large confidence in his sermons, in his essay on *The End of God in Creation,* in his chapter on the *Satisfaction of Christ* written in the very spirit of the *Cur Deus Homo,* in all his endeavors to quicken in reader and hearer the sense of guilt and the fear of its punishment, in his great discourse on *Spiritual Light,* and in his great volume on the *Religious Affections*. In all of them a consummate theologian of the reason distinctly appears. To this we must add his supremacy in the related gifts of clear exposition, subtle distinction, and acute polemic. To this supremacy the world has borne abundant testimony. If he is like Anselm in his high estimate of the reason, he is like Thomas Aquinas in his dialectical acuteness. Nor is this acuteness mere quickness of vision and alertness in logical fence. His two greatest polemic works are probably the essays on *Original Sin* and *The Freedom of the Will*. Both of them are profound as well as acute; both are large in their conception of the subject; and in both he is fair to his antagonist, and, though not so largely, yet as really constructive as he is polemic. To these we must add, finally, a consummate genius for theological construction. No one can go through his collected works even rapidly, as I was compelled to do this summer, without seeing that a self-consistent World-view or theory of the Universe was distinct and complete in the consciousness of Edwards, and that it is the living root out of which springs every one of his sermons and discussions. No theological writer is less atomistic. None is less the prey of his temporary impulses or aberrations. No theological essays less merit the name of *disjecta membra*. The joy of the completed literary presentation of this universal system, this spiritual and intellectual Cosmos, was denied him. But it is in his works, just as completely as Coleridge's system is in the *Biographia Literaria* and the *Table Talk*, just as clearly as Pascal's Pyrrhonism lies open to us in his fragmentary *Thoughts*. Had he lived to complete at Princeton his *History of Redemption*, his " body of divinity in an entire new method," it is my belief that the world would have seen in it the fruit of a constructive genius not less great than that which appears in the *Summa* of St. Thomas or in the *Institutes* of Calvin.

Though no theologian more habitually conceived the spiritual world as objective, yet his great powers and special talents wrought best, and he produced his best work, when he was writing on the religious life. That life he knew well, because of his own profound and vivid religious experience. But he never wrote out his experience alone. The spiritual universe as a whole is before him as he writes. It is always therefore the ideal religious life of the redeemed sinner he is describing. Hence its severity, its purity, its deep humility as it measures itself with the absolute ethical and spiritual perfection. If we do not wish to sink into despair, we must not forget this as we read the greatest of his tracts, the essay on *The Religious Affections.*

A theologian, so profound and so individual as Edwards was, could not but have made many contributions of the highest importance to theological science. Now whatever Edwards' distinctive contributions to theology were, it is important to notice that they were contributions to the historical theology of the Christian Church. He was in full concord with the great Ecumenical Councils on the Trinity and the Person of Christ. He thoroughly accepted the formal and material principles of the Reformation. And he was convinced of the truth of the great system known as Calvinism or the Reformed Theology. His greatness as a theologian and his fruitfulness as a writer are rooted in the consent of his heart, as well as the assent of his mind, to these historical doctrines. And though, as I have said, individually he was not distinctly informed by the historical spirit, yet he is in the line of the historical succession of Christian theologians.

Turning to these distinctive contributions I have time to name only one; but that one has been of immense historical importance in America. Jonathan Edwards changed what I may call the centre of thought in American theological thinking. There were great theologians in New England before Edwards. I mention only John Norton of Ipswich, and Samuel Willard of Harvard. They followed the Reformed School Divines not only in making the decree of God the constitutive doctrine of the system, but in emphasizing it. Edwards did not displace the eternal Decree as the constitutive doctrine; but by a change in emphasis he lifted into the place of first importance in theological thinking in America the inward state of man in nature and in grace. He appears to have been led strongly to emphasize these related themes, partly by the Great Awakening, and partly by the controversy on the Half-way Covenant which followed it. No one, however, but a man of genius could have made this change in emphasis so potent a fact in American Church history. It is impossible to exaggerate the influence thus exerted by Edwards on American theological and religious discussions and on American religious life. If I may so say, here is the open secret of the New England theology from Samuel Hopkins to Horace Bushnell. And more than to any other man, to Edwards is due the importance which, in American Christianity, is attributed to the conscious experience of the penitent sinner, as he passes into the membership of the Invisible Church.

Quite as important as this distinctive contribution is the tremendous stimulus and impetus he gave to theological speculation and construction. When I think of the Edwardean School of New England theologians from Samuel Hopkins to Edwards Park, between whom are included so many brilliant men, too many even to be named at this time; when I think of the Edwardean theologians in my own Church, like Henry Boynton Smith and William Greenough Thayer Shedd; when I think of the fruitful history of his works in Scotland and England, and recall his real mastery over the minds he influenced; it seems to me that it is not too much to say that, up to this time, his influence in the English-speaking world—not on all thinking, but on distinctively dogmatic thinking—has been as great as that of either Joseph Butler or Samuel Taylor Coleridge.

I have thus endeavored to set before you my impressions of Edwards' dominating quality, his intellectual gifts, and the kind of work he did; and to state the place which in my view he holds among the theologians of the Universal Church. I have refrained from eulogy. He is too consummate and sincere a master for us to approach with the language of compliment. But I should incompletely perform the duty you have devolved upon me, did I fail to speak of two of his works which have been violently and repeatedly attacked. One is the essay on *The Freedom of the Will*. The other is the *Sermons on the Punishment of the Wicked*.

The essay on the *Freedom of the Will* is essentially a polemic, and only incidentally a constructive treatise. As a polemic, therefore, it must be judged. He had before his mind, not the whole voluntary nature of man as a subject to be investigated, but the special Arminian doctrine of the liberty of indifference as an error to be antagonized. What, therefore, the essay shows is, not his constructive ability, but his ability as an antagonist. I have read carefully only one other treatise in which the propositions as obviously move forward in procession, with steps as firmly locked together. This other treatise is the *Ethics* of Spinoza. If you dare consentingly to follow Spinoza through his three kinds of knowledge up to his definition of substance—which, since it is thought not in a higher category but in itself, is self-existent; which is and can be one only; and whose known attributes " perceived to be of the essence of this substance " are infinite thought and infinite extension—if you follow Spinoza thus far; you will soon find yourself imprisoned in a universe of necessity, and bound in it by a chain of theorems, corollaries and lemmas impossible to be broken at any point. Your only safety is in obeying the precept, *Obsta principiis.* Quite equal to Spinoza's is Edwards' essay in its close procession of ordered argument. Like Spinoza he begins his treatise with definitions. And I cannot see how anyone, who permits himself to be led without protest through the first of the " Parts " of the essay, can refuse to go on with him at any point in the remaining three. In reading the treatise one should, above all, keep in view the fact that, though it is polemic against a particular theory, it was written in the interest of a positive theological doctrine. I think we shall do justice to this doctrine if we state it in terms like the following: " Man's permanent inclination is sinful; and his sinful inclination will certainly qualify his moral choices." This Augustinian doctrine Edwards defended by a closely reasoned psychology of the will. I am not sure that this great doctrine, which I heartily accept, was at all aided by Edwards when he involved it with and defended it by a particular psychology. And my doubt is deepened by what seems to me his unnecessary employment, in the spiritual sphere, of terms taken from the sphere of nature, like " cause ", " determination " and " necessity ". I can only call your attention to the fact that the defense of the religious doctrine, and not his psychology, was Edwards' deepest anxiety. And who of us is not prepared to say, that the bad man's badness is a permanent disposition certain to emerge in his ethical volitions, and that to revolutionize it there is needed the forth-putting of the power of the Holy Ghost?

But it is Edwards' sermons on *The Punishment of the Wicked* which have awakened the strongest enmity; an enmity expressed often in the most violent terms. The rational and Scriptural basis of the doctrine and the objections to it need not be set forth here. Edwards accepted, defended and proclaimed it, substantially in the form in which it has been taught in the Greek, the Latin and the Protestant Churches. It is the doctrine of the Fathers, the mediæval Schoolmen and the Protestant theologians. Edwards' doctrine of Hell is exactly one with the doctrine of Dante. Now it is of interest to note that there is a widespread revulsion from Edwards, considered as the author of these Sermons, which does not and so far as I am aware never did appear in the case of Dante, considered as the author of the *Inferno*. What is the explanation of the difference? Dante is praised and glorified by not a few of those to whom the name of Edwards is for the same reason a name of " execration and horror ". Indeed, Dante has been defended by a great American man of letters for rejoicing in the pain of the damned; while no one of Edwards' sermons, unless it is *Sinners in the Hands of an Angry God,* has been more severely criticised as inhuman than the discourse entitled, *The Torments of the Wicked in Hell no occasion of Grief to the Saints in Heaven.* We shall do well, therefore, to note the contrast between Dante's and Edwards' presentation of the same subject.

When Dante was sailing through the Lake of Mud in the Fifth Circle of Hell, there appeared before him suddenly Philippo Argenti, who in this world was full of arrogance and disdain of his fellowmen, now clothed only with the lake's muck. Pathetically he answers Dante's inquiry, "Who art thou that art become so foul?" with these words, "Thou seest I am one who weeps." And Dante replies, "With weeping and with wailing, accursed spirit, do thou remain, for I know thee although thou art all filthy." Then Virgil clasps Dante's neck and kisses his face and says, "Blessed is she who bore thee!" And Dante replies, "Master, I should much like to see him ducked in this broth before we depart from the lake." And Virgil promises that he shall be satisfied. "And after this", continues Dante, "I saw such rending of him by the muddy folk that I still praise God therefor and thank Him for it. All cried, 'At Philippo Argenti!' and the raging Florentine spirit turned upon himself with his teeth. Here we left him; so that I tell no more of him." This is one of the passages in Dante's poem of that Hell over whose entrance he read these words; "Through me is the way into eternal woe; through me is the way among the lost people. Justice moved my high creator; the divine Power, the supreme Wisdom, and the primal Love made me. Before me were no things created unless eternal, and I eternal last. Leave every hope, ye who enter here."

There is nothing in Edwards which, so far as I can judge, equals this in its horrid imagery and suggestion. And yet men enjoy Dante and the *Inferno*. They do not "execrate" him for a "monster", as Dr. Allen says they do Edwards. And in his great essay on Dante, Mr. James Russell Lowell makes this very scene the text of an eloquent laudation of Dante's moral quality, in which he says of him; "He believed in the righteous use of anger, and that baseness was its legitimate quarry." Why is it that the attitude of the general public, thus represented by Mr. Lowell, toward the Hell of Dante is so different from the attitude of the same public toward the Hell of Edwards? I think we shall find an answer to this question in what I may call Edwards' spiritual realism. Of course Dante is a realist also. How often this quality of his poem has been pointed out to us! But Dante's is the realism of the artist, the poet who appeals to our imagination. Our imagination being gratified, we enjoy the picture and even the sensations of horror which the picture starts. Of all this there is nothing in Edwards. There is no picture at all. There is scarcely a symbol. Here and there there is an illustration. But the illustrations of Edwards are never employed to make his subject vivid to the imagination. They are intended simply to explicate it to the understanding. The free, responsible, guilty and immortal spirit is immediately addressed; and the purely spiritual elements of the Hell of the wicked, separated from all else, are made to appear in their terrible nakedness before the reason and the conscience. The reason and the conscience respond. We are angry because startled out of our security. And we call him cruel, because of the conviction forced on us that we are in the presence of a terrible, even if mysterious, spiritual reality. Edwards always spoke, not to the imagination, but to the responsible spirit. Men realized when he addressed them that because they are sinners their moral constitution judicially inflicts upon their personality remorse; and that remorse is an absolute, immitigable and purely spiritual pain, independent of the conditions of time and space and, therefore, eternal.

The Nineteenth Century, in one of its greatest poets,[3] looking out on nature, sees no relief from this eternity of remorse; that is to say, it sees no evidence, in nature's " tooth and claw " that God will ever interfere to end this spiritual pain and punishment. It only "hopes " that, "at last, far off ", " Winter will turn to Spring." I shall not attack any man for a hope, maintained against the evidence of remorse within and nature without, that the mystery of pain and moral evil will be thus dissipated in their destruction. It is not my business to denounce a thoughtful and reverent spirit like Tennyson, because of any relief he may individually find, when facing the most terrible revelation of nature and of his moral constitution, in the " hope " which issues from our sensibility to pain and from the sentiment of mercy which God has implanted in us all. But I do say, that a man's private " hope " should never be elevated to the dignity of a dogma, or be made a norm of teaching, or be proposed as a rule of action. And I do protest that it is the height of literary injustice, while praising Dante, to con-

[3] *In Memoriam*, liii-lvi.

demn Edwards the preacher because, in his anxiety to induce men to " press into the kingdom," he preached, not the private hope of Lord Tennyson, but the spiritual verity to which the conscience of the sinner responds. Thus, in his treatment of this darkest of subjects, that spirituality which I have said was his dominant quality is regnant; and here, too, he should be called, " the friend and aider of those who would live in the spirit."

With this protest I conclude. Let me say again, that I am deeply grateful to you for the opportunity you have given me to unite with you in this commemoration of the man we so often call our greatest American Divine. He was indeed inexpressibly great in his intellectual endowment, in his theological achievement, in his continuing influence. He was greatest in his attribute of regnant, permeating, irradiating spirituality. It is at once a present beatitude and an omen of future good that, in these days of pride in wealth and all that wealth means, of pride in the fashion of this world which passeth away, we still in our heart of hearts reserve the highest honor for the great American who lived and moved and had his being in the Universe which is unseen and eternal.

THE SUPERNATURAL

WILLIAM BRENTON GREENE, JR.

I.—*Definition.* 1. Though spiritual, the Supernatural: a. Is not identical with all the spiritual, nor is it plural; b. Its distinction is that it is the Uncaused, the Self-Subsistent, the Autonomous.
2. The points specially to be guarded in this definition are: a. The separateness of the Supernatural from the natural; b. Its singleness as so separated.

II.—*Importance of this doctrine.* 1. In Christian Apologetics. 2. In Christian Dogmatics. 3. In Philosophy. 4. In Science. 5. In Ethics. 6. In Religion, Civilization and Human Achievement. 7. In the Christian Religion, according to its own claim. 8. With regard to the hope of the world.

III.—*The Reality of the Supernatural.* 1. The Question. 2. The Opposing Theories: a. *Positivism;* b. *Monism;* c. *Pluralism.* 3. The Argument: a. From the Consent of Philosophy; b. From the Necessity of Religion; c. From the Necessity in Thought.

IV.—*The Manifestation of the Supernatural.* 1. The Question, 2. The Opposing Theories: a. *Pantheism;* b. *Religious Positivism;* c. *Agnosticism.* 3. The Argument: a. From the standpoint of the reality of the Supernatural; b. From that of the reality of the natural.

V.—*The Personality of the Supernatural.* 1. Summary of opposing views. 2. Statement of true position. 3. Argument: a. The Supernatural can be personal; b. The Supernatural must be at least personal; c. The Supernatural cannot be higher than personal.

VI.—*The Personal, in the sense of Immediate, Manifestation of the Supernatural.* 1. What is meant by such manifestation. 2. The importance of the reality of such manifestation, not only to Christianity, but to all higher religion. 3. The denial of the possibility of miracles is based on the assumption that nature is and must be *uniform.* 4. Proof of the possibility and ,even of the probability of miracles, i. e., of supernatural interventions in the course of nature.

VII.—*Conclusion.* 1. Christianity is not established as the supernatural religion: this must still be decided by the appropriate evidence. But 2. the way, and the only way, for its establishment is laid open. 3. The reality of the Supernatural, of his manifestation through nature, of his personality, and of his personal intervention in nature—these are established or reason itself is denied.

THE SUPERNATURAL

I.

DEFINITION.

By the Supernatural we do not mean the spiritual. Yet this has been and is a common conception of it. The distinction between the Supernatural and the Natural is held to be the distinction between moral freedom and physical necessity, between spirit and matter. Such thinkers embrace within the Supernatural not only God, but angels and men. That is, all that is truly spiritual and so, because self-initiating, able to modify and even to break through the necessary succession of physical causes and effects they call supernatural. Thus Bushnell[1] defines the Supernatural as " Whatever it be that is, either not in the chain of material cause and effect, or which acts on the chain of causes and effects, in nature, from without the chain." So Hickok when discussing the " Valid Being of the Soul," says[2], " The facts of a comprehending—not merely conjoining, nor connecting—power over nature, and of an ethical experience, prove the soul to be supernatural." Thus, and in this representing many living and influential authors, William Adams Brown writes[3], " The insight that law is universal is matched by the higher insight that it is only in consciousness that we find law. Thus, the supernatural receives its true meaning of the personal, and the false antithesis between nature and the supernatural is removed. The supernatural is the natural seen in its spiritual significance." So, too, he says[4], " This sharp division between nature and the supernatural science no longer recognizes. It knows but one

[1] *Nature and the Supernatural,* p. 37.
[2] *Rational Psychology,* pp. 540, 541.
[3] *Christian Theology in Outline,* p. 229.
[4] *Methodist Review Quarterly,* Jan., 1911, p. 40.

world, both natural and supernatural, or, as we express it in the more familiar terms, both material and spiritual."

This way of thinking is, however, misleading, inadequate and untrue. It is misleading in that it assumes what is yet to be proved. As Henry B. Smith wrote,[5] " The implication or tacit assertion that the Supernatural and the spiritual are identical—that all which is truly spiritual is also supernatural, is the unproved and disputable position." It is a question, and a vital one, whether God and man are essentially the same. It is the question which divides the Old Theology from what is called the " New Theology." This definition, therefore, hides the issue. To accept it as a guide in controversy would blind us to the chief contention. Again, this mode of thinking is inadequate in that it does not reach to the heart of the question. This is not whether there is a kind of being above physical nature and so superior to the chain of necessary causes. There are many who deny even this; but there are many, too, who, while they admit both the reality and the transcendence of spirit as spirit, take, as we have seen, the ground that the human spirit and the Divine Spirit are essentially one. That is, the question is not whether man is above nature; it is whether there is anything above man. If there is not, then no argument is advanced by defining the Supernatural as the spiritual; if there is, then the definition contains no reply. Hence, it is inadequate. To get any where, we must ask, not is there being which is supernatural in the sense of spiritual, but is there being which is supernatural in the sense of absolute, that is, independent and self-existent because uncaused. Once more, the definition under consideration is untrue. It assumes, even when it does not assert, that human freedom and divine freedom are one and the same inasmuch as both are superior to physical or necessary causation. This is the reason why both should be classed as supernatural. The truth, however, is that, though both are alike with respect to this superiority, yet in another and more important respect they are radically unlike. The law of cause and effect, while it differs, does not break down when applied to the human will. As H. B. Smith

[5] *Apologetics*, p. 21.

says,[6] "If it did, then there would be pure contingence and the element of no law pervading the system." Physical and human nature, therefore, are alike in the most comprehensive and significant respect. They are both of them, though differently, yet really, caused and determined. They both of them presuppose a creator and reveal a preserver and governor. They are not, like that creator, preserver and governor, uncaused, self-subsistent and autonomous. This is the distinction in comparison with which all other distinctions are as nothing, and it is to this distinction that the definition of the Supernatural as the spiritual is untrue.

Again, by the Supernatural we do not mean being that, though uncaused, self-subsistent and autonomous, is plural, that is, made up of many such distinct and independent beings. Such a conception is on its face a contradiction. To go no further, what is autonomous must be single. Absolute sovereignty and a plurality of even federated gods are inconsistent.

By the Supernatural, then, we do mean, being that is above the sequence of *all* nature whether physical or spiritual; substance that is not caused, and that is not determined whether physically and necessarily as in the case of physical nature or rationally and freely as in the case of spiritual nature; in a word, unique reality the essence of whose uniqueness is that the reality is uncaused, self-subsistent and autonomous. We call this Supernatural the Infinite to denote the absence of limitation. We call it also the Absolute to express perfect independence both in being and action. We call it, too, the Unconditioned to emphasize freedom from every necessary relation. In short, we apply all three terms to it to affirm the absence of every restriction. Such is the Supernatural that we are about to consider. Does it exist? Does it manifest itself? What is its nature? If a person, can he reveal himself immediately as such? These are the inquiries which we shall raise. And the radical distinctness of the Supernatural from the natural, whether physical or spiritual; and the singleness of the Supernatural,—these are the two positions which our definition as it has been unfolded will call on us to guard most carefully.

[6] *Apologetics,* p. 22.

II.

Importance of the Inquiry.

Though as abstract and difficult as any, it is more important, because more fundamental, than all. This may be seen in the various departments of thought and life.

It is self-evidently so in Christian Apologetics. The subject-matter of this science is the proof, not of the superiority nor even of the uniqueness, but of the supernaturalness of the Christian religion. The aim of apologetics is to show that Christianity is supernatural and, therefore, superior to and unique among the religions of the world. Thus Christ is to be presented as the Saviour of men, not because he grew up out of the natural, but because he came down from the Supernatural. It is this that makes him, and it is only this that could make him, our almighty Redeemer. That is, apologetics presupposes the Supernatural. It would be as absurd were the the latter not real as would be the attempt on the part of one in Europe to prove that he was a citizen of the United States if there were no United States. Apologetics, therefore, cannot ignore our inquiry. Strictly speaking, it must begin with it. The first and the most necessary work of Fundamental Apologetics is to vindicate the Supernatural as a distinct and a single being.

Similar is its place in Christian dogmatics. Deny the Supernatural and the very substance of this science is evaporated. What it discusses is the Supernatural and the relation between it and the natural. Its chief topics are God, creation and providence, redemption, revelation and salvation: and God is the supernatural fact; creation and providence are supernatural acts; redemption involves a supernatural covenant, a supernatural gift and a supernatural sacrifice and victory; revelation is a supernatural communication of supernatural information; and salvation is the work of the Supernatural and issues in a supernatural transformation. Without the reality of the Supernatural, therefore, dogmatics would be as meaningless as astronomy would be if the stars were but spectres. Its subject-matter is the uncaused, the self-subsistent, the autonomous.

The case is much the same in philosophy. It must postulate, if it does not prove, the Supernatural. It fails to explain the reality in nature, if it denies or ignores the unique reality that is above nature. Thus positivism, in that it declines to go behind or beyond phenomena, ceases to be a false philosophy. It has no conception, not even a wrong one, of the aim of philosophy. Any explanation to be adequate must be ultimate, and no explanation can be ultimate till it rests on the uncaused, the self-subsistent and the autonomous.

It is so with science. This would observe, compare and classify phenomena. It would confine itself to giving an account of the outside of things. To do this, however, presupposes inquiry as to their inside. What a thing appears to be can be seen truly only in the light of what it is. To interpret the actions of a man, you must remember that he is not a stone nor even a dog. You will not see all that is to be seen in what he does, unless you regard it as the expression of a free self-conscious spirit. Precisely so, if science ignores what is above and behind nature, it fails to discern rightly and certainly to estimate justly what is in nature. The caused, the dependent, the determined must be read as a manifestation of the uncaused, the self-subsistent, the autonomous, the universe in its relation to its unique Creator, if it is to be understood or even if it is to be read as it really appears. Science's own development is establishing this most significant fact. " We can not overlook ", says Lindsay,[7] " how truly Spencerianism has been tending to prove that no progress of science shall be able to dispense with supersensible Reality, or to displace metaphysical intuition or belief;" and the fourteen years that have passed since the utterance of this judgment have only confirmed it.

Even more evidently is the Supernatural indispensable to morality. This presupposes a law above nature as well as objective to self. Its characteristic and unique sense of obligation can not be explained otherwise. This is not satisfied,

---

[7] *Recent Advances in Theistic Philosophy of Religion*, p. 74.

if regarded merely as expressing the demand of the constitution of things. The force even of the latter points to an authority above itself. Nature, spiritual no less than physical, is bound by the law of nature because this law has both its origin and sanction in that which is above nature. This is being appreciated as never before. As Lindsay says again,[8] " The moral problem is now more clearly seen to have its ultimate ground or metaphysical basis in the Absolute." Doubtless, a morality may be developed independently of this religious basis. It must, however, lack permanence as reared on a superficial foundation. It must also lack completeness; for[9] " the ideal law revealed in conscience is fully realized only as religion possesses the soul." This law must be the transcript of the nature and the revelation of the will of the being who is uncaused, self-subsistent, autonomous, that is, who is infinite and absolute and so unique in his holiness. In the sphere of moral law nothing short of this could be ideal. Fairly and fully interpreted, conscience itself affirms as much as this.

In view of all this, it should go without saying that religion and civilization and so human achievement depend directly on the conviction of the Supernatural. It is the heroes of faith who, as a rule, have been the men of action. In comparison with them what has been accomplished by the champions of unbelief? This is yet more evident in the case of the nation. Let a people, as the Anglo-Saxons, base their institutions on faith in the living God, and they move to the front and stay there. Let a race, as the Chinese, substitute agnosticism for religion, and they drop to the rear and keep there. Thus apologetics, dogmatics, philosophy, science, morality, religion, individual progress, civilization in general, presuppose and even demand the Supernatural. Of all truths the most metaphysical, no other is so intensely practical. Its atmosphere is necessary to life.

Beyond this, it should be observed that by its own claim the Christian religion must stand or fall with the reality of the Supernatural. Unless our religion express the intervention in nature, both physical and spiritual, of what is essentially un-

[8] *Ibid.*, p. 62.   [9] *Ibid.*, p. 62.

caused, self-subsistent and autonomous and, as and because
such, both radically distinct from the world and itself single,
it is of all frauds the most unblushing and stupendous.   It
presents itself to us, not as an evolution of the divine in nature,
but as a direct revelation of and from God, who, though in
nature, was alone before it and is also distinct from it and
alone above it.   Thus the new life that is characteristic of its
confessors it declares to be the result of a new birth, a birth
from above, a birth by the spirit of God (Jno. iii. 3), and to
be throughout a manifestation of his unique power (Gal. ii.
20).   The doctrine that it teaches it affirms to be "the wisdom of God" (1 Cor. i. 24) ; and, so far from admitting that
it may be known from nature, which does clearly reveal his
everlasting power and divinity, it insists that it was "kept
secret from the foundation of the world" (Mt. xiii. 35).   The
corner stone on which it rests, even the fact of Christ, it
declares to be both "the power of God and the wisdom of
God" (1 Cor. i. 24) : and it accounts for his person, by affirming that the eternal "Word was made flesh" (Jno. i. 14) ; for
his death, by teaching that God gave him (Jno. iii. 16) to be
"a ransom for many" (Mt. xx. 28) ; for his resurrection, by
ascribing it directly and solely to "the working of the strength
of the might of God himself" (Eph. i. 19, 20) ; and for the
power manifest in the church and in its members, by referring
it to the Holy Spirit as given by the exalted Christ and from
the throne of God (Eph. iv. 7-13).   In short, Christianity insists on nothing so strongly as on this, that it is not of this
world and so natural, but is directly of the sole because absolute
God and thus supernatural.   This is *the* message of its
Scriptures. Unless, therefore, its supernaturalness can be vindicated, it is discredited, and that, too, out of its own mouth.

Nor may we fail to observe that it is just this supernaturalness of Christianity which makes it the hope of the world.   It
is the "good tidings of great joy which shall be to all people"
because it is the way of salvation from the guilt and from the
power of sin.   It could not be this, however, were it not supernatural.   The condemned criminal cannot justify himself.
Another, and one not like himself under the curse of the

law, must bear his penalty. The diseased man can not cure himself. Another, and one not dying from his disease, must give to him of his blood and so of his life. Precisely thus, guilty human nature demands a supernatural redeemer, and corrupt human nature demands a supernatural regenerator and sanctifier; and under a moral government neither may come forward until authorized to do so by the absolute and so sole ruler. Our salvation in a word supposes a new start; and the possibility of this, whether for the race or for the individual, is conditioned on such supernatural intervention. If, as observation and experience no less than Scripture testify, we, as individuals and as a race, are " dead through trespasses and sins " (Eph. ii. 1), we can be quickened and raised up to heaven in the likeness of Christ only as God himself reaches down from heaven and himself lifts us up. The natural evolution of a corpse, even though nature be conceived, as we conceive it, as created and sustained and guided by God, can issue only in increasing corruption. That is precisely the result in which he intends that nature, since he has permitted it to become corrupt, should issue. Ours, therefore, is no ordinary contention. Not only the truth of Christianity, but the hope of the world is bound up with the question as to the Supernatural; and the question as to the Supernatural concerns both his distinctness from the natural and his singleness as regards himself.

III.

The Reality of the Supernatural.

The question is not whether the Infinite is, as many agnostics would hold, the all. Neither is it whether the Absolute exists and acts in entire isolation from the world. Nor yet is it whether the Unconditioned sustains no relation to anything. No one of these positions is essential to the conception of the Supernatural. The Infinite, because it signifies unlimited, need not mean the all. It may, at least as well, mean, not that it is not limited in the sense of being distinguished from other things, but that no limit is possible to it as so distinguished.

The Absolute need not mean that which exists and acts in isolation from the natural. It may as well mean that which is not dependent on the natural. The Unconditioned need not mean that which sustains no relations to anything. It may as well mean that which sustains no necessary relations.

Again, not only is no one of these positions of the agnostic essential to the conception of the Supernatural; no one of them is possible logically. The moral infinite can not be less than perfect. Hence, it can not be the all; for the all, to be the all, must be the sum of good and evil. The phenomenal universe demands the Absolute as its ground; but just because it is its ground, the Absolute, as regards some of its activity, cannot be existing in isolation from it. The order of the world implies an unconditioned governor; but if he be the governor of the world, the Unconditioned must have come into relation to it.

All this is confirmed by consciousness. Its clearest and strongest testimony, a testimony that must be accepted if we are to be justified in thinking, is to our individuality. That is, consciousness insists that the infinite does not embrace us and so that it is not the all. In a word, not only need not the Supernatural, if it be, be such as has been indicated; but in the nature of the case it could not be such, even if consciousness did not testify that it is not such.

The question, then, is, whether there is a being who, though he embraces nothing but himself, is in himself boundless; whether there is a being who, though now he exists in connection with nature and ordinarily acts through it, is in both his being and his action independent of it; whether there is a being who, though he is related to the universe as its creator and preserver and governor and redeemer, stands, so far as he himself is concerned, in no necessary relation to it—in short, whether there is a being who is supernatural in the sense that, though he has chosen to come into the closest relations to nature, he was before it and is above it and is unrestricted by it, being himself uncaused, self-subsistent, autonomous, and so distinct and single.

The reality of such a being is indicated by the untenableness of the opposing hypotheses. These are three: Positivism, Monism, Pluralism.

1. *Positivism.*—This is a negative and epistemological hypothesis rather than an affirmative and ontological one. It tries to explain why we cannot know and so should not believe in the Supernatural; it does not essay to provide a substitute for the Supernatural. Nevertheless, in spite of its negative character, it is prevalent enough, and it is important enough, both in itself and because of the degree to which monism incorporates and uses it, to demand separate statement and discussion.

By Positivism, then, we understand the doctrine that we can know phenomena and the laws by which they are connected, but nothing more. The reason assigned for this is that we have no knowledge prior to experience and all our knowledge is by induction from sensations. That is, the world of knowledge is that world, and only that world, which is revealed to us by sense-perception and so is the subject-matter of the Natural or Positive Sciences. Hence, as we cannot see, hear, touch, taste or smell the Supernatural, it must be incognizable; and if we thus do not know and can never know that it exists, what right have we to assert that it does or to believe that it does? Such is positivism. It denies, as must have appeared, both the positions which, as we have seen, it is incumbent on us to guard; namely, the distinctness of the Supernatural from the natural and the singleness of the Supernatural.

The theory of knowledge, however, on which it rests and in which it essentially consists is untrue. We have knowledge prior to experience and all our knowledge is not by induction from sensations.

The most extreme advocates of positivism virtually admit this. Thus Comte, at once the boldest and the most consistent of them, himself the father of positivism, says:[10] " If, on the one side, every positive theory must be necessarily founded on observation, it is, on the other side, equally plain that to apply itself to the task of observation our mind has need of some *theory*. If in contemplating the phenomena, we do not immed-

[10] *La Phil. Positive,* chap. i.

iately attach them to certain principles, not only would it be
impossible for us to combine those isolated observations, so
as to draw any fruit therefrom; but we should be entirely incapable of retaining them, and in most cases the facts would
remain before our eyes unnoticed. The need at all times of
some theory whereby to associate facts, combined with the evident impossibility of the human mind's forming, at its origin,
theories out of observations, is a fact which it is impossible to
ignore." What is this but an admission that, in order to experiential knowledge, there must be *à priori* knowledge; a
theory in the mind, if there is to be an induction from facts
outside of the mind? Of course, Comte does not mean this.
His explanation is that the mind invents its theory, and then,
when it has made its observations with its aid, rejects it.
Even this, however, allows that the mind must have a theory
in order to observe and that it can itself form a theory prior to
observation.

The necessity of these admissions appears in the nature of
induction. It proceeds in every case on the basis of an *à
priori* truth; namely, that the same causes under the same
circumstances produce the same effects. For example, you
conclude that ice will melt, should the temperature rise to 32°
F., because all observation has shown such to be the case.
But why should you so believe? From the mere fact that one
phenomenon always has followed another it may not be inferred that it always will. If such a conclusion may be drawn,
it is only because there is more in its premises than the observed
sequence. It must be because we know that there is power in
the antecedent, the temperature of 32°, to effect the consequent, the melting of the ice; and also because we know that,
the power and the conditions of its exercise continuing the
same, the consequent will be the same. These, however, are *à
priori* truths. They are not in any way the results of observation or of sensation. All that is given thus is the mere sequence
of the phenomena, the rising of the temperature to 32° and the
ice beginning then to melt. This the positivists maintain as
strenuously as any. This is all the explanation that they offer
of the principle of cause and effect. They reduce it to a se-

quence. Yet if they are to generalize with confidence from these sequences, they must admit the *à priori* truths that a cause is such because it has the power to produce its effect and that the same cause under the same circumstances must produce the same effect. And so it is that Comte speaks of the mind as obliged to invent a theory before it can observe profitably. Is it not more rational to believe that it finds itself furnished in advance with the true theory? Indeed, it is contradictory to speak of inventing something the elements of which are neither discovered without nor discerned within.

Moreover, in sensation itself there is given more than mere sensation. As H. B. Smith wrote,[11] " There is a material impact, *and also* a feeling of resistance, not material, but conscious—a resisting self, a person, an Ego—involved (whether or not this is given in the sensation itself is not material, it is certainly implied). And this *conscious knowledge* cannot be derived from the external phenomena, but is a distinguishable state of the ego. The ego cannot be derived from the non-ego." Even J. S. Mill confesses[12] that a series of sensations aware of itself is " the final inexplicability ". Positivism can describe the successive sensations, but that something whereby we know them as ours cannot come out of them. How can a mere sequence of feelings of pain generate the consciousness that it is I who feel the pain? Must there not be already the consciousness of self in order to the identification of the pain as my pain? I must recognize the particular peg as mine, if I am to hang my hat on my own peg. Admit that the sensation of pain may be the occasion of self-consciousness and even its necessary occasion, still, can it be its cause? A tree is the occasion of my seeing a tree. If no tree were presented to me, I should not see one. Yet who may say that the tree by itself produces the vision of a tree; or, if we speak strictly, that it produces it at all? What the tree does is to call the faculty of vision into exercise by furnishing it an appropriate object, and thus to show that the faculty in question existed prior to the presentation of the tree. It is the

[11] *Apologetics*, p. 53.
[12] *Ex. of Sir W. Hamilton's Phil.*, Vol. i, p. 262.

faculty of vision that produces the vision. Necessary though the tree is as an occasion, it is only an occasion. In like manner sensation is the occasion of self-consciousness. You may even argue that it is only in sensation that we become conscious of self. Yet who may maintain that sensation gives of itself the consciousness of self? All that it does is to call self-consciousness into exercise and so to reveal the self as existing prior to sensation and thus as independent of it. When Leibnitz was told that the gist of Locke's philosophy was, " Nihil est in intellectu quod non prius fuerit in sensu," he replied, " Etiam, nisi intellectus ipse."[13] Indeed, the intellect manifests itself in sense; à priori elements appear even in sensation itself.

Beyond this, if there be no knowledge except as the result of induction from individual sensations, we are involved by the very process of so-called knowledge in utter ignorance even of what we claim to know. The position is, that we know only what we can observe; that this is the mere sequence of phenomena, phenomena as antecedents and consequents; and that we know the consequents only as modes or forms of the antecedents. In a word, scientific knowledge is simply the knowledge of these differing modes. Suppose, then, that we trace back to the utmost point within our reach the last inspected consequents. These can be known " only as we know the antecedents," only as "modes of the antecedents." Then they cannot be known at all; for by the supposition, we cannot reach their antecedents, having already gone back as far as we can. Thus the whole process of knowing breaks down. As we do not know the ultimate antecedent, all our boasted knowledge becomes a chain of total ignorance. " It is a chain which ", as H. B. Smith wrote,[14] " is all hanging and nowhere hangs." What is beyond sense being absolutely unknown, we cannot know even what appears to sense. Hence, the positivist, to be consistent, ought to be agnostic as to every thing. If all that he can know be consequents of phenomena, he cannot know even this. Thus the denial of the Supernatural is the denial of the natural also. In a word, the refutation of

---

[13] *Nouv. Ess.* II, 1, 2.   [14] *Apologetics,* p. 55.

positivism is that it is a theory of knowledge which is destructive of all knowledge. Of course, this refutation does not prove the reality of the Supernatural. It does, however, dispose of the objection that because the Supernatural cannot be known by sensation it cannot be known at all. Such a theory of knowledge is contradictory and so must be untrue.

2. *Monism.*—This hypothesis, unlike that just considered, is affirmative and ontological. It offers a substitute for the Supernatural as we have described it. It does this by denying the first of the two positions which, as we have seen, must be guarded. That is, it ignores the distinction between the Supernatural and the natural: while either is to be conceived as single, this is so because they are both one and the same. This hypothesis itself assumes two forms according as the one absolute reality is regarded as essentially matter or spirit. In the one case we have Materialistic Monism; in the other, Idealistic Monism.

a. *Materialistic Monism.*—Of this Professor Ernst Haeckel is probably the representative exponent. " By Monism ", he says, " we unambiguously express our conviction that there lives ' one spirit in all things ', and that the whole cognizable world is constituted, and has been developed, in accordance with one common fundamental law. We emphasize by it, in particular, the essential unity of inorganic and organic nature, the latter having been evolved from the former only at a relatively late period. We cannot draw a sharp line of distinction between these two great divisions of nature, any more than we can recognize an absolute distinction between the animal and the vegetable kingdom, or between the lower animals and man. Similarly, we regard the whole of human knowledge as a structural unity; in this sphere we refuse to accept the distinction usually drawn between the natural and the spiritual. The latter is only a part of the former (or vice versa); both are one. Our monistic view of the world belongs, therefore, to that group of philosophical systems which from other points of view have been designated also as mechanical or pantheistic. However differently expressed in the philosophical systems of an Empedocles or a Lucretius, a Spinoza or a Giordano Bruno, a Lamarck or a David Strauss, the fundamental thought common to them all is ever that of the oneness of the cosmos, of the indissoluble connection between energy and matter, between mind and embodiment—or, as we may also say, between God and the world—to which Goethe, Germany's greatest poet and thinker, has given poetical expression in his Faust and in the wonderful series of poems entitled *Gott und Welt."* [15] This "confession of faith of a man of science," as Haeckel calls it, contains at least the following articles:

1. The universe or God, or, if you prefer, God or the universe, is infinite; for God "is the infinite sum of all natural forces, the sum of all atomic forces and all ether-vibrations."[16]

2. In the infinite God or the infinite universe there are no real distinctions. The organic is essentially one with the inorganic; the animal is essentially one with the vegetable; man is essentially one with the animal; God is essentially one with the world; in a word, the Supernatural is essentially one with the natural.

3. This supernatural or natural God or universe is to be understood in terms of matter. That is, Haeckel's monism is materialistic monism. This is what he affirms. "Even clearer does it become that all the wonderful phenomena of nature around us, organic as well as inorganic, are only products of one and the same original form, various combinations of one and the same primitive matter."[17] True, he would regard mind as well as matter as an aspect of what is most primitive and fundamental of all; namely, "substance": but that he would conceive of substance and so of mind mechanically rather than spiritually—this, too, is clear. Indeed, he says, Monism "strives to carry back all phenomena, without exception, to the mechanism of the atom." [18] In a word, materialistic monism starts with "animated atoms"; it would develop intelligent atoms; and it makes the Supernatural just "the infinite sum" of these atoms.

---

[15] *Monism,* pp. 3, 4, 5.
[16] *Ibid.,* p. 78.

[17] *Ibid,* p. 16.
[18] *Ibid.,* p. 19.

This hypothesis is invalid in at least the following three respects:

1. It begs the question. It starts with the life and consciousness and mind which are the very things to be explained. That is, it assumes what is to be proved. Thus Haeckel says: "The two fundamental forms of substance, ponderable matter and ether, are not dead and only moved by extrinsic force, but they are endowed with sensation and will (though naturally of the lowest grade); they experience an inclination for condensation, a dislike of strain; they strive after the one and struggle against the other."[19] "Every shade of inclination from complete indifference to the fiercest passion is exemplified in the chemical relation of the various elements towards each other."[20] "On those phenomena we base our conviction that even the *atom* is not without a rudimentary form of sensation and will, or, as it is better expressed, of feeling (æsthesis) and inclination (tropesis)—that is, a universal 'soul' of the simplest character."[21]

"Thus, then, in order to explain life and mind and consciousness by means of matter," Sir Oliver Lodge writes, commenting on this very passage, "all that is done is to assume that matter possesses these unexplained attributes."

"What the full meaning of that may be, whether there be any philosophic justification for any such idea, is a matter on which I will not now express an opinion; but, at any rate, as it stands, it is not science, and its formulation gives no sort of conception of what life and will and consciousness really are."

"Even if it were true, it contains nothing whatever in the nature of explanation; it recognizes the inexplicable, and relegates it to the atoms, where it seems to hope that further quest may cease. Instead of tackling the difficulty when it actually occurs; instead of associating life, will, and consciousness with the organisms in which they are actually in experience found, these ideas are foisted into the atoms of matter; and then the properties which have been conferred on the atoms are denied

---

[19] *The Riddle of the Universe*, p. 78.
[20] *Ibid.*, p. 79.
[21] *Ibid.*, p. 80.

in all essential reality to the fully developed organism which those atoms help to compose!" [22]

2. The hypothesis under consideration does not beg enough. Though it assumes what is to be proved, it must assume more to complete its proof. Starting with "animated atoms" "not without a rudimentary form of sensation and will," it develops out of them the inorganic world; then, the inorganic world into the organic; then, the vegetable into the animal; then, the animal into man; then, man into all that he has become and even into all that he will become. Not less than this is what materialistic monism undertakes to do; and, consequently, it is according to its ability by means of its assumption to explain how this can be done that it must stand or fall.

Now to do this, it has "animated atoms" "not without a rudimentary form of sensation and will." This is what it assumes and so is what it may work with; yet though big and utterly unwarranted as an assumption, this is all that it assumes and so is all that it may work with. But much more is needed. If this vast scheme of development is to be explained, intelligence, and not merely sensation and will, must come in, and must come in at the start. For feeling and inclination presuppose and are impossible without a condition or situation to be felt and to be inclined towards or against. As Haeckel says, " The two fundamental forms of substance, ponderable matter and ether, experience an inclination for condensation, a dislike of strain; they strive after the one and struggle against the other." Nor is this all. The result of an evolution starting with and proceeding by means of this striving and struggling must, in the nature of the case, depend on the kind and the degree of this condensation and of this strain, and on the kind and degree of them from the first instant of attraction and repulsion. Let there have been the smallest variation in these then from what there was, and it would be an entirely different universe that we should have now. How, then, came it about that the atomic feeling and inclination began to act under the one set of conditions that could have resulted in the existing state of things? By the law of probabilities, if it was

[22] *Life and Matter,* p. 42.

by chance, the chances were at least practically infinitely against it. But if not by chance, it must have been by design. That is, intelligence must have been not only implicit in but actually operative at the beginning of evolution. Whence, however, this intelligence? The hypothesis under criticism essays to show its development, but it does not assume it as already in exercise. Yet this it must go on and do, if it is to show anything but its own imbecility.

3. The hypothesis that we are considering, not only begs the question and still does not beg enough, but what it does beg and must beg, even to save its face, is impossible. It assumes that " the universe, or the cosmos, is eternal, infinite, and illimitable," " Its substance, with its two attributes (matter and energy), fills infinite space, and is in eternal motion". " This motion runs on through infinite time as an unbroken development, with a periodic change from life to death, from evolution to devolution." [23]　That is, as we have seen, it assumes that the sum of all atomic forces and of all ether vibrations is infinite and in that sense is God. This, moreover, must be assumed. As just indicated, there is no other way of escaping the necessity of positing an infinite intelligence distinct from the universe and operative at its origin. To do this, the cosmos must be regarded as itself " eternal, infinite, and illimitable." Evolution must be the ultimate fact; like God, it must have neither "beginning of days nor end of years; " it must itself be God himself, and so ultimate and thus beyond either explanation or the need of it, if that which is determinative of it be so rudimentary and inadequate as mere atomic feeling and atomic inclination. That is, we can get rid of the Supernatural only by putting the natural in its place. To do this, however, is impossible on any hypothesis, and it would seem to be specially so on the one under review. For the infinite substance which it assumes not only, as we have seen, " fills infinite space, but is in eternal motion." Now this is a contradiction. There are just two ways in which an infinite substance can be said to fill infinite space. It can really fill it.

[23] *The Riddle of the Universe*, p. 5.

That is, it can form a continuum. This, however, as Derr has pointed out, will mean " the annihilation of space." Indeed, there can be no space, if the ether of space be absolutely without pores or vacuities or parts; and this is just what a continuum is, and what it must be to be a continuum."[24] But " it is inconceivable that motion should take place in a continuum." [25] As Lucretius pointed out in his *De Rerum Natura* (II, 95 sqq.), if there were no void spaces in the universe, motion would be impossible. There would be no space to move in; there would be no parts to move. On the other hand, if ether does not form a continuum, if it does have pores, vacuities and parts, if in a word, there is either space within it for its parts to move in or, we may add, space without it for it as a whole to move in, then the cosmos can not be " eternal, infinite and illimitable." It could be conceived to be greater than it is. It would be greater than it is, if its pores and vacuities were filled and if it itself filled the infinitude of space. That is, from the physical standpoint the cosmos cannot both be conceived as " eternal, infinite, and illimitable " and at the same time be regarded as " in eternal motion " either with respect to its parts or with respect to it itself as a whole. The two conceptions are contradictory and so are mutually exclusive. Of course, it may be replied, and it is likely to be replied, to this argumentation that it is purely speculative. This is true. No scientist ever saw an atom or felt the ether. They are preëminently mental creations. We do not cognize them by the senses. As Ladd says, " It is only because of certain irresistable convictions or as symptoms of mind that we believe in their extra-mental reality." [26] Surely, then, criticism of inferences from these mental convictions and assumptions is in order. Thought-constructions must be tested by the laws of thought. If physicists will be metaphysicians, it is by metaphysics that they must be judged.

b. *Idealistic Monism.*—In this, as its name indicates and as has been pointed out, the one absolute reality is conceived, not

[24] *The Uncaused Being and the Criterion of Truth,* p. 72.
[26] *Elements of Physiological Psychology,* p. 677.
[25] *The Uncaused Being.* p. 73.

as matter or substance, but as spirit or subject. The world is not composed of atoms; but it is a system of thought relations, and God is just the unity and the identity of these relations. All existence, consequently, is regarded as a manifestation of the Absolute and the Universal Intelligence; and the inherent power of this "Absolute Idea" is conceived as the sole agency at work in all transformations. Thus, whatever is real is rational and whatever is rational is real; and the rational and real is neither more or less than the process of the logical unfolding of the "Absolute Idea." In a word, if materialistic monism makes the natural physical and puts it in the place of the supernatural, idealistic monism makes the Supernatural an idea and puts it in the place of the natural. That is, as represented by the philosophy of Hegel, in an important sense its source and type, it identifies the Supernatural and the natural in a universal syllogism. That this scheme has advantages over that just considered should go almost without saying. It escapes the embarrassments which, as we have seen, materialistic monism encounters from the start. Thus it does not have to begin by begging animation and mind for matter; for, as Balfour has well said, " it makes reason the very essence of all that is or can be: the immanent cause of the world-process; its origin and its goal." [27] Again, it does not have to beg further, in order to the evolution of the cosmos, the active and developed reason which it is the chief function of the evolution to evolve, for logical movement is of the essence of the Absolute Idea. Once more, it does not have to solve the insoluble problem how the physical universe can be infinite and yet in eternal motion; for it denies that there is a physical universe.

But in spite of these great advantages, this idealistic form of the monistic hypothesis has to encounter difficulties which would seem to be as fatal to it as are those that we have considered to materialistic monism.

1. As Balfour has written, " In all experience there is a refractory element which, though it cannot be presented in isolation, nevertheless refuses wholly to merge its being in a

[27] *The Foundations of Belief,* p. 143.

network of relations, necessary as these may be to give it ' significance for us as thinking beings.' If so, whence does this irreducible element arise? The mind, we are told, is the source of relations. What is the source of that which is related? "[28] We need not fall back on Kant's contradictory hypothesis of " a thing in itself ", but must we not admit his dictum that " without matter categories are empty?" [29] That is, there is reality which even idealistic monism must leave unexplained. As an hypothesis of the universe, therefore, it is at least inadequate.

2. Even where it should be strongest it will not work. That is, it breaks down also when it encounters the individuality of the self or ego. The reality of this individuality it denies. It does this by bringing all self-consciousnesses to identity in the divine self-consciousness. Because the self-consciousness of men reveals a similarity of type, the Hegelian infers unity of substance. This, however, is as much a non-sequitur as though we were to argue that all oak trees were one because they were all alike. Nay, it is a much more glaring non-sequitur; for the distinguishing characteristic of every self-consciousness is consciousness of itself as an individual. In the words of Seth, " Though self-hood involves a duality in unity, and is describable as subject-object, it is none the less true that each self is a unique existence, which is perfectly *impervious,* if I may so speak, to other selves—impervious in a fashion of which the impenetrability of matter is a faint analogue. The self, accordingly, resists invasion; in its character of self it refuses to admit another self within itself, and thus be made, as it were, a mere retainer of something else. The unity of things (which is not denied) cannot be properly expressed by making it depend upon a unity of the Self in all thinkers; for the very characteristic of a self is this exclusiveness."[30] Moreover, this fact is one with which an Hegelian specially is bound to reckon, because with him self-consciousness is the ultimate category. How, then, may he deny that exclusiveness, that individuality,

[28] *The Foundations of Belief,* p. 144.
[29] *Critique of Pure Reason,* Müller's translation, p. 45.
[30] *Hegelianism and Personality,* p. 216.

which, as we have seen, is the essence of self-consciousness? No hypothesis can work which thus repudiates the innermost content of that for which it assumes to account. It is not, therefore, too much to say that " the radical error of Hegelianism is the unification of consciousness in a single Self." Though it gave a valid explanation of self-consciousness in other respects, its breakdown in this would be fatal; for this is fundamental.

3. Its explanation, however, is invalid throughout. Even if it might explain away the individuality of the self, it would have to be set aside on other grounds, chief among them the following:

Man is put in the place of God. This is done by making, as we have seen, the human self-consciousness and the Absolute " identical quantities ". " God or the Absolute is represented in the system as the last term of a development into which we have a perfect insight; we ourselves, indeed, as absolute philosophers, are equally the last term of the development." Thus in the philosophy of law, of history, of æsthetics, and in the history of philosophy itself, the Absolute is attained, being simply man's record and ultimate achievement along these lines. Specially is this so in the " philosophy of religion," where we should naturally expect to meet it least. The self-existence of God seems to disappear; he has his only reality in the consciousness of the worshipping community. " God is not a spirit beyond the stars," says Hegel; " He is Spirit in all spirits ":[31] but this means, if not certainly to " the Master " himself, at least to many of his disciples, that anything like a separate personality or self-consciousness in the divine Being is renounced. In a word, we are put in the place of God. Can any such explanation of the human self be valid? It contradicts that which is scarcely less fundamental in our consciousness than the sense of individuality, and that is the feeling of dependence on the Supernatural. As Bacon has said, ' Man looks up to God as naturally as the dog does to his master;'[32] but this he could never do, were there no God save " his own great self ". Again, man as well as God is deprived of real

---

[31] *Werke*, xi. 24. [32] *Essay on Atheism.*

existence. After putting the former in the place of the latter, the hypothesis under review proceeds to destroy the former also. This it does by dividing and so, of course, killing him. His one concrete self is split into two. Of these that one of which each of us is conscious is the man: and the other, that which, according to Kant, unifies the former, and, according to Fichte, thinks it, and, according to Schelling, is the ground of it, and, according to Hegel, attains to self-consciousness, and so truly manifests itself, in it, is the Absolute or God. This division, however, does not more truly, as we have seen, undeify God by practically identifying him with the human self-consciousness than it dehumanizes man. Man is not " the empirical self "; or rather, the latter is only half the man, only the objective side of his consciousness. It is a half, too, that cannot exist, that cannot even be conceived, alone. If there are to be merely states of consciousness, there must be a subjective self of which they can be the states of consciousness. Nor does it help matters that the place of this subjective self is taken by what may be called the divine Self—a self identical in all men, a self, as we have seen, identical with man. " The individual seems thus to become no more than an object of the divine Self, a series of phenomena threaded together and reviewed by it—an office which it performs in precisely the same manner for any number of such so-called individuals." Surely this is to destroy man with a vengeance. He is made the mere object of an undeified God. Nothing in himself, he can be conceived to exist only in virtue of what cannot itself be regarded as self-conscious save in him and as far as he. As Seth puts it, " Human persons are, as it were, the foci in which the impersonal life of thought momentarily concentrates itself, in order to take stock of its own contents. These foci appear only to disappear in the perpetual process of this realization." [33]

This is to hypostalize an abstraction. " The impersonal life of thought ", which is admitted to constitute the subjective side of human consciousness, is, of course, such. Apart from a person, without a thinker, thought can not be, it cannot

<hr>

[33] *Hegelianism and Personality*, p. 190.

really be conceived as being; it is like an effect without a cause, it is an effect without a cause. But the empirical self, the phenomenal aspect of consciousness, is, by itself, equally an abstraction. States of consciousness presuppose and necessarily involve a subject of those states. As well think of qualities as existing save as the qualities of some substance. Nor will it help matters to take " the impersonal life of thought," as is done by at least the Hegelians of the Left, as the ground of the individual self-consciousness. The combination of two abstractions will not make one concrete reality any more than zero plus zero will make unity. Hence, Seth is correct when he says of the hypothesis under review: " It takes the notion of knowledge equivalent to a real knower; and the form of knowledge being one, it leaps to the conclusion that what we have before us is the One Subject which sustains the world, and is the real knower in all finite intelligences. It seems a hard thing to say, but to do this is neither more nor less than to hypostatize an abstraction." [34] Now to do this is, in plain English, to make something of nothing.

But this is not the worst. Having so deceived itself as to suppose that it has succeeded in working up mere abstractions into a real agent, the hypothesis goes on to ascribe to its absolute Nothing an absolutely impossible achievement. This is the creation as it were of reality. Though the Absolute is but an idea, though it is merely abstract thought, the logical unfolding of its categories is regarded as giving the whole actual world of nature and spirit. Hegelianism briefly expressed teaches, according to Schopenhauer, that the universe is a crystallized syllogism. This, however, cannot be. " There is no evolution possible of a fact from a conception." Logic can develop the meaning of nature, but it cannot originate it. " It cannot make the real, it can only describe what it finds." Indeed, it itself presupposes nature or reality; and without it, it is, as has been already observed, as powerless as it is empty. How, then, may we posit a mere nonentity like the " Absolute Idea " as the creator of such realities as the physical realm and

[34] *Hegelianism and Personality,* p. 29.

even the human soul? No hypothesis of the self can be tenable which leads to a result so irrational.

c. *Pluralism.*—This is the doctrine that reality consists of a plurality or multiplicity of distinct beings. It may be atomistic as with the atomists, or hylozoistic as with Empedocles, or spiritual as with Leibnitz, or indifferent as with Herbart, whose " unknowable reals " produce the phenomena of both mind and matter. Be its character, however, what it may, it is essentially the reverse of the hypothesis just considered. Monism, in both its materialistic and idealistic forms, admits that the Supernatural is single, but denies that there is any radical distinction between it and the natural. It is but the sum of the natural in materialistic monism; it is but the unity and identity of the natural in idealistic monism. Pluralism, on the contrary, denies the singleness and, consequently, the absoluteness of the Supernatural, but admits the reality of distinctions. " The atoms of the Atomist are endowed with perpetual motion which they do not receive from a transcendent principle, but which belongs to the essence ". We find no " notion of elementary unity " in " the four elements " of Empedocles, but they are equally " original ". The monads of Leibnitz are each of them " little divinities in their own department." The " reals " of Herbart are themselves " absolute ". That is, instead of one all-comprehending substance or one all-unifying subject, we have a plurality of independent, if not unrelated, substances or subjects.

This hypothesis, according to Ward the one now dominant (*The Realm of Ends,* p. 49), owes its special prominence and importance at present largely to the late William James. " Reality ", he says, " may exist in distributive form, in shape not of an all but of a set of eaches, just as it seems to."[35] God, then, is not " the absolute, but is himself a part when the system is conceived pluralistically. He has an environment, he is in time, he works out a history just like ourselves." [36] Distinct from us, he is not single among us or over us, being finite and relative as are we. That this view has not a little to commend it appears almost on its face. As William James

---

[35] *A Pluralistic Universe,* p. 129.   [36] *Ibid.,* p. 318.

points out, God, because finite and relative, " escapes from the foreignness from all that is human, of the static timeless perfect absolute." [37] Inasmuch as he is like us even to the extent of being limited as we are, we can feel that he is one with us. Again, the problem of evil becomes much easier from this standpoint. " The line of least resistance," says William James, " both in theology and in philosophy, is to accept, along with the superhuman consciousness, the notion that it is not all-embracing, the notion, in other words, that there is a God, but that he is finite, either in power or in knowledge, or in both at once." [38] We need not then explain his permission of evil : we may hold that he would conquer it, but cannot. Though indefinitely superior to us, he is no more absolute than are we. Hence, God and we are bound together in a bond of sympathy such as can bind those only who are fighting shoulder to shoulder in an as yet uncertain battle. Once more, reality seems to exist distributively. Though the universe may, in the last resort, be what William James calls " a block-universe," [39] that is, an absolute system; still, it is as " only strung along, not rounded in and closed," that we become aware of it. We know it simply as an aggregation of " eaches ". Why, then, should we admit more than this into any hypothesis with regard to it? That is, in not positing a single because absolute Supernatural, pluralism is at least true to what appears.

On the other hand, however, this hypothesis encounters difficulties neither few nor small. Among these are the following:

1. Pluralism, though true to what appears, is not true to all that appears. It may be true to the world of reality as the senses make that known to us, but it is not true even to our sensations and perceptions as these are interpreted to us by self-consciousness. For we find in the latter, and all men, in proportion as they develop mentally and their development is not biased by philosophy, find in the latter, the idea of the cosmos. That is to say, the human race, in so far as it thinks on these subjects, thinks naturally of the world as one system. Even

---

[37] *A Pluralistic Universe*, p. 318.
[38] *Ibid.*, p. 311.   [39] *Ibid.*, p. 328.

Zoroastrianism was not originally dualistic. Now there is no reason why this natural and well nigh universal belief in monism of some kind should not commend itself to us at least as much as the exceptional belief in pluralism. Indeed, the former stands better accredited. Pluralism in its denial of the cosmos denies one of those native principles of the mind which, as we saw in our discussion of positivism, must be admitted or knowledge even by sensation and perception becomes impossible.

Were this not so, however, the bare fact of science would establish that the world is not what William James describes as "only strung along", but is what he calls "a block universe" or what we prefer to term a cosmos. It is not, as the idealistic monist holds, only a system of thought-relations: but it is constructed throughout in accord with thought relations; and so it is one system, that is, a cosmos. The proof of this is that reason can and does interpret it and that mind can and does understand it. Were it otherwise, there could be no science as there can be no science of any jumble of independent facts. It is only as these can be viewed monistically rather than pluralistically that a science of them can be even conceived. The progress of science is, therefore, the denial of pluralism. Though this progress be small in comparison with the land yet to be possessed, enough has been systematized to warrant, if not to constrain, the belief that all can be possessed. Much of the universe may still, as William James would say, not be "closed in"; but what has been "closed in" indicates as the reason why more has not been "closed in", that our reason is limited, not that the world is not a rationalized whole.

2. Where pluralism claims to be strongest it is weakest. The doctrine of a finite God appears to commend itself to the heart. At first sight a God who would prevent evil, but cannot, is more attractive than one who permits it though, since he is omnipotent, he could prevent it. On second thought, however, not only is the mind unable to tolerate a finite God, but even the heart can "see no beauty in him that it should desire him". On the one hand, omnipotence and omniscience may be variously conceived; but, whether as held by the savage or by the

scholar, they are essential to his conception of God. The reason for this is that man has a primitive belief in the infinite. As, therefore, he must naturally believe in God, so he must naturally believe him to be infinite. He could not think of God as the greatest and the best that he knows unless he did so. On the other hand, it is precisely the omnipotence and the omniscience of God which give its unique worth to God's love for us and sympathy with us. These can be supremely precious because they differ from all other love and sympathy not only in degree but in kind. It is just because we can feel that God can do for us and can be to us all that " love which passes knowledge " can prompt that we stay our hearts on him and find perfect peace in him. It is easier far to trust that he loves us even when he chastens us and that he chastens us " for our profit that we may be partakers of his holiness " than it would be to rest our souls on him if we had even to suspect that, in spite of all his greatness, he was limited in power and wisdom as are we. There would always be the fearful possibility that at last we might be cast away. Even Paul, had he been a pluralist, could never have exclaimed, " For I am persuaded that nothing shall be able to separate us from the love of God which is in Christ Jesus our Lord " (Rom. viii. 38, 39). Thus pluralism fails just where it thinks itself the strongest. It compromises with the head for the sake of the heart only to be repudiated by the heart.

3. Logically, pluralism must give the lie to our religious nature and thus silence and at last destroy it. As Derr has written, " The religious implications of pluralism are obvious. All the various ' Eaches ' are coëternal and therefore coëqual, and enter into unions or combinations with one another of their own free will. Nothing can be compulsory amid the vast democracy of uncaused beings, for they are all independent of one another, and exist by the necessity of their own nature. They are all *finite* in power, for the sphere of activity of each is limited by each, hence a multitude of *infinite* beings is impossible. Nor can we, with any show of reason, assume that any one of these equal beings can lift itself so high above the rest as to assert sovereignty over them. All the eaches being

gods in their own right, there is no such a being as *A* God; the word, indeed, loses all its significance. And thus pluralism or modern polytheism ends in absolute nihilism, and the religious sentiment must necessarily go by default."[40] Can any hypothesis be true which thus destroys that which is noblest in the noblest being in the world that it is assumed to account for?

These, then, are the hypotheses which contradict that doctrine of the Supernatural which Christianity presupposes and which, accordingly, we would vindicate: positivism, which denies the Supernatural altogether, both its separateness and its singleness; monism, which, in either of its forms, admits its singleness but denies its separateness from the world; and pluralism, which denies its singleness but admits its separateness. Inasmuch as each one of these has been shown to be untenable, does it not follow that we should approach the only other hypothesis possible in the nature of the case, the hypothesis that there is a real Supernatural both separate from the world even as immanent in it and single in it and over it —does it not now follow that we should take up this hypothesis with a presumption at least that it is true? Some world-view that really explains the universe there must be, and this would seem to be the only other possible.

This presumption is strengthened by the fact that the Christian doctrine of the Supernatural would, if true, meet all the necessary conditions. Thus positivism, as we have seen, fails to interpret even the world as made known by the senses, through denying those innate ideas only under whose guidance can the senses conduct to knowledge: but the Christian doctrine of the Supernatural both recognizes and guarantees these ideas; as an idea it is one of them, and its subject, the supreme Intelligence, is the author of them, "the light that lighteneth every man coming into the world."

Again, if monism breaks down, in its materialistic form because it denies an absolute Spirit separate from the physical world, and in its idealistic form because it denies the separateness of such a Spirit from all finite spirits; so the view of the

[40] *The Uncaused Being and The Criterion of Truth,* p. 39.

Supernatural that we would vindicate supplies in both cases the deficiency by holding that God is not only single in himself, but absolutely distinct from the world whether of matter or of spirit.

Once more, if pluralism fails, and must fail, permanently to satisfy man's mental, emotional and religious natures for the reason that its Supernatural is not single and so cannot be absolute, the Christian doctrine of the Supernatural comes up to the requirements even in this respect; for it conceives of the Supernatural as him " by whom were all things created that are in heaven, and that are in earth, visible and invisible, whether they be thrones or dominions, or principalities, or powers: all things were created by him, and for him: and he is before all things, and by him all things consist" (Coll. i. 16, 17).

Moreover, the Christian doctrine of the Supernatural is a satisfactory hypothesis in fact as well as in logic. To prove and to illustrate this, it is necessary simply to recall what has been said with reference to the " Importance of the Supernatural ". As we have seen, not only do Christian apologetics and Christian dogmatics presuppose the Supernatural in the sense in which this paper conceives it as the end of the former and the subject of the latter; but philosophy, science, morality, religion, human progress and civilization,— all depend on its reality and, were there opportunity, could be shown to prosper in proportion as this reality is recognized. Could this be, if the Christian view of the Supernatural were untrue? That a doctrine will work does not of itself prove it to be true; but that it has worked well—this must, at any rate, raise a presumption that it is true, and must greatly strengthen any presumption of this sort already existing. Can less than this be meant by the Highest of all authorities when he says of false prophets, " Ye shall know them by their fruits " (Mt. vii. 16)? Clearly, then, the burden of proof is on those who would deny the existence of the Supernatural. It is for them to refute, it is not for us to establish, the Christian position. Strictly, according to the law of parsimony, no argument for the Christian hypothesis is called for. It is the only one that has not been proved to be untenable; it has been shown to be satisfactory in theory; it has been found to be indispensable in practice. Therefore, the threefold argument about to be advanced for it ought at least to be received with the highest respect and to be considered as from the start having everything in its favor.

1. The argument from the consent of philosophy.—Most schools of philosophy declare for the Supernatural. In a sense, all of them do. Thus Comte, the founder of positivism, repudiates the Supernatural avowedly, but he devises a very complicated system of worship and finds in " aggregate humanity " an object for it. Even this most significant concession does not satisfy his successors. Herbert Spencer, whether we regard him as a positivist or a monist or an agnostic, not unjustly represents them; and he comes out clearly and strongly for the Supernatural. " The axiomatic truths of physical science unavoidably postulate Absolute Being as their common basis. The persistence of the universe is the persistence of that Unknown Cause, Power or Force which is manifested to us through all phenomena. Such is the foundation of any possible system of positive knowledge. Deeper than demonstration—deeper even than definite cognition—deep as the very nature of the mind is the postulate at which we have arrived. Its authority transcends all other whatever; for not only is it given in the constitution of our own consciousness, but it is impossible to imagine a consciousness so constituted as not to give it . . . Thus the belief which this datum constitutes has a higher warrant than any other whatever." [41] Even Haeckel, the great exponent of monism, while repudiating all being above nature, concludes his " Monistic Confession of Faith " with the words: " May God, the Spirit of the Good, the Beautiful, and the True, be with us."[42] So, too, the first of modern pluralists, William James, even when arguing for a finite God, admits that the hypothesis of the absolute " must in spite of its irrational features, still be left open,[43] and seems to claim as the reason why it must be so that " it

[41] *First Principles*, pp. 256, 258, 98.   [42] *Monism*, p. 89.
[43] *A Pluralistic Universe*, p. 125.

gives peace ".[44] These concessions do not class their authors with the Supernaturalists; but are they not testimony, strong just because it was unexpected and is unwilling, to the truth of the supernaturalistic position? Thinkers can not leave this position and not try to find a substitute for it. Thus they prove at least its necessity and so indirectly its truth.

If such is the force of the teaching even of antisupernaturalists, it is not too much to claim that philosophy as a whole on the whole declares for the reality of the Supernatural, if not in the precise form of the Christian doctrine, yet in what approximates and tends towards it. Did not our limits forbid, nothing could be easier than to illustrate and establish this statement from such masters in philosophy as Plato, Aristotle, Cicero, Bacon, Descartes, Berkeley, Kant, Hamilton, Lotze, and many others. Indeed, as Lindsay writes, " We may surely say that it has become more clearly manifest that what thought as to the Primal Reality known as God testifies to is, above all else, the fact that such Inscrutable Reality, or the Unknowable, does undoubtedly exist." [45]

This amounts to a great deal. It shows that the ablest thinkers in all ages, though they may not speak as religious teachers and though some of them may speak even as the enemies of the Christian religion, nevertheless, give it as the last result of their deepest and best thinking that the Supernatural both does and must exist. This, of course, is not demonstration. The objective cannot be *deduced* from the subjective. The general consent, however, that we have been considering does prove that belief in the reality of the Supernatural is not the idiosyncrasy of some peculiar thinkers, and that we must grant it to be a true belief or allow the uselessness and even the folly of the best thinking in every age and the world over. But this is not sufficient. It may be urged that philosophy is the product of an artificial humanity, and that, consequently, it does not voice the natural and so best judgment of the race. We need, therefore, to appeal to,

2. The necessity of religion.—Religion is a universal phe-

[44] *A Pluralistic Universe,* p. 114.
[45] *Recent Advances in Theistic Philosophy,* p. 5.

nomenon. All men as men and because men are religious
in one way or another. Even those thinkers who have yielded
themselves to an intense and absorbing skepticism and whose
religious nature has in consequence become atrophied confess
the moral and spiritual necessity of religion, and their skepticism makes their reluctant confession all the more impressive. We have seen this to have been so in the case of Comte.
It might as readily have been shown to have been so in the
case of J. S. Mill and of many others. What is even more
to the point is that no tribe has been found so degraded as
not to evidence at least the beginnings of religion. The
claims that such had been discovered of scientists like Sir John
Lubbock and of travelers like Sir Samuel Baker have all
been refuted by wider and more careful investigation. For
example, Roskoff has declared that " no tribe has yet occurred
without trace of religious sentiments." Peschel has decidedly
denied " any tribe having been found quite without religious
emotions and ideas." In like vein, Hellwald affirms that " no
tribes completely without religion have thus far been met
with." [46]   The universality of religion would seem, therefore,
to be a commonplace of anthropological science; and the fact
that, no matter how debased, man is never observed to be
destitute of something which to him is religion would appear
to show that it belongs to his essence. In a word, religion
is so universal among men that it must be necessary to man.
As Kellogg puts it, " Its beliefs have been so universally accepted in all ages by men of both the highest and the lowest
degree of culture, that we can hardly avoid the conclusion that
they must be due to a certain instinct of man's nature." [47]
So far as can be seen, he can no more get away from religion
than a beast can escape the power of instinct. Indeed, the
religious feeling is man's instinct, and so the highest and
noblest of all instincts.

In the next place, religion is impossible, if there be no underlying sense of the reality of the Supernatural. Were this absent, whatever we might have, we should not have what we

[46] Lindsay's *Recent Advances in Theistic Philosophy*, p. 54.
[47] *Handbook of Comparative Religion*, p. 10.

recognize as religion. From the highest religion to the lowest, this belief in the reality of the Supernatural, of that which is above the world and which, in so far forth, is distinct from the world and itself single, is the one common and characteristic element. Let there be nothing left of religion but a vague sentiment, an undefined aspiration, an unintelligent impulse; still, so far as it goes, this is a belief in and a craving for a real Supernatural and such a Superntural as we would vindicate. "In most, if not in all cases where men worship gods many," says Kellogg, "there is discoverable in the background of the religious consciousness the dim outline of one sole Power, of which the many who are worshipped are either different manifestations, or to which they hold a position strictly subordinate." [48] Were this not so, however, our argument would not be weakened. What is significant is not that the Supernatural is conceived in all religions essentially as we have defined it, or that it is conceived at all; it is that all religions, even the lowest, reveal in their development the tendency toward such a conception: just as in appetite the significant thing is not that animals have from the first a clear idea of nourishment or that they have any idea of it; it is that the tendency to suck always develops into the desire for and the eating of what will nourish. That is, as Edward Caird has so well shown in his *Evolution of Religion,* it is the end and not the beginning of a process of development which reveals its nature. Hence, if religion be, as we have tried to make plain, the expression of man's distinctive instinct; so the religious instinct is the instinct for a true Supernatural just as the young animal's tendency to suck is because of an instinct for real food.

Now we find that every instinct has an object fitted to gratify it. According to all observation, the belief in the reality of the object that its craving implies is justified. There is its mother's milk to satisfy the sucking child. There is the southern land to satisfy the swallow's instinct in early autumn to fly to the southern land. There is the ocean to satisfy the young fish's instinct, which constrains it, though it has never

[48] *Handbook of Comparative Religion,* p. 7.

been away from the spawning grounds far up the stream, to swim toward the ocean. Hence, to prove the existence of an instinct is to prove the reality of the object fitted to gratify it. Why, then, should it not be so in the case of the instinct for the Supernatural? Nay, how could it not be so?

This does not demonstrate the reality of the Supernatural. It does, however, demonstrate that the Supernatural exists: or else, that there is an exception to the apparently universal and beneficent law of instinct; that this exception is in the case of the highest of all animals, man; and that it is in the instance of what in him is noblest. That is, the law of instinct breaks down, so far as we can see, only in the one creature that is capable of appreciating it, and with reference to that element of his nature which exalts him most. This is not demonstration, but is it not a reductio ad absurdum? This will be shown yet more clearly, if we consider,

3. The necessity in thought.—There is thought. This no one can deny. In denying it we should affirm it : the denial involves thinking, it is itself thinking. Thus thought itself is a necessity.

There is a necessity in thought. Not only can we not help thinking, but we must think in accord with certain rational principles. For example, if you think of finite being, you must believe in other being that is its ground. The former, because it is finite, cannot but be dependent; and what is conceived as dependent can be conceived only as we posit, definitely or not, that which can be its ground. We can no more think otherwise than we can think of a building that stands and yet has nothing on which to stand. There is a principle in the case that thought cannot set aside any more than it can cause itself to cease. Again, you cannot think of an event, a change, an effect, and not act on and thus really think in accord with the principle that everything that is finite, that begins to be, must have a cause. If you are in pain, you try to find out what produces it, and thus you show that, whatever may be your theory, you believe that there must be something or must have been something with power to produce it, that is, a real cause of it. You may even teach with Hamilton, that there is no positive power in a cause; that the cause of each and every phenomenon is " a negative impotence "; that we believe in the reality of causation, not because it is real, but because we cannot think it unreal. Still, even this theory will not make us any abler to think it unreal. Indeed, our denial of the principle of causation will only render more conspicuous and significant our practical recognition of it. We can no more help acting on it than we can cease thinking. Once more, we cannot think of acts and not regard them as the acts of some subject, of some agent. We can consider acts, as governing, as making, as upholding, as creating, by themselves; but we cannot conceive of them as taking place by themselves. Even when our abstraction of them as acts from their subject is complete, it never occurs to us to suppose that in reality they are either separated or separable from it. Though we may think of them singly we must believe the act to be impossible apart from its subject. This is a principle that thought is bound to observe. It can no more transcend this principle than it can arrest itself. Other necessary laws of thought might be mentioned, but these are sufficient for our purpose.

These principles reveal the necessity of the Supernatural. For example, the ground that, as we have seen, every thought of the finite presupposes is, in the last analysis, the Supernatural. Unless you posit this and thus find in it a self-subsistent ground of being, the finite universe, which cannot be conceived without a ground, is left without one. Thus this principle of thought discloses the necessity, if not the nature, of the Supernatural. Though it does not show us all that it is, it does show us that it must be. Only its real existence can satisfy the demands of thought. In like manner, the manifold changes and effects which make up the world require an absolute or uncaused cause, and so reveal the necessity of the Supernatural. Unless we assume this Supernatural cause, nature becomes at last a causeless effect; and this, because nature is essentially finite, is a contradiction. Nor will it help us to regard the series of finite causes and effects that constitute the world as infinite. This pushes the difficulty off where we cannot see it, but in so doing it only aggravates it. An infinite series of finite causes

and effects is as truly without a sufficient reason as is a finite
series of such causes and effects. The main difference between
the two is that the former is an infinite contradiction, whereas
the latter is but a finite one. Nor does the fact that we cannot
go back in the former case even in thought to the point at
which the series ends and where we discern the necessity of
the Self-subsistent Uncaused Cause render it less a necessity.
As vigorously as though it could discern just where such a
cause was required does the mind insist on its necessity. Only
in such a cause can it find the power that it cannot conceive of
the universe as not demanding. Thus this principle, too, makes
known to us the necessity of the Supernatural. It does not set
it before us as in a picture, but it will not suffer us not to
think of it as the painter of the passing world-picture that we
cannot help seeing. So also the Absolute Subject that such
acts as the creating and the upholding of the universe postulate is the Supernatural. As every act evinces a subject in
action, so these acts cannot but evidence an Unconditioned or
Supernatural Subject. The reason for this is that these acts
are and must be themselves unconditioned, and so can be the
acts only of an unconditioned subject. Nor may it be disputed
that these acts are and must be themselves unconditioned.
Let it be remembered that by the universe we mean the organism into the constitution of which enter all finite, related, conditioned beings and things, and this will at once appear. It is
not more evident that such a universe requires, because it is
finite, relative, conditioned, to be upheld than that the upholding of it cannot depend in any way on it, and so must itself be
essentially unconditioned. This should be as clear as that the
unfailing energizing of Atlas in the fable would have had to
be absolutely unconditioned by the world that he was supposed
to support on his broad shoulders. Thus this principle, as those
already noticed and as others that could be adduced, is not only
a necessity of thought, but necessarily makes known in thought
the Supernatural. If it does not unveil all its lineaments, it
does reveal its necessity in the necessity of its acts.

In short, the Supernatural is at the end of all thinking. Take
a blade of grass and think long enough and deeply enough with

reference to it, and you come up against the Supernatural. Every line of consistent thinking as to reality brings you to it as directly, as inevitably, as under the Roman Empire all roads led to the " Eternal City." If any do not find this to be so, it is not because it is not so; it is only because they do not follow their thought to its conclusion. Thought is not more a necessity than the Supernatural is *the* necessity in thought. We cannot think truly and deeply and not believe practically in its reality. Hence, again, the already noticed universality of religion. It is not only the manifestation of what we may call the instinct of humanity; it is also the expression of the most profound necessity of rational thought. As Calderwood puts it, "All intelligence moves toward the Absolute or Self-existent;" [49] and, " The essential implication of intelligence is that all finite being is traced to a self-existent fountain of Being." [50]

Now " we find that whatever is necessary to thought in the sphere of the natural has its correspondent reality in being." Does thought affirm that every finite object requires a ground of support? Scientific investigation discovers it: even the earth, that seems to hang unsupported in mid air, swings securely in an orbit made by the action of well-known forces. Does thought declare that every effect must have a cause? The scientist ferrets it out: though with the naked eye he cannot see the microbe that causes the pestilence, he detects and studies it with the microscope. Does thought refuse to conceive of acts save as the acts of some subject? We always find the subject, if we look long and carefully enough: by the ripple on the water far away we may know that it is blowing, though we neither hear nor feel the wind; but let us pull toward the ripple, and soon the breeze itself strikes our drooping sails. If, then, these principles are thus found to be trustworthy in the sphere of the natural or finite, why should we not trust them in the sphere of the Supernatural or Infinite?

Nay, we must trust them. Grant that they are " regulative principles." Still, it is not of intelligence in itself, but of intelligence as that concerns itself with *reality* that they are

[49] *Handbook of Moral Philosophy*, p. 257.   [50] *Ibid.*, p. 259.

regulative. As Calderwood puts it, " The whole force of
these principles is seen to be concerned with objective reality."[51] Whether there be reality or not outside of the thinking process, the significance of these principles is that they
point to it and insist on it. They would not be what they are,
they would not be at all, if they did not do this. This demand
of theirs for reality objective to themselves is what gives to
them their character. It *is* their significance. Moreover, as we
have already seen, the reality which they demand is, in the last
analysis, self-existent, uncaused and unconditioned. This, if
we may so speak, is the significance of their significance. If,
therefore, we verify or prove these principles on their lower
side, as we have seen that we do, we may not distrust them on
the higher. As Calderwood writes, " We cannot regard them
as trustworthy in their application to the concrete yet untrustworthy in their very significance."[52] Thus, though we
were not able to verify them on their higher or supernatural
side, verification on their lower or natural side would imply
verity on their higher. We should be bound to believe in the
objective reality as well as in the mental necessity of the
Supernatural, even though we had no faculties with which to
apprehend it; just as the astronomer without a telescope is
sure that, if he had a telescope, he would find a splendid planet
where his calculations, which hitherto have been invariably
sustained, tell him that one must be. That is, a principle could
not justify itself in every case within the limits of observation,
if in its very significance it were untrue; and the regulative
principles that we have been considering would be untrue in
their very significance, if the Supernatural, on whose objective
existence they insist as the reality of realities, were not itself
of all realities the most real.

It is not the fact, moreover, that the principles in question
have no verification when applied to the Supernatural. On the
contrary, there is a consciousness of God. As Shedd says,
it is " a universal and abiding form of human consciousness." [53] In addition to the craving after, the instinct for,

---

[51] *Handbook of Moral Philosophy*, p. 264.   [52] *Ibid.*, p. 264.
[53] *Dogmatic Theology*, Vol. i, p. 210.

the Supernatural, which has already been noticed as the universal and necessary root of religion, all men may know, and, as a matter of fact, most men do know, the Supernatural. Though they can neither see nor hear nor touch nor taste nor smell it, they are often awed by it; in their more serious moments they feel its presence; and so they must be conscious of it. Thus the principles which we have been considering are verified in the case of the Supernatural as in that of the natural. The telescope of Galle revealed the planet which the calculations of Leverrier and of Adams necessarily called for as the cause of certain perturbations of the solar system; and, in like manner, we are conscious of the Supernatural that reason with equal urgency demands as the ground and cause of the universe and the agent involved in its creation and preservation and government. Nor may it be said that this consciousness of the Supernatural is a mere hallucination. It is too general and especially too constant to be thus explained. Illusions vanish when the light is turned on them. The so-called illusion of the Supernatural, however, continues, though from the very first every effort has been made and is being made to expose it. Nor may it be urged either that some have lost this God-consciousness and some seem never to have had it. This amounts to nothing in view of its prevalence and persistence. He who does not use his eyes in the light will lose them, and the fish that are now hatched in the streams in the Mammoth Cave have none to lose. The significant fact is not that there are a few men who appear to have no consciousness of the Supernatural; it is rather that not a single individual was ever conscious that there was not a Supernatural. Says La Bruyère, " Je sens qu'il y a un dieu et je ne sens pas qu'il n'y en ait point." [54]

Beyond all this, the ultimate facts, the best attested realities, when considered objectively, that is, in themselves, quite as much as when viewed subjectively, that is, as necessities of thought, reveal the Supernatural as the fact which they all presuppose, as the reality which alone gives to them reality. Thus they evidence the Supernatural as truly as a building evi-

[54] *Les Caractères*, c. 16.

dences its foundation. For example, finite reality implies infinite or self-subsistent reality. But for this as its ground, it could not continue reality. The more real the world may appear the more deeply is this dependence written on it. In like manner, duality testifies to the reality of the Supernatural. How could real mind and real matter interact and together form the cosmos, did they not have a bond and controller as real as they, but superior to them and so supernatural? Such also is the witness of personality. The reality of the finite ego involves the Infinite Ego. As the human spirit, because finite, must depend on something; so because he is a spirit and thus a higher reality than matter, he can depend only on another and Infinite or Supernatural Ego. Hence, we observe that, in proportion as men come to know themselves, does their consciousness of the Supernatural develop. Indeed, self-consciousness cannot be true and not develop God-consciousness. As Calvin writes, " No man can take a survey of himself but he must immediately turn to the contemplation of God in whom he ' lives and moves '." [55] So, too, morality. Its objective obligatory ideal, its law, reveals a law giver and moral governor; and in the fact that his law is universal, eternal, and immutable, we see that he himself must be the Absolute, the Supernatural. Thus do these first and fundamental facts reveal the Supernatural. One and all, they involve it as the reality of realities.

It is possible to object that all this is only subjective delusion. We may affirm with J. S. Mill, that even the necessary principles of thought have no necessary validity; that, for example, from the fact that two and two make four in this world it does not follow that they do so in any other; and that consequently, the necessity to thought of the reality of the Supernatural argues nothing as to its actual reality. We may hold with Maudsley, that the individual consciousness is untrustworthy; that, therefore, though Maudsley, with blessed inconsistency, denied this, the general consciousness of the race is not to be depended on; and, hence, that the practically universal consciousness of the Supernatural affords no real verification of our necessary belief in its reality. We may

[55] *Institutes,* i. 1.

after the manner of Kant, in his Critique of the Pure Reason, declare that we see things, not as they are, but as our minds project themselves into them; and that thus we discern the Supernatural as implied in all the ultimate verities, only because of what we are, not because of what they are. All this we can do. But is it rational so to do? This is *the* question. Can we think thus and not commit intellectual suicide? That is, can we think thus and thought not contradict and so destroy itself? If its necessary principles, if its deepest consciousness, if its ultimate verities, are all to be set aside, it itself must be utterly discredited. This happening, what is left? Not the external world: we know it only as the object of thought. Not the knowing self: we know it only as it reveals itself in thought. Not even the certainty that we do not know the world without or the self within: to know even this involves the trustworthiness of thought. Thus the denial of the objective reality of the Supernatural issues in and so means absolute nescience and practical nihilism. In a word, as H. B. Smith says, "All minds believe and must believe in the Supernatural, unless they proclaim all Truth and all Being to be a mockery and a delusion." [56] It may still be replied that even this reductio ad absurdum is no formal demonstration. It should, however, be answered, What use for a demonstration of the Supernatural can they have whose position with reference to the Supernatural gives the lie to those very intellectual processes in which demonstration consists. Moreover, that we have not framed, and cannot frame, a formal demonstration of the objective reality of the Supernatural is itself confirmation of such reality. If we could ground it in any thing deeper and so prove its existence strictly, we should only prove that it was not the Supernatural whose existence we had proved. From its very nature the Supernatural must be incapable of formal demonstration.

[56] *Apologetics*, p. 26.

IV.

The Manifestation of the Supernatural.

The question is not whether the Supernatural has manifested itself fully nor whether it could so manifest itself. As the only manifestation with which we are concerned is to us, and thus to the natural, such manifestation of the Supernatural as the above must, in the nature of the case, be impossible and even inconceivable. Because infinite and absolute, the Supernatural cannot but be, in the most real sense, unknown and unknowable.

It is true that the pantheists dispute this. They hold, not only that the Absolue is known, but that knowledge of the Absolute is absolute knowledge. Their postulates are, that there is one Infinite Substance or Absolute Idea of which all relative and finite phenomena are but modifications; that, consequently, the development of the finite and relative from the Infinite and Absolute, inasmuch as it is a process necessarily implied in and resulting from the very nature of the Infinite and Absolute, must be demonstrable; and that thus man, because himself one with the Infinite and Absolute, and identical in his own consciousness and life with its processes, can and does know it. That is, since man's thinking is the immediate activity of the Supernatural, his knowledge of it is as direct and as complete as it is of himself. In knowing the latter he really knows the former. We have seen, however, that this position is contradicted by consciousness. Its deepest and most characteristic testimony is to the individuality of the self. So far from identifying it with the Supernatural, it affirms the sharpest distinction between them. Thus we cannot take the pantheistic standpoint and not invalidate consciousness; but consciousness is the foundation of philosophy, even the basis of knowledge. Still further, pantheism exposes weakness fatal to itself in the claim which it makes and must make. This claim is that the transition from the Infinite and Absolute to the finite and relative, from the Supernatural to the natural, can be demonstrated and explained. This cannot be done. As H. B. Smith says, "The real problem—equally a problem with pantheist and theist—is not to show that the one includes the other, but rather to show how the transition *must or may be made* from the one to the other." [57] On either system here is the mystery. Both find at this point a knot that cannot be untied. The difference between them is that theism need not untie it, whereas pantheism must. On the one hand, theism accounts for the natural as the creation of the Supernatural. It is the result of an infinite and absolute self-conscious Will. The method of this will's operation, however, the theist is not obliged to set forth. He need only show, as he can show, that creation is possible to an absolute will; and he may grant that the mode of creation is a mystery necessarily beyond the scrutiny of human science. We ourselves so often make what is other than we are that we should not stumble at the creation of the natural by the Supernatural. The latter act is one whose possibility does not depend on its comprehension by us. Nay, it is one that could not be the kind of act that it must be were it comprehended by us. On the other hand, however, pantheism would explain, and because it admits but one substance, must explain, the natural as an emanation from or an outgoing of, the Supernatural. That is, it may not, as we have just seen that theism may, leave the mode of transition from the Infinite and Absolute to the finite and relative a mystery : but it is *obliged* to explain the transition as a passing of the Infinite and Absolute into the finite and relative; as one thing, not making, but itself becoming, a radically different thing. Now this is not a mystery; it is a contradiction, an impossibility. We need not, therefore, and, indeed, may not, inquire as to the truth of the pantheistic position, that a knowledge of the Absolute is absolute knowledge. In view of what we have just seen that this position involves, such an inquiry becomes irrational.

The question, however, is, whether the Supernatural has so manifested itself that, though partially, it can be and is known by us.

[57] *Apologetics*, p. 69.

This is denied, at least in large part, by the school of Ritschl. In general, their position is that religious knowledge consists merely of value-judgments, while other knowledge consists of existential judgments. That is, knowledge in religion is not the recognition of what is; it is the experience of what is spiritually helpful: whereas knowledge elsewhere is real knowledge because composed of affirmations ascertained to correspond to actuality. Hence, this school claims to be independent of philosophy and denies the legitimacy of natural theology. Religion is wholly an affair of the heart. Science is wholly a matter of the head. The two spheres are distinct and exclusive. As Flint says, " no recognition of any revelation of God is granted except that in Scripture, and only there in so far as there is the revelation of God in Christ. Theology is represented to be incapable of attaining to any theoretic knowledge of God, and to have to do only with what God is felt to be in the religious experience of the Christian. That is to say, it is described as having for its task to set forth regarding God, not theoretical but practical judgments,—not affirmations which really apply to God in himself but affirmations which tell us what he is *worth to us*—that is, value-judgments, which, although they in no way express what God really is, may enable us to overcome the evil in the world and to lead a Christian life." [58] Thus this position, though it may not call itself agnosticism, is such. It would banish knowledge from religion and would reduce it to an affair of feeling only.

It may be refuted on the following grounds:

1. Its pretension to independence of philosophy and its consequent denial of natural theology are inconsistent in the extreme. It is on nothing but an unsound philosophy that this pretension bases itself. " It rests wholly on agnosticism as to reason and on the Kantian reduction of religion to a mode of representing the moral ideal. It assumes that Kants' philosophy as modified in certain respects by Lotze is the basis of theology." This, however, is an enormous assumption; it is an assumption wholly in the sphere of philosophy; and, last but not least, the epistemology assumed is wrong.

[58] *Agnosticism*, pp. 593, 594.

2. The school that we are examining proceeds on a false psychology. It presupposes that what are called man's different natures can operate in independence of each other. Hence, the religious and the theoretic spheres can be kept apart, and so a doctrine can have high religious value even though it have no foundation in objective fact. The truth, however, is that man's natures do not operate independently. They are not even separate themselves. Man's spiritual being is one and indivisible. It does not have even different powers. Its so-called faculties are but so many functions of one power, and these functions invariably involve each other. Intellect and will, for example, cannot be divorced, and thus the religious and theoretic spheres cannot be exclusive. That they could be, man would have to be other than he is.

3. The place assigned by this school to judgments of value is destructive of their value. That they have an important place in religion is not to be denied. Religion is animated by a practical motive. It does prize truth according to its effect on the heart. Further, religious judgment includes an element of ethical decision. It is he who wills to do the will of God who knows the doctrine. Finally, only the religious man can appreciate spiritual truth; for it is " spiritually judged ". In these ways religious judgment does differ from pure intellectual or theoretic judgment, as, for example, in geometrical demonstration. The element of value does enter into the former. In a true sense the head depends on the heart. ' No man can call Jesus Lord but by the Holy Ghost.' All this, however, implies that the judgment of value rests on a theoretic judgment; and not vice versa, as Kaftan holds and as Ritschl would seem to mean. The spiritual helpfulness of a doctrine depends on its truth; its truth is not proven by its apparent helpfulness. The deity of Christ is a precious doctrine, because it is the interpretation of a fact; and it would lose all its preciousness, if his body were still lying dead in a Syrian grave.

The position that we would establish as to the manifestation of the Supernatural is denied again by the avowed agnostics. They admit, and many of them strongly insist on, the objective reality of the Supernatural; but they hold yet more tenaciously that it is unknown and even that it must be unknowable. For example, Mansel, though he believes firmly in the reality of the Infinite and Absolute, denies that it can be present to us in consciousness; Max Müller, though he finds the principle of religion in the consciousness of the Infinite, holds that we are conscious of it only as the " Beyond ", as the mere negative of the finite, and so, of course, that we cannot know it; and Spencer, though he claims that we are conscious of the Infinite and Absolute as the positive basis of all our consciousness of the finite and relative, nevertheless, insists that we are conscious of this positive basis as without limits and thus as unknown and unknowable.

This theory whose chief forms in its distinctly religious reference have just been indicated is, generally speaking, exposed to the following objections:

1. It proceeds on a false theory of the nature of knowledge. This is, that to know anything we must know it in its essence and be able to define it itself. This, however, cannot be a true theory of knowledge. If it were, there could be no knowledge. Not even a blade of grass do we know absolutely; that is, in its essence and apart from its relations. Moreover, we often know certainly what we cannot define at all. You can be sure of your friend's handwriting, though you cannot give the marks by which it is distinguished from that of others. In short, knowledge may be real, though it is neither absolute nor definite. You can know something, though you do not know anything fully or exactly.

2. The denial that the Supernatural can so manifest itself as to be known by us proceeds on a false theory of the condition of knowledge. This condition is the identity of the subject knowing with the object known. " Quantum sumus scimus " and " Simile simili cognoscitur ". Hence, to know the Supernatural, we must be ourselves supernatural. While, however, in order to knowledge, there must be a kinship between subject and object, this is far from being, and, indeed, differs radically from, the identity claimed. We know the external world, though we are not the external world. Were the theory true, self-knowledge would be the only knowledge.

3. The denial that we are considering proceeds on a false view of the Infinite and Absolute. It is regarded as the all and the unrelated. Hence, as to know is to distinguish what is known from other things, the Infinite cannot be known; for if it could be so distinguished from other things as to be known, or even from the knowing self, it would no longer be the Infinite that was known: and as we can know only what has come into relation to us so as to be known, it would no more be the Absolute. That is, the Infinite and the Absolute, as regards the capacity for being known, is like a vase which is bound to go to pieces as you take hold of it.

As we saw, however, when we were considering just what was the question with regard to the reality of the Supernatural, there need not be, there is not, and there could not be, any such Infinite and Absolute as agnosticism presupposes. That is, the conception of the Supernatural on which it is founded is contradictory. Nor is this all. As should now be evident and as Flint has taught us in his classic work on Agnosticism, agnosticism as to the Supernatural must, unless inconsistent, become agnosticism as to everything ; and agnosticism as to everything, whether in the form of doubt or of disbelief, involves a fatal contradiction. In a word, together or singly, these objections are a reductio ad absurdum of the agnostic position; and thus, though they do not prove the reality of the manifestation of the Supernatural and of our knowledge of it, they do open the way for the following proof :

1. There is no à priori impossibility that the Supernatural should manifest itself and should be known as manifested. Admitting that only its bare existence has been established, it does not follow that no more can be established. Nay, that a thing is often raises a presumption or expectation that what it is will appear. This presumption or expectation is attested by the spirit of discovery which it produces. Nor may it be urged that all this applies only to the sphere of the natural. That is to beg the question. It is to assert the thing to be established.

2. The reality of the Supernatural cannot be known and its nature not be known also to some degree at the same time.

There is not anything the existence of which can be apprehended without an idea of at least some of its qualities. It is by means of the acts or the noises or the peculiarities in appearance of a strange beast that men in the first instance become aware of its existence, and there is no other way in which they can be assured of it. Knowledge that it is involves by a necessary law of thought some knowledge of what it is; and to this extent the establishment of its reality establishes also that it has, in so far forth, manifested itself and this manifestation been recognized. It cannot be otherwise in the case of the Supernatural. Because the law just referred to is a necessary law of thought as such, if we know the reality of the Supernatural, we know that to some degree it has manifested itself, and been recognized. We cannot know that it exists and not know something of what it is. Thus the mere question whether the Supernatural can manifest itself implies that it has done so sufficiently to be apprehended. But this raises the presumption at once, and it is from this presumption that our inquiry should proceed, the presumption that this manifestation of the Supernatural and the consequent recognition of it by us will keep on. Other things being equal, the antecedent likelihood is that what has been going on will continue.

3. In knowing the existence of the Supernatural we know it as that whose nature it is to manifest itself. For example, as we have seen, we know the Supernatural as Infinite Being and so as the ground of all finite being. Now it is not claimed that the former simply as being tends to manifest itself in the latter. In order to this, there must be, in addition to Infinite *Being,* a principle of movement, an act. Still, Infinite Being looks toward finite being, and thus toward manifestation in it, so far as this, that it can be the ground and condition of it. Again, as we have also seen, we know the Supernatural as the First Cause. It is not only Infinite Being. It is also a principle of movement; it has the power to act, to create. Now we do not hold that the First Cause must produce an effect and so manifest itself in it. The First Cause need not be, as we might show that it could not be, one that acts neces-

sarily. Yet, when there is nothing to the contrary, the presumption in the case of power is that it will exert and so manifest itself. Indeed, ordinarily, the power of self-manifestation implies a tendency toward it. Once more, as we have seen, too, we know the Supernatural as the Infinite Agent of the infinite acts that the universe, because finite, presupposes and thus itself evidences ; namely, creation, preservation and government. It must be, then, that in these acts, and so in their results, the Supernatural itself is really manifested. It is as impossible that an agent should not express himself in his acts as that these should not involve an agent. They are the agent himself in exercise. In simply knowing the existence of the Supernatural, then, we know it as that whose very nature it is to manifest itself. In the Supernatural as Infinite Being we have the necessary ground of the finite and to this extent the possibility of its manifestation in it. In the Supernatural as the First Cause we have the power of self-manifestation and in so far forth a tendency toward it. In the Supernatural as the Infinite Agent of the infinite acts that the finite universe implies, we have the actual manifestation of the Supernatural itself.

4. The same result may be reached, and just as conclusively, from the standpoint of the natural and phenomenal. This is the effect of the Supernatural. As we have already shown, we cannot really think otherwise, and it cannot be otherwise. See, however, what this law of cause and effect involves. The existence of the universe as an effect not only demands the existence of the Supernatural as its cause; but inasmuch as a cause must express itself more or less in its effect, it implies that the universe, though a partial, cannot but be a real manifestation of the Supernatural. In the natural, therefore, the Supernatural must appear and, in so far forth, must be known by us. We could no more avoid this than we could avoid seeing and knowing the artist in his work. This is true on any rational theory of the universe. Both the possibility and the fact of such a manifestation of the Supernatural must be conceded by all who hold to evolution as much as by those who believe in creation. Evolution—of what? Evolution in

the abstract is only a name for a possibility, a term descriptive of a process. There must be a Supernatural Something, an Absolute Reality; if the possibility named is to become actuality, if the process conceived is to operate. Darwin demands living germ cells if he is to work his development hypothesis. Huxley dispenses with life, but cannot get along without protoplasm. Lucretius does not require this, but even he must have atoms. Whence, however, the atom? Science says that it is evidently "a manufactured article." It, therefore, because an effect must be a manifestation of its cause. Whence protoplasm with its assumed power of generating life? Yet more, as being a more pregnant effect, must this be a more pregnant manifestation of its cause. Whence life? This is the highest and richest of all. Must not, then, its successive evolutions be a continuous as well as the fullest manifestation thus far considered of the First Cause and so of the Supernatural? As H. B. Smith says, " This cuts the roots of the theory that the Supernatural is simply something in itself inscrutable, remote, isolated—an unintelligible abstraction—for we have obtained not only *the Supernatural itself,* as a datum of reason and philosophy, but also *the Supernatural manifested,* as necessary to any evolution, development, progress, or construction of a universal system." [59] That is, the manifestation of the Supernatural in nature and our consequent knowledge of it is as much a necessity of thought and so as truly a reality as we have seen to be its objective existence. ' The heavens must declare its glory '. ' The firmament must show its handiwork '. ' Its everlasting power and divinity must be understood from the things that are made '. ' The spirit of man must be the candle of the Lord '. ' Christians must be epistles of Christ known and read of all men '. ' The church must make known the manifold wisdom of God.' ' The angels, since they are his ministers, must reveal his will.' In a word, all nature, both spiritual and physical, *must* manifest the Supernatural; and in all the universe we should discern the manifestation. In this nature finds the sufficient reason for its being, the ultimate condition of its existence. Throughout, as

[59] *Apologetics,* p. 41.

regards both its origination and its continuance, the workmanship of the Supernatural, it could not be otherwise. What,
then, does nature show the Supernatural to be?

V.

THE PERSONALITY OF THE SUPERNATURAL.

In affirming this we deny, on the one hand, the rude and
antisupernaturalistic materialism of Lucretius, which would
account for all things by means of atoms and motion; modern
materialism, which for atoms and motion would substitute
physical force; idealistic materialism or monism, as that of
Tyndall, Huxley and Mill, which in place of matter and force
would put an inscrutable mode of being whence they both
come; East Indian pantheism, which regards the Supernatural
as spirit abstract and undefined; materialistic pantheism, as that
of Spinoza, whose Supernatural is the absolute substance;
idealistic pantheism, as that of Hegel, which would conceive the
Supernatural as thought, with logical law, and as developing
by logical law the universe; the theory of the pessimistic philosophy of Schopenhauer, that the basis and cause of the universe is unconscious will: and, on the other hand, the position
of the " cosmic philosophy " of Spencer and Fiske, that the
Supernatural is " superpersonal "; that is, it is infinitely higher
than personal, and so is unknown and must be unknowable.
In opposition to all these views, on the criticism of which our
limits forbid us to enter, we hold that the Supernatural is an
identical, self-conscious, self-determining being; such as we
are, a person, only infinite and absolute and unconditioned.
This we would vindicate as follows:

1. The Supernatural can be personal. This is denied by
many, notably by Spinoza and by Fichte in his earlier teaching,
on the ground that personality is necessarily relative. The essence of it, it is said, is that it implies another outside of itself.
Hence, the Supernatural, because the Absolute, cannot be
personal. The condition of absoluteness is freedom from conditions of every kind. This position, however, confounds
personality with individuality. The latter is a mere relation.

It consists in separation from other things. It could not be if there were not other things. That is, its existence depends on its relation to other things. But personality is not a mere relation. As says H. B. Smith, "It is a point of fixed being."[60] Its essence is, not that it is marked off from other persons or things; for were this so, beasts would be persons. Its essence is self-consciousness and self-determination; for it is this internal distinguishing of the self as object from the self as subject, not any relation to other selves, or things, that constitutes personality. The objection, therefore, falls. Necessary relativity is inconsistent with the Absolute, but personality as such is entirely self-dependent and so altogether independent. As it appears in us it is relative. This relativity, however, is the result of our finiteness. We are persons, not because of it, but in spite of it. Indeed, the perfection of personality is possible only in the case of the Infinite and Absolute.

Nor may it be replied, that, though self-consciousness and self-determination do not involve any external relativity, they are determinations; that, according to the Spinozan maxim, "every determination is a negation;" and that on this ground, consequently, if on no other, the Supernatural or the Infinite and Absolute cannot be personal. This is to confound the laws of being with those of thought. That all determination or definition limits is true of mathematical quantities and of logical general notions, but it is not true of concrete beings. To hold that even Spinoza meant this is to misconceive him. As to beings, the opposite is true. As Harris says, "The more determined or specific a being is by the increase or multiplication of its powers, the greater and not the less or more limited, is the being." [61] Indeed, being without any determinations and specifications becomes an abstraction. We can conceive of it as real, and so as being rather than thought, only as we conceive of it as constituted in this way or in that. Thus do the laws of thought itself themselves witness to the difference between themselves and the laws of being. Hence, as we have all along insisted that we must do, we can be true to the

[60] *Introduction to Christian Theology*, p. 97.
[61] *The Philosophical Basis of Theism*, p. 29.

necessity in the former only as we recognize this difference. Indeed, as Lindsay puts it, " It is precisely in denying the Supernatural the power of being personal that his infinitude is parted with. This self-limitation of the Infinite—the great renunciation—is yet really its self-assertion and its self-revelation."[62] Evidently, therefore, the Supernatural can be personal: at least without some such determination as that of personality the Supernatural could not *be*.

2. As there must be a real Supernatural, so he must be at least personal. Three considerations will evince this clearly:

As much as this is involved in the nature of a first-cause. Whatever the Supernatural may not be, it is, as we have observed, of his essence that He should be the First-Cause. It is not more certain that there must be such a cause than it is certain that this cause cannot but be supernatural. " Now we have a real, though limited, experience of such a cause within ourselves, and there alone." We are conscious of being able to originate action, to initiate events, even in a measure to modify the processes of nature, in virtue of our free will or power of self-determination. That is, the only finite first-cause, if we may so speak, known to us is found to be such because of its personality. Its personality is what makes it, in spite of its limitations, a kind of first-cause. Would it, then, be otherwise were all restrictions to be removed? Nay, could it be so? It is of the essence of a first-cause that it should be personal. It could not originate action were it not self-determining. Unless, then, it continue such, it must cease to be a first-cause. And this will be true whether it be finite and natural or infinite and supernatural. The only difference between the two cases will be, not that in the latter it will not be personal, but that it will be the perfection of personality. This is so because even the transition from finite to infinite, while it must involve the perfection of what is under consideration, cannot change its essence and not destroy it itself. Hence, unless the Supernatural is to cease to be the First Cause, he must be at least a person as we are.

This follows as surely from the law of " causal resem-

[62] *Recent Advances in the Theistic Philosophy of Religion*, p. 315.

blance ". The gist of this law is that nothing can be in the effect which is not potentially in the cause; or that the cause must always be, in its nature and possibilities, superior to its effect. Thus, while we can believe that a man has made a machine, we could not believe that any mere machine could make a man. In the former case the cause would transcend the effect. In the latter the cause would fall below the effect, and for this reason would appear to be and would be impossible as its cause. Now the universe contains the personal. The personal or man is that in it which is highest. It is that toward the development of which all tends. In short, the personal is both the crown and the goal of the world considered by itself. As the evolutionists say, ' the personal is the meaning of the whole process of evolution.' How, then, can the First-Cause of the world, the originator, sustainer and director even of evolution itself, be himself less than personal? As the inspired psalmist says, " He that planted the ear, shall he not hear? " " He that formed the eye, shall he not see? " (Psalm xciv. 9) ; so consistent thought must decide that the source of that self-consciousness and self-determination in which creation culminates cannot himself be less than personal. If he were, the law of causal resemblance, elsewhere universally true, would break down precisely where, unless the world were a chaos, it should hold most strictly.

The law of universal development just referred to necessitates the same conclusion. In the words of Lindsay, " Do we not see the creation struggling toward personality, and mounting step by step through the preliminary stages of the vegetable and animal world, until in man it actually attains to individual personality, and becomes a self-conscious mind? Whence this universal tendency of all that lives toward personality, if it be not the law of the world; and whence this law, if the Principle of the world is an impersonal one? And if personality constitutes the preëminence of man over the inferior creation, can this preëminence be wanting in the highest Being of all? Can God, the most perfect Being imaginable, be devoid of personality the most perfect form of being? " [63] May it

[63] *Recent Advances in the Theistic Philosophy of Religion,* p. 329.

not be, however, it is replied, that the Supernatural is superpersonal? Hence, it should be observed, that,

3. The Supernatural, though he must be at least personal, cannot be higher than personal. This does not mean that man is the measure of the Supernatural. Because infinite and absolute, as we have already seen, the Supernatural must always be unknown and unknowable to even the highest form of the natural. Spinoza himself, though holding that the infinite Substance has infinite modes, teaches that we know but two of them, thought and extension. Even with respect to the essentials of personality the Supernatural Person must be infinitely higher than ourselves and so quite different from us. What self-consciousness is that has absolutely no limitations, what self-determination is that has absolutely no restrictions, we cannot imagine and we never shall be able to imagine. To the natural, even in the respects in which they are most akin, the Supernatural is the eternal as well as the supreme mystery. The very love of Christ, for example, " passes knowledge ". That the Supernatural cannot be higher than personal, however, does mean, on the one hand, that he cannot be higher in the sense of less determinate. The reason is that in the case of being, as we have already observed, highness is directly proportional to determinateness. Absurdity is inherent in the position of those thinkers who, as Spencer and Fiske, in postulating that the Supernatural, though personally non-existent, may yet be higher than personality, as Lindsay says, " place being plus intelligence below that which has it not, and who, in spite of the self-evidencing power of the theistic idea, assign that which is self-conscious and self-determining to a lower platform than that which blindly moves on to its end." [64] In a word, the Supernatural cannot be supernatural in the sense of impersonal, because the supernatural in this sense is really the sub-personal.

Nor, on the other hand, can the Supernatural be more determinate than personal, and so, in this way, if not in that just noticed, be superpersonal. Personality is of all possible modes of existence the highest. It is not simply the highest known

[64] *Recent Advances in the Theistic Philosophy of Religion*, p. 271.

to us, it is not merely the highest of which we can conceive; it reveals itself as finished, perfect, ultimate. It seems to say, not only has development never been traced beyond me, but development ends, and must end, with me. There may be higher and lower kinds of personality, but no other mode of being can be so high as personality. If the ground of this assertion be demanded, the one but the sufficient answer is that it is an ultimate truth. Just as in the sphere of thought reason reveals itself as alone because ultimate, so that we are sure that in thought there is not and could not be anything higher than reason; so in the sphere of being personality reveals itself as alone because ultimate, so that we are sure that in being there is not and could not be anything higher than personality. In self-consciousness and self-determination, that is, in personality, we meet determination which is as evidently ultimate as it is self-evident. Even the evolutionists would seem at least to have felt this. If not, why does Fiske say that the moral sense in which the reality of personality comes out most clearly—the moral sense is " the last and noblest product of evolution which we can ever know." [65] Thus the existence of the Supernatural and his manifestation in and through the universe of which he is the creator and preserver and governor are not more truly necessities of thought and so realities than is his personality. Not to admit this is to give the lie to our own personality, and, consequently, to all else; for it is in our intense consciousness of our own personality that the conception and conviction of reality arise. In a word, if there be reality, we must be real; if we are real, the Supernatural whom we presuppose must be so; if the Supernatural exists, as he cannot be less than self-conscious and self-determining, so he cannot be more. Such, that is, personal being is the apex and the foundation of all being. This is the last and highest testimony of our own personality, the most evidently real of all realities.

[65] *Outlines of Cosmic Philosophy,* Vol ii. p. 324.

VI.

The Personal or Immediate Manifestation of the Supernatural.

By this we mean, such a manifestation as would be such a direct communication from the Supernatural as it is claimed that the Decalogue is; such supernatural works as the miracles, if they were wrought, must have been; such a supernatural act as regeneration, if it be a real act, evidently is; such a supernatural person as Christ could not but have been, if he was, as he said, both " the Son of God " and " the Son of man." The characteristic of these manifestations of the Supernatural is not that they are more truly personal than is his manifestation of himself in and through the universe. No matter how many instruments a person may use, his action is always personal. No matter how numerous may be the media in and through which he reveals himself, his revelation is always personal. In the cases under consideration, however, no instruments are employed, no media intervene. God himself spoke and wrote the words of the Decalogue; God with his own arm, as it were, wrought the miracles; God by his own power alone quickens into newness of life the soul " dead through trespasses and sins;" Christ is " the image of the invisible God ", he reveals him by himself becoming " God manifest in the flesh." Such supernatural acts as these, then, are not simply truly personal; they are *only* personal: indeed, they appear conspicuously supernatural just because they are only personal; though they occur in nature, and though they need not and should not be conceived as violating or even as suspending any law of nature, they are so evidently not at all of nature, they are so manifestly due wholly to wisdom and power independent of it and superior to it, that they must proceed from the Supernatural Person alone. If they took place, they cannot but be interventions of his in the ordinary course of nature. Could they, then, take place? This is the question of questions to the Christian. If they could not, Christianity is a lie. Its most positive and characteristic claim is that it is based on the direct personal intervention of the Supernatural in the history of the race, in the development of the universe. As we saw when considering the importance of a true doctrine of the Supernatural, the New Testament cannot be honestly interpreted and yield any other teaching than this.

But this is not all. The question just raised is even more fundamental. Not only Christianity, but all higher religion is at stake. The reason for this is that the immediate knowledge of God as the supernatural Person is involved in the very conception of religion as based on the self-revelation of a personal God. The operatives in a factory may sustain a real and a conscious relation to the manager of it, though he never comes among them or speaks to them or interposes in the direction of affairs. He may have revealed himself so clearly in the plan of the factory, in sustaining it in operation, and in the orders of the foreman whom he has placed over it, that all in it can and, if rightly disposed, will, discern his wisdom and acknowledge his power and respect his authority. It will not, however, be nearly so natural and easy for them to do this as it would be if the manager came daily among his people and listened to them and himself personally took part in the control of the work; and if his people are not rightly disposed toward him, it is certain that they will not recognize him as they should, if there is no personal intervention on his part. They will lose sight of him himself in the machinery which he has designed and is operating.

Just so, there might be true religion, did we know of God only what is clearly seen from " the things that are made." That " we live and move and have our being in him " ought to dispose us to " acknowledge him in all our ways ", and the ' earth is so full of the goodness of the Lord ' that it would seem that we could not help loving him. All this, however, though true religion, would be only an undeveloped form of it. It is a form, too, which, it is certain, would not be attained by a sinful race. As already implied, not liking to retain God in their knowledge,' they would look only at his works, and so these works would in time even hide him himself from them. In order, therefore, to the higher exercises of religion and to

any true exercise of it in the case of sinners, we need to feel,
that God himself is in the midst of us; that he not only acts
through the laws of nature, but independently of them; and
that he can and, on occasion, does, put out his own hand and
solely by his own personal power effect what the forces of
nature though under his direction could not do and what may
even seem to set them aside.   In a word, as things are, in
order to the development of religion, we must not only recognize the Supernatural as the personal God, but we must recognize him also as only personal or as simply personal; that is,
as one who, in addition to presiding over nature and working
through it, can and does also manifest himself by interposing
personally in it and by operating independently of it, though
on it and in it.   Only thus can we appreciate sufficiently the
reality because the personality of God's revelation to us.

Even the impression of the Supernatural made in the creation, if it is to abide, needs to be deepened by supernatural
interventions in history.   Unbelief should not, but does, conclude that, if the Supernatural manifested himself immediately
and so simply personally only at the beginning, he does not
manifest himself as a person at all, and so did not even then.
This is substantially the position of the whole modern rationalistic school.   Not less truly do belief in a personal God and
in supernatural interventions stand or fall together than belief
in a true creation and in supernatural interventions stand or
fall together.   As there can not be true religion save as we
believe that God himself has spoken to us, so we shall not
long or truly believe thus save as we hold to an immediate
knowledge of God as only or simply personal.

The ultimate reason for this is that the self-revelation of a
personal God cannot be authenticated sufficiently as such, unless it be accompanied by supernatural interventions.   An effect,
reason dictates, can be assigned to a particular cause only as
it reproduces what is distinctive of that cause.   Hence, the
necessary inference is that if the Supernatural Person reveals
himself, the revelation will be, at any rate, at times, both above
nature and in contrast with, if not in opposition to, nature.
Accordingly, were such a revelation to be throughout natural,
though, as we have seen, necessarily presupposing and thus

indirectly revealing the Supernatural, reason would hesitate to recognize it as really supernatural. Though it would *be* such, it could not be certainly discriminated as such. Even, the cry of a man would seldom be mistaken for that of a beast: it always has a human quality. Nevertheless, it is only as it utters itself in speech that we can be altogether sure that it is a man whom we hear. Just so, the supernatural Person can, and ordinarily does, confine his manifestations within natural instrumentalities; but it is only as he breaks away from these and reveals himself both in contrast with nature and above it, that is, as only the supernatural Person could— that his revelation as a whole can be authenticated absolutely as being what it really is. Thus belief in the personal intervention in nature, and so above and in contrast with it, of the supernatural Person is indispensable to the highest conviction of the reality of his self-revelation. Without such interventions, the latter could not be recognized infallibly.

The proof of these conclusions is the history of religion. Whenever men have persuaded themselves that they are divine messengers they have adopted likewise the belief that they are able to work miracles. Among such in modern times are Swedenborg and Irving the Scotch preacher. Impostors also, perceiving that miracles are necessary in order that the human mind may receive a religion as divine, have invariably claimed miraculous powers. Such instances recur constantly from the days of Elymas the Sorcerer down to the Mormon Joseph Smith. Though, too, the founders of false religions have not themselves made these pretensions, their followers have made them for them. Witness the miracles that came to be attributed to Gotama and to Mohammed by their disciples. Thus it would appear that men are so constituted that if they are truly to see God in nature, they must recognize him as a person who can and, on occasion, does manifest himself immediately and in contrast with nature, and that even the revelation of himself in nature can be sufficiently authenticated only by such immediately personal and exclusively supernatural interventions. No question, therefore, can be more important that this, if so important as this. Are such interventions, that is, are miracles possible; and if so, can they be recognized? The very existence of all religion worthy of the name would seem to be suspended on the answer to this inquiry.

The denials of the possibility of supernatural intervention in the course of nature may be reduced to one. They all take their stand, whether positivistic or transcendental, on the position that the course of nature is and must be uniform. If they do not always hold that what has been is what will be, they do hold this to be true at least to this extent, that the order and method of the new will be the same with that of the old in that everything will still be accomplished through the forces of nature; there will not be, as there could not be, the personal intervention of the Supernatural. This hypothesis, however, prevalent though it is, is exposed to the following objections:

1. It may not be decided by à priori considerations. We can argue for or against the uniformity of nature only from what nature and the Supernatural have been found to be. Antecedently, there is as much reason to infer that nature must not be uniform as that it must be uniform; and that is no reason. In a word, the question is one of fact; it does not involve a necessary principle. There is no must in the case.

2. It begs the question. It is at any rate an open question whether the course of nature has been uniform. There is the best of testimony that it has not been. It is hard to see how the testimony for the resurrection of Christ, for example, can be set aside and all testimony not be invalidated.

3. It begs a question to beg which is for these theorists suicidal. As has just been implied, in doing so they knock the ground from under their own feet. Whether the course of nature has been violated or has not been violated, can be known only from testimony; there is and can be but negative testimony, that is, the absence of testimony, that it has not been; there is the most positive and the best testimony that it has been. To decide, therefore, that it has not been is to decide against the testimony, and this is to invalidate the one possible ground of judgment. It is like appealing to reason to disprove reason.

5. Nor may it be replied that the very point at issue is

whether any testimony can extend to the Supernatural. If this be so, it follows that we do not know that there have been supernatural interventions in the course of nature, but it follows just as surely that we do not know that there have not been any. The possibility of the personal manifestation of the Supernatural is left just where it was before.

5. Nor does the objector gain anything, if we concede that the uniformity of nature never has been interrupted. Were this so, we might not infer that it never could be. Induction from individual facts, however numerous or well attested, cannot give necessary truth. That things have been so and so does not prove that they will so continue. It is always possible that there are other facts which, if considered, would show the possibility, if not the certainty, of change.

6. This will appear more clearly when we remember just what the uniformity of nature is. It is not a principle; it is only the name of a mode of action. It does not state *why* things are as they are; it states only *how* they are, or rather how it is assumed that they have been. It amounts to no more than this, that the same causes acting under the same conditions produce the same results. This is the only principle, the only ultimate truth, the only immutable law, in the case. What is there in this to hinder at any time the personal intervention of the Supernatural? There is nothing in this principle to forbid the introduction of a new cause in the course of nature. All that it secures is that nature shall be uniform if no new cause be introduced. So far as the so-called principle of the uniformity of nature is concerned, the Supernatural may come in at any point, and when he does his strictly personal manifestation must ensue.

7. The modern doctrine of the conservation and the correlation of energy, so far from opposing, tends to confirm this position. Indeed, this doctrine implies the constant manifestation in nature of the Supernatural himself. The sum of force in the universe can continue the same only because the Infinite and Absolute Force is " ever reënforcing finite waste, change and decay." As Herschel has pointed out, " vital force " does pass away. When, for example, a beast dies, his chemical elements appear in other forms, but what becomes of

his life, his soul? Thus vital force, at least, would run out, if the Supernatural did not intervene to supply it. Even the modern " physicist proper declares that the laws of matter alone will not explain life." [66] In a word, the very uniformity of nature depends on the coming of the Supernatural into nature. It has been planned with reference to it. So far, then, from the objection based on the uniformity of nature, disproving the personal intervention of the Supernatural in nature, it would seem to suggest and demand the proof of its possibility and even probability.

The following mere outline of this proof is the utmost that our limits will permit.

1. The abstract possibility of supernatural interventions in the course of nature cannot be rationally questioned. Sir Oliver Lodge is reported to have said lately: " The possibility of what we call miracles has been hastily and wrongly denied. They are not necessarily more impossible or lawless than the interference of a human being would seem to a colony of ants. They should be judged by historical evidence and literary criticism." Indeed, the most consistent skeptics and agnostics have not denied them. J. S. Mill was ready to admit the Supernatural, if it could be found. Matthew Arnold, though he held that with the progress of science all miracles would be explained away, did not regard them inconceivable. Even Hume, though he was the author of the famous objection that no amount of testimony could prove a miracle, again and again allows its abstract possibility.[67] Beyond this, it could easily be shown that men generally and, as it would seem, naturally believe that there are such interventions. In a word, if the bare existence of the Supernatural be admitted, his intervention in nature must be possible à priori. Otherwise, he would not be the Supernatural.

2. This possibility becomes much clearer in view of the fact that the Supernatural, as we have already shown, is a person and is constantly acting in and through nature. This granted, no objection can be raised to strictly personal action on his

[66] Ward's *Naturalism and Agnosticism*, vol. ii, p. vi.
[67] *Essays,* ii, pp. 131, 132, Ed. ed., 1788.

part. As Mozley says, " The primary difficulty of philosophy
relating to Deity is action at all. . . . If action is conceded at all there is no difficulty about miraculous action." [68]
A being who can use tools can certainly work with his own
hands.

3. It is probable that the Supernatural will choose to do so.
This follows from the fact that he is a person. It is characteristic of a person, not only to manifest himself in action,
but also in strictly personal action. We see this in our own
case. It does not satisfy us to hold intercourse with others
by proxy alone. We wish to speak to them ourselves face to
face. It does not develop us to do nothing but tend a machine.
Unless there is room for handicraft, production will be at the
cost of manhood. Hence, it is only to be expected, that the
Supernatural would manifest himself in a strictly personal
way; that he would speak to us; that he would act directly on
us; that he would do something with his own hand alone in
the course of nature; that he would even himself come and
dwell among us, at least for a time, as a man with men. Were
the Supernatural Person not to do something of this kind, we
could scarcely conceive of him as the Supernatural *Person*.
So far as we know, a person will certainly choose to act thus.

4. This conclusion is much strengthened by the consideration that nature would seem to have been constituted with a
view to such action by the Supernatural Person. As Godet
says, " Nature is from, by, and for spirit ";[69] and, though, as
we have seen, the Supernatural and the spiritual are not identical, yet the Supernatural, because *the* Person, must also be *the*
Spirit. That is, as is involved in Godet's statement and as
this paper has tried to show, the Supernatural must be behind
nature; the Supernatural must uphold nature; the Supernatural must be the end of nature: that all this should be so
is the necessity of thought. This, however, implies that nature has been so arranged as to presuppose the personal intervention of the Supernatural. Otherwise, it would fetter him;
and depending on him and existing for him, as it does, that
it should fetter him is inconceivable.

[68] *On Miracles,* p. 84.
[69] *The Defense of the Christian Faith,* p. 127.

5. But we are not left to inferences like the above, trustworthy though these could be shown to be. We know that the Supernatural has acted in a purely personal manner. All historic time, whether of the heavens or of the earth, of the earth or of man, must have begun with such an act. Get rid of all miracles, if you please; admit only the uniform sequence of natural phenomena, if you will: and the great miracle of creation remains on any natural theory of the universe, evolutionary or not; and creation is an absolutely personal act. It must have taken place; the uniformity of nature, if nothing else, is the demonstration of that: and it could have taken place only by the immediate and so personal action of the Supernatural; for before the creation there was nothing in which and through which he could act. Whether, therefore, the Supernatural has so acted again or does so act to-day is for us candidly to inquire. His nature as a person renders it probable that he will; and the fact that he must have done so once, that is, at the creation, increases this probability.

6. The progressive development of religion is inexplicable unless the Supernatural does continue so to manifest himself. Religion, at least in all its higher forms, presupposes, not only the possibility or even the probability, but the fact of such personal manifestations of the Supernatural. It believes in communion with God himself. Were the reality of that to be disproved, its life would be destroyed. If God did not make himself known to those who are in sympathy with him save as the " heavens declare his glory and the firmament showeth his handiwork," if he could not himself dwell in us as " a principle of a new and a divine life "; the power of such religion as tends to persist as man develops would be gone. Can it be, then, that such personal manifestation of the Supernatural is not real? Can it be that religion is only the most solemn of all delusions? If so, there is no mystery so great as that of its persistence. Nothing has been able to overthrow it, yet it itself rests on nothing.

7. This conclusion is much strengthened by the fact that the course of human development, and specially of human religious development, has been interrupted and perverted by sin. Hence, though the normal religious needs of men did

not demand, as we have just seen that they do demand, the personal intervention of God in human life and history, his abnormal needs brought about by the entrance of sin would so require. Thus, because sin has marred the workmanship of God in physical nature and has defaced his image in the human soul and has deflected his development of the race, the revelation of the Supernatural in and through the natural is far from being as extensive as or what otherwise it would have been. Again, because of the noetic efforts of sin we can not discern fully or interpret truly even the partial and perverted revelation of the Supernatural which the natural still affords. Once more, and as what is most important, sin makes necessary the revelation of a new kind of knowledge, of that with regard to God which nature could by no possibility reveal. Nature can reveal only the essential attributes of God, only what he must be and, consequently, must require because he is God; but what guilty sinners need to know is his grace and how it can be obtained, that is, the free purpose of his heart, and this can be known only as he himself shall directly declare it. Therefore, even were we to allow that the personal intervention of the Supernatural in the natural would be unlikely, the world continuing to develop along its original and God-laid lines; the presumption would all be the other way, the world having been deflected from its first and true line of development. In a word, to quote B. B. Warfield, " Extraordinary exigencies (we speak as a man) are the sufficient explanation of extraordinary expedients."

8. Must not, then, directly and exclusively supernatural works, such as we designate miracles, be expected, both to call attention to the messengers bringing the good tidings of the grace of God and to authenticate them as his ambassadors and so to attest the truth of their proclamation? Moreover, as such supernatural interventions, because their purpose is as just stated, might not be expected when no new revelation was being made; so at the epochs characterized and constituted by such revelations, as, the age of Moses when God revealed himself as Jehovah the redeeming God, and, above all, in " the days of the Son of man " when the eternal " Word was made flesh and dwelt among us " and " fulfilled all righteousness "

in our behalf and " died for our sins " and " was raised again
for our justification " and ascended to the right hand of God to
be " head over all things to the church "—at such times and
under such circumstances would it not be the most difficult of
miracles in the sense of wonders, if we did not discern miracles? Thus, so far from their being credible only because
they occur in connection with Christianity, Christianity itself
would be incredible because impossible without them. To use
the thought and almost the exact words of Robert Hall, it
could not be supposed that God would give even his Son to
save us and not himself ring his bell for us to hear him.

9. Nor may it be replied that were the Supernatural thus
to intervene directly in nature, such manifestations could not
be recognized as such by us. This overlooks the fact that it is
the manifestation of a person to persons that is under consideration. Now personality is known immediately by personality,
and more especially if there be a moral affinity between the
persons. You do not need to see every beast to be sure that
a man is not a beast. You feel at once, and you can not help
feeling, a unique kinship between him and yourself. You
know directly what he is. And somewhat so, it is not necessary that you should have surveyed all nature in order to
recognize the Supernatural as supernatural. You feel immediately both the unique kinship between him and yourself,
and *also* the infinite difference. Because he is a person, you
recognize at once his personality *and* the supernaturalness of
his personality. You know directly what he is, if only a little
of all that he is. Of course, this will depend greatly on the
moral affinity between you and him. A bad man may become
insensible to the supernaturalness of the Supernatural, but he
becomes at the same time unconscious of the personality of
the Supernatural. Both go together; and the former reveals,
and cannot but reveal unmistakably, the latter. Hence, truly to
know the manhood of Christ is to feel him to be "the Son of
God." In a word, as persons we are too much like the Supernatural Person and too conscious of our superiority to all else
than ourselves in nature not to recognize at once his infinite
superiority. In the unique light of the kinship between us
and him we cannot but see his supernaturalness. Thus in

every respect is the reality of the strictly personal intervention of the Supernatural in the natural a real necessity of
thought.

VII.

CONCLUSION.

What, then, is the net result of the discussion? It is not
that Christianity is thereby established as the supernatural religion. This must still be decided by the appropriate evidence. The way, however, has been opened, and the only
way, for the fair consideration of this evidence; and this has
been done in that we have established the reality of the existence of the Supernatural, of his manifestation through nature, of his personality, and of the possibility and even probability of his personal intervention in nature. It is true that
no one of these has been in the strict sense demonstrated. But
in the nature of the case this is impossible. Himself the
ground and so proof of everything, there is nothing that can
be the ground and so proof of the Supernatural. Yet as the
building necessarily evidences the foundation on which it
rests; so all nature, and especially that in it which is highest
and surest, namely, reason, demands the reality in the above
respects of the Supernatural. This must be granted or reason
must be stultified. To have shown this is thus both the utmost
that could be shown and in itself enough.

THE ESCHATOLOGICAL ASPECT OF THE PAULINE CONCEPTION OF THE SPIRIT

GEERHARDUS VOS

Emphasis in recent biblico-theological discussion on the eschatological
outlook of the early church. Its influence traced in various aspects of the Pauline teaching. Abuse of the method and relative warrant for its application. Paul's conception of the Spirit
to be examined as to its eschatological affinities. Eschatological
aspects of the Spirit in the Old Testament. The inter-canonical
development of the doctrine. The Gospels. The early chapters
of Acts. Paul's statements: 1) As to the Spirit in connection
with the end; 2.) As to the relation of the Spirit to the exalted
Christ; 3.) As to the semi-eschatological character of the believer's state, both objectively and subjectively considered; 4.)
As to the Christian's connection through the Spirit with the
world of heaven; 5.) As to the Spirit's function in revealing the
eschatological content of "wisdom"; 6) As to the Spirit in opposition to evil spirits. Inferences drawn from the discussion:
The eschatological significance of the Spirit 1) throws light on
Paul's conception of the uniformly pneumatic character of the
Christian life at every point; 2) proves the non-availability of
the Spirit for explaining the personal constitution of the preëxistent Christ; 3) furnishes the most impressive witness for the
supernaturalism of Paul's view of the Christian life.

THE ESCHATOLOGICAL ASPECT OF THE
PAULINE CONCEPTION OF
THE SPIRIT

Like other parts of New Testament Theology the interpretation of Paul's teaching has strongly felt the influence of the emphasis placed in recent discussion upon the eschatological outlook of the early Church. It is said that, since the person of the Messiah and his work form already in the Old Testament part of an essentially eschatological program, and since the acceptance of Jesus as the Messiah was the distinctive feature of the new faith, therefore the whole perspective in which the content of this religion presented itself to the first Christians had of necessity to assume eschatological form. They could not help correlating more closely than we are accustomed to do their present beliefs and experiences with the final, eternal issues of the history of redemption, and interpreting the former in the light of the latter. To an extent we can hardly appreciate theoretically, far less reproduce in our mode of feeling, they were conscious of standing at the turning-point of the ages, of living in the very presence of the world to come.

It is true that contemporary Judaism had not consistently kept the Messiah and his work in that central place of the eschatological stage which the Old Testament assigned to him. From within the coming aeon he had been removed to its threshold, and his kingdom relegated to the rank of a mere provisional episode in the great drama of the end. This, however, was due to the inherent dualism of the Jewish eschatology. Because it was felt that the earthly and the heavenly, the sensual and the spiritual, the temporal and the eternal, the political and the transcendental, the national and the cosmical would not combine, and yet neither of the two could safely be abandoned, the incongruous elements were mechanically forced together in the scheme of two successive kingdoms, during the former of which the urgent claims of Israel pertaining to this world would receive at least a transient satisfaction, whilst in the latter the higher and broader hopes would find their everlasting embodiment. Under this scheme the Messiah and his work inevitably became associated with the provisional, temporal order of affairs and ceased to be of significance for the final state.

But no such necessity for keeping apart the Messianic developments and the consummated state existed for the Christian mind. Here from the outset the emphasis had been placed on the virtual identity of the blessings and privileges pertaining to the rule of Christ with the eternal life at the end. While as a matter of history the opening days of the Messiah are seen to lie this side of the ultimate world-crisis, this is much more a chronological than a substantial distinction, the Christ is not kept outside of the future world, nor is the future world regarded as incapable of projecting itself into the present life. On the contrary the whole Messianic hope has become so thoroughly spiritualized as to make it indistinguishable in essence and character from the final kingdom of God. Through the appearance of the Messiah, as the great representative figure of the coming aeon, this new age has begun to enter into the actual experience of the believer. He has been translated into a state, which, while falling short of the consummated life of eternity, yet may be truly characterized as semi-eschatological.

In view of this it can cause no surprise, we are told, when the mind of the New Testament writers in its attempt to grasp the content of the Christian salvation makes the future the interpreter of the present, eschatology the norm and example of soteriological experience. Strange as this movement of thought seems to us, it must have been to the believers of the apostolic age quite natural and familiar. The coming of the Christ had fixed their attention upon the eternal world in all its absoluteness and fulness and with this in mind they interpreted everything that through the Christ happened for them and in them. Even in our Lord's teaching we are invited to observe the influence of this factor. Not as if the kingdom proclaimed by him were altogether a kingdom of the future having no existence in the present. Such a view is too palpably at variance with his plain teaching to gain acceptance with any except a few " thoroughgoing eschatologists ". But the firmness with which the two aspects of the kingdom are held together under the same name and represented as one continuous thing and the absolute newness and incomparableness which are predicated of the whole as regards the Old Testament conditions, all this proves that Jesus viewed his work as in the most direct manner interlinked with the life to come, to all intents the beginning of a new creation. And in the early chapters of the Book of Acts the same thought is found to color the outlook of the mother-church, a feature which must be true to the facts, because it does not quite coincide with Luke's own point of view.

As for Paul, his attitude in regard to this matter was from the outset determined by the fact, that he views the resurrection of Christ as the beginning of the general resurrection of the saints. The general resurrection of the saints being an eschatological event, indeed constituting together with the judgment the main content of the eschatological program, it follows that to Paul in this one point at least the eschatological course of events had already been set in motion, an integral piece of " the last things " has become an accomplished fact. Nor does this remain with Paul an isolated instance of the principle referred to. We are asked to observe in several other connections that the Apostle thinks in eschatological terms even when speaking of present developments. The sending forth of Christ marks to him the πλήρωμα τοῦ χρόνου (Gal. iv. 4), a phrase which certainly means more than that the time was ripe for the introduction of Christ into the world : the fulness of the time means the end of that aeon and the commencement of another world-period. As the resurrection of Jesus anticipates and secures the general resurrection, so the death of Christ, usually represented by Paul as an atonement, occasionally appears as securing and embodying in advance the judgment and destruction of the spiritual powers opposed to God, thus bringing the other great eschatological transaction

within the scope of the present activity of Christ and the present experience of believers, Rom. viii. 3; I Cor. ii. 6 (where
notice the present participle καταργουμένων: "who are already coming to nought"). Even the idea of σωτηρία "salvation", which is to us predominantly suggestive of our Christian state and experience in this life, is shown to have been
with Paul in its original signification an eschatological idea
denoting deliverance from the wrath to come, salvation in the
judgment, and from this it is believed to have been carried
back into the present life, first of all to express the thought,
that even now the believer through Christ possesses immunity
from the condemnation of the last day.[1] The idea of "redemption", so closely associated with the death of Christ,
none the less has its eschatological application, although it is
not asserted that this is the older usage, Rom. viii. 23; I Cor.
i. 30; Eph. i. 14, iv. 30. Justification is, of course, to Paul
the basis on which the whole Christian state rests, and in so
far eminently concerns the present, and yet in its finality and
comprehensiveness, covering not merely time but likewise eternity, it presents remarkable analogies to the absolute vindication
expected at the end. And the subjective renewal of the believer likewise is placed by the Apostle in the light of the
world to come. The καινὴ κτίσις spoken of in 2 Cor. v. 17
means the beginning of that world-renewal in which all
eschatology culminates.

Undoubtedly in all this there is some one-sidedness and exaggeration. Altogether too much has been made, in calling
attention to the above and other allied facts, of the element of
time, as if the peculiar perspective in these matters could be

---

[1] Cf. the early passages 1 Thess. v. 8, 9; 2 Thess. ii. 13, 14, but also in
the later epistles, Rom. v. 9, 10, xiii. 11; Phil. i. 28, iii. 20; 2 Tim. iv. 18.
In all of these the σωτηρία is eschatological. Paul, however, knows also
of a "being saved" i. e. being in process of salvation, 1 Cor. i. 18, xv. 2;
2 Cor. ii. 15, in all of which the present tense is used, and of a "having
been saved", Eph. ii. 5; 2 Tim. i. 9, where the perfect and aorist occur.
From the original eschatological sense the fact may be explained that
σώζειν, σωτηρία stand regularly in Paul for the subjective side of salvation, what is dogmatically called the application of redemption. The
eschatological salvation lies in the subjective sphere.

explained from the early Christian belief in the nearness of the parousia. When this chronological element is unduly pressed, such monstrosities result as Schweitzer's construction of the life of Jesus. And the writers who are most enthusiastic about trying the key of eschatology upon the lock of every New Testament problem, are also the least apt to hold back with their conviction, that the eschatological frame of mind is a hopeless anachronism to the modern consciousness. Still the abuse made of the theory should not shut our eyes to whatever elements of truth it may have brought for the first time into focus. It can be shown, we believe, that the phenomena dwelt upon have their root in practical and theoretical premises, which were fixed in the minds of the New Testament writers altogether independently of the question of the relative nearness or remoteness of the parousia. In each case the consideration is not that in point of time, but that in point of causal nexus and identity of religious privilege, the present is most closely linked to the life of eternity. Not the belief in the nearness of the parousia first gave rise to this consciousness. On the contrary, there is reason to assume that the expectation of a speedy approach of the end which is reflected in the New Testament writings sprang, at least in part, from the consciousness in question. The early church lived to such an extent in the thought of the world to come, that it could hardly help hoping it to be near also in point of time. But this was a mere by-product of a much broader and deeper state of mind. Thus it happens that the principle to which the eschatological school has called attention may retain its ,validity, even though the present age and the life of eternity have become to our knowledge much farther separated than they were to the vision of the early church.

We propose in the following pages to investigate to what extent Paul's doctrine of the Holy Spirit shows interdependence with his eschatology. At this point better than at any other will we be able to test the relative warrant for the eschatological method of approach, and to understand the peculiar way in which it can contribute to an adequate appreciation of the fundamental structure of the great Apostle's teaching. Another reason for the selection lies in this, that in the treatment of Paul's pneumatology the new point of view has thus far been less thoroughly and systematically pursued than in regard to other aspects of his gospel. One reason for this is that the theological conception of the Spirit is chiefly regulated by the closing discourses of our Lord recorded in the Fourth Gospel. Here the Spirit seems to appear as merely the representative of Christ during his absence, and therefore confined in his operation to the intermediate period between the departure of Jesus and his return to the disciples. Thus restricted the Spirit would have no further significance for the consummated state, when Christ will resume direct intercourse with his own in a higher form. But even for John this would be a very one-sided statement of the facts. The Spirit does not abide temporarily with the disciples but " *forever* " Jno. xiv. 16, 17. It is the Spirit's specific function " to declare the things that are to come," xvi. 13. The Spirit " guides into all the truth ", and hence is called " the Spirit of truth ", xv. 26, xvi. 13, and this must be taken in connection with the peculiar Johannine objective conception of "truth" as designating the transcendental realities of the heavenly world, that truth of which Jesus is the center and incarnation, whence also the Spirit in supplying it takes of Jesus' own, xvi. 14, 15. Indeed so absolutely does the Spirit belong to the other world, that the kosmos is simply declared incapable of receiving, beholding, and knowing him, xiv. 17. Nor is the intermediate operation of the Spirit in the present meant to preclude his eternal significance as a factor in the life to come. That the latter idea is not more pointedly brought out in John is due to the thoroughgoing manner in which the Fourth Gospel eternalizes the present state of the believer, and emphasizes the identity rather than the difference between the life now possessed and the life to be inherited hereafter. Viewed in this light the prominence of the Spirit's activity now not only does not tell against, but distinctly favors the assumption that the Spirit has his proper sphere and a dominating part in the eschatological world.

But, even if the facts were different as regards the Fourth Gospel, this would not be decisive for the case of Paul. Our

Lord in John might have confined himself to pointing out one particular aspect of the Spirit's work, and Paul might teach the full-orbed doctrine of the Spirit, so as to bring the two hemispheres of his present and his eschatological activity under equal illumination. In how far this is actually the case we endeavor to trace in the following survey of Paul's teaching on the subject.

At the outset it will be well to remark that the connection of the Spirit with eschatology reaches back into the Old Testament. The fundamental sense of רוּחַ is in the Old Testament, that of air in motion, whilst that of air at rest seems to have been chiefly associated with the Greek πνεῦμα.[2] This rendered the word fit to describe the Spirit on his energizing, active side and falls in with his ultimate eschatological function, since the eschatological element in the religion of the Old Testament is but the supreme expression of its character as a religion of God's free historical self-assertion, a religion, not of nature-processes, but of redemption and revelation. Aside from this the Spirit and eschatology are linked together along four lines of thought. First we have the idea that the Spirit by special manifestations of the supernatural, by certain prophetic signs, heralds the near approach of the future world. Thus in Joel iii. 1 ff. (ii. 28 ff in English) the outpouring of the Spirit on all flesh and the subsequent prophesying and related phenomena are described as all taking place " before the great and terrible day of Jehovah comes " (verse 4). The idea is not that the Spirit will be characteristic of the eschatological state, but that it naturally falls to him to work the premonitions of its coming. This follows from the parallelism[3] between the Spirit-worked phenomena and the other cosmical signs enumerated. When this terrible castastrophe draws near, great prophetic excitement will lay hold upon men, even as the powers of nature will become moved in sympathy with what is approaching. It is not excluded by this that the Spirit will also have his place and role within the new era itself, but this is not indicated even indirectly. The Spirit works these signs, not because he

---

[2] Stade, *Bibl. Theol. d. Alt. Test.* I, p. 182, note 3.
[3] The two are parallel, not successive.

stands for the eschatological as such, but because the prophetic
and ecstatic experiences belong to his province.[4]

In the second place the Spirit is brought into the eschatological era itself as forming the official equipment of the Messiah.
This is done in a number of passages, Is. xi. 2, xxviii. 5, xlii. 1,
lix. 21 (?), lxi. 1.   It is to be noticed that the Messiah receives
the Spirit as a permanent possession, and not temporarily as
the prophets; further that the effects of this endowment lie in
the ethico-religious sphere.   By calling this equipment with the
Spirit official we do not mean to imply that it is externally attached to the Messiah and does not affect his own subjective religious life, for according to Is. xi. 2 he is not merely a " Spirit
of wisdom and understanding ", of " counsel and might ", but
also a " Spirit of knowledge and fear of Jehovah ".   Still
the prophet does not mean to describe what the Spirit is for
the Messiah himself, but what through the Messiah he is for
the people.[5]

---

[4] Volz, *Der Geist Gottes und die verwandten Erscheinungen im Alten
Testament und im anschliessenden Judenthum*, 1910 (p. 93), while explaining as above, thinks that Acts ii. 16-21 give a different exegesis of the
Joel-passage, because the disciples are represented as permanently possessed of the Spirit.   The contrary is true: Peter distinctly quotes the
entire passage, including the words which put the phenomena named before the coming of the day of Jehovah (v. 20), and which assign a
period of some length during which opportunity is given to call upon the
name of Jehovah in order to ultimate salvation in the day of judgment
(v. 21).   The Spirit's working is here no less sub-eschatological than in
Joel.   That it can be considered a gift of the exalted Jesus (v. 33)
and is perpetuated into the subsequent period does not alter its character.   Peter is even more explicit than Joel in regard to the point in
question, for he modifies the quotation by introducing into it the words
" in the last days ", a phrase which in the New Testament is everywhere
sub-eschatological.

[5] Volz op. cit. p. 87:   The Spirit "attaches less to the person than to
the office, for in connection with the Messiah Judaism is more interested
in what the Messiah accomplishes than in what he is."   Volz in this
recent book adheres to his earlier denial of the Isaianic origin of the
great Messianic prophecies, chs. ix. and xi., and finds further support for
this denial in the ethico-religious character of the effects here ascribed to
the Messianic Spirit.   This, he thinks, must point to a later date than
Isaiah, because the early prophets do not derive their own equipment
from the Spirit, p. 63.   In this last-named opinion Volz sides with

In the third place the Spirit appears as the source of the future new life of Israel, especially of the ethico-religious renewal, also as the pledge of divine favor for the new Israel, and as the author of a radical transformation of physical conditions in the eschatological era, and thus becomes characteristic of the eschatological state itself. To this head belong the following passages: Is. xxxii. 15-17, xliv. 3, lix. 21 (?); Ez. xxxvi. 27, xxxvii. 14, xxxix. 29. It will be. observed that in these passages the sending of the Spirit is expected not from the Messiah but from Jehovah directly, although the statements occur in prophecies that know the Messiah. The emphasis rests on the initial act as productive of new conditions; at the same time the terms used show that the presence and working of the Spirit are not restricted to the first introduction of the eschatological state but accompany the latter in continuance. The land or the nation becomes a permenent receptacle of the Spirit.[6] An individualizing form the promise assumes in Ez. xxxvi. 26.

In the fourth place we must take into account that in the Old Testament Spirit appears as the comprehensive formula for the transcendental, the supernatural. In all the manifestations of the Spirit a supernatural reality projects itself into the ordinary experience of man, and thus the sphere whence these manifestations come can be named after the power to which they are traced. This is in agreement with the twofold

Giesebrecht, *Die Berufsbegabung der A. T.-lichen Propheten*, 1897. The Spirit, he thinks, was for the prophets too materialistic, too unethical, too miraculous to allow of association with their own ideals. We can here once more observe how the ethical with the school to which this writer adheres drives out the supernatural even where the two seem most organically united. What happened formerly to the Messiah now happens to the Spirit of the Messiah.

[6] The figures used for the communication are those of "outpouring", שפך, יצק, נערה, words which imply the imparting of something that remains; also נתן "to give" and "to put into", are found, Ez. xxxvi. 27, xxxvii. 14. Notice the verbs expressing permanence in Is. xxxii. 16: "Then justice shall *dwell* in the wilderness, and righteousness shall *abide* in the fruitful field." According to Ez. xxxix. 29 the continuance of the favor of God is secure to the people, because they have received the Spirit: "Neither will I hide my face any more from them: for I have poured out my Spirit upon the house of Israel."

aspect of " the wind ", which is at the same time a concrete force, and a supernal element.[7]   But the Spirit stands for the supernatural not merely in so far as the latter connotes the miraculous, but also in so far as it is sovereign over against man: it " blows where it listeth ".   In man the pneumatic awakes the awe which pertains to the supernatural and its presence exposes to the same danger.   Because of this close association with the higher world the Spirit appears in closest conjunction with God, who is the center of that sphere.   Every bearer of the Spirit forms a link of connection between man and the higher world.   In the ecstatic state the Spirit lifts the prophet into the supernatural sphere which is peculiarly its own.   And even in his ordinary life the prophet is, on account of his pneumatic character, as it were concentrated upon a higher world, " he sits alone because of Jehovah's hand ", Jer. xv. 17.   All this, while not eschatological in itself, becomes of importance for our present purpose, because it is a recognized principle in New Testament teaching that in one aspect the eschatological order of things is identical with the heavenly order of things brought to light.   If the Spirit stands representatively for the latter, he will naturally reappear in the same capacity as regards the former.

In the apocryphal and pseudepigraphical literature and in the Rabbinical theology we meet again most of these ideas, and in one respect note a further development in the direction of the New Testament doctrine.   The Messiah becomes bearer of the Spirit not merely for the discharge of his own official functions, but also for the purpose of communicating the Spirit to others.   The Messiah pours out on men the Spirit of grace, so that henceforth they walk in the ways of God, Test. Jud. xxiv. 2.   In " the Elect ", i. e. the Messiah, " dwells the Spirit of wisdom, and the Spirit of him who gives understanding, and the Spirit of instruction and power, and the Spirit of those who are fallen asleep in righteousness ", En. xlix. 3.   Thus not merely the ethical but also the eschatological life of the resurrection is derived from the Messiah.

---

[7] Cf. Jno. iii. 8, where the wind comes from above, out of the region of mystery, and also Ez. xxxvii. 9: " Come from the four winds, O breath."

It will be observed, however, that the Spirit does not become any more than in the Old Testament the constituent principle of the Messiah's Person, he remains as before the Spirit of official endowment. Cf. further En. lxii. 2; Test. Lev. xviii. 7; Test. Jud. xxiv. 2; Or. Sib. iii. 655 ff.; Ps. Sol. xvii. 37. The possession of the eschatological Spirit is ascribed to the future saints also irrespective of Messianic mediation. It is in them a Spirit of life, En. lxi. 7,[8] a Spirit of faith, of wisdom, of patience, of mercy, of judgment, of peace and of benevolence, En. lxi. 11; a Spirit of eternal life, Or. Sib. iii. 771; a Spirit of holiness pertaining to paradise and named in connection with the tree of life, Test. Lev. xviii. 11. The Rabbinical Theology also brings the Spirit in connection with the resurrection: " Holiness leads to the Holy Spirit, the Holy Spirit leads to the resurrection ", R. Pinhas b. Ja'ir in B. Aboda s. 20ᵇ (quoted by Volz p. 114).[9] In comparison with the Old Testament period this thought of the Spirit's eschatological operation appears more developed and receives greater emphasis, a feature by some explained from the fact, that in the later times the present activity of the Spirit was felt to be rare or entirely in abeyance. What the present did not offer was expected from the future. None the less the fourth line of thought is as prominent as in the canonical literature. The impression that the period of Judaism was to itself an unpneumatic period is apt to be based on the comparison of these times with the immediately following Spirit-filled days of the early Christian church, rather than on an estimate of the period considered in itself. The " wise men " speak of themselves as " divine ", " immortal ", as the prophets of their age; Sap. Sol. vii. 27, viii. 13; Sir. xxiv. 33. The Apocalyptic writers also feel themselves men of a higher divine rank, in-

[8] Sokolowski, *Die Begriffe Geist und Leben bei Paulus,* 1903, pp. 201 ff. denies that pre-Christian Judaism associates the Spirit with the resurrection or the resurrection-life. On the other side cf. Slotemaker de Bruine, *De Eschatologische Voorstellingen in I en II Corinthe,* 1894, p. 57 and Volz, p. 114.

[9] Hence it is said that the people of the time of the deluge cannot attain unto the resurrection, because they are deprived of the Spirit (Gen. vi. 3) Sanh. xi. 3.

itiated into mysteries hidden even from the angels, capable of forecasting the future, the authors of inspired writings, En. xiv. 3, xxxvii. 3, lxxxii. 2, xci. 1, xcii. 1; 4 Ezra, xiv. 18 ff. 46; Slav. En. xviii. 8, xxiv. 3. We also read that the pneumatic state of these men assumed the specific form of a translation into the heavenly sphere[10] It is, however, difficult to determine how much in all this was actual, sincere experience, and how much was artificially conceived, or part of the traditional imagery of which all these writers availed themselves. The fact that the Pneuma is most frequently associated with the charisma of wisdom and general ethical virtue may be an indication that the specifically supernatural did no longer attest itself strongly to the consciousness of the period as a present possession.

In the Gospels the eschatological aspect of the Spirit is not much in evidence. This, however, is but part of the wider observation that the Spirit in general remains in the background. It is a striking proof of the high Christology of the Synoptical writers that they do not refer to the pneumatic equipment of Jesus in explanation of the supernatural character of his Person, and even make comparatively little of it in explanation of the supernatural character of his work. Obviously the Evangelists (Synoptics as well as John) had a higher, ontological aspect of the Person of Jesus in mind by which to account for the supernatural phenomena.[11] The Baptist makes the Holy Spirit the element wherein Jesus will baptize, and thus the distinctive element of the coming kingdom, Mk. i. 8. (= Mt. iii. 11 = Lk. iii. 16).[12] This implies

[10] The later Jewish tradition knows of four Rabbis who penetrated into Paradise, B. Chagiga 14ᵇ-15ᵇ, quoted by Volz p. 118. On the other hand, cf. the statement Tanchuma 114ᵃ: "In this world I impart wisdom through my Spirit, hereafter, I will myself impart wisdom."

[11] Cf. Joh. Weiss, *Das älteste Evangelium*, 1903, pp. 48, 49: "In Mark the representation that the Spirit is an equipment for Jesus' activity, receives very little prominence."

[12] For the combination ἐν πνεύματι ἁγίῳ καὶ πυρί in Mt. and Lk. cf. an interesting parallel in the statement of the Avesta (quoted by Volz p. 176): "Mazdah will prepare the recompense of blessedness and damnation through the holy spirit and fire." This favors the interpretation of the fire as an instrument of judgment.

that the Messiah imparts the Spirit. But in the Fourth Gospel the Baptist goes one step farther by bringing this baptism to be conferred by Jesus into connection with the descent of the Spirit upon Jesus, which is the first intimation in the New Testament, that the Spirit will rest on the Messiah and the members of his kingdom, passing over from him to them, i. 33. As the Spirit of the Messiah the Spirit appears in the accounts of the birth of Jesus, of the baptism and of the temptation; Cf. also Mt. iv. 14.[13] Our Lord himself refers to the Spirit in this capacity in the sayings of Mt. xii. 28 (=Lk. xi. 20) and Lk. iv. 18. Of the Spirit as communicable to the disciples in the kingdom speak Mt. x. 19 (= Lk. xii. 12) and Lk. xi. 13. It will be noted that here the giving of the Spirit is ascribed to God, not to the Messiah. To the closing chapters in John reference has been made above. The Spirit, while predominant in this intermediate period, is not confined to it, and the period, as well as the Spirit's operation in it, are conceived as semi-eschatological. Both the Father and Jesus send the Spirit, xiv. 16, 26, xv. 26, xvi. 7, xx. 22. In the earlier part of the Gospel the Messianic Spirit appears in i. 33, iii. 34, vi. 63; the future Spirit in vii. 39; the Spirit as representative of the supernatural, heavenly world in iii. 3, 5, 6, 8.

We have already seen that in the early Petrine teaching, traceable in Acts, the outpouring of the Spirit is, in dependence on the Joel-prophecy, represented as belonging to " the last days ", ii. 17.[14] It does not, however, follow from this, that the pneumatic phenomena appeared to the early disciples in the light of eschatological symptoms exclusively. It is evident from the whole tenor of the narrative that the possession of the Spirit had a subjective value for the disciples themselves. It is the sign of acceptance with God, of participation in the privileges of the Christian state, x. 45, 47. It is therefore represented as the fulfilment of the promise, which fulfilment Christ after his ascension received from the Father,

---

[13] Cf. also Acts i. 2, iv. 27, x. 38.

[14] Luke in his own narrative does not refer to the Spirit from this point of view, but speaks of him only in connection with the work of missions. Harnack appeals to this in proof of the accurate historical coloring of the Petrine speeches by the author of Acts.

i. 4, ii. 33.[15] It signalizes the present no less than it portends
the future. Still the characteristic feature, that the present
enjoyment of the Spirit's gifts is an anticipation of the world
to come seems to be wanting. The Spirit's work is prophetic
and at the same time symptomatic of salvation, but these two
ideas are not as yet organically connected, the intermediate
thought which would explain both features, viz. that the final
salvation consists in the full endowment with the Spirit, finds
no expression. The problems of the sphere to which the
operations of the Spirit belong and of the personal relation of
the Spirit to the exalted Messiah, can be more satisfactorily
dealt with at a subsequent stage in comparison with the Pauline
teaching on these points.

Coming to Paul himself we notice first that the Apostle explicitly links the Christian possession of the Spirit to the Old
Testament eschatological promise. This does not mean that the
presence and operation of the Spirit in the Old Testament are
denied.[16] Cf. Acts xxviii. 25; Rom. vii. 14; 1 Cor. x. 3, 4;
Gal. iv. 29 and 1 Tim. iv. 1. These things, however, so far as
they do not relate to the inspiration of the Scriptures, were of a
typical nature and therefore took place in the physical sphere.
The true era of the Spirit's activity was still outstanding. The
two aspects of the Messianic Person, that κατὰ πνεῦμα as well
as that κατὰ σάρκα were part of the prophetic promise in the
Holy Scriptures Rom. i. 1-4. The Spirit is an object of

[15] Harnack, *Die Apostelgeschichte*, 1908, p. 109 thinks that in ii. 33 the
promise of the Spirit (not the promised Spirit) is represented as having
been first given to Jesus after his ascension. But i. 4 shows that this is
a mistake, for here Jesus, before the ascension, speaks of "the promise
of the Father" for which they are to wait at Jerusalem. And in the
Gospel xxiv. 49 Jesus says: "I send forth the promise of my Father
upon you". In all three passages ἐπαγγελία is = "the thing promised",
cf. Gal. iii. 14 where the same phrase ἐπαγγελία τοῦ πνεύματος occurs in
the same sense. (For the variant reading see below.)

[16] 2 Cor. iv. 13 will also belong here, if τὸ αὐτὸ πνεῦμα be construed with
κατὰ τὸ γεγραμμένον i. e. the same Spirit of faith as finds expression in the
word of the Psalmist. But probably Paul means that the same Spirit
is in himself as in the Corinthians, although death works in him, life in
them, v. 12. Cf. Gloël, *Der Heilige Geist in der Heilsverkündigung des
Paulus*, 1888, p. 87.

ἐπαγγελία, Gal. iii. 14; Eph. i 13. While in the latter passage Paul probably has in mind the prophetic predictions of the outpouring of the Spirit, the context shows that in Gal. 3 he thinks of the εὐλογία given to Abraham as relating to the Spirit.[17]

We first examine the statements which introduce the Spirit in a strictly eschatological capacity, as connected with the future state. The Spirit and the resurrection belong together, and that in a twofold sense. On the one hand the resurrection as an act is derived from the Spirit, on the other hand the resurrection-state is represented as in permanence dependent on the Spirit, as a pneumatic state. In Rom. viii. 11 it is affirmed that God, διὰ τοῦ ἐνοικοῦντος αὐτοῦ πνεύματος (or τὸ ἐνοικοῦν αὐτοῦ πνεῦμα) ἐν ὑμῖν shall give life to their mortal bodies. In verse 10 the body and the Spirit are contrasted: the former is dead on account of sin, the latter is life on account of righteousness. Still πνεῦμα is here not the human spirit, psychologically conceived; it is the divine Pneuma in its close identification with the believer's person. Hence in verse 11 there is substituted for the simple τὸ πνεῦμα the fuller phrase " the Spirit of him that raised up Jesus from the dead ". The fact that God is thus designated is of importance for the argument. What God did for Jesus, he will do for the believer also.[18]. It is presupposed by the Apostle, though not expressed, that God raised Jesus through the Spirit. Hence

---

[17] So correctly Gloël pp. 96-97 against Meyer who finds the content of the εὐλογία in justification. But justification is proven from Abraham's case in so far as it is the indispensable prerequisite of receiving the εὐλογία . The latter =κληρονομία v. 18, and Rom. iv. 13 shows that with reference to the κληρονομία justification is a means to an end. Or εὐλογία = ζῆν vss. 10, 12 and life is based on justification, Rom. i. 17. The identification of the Spirit and εὐλογία is also found in Is. xliv. 3. If, with Zahn, on the basis of D. G d g and some patristic authorities, we read in Gal. iii. 14 εὐλογίαν τοῦ πνεύματος, we obtain an explicit identification of the blessing and the Spirit.

[18] It should be noticed how significantly Paul varies in this connection the name of Christ. First he speaks of the raising of *Jesus* from the dead. Here the Saviour comes under consideration as to his own Person. Then he speaks of the raising of *Christ Jesus* from the dead. Here the Saviour is considered as the Messiah in his representative capacity, which furnishes a guarantee that his resurrection must repeat itself in that of the others.

the argument from the analogy between Jesus and the believer is further strengthened by the consideration, that the instrument through which God accomplished this in Jesus is already present in the readers. The idea that the Spirit works instrumentally in the resurrection is thus plainly implied, altogether apart from the question whether the reading διά c. Gen. or διά c. Acc. be preferred in verse 11ᵉ.[19] As to 11ᵉ itself, when the textus receptus is followed, this part of the verse will only repeat in more explicit form the thought already implied in 11ᵃ: If the Spirit of God who raised Jesus dwells in you, then God will make the indwelling Spirit accomplish for you what he did for Jesus in the latter's resurrection. On the other reading we may paraphrase as follows: If the Spirit of God who raised Jesus dwells in you, then God will create for that Spirit the same bodily organisation, that he created for him in the resurrection-body of Christ. In the latter case there is added to the idea of the Spirit as the instrumental cause of the resurrection-act, the further idea of the Spirit as the permanent basis of the resurrection-state.

A second passage is Gal. vi. 8. Between verse 7 and verse 8 the figure varies, inasmuch as in the former the correspondence between the *seed* and the harvest, in the latter the correspondence between the *soil* and the harvest is affirmed. But the idea of correspondence is common to both forms of the figure. The reaping of eternal life follows from the sowing *into* the Spirit because the Spirit and eternal life belong together through identity of content, just as the σάρξ--soil is reproduced in the φθορά--harvest, because the σάρξ is inherently and necessarily the source of corruption. The phrase ζωή αἰώνιος, with Paul (in distinction from John) always strictly eschatological, proves that the reference is to the day of judgment. The future θερίσει is chronological. We, therefore, obtain the thought that the heavenly life, regarded as a reward for the believer, will essentially consist in pneuma, which, of course, extends to its bodily form, although it is

---

[19] The reading of the textus receptus διά c. Gen. rests on א, A, C, Clem. Al.; the other is supported by B, D, E, F, G, Orig. Iren. Tert. and the Old-Syriac and Old-Latin versions. Cf. Gloël, pp. 362 ff., who decides in favor of the latter.

not confined to this.[20]   Nothing is here said of the act of the resurrection and its dependence on the Spirit.   It is the harvest as a product, not the harvesting as a process, of which the pneumatic character is affirmed.

It might be said, however, that in these two passages the thought has its point of departure in the soteriological conception of the Spirit as a present factor in the Christian life and from here moves forward to the future, so that the eschatological function of the Spirit would be a doctrinal inference, rather than something inherent in the nature of the Spirit itself.[21]   We therefore turn to a third passage, which clearly starts from the eschatological end of the line and looks backward from this into the present life.   This is 2 Cor. v. 5. Here Paul declares that God has prepared him for the eternal state in the new heavenly body, as may be seen from this that he gave him the ἀρραβὼν τοῦ πνεύματος.   The ἀρραβών con-consists in the Spirit; " of the Spirit " is epexegetical, just as in Gal. iii. 14 the ἐπαγγελία τοῦ πνεύματος means the promised thing consisting in the Spirit.[22]   But the Spirit possesses this significance of an ἀρραβών because it is a preliminary instalment of what in its fulness will be received hereafter.   The analogous conception of the ἀπαρχὴ τοῦ πνεύματος, Rom. viii. 23, proves this.[23]   The figure of the ἀρραβών itself implies this

[20] For this aspect of the resurrection cf. 1 Cor. xv. 30-32, where it appears as a recompense for the κινδυνεύειν and daily ἀποθνήσκειν : "what doth it profit me?" and v. 58: "be ye steadfast. . . . forasmuch as ye know that your labor is not in vain in the Lord."

[21] This is the ordinary way of representing the matter.   Even Swete in his recent book *The Holy Spirit in the New Testament,* 1910, falls into it, when he puts the question as to the eschatological significance of the Spirit in this form: "Is the work of the Spirit preparatory only, or is it permanent, extending to the world to come?" p. 353.   That a movement of thought in the opposite direction may also have been familiar to the Apostle does not seem to suggest itself to the author.

[22] In Eph. i. 14 on the other hand the ἀρραβὼν τῆς κληρονομίας is the Spirit which pledges the inheritance, so that the construction is different, while the thought is the same; the pledge consists in the Spirit and assures of the inheritance.

[23] Another analogous conception, that of the σφραγίς, does not express the identity of the pledge and the thing pledged, cf. 2 Cor. i. 22; Eph. i. 13, iv. 30.

relation no less than that of the ἀπαρχή, for it means " money which in purchases is given as a pledge that the full amount will be subsequently paid ".[24]   In this instance, therefore, the Spirit is viewed as pertaining specifically to the future life, nay as constituting the substantial make-up of this life, and the present possession of the Spirit by the believer is regarded in the light of an anticipation.   The Spirit's proper sphere is according to this the world to come; from there he projects himself into the present, and becomes a prophecy of himself in his eschatological operation.[25]

Undoubtedly more statements to the same effect would be found, but for the circumstance that it was more natural for the Apostle to express the idea in connection with the eschatological life of Christ, as already a present reality, than in connection with the eschatological state of believers, which still lies in the future.   We, therefore, inquire in the second place to what extent eschatological side-lights fall on the resurrection and the resurrection-life of Christ.   We begin with Rom. i. 4.   Here, we read that Christ was ὁρισθεὶς υἱὸς θεοῦ ἐν δυνάμει κατὰ πνεῦμα ἁγιωσύνης ἐξ ἀναστάσεως νεκρῶν. The statement stands in close parallelism to verse 3 τοῦ γενομένου ἐκ σπέρματος Δαυεὶδ κατὰ σάρκα.   The following members correspond to each other in the two clauses:

γενόμενος	ὁρισθείς
κατὰ σάρκα	κατὰ πνεῦμα ἁγιωσύνης
ἐκ σπέρματος Δαυείδ	ἐξ ἀναστάσεως νεκρῶν.

[24] So Suidas sub voce.

[25] Charles, Teichmann and others assume that the derivation of the resurrection from the Spirit is a later development in the mind of Paul, that his earliest eschatology, represented by 1 Thess., was un-pneumatic, which involves that at this stage he expected the resurrection of the original body unchanged.   But this is an argument e silentio and not even quite that. To meet the difficulty of the Thessalonians the *fact* of the resurrection, not its mode, or the nature of the resurrection-life, had to be emphasized. Besides, the pneumatic character of the resurrection is clearly implied in Chap. iv. 14, for if the death and resurrection of Jesus *jointly considered* furnish the guarantee of the believer's resurrection, this must be understood on the principle that in Christ's experience that of the Christian is prefigured.   But of such reproduction of the experience of Christ in believers the Spirit is with Paul everywhere the mediating cause.   Cf. also the phrase οἱ νεκροὶ ἐν Χριστῷ, which has a pneumatic background.

The reference is not to two coexisting sides in the constitution of the Saviour, but to two successive stages in his life: there was first a γενέσθαι κατὰ σάρκα, then a ὁρισθῆναι κατὰ πνεῦμα. The two prepositional phrases have adverbial force: they describe the mode of the process, yet so as to throw emphasis rather on the result than on the initial act: Christ came into being as to his sarkic existence, and he was introduced by ὁρισμός into his pneumatic existence. The ὁρίζειν is not an abstract determination, but an effectual appointment; Paul obviously avoids the repetition of γενομένου not for rhetorical reasons only, but because it might have suggested, even before the reading of the whole sentence could correct it, the misunderstanding that at the resurrection the divine sonship of Christ *as such* first originated, whereas the Apostle merely meant to affirm this late temporal origin of the divine sonship ἐν δυνάμει, the sonship as such reaching back into the state of preëxistence. By the twofold κατά the mode of each state of existence is contrasted, by the twofold ἐκ the origin of each. Thus the existence κατὰ σάρκα originated " from the seed of David ", the existence κατὰ πνεῦμα originated " out of resurrection from the dead ". The point of importance for our present purpose lies in this last contrast. How can resurrection from the dead be the counterpart of an issue from the seed of David? There are in the Pauline world of thought but two answers to this question, and both will have to be combined in the present instance. The resurrection is to Paul the beginning of a new status of sonship:[26] hence, as Jesus derived his sonship κατὰ σάρκα from the seed of David, he can be said to have derived his divine-sonship-in-power from the resurrection. The implication is that the one working in the resurrection is God: it is

[26] Cf. Rom. viii. 23 where υἱοθεσία is equivalent to ἀπολύτρωσις τοῦ σώματος. In v. 29 the εἰκών of Christ unto conformity to which believers have been predestinated is the εἰκών of sonship (τοῦ υἱοῦ αὐτοῦ and " that he might be the first-born among many brethren ") and it is eschatologically conceived for the εἰκών looks forward to the ἐδόξασεν at the end of the catena. But the thought of eschatological sonship, and that specifically through the resurrection, is also met with in our Lord's teaching, cf. Mt. v. 9, xiii. 43; Lk. xx. 36.

his seed that supernaturally begets the higher sonship. And in all probability the Genitive ἀγιωσύνης which is added to " Spirit ", is meant as a designation of God from the point of view of his specific deity, sharply distinguishing him as such from David. Still, all this might have been expressed by Paul writing " effectually appointed according to the Spirit of Holiness the Son in power of God who raises the dead ". That, instead of doing this, he writes ἐξ ἀναστάσεως νεκρῶν must be explained from a second motive. He wished to contrast the resurrection-process in a broad generic way with the processes of this natural life; the resurrection is characteristic of the beginning of a new order of things, as sarkic birth is characteristic of an older order of things. What stands before the Apostle's mind is the contrast between the two aeons, for it was a familiar thought to the Jewish theology that the future aeon has its characteristic beginning in the great resurrection-act. This also will explain why in ἐξ ἀναστάσεως νεκρῶν both nouns are anarthrous. Paul is not thinking of *the* resurrection of Christ as an event, but of what happened to Christ in its generic qualitative capacity, as an epoch partaking of a strictly eschatological nature. From resurrection-beginnings, from an eschatological genesis dates the pneumatic state of Christ's glory which is described as a sonship of God ἐν δυνάμει.[27]

[27] For the justification of the above exegesis, which cannot here be given in detail, cf., besides the commentaries, especially Gloël, pp. 113-117; Sokolowski, pp. 56-62. According to our view the pneuma here spoken of begins with the resurrection. The other exegesis dates it back either to the state of preëxistence, so that it becomes the element which constituted the personality of the Son of God in that state, being identical with his sonship, or to his earthly life. Both these variations of the other view fall back, each after its own fashion, into the error of making the σάρξ and the πνεῦμα two coëxistent component parts in the Person of Christ instead of two successive states in the life of Christ. The main objections to this exegesis are: 1.) It would restrict the σάρξ spoken of to the body, because Spirit is already psychologically conceived and thus takes the place of the immaterial element. 2.) It is compelled to take the two κατὰ clauses in a different sense; the γενέσθαι κατὰ σάρκα means a genesis according to the σάρξ which first introduces Christ into the σάρξ, whereas in the ὁρισθῆναι κατὰ πνεῦμα the Spirit would appear as the preëxistent norm, in accordance with which the ὁρίζειν took place: a begin-

In 1 Cor. xv. 42-50 the Apostle contrasts the two bodies which belong to the pre-eschatological and the eschatological state respectively. The former is characterized as ψυχικόν, the latter as πνευματικόν. Here therefore, as regards the body, the eschatological state is the state in which the Pneuma rules, impressing upon the body its threefold characteristic of ἀφθαρσία, δόξα, δύναμις (verses 42, 43). And over against this, and preceding it, stands the "psychical" body characterized by φθορά, ἀτιμία, and ἀσθενεία. The proximate reference is to the body and the contrast is between the body in the state of sin and the body in the resurrection-state. It will be noticed, however, that in verses 45, 46 the Apostle generalizes the antithesis so that it no longer concerns the body exclusively, but the whole state of man, and at the same time enlarges the one term of the contrast, that relating to the pre-eschatological period, so as to make it cover no longer the reign of sin, but the order of things established in creation. Τὸ πνευματικόν and τὸ ψυχικόν in verse 46 are generalizing expressions, after which it would be a mistake to supply σῶμα ; they designate the successive reign of two comprehensive principles in history, two successive world-orders, a first and a second creation, beginning each with an Adam of its own.[28] Even apart from sin these two stand related to

ning-to-be- κατὰ σάρκα is contrasted with a beginning to be something else than pneuma in harmony with a given pneuma. Gloël himself acknowledges this difficulty on p. 115, note 1.

The above interpretation does not, of course, imply that Paul denied the presence of a pneumatic element in the pre-resurrection life of Jesus, in other words that he denied the supernatural conception and the equipment with the Spirit at baptism. Precisely, because he speaks of the pneumatic state in the absolute eschatological sense, he could disregard in this connection, the twofold supernatural equipment just named, for the reason that it did not give rise to a state ἐν δυνάμει κατὰ πνεῦμα such as characterizes the life of the risen Christ. He could equally well say here that Christ became κατὰ πνεῦμα at the resurrection, as he can say in 1 Cor. xv. 45 that Christ at the resurrection became a life-giving Spirit. As above stated, the emphasis rests not on the initial act of the resurrection but on the resulting state. In regard to the act as such Paul would not have denied that the entrance of Jesus upon the σάρξ was likewise κατὰ πνεῦμα.

[28] The question why Paul, after having up to v. 43 (incl.) constructed

each other, as the natural and the supernatural. This is expressed by the contrast ἐκ γῆς and ἐξ οὐρανοῦ. When it is said that the second man is from heaven, this has nothing to do with the original provenience of Christ from heaven; the ἐξ οὐρανοῦ does not imply a "coming" from heaven, no more than the ἐκ γῆς implies a coming of Adam from the earth at the first creation. To refer ἐξ οὐρανοῦ to the coming of Christ out of the state of preëxistence at his incarnation

his whole argument on the basis of a comparison between the body of sin and the body of the resurrection, substitutes from v. 44 on, for the body of sin, the body of creation, is both a difficult and interesting one. The answer cannot be found by ascribing to him the view that the creation-body and the body of sin are identical, in other words that the evil predicates of φθορά, ἀτιμία, ἀσθενεία enumerated in v. 42 belong to the body in virtue of creation. Paul teaches too plainly elsewhere that these things came into the world through sin. The proper solution seems to be to us the following: The Apostle was intent upon showing that in the plan of God from the outset provision was made for a higher kind of body than that of our present experience. From the abnormal body of sin no inference can be drawn as to the existence of another kind of body. The abnormal and the eschatological are not so logically correlated that the one can be postulated from the other. But the world of creation and the world of eschatology are thus correlated, the one points forward to the other; on the principle of typology the first Adam prefigures the second Adam, the psychical body, the pneumatic body (cf. Rom. v. 14). The statement of v. 44ᵉ is meant not as an assertion, but as an argument: if there exists the one kind of body, there exists the other kind also. This explains why the quotation from Gen. ii. 7, which relates only to the psychical state, can yet be treated by Paul as proving both, and as warranting the subjoined proposition: "The last Adam became a life-giving Spirit." The quotation proves this, because the psychical as such is typical of the pneumatic, the first creation of the second, the world that now is of the world to come. This disposes of the view that Paul meant to include v. 45ᵉ in the quotation, the latter being taken from Gen. i. 27 (man's creation in the image of God), which would then rest on the Philonic and older speculation of a twofold creation, first of the ideal, then of the empirical man. According to this speculation the ideal man is created first, the empirical man afterwards, as Gen. 1 comes before Gen. 2. Paul affirms the opposite: not the pneumatic is first, but the psychical is first. If there is reference to this Alexandrian philosophoumenon at all in v. 46, it is by way of pointed correction. Paul substitutes for the sequence of the idealistic philosophy, the sequence of historic unfolding: the categories of his thought are Jewish not Hellenic: he reasons in forms of time not of space.

would make Paul contradict himself, for it would reverse the order insisted upon in verse 46: not the pneumatic is first, but the psychical first.   Besides this, it would make the pneumatic the constitutive principle of the Person of Christ before the incarnation, of which there is no trace elsewhere in Paul. The phrase ἐξ οὐρανοῦ simply expresses that Christ after a supernatural fashion became " the second man " at the point marked by ἔπειτα.[29]   A " becoming " is affirmed of both Adams, the second as well as the first, for the ἐγένετο in verse 45 belongs to both clauses.[30]   How far in either case the subject of which this is affirmed existed before in a different condition is not reflected upon.[31]   The whole tenor of the discussion compels us to think of the resurrection as the moment at which τὸ πνευματικόν entered, the second man supernaturally appeared, in the form of πνεῦμα ζωοποιοῦν inaugurated the eschatological era.[32]   But besides identifying the eschatological and the pneumatic, our passage is peculiar in that it most closely identifies the Spirit with Christ. In the preceding passages the Spirit, who works and bears the future life was the Spirit of God.   Here it is not merely the Spirit of Christ, but the Spirit which Christ became.   And being thus closely and subjectively identified with the risen Christ the Spirit imparts to Christ the life-giving power which is peculiarly the Spirit's own: the second Adam became not

[29] Cf. for this use of ἐξ οὐρανοῦ 2 Cor. v. 2 " our habitation which is from heaven "; Mk. viii. 11, xi. 30; Jno. iii. 27, vi. 31; Apoc. xxi. 2.   The test of this interpretation of ἐξ οὐρανοῦ lies in the use of ἐπουράνιος in vss. 48, 49; this is applied to believers as well as to Christ and in the case of believers it cannot mean that they are at the time of writing " from heaven " or " in heaven ", cf. Lütgert, *Der Mensch aus dem Himmel*, in *Greifswalder Studien*, 1895, pp. 207-229.

[30] From this it follows that, if the ἐξ οὐρανοῦ of v. 47 were understood of the preëxistence, it would involve the Arian conception of a creation of Christ.

[31] The form of the quotation from Genesis made it easy for Paul thus to express himself, for according to it even of the first Adam it is said ἐγένετο εἰς ψυχὴν ζῶσαν " he was made *into* a living soul ", which in a certain sense presupposes (at least rhetorically) his previous existence.

[32] The Sept. expresses a similar thought in Is. ix. 6 where it renders אֲבִי עַד by πατὴρ τοῦ αἰῶνος μέλλοντος " father of the age to come ".

only πνεῦμα ζῶν but πνεῦμα ζωοποιοῦν. This is of great importance for determining the relation to eschatology of the Christ-worked life in believers, as we shall soon have occasion to show.

In a few other passages the resurrection of Christ is ascribed to the Spirit indirectly, being represented as an act of the δύναμις, the δόξα of God, both of which conceptions are regularly associated with the Spirit, cf. Rom. vi. 4; I Cor. vi. 14; 2 Cor. xiii. 4. In none of these, however, is any reference made to the permanent presence of the Spirit in Christ's life. But apart from the resurrection the δόξα is to Paul the specific form in which he conceives of the exalted state of Jesus, and this δόξα is so closely allied to the Spirit in Christ also, as to become almost a synonym for it. Thus, as God the Father is said to have raised Christ διὰ τῆς δόξης αὐτοῦ, believers are said to be transformed ἀπὸ δόξης εἰς δόξαν i. e. from the glory they behold in (or reflect from) Christ unto the glory they receive in themselves, 2 Cor. iii. 18.

We have found that the Spirit is both the instrumental cause of the resurrection-act and the permanent substratum of the resurrection-life. The question here arises: which of the two is the primary idea, either in order of thought or in point of chronological emergence. It might seem plausible to put the pneumatic derivation of the resurrection-act first, and to explain this feature from what the Old Testament teaches concerning the Spirit of God as the source of natural life in the world and in man, especially since in the allegory of Ezek. xxxvii. this had already been applied to the (metaphorical) resurrection of the nation of Israel. If the Spirit worked physical life in its present form, what was more reasonable than to assume that he would likewise be the author of the restoration of physical life in the resurrection? As a matter of fact, however, we find that the operation of the Spirit in connection with the natural world recedes into the background already in the intercanonical literature and remains so in the New Testament writings themselves. In reality Paul connects the Spirit with the resurrection not because he conceives of the future life in analogy with the present life, but from the very opposite reason, because he conceives of it as essentially distinct from the present life, as moving in a totally different element. It is more probable, therefore, that the thought of the resurrection-life as pneumatic in character is with him first in order, and that, in partial dependence on this at least, the idea emerges of the Spirit as the author of the act of the resurrection. For this there was given a solid Old Testament basis in trains of thought which had fully held their own, and even found richer development in the intermediate and in the early New Testament period. The transcendental, supernatural world is already to the Old Testament the specific domain of the Spirit. And, quite apart from references to the resurrection, this thought meets us again in Paul. The heavenly world is the pneumatic world, even irrespective of its eschatological complexion, 1 Cor. x. 3, 4; Eph. i. 3. From this the transition is not difficult to the idea that the eschatological state is preëminently a pneumatic state, since the highest form of life known, that of the world of heaven, must impart to it its specific character.

This will become clearer still, by inquiring in the next place to what extent the soteriological operations of the Spirit reveal eschatological affinity. Here a twofold perspective opens itself up to us. On the one hand in the forensic sphere all salvation is subsumed under the great rubric of justification. On the other hand in the pneumatic sphere the categories of regeneration and sanctification play an equally comprehensive part. The antithesis between the forensic and the pneumatic already indicates on which side the soteriological activity of the Spirit will chiefly lie and where we may expect traces, if such there be, of eschatological modes of approach to the subject. Still it would be rash simply to exclude on that account from our inquiry the topic of justification. Into the transaction of justification also the Spirit enters. In saying this we do not refer to the function of the Spirit in the production of faith on which as its subjective prerequisite the justifying act of God is suspended. Nor is it possible, contrary to Paul's plain and insistent declarations on this point, to assign the υἱοθεσία in part to the subjective sphere, making it consist in the impartation of the Spirit of sonship.[33]

[33] This Sokolowski attempts to vindicate as the true Pauline position,

Nor can the work of the Spirit in the subsequent production of
assurance come under consideration for our present purpose.
What we mean is something else than all this. The possession
of the Spirit is for Paul the natural correlate, the crown and
in so far the infallible exponent of the state of δικαιοσύνη.
This highly characteristic line of thought can perhaps most
clearly be traced in its application to Christ. For the same
reason that the resurrection of Jesus is in a very real sense
the justification of the Christ,[34] this can likewise be affirmed of
the resurrection-life which ever since that moment Christ lives.
The life and glory of the exalted Saviour are the product and
seal and exponent of his status of righteousness. Speaking
in our own terms, and yet faithfully rendering the Pauline
conception, we may say that in his resurrection-state Christ
is righteousness incarnate. Hence also justification is made
dependent on a faith terminating upon the living, glorified
Christ, for in this living, glorified state, his efficacious merit is
most concretely present to the believer's apprehension. Now
it must be remarked that the resurrection-state which is thus
exponential of righteousness is entirely based on the Spirit, cf.
1 Tim. iii. 16 ἐδικαιώθη ἐν πνεύματι. By becoming Pneuma
Christ has become the living witness of the eternal presence
of righteousness for us in the sight of God.[35] This will help
us to understand the association between the Spirit and righteousness where it appears in the case of believers. It

op. cit. pp. 67 ff. in opposition to Weiss and Pfleiderer, who both rightly
insist upon it, that the υἱοθεσία, like the δικαίωσις, is to Paul a strictly declara-
tive act.

[34] Rom. iv. 25 ἠγέρθη διὰ τὴν δικαίωσιν ἡμῶν probably refers tò our
representative justification in Christ as preceding his resurrection, just as
in the corresponding clause our παραπτώματα precede the παρεδόθη. According to 1 Cor. xv. 17, if Christ has not been raised, the faith of the
readers is vain, futile i. e. without effect of justification. Rom. viii. 34
teaches that the crowning reason, why, after God's justification of us,
no one can condemn, lies in Christ's resurrection. To ask in despair of
obtaining righteousness: "Who shall descend into the abyss?" is according to Rom. x. 7 tantamount to declaring the resurrection of Christ not
accomplished.

[35] Cf. for an admirable exposition of this whole train of thought:
Schäder, *Die Bedeutung des lebendigen Christus für die Rechtfertigung
nach Paulus*, 1893.

must here have the same significance, on the one hand that of a seal attesting justification as an accomplished fact, on the other hand that of the normal fruit of righteousness. And it is the former because it is the latter: the possession of the Spirit seals the actuality of righteousness, because in no other way than on the basis of righteousness could the Spirit have been bestowed. In this sense Paul says that the Pneuma is life διὰ δικαιοσύνην, Rom. viii. 10; and stakes the whole question as to the method by which the Galatians were justified on this, how the Spirit was supplied to them, Gal. iii. 5. The redemption from the curse of the law had the intent and effect of bringing to believers the promised Spirit, Gal. iii. 14. The status of sonship carries with it the mission of the Spirit into the heart, Gal. iv. 6. In Tit. iii. 5, 6 the gift of the Holy Spirit proves the connecting link between justification and renewal, being the effect of the former and the source of the latter. The πνεῦμα υἱοθεσίας in Rom. viii. 15 is a Spirit which results from (or goes with) adoption, not a Spirit which effects adoption. In 1 Cor. vi. 11 the washing, sanctifying and justifying of the Corinthians is attributed to the Spirit of God as well as to the name of the Lord Jesus Christ, and on the exegesis, which takes the ἁγιάσθητε in the sense of " ye were consecrated ", the whole transaction in its three stages belongs to the forensic sphere, and the Spirit receives a specific function within that sphere.[36]

It is plain, however, that all these statements with reference to the Spirit's presence in believers have for their background the presence of the Spirit in the same capacity as a seal and fruit of justification in the exalted Christ. And it is from this that they receive their eschatological coloring. For in Christ this Spirit which is the seal and fruit of righteousness is none other than the Spirit of the consummate life and the consummate glory, the circumambient element of the eschatological state in general. The conclusion, therefore, is fully warranted that the Spirit as a living attestation of the state of righteous-

[36] If ἁγιάσθητε be taken in its technical sense of " sanctification ", the two Datives ἐν ὀνόματι and ἐν πνεύματι will have to be chiastically distributed, the former going with " ye were justified ", the latter with " ye were washed ", " ye were sanctified ".

ness in the believer has this significance, because he is in principle the fountain of the blessedness of the world to come. And this is verified by observing how Paul combines with righteousness the peace and joy in the Holy Spirit, and finds in this Spirit-fed peace and joy the essence of the kingdom of God, Rom. xiv. 17; how the first-fruit of the Spirit looks forward to the eschatological υἱοθεσία Rom. viii. 23; how the καταλλαγή and the resulting justification (not first nor merely the subjective renewal) open up to the Christian a καινὴ κτίσις, that new world in which the old things are passed away and new things have come,[37] and which, as contradistinguished from the σάρξ, must be the κτίσις of the Pneuma. Finally, most instructive is here Gal. v. 5: πνεύματι ἐκ πίστεως ἐλπίδα δικαιοσύνης ἀπεκδεχόμεθα. Here the righteousness of the world to come which is to be bestowed in the last judgment is represented as a thing which the Christian still waits for.[38] This waiting, however, is determined by two coördinated factors: on the one hand it takes place ἐκ πίστεως, on the other hand πνεύματι,[39] and these two designate the subjective and the objective ground respectively on which the confident expectation is based. In the Spirit, not in the σάρξ, in faith, not in ἔργα νόμου, has the Christian the assurance that the full eschatological righteousness will become his. (Cf. also Tit. iii. 7.)

More specifically, however, the Spirit belongs to the other hemisphere of soteriology, that of the subjective renewal and the renewed state of man. It needs no pointing out how intimately this is associated with the Spirit. Πνεύματι περιπατεῖ is a comprehensive phrase for the God-pleasing walk of the Christian, Gal. v. 16; κατὰ πνεῦμα designates the standard of ethical normality, both as to being and striving, Rom. viii. 5.

---

[37] Thus γέγονεν καινά should be rendered, not: "they have become new".

[38] 'Ελπίς is here objective "the thing hoped for" and δικαιοσύνης is Gen. of apposition: "the hoped for thing consisting in righteousness."

[39] Πνεύματι and ἐκ πίστεως are not to be construed together, so as to make out the meaning "the Spirit received out of faith". Both go coordinately with the verb. Cf. for this passage the very lucid exposition of Zahn, in his *Commentary*, pp. 249 ff. He renders the verse as follows: "Wir erwarten im Geist im Folge Glaubens einen Hoffnungsgegenstand, welcher in Gerechtigkeit besteht."

The contrast between σάρξ and πνεῦμα is an ethical contrast, Gal. v. 17. Paul represents the Christian virtues and graces as fruits and gifts of the Spirit, Gal. v. 19 and Rom. xii. 8 ff. In particular love, which the Apostle regards as the essence of fulfilment of the law is derived from the Spirit, Rom. xv. 30; Col. i. 8. The whole range of sanctification belongs to the province of the Spirit, whence it is called ἁγιασμὸς πνεύματος, 2 Thess. ii. 13, and likewise, of course, the " renewal " at the beginning, Tit. iii. 5. But not only the specifically-ethical, also the more generally religious, graces and dispositions are the Spirit's work, such as faith,[40] 1 Cor. ii. 4, 5; 2 Cor. iii. 3 in connection with 1 Cor. iii. 5; 2 Cor. iv. 13; joy. Rom. xiv. 17; Gal. v. 22; 1 Thess. i. 6; peace Rom. viii. 6, xiv. 17, xv. 13; 1 Cor xiv. 33; Gal. v. 22; Eph. iv. 3; hope Rom. iv 5, xii. 12; Gal. v. 5; Eph. i. 18, iv. 4. Now the comprehensive conception under which Paul subsumes all these ethical and religious states, dispositions and activities is that of " life ". It is the " Spirit of life " which as a new principle and norm sets free of sin and determines the Christian, Rom. viii. 2. Whilst the letter kills, the Spirit gives life, 2 Cor. iii. 6, and that not merely in the forensic sense, but also in the ethico-religious sense (on account of verses 2, 3). Because believers live by the Spirit, they can be exhorted also to walk by the Spirit, Gal. v. 25. Life is to Paul by no means an exclusively physical conception,[41] as Rom. vii. 8-11; Eph. iv. 18 will show. The Apostle even approaches the conception that it springs from communion with God, Rom. viii. 7; Eph. iv. 18, and explicitly defines its goal as lying in God Rom. vi. 10, 11; Gal. ii. 19. We find then that on the one hand the renewal and the renewed state are derived from the Spirit, and that on the other hand they are reduced to terms of life. This certainly suggests the inference that the connecting link between the things enumerated and the Spirit lies in their being viewed as phenomena of life. The Spirit works all this, because he is

[40] So correctly Sokolowski pp. 71 ff. against Weiss and Pfleiderer; cf. also Titius, *Der Paulinismus unter dem Gesichtspunkt der Seligkeit*, 1900, p. 43, against Wendt.

[41] Against Kabisch, *Die Paulinische Eschatologie*, 1893. Kabisch is the Schweitzer of Paulinism.

the author of life. With this agrees the fact that in the passages cited above, where the ethical renewal of the Christian is attributed to the Spirit, Rom. viii. 2; 2 Cor. iii. 6; Gal. v. 25, the conception of " life " in each case accompanies the other two, being, as it were, the conception in which these meet and find their higher unity.

Our inquiry, therefore, resolves itself into this, whether when Paul calls the new state and walk of the believer life, a life by and in the Spirit, this has anything to do with or can receive any light from the eschatological aspect of the Spirit. It might be thought that the whole subsumption of the ethico-religious content of the Christian state under the category of the pneumatic, which is so characteristic of Paul, is nothing else but a simple working out of the prophetic teaching which, as we have seen above, derives from the Spirit the new heart, the new obedience, the state of acceptance with God. In that case the soteriological operation of the Spirit on its subjective side would not be in any way affected by his eschatological associations. Paul's movement of thought in conceiving of the Spirit as the new element of the Christian state would have been 'exclusively in the direction from the present to the future: because the Spirit is and does this now, he will also be operative after the same fashion in the future.[42] We do not mean to deny that this correctly reproduces a train of thought with which Paul was familiar. After once the Spirit was clearly apprehended as the substratum and element of the present Christian state it was inevitable that from this point of view the line of his characteristic activity should be prolonged into the future. Thus we find it in Rom. viii. 11. But this does not by any means exclude that alongside of this there may have been a perspective in the opposite direction, or that this may even represent the earlier and more fundamental mode of viewing the subject. Direct action and reflex action

[42] Thus Sokolowski thinks that the Pauline doctrine of the Spirit as the author of the resurrection arose, because to Paul the Spirit as the author of ethical processes on the one hand, and on the other hand the idea of the resurrection, stood equally in the foreground, " und das um so sicherer als sich seine " (d. h. des Geistes) " Fähigkeit physisches Leben zu wirken aus dem gegenwärtigen Dasein des Menschen ausweist ", p. 205.

here naturally go together as again Rom. viii. 11 strikingly shows.

Against exclusive insistence upon the former construction we would urge the following. First 2 Cor. v. 5 is one of the three directly eschatological passages where, as we have seen, the present Spirit is an anticipation of the future Spirit. Secondly, the close association of the ethico-religious function of the Spirit with life in itself creates a presumption in favor of the view that the future here in part at least colors the present. For "life" is undoubtedly with Paul, and before Paul with Jesus, especially in the Synoptical teaching, and idea that is in the first instance eschatologically conceived and thence carried back into the present. It is the ζωὴ αἰώνιος of the world to come. In the third place Paul speaks of the present pneumatic state in terms which are either directly borrowed from the eschatological vocabulary, or strongly reminiscent of it. The καινὴ κτίσις of 2 Cor. v. 17; Gal. vi. 15 is such a term, and also the καινότης πνεύματος of Rom. vii. 6 and the καινὴ διαθήκη πνεύματος of 2 Cor. iii. 6, may here be remembered. Fourthly, even in the Old Testament where the ethical operation of the Spirit is mentioned, this is done in the form of a promise, so that from the outset it appears in an eschatological environment.[43] Fifthly, here also, as before, we must take into account the Christological background of the soteriological process. The pneumatic life of the Christian is a product and a reflex of the pneumatic life of the Christ. It is a life ἐν πνεύματι to the same extent as it is a life ἐν Χριστῷ[44] It is important sharply to define the peculiarity

[43] In this connection it should be noted that the prophets, while ascribing to the Spirit the task of ethico-religious renewal, do not speak of the state thus produced in terms of life. The combination between the two ideas Paul did not borrow from the prophets.

[44] It is not essential to the above position to assert that the two formulas are entirely synonymous and coëxtensive, or that the formula ἐν Χριστῷ is formed after the analogy of ἐν πνεύματι, as Deissman, *Die Neutestamentliche Formel in Christo-Jesu*, 1892, thinks. Walter, *Der religiöse Gehalt des Galaterbriefs*, 1904, pp. 122-144, has, in our opinion, convincingly shown that the usage of ἐν Χριστῷ considerably overlaps the limits within which ἐν πνεύματι would be applicable. It has a large forensic connota-

on this point of the Pauline doctrine on the relation between
the Spirit bestowed by Christ and the Saviour's own glorified
life, and the extent to which it marks a development beyond
the pre-Pauline teaching.   In the Petrine speeches recorded
in the earlier chapters of Acts the Spirit indeed appears as a
gift of the glorified Christ.   It was given to Jesus in fulfilment
of the promise of the Father and having received the promised
Spirit he immediately poured it forth upon the disciples, Acts
ii. 33.   But according to Paul Jesus at the resurrection receives
the Spirit not merely as an objective gift, something that he
can dispense; the Spirit becomes his own subjective possession,
the Spirit dwelling in him, the source of his own glorified life,
so that when he communicates the Spirit he communicates of
his own, whence also the possession of the Spirit works in the
believer a mystical, vital union with Christ.   While Peter's
teaching leaves full room for this whole rich Pauline development, it does not yet contain this development.[45]   Paul emphasizes repeatedly that the Spirit who works life in believers
is the identical Spirit who wrought and still is life for the exalted Lord, Rom. viii. 9, 11; 2 Cor. xiii. 4.   When Jesus was
raised from the dead, he did become Pneuma, but this Pneuma
was more than ζῶν he was ζωοποιοῦν, communicating himself

tion. But where ἐν Χριστῷ relates to the mystical sphere, the two formulas
are practically interchangeable.

[45] A point of contact for it has been found in Acts iv. 2. When it is
said that the Apostles "proclaimed in Jesus the resurrection from the
dead", this might, so far as the words are concerned, have the pregnant
Pauline meaning, to the effect that the general resurrection (of the members of the kingdom) was potentially given in Jesus' resurrection. The
opposite extreme is to understand the Apostolic preaching as a simple
affirmation of the possibility of the resurrection as illustrated in the
concrete case of Jesus, with an anti-Sadducaeic point. But there can be
no doubt that from the beginning the resurrection of Jesus was apprehended in its eschatological as well as in its Christological importance.
The best view is to find in the words the affirmation by the Apostles that
the resurrection of Jesus guaranteed the resurrection of believers in
general, without reflection upon the vital connection between the two. The
same idea of the typical significance of the resurrection of Jesus finds
expression in the phrases ἀρχηγὸς ζωῆς iii. 15 and ἀρχηγὸς καὶ σωτήρ in
v. 31, if at least ἀρχηγός be given the pregnant sense of one who first
experiences in himself what he effects for others.

to others, 1 Cor. xv. 45. This only will explain why Paul cannot merely say Christ *has* the Spirit but can say: ὁ δὲ Κύριος τὸ πνεῦμά ἐστιν and can speak of Christ as Κύριος πνεύματος , 2 Cor. iii. 17, 18.[46] The gospel is the gospel of the glory of Christ, 2 Cor. iv. 5. And in the light of all this it must be further interpreted when Paul speaks of the process of renewal and sanctification in terms which are not merely derived from the death and resurrection of Christ, for this might be a purely figurative usage, but in terms which posit a real, vital connection between the two, so that what takes place in the believer is an actual self-reproduction of what was transacted in Christ. To be joined with the Lord is to be one Spirit with him, 1 Cor. vi. 17. Now all this tends to confirm the conclusion already drawn from the four preceding considerations. If the pneumatic life of the Christian bears this relation to the pneumatic life of the exalted Lord, then it must to some extent partake of the eschatological character of the latter.[47]

It will perhaps repay us to pursue this thought somewhat further from a different angle. Especially in the later epis-

---

[46] In ἀπὸ Κυρίου πνεύματος the preposition governs Κυρίου and πνεύματος is Genit. qualitatis. It means "from the Lord of the Spirit" not "from the Spirit of the Lord". Gloël, p. 123: "Geistes Herr ist Christus sofern er als Herr zu einem Stand erhoben ist im welchem Geist den Charakter seines Wesens ausmacht." An interesting parallel to 1 Cor. xv. 45 and 2 Cor. iii. 17 is Is. xxviii. 5, 6 "Jehovah will become a Spirit of justice." The parallel shows how close the identification between the Spirit and Christ is; it is in some respects like unto that between Jehovah and the Spirit in the Old Testament. Parallel with the union between the Spirit and Christ's human nature runs that of the believer and the Spirit. Hence the peculiar phraseology τὸ Πνεῦμά μου, τὸ Πνεῦμά σου.

[47] There is only one qualification to be added to the above statement. When Paul conceives the present life of the Christian as semi-eschatological, this does not extend to the body. Rom. viii. 18; 2 Cor. iii, 18, iv. 17, 18, v. 3, 4; Col. iii. 3 do not teach that a change in the body is now taking place, or a new pneumatic body now being formed underneath the sarkic body. Cf. Titius, *Der Paulinismus*, pp. 58 ff., as against Schmiedel. Reitzenstein, *Die Hellenistischen Mysterienreligionen* pp. 175 ff. would even find in ἐπενδύσασθαι of 2 Cor. v. 2, 4 the idea that, after divestment of the earthly body, Paul will not be found naked but in possession of an interior body.

tles, but also to some extent already in the earlier ones, the
Christian state is represented as a belonging to and participation in the sphere of heaven and the heavenly order of
things. The principle is, of course, implied in everything
taught about communion with the heavenly Christ. But in the
representation we have now in mind it assumes a broader, less
personal, so to speak, more local form of expression. There
are two worlds the lower and the higher, and it is affirmed
of the believer that he belongs to the latter and no longer to
the former temporal, the latter eternal, 2 Cor. iv. 18. The
reality. Each has its own σχῆμα, but the σχῆμα after which
the Christian patterns himself is that of the other world not
that of this world, Rom. xii. 2. There is a system of things
that are seen, and a system of things that are not seen,
the former temporal, the latter eternal, 2 Cor. iv. 18. The
world has been crucified to the Christian and he unto the world,
Gal. vi. 15. There is a sphere of the heavenly, far above
all rule and authority and power and dominion, Eph. i. 20,
21. Believers have been made to sit in heavenly places, Eph.
ii. 6. The Christian has his πολιτεία in heaven, not upon
earth and therefore should not mind earthly things, Phil. iii.
19, 20. Being raised with Christ he must seek and set his
mind upon the things that are above, not upon the things that
are upon the earth, Col. iii. 1. 2. Sometimes this higher
heavenly order of things is centered in the risen Christ, but it
is also identified with the realm of the Spirit. The πνευματικόν
is the heavenly. God has blessed us ἐν πάσῃ εὐλογίᾳ πνευμ-
ατικῇ ἐν τοῖς ἐπουρανίοις, Eph. i. 3. The πνευματικός is also the
ἐπουράνιος, 1 Cor. xv. 40, 50, (Cf. 1 Cor. x. 3) When
speaking of "the things not seen" and "eternal", Paul
undoubtedly has in mind the Pneuma as the category to which
these belong, 2 Cor. iv. 18 (cf. the ἀνακαινοῦται in verse 16
and the αἰώνιον βάρος δόξης in verse 17, the ἐπίγειος in
v. 1 and the ἀρραβὼν τοῦ πνεύματος in verse 5.) The same
applies to the distinction between the spheres of faith and
sight in 2 Cor. v. 7. And somewhat of the contrast between the
earthly and the heavenly enters into the great Pauline antithesis
of σάρξ and πνεῦμα, a point to which we shall presently revert.
What interests us here is that this whole opposition between a

heavenly and an earthly order of things and the anchoring of the Christian life in the former is a direct offshoot of the eschatological distinction between two ages. The eschatological point of view is, of course, originally historical and dramatic; a new world can come only with the new age and therefore lies at first in the future. But the coming age has begun to be present with the death and resurrection of Christ. From this it follows that of the coming world likewise a present existence can be affirmed. Here then the scheme of two successive worlds makes place for the scheme of two coexisting worlds. Still further it must be remembered that Christ has through his resurrection carried the center of this new world into heaven where he reigns and whence he extends its influence and boundaries. The two coexisting worlds therefore broadly coincide with the spheres of heaven and earth. If now the higher, heavenly world to which the Christian belongs is that of the Spirit, it must always be remembered that it has become this in virtue of the progress of the eschatological drama and will become so more in the same degree that this drama hastens on to its final dénouement. The pneumatic life of the believer, while centered in heaven, loses none of its eschatological setting. Back of the static continues to lie the dramatic; the distinction between the earthly and the heavenly is not cosmologically but eschatologically conceived. By the pneumatic as a synonym of the heavenly Paul does not mean heaven or the spiritual in the abstract, but heaven and the spiritual as they have become in result of the process of redemption. Τὸ πνευματικόν is " second " (εἶτα) and Christ as Πνεῦμα ζωοποιοῦν " became " (ἐγένετο).[48] This will also explain why the new contrast between two simultaneous worlds does not supersede the eschatological perspective for the future. The two spheres still are in conflict, the two ages still labor to bring forth their respective worlds, a crisis is still outstanding. Cf. Eph. i. 14, i. 21, ii. 7, 12, iv. 4, 30, v. 6; Col. iii. 4, vi. 24; Phil. i. 6, ii. 16, iii. 20. Precisely here lies the point in which the Pauline doctrine of the Spirit and the

[48] Here the difference between Philo and Paul is very striking, for according to Philo Adam already possessed the Pneuma-power, Opif. 144 quoted by Volz, p. 106.

Hellenic or Hellenistic conception of the pneuma are sharply differentiated, striking though their similarity in some other respects may be. The Greek philosophical pneuma, whether in its dualistic Platonic or neo-Platonic form, or in its hylozoistic Stoic form, lacks every historic significance, it is, even where it appears in contrast to an opposing element, the result of a bisection of nature, not the product of a supernatural divine activity. With Paul, both in regard to the σάρξ and the πνεῦμα, the historical factor remains the controlling one. If the sphere of the σάρξ is evil, this is not due to its natural constitution, because it is material or sensual, but because it has historically become evil through the entrance of sin.[49] And when Paul views the pneumatic world as the consummated world, this also is not due simply to its natural constitution as the ideal nonsensual world, but because through the Messiah it has become the finished product of God's designs for man.[50]

Even into the revealing work of the Spirit the eschatological associations enter. From the nature of the case this has its primary reference to the present life, just as the glossolalia and the cognate phenomena are rather premonitions of the world to come than constituent elements of that world itself, sub-eschatological rather than semi-eschatological manifestations.[51] Revelation, however, while providing for a present need, may have for its object the realities of the future life, and thus the thought emerges that the Spirit, who is so closely identified with the future life in general, when thus disclosing the things to come, discloses what in a very special sense is his own. With this thought we actually meet in 1 Cor. ii. The wisdom which Paul speaks among the τέλειοι, verse 6, but which he could not speak among the Corinthians (iii. 1 πνευματικοί = τέλειοι), a wisdom therefore to be distinguished from his ordinary preaching, God's wisdom ἐν μυστηρίῳ (ii. 7) is according to verse 10 derived from the Spirit. The point of

---

[49] Notice the studied avoidance of the term σαρκικός in the context of 1 Cor. xv. 44 ff., where Paul wishes to contrast the pneumatic with the natural-as-such, irrespective of its sinful quality.

[50] Cf. Titius, *Der Paulinismus*, pp. 242-250.

[51] Cf. 1 Cor. xiv. 22, xiii. 10-13; but, on the other hand xiii. 1 "the tongues of angels".

view from which Paul makes this last affirmation is partly theological: the Spirit is the appropriate organ for revealing such things, because he stands in as intimate a relation to God as the spirit of a man to man. He can search all things, even those deep things of God with which the higher σοφία deals, for he is the *Spirit of God*. Intertwined with this, however, appears the other consideration, that the " wisdom " has to do with eschatological facts and that for this reason it belongs to the particular province of the Spirit to reveal it. It relates to something that has been hidden, which God foreordained before the aeons, and which concerned the δόξα of believers, verse 7. More particularly it is defined as that " which eye saw not and ear heard not, and which entered not into the heart of man, whatsoever things God prepared for them that love him ".[52] It comprises " the things that were freely given to us of God ", verse 12. In contrast to it stands a wisdom τοῦ αἰῶνος τούτου " of this age " and of " the ἄρχοντες of this age " who are already coming to nought, verse 6. Those who belong to " this age " can not know it, verse 8. Obviously this implies that believers can know it because they belong to " the age to come."[53] Because they have part in the future world, the mysteries of the future world are communicable to them. Now, it should be noticed that Paul expresses the same idea also in the other form that the Christian is, or may be πνευματικός, whereas the man who belongs to the present age is ψυχικός, ii. 14-16, iii. 1. It is as πνευματικός that he has access to these transcendental things from which the ψυχικός is by his very constitution excluded. To belong to the world to come and to be πνευματικός are used as interchangeable conceptions. Not merely, therefore, because the Christian is the recipient of revelation, but for the further and more speci-

---

[52] According to Origen *Comm. ad Matth.* xxvii. 9 these words stood in *the Secreta Eliae Prophetae* which tends to confirm their eschatological reference (cf. Schürer, *Gesch. des. Jüd. Volk.* III, pp. 361 ff.). Dibelius, *Die Geisterwelt im Glauben des Paulus,* 1909, p. 91 note 1.

[53] In the reading ἡμῖν γάρ (v. 10) the γάρ is highly significant, because it attaches itself to the intermediate (unexpressed) thought: " We do not share in the ignorance of the αἰὼν οὗτος "—" for *to us* God has revealed them through his Spirit."

fic reason, that he already partakes of that which is the distinctive quality of the future life, can he be initiated into the mysteries of the latter. The spirit is the source of the eschatological μυστήριον both in the sphere of being and in the sphere of revelation. Hence also in verse 11 Paul draws a formal distinction between the πνεῦμα of the κόσμος and the πνεῦμα τὸ ἐκ τοῦ θεοῦ which once more shows that the Spirit is considered not exclusively as a *principium revelations,* but as the determining principle of an order of things, and *therefore* as the natural organ for disclosing its content.[54] The passage also furnishes a parallel to the eschatological interpretation of the contrast between ψυχικός and πνευματικός met with in 1 Cor. xv. 44 ff. Very sharply Paul distinguishes in iii. 1-4 not merely between πνευματικός and σάρκινος (verse 1 ; in verse 3 σαρκικός) or between κατὰ ἄνθρωπον περιπατεῖν and its opposite, (verse 3) but also between the mere ἄνθρωπον εἶναι and the being something more than a mere man (verse 4 οὐκ ἄνθρωποί ἐστε;). It goes without saying that a rhetorical form of statement like the last-mentioned ought not to be pressed, as if Paul meant to represent the Christian pneumatic state as something super-human. What he means is evidently that the Corinthians had behaved as ordinary men, who were no more than what man is by nature. Still the paradoxical form in which the thought finds expression bears strong witness to the fact that Paul looked upon the Christian state as something belonging to a totally different order of affairs from the state of nature, and that the eschatological contrast was to him the only category which could adequately convey this difference.[55]

[54] Notice how in the context ὁ κόσμος οὗτος and ὁ αἰὼν οὗτος are used promiscuously, 1 Cor. i. 20, ii. 6, 12, iii. 18, 19.

[55] Reitzenstein, *Die Hellenistischen Mysterienreligionen,* 1910, proposes an interpretation of the antithesis ψυχικός—πνευματικός. which would detach it altogether from its eschatological background, and in the place of this make it a form of expression of the essentially Hellenistic and Gnostic contrast between the supernatural world of the spiritual and the natural world of sense. According to him the technical sense of ψυχικός arose from the belief that in the mysteries through regeneration a new ego is created which traverses the heavens and attains to the vision of God. This new ego is distinct from and replaces the old self =ψυχή, because it is deified. Holy Spirit has entered into such an one, his own person he

The passage just examined suggests the query to what extent, if to any, the Holy Spirit is by Paul placed in contrast to Satan and evil spirits in general. Inasmuch as evil spirit-powers undoubtedly play a rôle in connection with the present aeon and their conquest is plainly a considerable part of its passing away, every pointed opposition of the Spirit to such powers

has left behind. In the ecstatic state also the God who enters, *mentem priorem expulit, atque hominem toto sibi cedere jussit pectore* (quoted from Lucanus). Here $ψυχή =$ self and $πνεῦμα$ are mutually exclusive (pp. 44-46). What the pneuma produces is a " Gottwesen " (p. 55), the process is an $ἀποθέωσις$, and in this sense Reitzenstein interprets the Pauline terms $δοξάζειν$ and $μεταμορφοῦν$ (p. 168.)   The $πνευματικός$ is "überhaupt nicht mehr Mensch " (p. 168). Pfleiderer's quotation from Rohde's *Psyche*, in *Urchristenthum*[2] *I*, p. 266, also suggests the same solution. Reitzenstein is well aware that such ideas must have stood in flagrant contradiction to Paul's fundamental type of thought, because, as he himself admits, the magical transformation of a sinful man into a " Gottwesen " runs contrary to the profound moral earnestness of the Jewish religion (p. 56.) He further admits that Paul has not been able to surmount this contradiction (ib.). The only thing that might commend this hypothesis it that it seems to offer a plausible explanation of the technical use of $ψυχικός$. But even if this could not be explained in any other way, it would not be permissible on that account to entertain a solution so flagrantly at variance with Paul's fundamental religious convictions. As to the passages themselves which Reitzenstein discusses at great length (*Paulus als Pneumatiker* pp. 160-204), there is only one expression that seems to favor his proposal, viz. the depreciatory characterization of the Corinthians as $ἄνθρωποι$, 1 Cor. iii. 4. But, as has already been said, it would be absurd to press this to the extent of finding in it the deification of the Christian and the denial of his true humanity. Nor can the fact that in contrast to $ψυχικός$ $ἄνθρωπος$ Paul puts the simple $πνευματικός$ (without $ἄνθρωπος$) in ii. 15 be appealed to in proof of such a view, for in iii. 1, 3 both $σαρκίνοις$ and $πνευματικοῖς$ occur without the noun. Reitzenstein also argues from the phrase $τὰ τοῦ πνεύματος τοῦ θεοῦ$ in ii. 14, because the addition of $τοῦ θεοῦ$ is in his view intelligible only on the supposition that "previously to the miraculous transmutation of being man and God belong to two different worlds". But the thought is all the time that the wisdom of man is a wisdom of the $κόσμος$ and of a definite $αἰών$ of the $κόσμος$, so that its counterpart, the wisdom of God will also have its own domain in a definite sphere and period. It can be called the wisdom of God, because God is supreme in that sphere and age. What Paul, therefore, means is not that man must become God, but that he must be translated from the $κόσμος$ into the world of God. The true contrast to " ye are men " in iii. 4 is not " ye are divine " but " ye

would carry with it more or less of an eschatological atmosphere.[56] As a matter of fact, however, not much material of

are of God and of Christ ", v. 22, and the same is implied by way of contrast in the clauses " I am of Paul ", " I am of Apollos " iii. 4. The absurdity of this nomenclature does not lie in the fact that they act like men while being divine, but is that they act as belonging to men, while being the property of God. And, what decides everything, in 1 Cor. xv. 45, 47 the pneumatic Christ is distinctly called " man ". Reitzenstein gets around this only by altering the text. He proposes (p. 172) to read in v. 45 ἐγένετο ὁ ἄνθρωπος (instead of ἐγένετο ὁ πρῶτος ἄνθρωπος ᾿Αδαμ), which not only eliminates, through the omission of πρῶτος, the implication that there is a *second man*, but also imparts the idea that the second Adam is *not man*, because the first is called " the man " specifically. It might, of course, be said, that the true manhood of Christ even so is presupposed in his being called ὁ δεύτερος ἄνθρωπος in v. 47, but Reitzenstein interprets this on the basis of a belief on Paul's part in a God named ᾿Ανθρωπος (with a capital), which God is identified with Christ, so as to warrant the conclusion, that the latter is πνεῦμα ζωοποιόν (p. 173.) This change of the text is absolutely uncalled for, and the introduction of a God ᾿Ανθρωπος entirely foreign to the Apostle's trend of thought, which is throughout governed by the principle of the true unity and parallelism between Christ's human nature and ours as appears with sufficient clearness from v. 21: " For since δι' ἀνθρώπου came death, δι' ἀνθρώπου came also the resurrection of the dead." The " mere man " who is transcended by the " deified man " Reitzenstein also would find in 2 Cor. xii. 4: " which it is not lawful for a man (i. e. 'a mere man') to utter." This may be answered by pointing to v. 2 where the recipient of the revelation described, i. e. a highly pneumatic subject, is spoken of as " a man in Christ ". Reitzenstein, to be sure thinks he can escape the force of this by taking " a man in Christ " as one idea = a pneumatic person. Still even so he remains to Paul a man, and besides in v. 3 we have the simple " such a man " (without ἐν Χριστῷ). The whole explanation of ψυχικός from the ecstatic state breaks down, because in ecstasy, as defined by Philo and others, the ψυχή of man simply vacates and, far from forming a new divine subject, the man becomes a receptacle for the divine Pneuma. The man disappears and God takes his place: the technical phrase is κατέχεσθαι ἐκ θεοῦ. The contrast between a " psychical " and a " pneumatic " man cannot have arisen through reflection upon this. As to the impossibility of πνευματικός meaning in contrast to ψυχικός " one who has not only a ψυχή but also the Πνεῦμα," to which Reitzenstein appeals in support of his view, we may refer to Zielinski in *Theol. Literaturz.* 1911, no. 24, col. 740, who shows that the contrast between *proletarius* and *assiduus* is of precisely the same nature, the former being one who has only children, the latter one who has landed property, but is not necessarily childless.

[56] Cf. the Synoptical statement, Mt. xii. 28 = Lk. xi. 20 (where, however, ἐν δακτύλῳ θεοῦ takes the place of the ἐν πνεύματι θεοῦin Mt.).

this nature can be gleaned from the Pauline epistles. As we have seen in 1 Cor. ii. 12 the kosmos has its own spirit which governs the psychical man. At the same time the kosmos has its own rulers in the supernatural sphere, for of such the ἄρχοντες τοῦ αἰῶνος τούτου in verse 6 will probably have to be understood. It is not clear whether in verse 12 the conception of "*receiving*" the spirit of the kosmos points to a transcendental influence brought to bear upon men from the outside. If so, it will be natural to connect this πνεῦμα τοῦ κόσμου with the ἄρχοντες τοῦ αἰῶνος τούτου . It must also be remembered that Satan is called in 2 Cor. iv. 4 ὁ θεὸς τοῦ αἰῶνος τούτου , and the very point of this bold comparison seems to lie in this that, as the true God by his Spirit illumines the minds of believers enabling them to behold the glory of Christ in the gospel, so the false God of the present age, has a counter-spirit at work (or is a counter-spirit) which blinds the minds of the unbelieving that the light of the gospel of the glory of Christ should not dawn upon them. Here both the conception of δόξα as the content of the gospel and the parallelism between the first and the second creation in verse 6 impart an unmistakable eschatological flavor to the comparison. Where the thought of the wisdom-passage in 1 Cor. ii. recurs later in Col. ii. 2 ff. with many striking reminiscences even as to the form, the contrast becomes one purely between Christ and the spirits, and the conception of the πνεῦμα τοῦ κόσμου in its opposition to the πνεῦμα τὸ ἐκ τοῦ θεοῦ does not reappear. This suggests that the relative absence of the antithesis between the Holy Spirit and the evil spirits is largely due to the fact that, wherever such comparisons occur with Paul, Christ himself is personally opposed to the Satanic power and the Spirit not explicitly mentioned.[57] In Eph. ii. 2 on the other hand we read again, as in 1 Cor. ii. 12, of a "pneuma that now works in the sons of disobedience", which pneuma is moreover distinctly associated with the aeon of this present kosmos, so that the corresponding conception

---

[57] Cf. Col. i. 11, where the ἐξουσία τοῦ σκότους is contrasted with the βασιλεία τοῦ υἱοῦ and only the characterization of the inheritance of the saints as a κλῆρος ἐν τῷ φωτί reminds of the domain of the Spirit. Cf. further ii. 9, 15.

of a Spirit belonging to the age to come inevitably obtrudes itself, a point further favored by the fact that the formula elsewhere characteristic of conformity to the Holy Spirit as an ethical power here occurs of conformity to the opposite principle, περιπατεῖν κατὰ τὸν αἰῶνα τοῦ κόσμου τούτου, κατὰ τὸν ἄρχοντα τῆς ἐξουσίας τοῦ ἀέρος. Also the ἐνεργεῖν ascribed to the evil spirit reminds of the energizing of the Holy Spirit, cf. 1 Cor. xii. 11; Eph. iii. 20. Finally the κοσμοκράτορες τοῦ σκότους τούτου, τὰ πνευματικὰ τῆς πονηρίας ἐν τοῖς ἐπουρανίοις of Eph. vi. 12 may be mentioned here, although the implied contrast to the Spirit of God is not so clearly present.

Quite a large sphere would have to be annexed to this rubric, if it could be proven on the one hand that the στοιχεῖα τοῦ κόσμου appearing in Galatians and Colossians are meant by Paul as world-spirits or spirits of the elements, and on the other hand that Paul connects the σάρξ directly with the rule of evil spirits. In the case of the στοιχεῖα the opposition to the Holy Spirit would be of an implied nature, rather than explicit: still Gal. iii. 3 compared with iii. 6 might be quoted in support of this. In Colossians it is Christ, not the Spirit who forms the contrast to the στοιχεῖα, ii. 8, 20.[58] In regard to the σάρξ the correlation with the Pneuma is undisputed, but here no proof can be adduced of any constant association in the mind of Paul between it and the world of evil spirits. This could be done only by connecting the σάρξ with the στοιχεῖα, a connection in no wise indicated by any Pauline passage.[59]

[58] For the modern discussion on the στοιχεῖα cf. Hilgenfeld, Der Galaterbrief, 1852, pp. 66 ff., and ZWTh., 1858, pp. 99 ff.; 1860, pp. 208 ff.; 1866, pp. 314 ff.; Schaubach, Commentatio qua exponitur quid στοιχεῖα τοῦ κόσμου in N.T. sibi velint, 1862; Schneckenburger, Theol. Jahrb. 1848, pp. 445 ff.; Klöpper, Der Brief an die Kolosser, 1882, pp. 361 ff., Blom, Theol. Tydschr., 1883, pp. 4 ff.; Spitta, Der zweite Brief des Petrus, 1885; Everling, Die Paulinische Angelologie und Dämonologie, 1888, pp. 65 ff.; Diels, Elementum, 1899; Deissman's art. Elements in Enc. Bib.; Dibelius, Die Geisterwelt im Glauben des Paulus, 1909, pp. 78 ff., 136 ff., 227 ff.

[59] Gal. iii. 3 stands too far removed from iv. 3, 9 to come under consideration here, and besides too plainly refers to "works of the law", as the concrete form of the σάρξ. Brückner, Die Entstehung der Paulinischen

The above discussion, aside from its inherent interest has a bearing on certain important Biblico-theological problems. This we briefly indicate in conclusion.

In the first place the eschatological conception of the Spirit and his work is perhaps adapted to throw light upon what is most striking and characteristic in Paul's entire treatment of the subject of the Spirit. This consists in the thoroughness with which the pneumatic factor is equally distributed over the entire range of the Christian life, so that from the subjective side the Christian and the pneumatic become interchangeable, and especially in the emphasis with which the center of the Spirit's operation is placed in the ethico-religious sphere. Wth such thoroughness and emphasis this had not been done before Paul. Gunkel[60] has no doubt exaggerated

Christologie, 1903, pp. 210 ff. attempts to establish a connection between demoniacal powers and the σάρξ as the principle of sin. He is not, however, able to quote anything in support of this except 2 Cor. xi. 3, which proves nothing, and the general observation that the ματαιότης and φθορά to which the creation is subject have a demoniacal background, which does not appear either in Rom. viii. 20, 21 or anywhere else. Dibelius, who carefully traces all the demonological references and allusions in Paul, and even recognizes in Ἁμαρτία and Θάνατος personal spirits, is entirely silent about the σάρξ .

[60] *Die Wirkungen des Heiligen Geistes nach der populären Anschauung der apostolischen Zeit und nach der Lehre des Apostels Paulus,* 1888, 2d ed. 1899. Sokolowski, p. 199 is more fair in the estimate placed upon the Old Testament statements in regard to the ethical functions of the Spirit; as to the early apostolic teaching he throws out this caution that much may have existed in the minds of the first Christians, of which no record is made in Acts, and so with reference to Jesus. Still, where the sources do not speak, he deems it scientifically more correct " vor der Hand " to deny to Jesus and the early church the specific Pauline conceptions than the reverse, p. 196. Volz, pp. 194 ff. thinks that the contrast as usually drawn between Synoptics-Acts and Paul is wrong, that there should be substituted for it the contrast between Matthew and Mark on the one hand and Luke and Paul on the other hand, that is, the contrast between Palestinian Christianity and Pauline-Hellenic world-Christianity. But why not say that it is simply a contrast between the records of the earlier and the records of later history, so that the prominence of the Spirit in the documents reflects the lesser or greater prominence of the Spirit in the development of events? That Luke in the Gospel makes more of the Spirit than Matthew is contraindicated by his substituting xi. 20 ἐν δακτύλῳ for ἐν πνεύματι Mt. xii. 28.

the originality of Paul in this respect and underestimated the
preparation made for this development by the Old Testament
prophetic and earlier New Testament teaching.   Still a simple
comparison between the Petrine speeches in Acts and the Pauline statements abundantly shows, that Paul was the first to ascribe to the Spirit that dominating place and that pervasive uniform activity, which secure to him alongside of the Father and
the Son a necessary relation to the Christian state at every
point.   The question arises whether we can trace in Paul's
teaching the roots out of which this conception of the Spirit
grew, or at least the other elements in his thought to which it
sustained from its very birth a relation of interdependence and
mutual adjustment.   Probably more than one factor will here
have to be taken into account.   The theocentric bent of Paul's
mind makes for the conclusion that in the Christian life all
must be from God and for God, and the Spirit of God would
be the natural agent for securing this.   The impotence of sinful human nature for good, one of the Apostle's profoundest
convictions, would likewise postulate the operation of the
Spirit along the whole range of ethical movement and activity.
The marvellous efflorescence of a new ethical life among the
early Christians in its contrast with pagan immorality, and
its impulsiveness and spontaneity as compared with Jewish
formalism, would of themselves point to a miraculous, supernatural source, which could be none other than the Spirit of
God. Still further, the fact that to Paul the Spirit is preëminently the Spirit of Christ and therefore as thoroughly equable
and ethical in his activity as the mind of Jesus himself, will
have to be remembered here.   But, alongside of all these motives, there worked probably as the first and most influential
cause the idea that it is the Spirit of God who gives form and
character to the eschatological life in the broadest and most
pervasive sense, that the coming age is the age of the Spirit
par excellence, so that all that enters into it, forms part of it,
or takes place in it, must necessarily be baptized into the
Pneuma as into an omnipresent element and thus itself become
" spiritual " in its mode of existence and quality.   This will
explain not only the uniform and equable infusion of the Spirit
into the Christian life at every point; it also accounts for the

strong emphasis thrown upon the ethico-religious life as within the larger sphere the most characteristic of all the Spirit's products. For if the Spirit be the Spirit of the αἰὼν μέλλων, then his most distinctive task must lie where the coming aeon is most sharply differentiated in principle from the present age. And this, as all the Pauline references to the two aeons go to prove, is the ethical quality of both. The αἰὼν ἐνεστώς is before all other things an αἰὼν πονηρός, Gal. i. 4. One to whom this ethical contrast stood in the foreground, and who was at the same time accustomed to view the future aeon as the world of the Spirit, would of necessity be thereby led to place the ethico-religious transformation at the center of the Spirit's activity. He would interpret not only the whole Christian life in terms of the Spirit, but would also regard the newness of the moral and religious life as a fruit of the Spirit in its highest potency.[61]

Our second inference concerns the Apostle's Christology. A widely current modern construction of the Pauline doctrine

[61] The question may properly be raised at this point whether Paul's characteristic conception of the σάρξ does not likewise have its eschatological antecedents. It is so antithetically determined by its correlative, the Pneuma, that a certain illumination of the one must more or less affect the coloring of the other. To discuss the question here would lead us too far afield. We confine ourselves to the following. While the σάρξ chiefly appears as a power or principle in the subjective experience of man, yet this is by no means the only aspect under which Paul regards it. It is an organism, an order of things beyond the individual man, even beyond human nature. It is something that is not inherently evil, the evil predicates are joined to it by means of a synthetic judgment. Still further it has its affiliations and ramifications in the external, physical, natural (as opposed to supernatural) constitution of things. Now if σάρξ was originally the characteristic designation of the first world-order, as Pneuma is that of the second, all these features could be easily accounted for without having recourse to Hellenistic-dualistic explanations. From its association with the entire present aeon, the σάρξ could derive its pervasive, comprehensive significance, in virtue of which a man can be ἐν σαρκί as he can be ἐν πνεύματι; like the aeon it lends a uniform complexion to all existing things. It would also derive from this its partial coincidence with the somatic, because the whole first aeon moves on the external, provisional, physical plane. Finally it would derive from this its synonymy with evil, for according to Paul, the present aeon has become an evil aeon in its whole extent.

of Christ finds in the Spirit that element which formed the
true inner essence of the Son of God in his preëxistent state,
so that his being the Son of God, and his being the Spirit come
to express the·same thing, the one from a formal the other
from a material point of view.   Christ carried over this original pneumatic character from the preëxistent state into his
earthly life and from his earthly life again into the post-resur-
rection state, the only difference being that, while in the first
and the third stages the Spirit ruled supreme, in the intermediate stage his presence was obscured and his activity repressed by the σάρξ .   In this construction the place of the
divine nature is taken by the pneumatic personality.   The absolute sense of the μορφὴ θεοῦ of Phil. ii. 6 is weakened so
as to make it appear the equivalent of the εἰκὼν θεοῦ or the
δόξα θεοῦ of which elsewhere Paul represents Christ as the
bearer.   For the divine Christ is substituted a Spirit-being, a
creature of high rank but still a creature.[62]   Now, if we have
succeeded to any degree in elucidating the actual perspective
in which the Christ-Pneuma appears with Paul, it will be easily
felt what gross violence this modern construction does to the

[62] Especially Brückner in his work *Die Entstehung der Paulinischen
Christologie,* 1903, has strenuously advocated this theory, in the special
form that he places the origin of this pneumatic Christology back of
Paul in Judaism.   According to him the " Wesensveränderung " of the
Messiah into a pneumatic person was due to this that the enemies of the
Messiah had come to be regarded as celestial powers, angels and demons, no longer as mere men p. 116.   In order to make him equal to the
requirements of a conquest of these, it was necessary to believe him super-
human.   But it is far from clear why pneumatic endowment should not
have been thought sufficient for this.   As a matter of fact all that Brückner
succeeds in gleaning from the apocalyptic literature amounts to no more
than this.   Of equipment we read in Psalt. Sol. xvii. 37; xviii. 7.   As to
Enoch (Similit.) Brückner himself admits, that the author does not reflect
upon the relation between the Messiah and God, p. 140.   Here also we
meet with the idea of equipment, xlix. 3.   To be sure he thinks that
here the endowment with the Spirit is more of a " Wesensbestimmung "
than in Psalt. Sol., but this is scarcely borne out by the facts p. 144.
The only thing Brückner can find in 4 Ezr. to connect the Messiah with
the Spirit is the stream of fire proceeding from him for the destruction
of his enemies, xiii. 9-11, p. 156, but this is rather far-fetched.   In the
Ap. of Bar. there is no reference to the Messianic Spirit at all.   In
Test. XII Pat. we have again the idea of endowment, Test. Lev. 18.

main principle which governs that part of the Apostle's teaching. For we have found that the peculiar identification between Christ and the Spirit, on which the construction depends, is dated by Paul from the resurrection, that it has a strictly eschatological significance, that it is used exclusively to describe what Christ is in his Messianic capacity with reference to believers, and never recurred upon to define the original constitution of Christ's Person as such. Paul everywhere approaches the endowment of Christ with the Spirit from an eschatological-soteriological point of view, and the fundamental error of this modern reproduction of his Christological teaching arises from its failure to appreciate that fact. What the Apostle places at the end of the Messianic process is mistakenly carried back into the earlier life of the Messianic Person and there made to do service for explaining the mystery of the origin of the Son of God. The fallacy of this procedure will become doubly apparent by observing, that on the one hand, where Paul introduces the pneumatic Christ he uniformly refers to the state of exaltation, and on the other hand, where he speaks of the preëxistent Christ every reference to the Pneuma is conspicuously absent. Paul himself did not confound, as his modern interpreters do, what belongs to Christ as a Person and what belongs to him in virtue of his office.

The third and last observation suggested by our inquiry touches the heart of the Pauline pneumatology itself. It is often asserted by representatives of a certain school of theological thought, that the development of New Testament doctrine moves along the line of " deëschatologization." The great service rendered both by Jesus in his teaching on the present kingdom and by Paul in his teaching on justification and the life in the Spirit is held to consist in this, that they translated the transcendental blessedness expected from a future world into experiences and privileges of a purely immanent character to be enjoyed now and here below. To the same degree as they succeeded in doing this they divested the eschatological of its intrinsic importance and made it a mere fringe or form to the true substance of Christianity which can and does exist independently of it. It would seem to us that in most representations of this kind the dislike of the eschatological revealed springs from a suspicious motive. It is easy to speak disparagingly of the gross realistic expectations of the Jews, but those, who do so, often under the pretense of a refined spiritualism attack the very essence of Biblical supernaturalism. At bottom it is the spirit of the evolutionary philosophy, which here voices its protest against the idea of consummation, as at the other end of the line of Biblical history it protests against the idea of creation. Besides the supernatural it is the soteriological that is resented in eschatology. The eschatological is nothing else but supernaturalism and soteriology in the strongest possible solution.[68]   Hence the religion of the present, what is so highly extolled in Jesus and Paul, is depicted largely in the colors of an ideal natural religion. The eschatological kingdom not merely becomes present, but the present kingdom becomes a mere matter of sonship and righteousness without redemptive setting and realized by subjective internal processes. And the essence of the Christian state, as Paul describes it, is sought in much the same things. The " Spirit " is supposed to stand for that side of the Apostle's conception of religion, on which it is least affected by the abnormal, the miraculous, in a word for the " spiritual " in the conventional sense of that term. We, therefore, have to do here not with an innocent shift from the future to the present, but with a radical change from one clearly defined type of religion to another.[64]   With the setting aside of the eschatological something else of inestimable value and importance that lies enshrined in it and cannot exist without it, evaporates.

[68] This goes far to account for the modern dislike of the Messianic consciousness of Jesus and the doubt of its historicity. Messianism is the most typical expression of an eschatological world-view and carries with it all the implications of the latter.

[64] In a recent work by Von Dobschütz, *The Eschatology of the Gospels,* 1910, this tendency finds typical expression. The author speaks of Jesus' doctrine of the present kingdom as "transmuted eschatology". Transmutation implies that a change in character and tone, not in mere chronology, has taken place. "Anticipation of eschatology" would far more accurately describe the actual process both in the mind of Jesus and of Paul.

If our investigation has shown anything, it has shown how utterly foreign all this is to the plain intent of the Apostle's teaching on the Spirit. For Paul the Spirit was regularly associated with the world to come and from the Spirit thus conceived in all his supernatural and redemptive potency the Christian life receives throughout its specific character. In the combination of these two ideas, that the Spirit belongs to the αἰὼν μέλλων and that he determines the present life, we have the most impressive witness for the thoroughgoing supernaturalness of Paul's interpretation of Christianity. In its origin and in the source from which in continuance its life is fed Christianity is as little of this world as the future life is of this world. The conception of the Spirit proves that what Paul meant to do is precisely the opposite of what is imputed to him. Not to " transmute " the eschatological into a religion of time, but to raise the religion of time to the plane of eternity—such was the purport of his gospel.

THE ARAMAIC OF DANIEL

Robert Dick Wilson

Purpose of the article is to review certain statements of Dr. Driver about the Aramaic of Daniel.

Citation of Dr. Driver's statements.

The four propositions contained in these statements.

A. Discussion of the first proposition, that Daniel belongs to the Western Aramaic.

    1. Proof that the preformative '*y*' was not in Daniel's time a distinctive mark of Western Aramaic.

    2. Proof that the ending *ā* retained its definite sense up to 400 B. C. among the Eastern Arameans.

B. Discussion of the second proposition, that the Aramaic of Daniel is all but identical with that of Ezra.

C. Discussion of the third proposition, that it is nearly allied to that of the Targum of Onkelos and Jonathan and to that of the Nabateans and the Palmyrenes.

    I. Signs and sounds.

        1. Use of Aleph.   2. Use of Wau.   3. Use of He.
        4. Use of Lomadh.   5. Use of d and z.   6. Use of m and n.
        7. Further discussion of n.
        8. Interchange of Sadhe, Ayin and Qoph.
        9. Use of other letters.

    II. Forms and Inflections.

        1. Pronouns. 2. Nouns. 3. Particles. 4. Verbs.

        a. Imperfect of the Lomadh Aleph (Hê) verbs.
        b. The Hophal.   c. The Pe'il.
        d. The 3rd pl. fem. perfect.
        e. The Nun of Pe Nun verbs in the imperfect.
        f. איתי   g. Shaphel.
        h. The preformative He in the causative stem.

    III. Syntax: the manner of denoting the direct object.

    IV. Vocabulary.

        a. Of Onkelos.
        1. Verbs denoting the idea "to put".
        2. Foreign words employed.
            (1) Greek. (2) Persian. (3) Babylonian.
        b. Of the Nabateans.
        c. Of the Palmyrenes.
        d. Of the Targum of Jonathan.

D. Discussion of the fourth proposition, that the Aramaic of Daniel is that which was spoken in or near Palestine at a date after the conquest of Palestine by Alexander the Great.

Conclusion: The evidence points to Babylon as the place and the latter part of the 6th century B. C. as the time of the composition of Daniel.

THE ARAMAIC OF DANIEL

Every student of the Old Testament who has read the chapter on Daniel in Dr. Driver's *Literature of the Old Testament* (*LOT* latest edition 1910) must have been forcibly struck by the arguments presented in favor of a late date for the book which are based upon the alleged agreement between the Aramaic contained in it and that found in the dialects of the Nabateans, of the Palmyrenes, and of the Targums of Onkelos and Jonathan. So impressed was the writer of this article by the significance of these statements, backed up as they are by an imposing array of evidence, that he determined to undertake a new investigation of the whole problem of the relations existing between the various dialects of Aramaic. Such an undertaking necessarily involved as complete an investigation as was possible of the documents which constitute the extant literature of these dialects, in so far as they bear upon grammar and lexicography. Fortunately, a large part of the work involved in the investigation had already been completed by him. But, needless to remark, the accomplishment of such a task—and the writer does not regard it as yet accomplished, although he is firmly convinced that further investigation will only serve to strengthen and confirm the conclusions which he has put forward in this article— would have been utterly impossible, had there not been already to hand so many grammars, lexicons, and texts, of scientific value. Largely for convenience of treatment the writer has divided the material into ten parts, each of which he calls a dialect. These dialects are (1) Northern Aramaic, embracing all inscriptions found outside of Egypt down to the year 400 B.C., (2) Egypto-Aramaic, (3) Daniel, (4) Ezra, (5) the Nabatean inscriptions, (6) the Palmyrene, (7) the Targum of Onkelos, (8) the Syriac, (9) the Mandean, and (10) the

Samaritan. The works to which he has been most indebted are the *Corpus Inscriptionum Semiticarum* and the works of De Vogué, Euting, Pognon, Sayce-Cowley, Sachau, Littmann, Cooke, Lidzbarski, Brederek, Nöldeke, Petermann, Kautzsch, Strack, Marti, Brockelmann, Norberg, Levy and Dalman. The invaluable Sachau papyri (Leipzig, Heinrichs 1911) arrived in time to be made available in their bearing upon most of the points discussed.

The views advanced by Dr. Driver to which the writer takes exception will be found on pages 502-4, and 508 of his *LOT,* where we read as follows:

" The *Aramaic* of David (which is all but identical with that of Ezra) is a *Western* Aramaic dialect, of the type spoken in and about *Palestine.*[1] It is nearly allied to the Aramaic of the Targums of Onkelos and Jonathan; and still more so to the Aramaic dialects spoken E. and SE. of Palestine, in Palmyra and Nabatæa, and known from inscriptions dating from the 3rd cent. B.C. to the 2nd cent. A.D. In some respects it is of an earlier type than the Aramaic of Onkelos and Jonathan; and this fact was formerly supposed to be a ground for the antiquity of the Book. But the argument is not conclusive. For (1) the differences are not considerable,[2] and largely ortho-

---

[1] Nöldeke, *Enc. Brit.*[9] xxi. 647[b] — 8[a] = *Die Sem. Sprachen*[2] (1899), 35, 37; *Enc. B.* i. 282. The idea that the Jews forgot their Hebrew in Babylonia, and spoke in "Chaldee" when they returned to Palestine, is unfounded. Haggai, Zechariah and other post-exilic writers use Hebrew: Aramaic is exceptional. Hebrew was still normally spoken *c.* 430 B. C. in Jerusalem (Neh. xiii. 24). The Hebrews, after their Captivity, acquired gradually the use of the Aramaic *from their neighbours* in and about Palestine. See Nöldeke. *ZDMG.* 1871, p. 129 f.; Kautzsch, *Gramm. des Bibl. Aram.* § 6; Wright, *Compar. Gramm. of the Semitic Languages* (1890), p. 16: " Now do not for a moment suppose that the Jews lost the use of Hebrew in the Babylonian captivity, and brought back with then into Palestine this so-called Chaldee. The Aramean dialect, which gradually got the upper hand since 5-4 cent. B. C., did not come that long journey across the Syrian desert; it was *there,* on the spot; and it ended by taking possession of the field, side by side with the kindred dialect of the Samaritans." The term "Chaldee" for the Aramaic of either the Bible or the Targums is a misnomer, the use of which is only a source of confusion.

[2] They are carefully collected (on the basis, largely, of M'Gill's investigations) by Dr. Pusey, *Daniel,* ed 2, pp. 45 ff., 602 ff. (an interesting lexi-

graphical: the Targums of Onkelos and Jonathan did not
probably receive their present form before the 4th cent. A.D.:[3]
and we are not in a position to affirm that the transition from
the Aramaic of Dan. and Ezra to that of the Targums must
have required 8-9 centuries, and could not have been accomplished in 4-5; (2) recently discovered inscriptions have shown
that many of the forms in which it differs from the Aramaic
of the Targums were actually in use in neighbouring countries
down to the 1st cent. A.D.[4] "

Thus the final ה (for א) in verbs ל״א, and in חֹזֶה, מָה, אֲנָה &c., occurs
often in Nab.; the Hofal (*not* a Hebraism: Nöld. *GGA.*, 1884, 1015;
Sachau; Wright), and in the pass. of Pe'al (Dan. iii. 21 *al.*: Bev. pp. 37,
72), in the Palm. Tariff (Sachau, *ZMDG.* 1883, p. 564 f.; Wright, *Comp.
Gr.* p. 224 f.; otherwise Cooke, 334); note also עֲבִידָה *was made* in Cooke,
No. 96[8] (Nöld. *Z. f. Ass.*, 1890, p. 290; cf. Dalman, *Gram. des Jüd.-Pal.
Aram.* 202 ([2]253) *n.*); the א in the impf. of verbs ר״א not changed to
י, repeatedly in Nab. and the Tariff; מְרָאנָא (with א) Dan. iv. 16, 21; Kt.
Nab, Cooke 81[8], 82[4], 94[3], Eut. 27 (= *CIS.* ii. 224)[13]; אִיתַי (Tg. אִית) Nab.
Cooke 80[7] 81[7] 85[9] 86[2·7] &c.; דִי·(Tg. דִ) and דְּנָה (Tg. דֵּין), both regularly
in Palm. Nab.; אֲנוּשׁ Dan. iv. 13, 14; Kt., Nab. *ibid.* 79[7] 86[8 5 6] &c.; נ retained in the impf. of verbs פ״י, Nab. *ibid.* 79[2] 80[5 9] 86[5] 87[8] יִנְפַּק, 79[8 6] 80[5]
יִנְתֵּן; the 3 pl. pf. *fem.* in נ-, as Dan. vi. 5, vii. 20; Kt., Nab *ibid.* 80[1] 85[1].
For the suff. of 3 ps. pl., Nab. has הֹם- (the more original form), Palm.
הוֹן- ; Dan. agrees here with Palm., Jer. x. 11 with Nab.; Ezr. has both
forms.

It is remarkable that—to judge from the uniform usage of the inscriptions at present known from Nineveh, Babylon, Têma, Egypt, and even
Cilicia (coins of Mazæus: Cook 149 A 6, cf. on A 5), Cappadocia (Lidzbarski, *Ephem. Epigr.* i. 67, 323, 325), and Lycia (*CIS.* II. i. 109,—with

cal point is that the vocabulary agrees sometimes with Syriac against the
Targums). But when all are told, the differences are far outweighed by
the *resemblances;* so that relatively they cannot be termed important or
considerable. (The amount of difference is much exaggerated in the
Speaker's Comm. p. 228. The statement in the text agrees with the judgment of Nöldeke, *l.c.* p. 648[b]; *Enc. Bibl.* i. 283.)

[3] Deutsch in Smith's *DB.* iii. 1644, 1652; Volck in Herzog,[2] xv. 366,
370; Nöldeke, *Enc. Bibl.* i. 282.

[4] See (chiefly) De Vogüé, *La Syrie Centrale* (1868), with inscriptions
from Palmyra, mostly from 1-3 cent. A. D. (an excellent selection in Cooke,
N.-Sem. Inscr. Nos. 110-146), the long bilingual Tariff of tolls from Palmyra, of A. D. 137 (*ibid.* No. 147); Euting, *Nabatäische Inschriften* (1885),
with inscriptions (largely of the reign of חרתת = 'Ἀρέτας, 2 Cor. xi. 32)
from B. C. 9 to A. D. 75 (Cooke, Nos. 78-102).

זנה for דנה)—in the Aramaic used officially (cf. p. 255; Isa. xxxvi. 11) in the Ass. and Persian empires, the relative was וי,[5] not, as in Dan. Ezr., and Aram. generally, די (ד). וי thus occurs on weights and contract-tablets from Nineveh (*CIS.* 11. i. 2-5 [cf. Cooke, No. 60], 17, 20, 28, 30, 31, 38, 39, 41, 42, all of 8-7 cent B. C.; rf. Cooke 150. 2); and Babylon (*ibid.* 65, B. C. 504, 69-71, B. C. 418, 407, 408; Clay, in *OT. and Sem. Studies in memory of W. R. Harper,* 1908, ii. 299 ff., Nos. 2, 3, 5, 6, 8, 9, 11, 33 from the reign of Artaxerxes, B. C. 464-424, and Nos. 23, 26, 28, 29, 33, 35, 40 from that of Darius II.. B. C. 424-404; cf. Cooke, No. 67: ארק (א) *earth* for ארע(א) (Dan., Ezr.) also occurs regularly in the same inscription, *CIS.* 1-4 [Cooke, No. 66], 7, 11, 28, 35 from Nineveh, Clay, Nos. 5. 8, 11, 29, 40 from Babylon. These differences are cogent evidence that the Aramaic of Daniel was *not* that spoken at Babylon in Daniel's age. Its character in other respects apart from the Persian and Greek words which it contains, cannot be said to lead to any definite result: its resemblance with the Aramaic of Ezra (probably *c.* 400 B. C.) does not prove it to be contemporary.

Again Dr. Driver says on page 508 of the same work: "The verdict of the language of Daniel is thus clear. The *Persian* words presuppose a period after the Persian empire had been well established: the Greek words *demand,* the Hebrew *supports,* and the Aramaic *permits,* a date *after the conquest of Palestine by Alexander the Great* (B.C. 332). The Aramaic is also that which was spoken *in or near Palestine.* With our present knowledge, this is as much as the language authorizes us definitely to affirm." [6]

There are four main propositions contained in these citations from Dr. Driver: first, that the Aramaic of Daniel is Western; second, that it is all but identical with that of Ezra; third, that it is nearly allied with that of the Targums of Onkelos and Jonathan and to that of the Nabateans and Palmyrenes; and fourth, that it was "spoken in and about

[5] So in the Aram. of Zinjirli (p. 255 *n.*): Cooke, Nos. 61-65.
[6] In justice to Dr. Driver we have cited the above statements in full. In justice to the writer of this review it should be said that he has reserved for a future article the words in the second citation, "The Hebrew supports"; and that the word "thus" of the first sentence in so far as it refers to Dr. Driver's discussion of the Hebrew of Daniel on page 504-8 has not been considered in this article. Hebrew is brought into the present treatment only in so far as it is a constituent part of the Aramaic portion of Daniel.

Palestine ", "at a date after the conquest of Palestine by Alexander the Great ".

A. Taking these propositions up in order, we would like to ask in the first place, in view of the inscriptions that have been lately published, what foundation still exists for designating the Aramaic of Daniel as Western.

The only reasons given by Prof. Theodor Nöldeke, who is generally recognized as the highest authority in this field, for the distinction between Eastern and Western Aramaic are that the third person masculine of the Imperfect of the Eastern type has the preformative n (or l), whereas the Western has y; and that the Eastern has ceased to attach the sense of the definite article to the ending $\bar{a}$ of the status emphaticus. (See also Margoliouth in *Encyc. Brit.* 24:625). It is undoubtedly true and must be readily admitted by all that these distinctions are perfectly clear and undeniable in all works which have come down to us that were written subsequent to the year 200 A.D. But all the documentary evidence that we possess shows that in earlier times, down at least to 73 A.D., the Eastern Aramaic did not differ in these two respects from the Western. According to Nöldeke himself the evidence of the Babylonian Talmud does not go back beyond the period from the fourth to the sixth century A.D., and the Mandean writings belong to a somewhat later period.[7] The earliest Syriac writing known is the inscription of the tomb of Manu near Serrin in Mesopotamia, which was discovered and published by H. Pognon, the erudite French consul, in his work called *Inscriptions Sémitiques de la Syrie, de la Mésopotamie et de la Région de Mossoul, Paris, 1907.* (Part First, page 15, seq.) All of the imperfects of the third person in this inscription, and there are six of them, have the performative y; so that it is certain that as late as the end of the 1st century A.D., the preformative that has hitherto been looked upon as at all times a characteristic of the Western Aramaic was also in use in the Eastern. Whether the other preformative was also in use so early is an interesting question, but one

---

[7] In his Mandean Grammar, page 22, he states that the earliest of the Mandean writings that are known was composed in the 7th century A. D.

which cannot be answered at present, since no further data exist. It ought, however, certainly to be admitted, that if one writer of Eastern Aramaic could and did use the preformative *y* at the end of the first century A.D., another writer of Eastern Aramaic might have used it at the end of the sixth century B.C. That is, if Manu, son of Darnahai, used it in 73 A.D., Daniel *may* at least have used it in 535 B.C., despite the fact that from the second century A.D. on, other forms are found to have been used universally and exclusively in all the East-Aramaic documents that have been discovered.

But the inscription of Manu is not the only evidence that the preformative *y* was used in pre-Christian times in Eastern Aramaic. In CIS43 we find the form ya'al " let him bring ", and also יכלא in CIS106, both of the 7th century B.C. Furthermore, in all of the old Aramaic names that have so far been published in the *Corpus Inscriptionum Semiticarum* and elsewhere, which contain this form of the verb as a component part, the preformative is inveriably *y*. All of these names are indisputably from the regions occupied by the Eastern Arameans. These names are Yirpeel, (CIS77) from the eighth or seventh century B.C.; Neboyirban (CIS39) from the year 674 B.C.; Yibcharel (CIS47) from the seventh century B.C.

Finally, the third person masculine of the imperfects in the Aramaic version of the Behistun Inscription published in Sept. 1911 by Prof. Sachau of Berlin, have invariably the preformative *y*. Of course, this may represent a West-Aramaic rescension; but, inasmuch as the kings of Persia had their court in the midst of the East-Arameans and since the Behistun Inscription was in the neighborhood of the regions occupied by the East-Arameans, it is fully as probable that the Aramaic version preserved in these particular papyri represents the Eastern Aramaic of that time.

Inasmuch, then, as it has been shown that the preformative *n* to denote the third person masculine of the imperfect was never employed by any of the oldest Arameans, East or West, the assertion that the book of Daniel (whether it was written in the second or in the sixth century B.C., is not here the question) was written in a Western dialect and the consequent implication that it cannot have been written in Babylon, are both shown to be without any foundation in the facts as known.

With regard to the use of Lomadh as a preformative of the jussive form of the imperfect, the fact that it has been found in the Hadad inscription from the 8th century B.C. shows that it may well have been used in a document coming from the 6th century B.C. The fact that in later times it occurs only in the Babylonian Talmud and in the Mandean,[8] both written in or about Babylon, shows as far as it shows anything, that Daniel was written in the East rather than in the West.

With regard to the second distinction between the Western and Eastern Aramaic (that the former employs the ending $\bar{a}$ to denote the definite or emphatic state, whereas the latter has come to use the emphatic in the same sense as the absolute), a study of the earlier East-Aramaic inscriptions would indicate that in the usage of the period from 800 B.C. to 400 B.C. the distinction between the two states was just as closely preserved in the Eastern as in the Western Aramaic. Thus in the Aramaic inscriptions from the 8th to the 6th century B.C. the ending $\bar{a}$ to represent the emphatic state is employed in the following phrases:

" of the land ", CIS Nos. 1, 2, 3, 4, 7.
" sale of the handmaid Hambusu ", id. 19.
" sale of the field ", id. 24, 27, 53.
" book of the silver ", id. 30.
" son of the king ", id. 38, 39.
" the barley ", id. 42.
" the silver ", id. 43, 70, 71, 108.
" the scribe ", id. 46, 84.
" the pledge ", id. 65.
" the house ", id. 65.
" the eunuch ", id. 75.
" the guards ", id. 108.

[8] Dalman says on p. 264 of his Grammar, that in Onkelos and the Targum of Jonathan the form never is found except in additions (abgesehen von Zusätzen) to the text.

So in Clay's Aramaic Indorsements, some of which reach as late as 400 B.C., we find the same usage, viz., " the rent of the land ", No. 5, 8, 11, cf. 21; " document concerning the house ", 17; " Darius the king ", 22; " document of the lands of the Carpenter ", 29.

When it is remembered that all the inscriptions here cited are from the provenience of the Eastern Aramaic, that they cover the period from the 8th century B.C. to the 5th Century B.C. inclusive, and that in every one of the cases given in the CIS and in Clay's Indorsements the emphatic state is used in a definite and proper sense, it will be evident that in the 6th century B.C., a writer composing a work at Babylon might have employed the emphatic state in its definite sense. For there is no proof that in the 6th century B.C., any dialect of the Aramaic did not use the emphatic state to denote what the Hebrew denoted by the definite article. The Eastern as well as the Western Aramaic documents alike employ the emphatic state, ending in $\bar{a}$, and they both alike employ it correctly and in the same sense.

There is therefore no evidence that in the 6th century B.C., either of these two features, which at a later time make the distinction between the Eastern and Western Aramaic, was in existence; and hence it is wrong to say that the book of Daniel was written in Western Aramaic as distinguished from Eastern.

B. The second statement of Dr. Driver to the effect that the Aramaic of Daniel is all but identical with that of Ezra may be accepted as in most respects correct. This is what we might have expected, if Daniel was written in the 6th and Ezra in the 5th century B.C. But since they are almost identical, it would follow that if the Aramaic of Daniel were late, the Aramaic of Ezra would be late also. That is, this would follow if Dr. Driver's argument be correct and if it were true that a proved similarity between the Aramaic of Daniel and that of the Nabateans, Palmyrenes, and the Targums, would prove the late date of Daniel. By parity of reasoning, if Daniel be late because its language is like that of the Nabateans, Palmyrenes, and the Targums; then it is early because it is like that of Ezra, or Ezra is late because its language is like that of Daniel. According to Dr. Driver's own argument, either Daniel and Ezra are both early or both late. In the sequel we shall endeavor to show that the language of Daniel is not like that of either the Nabateans, the Palmyrenes, or the Talmuds, and that the language of Daniel is early rather than late.

C. In the third place, Dr. Driver says, that the Aramaic of Daniel is "nearly allied to the Aramaic of the Targums of Onkelos and Jonathan; and still more so to the Aramaic dialects spoken East and Southeast of Palestine, in Palmyra and Nabataea, and known from inscriptions dating from the 3rd century B.C. to the 2nd ceutury A.D."

The obvious intention of this statement is to leave the impression on the mind of the reader that the book of Daniel is late, because the Aramaic dialect in which a part of it is written resembles the Aramaic contained in writings that are known to have been composed long after the 6th century B.C. We judge that it was a slip of the pen that caused Dr. Driver to say that the Palmyrene and Nabatean inscriptions are dated from the 3rd century B.C. to the 2nd century A.D. It would be more exact to say that the Nabatean inscriptions whose date is known extend from 70 B.C. to 95 A.D. and the Palmyrene from 9 B.C. to 271 A.D. This correction of Dr. Driver's statement merely brings it into harmony with the generally accepted view, that there are no Aramaic inscriptions of any kind from what is called the Greek period, except the bilingual proper name from Tello. But passing by this statement as a mere inadvertence, we shall address ourselves to the main issue, stating the question to be considered as follows: Is it true that the Aramaic of Daniel is *nearly allied* to that of the Targums of Onkelos and Jonathan and to that of the Palmyrene and Nabatean inscriptions?

Before attempting to answer this question, it may be well to define what we mean by " nearly allied ". All dialects of a given language are allied and always more closely allied to one another than they are to the dialects of any other language. When it is said that one dialect of a language is *nearly* allied to one or more other dialects, it means that it resembles it or them more closely than it resembles certain others. In other words, it is a comparative statement. In the particular case before us, it can only mean that the Aramaic of Daniel is more nearly allied to those dialects mentioned than it is to the Northern Syriac of the Sendshirli inscriptions, or to the Egyptian Aramaic, or to the Mandean and Syriac. And the purpose of the statement is, that, if it were true, it would make a presumption, almost equivalent to a demonstration, that the Aramaic of Daniel was written in or about Palestine and at a date not far removed from that at which the documents which it resembles were written.

If it can be shown that the Aramaic of Daniel resembles the Aramaic from the 8th to the 5th century B.C. as much as it resembles that of these later documents, no conclusion as to the date of the Aramaic of Daniel could be drawn from its resemblances to these other Aramaic dialects. If it can be shown that it more closely resembles the language of the ancient documents than it does that of the later, there would be a strong presumption for an early date for the Aramaic of Daniel. And *vice versa*.

But, while paying due attention to the resemblances between the dialects, we must not fail to keep in mind, that after all it is the *differences* between the dialects that constitute their essential characteristics. The Aramaic of Daniel, for example, is not a *dialect* because of those parts which are common to it with other dialects, but because of its differentia. And the question to be asked with regard to these differentia in determining the date and provenience of a dialect is: At what time and place would a dialect possessing them have been produced? If the dialect is preserved in a single work, we may further ask, whether the personality, education, and circumstances, of the presumptive author might have influenced him in certain pecularities of language, making them personal rather than dialectic.

Furthermore, in discussing the question of the date and provenience of a work, and the pecularities and alliances of a dialect, it is proper to consider not merely the grammar of each but also the vocabulary. And again, in respect to the vocabulary, it is not so much to the use of different words that are possibly of pure Aramaic origin or use, as to the admixture of foreign vocables, that attention must be directed, inasmuch as almost every work, especially if it be on a new subject, will contain words not found elsewhere in the written language. Foreign terms, however, almost infallibly indicate the location and time that the work was written, especially in their earliest occurrence, or if they be found nowhere else.

With these preliminary remarks, let us proceed to a discussion of the relations of the Aramaic of Daniel to that of the other dialects, first as to its grammar and secondly as to its vocabulary. We shall study these relations under the headings of signs and sounds, forms and inflections, syntax and vocabulary.

I. SIGNS AND SOUNDS

The dialects agree in general in the use they make of the signs *b, g, ḥ, ṭ, k, l, p,* and *r.* That is, where we find *b* or *g* in one dialect we may expect to find them in all, since they always denote the same sound. But on the other hand, the use of Aleph and *h* varies frequently in the different dialects or even in the same dialect; as does also that of *d* and *z; w, y* and Aleph; *m* and *n;* Semkath and Sin; Sodhe, 'Ayin, and Qoph; and of Shin and Tau. Sometimes these differences are simply variant ways of spelling, no difference in sound being presupposed. At other times, however, a variation in the sound lies at the foundation of the variation of the sign.

1. *Use of Aleph.* Giving our attention first to the letter Aleph, we shall take as an example of the variation in the use of it the word מרא "lord". The fact that this word retains the Aleph in the Nabatean, just as we find it in the Kethiv of Dan. iv. 16, 21, is used by Dr. Driver as evidence that Daniel may have been late in spite of the fact that the Aramaic of the Targums has dropped the Aleph. The evidence with regard to the writing of מרא is as follows:

a. In the Sendshirli inscriptions we find it in the const. sing. מרא B. R. 3, מר[א]ה Pan. 11, מראי Pan. 19, B. R. 5, 6.

b. In the Egypto-Aramaic, מרא in Sach. 15.15.6, 35.37.2; 50a. 2, 61R. 9 in the absolute; 2.15 in the construct; מראי

7.8, 11. 17, 12.2 (?), 13.12V.2, 36.39R.1, 43.2.10, 60.7.2; מראך 49.2 and CIS144A.1,2; מראה 49.2 and CIS145AF; מראן 1.1, 2.18, 23, 3V.17, 22, 4.5.7, 12, 12, 5. 1, 5; מראי 11.1, 12.1, 12; מראתי 13.12V.1.2.3. Without Aleph, מריהם ? 15,15.6; in SC possibly מרי M.a.2(?) and מרן P.2.

c. In Daniel מרא in the construct ii. 47, v. 23; מראי iv. 16, 21.

d. In Ezra, no form found.

e. In Nabatean, מרא in the construct CIS235A2; מראנא Pet. i. 3. CIS199.8, 201.4.

f. In Palmyrene, מרא in the construct, Vog.73.1, Tay.1; מרהון Vog.28.4, מרן Vog.23.2, 25.3; מרוהי Vog. 103.6; מרתהון Vog.29.4(?)

g. In all the Targums, we have מר, in the construct מרי but never מרא .

h. In Syriac, Mandean, and Samaritan, the Aleph is always dropped.

From the above examples it will be seen that while a late writer of Aramaic might have written the word as Daniel does, the almost universal usage is against it. The Nabateans and Palmyrenes in the central desert still employed it, but to the east, north and west of them it was dropped by all. Among the older writings, however, it was almost as universally employed, but one certain example of its omission being known.

2. *Use of Wau.* Every student of ancient Aramaic texts knows that variations in the use of Wau and Yodh are no sure indications of the age of a document. In inscriptions from the same age and dialect, we frequently find the same word written both with and without one or the other of these letters. For example, take in Palmyrene the word " to save ". It is written שיזב in Cooke No. 101, from A.D. 45, and שזב in another document from 96 A.D. (*id.* note). Take also ימא (Sachau papyri 64.2) instead of the usual יומא (*id.* 2.20; 3V.19; 20.K.7.1; 33.33.4; 45.1; 63.Ib.2).

Further, it must be kept in mind in discussing Wau and Yodh, that thousands of variations in the use of them are to be found in the Hebrew MSS. of the Old Testament. We should remember also that the vowel signs now in the Hebrew

and Aramaic texts of the Bible do not antedate the 6th century
A.D.

Bearing these facts in mind we shall enter upon a discussion of Dr. Driver's statement on page 504 of LOT, that we
have the same manner of writing אנוש in the Kethiv of
Daniel iv. 13, 14 and in the Nabatean (Cooke 79.7, 86,3,5,6,
etc.). This remark must refer to the spelling, since the use
of the word in the sense of "one" is found in Palmyrene
(Cooke p. 311) and we may add, in SC, K8, 10, and in Sach.
36.39 and 46.14; but in Daniel it means "men, mankind,
Menschheit" just as in Sach. Pap. 46.6 and 48.1.4. The
papyri distinguished between אנש and אנשא using the
former for "one" and the latter for "mankind", just as
Daniel does, for in iv. 13, 14 the latter writes אֲנוֹשָׁא (or אֲנָשָׁא
if we follow the Qrê), while the Nabatean has אנוש. In
other words, the meaning of the form used in Nabatean
differs from that used in Daniel in the verses cited. Still, as
Daniel does elsewhere use אנש in the sense of "one", we
may waive this point.

It has been customary to call these two cases Hebraisms, as
Marti did in the first edition of his Aramaic Grammar. This
would seem probably correct, in view of the fact that Daniel
eight times elsewhere in the Aramaic portions spells the word
אֲנָשָׁא and that the word is spelled with the ô 42 times in
the Hebrew portion of the Bible. The Massoretes have considered the ô to be a mistake in the text of iv. 13, 14 and have
corrected it by changing the vowel from ô to â in harmony with
the usual spelling elsewhere in Daniel. In view of the fact
that the Hebrew in nearly all cases has changed an â to ô, and
especially in view of the further fact that in the West Syriac
an East Syriac â is pronounced as ô, it is easy to see how a
writer or copyist might vary in the spelling of a word containing a sound that shifted from â to ô. Especially would
this be true of a Hebrew writing Aramaic. This variation of
sound may account also for the fact that the Palmyrene has
אנש while the Nabatean has אנוש. For ourselves, we
prefer to consider it an error of a Hebrew scribe, just as the
Massoretes have done. But at any rate, that the writer of

Daniel should have spelt the word twice with an *â* as against eighteen times with an *ô* does not show a very close relation between him and the Nabatean scribes who wrote the inscriptions in that language in the first century A.D.; for they always write it with an *ô*.

3. *Use of He.* Dr. Driver says that Daniel may have been late, because a final He in verbs Lomadh Aleph occurs often in Nabatean, although the Targums have uniformly employed Aleph. This statement is ambiguous. No verb that had originally an Aleph as its third radical has been found either in Nabatean, or Palmyrene. What Dr. Driver means us to understand is, that verbs whose third radical was Wau or Yodh have had this third radical elided and that its place is taken by the vowel letter He, instead of by Aleph as in the Targums. How a verb whose third radical was Aleph could have been written in Nabatean or Palmyrene, we do not know, because no such verb has yet been found. The evidence for the use of the final He, or Aleph, in the verbs whose third radical was originally Wau, Yodh, or Aleph, is as follows:

a. The Syriac, Mandean, and the Aramaic of the Targums never use He.

b. The early inscriptions always use He for verbs whose third radical was Wau or Yodh and Aleph for those whose third radical was Aleph.

c. The Nabatean and Palmyrene and the book of Ezra have no verbs whose third radical was originally Aleph. In writing those which had originally Wau or Yodh, they sometimes employ He, sometimes Aleph.

d. Samaritan commonly employs Aleph for verbs that originally had Aleph and He for those that had Wau and Yodh, though for the latter Wau and Yodh are sometimes employed, perhaps in imitation of the Arabic method of writing them.

e. The text of Daniel presents a method of writing different from that found elsewhere.

(1) The originally Lomadh Aleph verb נשא is written with an Aleph.

(2) The verb מטא which the Sachau papyri treat as an

originally Lomadh Aleph verb, Daniel writes מטא once
and twice, מטה.

(3) שרא is written with an Aleph, (once only). Possibly this verb is found in the עבדשרא of CIS696.3.

(4) מנה, רבה and אתה are written with a He, though Ezra
writes the latter with an Aleph.

(5) חזא and בעא are written once each with Aleph
and once each with He. Marti's text reads חזה both times
and בעא both times. הוה is written seven times and הוא four
times without variants, and once we find each one in the
Kethiv and the other in the Qrê. Since the latter two verbs
are always written with a He in Egypto-Aramaic and מטא
with an Aleph, it would require merely the harmonizing of
these variant readings of Daniel to bring his text into complete
accord with the spellings of the Aramaic Egyptian documents
of the 5th century B.C. The same may be said of אנה,
מה, and חדה which is Egypto-Aramaic and always spelled
with a He.

4. *Use of Lomadh.* a. In Daniel. In the verb סלק the ל
is assimilated backwards whenever the ס comes at the end
of the syllable; e. g., a. הֻסָּקָ iii. 22, חְסַק vi. 24.

Instead of the doubling of the ס, the Inf. Hoph. inserts a
Nun before it. e. g. הַנְסָקָה vi. 24. But מַהְלְכִין iii. 25, iv. 34.

b. In Ezra, the ל of הֲלַךְ is dropped. e. g., יְהָךְ v. 5, vii. 13,
לִמְהָךְ vii. 13.

c. In N. Syr. the verbs containing these peculiarities have
not been found.

d. In Egyptian Aramaic, we have תהך Sak. B.4 C6
(= CIS145 B4C6) and SCG 25, 28; אהך SC.D22; מהך
Sach. 63.5.2, but מהלך 42.9; יהכון Sach. 29.19.

e. In Nabatean the verbs containing these peculiarities have
not yet been found.

f. In Palmyrene we find אסקו T. 1.5, מסק T. 1.8; אסק
Vog. 74. We find in Pal. also כלדיא Sem. vi. 4 for BAכשדיא.

g. In Onkelos ל is (1) dropped in the Imv. Peal of סלק
and in the Impf. and Inf. Peal of הלך (Dalm. 66.1, 70.9.),
e. g. סקו N. xiii. 17, סק G. xxxv. 1, סקי N. xxi. 18, יהך
D. xx. 6, יהכון E. xxxii. 1, למהך D. xxix. 17.

(2) Assimilated in מסך N. xiii.31, אסק E. xxxii. 38, אסיך G. viii. 20.

h. In Sam. ל is dropped in the Imv. Peal of הלך and סלק e. g., אהך G. xxviii. 2, סוק N. xxxiii. 17, סק G. xxxv. 1; but סלקי N. xxi. 18. It is assimilated in אסק G. viii. 20, מסק E. xix. 23.

i. In Syriac (see Nöldeke § § 29 and 183 (5)) the first ל is not pronounced in ממללא and ממללא׳ and falls away in some forms of אזל and in the Peal and Aphel of סלק.

j. In Mandean we have מאסק, אסיק, מימאק, עמאק, נימאק, סיק, סאק.

From the above collection of facts as to the manner of writing Lomadh we find that it is assimilated backwards in all the forms of Peal and Aphel perfect and imperfect which have a preformative. Unfortunately, such forms are found only in Daniel, Onkelos, Syriac, Mandean and Samaritan. Daniel is peculiar in inserting a dissimilative Nun in the infinitive of the causative active stem of this verb.

Further, Daniel agrees with the Egypto-Aramaic in retaining the Lomadh in forms of הלך in which the preformative is Mem.

5. *Use of d and z.* The primitive Semitic seems to have had three sounds corresponding to our *d, dh,* and *z.* From whatever source they adopted their alphabet there seem to have been but two signs to express the three sounds. One of these signs was used exclusively to denote *d* and another to denote *z.* There being no sign for the third sound, three methods were followed. The Arabs invented a third sign. Hebrew, Ethiopic and Babylonian expressed *dh* prevailingly by the *z* sign but sometimes by the *d* sign. The old Aramean inscriptions of Northern Syria and of Assyria from the 9th to the 7th century inclusive always use *z.* The Palmyrene, the Syriac and the Targums of Onkelos and Jonathan always use *d.* The Aramaic papyri use either with almost equal frequency. The Samaritan Targum and the Mandean dialect also, vary in their use even in writing the same words. The earliest Nabatean inscription, dating from 70 B.C. (CIS I 349) always uses *z*, but all the other inscriptions regularly use *d.* In the Assyrian transliterations of Aramean names

as early as 855 B.C., Hadadezer is rendered by Dad-idri.
Daniel and Ezra always use *d* for this sound except in Ezra's
writing of גזבר where Daniel has גדבר.

This variety of sign to express the same original sound
would seem to confirm the opinion that we have here to deal
not with a linguistic or dialectic change of sound but with
the endeavor to compel two signs to serve for three sounds.
The Arabic denotes it by putting a dot over the ordinary
sign for *d*. The other dialects avail themselves of the usual
sign for *d* or *z*, just as we English avail ourselves of the
sigh *th* in *thin* and *that*. The oldest Arameans consistently
used *z*. The book of Daniel, if written in the latter part of
the 6th century B.C., would be the first known document to
use the sign *d* for *dh*. Being an educated man the author
used it consistently and exclusively. After his time, the
writers in Egypt and the Samaritans and Nabateans wavered
in their usage; but the Targums and those books whose writers were under the influence of Daniel came to use *d* exclusively. The Arabs not being under this influence pursued their
own way of expressing *dh*. In studying this difficult question
we must keep two matters in mind; first, that Daniel had studied both Hebrew and Babylonian and in each of these *dh* was
written by means of both *d* and *z;* and secondly, that somebody
must have started this spelling reform and Daniel's position
would have enabled him to do it.

6. *Use of Mem and Nun*. These two letters vary in the
different languages and dialects of the Semitic family in the
absolute masc. plural of the noun and in the second and third
personal pronouns. The latter only enters into the discussion
of Daniel because he always uses the forms kon and hon
where some other Aramaic dialects use kum and hum, or hon
and kon. The question is: Can the book of Daniel have been
written in the 6th century B.C. and yet have used *n* instead of
m in these cases? We think it can.

(1) Because all Aramaic documents of any age written in
the East have used *n* instead of *m*. This is true of everything
in Syriac, Mandean, and the Talmud as well as of Palmyrene.

(2) It is true of all documents in Assyrian and Babylonian.

(3) Ezra, whose composition Dr. Driver puts at 400 B.C., uses *n* as well as *m*.

(4) The Samaritans used *m* as well as *n*.

(5) While it may be said, that the Sendshirli and other early Western documents used *m* in imitation of the Hebrews and Phenicians, or in the case of the Nabateans, of the Arabs; so it may be said, that the eastern dialects used *n* in imitation of the Assyrio-Babylonians. Ezra being composed largely of letters between the eastern Arameans and the western uses both.

(6) The variations in the transliteration of proper names in the use of *m* for *n* and *n* for *m,* and between mimmation and nunnation present a problem that cannot yet be solved and that should make us hesitate to dogmatize on the reasons for the variations in the different dialects and languages in the use of these letters.

(7) The earliest document outside the Scriptures and the Assyrio-Babylonian to make use of *n* is the Palmyrene inscription of 21 A.D. The earliest Syriac is from 73 A.D. The latest Nabatean inscription to use these suffixes uses the form with *m*. It is dated according to Cooke (North Semitic Inscriptions p. 252) in 65 A.D. If the writer of Daniel could have used the *n* in 165 B.C. in Palestine, as his critics would have us believe, although those " in and about Palestine " were using *m,* why may he not have used *n* in Babylon in 535 B.C. where all in and about Babylon were using *n*?

7. *Further use of Nun.* The following uses of Nun are to be noted.

(1) It is dropped :

    a. In Daniel, פּוּקוּ iii. 26.

    b. In Ezra, שֵׁא v. 15.

    c. In No. Syr., תְּנִי CIS.150[6].

    d. In Eg. Ar., חת, טר, שׁא. See Sach. Pap.

    e. Nabatean, no form occurs.

    f. Palmyrene, no form occurs.

    g. In Onkelos, פוּק, חות. See Dalman p. 293.

    h. In Syriac, פוּק, חות, טר, and many others. See Nöldeke pp. 22, 115.

i. In Mandean, only in סאב, פיל, הות and פאק. Nöldeke
p. 240.

j. In Sam., סב, אחת. See Petermann pp. 8 and 34.

(2) It is assimilated:

a. In Daniel, יִפֵּל iii. 6, 10, 11, תִּפְּלוּן iii. 5, 15, מַצֵּל vi. 28,
הַצָּלָה iii. 29, הַצָּלוּתֵהּ vi. 15, יתנגח iv. 14, 22, 29,
מַתְּנָן ii. 6, 48, מַתְּנָתָךְ v. 17.

b. In Ezra יפל vii. 20, תחת vi. 5, אחת v. 15, מהחתין vi. 1.

c. In N. S. יתן Hadad 23 ; יתנו Hadad 4 ; אשא Zakir i. 11 ;
יסחו Ner i. 9.

d. In Eg. Ar. יתן CIS149 BC12 ; [י]תנון CIS138 B2;
יחתון CIS145 B6; מתנא Sach. Pap. vi. 2, 7, 11, 12.

e. In Nabatean [מטר]תא Litt. i. 3; אתתה CIS, 158⁴.

f. In Pal. אפק Tɪɪ b43, מאפק Tɪɪ c12; אסם Vog. 74,
מסק Tɪ8, יתן Tɪɪ a5, b20, מדיתהון Eph. ɪɪ 278⁶, אחת
id. 298⁵.

g. In Onkelos the Nun is almost always assimilated,
except when before He or Ayin. Dal. p. 101.

h. In Syr. "almost always", Nold. § 28, except before He.

i. In Mandean "often". נִיפִיל, אפיק, שיתא "year", Nol-
deke §§ 56, 178.

j. In Sam. נתת, יסב. See Petermann pp. 8 and 34.

(3) It is inserted:

a. In Daniel, תנדע iv. 22, 23, 29, 30; אנדע ii. 9; ינדעוּן
iv. 14; מנדע ii. 21, iv. 31, 33, v. 12; הנסקה vi. 24;
הנעל ii. 25; הנעלה iv. 3.

b. In Ezra, תנדע iv. 15.

c. In N. S. No examples.

d. In Eg. Ar. מנדעם Sach. often ; מנדע Sach. 43.1.5;
כנכר Sach. ix. 17, ii. 28, 3R27 ; צנפר Sach, ter.

e. In Nab. No examples.

f. In Pal. No examples.

g. In Onkelos. Only in חנגין Ex. xxxii. 19. See Dalman,
p. 102.

h. In Syr. only in ננברא; but "Nun stroked out later",
Nöldeke §28.

i. In Man. "manchmal", and especially nd for dd, ng for
gg, mb for bb. Nöldeke, §68.

j. In Sam. apparently never. The so-called Nun epenthetic is not an insertion. See Petermann, p. 9.

(4) It is epenthetic:
  a. Always with the impf. before suffixes. Marti §52b.
  b. Always with the impf. before suffixes. *id.*
  c. In N. S. לכתשנה Had. 31; but, לכתשה without Nun
   in the same line, ויהנסנה Zakir II 20.
  d. In Eg. Ar., it is frequent, יתקלנהי Sak. A6 [ת]תלנה
   id C3 (unsicher, Lidg). And almost always in the
   Sachau papyri. (See *id.* p. 272).
  e. In Nab. no examples have been found.
  f. In Palm. יכילנה T II. b23; but יפתחיהי Cl. Gan. I⁶.
  g. In Onk., always with impf. before suffixes. See Dalman pp. 368–374.
  h. In Syriac it is not found. See Nöldeke §28.
  i. In Mandean it is apparently not used. See Nöldeke
   §200.
  j. The Samaritan often employs it. See Petermann p. 9,
   and numerous examples on p. 32.

(5) It is retained at end of syllable:
  a. In Dan. הנפק v. 2, הנפקו v. 3, ינתן ii. 16, אנבה iv. 9,
   הנחת v. 20, אנפוהי ii. 46, אנתון , אנתה .
  b. In Ezra הנפק v. 14 *bis.*, vi. 5, הנזקת iv. 22, תהנזק iv. 13,
   מהנזקת iv. 15, מנתן vii. 20, תנתן vii. 20, ינתנון iv. 13,
   הנטין vi. 9.
  c. In N. S. ינסחוהי Tay. 14, [ו]יהנ[פק] Tay. iii. 21, ינצר Ner.
   i. 13, תנצר Ner. i. 12.
  d. In Eg. Ar., almost always. In Sayce–Cowley 34 exs;
   in Sachau pap. 34 exs. See SC, p. 18, and
   Sachau p. 271.
  e. In Nab., ינפק CIS.197², ינתן CIS.197³,⁶, 198⁵, אנתתה
   Litt. ii. 8.
  f. In Palm., never in examples found.
  g. In Onk., מינסב, גינתא, שינתא and before and ה and ע,
   Dalm. p. 101, and often at end of word. *id.* 102, e. g.
   תמן for תמה.
  h. In Syr., גנתא, שכינתא, מדינתא and before He. See
   Nöldeke §28.

i. In Mand., אופיא, שכינתא, מדינתא, נינתא. See Nöldeke
   Gr. p. 52.

j. In Sam. הנפק, and often. See Pet. p. 35.

It will be noted that so far as examples are found there is an
exact agreement in the use of Nun between Daniel and the
North Syrian and Egypto-Aramaic. The latter is in perfect
agreement with Daniel in every one of the five particulars.
The examples of the uses of Nun are extremely rare in the
Nabatean and Palmyrene, so that no comparison can be made.
The agreement in the Onkelos is close, but an agreement for
a late date and a "near alliance" of the dialect of Onkelos
with that of Daniel loses its force in view of the like close
agreement between the dialect of Daniel and that of the inscriptions of Northern Syria and of Egypt.

8. *Use of Sodhe, 'Ayin and Qoph.* The fact that Daniel
writes the word for "earth, land" with an 'Ayin instead of a
Qoph is taken by Dr. Driver as a positive proof that "the
Aramaic of Daniel was not that spoken at Babylon in Daniel's
age". In support of this position he cites the fact that in
CIS 1-4, 7, 11, 28, 35 from Nineveh and in Clay's Aramaic
Endorsements, Nos. 5, 8, 11, 29, 40 from Babylon the word
is written ארקא and in Daniel ארעא. He might have added,
that in the Sendshirli inscriptions in like manner this is
the case not merely for this word but for two others; and that
the inscription from Zakir, also writes 'arqa. Further, he
might have said that in some of the Aramaic papyri from
Egypt the word is written with a Qoph.

But, he should have added, also, in order that we should
have a fair statement of the case, first, that the papyri of the
5th century B.C. have already begun to write this word with an
'Ayin. Some of them use 'Ayin alone, as for example, the
Sachau papyri and Sayce-Cowley A and G. Some use Qoph
alone, as C, D, E, of Sayce-Cowley and B uses both.

Secondly, it might be added that the papyri also write
קמרא for צמר "wool" and עק for עץ Bib. Aram. אע as
also both ערק and ערע where the Targum and Syriac have
ארע "to meet".

Thirdly, it should be added that the Targum of Onkelos
writes דעדק where the Syriac has דקדק.

Fourthly, that the Nabatean inscription of El-Hejra A.D.1. has קנם for the Phoenician and Hebrew עָנָשׁ " fine ".

Fifthly, that the Samaritan Targum has יעד (e. g. Lev. ix. 10) where the Syriac has יקד . Further, it often writes שׂמק for שׁמע.

Sixthly, the Mandean writings (6th to 9th cent. A.D.) still write ארקא. They also write אקמרא for צמר, אקאפרא for עפר, אקנא for עאנא = צאן (See Nöldeke Mand. Gram. p. 72) ; but they use the Hebrew spelling for עץ " tree ".

Seventhly, in the Aramaic verse in Jeremiah (x. 11) both writings of the word for earth occur.

Eighthly, Ezra always uses 'Ayin just as Daniel does.

From the above statements it will be seen that Qoph was used to denote this sound from the 9th century B.C. to the 9th century A.D., and 'Ayin from the 5th century to the present. It is true that if Daniel were written in the 6th century B.C., it will have been the first record known in which 'Ayin was used. But it must be borne in mind, first, that in the 5th century Ezra also uses it always just as Daniel does; secondly, that in the same century the Aramaic papyri use both; thirdly, that there may have been two uses side by side at Babylon in the 6th century B.C. as well as at Syene in the 5th; and lastly, that someone must have used this writing first, and why not Daniel?

9. *Use of Other Letters.* With regard to the letters, Teth, Tau, Shin, Sin and Samekh, it is only necessary to say that they are written in general in the same way as in the Aramaic papyri and in Ezra, both from the 5th century B.C.

II. FORMS AND INFLECTIONS

1. With regard to the pronouns of Daniel, it may be said, that with the exception that *dh* is written with Dolath instead of with Zayin, they agree more closely in writing, form and inflection with those of the old Aramaic dialects found in the papyri and in the inscriptions of Syria than they do with those of the later inscriptions and Targums, or with those of the Syriac, Mandean and Samaritan documents.

2. With regard to the nouns, also, not merely in the forms

found but in the way they are written and in the inflection, they show an almost exact resemblance to the Northern Syrian inscriptions from the 9th to the 7th century B.C., and to the nouns found in the Egyptian papyri from the 5th century B.C.

3. With respect to the particles, the dialects differ so much both in the character and number of the particles used and in the meanings attached to them, that we shall have to postpone treatment of them to another time. Suffice it to say that with regard to the writing, forms, inflection and use, of those found in Daniel there is no good reason for supposing that they may not have characterized a dialect written at Babylon in the 6th century B.C.

4. With regard to the verbs used in Daniel, we shall go more into particulars. Next to the spelling of words in general the forms of the verbs and the spelling of them are made by Dr. Driver the principal ground upon which he bases his conclusion that the Aramaic of Daniel is late.

As to agreements in forms, all of the old Aramaic dialects, from the earliest to the old Syriac and Mandean inclusive, have the three active stems Peal, Paal, and Aphel or Haphal, and the two reflective or passive stems Ethpeel and Ethpaal, varying mostly only in certain particulars of spelling. We shall not go into these variations except as it is necessary to make clear the three points specified by Dr. Driver in *LOT* p. 504.

a. His first point is, that the imperfect of Lomadh Aleph verbs in Nabatean and in the Palmyrene Tariff is found with Aleph and not with Yodh. The inference that we are intended to draw is, that inasmuch as Daniel has in like manner Aleph and not Yodh, therefore it is from the same region and age.

But, first, while it is true that Yodh alone has thus far been found in the inscriptions antedating 600 B.C. as the concluding consonant of Lomadh He verbs, it is questionable if they should be brought into this comparison. For in Egypto-Aramaic, the forms ending in Yodh are all apparently Jussive forms, (See Sachau p. 270) and these forms are carefully distinguished from the forms ending in He which are the regular indicative forms. In the Sendshirli inscriptions also,

three of the forms are also certainly Jussives, one of them occurring with the negative 'al as in the Sachau papyri; and the
fourth follows a Wau that is probably a Wau conversive,
since it follows a perfect and is used in the same sense. Following the analogy of the Hebrew, which uses the Jussive,
or a form like it, after Wau conversive, we would classify
this fourth imperfect in the Hadad inscription as a Jussive
also. The use of a Wau conversive in the Aramaic of the
Hadad inscription is rendered probable by its certain use in
the Zakir inscription, where we have ויאמר, ואמא and ויענני.

The forms in Yodh of the early inscriptions being thus
ruled out of the discussion, we find that the Egypto-Aramaic
except in the Jussive employs consistently a He at the end of
the imperfect of Lomadh He verbs and Aleph at the end of
Lomadh Aleph verbs; whereas Daniel employs Aleph usually
for both and exceptionally He for both. Nabatean goes one
step further and never employs anything but Aleph for both.
The Palmyrene Tariff uses He once; but everywhere else,
both in the Tariff and elsewhere uses Aleph. The Aramaic
of the Targums and Talmud has uniformly a Yodh at the
end. The Syriac as uniformly has Aleph, while the Mandean
has Yodh followed by Aleph. The Samaritan commonly employs Yodh, but He is occasionally found.

From all which it appears: First, that the only Aramaic
that employs He at the end of its Lomadh He verbs in the
imperfect is the Aramaic that was written by Jews, or those
directly influenced by Jews, such as the Aramaic papyri of
Egypt, and the works of Daniel and Ezra. The few sporadic
cases of its employment in Samaritan and the òne instance of
its use in Palmyrene may be attributed to the same influence.
Secondly, it appears that Yodh was used by the Arameans
who lived and wrote in Palestine after Ezra's time as is evident from the usage of the Jewish Targums and of the Talmud and of the Samaritans. It was used, also, by the Jews
who wrote the Babylonian Talmud; and in the forms of the
imperfect used in the Hadad inscription from Northern Syria.
Thirdly, Aleph was, with the one exception in Palmyrene noted
above, the universal ending in the dialects between Palestine
and Syria on the one hand and the Mandeans on the other,

i. e., among the Nabateans, the Palmyrenes, and the so-called Syrians. Fourthly, the Mandeans used both at once and together, i. e. a Yodh followed by an Aleph. Fifthly, Daniel being in the central country between the two extremes may well have used Aleph, as all other dialects in the central zone have done, his exceptional use of He being due to Hebrew influence.

b. Dr. Driver's second point is, that the Aramaic of Daniel is late, because a Hophal has been discovered in the Palmyrene Tariff, written in 137 A.D. He might have added, because another is found in the Targum of Onkelos, and two in the Jerusalem Targum I. (See Dalman p. 253). These last are probably not mentioned by him because they are so sporadic and obviously due to Hebrew influence. As to the first point, it may be said,

(1) That it is doubtful if there be a Hophal form in the Tariff. The words יכתב and יובן may be otherwise explained in perfect harmony with common Aramaic usage, and are so explained by Duval and Cooke. If אשׁר be a passive of the causative stem and not the active, it is formed rather after the analogy of the Arabaic 4th stem than after that of the Hebrew, or Bib. Aramaic Hophal. Our readers will notice that these verbal forms are without any vowel, or other points that distinguish species or stem. Whether they be Hophals or not depends upon the pointing that you insert.

(2) That in this same Tariff, we find the Ittaphal used six times in the passive of the causative stem. Now, it is a noteworthy fact that no dialect that uses the Hophal uses the Ittaphal also, and vice versa. The Sendshirli inscriptions have the Hophal once in the participle מימת from מות. Daniel has the Hophal of nine verbs in eleven different forms. Ezra has but one Hophal. But none of these three dialects (or two, if you put Ezra in the same dialect with Daniel) has an Ittaphal.

On the other hand, the Aramaic of the Talmud and Targums, of the Palmyrene inscriptions, of Syriac and Mandean, and Samaritan, employs the Ittaphal to the entire exclusion of the Hophal or Ophal, unless these unpointed Palmyrene words be treated as such. The Targum of Onkelos has 20 verbs in the Ittaphal and not one case of the Hophal, unless a variant reading in Ex. xix. 13 be classed as such (See Dalman Gram. der jüd.-pal. Aram. § § 59.6 and 64).

(3) If it is right for Dr. Driver to make as much as he does of the agreements between Daniel and the Nabatean and Palmyrene inscriptions as regards the writing of Aleph and He in certain forms in order to prove that they are or may have been written near the same time, it is no more than fair to suggest that the fact that Daniel uses a Hophal while in Palmyrene we find an Ophal might better be regarded as supporting the theory that the two dialects were spoken at different dates. In fact, since the bulk of the population of Palmyra was Arab and since many proper names, especially of gods, and several common names of Arabic origin appear in their literature, we might expect to find in the Palmyrene traces of Arabic grammatical usages. (Cooke N. S. Insc. p. 264). This אשר might indeed be the passive of the 4th stem 'ushira and be due to Arabaic influence; just as the Hophals in Daniel and the Niphals in Samaritan are due to Hebrew influence.

The relations of the dialects, so far as the forms of the verbs are concerned, will be best seen from the series of tables to be found in the Appendix. From these tables it will appear that no two dialects agree exactly in the forms used by them. As to forms in general it appears that Daniel agrees more nearly with Ezra and Egypto-Aramaic than with any later dialects. As to the Hophal, the possible use of one form of it in Pal. and Onk. is offset by the certain use of the Hophal in Ezra and its probable use in Hadad 24 and 26.

c. Dr. Driver uses the fact that עבידת, the third singular feminine perfect passive, is found in CIS 196:7, a Nabatean inscription from 37 A.D., to show that Daniel may have been written late. We, also, think that this is a perfect passive; though in regard to the other example cited, the כתב of the Palmyrene Tariff, we agree with Prof. Cooke (NSI p. 334), that it is not necessary to treat it as a passive, whether Pual, or Peîl. We do think, however, that it would have been right for Dr. Driver to have cited the Samaritan נסבת the translation in Gen. iii. 19 of the Hebrew לקחה " was taken"; as also the אחידת of Meg. Taan. (See Dalman p. 253).

But that our readers, most of whom are not specialists, may be able to estimate these facts at their true value in their relation to the question of the date of Daniel, it may be well to add, that not merely Ezra but the Aramaic papyri also, make use of this form. Ezra has יהיבו in v. 14 and the Sachau papyri have קטילו in i. 17 and ii. 15, לקיחת in 56 V.I.1; שאילתם in SC, 11 8; all of which are certainly true Peïl forms. Prof. Sachau adds further the forms עביד, קטיר, כתיב, and שליח. So that while admitting that this perfect passive *may* have been written late, the arguments from analogy and from frequency of use are decidedly in favor of an early date, inasmuch as Ezra and the Aramaic papyri are admittedly from the 5th century B.C. Further, the argument that the late isolated forms (one each in Nabatean, Samaritan and the Talmud) may have been used through imitation of, or under the influence of, the Arabic, which forms its passive regularly in this way, cannot be used with regard to the Aramaic of Egypt in the 5th century B.C.

d. The third plural of the feminine of the perfect ends in Wau in Daniel v. 5, vii. 20 and also in Nabatean in Cooke 80:1 and 85:1.

It is well known that in Hebrew the one form קטלו serves for the third feminine plural as well as for the masculine. In Daniel, this usage may have been derived from the Hebrew. Unfortunately, the old Aramaic inscriptions have no example of the feminine plural of the perfect.

The best possible explanations of the form עבדו in Nabatean are (1) that, like the Hebrew, there was no feminine form, or (2) that the sculptor followed the common manner in other inscriptions, where the masculine form is always used, or (3) that he used the masculine, because the nearest noun in each of the two cases is masculine in form, although the name of a woman.

The Sachau papyri, however, give us one form of the feminine plural imperfect and it agrees with the form in Daniel. I refer to ירוקן, p. 169 of Sachau's papyri. This is exactly like the ישכנן of Dan. iv. 18. The Nabatean gives us but one example of the imperfect third plural feminine and it has the same form as the masculine, i. e. יתקברון (See Cooke NSI p. 221 and p. 240).

It will be noticed, that the Qrê in Daniel has corrected the ending ו to הָ , in all cases in the perfect where it has a feminine subject. This harmonizes the form with that in use in the Assyrian and in the Targums of Onkelos and Jonathan. In the Jerusalem Targum, the third feminine perfect plural ends in *an;* in Syriac in *ên* or a silent Yodh, or the ending has disappeared; in Mandean, in יאן or א, but usually the ending has entirely disappeared; in Samaritan, in י, ין, or ן.

To sum up, the third feminine plural in the Kethiv of Daniel agrees with the form found in Nabatean, and the Qrê agrees with the forms found in the Targums of Onkelos and Jonathan.

The third feminine imperfect plural in Daniel agrees with that found in the Sachau papyri but differs from that found in Nabatean. In this case, all the other dialects agree with Daniel, the Nabatean standing alone.

e. The Nun, says Dr. Driver, is retained in the imperfect of Pe Nun verbs in the Nabatean just as in Daniel. A more exact statement of the case would be, that the Nun has been retained in *all* of the examples of the imperfect of Pe Nun verbs thus far found in Nabatean, agreeing in this respect with the comparatively few examples found in Daniel where Nun is not assimilated. A fuller statement of the facts with regard to the writing of Nun in all the dialects will give our readers an opportunity of judging for themselves as to the relation in this regard between the Aramaic of Daniel and of the other dialects.

1. As to the retention of a Nun in the imperfect of verbs Pe Nun, Daniel retains once only, Nabatean always, whereas Daniel assimilates eight times and Nabatean never. In Ezra, the Nun is retained three times, assimilated once. In Northern Aramaic (Sendshirli *et al.*) Nun is retained four times, assimilated four. In Egypto-Aramaic, Nun is retained about seventy times, assimilated about three. In Palmyrene, it is assimilated almost always, except before He or Ayin. In Samaritan, Nun is often retained, but most frequently assimilated. In

Syriac it is assimilated almost always and in Mandean often.

2. Nun is inserted often in Daniel and Mandean and not infrequently in Egypto-Aramaic; never in Nabatean, Palmyrene and Samaritan, nor in the North Syrian inscriptions; in Onkelos, Ezra, and Syriac, in only one word for each. Daniel here agrees on the one hand with the dialect nearest his own time and on the other with that nearest to Babylon.

3. In regard to dropping the Nun in the imperative Peal, all of the dialects in which imperatives are found agree. No examples have been found in Nabatean or Palmyrene.

4. In regard to Nun epenthetic, it is always found with the imperfect before suffixes in Daniel, Ezra, and Onkelos; never in Syriac and Mandean and there are no examples of it in Nabatean; nearly always in the North Syrian inscriptions and in Egypto-Aramaic and in Samaritan; and once in Palmyrene and once not.

f. Dr. Driver suggests that Daniel may be late because the word for "there is" is written the same way in Nabatean as in Daniel, i. e. איתי. This he says to overthrow the supposition that Daniel cannot be late because Onkelos has אית. A fuller statement with regard to איתי may be made so as to avoid misunderstandings. The long form is used in Daniel without suffixes, ten times; in Ezra, twice; in Sayce-Cowley, fifteen times; in Sachau papyri, six times; in Nabatean, twice. The short form is used in the Targums always; in Palmyrene once (the only time found); in Syriac and Mandean always; in Egypto-Aramaic once only. (i. e. in Sachau xxxi. 3).

g. Dr. Driver might well have added to his collection of similarities in the use of verb forms between the Nabatean and Daniel the remarkable fact that each of them has but one Shaphel form and that from the same root, i. e., שיזב Cooke No. 101:12 (or שיזב in one other insc. Duss and Macleane, No. 62). To be sure, this form is found in other late dialects, but not from this verb exclusively. The Galilean dialect has also שעבד, שיצי and שלהי. Onkelos has all of these and in addition שכליל and שלהב. The Targum of Jonathan adds שעמם and שחביב. The Jerusalem Targums use seven additional forms. The Syriac has at least twelve of these forms; the Mandean, six; and the

Modern Syriac, four. Besides these, we find half a dozen forms in New Hebrew.

In the Bible, Ezra has the form from two verbs, to wit שיצי and שכלל.

Fortunately, the form שיזב the only one that Daniel employs, is found also in the old Aramaic inscriptions and it is the only form yet found. It occurs in the Sachau papyri xxxxii. 14, xii. 5 and 56 obv. i. 6. So that the use of this form in Aramaic documents can now be traced back to a time when men who may have known Daniel were still living.

h. Dr. Driver might also have mentioned the fact that the preformative He in the causative stem, which Daniel employs so often, is no evidence of an early date, because it is found, also, in Nabatean in the form הקים CIS 161.1.1 and 349.2. To be sure, he may have thought this to be unnecessary, because Onkelos also has He in the causative of the verb to know (הודע) and in the borrowed Hebrew word הימין. As we, however, think that Daniel's use of He in this form is one of the strongest proofs of its early date, we shall present the facts as to the preformative of the causative stem in the Aramaic dialects.

1. The Syriac and Palmyrene always have Aleph.

2. The early inscriptions of Zakir, Sendshirli and Assyria and the Aramaic papyri always have He.

3. The Nabatean always has Aleph except in two cases, both from the same verb; the Targum of Onkelos has Aleph in scores of cases, He in but two verbs, one of them certainly borrowed from the Hebrew; the Mandean uses He nearly always, Aleph only occasionally; the Samaritan usually has Aleph, but sometimes He; the Targum of Jonathan uses He in the one form הופע and the Jerusalem Targums have He in eight or nine verbs, manifestly under the influence of Hebrew, as is doubtless the case in the Samaritan also.

4. Ezra has Aleph once only and He everywhere else.

5. Daniel has Aleph but twice and He in numerous instances.

It will thus be seen, that in this respect, the usage of Daniel is decidedly with the earlier dialects and against the later ones.

III. Syntax

We shall not have space here to discuss fully the syntactical relation of Daniel to the other dialects. As an example of the importance of this subject in determining the dialectical affinities, we shall mention only the manner of denoting the accusative.

1. All of the dialects agree in that they employ no particle before the indefinite direct object and in that they frequently omit it before the definite direct object as well.

2. Regarding the use of the particles, the following points are to be noticed:

a. Daniel, the Egyptian papyri, the Syriac and the Mandean, frequently employ Lomadh before the definite direct object, but not without many variations of usage one from the other, especially in the case of the Mandean. The Zakir, Sendshirli and Nabatean inscriptions never employ Lomadh with the direct object, and Palmyrene but once only. Ezra and the Samaritan seldom employ it. Onkelos sometimes uses it, but preceded by a pronominal suffix after the verb. In this respect it agrees with the common usage in the Mandean.

b. The Zakir inscription always uses אית before the definite direct object except when it is accompanied by a demonstrative pronoun.

Onkelos, the Samaritan, and the Nabatean often use it (written ית).

Palmyrene, Daniel and the Sendshirli inscriptions have it once each.

In Syriac it is seldom employed, and then mostly in the Bible to render the Hebrew את.

Ezra, the Egyptian papyri, and the Mandean, never employ it.

It will be seen from the above that in respect to the use of Lomadh Daniel disagrees with all the dialects with which Dr. Driver says it is "nearly allied", and that it agrees most nearly with the Egypto-Aramaic, the one written just about the time that Daniel is said to have lived, and with the Syriac and Mandean, that were written in the regions the nearest to Babylon.

With regard to the use of ית as the sign of the definite object, Daniel employs it but once. In this respect he differs decidedly from Onkelos and the Nabatean, and agrees most nearly with the Sendshirli of the 8th century B.C., and with the Palmyrene. That it is employed so frequently in the earliest of all the inscriptions, that of Zakir and also in the Sendshirli, permits of its use by Daniel in the 6th century B.C.

IV. VOCABULARY

In discussing the vocabulary of Daniel we shall consider in order the relation that it bears to the vocabularies of Onkelos, the Nabateans, the Palmyrenes, and the Targum of Jonathan.

a. Onkelos. As a matter of fact, the vocabulary of Daniel is not "nearly allied" to that of Onkelos as will sufficiently appear from the following evidence which the writer has selected from a large number of similar proofs.

1. Let us call up the testimony of the verbs employed in the two dialects to denote the idea "to put, to set".

Daniel employs שים ten times in this sense. It is the only word used by him to express this idea. Ezra uses it sixteen times; Zakir four times; Sendshirli, four; Nerab, three; the Sachau papyri, thirteen times; and Teima, once. Onkelos never uses it but once for certain (Ler. 1914) and perhaps in one other place (Gen. 1. 26) where the text is disputed. This is most noteworthy inasmuch as שים "to put" occurs in the Hebrew Pentateuch 151 times and שית of like meaning, eighteen times. The common word in Onkelos to render these words is שוא by which he translates the Hebrew שים 130 times and שית fourteen times. The Hebrew שים he renders also by מנא twelve times; שרא and סדר three times each; גזר, עבד and אסר once each. The Hebrew שית he renders also by מנא, יהב, and ערב once each. The one time that Onkelos does use שים (Lev. xix. 14), it is a translation of נתן.

Further, it should be remarked with regard to שים, that neither the Targum of Jonathan, nor the Nabatean nor the Palmyrene uses it at all.

And again, it should be observed, that in Syriac and Mandean, both belonging to what is called Eastern Aramaic, שׁים
is the ordinary verb for " to put " just as it is in the North
Syrian and Egypto-Aramaic inscriptions and in Ezra and
Daniel.

Again, it should be observed on the other hand, that Daniel
does use שׁוא twice (iii. 29, v. 21), but never in the sense in
which it is employed in Onkelos. In Onkelos it always means
" to set, to put, to make "; but in Daniel it means " to be or
make like ". This meaning in Daniel is like that found in the
Egypto-Aramaic, the Syriac, and the Mandean, where the
primary meaning was " to be at par ", " to be equal to "; hence,
" to be worth " in a business sense and " to be worthy " or
" to agree " in a moral sense. It is so used seven times in the
SC papyri and frequently in both Syriac and Mandean.

Finally, of the other eight verbs which Onkelos uses to
translate שׁים and שׁית Daniel employs all but סדר and אסר; but
all of them only and always in a sense different entirely
from that in which they are employed in Onkelos as a rendering for the two Hebrew words for " to put ", except in the
case of the one word עבד which Onkelos uses for שׁים but
once and for שׁית not at all. Thus מנה is used in Daniel
in the sense of " to number " (three times), Pa. " to appoint "
(three times). So also in Dan. vii. 25, שׁרא " to loose "
(five times); נזר " to cut out ", (twice); יהב " to give,
deliver over " (twenty times, in Ezra eight times); ערב " to
mix ", (four times).

We hope our readers will peruse the preceding paragraphs
twice at least, that they may fully appreciate the data therein
presented. Here is an idea for the expression of which the
Hebrew Pentateuch uses two words 169 times. That one of
these two words which the Hebrew employs 151 times is rendered in Onkelos by a word that is never used in this sense
in Daniel, whereas Daniel uses to denote the idea the same
word that is found in Hebrew. Further, the Targum of Jonathan, the Nabatean, and the Palmyrene agree with Onkelos in
not using שׁים while the old inscriptions on the one hand and
the eastern dialects on the other, agree with Daniel in using it
and also in their use of שׁוא. Lastly, of the eight other words

found in Onkelos to render שׁים and שׁית, Daniel uses six, but only one of them in a sense that might be deemed equivalent to that of the verb " to put ".

If we had space, we would like to add a number of other demonstrations of like character with the above, some of which would be almost or quite as convincing. We hope that this one will be sufficient to make the reader pause at least for further light upon the subject before accepting the statement that the Aramaic of Daniel is " nearly allied " to that of Onkelos.

2. Not merely, however, in the pure Aramaic words employed, but also in the foreign words that are found in them, do the dialectical differences between Daniel and Onkelos appear.

(1) Daniel uses three words which seem to be Greek. These words are names of musical instruments, and things of this kind nearly always even to this day bear names which indicate more or less definitely the source, national or personal, from which they came. We are not going to discuss at this time the possibility of Greek words having been found in Aramaic in the 6th century B.C. We shall only remark in this connection, that Prof. Sachau thinks he has discovered three Greek words and one Latin one in the papyri of the 5th century B.C. But, when comparing the vocabulary of Daniel with that of Onkelos with which it is said to be " closely allied ", the great question is not how does it happen that there are three Greek words in Daniel, but rather why are there no more than three. Dalman in his Grammar of the Jewish-Palestinian Aramaic, pages 184-187, gives a list of twenty-five Greek nouns that occur in Onkelos. On page 183, he gives two denominative verbs found in Onkelos that are derived from Greek nouns that had been taken over into the dialect of the people from among whom the Targum originated. Moreover, these Greek words do not all occur in one section and in one phrase as in Daniel, but they are scattered all through the Pentateuch from the first chapter of Genesis to the latter part of Deuteronomy. These words do not denote articles of commerce merely, as is the case in Daniel, but governmental, geographical, and scientific terms, such as could

have come into use only after the conquest of Alexander. So that, as far as Greek words are concerned, the dialect of Onkelos differs from that of Daniel:

a. In the number of words that occur.

b. In the frequency of their occurrence.

c. In that they are scattered through the whole book in one case and confined to a single section and phrase in the other.

d. In that one borrows names of musical instruments merely, whereas the other has borrowed names of stuffs, stones, colors, and geographical, commercial, governmental and scientific terms. In Daniel, such borrowed terms are prevailingly Babylonian and Persian, never Greek.

e. In that the dialect of Onkelos has verbalized two Greek nouns at least, whereas all of Daniel's verbs are Aramaic (or Hebrew), except one, and it is Babylonian.

(2) The Aramaic of Daniel, according to Dr. Driver, has thirteen Persian words. We think this estimate is probably correct. The Targum of Onkelos, however, has but five Persian words. The most common of these, פתגם, occurs in the Hebrew of Esther and Ecclesiastes, once in each, and four times in the Aramaic of Ezra and twice in that of Daniel. Another, פרשגן, occurs also in the Hebrew of Ezra once and in the Aramaic three times. In Onkelos, it occurs only in Deut. xvii. 18. The other three are found in Onkelos once each. The Egyptian papyri have ten to fifteen Persian common names besides a large number of proper names. Ezra has at least ten. The Greek and Babylonian writers of the Persian period have also a large number of persian words (See Prof. John D. Davis in the Harper Memorial Volume). The Nabatean, on the other hand, has no Persian word and the Palmyrene only one common name (from 264 A.D.) and one proper name (from 125 A.D.) In the Targum of Jonathan there are but a very few Persian words.

So that in regard to the Persian words employed, Daniel is seen to agree with the writings from the Persian period, and not as Dr. Driver suggests with the Targums of Onkelos and Jonathan and with the Nabatean and Palmyrene inscriptions.

(3) An important element in the vocabulary of Daniel, to

which, however, Dr. Driver pays no attention, are the Babylonian words contained in it. The lately discovered documents of
this once important language have enabled us to explain a
number of words as of genuine Semitic origin, which were
formerly supposed to be of Persian origin, or to be Aramaic
words peculiar to Daniel. Of the former kind are many proper
names such as Ashpenaz, Beltshazzar, Abednego and others.
Of the latter class are אתּוּן, זִיו, חֲשַׁח, אֶשַׁף, שֵׁיזֵב, כֹּתֶל, and
perhaps נְסָךְ and רְחַץ. Of these Babylonian words, Ezra has
about eight common names and a number of proper ones, such
as Sheshbazzar and Zerubbabel. The Egypto-Aramaic, also,
is rich in Babylonian terms of both kinds, there being from
eleven to sixteen Babylonian common names and a large number of proper names in the Sayce-Cowley papyri alone.

On the other hand, the Targum of Onkelos has probably
only six or seven words of Babylonian origin and all of them
are found in, and perhaps most if not all of them derived by,
Onkelos from the Babylonian through the earlier works of
Daniel and Ezra.

b. Vocabulary of the Nabateans. It is impossible for the
writer to conceive how anyone who had read the Nabatean
inscriptions could assert that, so far as vocabulary is concerned,
the language is " nearly allied " to that of Daniel. Take for
the sake of comparison with Daniel the El Hejra inscription of
A.D.1 (Cooke p. 220). There are sixty-three words in this
inscription. Fourteen of these are proper names, of which
one is the name of a place, one of a month, five the names of
gods, and seven the names of persons. All of these are Arabic
except the name of the month Tebeth which is Babylonian.
There are forty-nine other words, twenty-five of which are
found in Daniel. But of these three are pronouns and eleven
are particles. The five verbs are עֲבַד, נְתַן, כְּתַב, נְפַק and זְבַן,
to which may be added אִיתַי " there is ", all of which are
found in Egypto-Aramaic and all but זְבַן in Ezra. They are
found in Syriac, Mandean, and all in Onkelos, except
זְבַן (one or two derivatives of which are found, however).
Palmyrean, also, has all of them. The nouns are אֱלָף, יַד,
יְרַח שְׁנָה, and מֶלֶךְ, all words that are found in Babylonian and
Hebrew as well as in Egypto-Aramaic and all later Aramaic

dialects. As to the twenty-four words that are not found in Daniel five are Arabic nouns and two are Arabic verbs, i. e., Arabaic roots in Aramaic forms. Moreover one word is possibly Babylonian and one possibly Latin; six are particles, one of which is probably Arabic; one is of doubtful origin and meaning; and the others are the words for "nine", "self", "posterity", "daughter", "good", "love", and for "to bury".

This is a fair sample of the longest and most distinctively Nabatean inscription. Occasionally, we meet with a Greek word, or even a Latin word, and there is possibly one Babylonian word, but there are no Persian words and no Hebrew ones. The distinctive feature of this dialect is its Arabisms. We leave the intelligent reader to form his own judgment as to whether the Nabatean dialect is "nearly allied" to that of Daniel, in which there are *no* Arabic words, but many Hebrew, Persian, and Babylonian ones.

c. The Vocabulary of the Palmyrenes. As an example of the Palmyrene inscriptions, we shall give an analysis of No. 129 in Cooke's NSI. p. 249, (A.D. 264). The first line has one Aramaic, one Latin and two Greek words; the second, one Aramaic, two Latin, and one Persian word; the third, one Aramaic, two Latin, and one Greek word; the fourth, three Aramaic, one Greek, and two Arabic words; the fifth, five Aramaic, and one Babylonian word; the sixth, one Aramaic word followed by the date.

We shall give also a translation of No. 127. "*Septimius Worod, most excellent* (Gk) *procurator* (Gk) *ducenarius* (Lat) which has been set up to his honor, by *Julius Aurelius Nebu-bad,* son of *So'adu* (son of) *Haira, strategos* (Gk) of the *colony* (Lat), his friend. The year 574 (i. e. 263 A.D.), in the month *Kislul.*"

Finally, we shall give a translation of No. 121. " Statue of *Julius Aurelius Zabd-ile,* son of *Maliku,* son of *Maliku,* (son of) *Nassum,* who was *strategos* (Gr) of the *colony* (Lat) at the coming of the good *Alexander Caesar;* and he served when *Crispinus* the *governor* was here and when he brought here the *legions* (Lat) many times; and he was chief of the market and spent *money* (Arab) in a·most generous manner; and he

led his life peaceably (?) ; on this account the good Yarhibal
has borne witness to him, and also *Julius,* who fosters and
loves the city; the *council* (Gk) and *people* (Gk) have set up
(this) to him to his honor. The year 554." (i. e. AD. 242-3).

The above are good examples of the composition of the
Palmyrene Aramaic dialect. Our readers will perceive that
the language is a mixture of pure Aramaic with Greek, Latin,
Arabic, and (in the case of proper names and names of
months) of Babylonian. Only one Persian word is here; but
this word is the title of a governmental official and was taken
over from the Sassanian Persians and not from the old Achae-
menids of Daniel's time.

Our readers will please notice that in the Palmyrene we
have a conglomerate of very different composition from that in
Daniel, which, as we saw above, is composed of Aramaic, He-
brew, Old Persian, Babylonian and Greek (3 words) ; whereas
Palmyrene is composed of Aramaic, Greek, Arabic, Latin,
Babylonian and New Persian (one word) with no Hebrew.

We have placed the names of the languages making up the
two dialects in the order of their relative frequency of occurrence. The reader may make his own conclusion as to
whether they are " nearly allied ".

d. The Targum of Jonathan. What we have said above
about the Targum of Onkelos is even more true of that of
Jonathan. See especially Dalman's Grammar and Levy's Dictionary.

D. As to Dr. Driver's fourth proposition, that the Aramaic
of Daniel is " that which was spoken in or near Palestine "
and " at a date after the conquest of Palestine by Alexander
the Great ", we shall address our remarks first to the statement
that such a dialect was spoken *near* Palestine, and we shall
begin by asking when was it spoken near Palestine and by
whom. The only evidence we have is (1) that from the North
Syrian inscriptions, but this language is not like that of
Daniel, for it has no Persian, no Babylonian, no Greek; (2)
that from the Nabateans, but we know that they were an Arab
people speaking or at least writing Aramaic and that of a
kind, as we have seen, unlike that found in Daniel; (3) that
from the Palmyrenes, but we have seen that the language of

the Palmyrenes was *not* like that of Daniel; (4) that of the Syrians, but their earliest document goes back only to 73 A.D. and the next to 201 A.D.; besides, as is well known, Syriac is not written in the dialect of Daniel. In other words, there is no evidence, that any dialect resembling Daniel's was ever spoken by anybody *near* Palestine.

Nor have we any evidence from *in* Palestine. Dr. Driver says that the Targums of Onkelos and Jonathan received their present form between the 4th and 6th century A.D. Now between the time of Ezra which he places in Palestine at 400 B.C. (probably c. 400 B.C., *LOT* p. 504) and that of the Targums, what evidence can be produced to show what the people living in Palestine spoke? There are no Aramaic inscriptions from Palestine from any time. The other Targums are certainly later than those of Onkelos and Jonathan. Besides, if anything earlier than these were forthcoming, we doubt not Dr. Driver would have produced it. Of course, there are the writings of the Samaritans; but in the first place, they are not written in a dialect resembling that of Daniel, and secondly, no one probably would contend that they reached their present form until long after the year 400 A.D.

But perhaps by *near Palestine,* Egypt might be meant. Here, however, we are met by two serious objections to Dr. Driver's proposition. First, the latest dated document from Egypt is from the year 400 B.C.; and secondly, the Aramaic of Egypt differs in some very important respects from that of Daniel. For example, it has no Hophal, nor is it full of Hebrew common words as Daniel is. Besides, it has Egyptian words, both proper and common, and Daniel has neither.

But, perhaps, *Babylon* is *near* Palestine. We are of the opinion that it is near enough for the dialect in which Daniel is written to have been spoken there. This provenience and this alone would in our opinion suit the peculiarities of the dialect of the book of Daniel. This would account for the absence of Egyptian words. This would account for the Persian and Babylonian and Hebrew elements that mix in with the pure Aramaic to form this dialect. Then, also, 150 years after Sennacherib had conquered the Greeks of Cilicia, thirty years after Nebuchadnezzar had conquered the Greek mercenaries of the king of Egypt, and long after he had taken Greek hirelings into his own service, we might expect to find the names of three Greek musical instruments in the language spoken by probably the major part of his subjects.

But how about the Persian words? There is no difficulty whatever about them. The children of Israel had been settled in the cities of the Medes for almost 200 years before Daniel is supposed to have been written. Some of these Israelites and many of the Jews were settled in Assyria and Babylonia where most if not all of the people spoke Aramaic. Nineveh and northern Assyria were conquered by the Medes about 606 B.C. Here were seventy years before Daniel was written for Israelites and Jews and Arameans to adopt Medo-Persian words. All the witnesses from antiquity unite to prove that the Medes and Persians were akin and spoke dialects of the same language. The Greeks and the Hebrew prophets use their names at times interchangeably. The proper names of gods and persons used among them are the same, or similar. No one can affirm with any evidence to support him that the words in Daniel called by us Persian might not rather be called Median. The difficulty arising from the way in which the author of Daniel writes a few of the sounds is more than offset by the fact that nowhere else than in Babylon at about the year 500 B.C. could such a composite Aramaic as that which we find therein have been written. Grammar and vocabulary alike can be best accounted for by supposing that the book was written by a Jew living in Babylon at about that time, that is, when Aramaic was the common language of the world of commerce and diplomacy and social intercourse, when Babylonian and Medo-Persian were contending for the universal dominion over the nations, and when Greek words were just beginning to appear in the Lingua Franca of international commerce.

CONCLUSION

In conclusion, we would express the hope that we have been able to convince our readers that in so far as philology is concerned there is no such evidence existing as Dr. Driver alleges, in support of the late date and western provenience of the book of Daniel. The evidence for the early date derived from the orthography is not as convincing in the case of every individual letter as could be desired; but taken as a whole, it is in favor of an early rather than of a late date. The evidence derived from forms and inflections and syntax is decidedly, and that from the vocabulary is overwhelmingly, in favor of an early date and of an eastern provenience. What may be called the pure Aramaic matrix of this unique conglomerate, which we call the dialect of Daniel, presents evidence in the words that it used to express the most common ideas that it differed materially from the dialects with which Dr. Driver affirms that it was " nearly allied ". These same words show that a close relationship existed between it and the dialect of Egypto-Aramaic of the 5th century B.C., and also a remarkable agreement with the Syriac and Mandean, among the most eastern of all the dialects. So that the evidence of the strictly Aramaic vocabulary of the dialect of Daniel is predominantly in favor of the early date and of the eastern provenience.

But, it is when we consider the foreign elements in the language, that we must be convinced that the evidence for the composition of the book at or near Babylon at some time not far removed from the founding of the Persian empire is simply overwhelming. At no other time could such a conglomerate have been composed. The nearest dialects to it in variety and kind of commingling elements are those of Ezra and of the Egyptian papyri, both from the 5th century B.C. At a time later than this, there is no evidence that any such dialect was in use. At a place far removed from Babylon, a composition of such heterogeneous elements could never have been produced. For there never has been a time and place known to history save Babylon in the latter half of the 6th century B.C., in which an Aramaic dialect with just such an admixture of foreign ingredients and in just such proportions could have been brought into existence. For, it must be borne in mind, that the place and time of all the Aramaic dialects can be determined approximately by the kinds and proportions of extraneous elements contained in them. Thus the Zakir inscription of 850 B.C. has no foreign elements, except perhaps Hebrew. The Sendshirli inscriptions of the latter part of the 8th century B.C. have Assyrian ingredients. The Egypto-Aramaic of the 5th century B.C. has Persian, Babylonian, Hebrew, and Egyptian terms, and perhaps one Latin and three Greek words. Ezra has Persian, Babylonian and Hebrew. The Nabatean has Arabic in large measure, one Babylonian word and a few Greek ones. The Palmyrene has Greek predominantly, some Arabic, and two Sassanian, or late Persian words. The Targum of Onkelos has mainly Greek words, (two of which have been verbalized after Aramaic forms), five Persian words, and some Hebrew and Babylonian elements. The Targum of Jonathan has yet more Greek nouns and three verbs likewise Aramaic in form derived from Greek nouns, at least one Latin word, apparently no Persian words, and only one Babylonian word or form, except such as are found in the Scriptures, and a considerable number of Hebrew words. The Syriac (Edessene) has hundreds of Greek words, a considerable number of which are verbalized; scores of Latin words; many Hebrew words, a few of them verbalized; a few Babylonian words and forms; many late Persian nouns, perhaps none of which are verbalized; a little Sanskrit, and in later works many Arabic nouns, especially names of persons and places. In New Syriac the foreign elements are predominantly Turkish, Arabic and Kurdish loan words.

Therefore, it being thus apparent that on the basis of foreign elements imbedded in Aramaic dialects, it is possible for the scholar to fix approximately the time and the locality in which the different dialects were spoken; all the more when as has been shown in the case of Daniel such a date and locality are required by the vocabulary of the pure Aramaic substratum and favored or at least permitted by its grammati-

cal forms and structure, we are abundantly justified in concluding that the dialect of Daniel containing, as it does, so many
Persian, Hebrew, and Babylonian elements, and so few Greek
words, with not one Egyptian, Latin or Arabic word, and
so nearly allied in grammatical form and structure to the
older Aramaic dialects and in its conglomerate vocabulary
to the dialects of Ezra and Egypto-Aramaic, must have been
used at or near Babylon at a time not long after the founding
of the Persian empire.

APPENDIX.

The verbal forms used by the Arameans may be denoted to the eye by three tables, giving the forms used between 900 and 400 B. C., between 400 B. C. and 700 A. D., and by the writers of Daniel and Ezra and the dialects of the Nabateans and Palmyrenes respectively.

TABLE I.

ZAKIR	SENDSHIRLI & NERAB	EG.-ARAMAIC
Peal	Peal	Peal
Paal (?)	Paal (?)	Paal
Hafal	Hafal	Hafal
	Ethpeel	Ethpeel
	Hafal (?)	Ethpaal
	Peil	Peil
		Shafel

TABLE II.

TRG. ONKELOS.	TRG. JNO.	SYRIAC	SAM.	MANDEAN
Peal	Peal	Peal	Peal	Peal
Paal	Paal	Paal	Pail	Pail
Afal	Afal	Afal	Afal	Afel
Ethpeel	Ethpeel	Ethpeel	Ethpeel	Hafel
Ethpaal	Ethpaal	Ethpaal	Ethpaal	Shafel
Ittafal	Ittafal	Ettafal	Ittafal	Safel
Pael	Ishtafal	Shafel	Nifal	Ethpeel
Pāel	Pāel	Safel	Pual (?)	Ethpael
Pālel	Pālel	Ethpauel (?)	Hafal' (?)	Ettafal
Palpel	Palpel	Palpel	Peil 1	Eshtafal
	Palel	Ethpaulel (?)		
Hofal 1 (?)	Ithpalpel	Paiel (?)		
	Hofal 1 (?)	Eshtafal		

TABLE III.

DANIEL	EZRA	NABATEAN	PALMYREAN
Peal	Peal	Peal	Peal
Paal	Afel	Paal	Paal
Hafel	Afel	Paal	Paal
Afel	Hafel	Afel	Afel
Shafel 1	Shafel 2	Hafel	
Ethpeel	Ethpeel	Shafel 1	
Ethpaal	Ethpaal	Ethpeel	Ethpeel
Palel 1	Pail	Ethpaal	Ethpaal
	Hafal 1	Peil 1	
Hofal 9	Hishtafal 1		
Hithpolel 1	————		
Hithpoal 1	————		
Peil	Peil		

THE PLACE OF THE RESURRECTION APPEARANCES OF JESUS

WILLIAM PARK ARMSTRONG

THE PLACE OF THE RESURRECTION
APPEARANCES OF JESUS

The early Christian community in Jerusalem believed that
Jesus of Nazareth, who had been crucified under Pontius Pilate, was the Messiah. This belief according to the earliest
tradition had its origin in the consciousness of Jesus himself,
for he both accepted the expression of it from others[1] and
gave explicit witness to it by his own words[2] and actions.[3]
It was shared by his disciples. Through his death an element
quite incongruous with their expectations was introduced into
it.[4] Yet the belief persisted and became a world-historic force.
In the earliest form of which we have knowledge,—that is, of
the faith of the primitive Christian community—it included
two distinctive features:—the death and the resurrection of
Jesus. There are clear indications in the Gospels that both
of these elements entered into Jesus' conception of his Messiahship;[5] but even if these indications be regarded merely as
reflections of early Christian faith they imply by contrast a

[1] Mt. xvi. 16; Mk. viii. 29; Lk. ix. 20.

[2] Especially in the self-designation "Son of Man"; cf. Holtzmann, *Das
mess. Bewusstsein Jesu*, 1907; *Lehrbuch d. neutest. Theologie*,[2] i, 1911,
pp. 295 ff.; Pfleiderer *Das Urchristentum*[2] usw. i, 1902, pp. 660 ff. Tillmann,
Der Menschensohn, BSt. xii. 1-2, 1907; Schlatter, *Der Zweifel an der Mes-
sianität Jesu, BFTh.* xi. 4, 1907; E. Klostermann, *Markus, HB.* ii. 1907,
pp. 67 f.; B. B. Warfield, *The Lord of Glory*, 1907, pp. 23 ff., etc.

[3] Mt. xxi. 1 ff; Mk. xi. 1 ff; Lk. xix. 29 ff.

[4] Mk. viii. 32, ix. 10, 32, x. 35 ff., xiv. 27 ff., 51; Lk. xxiv. 21;
cf. 1 Cor. i. 23; Gal. vi. 12ff; on the idea of a suffering Messiah in Judaism
cf. Bousset, *Religion d. Judentums*[2], 1906, p. 265; Schürer, *Gesch. d. jüd.
Volkes*[4] usw. ii, 1907, pp. 648 ff.; J. Weiss, *SNT.*[2] i, 1907, pp. 148 ff.;
Schweitzer, *Von Reimarus zu Wrede*, 1906, pp. 368 f., 383 ff.; Volz, *Jüdische
Eschatologie* usw, 1903, p. 237; Bertholet, *Biblische Theologie d. Alten
Testaments*, ii. 1911, p. 450.

[5] Mk. viii. 30 f, etc.

change in the content of faith which was not without a cause. And if this cause be not, or not alone, in the consciousness of Jesus and his teaching, it must be sought in the experience of the disciples subsequent to his death. How then did the faith in Jesus as the Messiah, which embraced his death and resurrection, emerge in the consciousness of the disciples? There can be no doubt that it did emerge and that it did contain these elements. This is proven by the testimony of Paul.[6] Converted to this faith within a few years after Jesus' death, he not only shared it from the beginning of his missionary activity,[7] but in it knew himself to be in full accord with the early Christian community in Jerusalem.[8] There is no trace of any difference of opinion on this subject.[9] The difficulties in Corinth about the resurrection concerned not Jesus but believers.[10] There is every reason to think that it had its origin

[6] 1 Cor. xv. 2–8: παρέδωκα γὰρ ὑμῖν ἐν πρώτοις, ὃ καὶ παρέλαβον, ὅτι Χριστὸς ἀπέθανεν ὑπὲρ τῶν ἁμαρτιῶν ἡμῶν κατὰ τὰς γραφάς, καὶ ὅτι ἐτάφη, καὶ ὅτι ἐγήγερται τῇ ἡμέρᾳ τῇ τρίτῃ κατὰ τὰς γραφάς, καὶ ὅτι ὤφθη Κηφᾷ, εἶτα τοῖς δώδεκα· ἔπειτα ὤφθη ἐπάνω πεντακοσίοις ἀδελφοῖς ἐφάπαξ, ἐξ ὧν οἱ πλείονες μένουσιν ἕως ἄρτι, τινὲς δὲ ἐκοιμήθησαν· ἔπειτα ὤφθη Ἰακώβῳ, εἶτα τοῖς ἀποστόλοις πᾶσιν· ἔσχατον δὲ πάντων ὡσπερεὶ τῷ ἐκτρώματι ὤφθη κἀμοί.

[7] It appears definitely in his earliest Epistle (1 Thess. i. 10, iv. 14); and it is impossible to suppose that so fundamental an element in his thought could have been absent prior to this and the fact of its subsequent introduction have left no trace in his Epistles. The character of his pre-Christian activity (Gal. i. 14, 24; 1 Cor. xv. 9), the manner of his conversion (Gal. i. 16, cf. i. 2; 1 Cor. ix. 1, xv. 8; cf. Acts ix. 3 ff.; xxii. 6 ff.; xxvi. 12 ff.) and the close association of the resurrection and the exaltation of Jesus (Rom. i. 4; viii. 34) require the presence of this element in Paul's faith from its inception.

[8] 1 Cor. xv. 1 ff.; Gal. i. 18 f.

[9] As there was about other matters touching the relation of the Gentile Christians to the ceremonial law; cf. the significant statement of Weizsäcker (*Das apostolische Zeitalter der christlichen Kirche*², 1892, pp. 16f) in regard to the fundamental agreement of Paul and the early Church in the christology which grew out of the common belief in the resurrection; cf. also F. Dibelius, *Das Abendmahl*, 1911, pp. 1 ff.

[10] Paul's argument for the resurrection of believers in 1 Cor. xv. is based upon the resurrection of Jesus as a premise of fact about which all were agreed. Kirsopp Lake says (*The Earlier Epistles of St. Paul*, 1911, pp. 215 f); " It is clear from 1 Cor. xv. that there was a party at Corinth which denied that there would ever be a resurrection of the dead. It is also plain that there was nevertheless no dispute as to the resurrection of

on the third day after Jesus' death,—on the first Easter Sunday, when the sepulchre of Jesus was found empty[11] and Jesus appeared to Peter and to others.

In the earliest documentary evidence Jesus himself is represented as the cause of this faith. His death was a well accredited fact. Belief in his resurrection is attributed to the self-manifestations of Jesus to his disciples and others by which he convinced them of his triumph over death; and this in turn gave to the empty tomb—a fact of their experience[12]— its true explanation.

The New Testament accounts of the self-manifestations or appearances of Jesus constitute an important element in the ex-

Christ, for the whole argument of St. Paul is based on the fact that there was a general consent on that subject. It has sometimes been thought that this implies that the Corinthians had no hope of any future life beyond death. But this view is an unjustified conclusion from I Cor. xv. 17-19. St. Paul is here arguing that there must be a resurrection, because a future life is impossible without one, and that the hope of the Christian to share in the life of Christ necessitates that he should rise from the dead just as Christ did. Moreover, the idea that there was no future life is as wholly foreign to the point of view of the "Mystery Religions" of the Corinthian world, as it was to that of Jewish theology. The question was not whether there would be a future life, but whether a future life must be attained by means of a resurrection, and St. Paul's argument is that in the first place the past resurrection of Christ is positive evidence for the future resurrection of Christians, and in the second place that the conception of a resurrection is central and essential in Christianity, which offers no hope of a future life for the dead apart from a resurrection." Cf. also Lake's estimate of the significance to be attached to the elements of Christian faith held in common by Paul and his readers and therefore presupposed in his Epistles, ibid., pp. 115, 132 f., 233 n., 277, 424, 437, and Exp. 1909, i, p. 506.

[11] This is witnessed by all the Gospels and is implied in I Cor. xv. 3 f. by the close association of the burial and the resurrection on the third day. It was thus part of the primitive apostolic tradition. On the recent discussion of the empty tomb cf. A. Meyer, Die Auferstehung Christi usw. 1905, pp. 106ff; K. Lake, The Historical Evidence for the Resurrection of Jesus Christ, 1907, pp. 240 ff.; H. J. Holtzmann, ThR. 1906, pp. 79 ff., 119 ff., ThLz. 1908, pp. 262 f.; P. W. Schmiedel, PrM. 1908, pp. 12ff; Korff, Die Auferstehung Christi usw. 1908, pp. 142ff; W. H. Ryder, HThR. 1909, pp. 1 ff.; C. R. Bowen, The Resurrection in the New Testament, 1911, pp. 204 ff.

[12] Cf. Lk. xxiv. 23; Jno. xx. 3 ff.

planation which the early Christians gave of an essential feature of their faith. If these accounts are trustworthy, there can be no reasonable doubt concerning the ground upon which the primitive faith in the resurrection rested. Undoubtedly they reflect the belief of the early Christians. But are they for this reason or because of their contents and mutual relations witnesses only to faith and not to fact? Historical criticism, it is true, is concerned primarily with the narratives, —their exact content, mutual and genetic relations, and their value; but the final judgment which it must render concerning the truthfulness of the narratives, their correspondence with reality,—involving as this does the idea of causation—cannot be made apart from a general world-view or ultimate philosophical theory.[18] And since the end of the process may be first in thought, the process itself will sometimes disclose the influence of theoretical considerations.

In considering the relation of early Christian belief to historical fact, critical investigation enters upon a historico-genetic analysis of the documentary evidence in which search is made in the details of the different narratives for traces of the stages through which the final result,—i. e. the belief whose origin the narratives professedly set forth—was attained. Among the details which may be expected to throw light on this process the indications of place or locality in the narratives of the appearances are not only important in themselves but have, since the time of Reimarus, Lessing, and Strauss, held a central place in modern discussion of the subject.

The witness of the New Testament to the place of the appearances is in general quite plain. In the list of appearances which Paul gives in 1 Cor. xv. 5-8 no mention is made of

[18] On this aspect of historical criticism cf. *PrThR.* 1910, pp. 247 ff.; Kiefl, *Der geschichtliche Christus und die moderne Philosophie,* 1911; and the discussions of the "religious à priori" by Bousset, *ThR.* 1909, pp. 419 ff., 471 ff. (cf. *ZThK.* 1910, pp. 341 ff.; 1911, pp. 141 ff.) ; Dunkmann, *Das religiöse Apriori und die Geschichte, BFTh.* xiv. 3, 1910; Wobbermin, *ZThK.* 1911, *Ergänzungsheft* 2; Troeltsch, *RGG.* ii. pp. 1437 ff., 1447 ff.; *Die Bedeutung der Geschichtlichkeit Jesu für den Glauben,* 1911; Mackintosh, *Exp.* 1911, i. pp. 434 ff.; Beth, *ThR.* 1912, pp. 1 ff.; also C. H. Weisse, *Evangelische Geschichte,* ii. 1838, pp. 441 ff.

place, although the Apostle incidentally alludes elsewhere to the place of one of them in a manner which presupposes knowledge of it.[14] In Mt. xxviii two appearances are narrated,— one to certain women in Jerusalem on Easter Sunday,[15] and one at a later time to the disciples in Galilee.[16] Mark in its earliest transmitted form ends abruptly at xvi. 8 without mention of an appearance; but the message of the young man at the sepulchre gives promise of an appearance in Galilee.[17] Lk. xxiv records at least two appearances,—one to Cleopas and his companion at Emmaus,[18] and one to the disciples in Jerusalem on the evening of Easter Sunday[19]—allusion being made also to a third, the appearance to Peter on Easter Sunday and by necessary implication in or near Jerusalem.[20] Jno. xx relates an appearance to Mary Magdalene at the sepulchre,[21] an appearance to the disciples—Thomas being absent—on Easter Sunday and in Jerusalem,[22] and an appearance to the disciples again—Thomas being present—a week later and most probably in Jerusalem.[23] Jno. xxi describes an appearance to

[14] Gal. i. 15 f. and 17 (καὶ πάλιν ὑπέστρεψα εἰς Δαμασκόν).

[15] xxviii. 9–10. καὶ ἰδοὺ Ἰησοῦς ὑπήντησεν αὐταῖς λέγων χαίρετε. αἱ δὲ προσελθοῦσαι ἐκράτησαν αὐτοῦ τοὺς πόδας καὶ προσεκύνησαν αὐτῷ. τότε λέγει αὐταῖς ὁ Ἰησοῦς μὴ φοβεῖσθε· ὑπάγετε ἀπαγγείλατε τοῖς ἀδελφοῖς μου ἵνα ἀπέλθωσιν εἰς τὴν Γαλιλαίαν, κἀκεῖ με ὄψονται.

[16] xxviii. 16–20 : οἱ δὲ ἔνδεκα μαθηταὶ ἐπορεύθησαν εἰς τὴν Γαλιλαίαν, εἰς τὸ ὄρος οὗ ἐτάξατο αὐτοῖς ὁ Ἰησοῦς, καὶ ἰδόντες αὐτὸν προσεκύνησαν, οἱ δὲ ἐδίστασαν. καὶ προσελθὼν ὁ Ἰησοῦς ἐλάλησεν αὐτοῖς λέγων ἐδόθη μοι πᾶσα ἐξουσία κτλ.

[17] xvi. 7 : ἀλλὰ ὑπάγετε εἴπατε τοῖς μαθηταῖς αὐτοῦ καὶ τῷ Πέτρῳ ὅτι προάγει ὑμᾶς εἰς τὴν Γαλιλαίαν· ἐκεῖ αὐτὸν ὄψεσθε, καθὼς εἶπεν ὑμῖν (cf. Mk. xiv. 28).

[18] xxiv. 13–35 : καὶ ἰδοὺ δύο ἐξ αὐτῶν αὐτῇ τῇ ἡμέρᾳ ἦσαν πορευόμενοι εἰς κώμην ἀπέχουσαν σταδίους ἑξήκοντα ἀπὸ Ἰερουσαλήμ, ᾗ ὄνομα Ἐμμαούς, καὶ αὐτοὶ ὡμίλουν πρὸς ἀλλήλους περὶ πάντων τῶν συμβεβηκότων τούτων. καὶ ἐγένετο ἐν τῷ ὁμιλεῖν αὐτοὺς καὶ συνζητεῖν, καὶ αὐτὸς Ἰησοῦς ἐγγίσας συνεπορεύετο αὐτοῖς κτλ.

[19] xxiv. 36 ff. : ταῦτα δὲ αὐτῶν λαλούντων αὐτὸς ἔστη ἐν μέσῳ αὐτῶν κτλ.

[20] xxiv. 33ᵇf. : καὶ εὗρον ἠθροισμένους τοὺς ἔνδεκα καὶ τοὺς σὺν αὐτοῖς, λέγοντας ὅτι ὄντως ἠγέρθη ὁ κύριος καὶ ὤφθη Σίμωνι.

[21] xx. 11–18 : Μαρία δὲ εἰστήκει πρὸς τῷ μνημείῳ ἔξω κλαίουσα . . . . ἐστράφη εἰς τὰ ὀπίσω, καὶ θεωρεῖ τὸν Ἰησοῦν ἑστῶτα κτλ.

[22] xx. 19–23 [24] : οὔσης οὖν ὀψίας τῇ ἡμέρᾳ ἐκείνῃ τῇ μιᾷ σαββάτων . . . ἦλθεν ὁ Ἰησοῦς καὶ ἔστη εἰς τὸ μέσον . . . Θωμᾶς δὲ εἷς ἐκ τῶν δώδεκα . . . οὐκ ἦν μετ' αὐτῶν ὅτε ἦλθεν Ἰησοῦς.

[23] xx. 26–29 : καὶ μεθ' ἡμέρας ὀκτὼ πάλιν ἦσαν ἔσω οἱ μαθηταὶ αὐτοῦ, καὶ Θωμᾶς μετ' αὐτῶν. ἔρχεται ὁ Ἰησοῦς κτλ.

seven disciples by the Sea of Tiberias in Galilee.[24]   Acts states that the period during which Jesus appeared to his disciples extended over forty days,[25] and records words of Paul which point to Jerusalem as the scene of the appearances.[26]

The most natural interpretation of this evidence in its entirety favors the view that there were appearances first in or near Jerusalem, then in Galilee, and finally in or near Jerusalem,—neglecting for the purpose of this discussion the place of the appearance to Paul.

Tradition later than the New Testament yields little or nothing of a trustworthy character. Of the endings which have been added to Mark, the longer[27] is composite in form, dependent on Luke and John,[28] and mentions appearances in or near Jerusalem—to Mary Magdalene, to two walking in the country, and to the Eleven. This ending must have been added to the Gospel in the second century,—probably before the middle of the century and in Asia Minor.[29] The short ending[30] is still later. It reports in a summary manner the delivery by the women of the message of the young man to "those about Peter", and then records an appearance in

[24] xxi. 1 ff.: μετὰ ταῦτα ἐφανέρωσεν ἑαυτὸν πάλιν Ἰησοῦς τοῖς μαθηταῖς ἐπὶ τῆς θαλάσσης τῆς Τιβεριάδος κτλ.

[25] i. 3: οἷς καὶ παρέστησεν ἑαυτὸν ζῶντα μετὰ τὸ παθεῖν αὐτὸν ἐν πολλοῖς τεκμηρίοις, δι' ἡμερῶν τεσσεράκοντα ὀπτανόμενος αὐτοῖς.

[26] xiii. 31: ὃς ὤφθη ἐπὶ ἡμέρας πλείους τοῖς συναναβᾶσιν αὐτῷ ἀπὸ τῆς Γαλιλαίας εἰς Ἰερουσαλήμ κτλ. cf. x. 40: τοῦτον ὁ θεὸς ἤγειρεν ἐν τῇ τρίτῃ ἡμέρᾳ καὶ ἔδωκεν αὐτὸν ἐμφανῆ γενέσθαι, οὐ παντὶ τῷ λαῷ, ἀλλὰ μάρτυσιν τοῖς προκεχειροτονημένοις ὑπὸ τοῦ θεοῦ, ἡμῖν, οἵτινες συνεφάγομεν καὶ συνεπίομεν αὐτῷ μετὰ τὸ ἀναστῆναι αὐτὸν ἐκ νεκρῶν.

[27] xvi. 9-20: ἀναστὰς δὲ πρωῒ πρώτῃ σαββάτου ἐφάνη πρῶτον Μαρίᾳ τῇ Μαγδαληνῇ . . . μετὰ δὲ ταῦτα δυσὶν ἐξ αὐτῶν περιπατοῦσιν ἐφανερώθη ἐν ἑτέρᾳ μορφῇ πορευομένοις εἰς ἀγρόν . . . ὕστερον δὲ ἀνακειμένοις αὐτοῖς τοῖς ἕνδεκα ἐφανερώθη κτλ.

[28] xvi. 9—Jno. xx. 1, 14-17, Lk. viii. 2; xvi. 10—Lk. xxiv. 11; xvi. 12—Lk. xxiv. 12-31; xvi. 14—Lk. xxiv. 41 ff.; xvi. 15—Lk. xxiv. 47; Mt. xxviii. 19; cf. Zahn, Einleitung³, ii. 1907, pp. 234, 244 f.; E. Klostermann, Markus, HB. ii. pp. 147 f.; Wohlenberg, Evang. d. Markus, ZK. ii. 1910, pp. 386 ff.

[29] Cf. Zahn, Gesch. d. nt. Kanons, ii. pp. 910 ff.; Einleitung, ii. pp. 232 ff.; Westcott and Hort, The New Testament in Greek, 1882, ii, Appendix, pp. 29 ff.; Swete, The Gospel according to St. Mark, 1898, pp. xcvi. ff.

[30] Πάντα δὲ τὰ παρηγγελμένα τοῖς περὶ τὸν Πέτρον συντόμως ἐξήγγειλαν. Μετὰ δὲ ταῦτα καὶ αὐτὸς ὁ Ἰησοῦς ἀπὸ ἀνατολῆς καὶ ἄχρι δύσεως ἐξαπέστειλεν δι' αὐτῶν τὸ ἱερὸν καὶ ἄφθαρτον κήρυγμα τῆς αἰωνίου σωτηρίας.

which Jesus sends forth through them—i. e. those about Peter—" the holy and incorruptible preaching of eternal salvation ". No mention is made of the place or the time but it is natural to infer from the preceding context, which this ending was intended to supplement and complete, that the place was Jerusalem and the time Easter Sunday. A quotation from the Gospel according to the Hebrews[31] (2nd century) tell of an appearance to James, the brother of the Lord, and to others,—probably in Jerusalem—but its description of the attendant circumstances is plainly secondary. The Gospel of Peter[32] (2nd century) is dependent on the canonical Gospels and distinctly secondary in its account of the resurrection. It does not record an appearance to the women or to the disciples, but seems on the point of narrating an incident not unlike the appearance to the seven by the Sea of Tiberias[33] when the fragment ends abruptly. Its most distinctive feature is the description of the return of the disciples to Galilee at the end of the feast in sorrow, apparently without knowledge either of the experience of the women at the sepulchre as recorded in the canonical Gospels or of the resurrection. A Coptic document[34] (4th or 5th century, but thought to embody a second century narrative[35]) contains in fragmentary form an account of an appearance to Mary, Martha and Mary Magdalene at the sepulchre and then to the disciples,—by plain implication, in Jerusalem. The Syriac Didascalia[36] (4th century) records an appearance to Mary Magdalene and Mary, the daughter of James, then an appearance in the house of Levi, and finally an appearance to us (i. e. the disciples),—certainly at first

[31] Hieronymus, *Liber de viris inlustribus,* in Gebhardt u. Harnack, *TU.* xiv. 1896, p. 8; cf. Appendix, p. 351, I.

[32] Cf. Appendix, p. 351, II.

[33] Jno. xxi. 1 ff.

[34] C. Schmidt, *SAB.* 1895, pp. 705-711; Harnack, *Theologische Studien B. Weiss dargebracht,* 1897, pp. 1-8, cf. Appendix, p. 352, III.

[35] Schmidt *Ibid.;* Harnack *Ibid.;* cf. Ehrhard, *Die altchrist. Literatur und ihre Erforschung von 1884-1900,* in *Strassburger Theologische Studien,* 1900, p. 146.

[36] Achelis und Flemming, in Gebhardt u. Harnack, *TU.* NF. x. 1904, cap. xxi; cf. Hennecke, *Neutest. Apokryphen,* 1904, pp. 292 ff.; Preuschen, *Antilegomena²,* 1905, p. 81; and Appendix, pp. 352 f., IV.

near Jerusalem and subsequently in the place where this document located the house of Levi, probably in Jerusalem. Tertullian[37] speaks of appearances in Galilee in Judea; the Acts of Pilate[38] (4th century) of an appearance to Joseph of Arimathea in Jerusalem and to the disciples on the Mount of Olives in Galilee.

No theory of the place of the appearances can be based solely on the extra-canonical tradition. Appeal is generally made to this tradition in support of a particular interpretation of the primary evidence. Critical analysis of the primary evidence has yielded but three theories. The appearances—however conceived—may be held to have occurred in Galilee, in or near Jerusalem, or in both places.

THE GALILEAN THEORY

The view that the first and only resurrection-appearances of Jesus took place in Galilee is not merely wide-spread but has attained the status of a " critical tradition ". It is closely associated with the theory of a " flight of the disciples to Galilee " on the night of Jesus' arrest or not later than Easter morning and without knowledge of the empty tomb or news of the resurrection.[39] The advocates of this view usually

[37] *Apol.* xxi.; cf. Appendix, p. 353, V.

[38] Tischendorf, *Evangelia Apocrypha*[2], 1876, *Acta Pilati;* cf. Appendix, pp. 353 f., VI. Justin, *Dial.* li. 271 A, mentions the intention to appear again in Jerusalem (πάλιν παραγενήσεσθαι ἐν Ἱερουσαλήμ) as part of Jesus' prophecies of his passion; the scattering and flight of the disciples (Mk. xiv. 27; Mt. xxvi. 31; Mk. xiv. 50; Mt. xxvi. 56) is retained but without intimation of a "flight to Galilee": *Apol.* i. 50, 86 A μετὰ οὖν τὸ σταυρωθῆναι αὐτὸν καὶ οἱ γνώριμοι αὐτοῦ πάντες ἀπέστησαν, ἀρνησάμενοι αὐτόν· ὕστερον δέ, ἐκ νεκρῶν ἀναστάντος καὶ ὀφθέντος αὐτοῖς κτλ: *Dial.* 53, 273 C μετὰ γὰρ τὸ σταυρωθῆναι αὐτὸν οἱ σὺν αὐτῷ ὄντες μαθηταὶ αὐτοῦ διεσκεδάσθησαν, μέχρις ὅτου ἀνέστη ἐκ νεκρῶν καὶ πέπεικεν αὐτοὺς ὅτι οὕτως προεπεφήτευτο περὶ αὐτοῦ παθεῖν αὐτὸν κτλ: *Dial.* 106, 333 C μετενόησαν ἐπὶ τῷ ἀφίστασθαι αὐτοῦ ὅτε ἐσταυρώθη κτλ. Tatian, beside Jerusalem and Galilee, names Capernaum (cf. Zahn, *Forschungen*, i. 1881, pp. 218 f; Bowen, *Resurrection in NT*, p. 426) ; for still later literature cf. W. Bauer, *Leben Jesu im Zeitalter der neutest. Apokryphen*, 1909, pp. 265 f.

[39] J. Weiss, *Der erste Korintherbrief*[9], MK. v. 1910, p. 350, characterizes the " flight" theory as a " scientific legend "); cf. Schwartzkopff, *Die Weissagungen Jesu Christi* usw, 1895, pp. 70 f., *The Prophecies of Jesus Christ*, etc. 1897, pp. 113 f.; J. A. Cramer, *ThT.* 1910, pp. 192 ff.

seek to distinguish a primary from a secondary tradition in the Gospels,—Matthew and Mark being the representatives of the one, Luke and John of the other.

Strauss says:[40] " The most important of all the differences in the history of the resurrection turns upon the question, what locality did Jesus design to be the chief theatre of his appearances after the resurrection? " After reviewing the contents of the Gospel narratives, he continues:[41] ." Here two questions inevitably arise; 1st, how can Jesus have directed the disciples to journey into Galilee, and yet at the same time have commanded them to remain in Jerusalem until Pentecost? and 2ndly, how could he refer them to a promised appearance in Galilee, when he had the intention of showing himself to them that very day in and near Jerusalem? " He quotes the Fragmentist [Reimarus] :[42] " If the disciples collectively twice saw him, spoke with him, touched him, and ate with him, in Jerusalem; how can it be that they must have had to take a long journey into Galilee in order to see him? "[43] " According to this ", continues Strauss,[44] " we must agree with the latest criticism of the gospel of Matthew, in acknowledging the contradiction between it and the rest in relation to the locality of the appearances of Jesus after the resurrection; but, it must be asked, can we also approve the verdict of this criticism when it at once renounces the representation of the first Gospel in favor of that of the other Evangelists." He then asks the question:[45] " which of the two divergent accounts is the best adapted to be regarded as a traditional modification and development of the other? ", and answers by maintaining the primitive character of the Matthæan account. The possibility[46] " that perhaps originally only Galilean appearances of the risen Jesus were known, but that tradition gradually added appearances in Judea and Jeru-

---

[40] *The Life of Jesus,* translated from the fourth German edition by George Eliot, fifth ed. in one vol. 1906, p. 718.

[41] *Ibid.* p. 719.   [42] *Ibid.* p. 720.

[43] Cf. also the statement (p. 724) that the appearance before the Apostles in Jerusalem could not have happened because Matthew makes the eleven journey to Galilee in order to see Jesus.

[44] *Ibid.* p. 721.   [45] *Ibid.* p. 721.   [46] *Ibid.* pp. 722 f.

salem, and that at length these completely supplanted the
former, may on many grounds be heightened into a probability ",—but chiefly on the ground that it seems to be " a
natural idea ".

Better knowledge of the history of the text of the New
Testament has eliminated certain features of Strauss' criticism of the Gospels, but in his central contention and in some
of his principles he has had many followers.

Weizsäcker[47] argues that if the disciples of Jesus withdrew
after his death to Galilee, then it was there that the faith in
which they returned to Jerusalem had its origin. This faith
that Jesus lives, that he is risen, which furnished for Peter as
it did for Paul the motive power of a life-work, originated in
an appearance to Peter in Galilee. This view, he admits, is not
in accord with the representation of the Gospels, but these are
held to be only secondary sources in comparison with Paul's
account since they are dominated by a tendency to accentuate
the physical reality of the resurrection. This tendency manifests itself especially in their account of the empty grave, in
the report of appearances in Jerusalem and in the ascription
of bodily or physical functions to the risen Jesus. All of
this is in conflict with Paul who knows nothing of the empty
grave or of the appearances to the women in Jerusalem. Paul
moreover gives a different description of the form of the appearances. From the fact that Paul does not mention the appearances in Jerusalem which are reported in the Gospels
Weizsäcker infers ignorance of them not merely on Paul's
part but on that of the leaders of the Jerusalem Church as
well, for it was from them that Paul received his information
about the appearances. In the earlier form of Gospel tradition (Mt.-Mk.) appearances in Galilee are reported, and
only in the later form (Lk.-Jno.) are they located in Jerusalem, with ever increasing emphasis of their physical, sensible
aspects. The first appearance to Peter finds only an echo in
Mark[48] and is mentioned by Luke[49] in evident dependence on
Paul. The Fourth Gospel mentions Peter's visit to the grave

[47] *Apos. Zeitalter*, pp. 3ff; cf. *Untersuchungen über d. evang. Geschichte*[2],
1901, pp. 363 ff.
[48] xvi. 7.   [49] xxiv. 34.

and only in the last chapter an appearance to him, but even then, not to him alone. Yet the fact that the first appearance was made to Peter, Weizsäcker regards as historically the most certain event in the whole of this dark period, for it alone explains the historical position of Peter who was undoubtedly the first man of the early Church.

Weizsäcker's statements characterize rather than ground the Galilean theory of the appearances; and this is true likewise of Wernle's more impassioned argument. Wernle[50] too takes as his starting point the flight and scattering of the disciples on the night of Jesus' arrest. The death of Jesus seemed for the moment to signalize the triumph of his enemies and the destruction of his cause. This appeared at first to have been realized in the scattering of the disciples. Contrary to expectation however the disciples soon assembled again, first in Galilee and then in Jerusalem. In the face of the murderers of Jesus they gave utterance to the enthusiastic cry " He is not dead; he lives!" The clever reckoning of the Sanhedrin overreached itself. The faith in the crucified and risen accomplished what the faith in the living had not been able to effect,—the founding of a new Church, the separation from Judaism and the conquest of the world. Whence came this change? The answer of the disciples was: The Lord has appeared to us, first to Peter, then to the Twelve, then to more than five hundred brethren at once, then to James, then to all the Apostles.[51] From these appearances—and the first must according to the oldest account have occurred in Galilee —they inferred the resurrection of Jesus and his continued

[50] *Die Anfänge unserer Religion*[2], 1904, pp. 81 f.; cf. *Die syn. Frage*, 1899, pp. 246 f. Bowen's view is not unlike Wernle's. He says (*Resurrection in NT.* p. 456) : " And the fact that the disciples' first feeling of amazement and terror was immediately swallowed up in the glad faith that their dear Master is alive forevermore, their heavenly friend and God's Messiah, is ' the perfect tribute' to the marvelous impression his loving personality had made on them. This is, after all, the great miracle, the impress of Jesus' personality on his disciples. It was so deep and strong, in a word, that they saw him after he had died. This is the real secret of the ' appearances ' ".

[51] 1 Cor. xv. 5-8.

existence in a glorious state of being. The new faith thus stood on the appearances alone. Our judgment concerning these appearances will depend in a measure on our confidence in Paul and his informer; but ultimately on our philosophical and religious standpoint—on our faith. Purely scientific considerations cannot decide in a matter that concerns the invisible world and the possibility of a communion of spirits; and, since for Christian faith the spiritual world is a reality transcending the sensible, material world, there should be no difficulty in believing that the real intervention of Jesus, though mediated by a vision, is the ground of the belief in the resurrection. The historian however cannot rest here, even though he concur in this judgment, since this would make the origin of Christianity dependent on chance, as if the cause of Jesus would or could have failed apart from this vision. In the person of Jesus was manifested a redeeming power too great and too triumphant to have been destroyed by a shameful death. Thus the appearances accomplished their far reaching effect not accidentally but because of the earlier redemptive impression of Jesus.

P. W. Schmiedel has given a fuller statement of the grounds upon which the Galilean theory is based. He says:[52] " An equally important point is that the first appearances happened in Galilee." For[53] " the most credible statement in the Synoptics is that of Mt. (and Mk.) that the first appearances were in Galilee. The appearance in Jerusalem to the two women (Mt. xxviii. 9 f.) is almost universally given up—not only because of the silence of all the other accounts, but also because in it Jesus only repeats the direction which the women had already received through the angel. If the disciples had seen Jesus in Jerusalem as Lk. states, it would be absolutely incomprehensible how Mk. and Mt. came to require them to repair to Galilee before they could receive a manifestation of Jesus. The converse on the other hand is very easy to understand; Lk. found it inconceivable that the disciples who, according to him, were still in Jerusalem, should have been unable to see Jesus until they went to Galilee. In actual fact the

---

[52] *EB.* iv. col. 4063.   [53] *EB.* ii. col. 1878 f.

disciples had already dispersed at Gethsemane (Mk. xiv. 50,
Mt. xxvi. 56) ; this Lk. very significantly omits. Even Peter,
after he had perceived, when he denied his Master, the dangers
he incurred, will hardly have exposed himself to these, gratui-
tously, any longer. At the cross only women, not disciples,
were present. Whither these last had betaken themselves we
are not told. But it is not difficult to conjecture that they had
gone to their native Galilee. The angelic command, therefore, that they should make this their rendezvous, may reasonably be taken as a veiled indication that they had already gone
thither. The presupposition made both by Mk. and by Mt.
that they were still in Jerusalem on the day of the resurrection is accordingly erroneous. It was this error of theirs
that led Lk. to his still more erroneous inversion of the actual
state of the facts." But[54] " if Galilee and Jerusalem were at
first mutually exclusive, both cannot rest upon equally valid
tradition; there must have been some reason why the one
locality was changed for the other. . . . if Mk. and
Mt. had to fall back on their own powers of conjecture,
where else were they to look for appearances if not in Jerusalem where the grave, the women, and the disciples were?
Thus the tradition which induced them to place the appearances in Galilee must have been one of very great stability."
And again[55] " As long as there was still current knowledge
that the first appearances of the risen Jesus were in Galilee,
the fact could be reconciled with the presence of the disciples
in Jerusalem on the morning of the resurrection only (a) on
the assumption that they were then directed to go to Galilee.
The natural media for conveying such a communication must
have seemed to be the angels at the sepulchre in the first instance, and after them the women. So Mk. and Mt.
So far as Mt. is concerned this direction to be given to
the disciples was perhaps the [or a] reason . . . why the
women should be made to go to the grave so early as the
evening ending the Sabbath, so that the disciples might still in
the course of the night have time to set out and if possible ·
obtain a sight of Jesus within three days after his crucifixion.

[54] *EB*. iv. col. 4064.   [55] *EB*. iv. col. 4072.

(b) Yet such a combination as this was altogether too strange. Why should Jesus not have appeared forthwith in Jerusalem to the disciples? Accordingly Lk. and Jn. simply suppressed the direction to go to Galilee, finding themselves unable to accept it, and transferred the appearances to Jerusalem. Or, it was not our common evangelists who did both things at one and the same time, but there had sprung up, irrespective of Mk. and Mt., the feeling that Jesus must in any case have already appeared to the disciples in Jerusalem; it presented itself to Lk. and Jn. with a certain degree of authority, and these writers had not now any occasion to invent but simply to choose what seemed to them the more probable representation, and then, when in the preparation of their respective books they reached the order to go to Galilee, merely to pass over it or get around it as no longer compatible with the new view."

This argument is interesting as a highly subjective reconstruction of a possible development of Gospel tradition regarding the place of the appearances on the hypothesis of a "flight of the disciples to Galilee." This hypothesis is maintained against all the documentary evidence,—the earlier (Mk. and Mt.) as well as the later (Lk. and Jno.), on Schmiedel's own analysis. The appearance to the women in Jerusalem—also contained in a representative of the earlier form of Gospel tradition (Mt.)—is rejected on equally subjective grounds; while the exposition of the origin and growth of the later form of Gospel tradition as embodied in Luke and John is little more than an elaboration of Strauss' principle that the tradition which reflects a "natural idea" is secondary. Of actual evidence in support of the Galilean theory Schmiedel offers nothing.

The advocates of the Galilean theory, finding so little in the Gospels that is favorable to their view and much that is opposed to it, have had recourse to later extra-canonical literature. When a fragment of the Gospel of Peter was discovered and published in 1892, Harnack[56] sought to show

---

[56] *Bruchstücke des Evangeliums und der Apokalypse des Petrus*[2]. 1893, pp. 31 ff., 62.

that it contained valuable material from which the character and probable contents of the original ending of Mark might be ascertained. This view was developed by Rohrbach[57] in a form subsequently approved in its essential features by Harnack himself.[58] From Mk. xiv. 28, xvi. 7 it is inferred that the Gospel in its original form narrated an appearance in Galilee, the ending having been removed before the Gospel was used by Matthew and Luke. From internal indications it is inferred that the original ending probably contained the following: an appearance to the disciples in Galilee, some word of Jesus in reference to the continuation of his work, ignorance on the part of the disciples of the resurrection until the appearance in Galilee, and an unpreparedness of the disciples for the first appearance. The other Gospels contain no trace of the existence of such an ending, for they all imply knowledge of the resurrection before the return of the disciples to Galilee. The literary phenomena of the Gospel of Peter however show that Mk. xvi. 1-8 is the source of its narrative in verses 50-57 and it is thought probable therefore that verses 58-60 depend on the lost ending. In these verses the disciples are represented as returning to Galilee at the end of the feast in sorrow and therefore without knowledge of the resurrection. Levi is called the son of Alphaeus,—a designation found only in Mk. ii. 14. And finally the Gospel of Peter breaks off just as it is about to narrate an appearance in Galilee. The character of the original ending of Mark thus explains its loss, and the circumstances of its loss explain the fact that it was not known to Matthew or Luke; for, because it did not agree with the tradition regarding the appearances which was current in Johannine circles in Asia Minor, it was intentionally removed and the secondary ending ([Mk.] xvi. 9-20) substituted for it,—although not necessarily at just the same time. The central point in the original ending must have been the restoration of Peter. This is equally central in Jno.

[57] *Der Schluss des Markusevangeliums* usw. 1894; *Die Berichte über die Auferstehung Jesu*, 1898.

[58] *Gesch. d. altchr. Lit. bis Eusebius*, ii. *Die Chronologie*, i. 1897, pp. 696 f.; *ThLz.* 1899, pp. 174 ff.; *Lukas der Arzt*, 1906, pp. 158 f.; *Neue Untersuchungen zur Apostelgeschichte*, 1911, pp. 110 ff.

xxi. But this chapter does not fit well after chapter xx, for it represents the disciples as returning to their fishing and this suits only a time before they had learned of the resur-rection—as in the Gospel of Peter and the original ending of Mark. The Gospel of Peter however is not dependent on Jno. xxi. The names Andrew and Levi and the designation of the appearance by the Sea as the third—manifestly a polemic against its representation as the first in the original ending of Mark—make the theory of dependence unlikely. Jno. xxi (but not verse 7 or the narrative about John at the close) is either a paraphrase of the original ending of Mark or an express criticism of it. According to Lk. xxiv. 34, 1 Cor. xv. 5 the first appearance was made to Peter; and it is probable therefore that in the original ending of Mark the first appearance in Galilee was represented as made to Peter alone. This was doubtless followed by an appearance to the Twelve (1 Cor. xv. 5) in Galilee (implied in Mark) and possibly in the evening at a meal (Lk.-Jno.). The alteration to which Mark was subjected moreover is not isolated but has in the other Gospels parallels which probably had their origin in the same circles.[59] This process of alteration was dominated by the tendency to substitute another tradition of the appearances for that of the original ending of Mark, that is,—to substitute Jerusalem for Galilee as the place of the first appearances, and to subordinate the appearance to Peter.

The central contention of this theory is the knowledge and use of the original ending of Mark by the Gospel of Peter. But the evidence for this is far from being conclusive. The return of the disciples to Galilee without knowledge of the resurrection is implied in the Gospel of Peter, but this is certainly a secondary feature closely connected with the tendency which characterizes its description of the resurrection.[60] The coincidence with Mk. ii. 14 does not prove knowledge and use of an original ending; while Luke by mentioning the appearance to Peter[61] falls out of its rôle, and John's

[59] Jno. xxi.; Mt. xxviii. 9-10; Lk. xxiv. 12; [Mk.] xvi. 9-20.

[60] Schubert, *Die Composition des pseudopetrinischen Evangelienfragments,* 1893, pp. 140 ff.

[61] xxiv. 34.

" polemic " third receives its character from the theory.[62]
W. Brückner[63] maintains against Rohrbach the dependence
of [Mk.] xvi. 9-20 on Luke and John. Lk. xxiv with its bold
transfer of the appearances from Galilee to Jerusalem is older;
but it is dependent on Mk. xvi. 1-8. In Lk. xxiv. 6, Mk. xvi.
7 (xiv. 28) is intentionally changed. The narrative of the
appearance to the disciples at Emmaus has its origin in the
dogmatic reflection and poetic art that created the allegories in
iv. 16-30, v. 1-10, vii. 36-49. Jno. xx is dependent on Lk.
xxiv and Mk. xvi, but its narrative is purely allegorical, the
different characters being merely typical stages of the faith in
the glorified Christ. Thus the tradition which locates the appearances in Jerusalem is Lucan rather than Johannine. The
Gospel of Peter and Jno. xxi furnish no support to the
Galilean localization, for it is not certain that the former
depends on the lost ending of Mark and the latter occupies
its proper place in an allegorical narrative. Matthew indeed
is dependent on Luke but its rejection of the Jerusalem for
the Galilean localization is deliberate.

The theory of a Lucan transformation of the primitive
Galilean localization of the appearances is carried forward by
Völter in his analysis of the Emmaus narrative.[64] Völter
holds that Jno. xxi and the last verses of the Gospel of Peter
are derived from the lost ending of Mark which contained
not only an appearance to Peter but also an appearance to the
disciples in Galilee, in both of which Jesus was made known
in the breaking of bread. The Galilean location of the appearance to Peter is implied in Mark, Luke, the Gospel ac-

---

[62] Cf. L. Brun, *ThStKr.* 1911, p. 167. Spitta, *Das Johannes-Evangelium*
usw. 1910, pp. 3 ff., explains τοῦτο ἤδη τρίτον of xxi. 14 by coördination
in the series ii. 11 (ταύτην ἐποίησεν ἀρχὴν τῶν σημείων at Cana) and iv.
54 (τοῦτο (πάλιν) δεύτερον σημεῖον ἐποίησεν at Cana-Capernaum). Chapter xxi
was added and transformed by a " Bearbeiter " from a document which
recounted the incident of Peter's call in the beginning of Jesus' Galilean
ministry. But much of Spitta's literary analysis is over subtle and its
subjectivity here is not transcended by the proposed—but extremely improbable—coördination and the hypothesis of redaction.

[63] *PrM.* 1899, pp. 41 ff., 76 ff., 153 ff.

[64] *Die Entstehung des Glaubens an die Auferstehung Jesu,* 1910; *PrM.*
1911, pp. 61ff.

cording to the Hebrews, and the Didascalia. Luke indeed locates this appearance near Jerusalem, but Cleopas is simply a transformation of Clopas[65] and his unnamed companion is no other than Peter[66] while Emmaus was a town in Galilee between Tiberias and Tarichäa.[67] The Gospel according to the Hebrews has also transformed this appearance, substituting, under the influence of its Jewish Christian tendency, James for Peter and Jerusalem for Galilee. The Didascalia witnesses to it by its account of an appearance in a house [of Levi] in Galilee. The second appearance was also in Galilee and to the Apostles. This is implied in Mark and witnessed to by Matthew, Luke, the Gospel according to the Hebrews in Ignatius,[68] the Didascalia, the Gospel of Peter, and Jno. xxi. Luke transferred this appearance also to Jerusalem. The appearance to the Apostles in the Gospel according to the Hebrews is parallel with Lk. xxiv. 36ff but is drawn from Luke's source, in which the location was Galilee and the occasion at a meal. This is the situation implied also in the Didascalia where the appearance " to us " is followed by instructions regarding fasting. This is the appearance implied likewise in the Gospel of Peter, for the mention of others beside Peter shows that the appearance was not to Peter alone. Jno. xxi depends on the same source and describes this appearance with addition of distinctively Johannine elements.[69]

The subjectivity of Völter's criticism by which Luke is transformed into a witness to the Galilean localization of the appearances reaches its climax when, in the attempt to forestall an impression of arbitrariness, it is said:[70] " If any one be disposed to call this criticism of the Lucan narrative of the Emmaus disciples arbitrary, we reply that it is absolutely necessary and that the Apostle Paul,—the author of 1 Cor. xv. 5—had he been able to read the narrative of Lk, would have subjected it to similar treatment. If arbitrariness is to be found at all, then it is certainly on the side of Luke."

[65] Identified with Peter in *Die Entstehung* usw. p. 39.
[66] *PrM*. 1911, p. 64.　　　　　[67] *PrM*. 1911, p. 64.
[68] *Ad. Smyrn.* iii. 1, 2; cf. Appendix, pp. 352 f., IV.
[69] *Die Entstehung* usw. p. 52.　　　[70] *PrM*. 1911, p. 65.

Völter thought it strange that no account of the appearance to Peter should have been preserved in Gospel tradition, and upon investigation was persuaded that it lay hidden in the story of the walk to Emmaus. His hypothesis however was beset with local diffculties, for this appearance—on the Galilean theory—must have occurred in Galilee. It was not unnatural therefore that some incident with a distinctly Galilean setting should prove more enticing to independent and hardy discoverers. Mt. xxviii. 16 mentions a mountain as the scene of the Galilean appearance, and the Synoptic Gospels locate the transfiguration of Jesus on a mountain. Moreover the narratives of the transfiguration have been interpreted as merely symbolical[71] or as reflecting a faith already influenced by belief in the resurrection.[72] It was not surprising therefore, that Wellhausen[73] should venture upon the supposition that the transfiguration story is actually a resurrection narrative and perhaps the oldest in the Gospels,—Peter being the first to recognize the transfigured Christ.

But this view does not satisfy the statement of Paul,[74] which implies an appearance to Peter alone; and it leaves no place for the doubt of the disciples.[75] The narrative clearly reflects some other incident in the experience of Peter.[76] For these reasons Kreyenbühl[77] rejects Wellhausen's theory in part.

[71] C. H. Weisse, *Die evangelische Geschichte,* 1838, i, p. 541; ii. p. 400; *Die Evangelienfrage,* 1856, pp. 255 ff.; Weizsäcker, *Apos. Zeitalter,* p. 397; Loisy, *Les Évangiles synoptiques,* ii. 1909, p. 29.

[72] Holtzmann, *HC.* i. *Die Synoptiker³.* 1901, p. 86; Bacon, *AJTh.* 1902, p. 259; Goodspeed, *AJTh,* 1905, p. 448; Case, *AJTh.* 1909, p. 184; cf. Loisy, *Évang. syn.* ii. p. 40; Bowen, *Resurrection in NT.* pp. 419f; H. Meltzer, *PrM.* 1902, pp. 154 ff. (locating the first appearance to Peter on Tabor, the traditional mount of the transfiguration, where Peter and John and Levi had stopped over night on their flight from Jerusalem to Galilee).

[73] *Das Evangelium Marci,* 1903, p. 77; cf. van den Bergh van Eysinga, *Indische Einflüsse auf die evangelischen Erzählungen,* 1904, pp. 62 f.; Loisy, *Évang. syn.* ii. p. 39; identified by W. Erbt, *Das Marcusevangelium usw.* 1911, p. 35, with the ascension; cf. also the criticism of this view by Spitta, *ZwTh.* 1911, p. 165.

[74] 1 Cor. xv. 5; cf. Lk. xxiv. 34.

[75] Mt. xxviii. 17.

[76] Identified by Kreyenbühl with Acts ii. 1 ff.

[77] *ZNW.* 1908, pp. 257-296; van den Bergh van Eysinga, *Indische Ein-*

The transfiguration story was originally a resurrection narrative, but it does not recount the first appearance to Peter. The oldest narrative of this incident is rather to be found in the description of Jesus' walking on the water[78] and its variants.[79]   The story in its original form is thought to have come from Peter and to have formed part of the primitive Gospel of the Jerusalem Church.[80]   It describes in the language of fantasy the experience through which Peter passed from popular ghost-fear to belief in the resurrection, i. e. to the eschatologico-apocalyptic belief that Jesus was the exalted Messiah.   This belief transformed both Peter and Jesus.   Through Peter's influence others were led to a similar faith, first the Twelve, then more than five hundred. This is the meaning of the two narratives of Jesus' walking on the water and the transfiguration on the mount.   Both are resurrection narratives and recount the genesis and growth of the resurrection-faith first in Peter and the other disciples in Galilee and then in the five hundred or more in Jerusalem,—the mount in the transfiguration narrative being merely the figurative mount of revelation.[81]

flüsse, p. 47; O. Schmiedel, *Die Hauptprobleme der Leben-Jesu-Forschung*², 1906, pp. 81 f.; cf. Bowen, *Resurrection in NT.* p. 417 n. 1.

[78] Mt. xiv. 22-23.

[79] Mk. iv. 35-41; vi. 42-52; Mt. viii. 23-27.

[80] The relation of the variants to the original is conceived as follows: Peter first told the story in Aramaic; this was translated into Greek by John Mark and formed the concluding part of the primitive Gospel of the Jerusalem Church before 70 AD; it was then transformed by a Gentile Christian of the West into a magical stilling of a sea storm; the redactor of Mark's Gospel took the story of the storm from oral tradition (Mk. iv. 35-41) and himself produced another ·variant of the original (Mk. vi. 42-52); finally the redactor of Matthew both preserved the original, which he inserted in Mark's order (Mt. xiv. 22-23), and added in dependence on Mark his variant of the storm (viii. 23-27).

[81] On the Galilean theory cf. C. H. Weisse, *Evang. Gesch.* ii. 349 ff., 358 f., 386, 416; Keim, *Geschichte Jesu von Nazara*, iii. 1872, pp. 533ff; W. Brandt, *Evangelische Geschichte*, 1893, pp. 337 ff.; Pfleiderer, *Urchristentum*, i. pp. 2 ff., 395; P. W. Schmidt, *Die Geschichte Jesu*, ii. 1904, pp. 401 ff.; O. Holtzmann, *Leben Jesu*, 1901, pp. 390 ff.; N. Schmidt, *The Prophet of Nazareth*, 1905, pp. 392 ff.; A. Meyer, *Auferstehung*, usw. pp. 127 ff.; Bousset,

THE JERUSALEM THEORY

In opposition to the theory which locates the first appearances in Galilee, Loofs,[82] in dependence on the Luke-John tradition, seeks to establish the theory of localization in and about Jerusalem. He argues that the theory which locates the appearances in Galilee, in the form which denies as in that which accepts the historicity of the empty grave on the third day, is untenable. For the flight of the disciples[83] was not a "flight to Galilee." On the contrary Mk. xvi. 7[84] implies their presence in Jerusalem on Easter morning. This theory moreover finds no support in Justin.[85] It rests chiefly on Mark. But Mark was not written by an eye-witness, and the lost ending is an unknown quantity. The Papian tradition regarding the Petrine source of Mark may have had no other basis than 1 Pet. v. 13, and there is no sufficient reason for supposing that the contents of the lost ending are preserved in Jno. xxi. 1 Cor. xv. 5 favors Jerusalem as the place of the appearance to Peter. It is more probable therefore that the Matthew-Mark tradition is, like the Synoptic account of Jesus' public ministry, one-sidedly Galilean. And finally Mark is the only source of this tradition; for there is no proof that Matthew had any other basis for the Galilean localization. The Gospel of Peter depends on Mark. Lk. xxiv. 34 cannot be

SNT. ii. p. 148; Loisy, *Évang. syn.* ii. pp. 741ff; Bacon, *The Founding of the Church,* 1909, pp. 25 ff., *The Beginnings of Gospel Story,* 1909, pp. xvii f., xl, 190 ff.; Edmunds, *OC.* 1910, pp. 130 ff.; Bowen, *Resurrection in NT.* pp. 150 ff., 430, 432 f., 440 n. 1; Conybeare, *Myth, Magic and Morals,* 1909, pp. 291 f., 301 ff.

[82] *Die Auferstehungsberichte und ihr Wert,* 1908; cf. the account of the origin of the Galilean tradition by Holsten, *Zum Evangelium des Paulus und des Petrus,* 1868, pp. 119, 156 ff.—under the influence of an anti-Pauline polemic; by Hilgenfeld, *ZwTh.* 1868, pp. 73f, *Nov. Test. ex. Can.* iv. *Evang. sec. Heb.* 1866, pp. 29 ff.—under the influence of a redaction favorable to the Gentile Christian Church; by Korff, *Auferstehung Christi* usw. pp. 47 ff., 92, 104 f.—under the influence of a Marcan apologetic against the derivation of the appearances from the empty tomb.

[83] Mk. xiv. 50.　　　　[84] Also Mt. xxviii. 10.

[85] *Dial.* 53 p. 180 C; 106 p. 378 C; *Apol.* i. 50 p. 136 A; cf. above note 38.

separated from its context and assigned to another (Galilean) source; and Jno. xxi, although it describes the first appearance, is proven to be inaccurate by 1 Corinthians and may well be dependent on the Synoptic tradition. On the other hand the tradition of Luke-John is commended as trustworthy by its agreement with Paul, although Luke adds the appearance to the disciples at Emmaus and John the appearance to Mary Magdalene. Luke moreover shows by his narrative of the last journey to Jerusalem that he had access to a special source, and John embodies Johannine tradition. Mt. xxviii. 16ff may correspond with 1 Cor. xv. 6, but Lk. xxiv. 49 excludes the Galilean localization. The Galilean appearance in Jno. xxi is discredited on the same ground and also by internal inconsistency. The rehabilitation of Peter[86] manifestly belongs to the first appearance. Its Galilean setting is due to its false connection with xxi. 1-14,—a connection which is shown to be unhistorical by Paul's silence and may have had its origin in Lk. v. 1-4.

The two principal pillars upon which this theory rests—the reference of Lk. xxiv. 49 to the whole period between Easter and Pentecost, and the silence of Paul—are weak in themselves and quite insufficient to support the structure that is built upon them. The Marcan tradition, with its indication of Galilee, cannot be discredited by a vague suspicion regarding its ultimate Petrine source or by the argument from silence since the Gospel in its earliest transmitted form is incomplete. There is no evidence for rejecting the Galilean location of the appearance recorded in Mt. xxviii. 16 ff, for Paul is equally silent about Jerusalem. And if the Mark-Matthew tradition gives evidence of an appearance in Galilee no reason remains for the proposed transformation, analysis and derivation of Jno. xxi.[87]

---

[86] xxi, 15-19 (23).

[87] J. A. Cramer's advocacy of the Jerusalem tradition (*ThT.* 1910, pp. 189-222) is scarcely less negative in its treatment of the Galilean tradition. The two traditions are thought to be mutually exclusive. All the documentary evidence, it is held, witnesses to the presence of the disciples in Jerusalem on the day of the resurrection, and the theory both of the flight to Galilee and of the first and special appearance to Peter in Galilee is

In the interest of the Jerusalem localization of the appearances appeal has been made to a geographical tradition in which mention is made of a Galilee near Jerusalem. According to this tradition the peak to the north of the Mount of Olives or the entire region including the Mount of Olives bore the name Galilee in the time of Jesus. The words of Jesus and of the angel [88] have reference to this Galilee and were so understood by the disciples. The appearances therefore, with the exception of the one described in Jno. xxi, occurred in or near Jerusalem. Evidence for this view is sought in the Old Testament, especially in Joshua[89] and Ezekiel;[90] but even if the word was used of different parts of Palestine in the sense of boundry and in particular of the boundary of the territory of Benjamin near Jerusalem, this usage would require other evidence to prove its influence in the time of Jesus. For this, appeal is made to the Acts of Pilate[91] and to Tertullian.[92] According to the one the Mount of Olives was in Galilee; according to the other Galilee was in Judea. If Tertullian knew the Acts of Pilate, they must belong in some form at least to the second century. His language[93] however finds a natural explanation in the usage of the time.[94] No other trace of this tradition appears until the Pilgrim literature of the middle

opposed by intrinsic and traditional probability. The Jerusalem tradition is well accredited and explains the character of early Christian faith and the origin of the Church in Jerusalem. Two possibilities are proposed for the origin of the Galilean tradition: either (a) from appearances there such as the appearance to more than five hundred of which very little is known—Mt. xxviii. 16ff reflecting a vague Galilean tradition but freely supplying details of place and persons; or (b) from an erroneous combination of the call (Mk. i. 16-20) and restoration (Jno. xxi. 11-19) of Peter with a wonderful catch of fish (Lk. v. 1-11; Jno. xxi. 2-11). If the second of these possibilities be true, the whole Galilean tradition must, as Cramer says (p. 218), be consigned to the realm of legend. This argument, however, in its negative aspect, like the argument of Loofs, suffers from its insistence on the exclusive character of the Jerusalem tradition.

[88] Mt. xxvi. 37; Mk. xiv. 28; Mt. xxviii. 7, 10; Mk. xvi. 7.

[89] xviii. 11-20, xv. 1-15.   [90] xlvii. 8.

[91] Tischendorf, *Evangelia Apocrypha;* cf. Appendix, pp. 353 f., VI.

[92] *Apol.* xxi.; cf. Appendix, p. 353, V.

[93] Apud Galilæam Iudæae regionem.

[94] Schürer, *ThLz.* 1897, pp. 187 f.

ages. Use of it to interpret the tradition of the Gospels in regard to the place of the appearances had a beginning in the eighteenth century. In 1832 Thilo[95] reviewed the evidence and literature. Impressed by Thilo's note, R. Hofmann[96] increased the references to the mediæval Pilgrim literature and A. Resch[97] has sought to bridge the chasm between the Acts of Pilate and the New Testament times by investigating the Old Testament usage. The theory has found advocates in Lepsius,[98] Thomsen,[99] and Kresser;[100] but there has been no increase in the evidence,—which is ultimately reducible to the Acts of Pilate. Until these are shown to contain a trustworthy tradition of the geography of Palestine in the time of Jesus the theory must inevitably yield before the plain implications of a uniform New Testament usage.[101]

THE DOUBLE TRADITION

The Gospels witness plainly to appearances of Jesus in or near Jerusalem and in Galilee. This is true both of the Synoptic and of the Johannine tradition. Even among the separate Gospels, Luke alone records appearances only in one general locality. It is therefore highly probable that the appearances were not restricted to a single place and that consequently the two traditions should not be set over the one against the

[95] *Codex Apocryphus Novi Testamenti,* i. 1832, pp. 617 ff.

[96] *Das Leben Jesu nach den Apokryphen,* 1851, pp. 393 ff.; *Ueber den Berg Galiläa,* 1856; *Auf dem Oelberg,* 1896.

[97] Gebhardt und Harnack, *TU.* 1894, x. 2, pp. 381 ff.; *Das Galiläa bei Jerusalem,* 1910; *Der Auferstandene in Galiläa bei Jerusalem,* 1911.

[98] *Reden und Abhandlungen,* iv. *Die Auferstehungsberichte,* 1902.

[99] *BG.* 1906, pp. 352 ff.

[100] *ThQ.* 1911, pp. 505 ff.; cf. Zimermann, *ThStKr.* 1901, p. 447.

[101] Cf. Romberg, *NkZ.* 1901, pp. 289 ff.; Zahn, *Gesch. d. nt. Kanons,* ii. pp. 937 f.; *NkZ.* 1903, pp. 770 ff.; Edgar, *Exp.* 1897, ii. pp. 119 ff.; Conybeare, *StBE.* iv. 1896, pp. 59 ff.; Voigt, *Die aeltesten Berichte über die Auferstehung Jesu Christi,* 1906, p. 81; A. Meyer, *Auferstehung* usw. pp. 95 ff.; Harnack, *Chronologie,* i. pp. 603 ff.; Schubert, *Pseudopetrin. Evang.* pp. 176 ff., 185; Stülcken, in Hennecke, *Handbuch z. d. nt. Apokryphen,* 1904, pp. 143 ff.; Riggenbach, *ThLBl.* 1910, pp. 537 f.; Bowen, *Resurrection in NT.* pp. 350 ff., 440 n. 1; Moffatt, *Introduction to the Literature of the New Testament,* 1911, pp. 254 f.; cf. below note 134.

other as mutually exclusive. It has indeed been affirmed that the opposition of the Galilean and the Jerusalem tradition constitutes the primary condition of an intelligent criticism of the narratives of the resurrection,[102] and undoubtedly this opinion seems to have become so axiomatic an historical premise that its acceptance is no longer felt to constitute a peculiar virtue. Certain even of those who admit a factual basis underlying the two-fold tradition of the Gospels do not hesitate to speak disparagingly of the " usual harmonistic method of addition ".[103] The denial of the critical basis of the Galilean theory is of course destructive of that theory, and the method of addition—however good in itself—can serve no useful purpose for those who are persuaded that the problem demands a different process for its solution.

Just as the tradition of the empty sepulchre is retained by certain representatives of the Galilean theory to explain the form of the disciples' faith,[104] so appearances in Jerusalem are admitted to explain the origin of the Lk.-Jno. tradition by a writer who still adheres to the priority of the Galilean appearances. Von Dobschütz[105] holds that the first appearance was made to Peter in Galilee. The disciples had returned in deep despondency and were about to take up again their old trade. They had dreamed a dream,—a beautiful dream with its vision of thrones and judgment; but it was only a dream, and back they must go to their fish-nets, when suddenly—at the psychological moment—the Lord intervenes (Jno. xxi) and, by quickening again their faith in his Messiahship, makes them fishers of men. Their mission leads them to Jerusalem where they are met by some who had seen Jesus.[106] Subsequently Jesus appears to the five hundred at Pentecost.[107]

[102] Bousset, *ThLz.* 1897, p. 73.

[103] von Dobschütz, *Probleme des apostolischen Zeitalters*, 1904, p. 10.

[104] Völter, *Die Entstehung* usw.; cf. Loofs, *Auferstehungsberichte* usw. ·pp. 18.

[105] *Probleme* usw.; cf. Clemen, *Paulus* usw. i. 1904, pp. 204 ff.; Lake, *Hist. Evidence*, etc., p. 212.

[106] Lk. xxiv. 13 f.; cf. also Réville, *Jésus de Nazareth*, ii. 1906, pp. 426 ff.; Stapfer, *La mort et la résurrection de Jésus Christ*, 1898, pp. 231 ff.

[107] Jno. xx. 21-23; Acts ii. 1 ff.; cf. *Ostern und Pfingsten*, 1903; Weisse, *Evang. Gesch.* ii. p. 417; Steck, *Der Galaterbrief*, 1888, p. 186; Pfleiderer,

A less dramatic but more penetrating discussion of the double tradition is given by T. S. Rördam.[108] Two principal difficulties confront the theory of a twofold location,—the apparent exclusion of appearances in Galilee by Luke, and the apparent exclusion of an appearance to the disciples in Jerusalem by Matthew-Mark. Rördam seeks to meet these difficulties by literary analysis. Luke is thought to have followed a source of Jerusalem origin in which two Jerusalem appearances—one on Easter Sunday and one at the time of the ascension some forty days later—had been combined. The combination was not made by Luke but had already taken place in the oral tradition, so that verse 47 appears as the natural continuation of verse 46; whereas the proper place for the Galilean appearance implied in Mark is immediately after verse 46. As the result of this the command to tarry in Jerusalem[109] seemed to exclude the Galilean appearances, and the reference to Galilee[110] assumed its vaguer form. The occasion of the Jerusalem appearances was the unbelief of the disciples.

But are such appearances really excluded by the contents of the lost ending of Mark? If Matthew and Luke used Mark, and Luke follows another source in chapter xxiv, the contents of the Marcan ending must be sought in Matthew.[111]

Urchristentum, i. pp. 10 f.; Harnack, *Chronologie*, i. pp. 707 f.; Bowen, however (*Resurrection in NT*. pp. 430 n. 1, 433) more logically—but without evidence—locates the origin of the Church in Galilee.

[108] *HJ*. 1905, pp. 769-790; cf. also Feine, *Eine vorkanon. Überlieferung d. Lukas*, 1891, pp. 72 ff., 160 ff.; Zimmermann, *ThStKr.* 1901, pp. 438 ff.; Allen, *St. Matthew, ICC.* 1907, pp. 302 ff.; B. Weiss, *Die Quellen d. Lukas-evangeliums*, 1907, pp. 230 ff.

[109] xxiv. 49.   [110] xxiv. 6; cf. Mk. xvi. 7.

[111] Cf. Weisse, *Evang. Gesch.* ii. p. 359 f.; Volkmar, *Die Evangelien usw.* 1870, pp. 241, 608 ff.; Wright, *Some New Testament Problems*, 1898, pp. 122 f.; Goodspeed *AJTh.* 1905, pp. 484 ff. says (p. 488) : " The narrative of Mark, when it breaks off with 16 : 8, evidently demands just two things for its completion ; the reassurance of the women, and the reappearance of Jesus in Galilee. These two things Matthew records, and the conclusion seems inevitable that he derived them from his chief narrative source, the gospel of Mark." Cf. also Plummer, *Commentary on St. Matthew*, 1910, pp. 412 f.; 421 f.; and on the other hand Bowen, *Resurrection in NT*. pp. 164 ff., 166 n. 2 and, for reconstruction of the contents of the lost ending, pp. 161 f.

Mark cannot have intended his Gospel to end with the words
ἐφοβοῦντο γάρ, and neither can he have intended to say that
the women never told of their experience. But as it is unlikely that the women were afraid of the angel, we may complete the unfinished sentence: " for they were afraid that it
might not be true ". Consequently an appearance of Jesus
to confirm the message of the angel is not only probable in itself but is recorded by Mt. xxviii. 9-12.[112] Mk. xvi. 7 implies an appearance to Peter and in Galilee. But as the disciples, according to Mark, were still in Jerusalem, their unbelief
may have caused an appearance there. Matthew indeed represents the appearance to the Eleven in Galilee as the fulfilment
of the promise in xxviii. 7 (Mk. xvi. 7) ; but the definite mountain in xxviii. 16 implies an appearance to the Eleven in Jerusalem, and the doubt of some in xxviii. 17 suits this better
than a later occasion. This allusion to an appearance to the
disciples in Jerusalem Matthew derived from Mark,[113] the

---

[112] Spitta, *Zur Geschichte und Litteratur des Urchristentums,* iii. 2, 1907,
pp. 112 ff., argues that inasmuch as Mk. xiv. 28, xvi. 7 imply an appearance in Galilee, the author must have intended to conclude his Gospel with
a narrative similar to Mt. xxviii. 16-20. But Mk. xvi. 7 contains also a
message to be delivered by the women to the disciples. Luke and John
report its delivery but Mark closes with the statement of a hindrance,
which can, however, have been only the introduction to an account of its
removal, and most naturally by an appearance of Jesus. General recog-
ition of this has been hindered by the hypothesis that the oldest tradition—represented in Mark—reported appearances only in Galilee. As the
Marcan text demands even more plainly than Matthew an appearance to
the women in Jerusalem, Matthew must have known the original ending
of Mark and furnishes—rather than Jno. xxi—information concerning its
contents. Cf. also *Streitfragen der Geschichte Jesu,* 1907, pp. 78 f. where the
literary parallels are given, especially the Marcan ἔφυγον, τρόμος, καὶ ἔκστασις
with Mt. ἀπελθοῦσαι ταχύ, μετὰ φόβου καὶ χαρᾶς μεγάλης; the Marcan ἐφοβοῦντο γάρ
with Mt. μὴ φοβεῖσθε. The criticism of Brun, *ThStKr.* 1911, pp. 168 f., does
not break the force of Spitta's argument in so far as it concerns the implications of the closing verse of Mark and the support that it lends to
Matthew's report of the appearance to the women. Cf. also Stanton, *The
Gospels as Historical Documents.* ii. 1909, pp. 201 f.

[113] This is seen also in the fact that Matthew does not mention the delivery of the women's message to the disciples, and in the fact that the
mountain in Galilee is said to have been appointed—not to the women—
but to the disciples. This allusive or "hinting" feature of the narrative

Marcan account being omitted because of an unwillingness to chronicle the doubts of the disciples.[114]　The original conclusion of Mark thus contained, according to Rördam, three appearances in Jerusalem,—to the women, to Peter, and to the Apostles.　Then followed an appearance to the disciples generally in Galilee,—agreeing in order with the source of Luke.　Mark probably contained also some parting appearance of Jesus similar to that described in Lk. xxiv. 47-53, Acts i. 4-12, 1 Cor. xv. 7,—for this was part of the apostolic tradition.　It is not contained in Matthew because it was probably lost from the copy of Mark used by Matthew.

Rördam's theory depends mainly on two things: his reconstruction of the source of Lk. xxiv and his conception of the contents of the lost ending of Mark.　Of these the latter is the more crucial.　Is the method which follows Matthew as guide more satisfactory than that which follows the Gospel of Peter? Must we be content with a non liquet, or is there a reasonable minimum of inference from Mk. xvi. 7-8 that may be safely made?　To this minimum Lyder Brun[115] reckons an appearance before the disciples in Galilee, but prior to this an appearance to Peter in Jerusalem—possibly also an appearance to the disciples in Jerusalem.　In agreement with Spitta[116] it is maintained that the meaning of προάξω in Mk. xiv. 28, Mt. xxvi. 32 is dètermined by the reference in the context to the shepherd and the scattered sheep.　After his resurrection Jesus is to gather his scattered disciples and lead them back to

[114] is responsible for the impression, produced by xxviii. 17, that some of the Apostles doubted, " though the narrator clearly meant to say that the apostles adored, but some of the other disciples doubted " (p. 785).

[114] This appears in the silence of Matthew about the doubt of the women which is thought to have been the occasion of the appearance in xxviii. 9-10.

[115] *ThStKr.* 1911, pp. 157-180.

[116] *Zur Gesch. u. Lit. d. Urchristentums*, iii. pp. 111 ff.; *Streitfragen der Gesch. Jesu*, pp. 74 ff.; cf. also Zimmermann, *ThStKr.* 1901, pp. 446 f.; Riggenbach, *Aus Schrift u. Geschichte*, 1898, p. 138; J. Weiss, *SNT.* i. p. 208; Cramer, *ThT.* 1910, pp. 200 ff.; on the other hand Bowen, *Resurrection in NT.* p. 196, sees in προάξω of Mk. xiv. 28 a prophecy ex eventu which witnesses to the " flight of the disciples to Galilee "; cf. pp. 148, 200 f.

Galilee. Mk. xvi. 7 adds to this the promise that the disciples would see Jesus in Galilee. The special mention of Peter is due to the interpretation of Mk. xiv. 28 as a call to go to Galilee. But the silence of the women prepares for an appearance to Peter in Jerusalem, that, being himself strengthened, he might gather the scattered disciples and lead them back to Galilee.[117]

In the light of Mk. xvi. 7 there are four possible inferences regarding the contents of the lost ending:

(1) The women say nothing and the disciples return to Galilee without knowledge of the empty grave or the message of the angel,—as in the Gospel of Peter.

(2) The silence of the women, caused as it was by fear, lasted but a short time, after which,—having recovered self-possession—they delivered the message of the angel,—as in the short ending of Mark.[118]

(3) The fear of the women was overcome by an appearance of Jesus, after which they delivered their message,[119]—in which case there seems to be no place for a special appearance to Peter, unless the message met with unbelief[120] and this was overcome by the appearance to Peter.[121]

(4) Since the women said nothing to the disciples or to Peter, Jesus appeared to Peter in Jerusalem[122] and directed the disciples to go to Galilee.[123]

The second of these possibilities is set aside because it weakens the force of οὐδενὶ οὐδὲν εἶπον; the first because the " flight " theory is excluded by Mark and there is no conclusive evidence that the Gospel of Peter knew the original ending of Mark; the third because there is no sufficient evidence that Matthew knew the original ending of Mark. The fourth possibility however avoids both the weakening of οὐδενὶ οὐδὲν εἶπον and the doubling of the message to the women.

---

[117] Cf. Lk. xxi. 32, xxiv. 34; 1 Cor. xv. 5.

[118] πάντα δὲ τὰ παρηγγελμένα τοῖς περὶ τὸν Πέτρον συντόμως ἐξήγγειλαν κτλ. Cf. Mt. xxviii. 8; Lk. xxiv. 9.

[119] Mt. xxviii. 9-10.

[120] Lk. xxiv. 11, 22-24; [Mk.] xvi. 10.   [121] Lk. xxiv. 34.

[122] Lk. xxiv. 34; cf. xxii. 32.   [123] Mt. xxviii. 16.

The appearance to Peter corresponds also with the special reference to him in the message of the angel and with the place assigned to it by Paul. The parallel with Luke is close; and it is not improbable that the appearance to James in the Gospel according to the Hebrews is simply a transformation of the appearance to Peter. The reference to Galilee in Mark and Matthew is to be explained by the prominence assigned to Galilee in their account of the ministry of Jesus,[124] by the prophecy in Mk. xiv. 28, and by the significance of the Galilean appearances for the vocation[125] of the Apostles. In Luke the intervening step between the first and the last appearances in Jerusalem—the appearances in Galilee—fell away because the later activity of the Apostles, in which Luke was particularly interested, was connected with Jerusalem.

Even a minimum of inference from Mk. xvi. 7-8 regarding the contents of the original ending of the Gospel is rejected by those who maintain that the Gospel ended originally—whether in intention or in fact—with xvi. 8.[126] The statement of

[124] Spitta, *Streitfragen*, p. 81, formulates the problem concerning the place of the appearances as follows: The question is not, Did the earliest tradition know of appearances in Judea?—all the sources agree in this—but, Did Galilee originally come into consideration in this part of the history of Jesus? He concludes from his investigation of the geographical disposition of the life of Jesus in the Synoptic Gospels that the underlying document (Grundschrift) did not contain the Galilean appearances,—which were first added in their recension of this document by Mark-Matthew.

[125] Berufsbewusstsein.

[126] B. Weiss, *Die Evangelien des Markus und Lukas,*[6] 1901, *MK*. i. 2, p. 245. Zahn, *Gesch. d. neutest. Kanons*, ii. p. 930; *Einleitung*, ii., pp. 238 ff.; Riggenbach, *Aus Schrift und Geschichte*, p. 126; so also Wellhausen, *Das Evangelium Marci*, 1903, p. 146—though from a different point of view and for a different reason; cf. H. J. Holtzmann, *HC*. i.[3], 1901, p. 183; O. Holtzmann, *Leben Jesu*, 1901, p. 390; R. A. Hoffmann, *Das Marcusevangelium*, 1904, p. 641; Wendling, *Die Entstehung des Marcus-Evangeliums*, 1908, p. 201—the earliest form of the narrative ends with ἐξέπνευσεν Mk. xv. 37; cf. the text in his *Ur-Marcus*, 1905, p. 59; Zimmermann, *ThStKr*. 1901, p. 148, ends his AQ source with Mk. xvi. 8 and thinks that the reference to the silence of the women not only indicates the absence of their story from earlier tradition but explains its first appearance in this source (cf. Bowen, *Resurrection in NT*. pp. 157 f., 180 ff.). J. Weiss, *Das älteste Evangelium*, 1903, pp. 340 ff., explains the silence of the women about the empty tomb from the apologetic reference of the story to the Jews (p. 340) and

Riggenbach[127] that there is no tradition which relates exclusively Galilean appearances seems to be true of the later as of the earlier tradition.[128]   The Galilean theory rests entirely, in the last analysis, on an inference, for the sake of which practically all the documentary evidence is traversed.

There is indeed some difference of opinion among the advocates of the double tradition about the duration of the first appearances in Jerusalem.   Zahn[129] locates the appearance described in Jno. xx. 26-29 in Galilee because it is not explicitly said to have occurred in Jerusalem, and the stay of the disciples in Jerusalem for a week after Easter Sunday is thought improbable.[130]   Appeal is made also to the patristic association of the doubt of Thomas with Mt. xxviii. 16 f.[131]   The implications of the context, however, strongly favor Jerusalem as the scene of Jno. xx. 26-29.   Moreover the time of the departure to Galilee is not fixed by the Synoptic tradition.   It may not be possible fully to explain this stay in Jerusalem. There was need to gather the scattered disciples, inform them of the command to go to Galilee and of the appointed meeting-place.   Their hopes for the restoration of the kingdom

holds that the Gospel may have ended with xvi. 8 (p. 345); *SNT*. I. p. 227.   This theory of an anti-Jewish apologetic motive dominating the Gospel of Mark, applied by Wrede (*Das Messiasgeheimnis*, 1901) to a particular feature of the Marcan narrative, is generalized by Baldensperger in relation to the resurrection-narratives in *Urchristliche Apologie, die älteste Auferstehungskontroverse*, 1909.   Cf. also Louis Coulange, *RHLR*. 1911, pp. 145 ff., 297 ff.; Bowen *Resurrection in NT*. p. 159 n. 4.

[127] *Aus Schrift* usw. p. 142.

[128] The Gospel of Peter may constitute an exception, if not in fact, at least in the natural inference from its fragmentary conclusion; yet even this Gospel makes of Jesus' enemies witnesses of his resurrection in Jerusalem (cf. Schubert *Pseudopetrin. Evang.* p. 96; W. Bauer, *Leben Jesu* usw. pp. 256 f).

[129] *Evang. des Joh. ZK.* iv. 1908, p. 672.

[130] Cf. Mt. xxvi. 32, xxviii. 7, 16; Mk. xiv. 28, xvi. 7.

[131] *NkZ*. 1903, p. 806 n. 1, citing a scholion attributed to Origen in Cramer, *Cat. in Ev. Matt. et Marci*, p. 243, and Jerome.   The addition however of εἴτε Φίλιππος (cf. also *Petrus von Laodicea*, ed. Heinrici, 1908, pp. 343 f) and the differentiation of the two incidents in Chrysostom weaken the force of this appeal.

to Israel[132] would readily center in Jerusalem, and the command to go to Galilee—repeated as it was—may suggest that this was not the natural thing for them to do. Doubt had to be overcome,—in particular the doubt of Thomas. The Jerusalem appearances moreover may well have been intended to serve particularly in confirming the disciples' faith in the resurrection, the Galilean to give fuller instruction regarding their subsequent mission. The doubt of some in Mt. xxviii. 17 scarcely suggests the scene of Jno. xx. 26ff. It may have had its occasion in the form of the appearance, or it may indicate the presence of others beside the Eleven.[133]

Voigt transfers the ascension from the Mount of Olives to the mount in Galilee, north-west of Capernaum,—the scene of the beatitudes and of the calling of the Twelve.[134] Luke is supposed to have identified the mountain of his Jerusalem source with the Mount of Olives and to have interpreted the separation there of Jesus from his disciples as final, in consequence of which the command to remain in the city was introduced.[135] The appearance to Peter, implied in Mark and

[132] Acts i. 6; cf. Lk. xxiv. 21.

[133] Cf. Riggenbach, *Aus Schrift* usw. p. 150; Voigt, *Die aeltesten Berichte über die Auferstehung Jesu Christi*, 1906, pp. 63 f.; on the summary character of the description cf. C. H. Weisse, *Evang. Gesch.* ii. pp. 415 ff.; Steinmeyer, *Apologetische Beiträge*, iii. 1871, p. 153, and J. Denney, *Jesus and the Gospel*, 1908, pp. 155 ff.; Korff, *Auferstehung* usw. pp. 29 ff.; Plummer, *St. Matthew*, p. 426.

[134] *Berichte* usw. pp. 79 ff—although rejecting the reference of οὖ ἐτάξατο αὐτοῖς ὁ Ἰησοῦς (Mt. xxviii. 16) to the mount of the beatitudes; cf. Volkmar, *Die Evangelien* usw. 1870, p. 609; Westcott, *Introduction to the Study of the Gospels*, 1860 (1887), p. 330; B. Weiss, *Das Matthäus-Evangelium*, 1898, *MK.* i. 1. p. 506; Bowen, *Resurrection in NT.* pp. 275 f. The identification with Thabor is combined with rejection of " Galilee on the Mount of Olives " by Ludolphus de Saxonia, *Vita Christi*, ed. Rigollot, iv. 1878, p. 237, par. ii. cap. lxxx, 1: " Et sciendum, quod prope montem Oliveti ex parte boreali ad unum milliare est mons, qui appellatur Galilæa: et dicunt quidam quod ille est mons praedictus ad quem discipuli undecim abierunt, non quia mons sit in Galilæa, cum sit in Judæa, sed quia mons iste appellatur Galilæa; alii, quod magis videtur, dicunt hoc fuisse in monte Thabor, in quo Dominus transfiguratus fuit, qui vere in Galilæa consistit."

[135] *Ibid.* pp. 102 ff.

described in the appendix added to the Fourth Gospel by a disciple of John, occurred on the western slope of the Mount of Olives.[136] Emmaus is identified with Ensemes between Bethany and Jericho. Eight days after the appearances on Easter Sunday—to Mary Magdalene, to the women, to Peter, to Cleopas and his companion, and to the disciples in Jerusalem, Thomas being absent—Jesus appeared again to the disciples now about to depart to Galilee, Thomas being present; he then led them out to the Mount of Olives where he was separated from them, going before them, though now unseen, in the way to Galilee. On this journey he appeared to the five hundred; then in Galilee to the seven by the Sea, and finally on the mount where he gave commission to the disciples and was received up into heaven.[137]

The plain statements of the Third Gospel and of Acts oppose this construction, and the transposition of the restoration, of Peter from the place assigned to it in Jno. xxi depends wholly on an individual sense of fitness. The view of Riggenbach[138] is simpler and in closer accord with the evidence. The Jerusalem appearances, including an appearance to Peter and the appearance to the disciples after eight days,—Thomas being present—were followed by Galilean appearances, the appearance to the seven by the Sea including the restoration of Peter, and the appearance on the mountain—identified probably with the appearance to the five hundred—and finally in Jerusalem again, the appearance to James, and the farewell appearance terminated by the ascension from the Mount of Olives toward Bethany.[139]

[136] *Ibid.* pp. 74 ff.   [137] Cf. *ibid.* pp. 111 ff.

[138] *Aus Schrift und Geschichte,* pp. 151 ff.

[139] On the double tradition cf. Romberg, *NkZ.* 1901, pp. 315 ff.; B. Weiss, *Leben Jesu,*[4] ii. 1902, pp. 507 ff.; Beyschlag, *ThStKr.* 1899, pp. 507 ff.; *Leben Jesu,*[4] i. 1902, pp. 433 ff.; Horn, *NkZ.* 1902, pp. 349 ff.; *Abfassungzeit, Geschichtlichkeit und Zweck von Evang. Joh. Kap. 21,* 1904, pp. 94 ff.; Belser, *Geschichte d. Leidens u. Sterbens, d. Auferstehung u. Himmelfahrt d. Herrn,* 1903, pp. 454 ff.; Wabnitz, *Hist. de la Vie de Jésus,* 1904, pp. 408 ff.; Sanday, *Outlines of the Life of Christ,* 1905, pp. 170 ff.; D. Smith, *The Days of His Flesh,* 1905, pp. 508 ff.; an article in *ChQuRev.* Oct. 1905-Jan. 1906, pp. 323-355, especially pp. 347 ff.; Swete, *The Appearances of our Lord,* etc., 1907; Westcott, *The Gospel according to St. John,* 1908, ii. pp.

It may be difficult to solve in detail all the problems which arise on this general view of the relation of the narratives; but this should not affect our confidence in its validity. There will of necessity enter into every reconstruction of the course of events a subjective element which will preclude the attainment of more than a certain degree of probability. Paul's account is favorable to the tradition which locates the first appearances—including the appearance to Peter—in Jerusalem and on Easter Sunday; but the identification of the appearances which he mentions with particular appearances described in the Gospels is less certain. Judging from the order in which the appearance to James occurs in his list,[140] the place assigned to it in the Gospel according to the Hebrews cannot be historical.[141] The fact however underlies and explains the position of James and the other brethren of the Lord in the early Church.[142] It is perhaps more natural therefore, as the Jerusalem setting seems to be excluded, to locate this appearance in Galilee.

As Paul is silent about the appearances to the women, knowledge of them must be derived from the Gospels. The presence of women at the sepulchre on Easter morning is witnessed by all the Gospels,[143] and appearances of Jesus to them by two,—an appearance to Mary Magdalene at the sepulchre by John,[144] and an appearance to certain women on their way from the sepulchre by Matthew.[145] As John's narrative is the more graphic and the Fourth Gospel elsewhere presupposes knowledge of the Synoptic tradition, the appearance to Mary Magdalene is probably to be separated from the appearance to the women, Mary having left the others when she went to bring Peter and John word of the empty tomb.

333 f; J. Orr, *The Resurrection of Jesus,* 1909, pp. 149 ff; E. Mangenot, *La Résurrection de Jésus,* 1910, pp. 240 ff.; W. J. Sparrow Simpson, *DCG.* ii. p. 508; *The Resurrection and Modern Thought,* 1911, pp. 70 ff.

[140] Κηφᾷ, τοῖς δώδεκα, ἐπάνω πεντακοσίοις ἀδελφοῖς, Ἰακώβῳ.

[141] Cf. Appendix, p. 351, I.

[142] Gal. i. 19, ii. 9, 12; 1 Cor. ix. 5; Acts i. 14, xii. 17, xv. 13, xxi. 18; cf. Jno. vii. 3, 5.

[143] Mt. xxviii. 1 ff; Mk. xvi. 1 ff; Lk. xxiii. 55 f, xxiv. 1 ff, 10 f, 22; Jno. xx. 1 ff.

[144] Jno. xx. 1 ff.   [145] Mt. xxviii. 9-10.

Upon her return and after the departure of Peter and John, Jesus appeared to her. The appearance to the other women[146] followed as they went to tell to the disciples the message of the angel. The silence of the women as they left the sepulchre[147] cannot have continued indefinitely; for Mark shows knowledge of their experience and Matthew and Luke alike imply the breaking of what must have been a temporary state induced by fear.[148] The mingling of fear and joy[149] in their experience is not incongruous, nor does the appearance of Jesus to the women render an appearance to Peter superfluous. This may well have served the purpose of reëstablishing Peter's faith and of fitting him to become a center of influence in gathering the scattered disciples and, eventually, their leader on the journey back to Galilee: for the Gospels imply the presence of the disciples in Jerusalem on Easter Sunday[150] and their scattering at Gethsemane[151] cannot have been a " flight to Galilee ".

There is no intimation in Luke that Cleopas and his companion were on their way to Galilee; and the isolated allusion to Emmaus is plainly indicative of authentic reminiscence.[152]

[146] Mk. xvi. 1 Mary Magdalene, Mary [the mother] of James, and Salome; Lk. xxiv. 10 Mary Magdalene, Joanna, Mary [the mother] of James, and the others with them.

[147] Mk. xvi. 8.

[148] Mt. xxviii. 8 ff; Lk. xxiv. 9, 22 f.

[149] Mt. xxviii. 8; cf. the description of the mental state of the disciples in Lk. xxiv. 37 and 41: πτοηθέντες δὲ καὶ ἔμφοβοι γενόμενοι . . . ἔτι δὲ ἀπιστούντων αὐτῶν ἀπὸ τῆς χαρᾶς καὶ θαυμοζόντων κτλ.

[150] After the scattering at Gethsemane the presence of the disciples in or near Jerusalem is implied in Mt. xxviii. 7 f., 10 f.; Mk. xvi. 7; Lk. xxiii. 49 (οἱ γνωστοὶ αὐτῷ); xxiv. 9 f., 24, 33 ff.; Jno. xx. 18, 19 ff.; the presence of Peter in Mt. xxvi. 57 ff.; Mk. xiv. 53 ff.; Lk. xxii. 54 ff.; xxiv. [12], 34; Jno. xviii. 15 ff., 25 ff., xx. 3 ff.; of John in Jno. xviii. 15 f., xix. 26 f, xx. 3 ff.

[151] The scattering of the disciples is witnessed by Mt. xxvi. 56; Mk. xiv. 50, and was predicted in Mt. xxvi. 31; Mk. xiv. 27; Jno. xvi. 32; cf. Justin, Apol. i. 50; Dial. 53; 106; see above note 38.

[152] On the location cf. Schürer, Gesch. d. jüd. Volkes usw. i. pp. 640 ff.; on the similarity of the narrative with Acts viii. 26-40 and possible derivation from the family of Philip cf. M. Dibelius, ZNW. 1911, p. 329.

An appearance to the disciples in Jerusalem[153] seems to be implied in Matthew.[154] Luke describes an appearance to the disciples and others as occurring late on the evening of Easter Sunday, after the return of Cleopas and his companion. This is probably identical with the appearance to the Twelve, which follows the appearance to Peter in Paul's list, and with the appearance to the disciples when Thomas was absent, which is recorded by John.[155]

The hesitation or doubt of some when they heard the story of the women[156] and witnessed or learned of an appearance[157] shows a desire for tangible, sensible evidence which was not unnatural under the circumstances and is not an indication of a late stage in the development of Gospel tradition. Its exaggeration in later narratives[158] may have had an apologetic or an antidocetic motive, but there is no reason to question its existence. Its duration in individuals can be fixed if definitely indicated,[159] but its presence is not in itself proof of an initial experience. Those who doubted on the mountain in Galilee may have been among the disciples to whom Jesus had already appeared; but it is quite possible that Matthew in following a source[160] has mentioned the Eleven specifically as present for the purpose of reporting the carrying out of Jesus' direction and the fulfilment of his promise, without noting the presence of others. Certainly the whole incident cannot be assigned to an earlier period on the ground of Matthew's unwillingness to record the doubts of the disciples.[161]

[153] Lk. xxiv. 36 ff.

[154] Mt. xxviii. 16 (οὗ ἐτάξατο αὐτοῖς).

[155] I Cor. xv. 5; Jno. xx. 19 ff.

[156] Lk. xxiv. 11.

[157] Mt. xxviii. 17; Lk. xxiv. 37; Jno. xx. 24 ff.

[158] [Mk.] xvi. 11, 14 ff, the addition in the Freer Ms.—cf. Gregory, *Das Freer Logion,* 1908—and the Coptic Document; cf. Appendix, p. 352, III.

[159] Jno. xx. 26 ff.

[160] In xxviii. 17 οἱ δέ is introduced abruptly and the οὗ ἐτάξατο αὐτοῖς is not adequately grounded in the preceding context. Likewise in verse 9 the antecedent of αὐταῖς is Μαριάμ ἡ Μαγδαληνὴ καὶ ἡ ἄλλη Μαρία (verse 1), although it seems probable that Mary Magdalene was not actually present on this occasion.

[161] Cf. above p. 336.

Jesus' promise before his death, repeated in the message of the angel and of Jesus to the women, that he would "go before his disciples into Galilee" seems to imply personal leadership rather than temporal precedence or prior arrival.[162] The changed form of the message in Luke,[163] even if it be based on Mark, is intended to introduce another feature, to doubt the authenticity of which there is no other ground than the suspicion that Luke begins at this point an unhistorical elimination of the Galilean appearances. But this elimination is unhistorical in Luke, as the elimination of the Jerusalem appearance to the disciples is unhistorical in Matthew, only when the narratives are held to be exclusive of facts which they do not record. Luke's narrative is plainly determined by interest in the Jerusalem appearances. It is greatly condensed. Whether or not it be possible to show that Luke's source contained an account of Galilean appearances, some break in the temporal order[164] is demanded in the interest of a rational interpretation of the closing scene. Luke cannot have meant[165] or intended his readers to think of Jesus' final separation from the disciples as occurring late at night. And if such a break be admitted, the words of Jesus bidding the disciples "tarry

[162] Mt. xxvi. 32; Mk. xiv. 28: προάξω ὑμᾶς εἰς τὴν Γαλιλαίαν; cf. Mt. xxviii. 7; Mk. xvi. 7 (προάγει). This interpretation is commended both by the context of the original promise and by the usage in Mk. x. 32: ἦσαν δὲ ἐν τῇ ὁδῷ ἀναβαίνοντες εἰς Ἱεροσόλυμα, καὶ ἦν προάγων αὐτοὺς ὁ Ἰησοῦς κτλ. Cf. also Mt. ii. 9, xxi. 9; Mk. xi. 9; Lk. xviii. 39; Acts xii. 6, xvi. 30; but on the other hand, Mt. xiv. 22; Mk. vi. 45; Mt. xxi. 31.

[163] xxiv. 6: μνήσθητε ὡς ἐλάλησεν ὑμῖν ἔτι ὢν ἐν τῇ Γαλιλαίᾳ λέγων τὸν υἱὸν τοῦ ἀνθρώπου ὅτι δεῖ παραδοθῆναι κτλ.

[164] Either after verse 43, 45, or 48; cf. Plummer, St. Luke, ICC. pp. 561, 564.

[165] This follows not only from a careful examination of Lk. xxiv but from the definite statement in Acts i. 3 that the appearances continued during forty days. To those who admit the Lukan authorship of the Third Gospel and Acts this should be conclusive, even if the consequences do not contribute to the stability of the Galilean theory of the appearances. Harnack however having characteristized the "forty days" as a myth (Apostelgeschichte, 1908, p. 129) is disposed to admit its early origin [uralt] only as a messianic-apocalyptic theologoumenon (Neue Untersuchungen zur Apostelgeschichte, 1911, pp. 113 f). For a different view of the "forty days"—by which the appearance to Peter is dated—cf. B. W. Bacon, AJTh. 1911, p. 402.

in the city " [166] will not exclude the appearances in Galilee which are implied in Mark and recorded in Matthew and John.

Following the appearance on the eighth day after Easter,[167] the disciples went to Galilee. The appearance to the seven by the Sea probably preceded the appearance on the mountain.[168] The fishing scene may imply in the Gospel of Peter the taking up again of an old occupation in the despondency and despair which followed the dissipation of cherished hopes;[169] but such an interpretation of it is excluded in John. The disciples are in Galilee at Jesus' command—as John and his readers would know from Matthew[170]—and they could not have been in despair of Jesus' cause in the thought either of the author or of the reader of Jno. xx. The commission of Peter which is connected with this incident, like the commission of the disciples,[171] is not necessarily connected either logically or temporally with the first experience of an appearance of Jesus. The author of Jno. xxi not only felt no incongruity in the order but specifically calls this the third time that Jesus appeared to his disciples. To insist that it must have been the first because the author calls it the third is arbitrary;[172] and there is no adequate literary justification for the separation of the two incidents of this scene.

The identification of the appearance to the five hundred with the appearance to the Eleven on the mountain in Galilee and of that to all the disciples—in Paul's list—with the final appearance in Jerusalem at the time of the ascension from the Mount of Olives toward Bethany is both natural and highly probable.

Of the three views concerning the place of the appearances the Jerusalem theory has least to commend it and the evidence

---

[166] xxiv. 49; cf. Acts i. 4.

[167] Jno. xx. 26 ff.

[168] Cf. Jno. xxi. 14: τοῦτο ἤδη τρίτον ἐφανερώθη ᾽Ιησοῦς τοῖς μαθηταῖς ἐγερθεὶς ἐκ νεκρῶν.

[169] Cf. above p. 333.

[170] On the relation of the Fourth Gospel to the Synoptic Gospels cf. Zahn, Einleitung. ii. pp. 507 ff..

[171] Mt. xxviii. 18 ff.

[172] Cf. Lyder Brun, ThStKr. 1911, p. 167.

against it is clear and convincing. For this and other reasons
the Galilean theory is generally considered the critical alternative to the double tradition. It is however closely associated
with the " flight to Galilee " theory; and this is contrary to the
historical evidence. Even the Gospel of Peter represents the
disciples as present in Jerusalem until the end of the feast, and
certainly therefore until the third day, if not longer. This
being true, it is impossible to hold against all the evidence except the Gospel of Peter that the journey to Galilee was made
in ignorance of the empty tomb and the message of the angel.
The transfer to Galilee of the appearance to Peter—recorded
by Luke in a Jerusalem setting—is arbitrary and made in the
interest of the general theory. This theory moreover is not
adequately supported by inference from Mark, by the hypothetical contents of the lost ending of Mark, by the Gospel of
Peter, and by a critical transformation of Jno. xxi. Its treatment of the Gospels as literary embodiments of a twofold,
but mutually exclusive tradition, is supported indeed by the
affirmation of axiomatic validity for its own historical premise,
but this only discloses the intrusion of an unsound skepticism
between the interpreter and his sources,[173] the deepest roots of
which are not historical but philosophical. The close association of this theory with the interpretation of the appearances
as visionary experiences—whether objectively or subjectively
occasioned—is of course not accidental.[174] Its bearing on the
resurrection itself and the transformation of Christianity,
which the elimination of this element from its historic faith
involves, are not concealed.

The theory that maintains the validity of the double tradition offers an explanation of the documentary evidence by at-

[173] Cf. J. Weiss, *Jesus von Nazareth, Mythus oder Geschichte,* 1910, pp.
84 f. This attitude toward the sources is not confined to the radical type
of criticism; and Weiss' statement is made in a form broadly applicable
to contemporary historical method; cf. also p. 93.

[174] Kreyenbühl's repudiation and criticism of the vision hypothesis is
interesting but not significant, for his own theory of the psychological
genesis of the resurrection faith in the triumph of the messianic-apocalyptic idea over popular ghost-fear is equally naturalistic and opposed to the
plain implications of the historical sources (*ZNW.* 1908, pp. 273 ff); cf.
J. A. Cramer, *ThT.* 1910, p. 213.

tempting an interpretation of it in accordance with the prem
ises of the documents.   Both Paul and the primitive Christian
community believed that Jesus rose from the dead and that he
appeared to certain persons.   The records of fact underlying
this belief are consistent in regard to its essential features,
though no one of them attempts to set forth the different elements in their various relations.   Concrete events have influenced the narratives, but here as elsewhere the Gospels are
not dominated by the modern interest in exact sequence in time
or minute local description.   They record enough to make
their witness quite plain in its broad aspects and not intract-
able to a constructive treatment which shares their premises.
But when these premises are rejected, the effort to discover a
different factual basis for the belief which the documents reflect necessarily results in a treatment of the sources, the violence of which is less apparent but not justified because it
forms part of a particular theory of the character and development of early Christianity.[175]

The method which treats the Gospel narratives as supplementary[176]—the so-called " method of addition "—yields a result that fairly interprets and is supported by the objective
evidence of the documents.   With the increasing recognition
of the evidence for the early date of the Synoptic Gospels,
their sources,—of whatever kind and constitution—being still
earlier,—carry back the witness of the documents to the time of
the eye-witnesses.   And among these there was no difference
of opinion concerning the factual basis which underlies the
tradition recorded by the Gospels in concrete and varying
forms.   To admit with Harnack that the Gospel of Luke was
written before 70 A.D. and early in the sixties,[177] is to accept
a fact which has an important bearing on the origin of the
sources of the Synoptic Gospels,—a fact which makes it difficult, as Harnack himself foresaw,[178] to regard as legendary
their accounts of supernatural events.   For if the Gospels em-

---

[175] Cf. B. B. Warfield, *AJTh.* 1911, pp. 337 ff., 546 ff., and J. A. Cramer,
ThT. 1910, pp. 217 ff.

[176] Barth, *Hauptprobleme d. Lebens Jesu,*[2] 1903, p. 218.

[177] *Neue Untersuchungen zur Apostelgeschichte,* pp. 81 ff.

[178] *Die Apostelgeschichte,* p. 221, n. 2.

body the view of Jesus which was current in the primitive Christian community about 60 A.D.—as Heitmüller admits[179] —or earlier—as Harnack's dating of Luke requires—the rejection of their witness cannot be based upon their differences or upon purely historical considerations. Recourse must be had to a principle springing ultimately out of philosophical conceptions by which their unanimous witness to essential features in their portraiture of Jesus may be set aside.[180] It is not strange therefore that this type of Gospel criticism finds itself confronted by a still more radical type[181] against which it can with difficulty defend the historical minimum permitted by its premises.[182] And this only raises more acutely the issue concerning the validity of the premises upon which an attitude

[179] Cf. the following note.

[180] Cf. the principle formulated and applied to the Gospels by Schmiedel in *EB.* ii. col. 1839-1896, and more recently by Heitmüller in *DGG.* iii. 1911, pp. 359-362. After pointing out that the earliest sources of the Synoptic Gospels do not go back of but reflect merely the view of Jesus which was current in the Palestinian community from 50-70 and formulating as the canon of historical trustworthiness the generally accepted [allgemein anerkannten] principle of contradiction—that those elements of Gospel tradition may be accepted as surely trustworthy which are not in accord with the faith of the community to which the general representation belongs—Heitmüller says (p. 361): Our scrupulousness [Skrupulosität, or Bedenken (p. 377), or Vorsicht (p. 396)] "must be especially active against all the things that were especially dear to the early Christians; to which belong the faith in Jesus' Messiahship, his near return, the whole subject of so-called eschatology (kingdom of God), the passion and resurrection, and the miraculous power of Jesus; where the heart and the theology or the apologetic of the early Christians were especially interested, an influence on historical tradition or construction must be feared"; cf. also an exposition of the "ætiological" principle or the "method of pragmatic values" by B. W. Bacon, *HThR.* 1908, pp. 48 ff.—privately endorsed by Harnack, cf. *AJTh.* 1911, p. 374, n. 4—and *JBL.* 1910, i. pp. 41ff; and the theory of the "messianisation" of the earthly life of Jesus in Bowen, *Resurrection in NT.* pp. 402 ff., 421 ff., 439. On the other hand cf. the acute criticism of the literary and historical methods which characterize this point of view by Franz Dibelius, *Das Abendmahl*, 1911, pp. 1 ff.

[181] Kalthoff, J. M. Robertson, W. B. Smith, Jensen, A. Drews, etc.

[182] Cf. Bousset, *Was wissen wir von Jesus*, 1904; *ThR.* 1911, pp. 373 ff.; J. Weiss, *Jesus von Nazareth, Mythus oder Geschichte,* 1910; a review of Weiss by B. B. Warfield in *PrThR.* 1911, pp. 332 ff.; M. Dibelius in *ThLz.* 1910, pp. 545 ff.; Windisch in *ThR.* 1910, p. 163 ff., 199 ff.; 1911, pp. 114 ff.

of distrust toward the early Christian view of Jesus as recorded in the Gospels and embodied in the earliest sources
which they incorporate is maintained.   But if the early Christian view of Jesus be true in its essential features—and it is
attested by all the historical evidence—it may confidently be
expected that the totality of the Gospel witness in its concrete
details will come into its rights, which are the rights—as its
witness is true—of Jesus, the Christ, who by his resurrection
and appearances became the author of Christian faith at the
inception of the Church's life, and who is still the ever living
source of faith, the Lord of life and glory.

199 ff.; A. Drews, *Die Christusmythe,* ii. 1911—*Ein Antwort an die Schrift-
gelehrten* usw.; Holtzmann, *PrM.* 1900, pp. 463 ff.; 1907, pp. 313 ff,; *ChrW.*
1910, pp. 151 ff.; Case, *AJTh.* 1911, pp. 20 ff., 205 ff., 265 ff.; *The Historicity of Jesus,* 1912.

APPENDIX.

I. Gospel according to the Hebrews: Hieronymus, Liber de viris inlustribus, Gebhardt u. Harnack, *TU.* xiv. 1896, p. 8.

'Dominus autem cum dedisset sindonem servo sacerdotis, ivit ad Iacobum et apparuit ei', (iuraverat enim Iacobus se non comesurum panem ab illa hora qua biberat calicem Domini, donec videret eum resurgentem a dormientibus) rursusque post paululum, 'Adferte, ait Dominus, mensam et panem', statimque additur: 'Tulit panem et benedixit et fregit et dedit Iacobo Iusto et dixit ei: 'Frater mi, comede panem tuum, quia resurrexit Filius hominis a dormientibus'. Cf. 1 Cor. xv. 7. The secondary character of this narrative is plain even if "dominus" be read with the Greek translation (ὁ κύριος) for "domini" in the clause "qua biberat calicem"; cf. Lightfoot, *St. Paul's Epistle to the Galatians,* 1892, p. 274; Harnack, *Gesch. d. altchr. Lit. bis Euseb.* i. 1, p. 8; ii. 1, p. 650 n. 1; Resch, *Agrapha,*[2] Gebhardt u. Harnack, *TU.* NF. xv. 3-4, 1906, pp. 248 ff; Handmann, *Das Hebräer-Evangelium,* 1888, pp. 77 ff.; Schmidtke, *Neue Fragmente u. Untersuchungen z. d. jüdenchr. Evangelien,* Harnack u. Schmidt, *TU.* 3. Reihe, vii. 1, 1911, p. 37; on the other hand cf. Zahn, *Gesch. d. nt. Kanons,* ii. pp. 700 ff.; *Forschungen,* vi. 1900, p. 277; W. Bauer, *Leben Jesu* usw. p. 164; Bowen, *Resurrection in NT.* p. 424 n. 2.

II. Gospel of Peter: Klostermann, *Apocrypha,*[2] Lietzmann, *KlT.* 3, 1908, pp. 7 f.

xii 50 Ὄρθρου δὲ τῆς κυριακῆς Μαριὰμ ἡ Μαγδαληνή, μαθήτρια τοῦ κυρίου ([ἦ] φοβουμένη διὰ τοὺς Ἰουδαίους, ἐπειδὴ ἐφλέγοντο ὑπὸ τῆς ὀργῆς, οὐκ ἐποίησεν ἐπὶ τῷ μνήματι τοῦ κυρίου ἃ εἰώθεσαν ποιεῖν αἱ γυναῖκες ἐπὶ τοῖς ἀποθνήσκουσι τοῖς καὶ ἀγαπωμένοις αὐταῖς) 51 λαβοῦσα μεθ' ἑαυτῆς τὰς φίλας ἦλθεν ἐπὶ τὸ μνημεῖον ὅπου ἦν τεθείς. 52 καὶ ἐφοβοῦντο μὴ ἴδωσιν αὐτὰς οἱ Ἰουδαῖοι καὶ ἔλεγον· " εἰ καὶ μὴ ἐν ἐκείνῃ τῇ ἡμέρᾳ ᾗ ἐσταυρώθη ἐδυνήθημεν κλαῦσαι καὶ κόψασθαι, κἂν νῦν ἐπὶ τοῦ μνήματος αὐτοῦ ποιήσωμεν ταῦτα. 53 τίς δὲ ἀποκυλίσει ἡμῖν καὶ τὸν λίθον τὸν τεθέντα ἐπὶ τῆς θύρας τοῦ μνημείου, ἵνα εἰσελθοῦσαι παρακαθεσθῶμεν αὐτῷ καὶ ποιήσωμεν τὰ ὀφειλόμενα ; 54 μέγας γὰρ ἦν ὁ λίθος, καὶ φοβούμεθα μή τις ἡμᾶς ἴδῃ. καὶ εἰ μὴ δυνάμεθα, κἂν ἐπὶ τῆς θύρας βάλωμεν ἃ φέρομεν εἰς μνημοσύνην αὐτοῦ,[καὶ] κλαύσωμεν καὶ κοψώμεθα ἕως ἔλθωμεν εἰς τὸν οἶκον ἡμῶν." xiii 55 καὶ ἐπελθοῦσαι εὗρον τὸν τάφον ἠνεῳγμένον· καὶ προσελθοῦσαι παρέκυψαν ἐκεῖ, καὶ ὁρῶσιν ἐκεῖ τινα νεανίσκον καθεζόμενον [ἐν] μέσῳ τοῦ τάφου ὡραῖον καὶ περιβεβλημένον στολὴν λαμπροτάτην, ὅστις ἔφη αὐταῖς· 56 " τί ἤλθατε ; τίνα ζητεῖτε ; μὴ τὸν σταυρωθέντα ἐκεῖνον ; ἀνέστη καὶ ἀπῆλθεν· εἰ δὲ μὴ πιστεύετε, παρακύψατε καὶ ἴδετε τὸν τόπον ἔνθα ἔκειτο, ὅτι οὐκ ἔστιν· ἀνέστη γὰρ καὶ ἀπῆλθεν ἐκεῖ ὅθεν ἀπεστάλη." 57 τότε αἱ γυναῖκες φοβηθεῖσαι ἔφυγον.

xiv 58 Ἦν δὲ τελευταία ἡμέρα τῶν ἀζύμων, καὶ πολλοί τινες ἐξήρχοντο ὑποστρέφοντες εἰς τοὺς οἴκους αὐτῶν τῆς ἑορτῆς παυσαμένης. 59 ἡμεῖς δὲ οἱ δώδεκα μαθηταὶ τοῦ κυρίου ἐκλαίομεν καὶ ἐλυπούμεθα, καὶ ἕκαστος λυπούμενος διὰ τὸ συμβὰν ἀπηλλάγη εἰς τὸν οἶκον αὐτοῦ. 60 ἐγὼ δὲ Σίμων Πέτρος καὶ Ἀνδρέας ὁ ἀδελφός μου λαβόντες ἡμῶν τὰ λίνα ἀπήλθαμεν εἰς τὴν θάλασσαν· καὶ ἦν σὺν ἡμῖν Λευεὶς ὁ τοῦ Ἀλφαίου, ὃν κύριος. . . . .

III. Coptic Document: translated from Schmidt, *SAB.* 1895, pp. 707 f.

"Mary, Martha and Mary Magdelene go to the grave to anoint the body. Finding the grave empty, they are sorrowful and weep. The Lord appears to them and says: 'Why do ye weep, cease weeping, I am [he] whom ye seek. But let one of you go to your brethren and say: 'Come, the Master is risen from the dead.' Martha went and told it to us. We spake to her: 'What hast thou to do with us, O woman? He who died is buried and it is not possible that he lives.' We did not believe her, that the Redeemer was risen from the dead. Then went she to the Lord and spake to him: 'None among them believe me, that thou livest.' He spake: 'Let another of you go to them and tell it to them again.' Mary went and told it to us again, and we did not believe her. She returned to the Lord, and she likewise told it to him. Then said the Lord to Mary and her other sisters: 'Let us go to them.' And he went and found us within and called us outside. But we thought that it was a spirit (φαντασία) and believed not, that it was the Lord. Then spake he to us: 'Come and . . . Thou, O Peter, who hast denied his [Preuschen, <me>] thrice, and dost thou deny even now?' We drew near to him, doubting in our hearts that perhaps it might not be he. Then spake he to us: 'Why do you still doubt and are unbelieving? I am he who spake to you about my flesh and my death and my resurrection, that ye might know that I am he. Peter, lay thy finger in the nail-prints in my hands, and thou Thomas lay thy finger in the spear-thrust in my side, but do thou Andrew touch my feet, thus thou seest that she . . . to those of earth. For it is written in the prophet, 'fantacies of dreams . . . on earth.' We answered him: 'We have recognized in truth, that . . . in the flesh.' And we cast ourselves on our face[s] and confessed our sins that we had been unbelieving."

Schmidt (*SAB.* 1908, p. 1055) thinks that the author of the Greek original knew the passage in Ignatius *ad Smyrn.* iii: ἐγὼ γὰρ καὶ μετὰ τὴν ἀνάστασιν ἐν σαρκὶ αὐτὸν οἶδα καὶ πιστεύω ὄντα. καὶ ὅτε πρὸς τοὺς περὶ Πέτρον ἦλθεν, ἔφη αὐτοῖς· λάβετε, ψηλαφήσατέ με καὶ ἴδετε, ὅτι οὐκ εἰμὶ δαιμόνιον ἀσώματον. καὶ εὐθὺς αὐτοῦ ἥψαντο καὶ ἐπίστευσαν, κραθέντες τῇ σαρκὶ αὐτοῦ καὶ τῷ πνεύματι (cf. *ad Trall.* ix). Cf. also Hier. *de vir. ill.* xvi; Schmidt, *SAB.* 1908, pp. 1047-1056 and *ThLz.* 1910, p. 796; Harnack, *Theologische Studien B. Weiss dargebracht,* pp. 1-8; A. Meyer, *Auferstehung* usw. pp. 81 f.; M. R. James, *JThSt.* 1909-10, pp. 101, 290, 569; 1910-11, pp. 55 f.; D. P. Bihlmeyer, *RBd.* 1911, pp. 270 ff; Hennecke, *Neutest. Apokryphen,* pp. 38 f; Preuschen, *Antilegomena,* pp. 83 f; W. Bauer, *Leben Jesu* usw. p. 262.

IV. The Syriac Didascalia: translated from Achelis und Flemming in Gebhardt u. Harnack, *TU.* NF. x. 1904, p. 107.

"Because then these days and nights were short, therefore it is written thus [in the Old Testament quotation which precedes]. In the night therefore, as Sunday was breaking, he appeared to Mary Magdalene and Mary the daughter of James, and in the morning-dawn of Sunday he entered into [the house of] Levi, and then he appeared also to us."

The account of the appearances follows an explanation of the manner in which the word of Jesus in Mt. xii. 40—the Son Man must be three days in the heart of the earth—was fulfilled; afterwards Jesus gives instructions concerning fasting.

V. TERTULLIAN, APOLOGETICUM, XXI: Oehler, i. pp. 201 ff.

Ad doctrinam vero eius, qua revincebantur magistri primoresque Iudæorum, ita exasperabantur, maxime quod ingens ad eum multitudo deflecteret, ut postremo oblatum Pontio Pilato, Syriam tunc ex parte Romana procuranti, violentia suffragiorum in crucem Iesum dedi sibi extorserint . . . Sed ecce tertia die concussa repente terra, et mole revoluta quae obstruxerat sepulchrum, et custodia pavore disiecta, nullis apparentibus discipulis nihil in sepulchro repertum est praeterquam exuviae sepulti . . . Nam nec ille se in vulgus eduxit, ne impii errore liberarentur, ut et fides, non mediocri praemio destinata, difficultate constaret. Cum discipulis autem quibusdam apud Galilæam, Iudæam regionem, ad quadraginta dies egit docens eos quae docerent. Dehinc ordinatis eis ad officium praedicandi per orbem circumfusa nube in caelum est receptus . . . Ea omnia super Christo Pilatus, et ipse iam pro sua conscientia Christianus, Caesari tunc Tiberio nuntiavit.

VI. ACTA PILATI: Tischendorf, *Evangelia Apocrypha,*[2] 1876.

B xv. 5 (p. 321) ἔφη πρὸς αὐτοὺς ὁ Ἰωσήφ· κατὰ τὴν ἑσπέραν τῆς παρασκευῆς, ὅτε με ἐν φυλακῇ κατησφαλίσατε, ἔπεσον εἰς προσευχὴν δι' ὅλης τῆς νυκτὸς καὶ δι' ὅλης τῆς ἡμέρας τοῦ σαββάτου. καὶ τοῦ μεσονυκτίου ὁρῶ τὸν οἶκον τῆς φυλακῆς ὅτι ἐσίκωσαν αὐτὸν ἄγγελοι τέσσαρες, ἀπὸ τῶν τεσσάρων γονιῶν κατέχοντες αὐτόν. καὶ εἰσῆλθεν ὁ Ἰησοῦς ὡς ἀστραπή, καὶ ἀπὸ τοῦ φόβου ἔπεσον εἰς τὴν γῆν. κρατήσας οὖν με τῆς χειρὸς ἤγειρε λέγων· μὴ φοβοῦ, Ἰωσήφ. εἶτα περιλαβὼν κατεφίλησέ με καὶ λέγει· ἐπιστράφου καὶ ἴδε τίς εἰμι. στραφεὶς οὖν καὶ ἰδὼν εἶπον· κύριε, οὐκ οἶδα τίς εἶ. λέγει ἐκεῖνος· ἐγώ εἰμι Ἰησοῦς, ὃν προεχθὲς ἐκήδευσας. λέγω πρὸς αὐτόν· δεῖξόν μοι τὸν τάφον, καὶ τότε πιστεύσω. λαβὼν οὖν με τῆς χειρὸς ἀπήγαγεν ἐν τῷ τάφῳ ὄντι ἠνεῳγμένῳ. καὶ ἰδὼν ἐγὼ τὴν σινδόνα καὶ τὸ σουδάριον καὶ γνωρίσας εἶπον· εὐλογημένος ὁ ἐρχόμενος ἐν ὀνόματι κυρίου, καὶ προσεκύνησα αὐτόν. εἶτα λαβών με τῆς χειρός, ἀκολουθούντων καὶ τῶν ἀγγέλων, ἤγαγεν εἰς Ἀριμαθίαν ἐν τῷ οἴκῳ μου, καὶ λέγει μοι· κάθου ἐνταῦθα ἕως ἡμέρας τεσσαράκοντα. ἐγὼ γὰρ ὑπάγω εἰς τοὺς μαθητάς μου, ἵνα πληροφορήσω αὐτοὺς κηρύττειν τὴν ἐμὴν ἀνάστασιν [A. xv. 6 (p. 274): ἰδοὺ γὰρ πορεύομαι πρὸς τοὺς ἀδελφούς μου εἰς τὴν Γαλιλαίαν]. Cf. A xv. 6 (pp. 272 ff.); *Gesta.* xv. 5 (pp. 381 f.); *Narratio Iosephi,* iv. 2 (pp. 467 ff.).

B. xiv. 1 (p. 318): μεθ' ἡμέρας δὲ ὀλίγας ἦλθον ἀπὸ τῆς Γαλιλαίας εἰς τὰ Ἱεροσόλυμα ἄνθρωποι τρεῖς· ὁ εἷς ἐξ αὐτῶν ἦν ἱερεὺς ὀνόματι Φινεές, ὁ ἕτερος λευίτης ὀνόματι Ἀγγαῖος, καὶ ὁ ἕτερος στρατιώτης [A. xiv. 1 (p. 259) διδάσκαλος] ὀνόματι Ἀδᾶς. οὗτοι ἦλθον πρὸς τοὺς ἀρχιερεῖς καὶ εἶπον αὐτοῖς καὶ τῷ λαῷ· τὸν Ἰησοῦν, ὃν ὑμεῖς ἐσταυρώσατε, εἴδομεν ἐν τῇ Γαλιλαίᾳ μετὰ τῶν ἕνδεκα μαθητῶν αὐτοῦ εἰς τὸ ὄρος τῶν ἐλαιῶν [A. xiv. 1

(p. 259) τὸ καλούμενον Μαμῖλχ.   v.l. Μαμβήχ, Μαλήκ, Μοφήκ, Μομφῆ, *Manbre sive Malech, Manbre sive Amalech, Mambre, Mabrech*], διδάσκοντα πρὸς αὐτοὺς καὶ λέγοντα· πορεύθητε εἰς πάντα τὸν κόσμον καὶ κηρύξατε τὸ εὐγγέλιον, καὶ ὅστις πιστεύσει καὶ βαπτισθῇ σωθήσεται, ὅστις δὲ οὐ πιστεύσει κατακριθήσεται. καὶ ταῦτα λέγων ἀνέβαινεν εἰς τὸν οὐρανόν. καὶ ἐθεωροῦμεν καὶ ἡμεῖς καὶ ἄλλοι πολλοὶ τῶν πεντακοσίων ἐπέκεινα.   Cf. A. xiv. 1 (pp. 259 f.), *Gesta,* xiv. 1 (p. 372) ; B. xvi. 2 (p. 322), A. xvi. 5 (p. 279), *Gesta,* xvi. 3 (p. 386) ; *Descensus Christi,* B. i. [xvii.] (p. 417). In A. xiii. 1 (p. 255) the message of the angel to the women at the sepulchre concludes : καὶ ταχὺ πορευθεῖσαι εἴπατε τοῖς μαθηταῖς αὐτοῦ ὅτι ἠγέρθη ἀπὸ τῶν νεκρῶν, καὶ ἔστιν ἐν τῇ Γαλιλαίᾳ.. Cf. also xiii. 2 (p. 257), B. xiii. 1 (p. 317), *Gesta,* xiii. 1 (p. 369) ; *Anaphora Pilati,* A. 9 (p. 441).

VII. ABBREVIATIONS.

AJTh.	The American Journal of Theology: Chicago University.
BG.	Beweiss des Glaubens: Zöckler und Steude.
BFTh.	Beiträge zur Förderung christ. Theologie; Schlatter u. Lütgert.
ChQuRev.	Church Quarterly Review; A. C. Headlam.
ChrW.	Christliche Welt: Rade.
DCG.	Dictionary of Christ and the Gospels: Hastings.
EB.	Encyclopedia Biblica: Cheyne and Black.
Exp.	Expositor: R. Nicoll.
HB.	Handbuch zum Neuen Testament: Lietzmann.
HC.	Hand-Commentar zum Neuen Testament: H. J. Holtzmann.
HJ.	Hibbert Journal: L. P. Hicks.
HThR.	The Harvard Theological Review: Harvard University.
ICC.	International Crit. Commentary: Briggs, Driver and Plummer.
JBL.	Journal of Biblical Literature: Society of Bibl. Lit. and Exeg.
JThSt.	Journal of Theological Studies: Bethune-Baker.
KlT.	Kleine Texte: Lietzmann.
MK.	Kritisch-exegetischer Kommentar über das Neue Testament begründet von H. A. W. Meyer.
NkZ.	Neue kirchliche Zeitschrift: Engelhardt.
OC.	The Open Court: Open Court Publishing Company.
PrM.	Protestantische Monatshefte: Websky.
PrThR.	The Princeton Theological Review: Princeton.
RBd.	Revue Bénédictine: Maredsous.
RGG.	Religion in Geschichte und Gegenwart: Schiele u. Zscharnack.
RHLR.	Revue d'Histoire et de littérature religieuses: Émile Nourry.
SAB.	Sitzungsberichte d. königl. preuss. Akad. d. Wiss. zu Berlin.
SNT.	Die Schriften des Neuen Testaments: J. Weiss.
StBE.	Studia Biblica et Ecclesiastica: Clarendon Press.
ThLBl.	Theologische Literaturblatt: Ihmels.
ThLz.	Theologische Literaturzeitung: Schürer und Harnack.
ThQ.	Theologische Quartalschrift: Belser.
ThR.	Theologische Rundschau: Bousset und Heitmüller.
ThStKr.	Theologische Studien und Kritiken: Kattenbusch und Loofs.
ThT.	Theologisch Tijdschrift: B. D. Eerdmans.
TU.	Texte und Untersuchungen: Gebhardt und Harnack.
ZK.	Kommentar zum Neuen Testament: Th. Zahn.
ZNW.	Zeitschrift für die neutest. Wissenschaft: Preuschen.
ZThK.	Zeitschrift für Theologie und Kirche: Herrmann und Rade.
ZwTh.	Zeitschrift für wissenschaftliche Theologie: A. Hilgenfeld.

MODERN SPIRITUAL MOVEMENTS

CHARLES ROSENBURY ERDMAN

MODERN SPIRITUAL MOVEMENTS

The last century of Christian history has been characterized by notable achievements in various spheres of religious thought and endeavor. It has been an era of great activity in biblical and theological science, of marked development in philanthropic and social service, of unequalled progress in evangelistic and missionary work. All these activities have been manifestations of the spiritual life of the church. In its essence this life has been the same in all ages, however varied may have been its providential expressions and embodiments. The absolute necessity of maintaining this life in vigor is quite obvious. Upon it depends not only the service, and the growth of the church, but its very existence. In these days of vast and complicated religious enterprises there should be proportionate efforts to insure the growth and development of this essential energy. There is a temptation to attempt service without strength, to project great movements without the supply of power, to expect activities without life. It is therefore encouraging to find, even in days of reputed spiritual indifference, large groups of Christians who are facing the problems of Christian experience, and, to use a conventional phrase, are striving for " the deepening of the spiritual life ". Obviously " the means of grace " and the processes of spiritual growth are the same for all generations, yet it is helpful and stimulating to note the phases of spiritual life which have been emphasized by certain modern movements. Few of these movements have been definitely organized or clearly defined, yet they have expressed the aspirations of sincere souls for something higher in Christian attainment, for something deeper in Christian experience; and their influence has resulted in the elevation and maintenance of truer ideals of Christian living. Many of them have been attended by extravagances and misconceptions, but these have been like waves which, as they break above the surface, show the direction and power of currents hidden and silent and strong. These movements draw attention to elements which have never been wanting in the true life of the church, but which need to be recognized and developed continually if this life is to be maintained in purity and developed in power.

I

HOLINESS

Among the essential characteristics of the followers of Christ, personal holiness has ever been regarded as of first importance. Christians are " called to be saints ". Hence there is a deep interest and significance in the " holiness movements " which, under various names and in differing forms, have appeared during the past century. Among their leaders are many types, from the advocates of " sinless perfection " on the one extreme, to the mild advocates of " ethical revival " on the other; yet all have emphasized the Christian duty of closer conformity to the will and character of God.

Occasionally those have appeared who claimed absolute sinlessness; they confessed no further need of penitence and forgiveness; they claimed to have perfectly fulfilled the law of God; but they exerted slight influence and aroused little interest, possibly because their impeccability was a phenomenon discovered by none save themselves, while to unbiased observers there was much in their ideals and actions which apparently fell below a divine standard. This was notably the case with the American " Perfectionists ", the followers of Noyes, who held that Christ had returned to earth in the Apostolic age, and so completed his saving work that all who accepted his rule were no longer under law but under grace and could do no wrong; but their conduct so far invalidated their claims that unsympathetic neighbors broke up their community in 1847, after an experiment of little more than ten years. " Absolute perfection " does not seem to make a very serious appeal to the modern imagination.

More commonly, however, the claim has been made of a relative holiness, or of " Christian Perfection ". This doctrine is of course associated with the name of John Wesley, who, in the previous century, had advocated the theory, but had carefully limited his statement by declaring that it was neither a divine, nor an angelic, nor an Adamic perfection; but such as is possible for fallen but regenerated man. It does not exclude ignorance and errors of judgment with consequent wrong affections. " It needs the atoning blood for both words and actions which are, in a sense, transgressions of the perfect law ". As Wesley declared " it is the perfection of which man is capable while dwelling in a corruptible body;—it is loving the Lord his God with all his heart and with all his soul, and with all his mind." While this doctrine has been subsequently misrepresented, and has led to delusions and self-deceptions, while even in its original form it is open to serious question and criticism, yet there can be no doubt that it has been of wide and helpful influence, and that the teachings of Methodism have stimulated the desire for holier living, and have led many to higher levels of Christian experience.

About the middle of the century there appeared a curious phase of holiness doctrine, which was first advocated by two theological students of Oberlin. According to the theory of " the simplicity of moral action " it is impossible that sin and virtue should coexist in the human heart at the same time. "All moral action is single and indivisible; the soul is either wholly consecrated to Christ or it has none of his spirit. The two states may alternate. The man may be a Christian at one moment, and a sinner the next, but he cannot be at any moment a sinful or imperfect Christian ". Dr. Finney seems to have accepted the logical conclusions of the theory and to have taught that regeneration involved complete sanctification.

The errors in such a system it may not be difficult to discover; yet at the same time it is not to be denied that Dr. Finney proved to be a great power in promoting personal holiness. While undoubtedly carrying his doctrine too far and suggesting that a perfect choice of God is essentially a perfect life, he did emphasize the responsible activity of the human will. While Christians were apparently waiting for some mysterious, divine impulse, and meanwhile were living carnal lives of selfish indulgence, he sounded out his commanding message of responsibility, of the duty of moral choice, of the absolute necessity of immediate and continual effort to attain the holiness which is possible for the believer and is demanded of the follower of Christ.

An equally curious theory of holiness, which has had a wider acceptance than is usually realized, has been falsely attributed to the Plymouth Brethren. It was a perversion of "Plymouthism" and should never be regarded as forming a part of that system. According to this peculiar theory, regeneration consists in the creation of a "new nature" which is sinless, and which constitutes the "real self". Meanwhile the "old nature" still exists, but is no longer identified with the "Ego". Whatever this "old nature" may do involves the believer in no sin, for he is identified with the new nature which does no sin. Every Christian therefore possesses a dual personality; he is a veritable "Doctor Jekyll and Mr. Hyde", only, no matter what may be done by him, he is accountable only for the actions of the genial Doctor. This would be a comfortable doctrine, if we could only persuade ourselves of its truth; but most of us are compelled to believe that the continuous identity of personality is a fundamental fact in all human consciousness and experience.

What the Plymouth Brethren actually taught was the contrast between the tendencies, motives and inclinations of the regenerate and unregenerate soul, and not a transferred nor a dual personality. They continually exhorted believers to "identify themselves" with the "new nature", or in Pauline phrase, "to reckon themselves dead unto sin", "knowing that the old man was crucified with Christ". It was this scriptural doctrine, or their possibly imperfect statement of this doctrine, which was perverted into the theory of the "transferred self". "Plymouthism", whatever its faults, never made for antinomianism. It arose as a protest against the worldliness of the church and the unscriptural practices of professing Christians. Its adherents advocated absolute submission to the scriptures, and proclaimed with clearness and fidelity the great truths concerning the work of Christ, the justification and

standing of believers, and the absolute need of continual identification with Christ. To this movement more than to any
other one influence the church is indebted for the teachings
and work of the late D. L. Moody. He was never identified
with the " Brethren ", yet he was fully imbued with their
doctrines and they formed the substance of his message.
Such an example may suggest the general relation of Plymouth
teachings to evangelical truth in general; but it is in the specific
matter of the promotion of holiness that these teachings had
their most helpful influence, an influence extending widely beyond the circles of the Brethren. According to these tenets,
the justified soul is free from the guilt both of " sins " and of
" sin ", from condemnation not only for actual transgressions
but also for the possession of an evil nature, and so of a tendency to sin. Of course if one allows that nature to express
itself in acts, those acts are sins, and bring with them guilt and
separation from God. But the mere possession of these evil
tendencies is not sin. " There is no condemnation for them
that are in Christ Jesus." The apprehension of such a truth
has lifted a crushing burden from many a soul and resulted in
immediate and unprecedented progress in holiness. The result has been like the difference between the experiences described in the seventh and in the eighth chapter of Romans.
It has come from the fuller understanding of what is involved
in the pregnant statement: " What the law could not do in
that it was weak through the flesh, God sending his own Son
in the likeness of sinful flesh, and for sin, condemned sin in
the flesh, that the righteousness of the law might be fulfilled in
us who walk not after the flesh but after the Spirit." It is
this very truth of " the standing " of the believer, in spite of
his possession of evil tendencies, as stated by the Plymouth
teachers, which was perverted into the doctrine of the " transferred self ". Possibly as stated by these teachers,—who were
not usually expert in metaphysical distinctions, and who often
were unconscious of the psychological implications of their
own statements as they spoke of old and new " natures ", of
identification with " the new man ", and identification with
Christ,—the propositions may have been open to such perversion; yet none can sympathetically review the Plymouth teach-

ings without gaining a fuller apprehension of our relation to God through Christ. In spite of their divisive tendencies, their occasional misinterpretations of scripture and their fondness for controversy, the Plymouth Brethren have been examples to their fellow Christians in practical separation from the world, in loyal adherence to the great doctrines of grace, and in personal holiness of life.

Another phase of holiness teaching with even less apparent foundation in Scripture than could be found for the theory of the "transferred self" was advanced by the advocates of "The Higher Life". While this movement had various forms, and was indicated by different phrases, as "the second blessing", "entire sanctification", or "complete salvation", its essential teaching was that absolute sinlessness might be attained by a single act of complete consecration to God. It was held that as a result of such a dedication of self and of a simultaneous act of appropriating faith, a state could be attained where henceforth the believer would be kept from sin. This extreme and obviously untenable position was soon modified by suggesting that the experience to be secured was not absolute sinlessness, but a perfection of Christian love, and a relative holiness, which was later defined as a "deliverance from known sin". In this modified form the movement exerted wide influence. Among its leaders will be remembered the name of R. Pearsall Smith, whose rather pathetic story reminds us of the powerful and effective appeals made by these teachers for the abandonment, not only of positive sins, but of all "weights", and hindrances to Christian progress, and for a definite and complete consecration to Christ. It is to the meetings held for such consecration, and to the suggestion of the possibility of attaining a truer Christian experience, that we are to trace the inception of the movement associated with the names of Oxford, and Brighton and Keswick.

This last is the most definite and powerful and familiar of all the movements for holiness which the century has witnessed. Like the advocates of "The Higher Life", its early leaders insisted upon an experience in the nature of a "crisis", and aimed to secure "freedom from sin". Yet this crisis was such, in its essence, as most believers needed to experience,

and the deliverance promised was from "known and discovered sin ". Some of these teachers insisted that the
" crisis " must be obtained by a mechanical process, involving
" seven steps ", which were to be taken by all, and in an in-
variable order, to secure " the fullness of blessing ". Keswick teachers no longer hold such a stereotyped form of experience to be essential or requisite. In fact the peculiarity of
the Keswick movement is that its true helpfulness has been
found, not in changing the doctrinal beliefs of its adherents,
but in aiding them to appreciate and appropriate the riches of
grace in Christ Jesus which are offered in common to all believers. Its supreme aim is indicated in the invitation to the
original Oxford meetings in 1874, " For the Promotion of
Scriptural Holiness ", or in the title of the first Keswick gathering, in 1875, a " Convention for the Promotion of Practical
Holiness." The purpose therefore has been to make men holy.
It has never suggested " sinless perfection "; it has advocated
no new doctrines of theology; but it has insisted upon the
necessity of abandoning all known sin, of complete dedication
to Christ, and of appropriating, for holy living, the power of
God in Christ.

Such a message the church needs to-day; such a movement,
in some form, it should welcome and promote. Too long has
the mere mention of " holiness " awakened suspicion and a
conscious contempt for theories of " sinless perfection " on
the part of those who feel content with practices of sinful imperfection. It is no new doctrine to declare that Christ came
to save us from the power as well as the guilt of sin; but it
comes like a divine revelation to many, who are in bondage
to some particular form of evil, to be assured that they may
enjoy and should expect continual victory. Every Christian
is familiar with the divine command: " Be ye holy for I am
holy "; yet by what qualifications and excuses do we allow
ourselves to be guilty of pride and indolence, and covetous-
ness and censoriousness, of self-indulgence and spiritual indifference! Conscious of secret faults, yet facing our serious
tasks, we need to be reminded anew that our Lord will use
only clean vessels. Let us review the written pledges of divine help and divine fellowship, and " having these promises,

let us cleanse ourselves from all defilement of flesh and spirit perfecting holiness in the fear of God ".

II

PEACE.

A second element of spiritual life, which these movements have emphasized, is the possibility of rest and peace of soul and heart. This was the promise of the Master, " Come unto me and I will give you rest ". This was his legacy: " Peace, I leave with you, my peace I give unto you." This was the continual salutation of the apostles: " Peace be multiplied unto you ". Yet in how few lives is unbroken peace either an habitual experience or a recognized possibility. In its place are doubts as to acceptance with God, the distraction of pressing duties, the depression of conscious and continual moral failure, worry in the present and anxiety for the future. Yet the leaders of these various movements speak, with an unquestioned sincerity, of their experience of " perfect peace and rest ". It is noticeable that the Brethren, the advocates of " The Higher Life ", and the Keswick teachers have this in common, that they have laid great stress upon the experience of an abiding tranquility of soul. It is described by different phrases, as " assurance ", or " the rest of faith ", or the " fullness of blessing "; but it seems to indicate an element of life noticeably lacking in the modern church. The experience was said to arise from different sources, and was explained on different grounds, and in all cases was evidently distinct from the Quietism of earlier centuries. According to the tenets of the many sects who have been classed under this general term, the perfect state of the soul is one of perfect quiet in which it ceases to reason or to reflect either upon itself or upon God, or to exercise any of its faculties, being completely under the influence of God's Spirit, without performing the ordinary acts of faith or hope or love. Modern spiritual movements have known but little, if anything, of such speculative errors; and yet when open to criticism in their suggestions as to the means of securing peace, it has been along a closely related line of indicating a too passive acceptance of supernatural influences. Unlike the " Quietists ", modern teachers have always insisted upon faith, and consciousness, and the active states of the soul. If peace has come it has been the " peace of believing ", if rest has been enjoyed it has been the " rest of faith ".

Among the Plymouth Brethren the experience has been known as " the assurance of salvation ". It has sprung from confidence in a divinely wrought work of regeneration, in the possession of a new nature, and in the promises of scripture. It has been inseparable from belief in the atoning work of Christ, in the renewing and sanctifying power of the Holy Spirit, in the changeless love of God. Even though there were, in the minds of many, certain mistaken conceptions as to the " new nature ", this experience was evidently based on the acceptance of truths which have been the common possession of the church of all ages. There was nothing novel in this aspect of their teaching; they were enjoying a peaceful assurance, perfectly possible for all, but utterly unknown by vast multitudes of the professed followers of Christ. Nothing would be more helpful in preparing the modern church for service than the possession of this confident " assurance of faith ".

In the case of the advocates of " The Higher Life " the experience was not so much a peace born of a conscious acceptance with God as a joyful but passive reception of deliverance from sin. If we associate the name of R. Pearsall Smith with a call to holiness, we cannot fail to remember Hannah Whitall Smith as an advocate of " the rest of faith ". When reading " the Christian's secret of a happy life " one cannot but feel that too little stress is laid upon the need of human effort, of resolution, determination, conflict; yet none the less there is awakened a hunger of heart for the peace and rest and joyous confidence which the writer shows to be the rightful experience of every Christian, but which the average reader regards with the yearning of one who is tossing upon a troubled sea, but dimly discerning the distant quiet haven he seems unable to reach. The Christian life is of course a struggle, a contest, a buffeting of the body, a warfare; and any theory is to be deprecated which makes us less mindful of the necessity which is ever upon us to " watch and pray lest we fall into temptation ". It is just possible that the very phrase " the rest of faith " has at times concealed this aspect of truth. It has come to us from the fourth chapter of the Epistle to the Hebrews and has usually been employed, not only by advocates of the " Higher Life ", but by many other teachers, in a sense rather at variance with the usage of the author of the Epistle. It appears that he is speaking, not of a present rest, but of a future experience, which he finally describes as " a Sabbath rest " which yet " remains for the people of God ". For the present there is continual conflict, yet there may be continuous victory. " The rest of faith " should never denote a state of inactivity. As a scriptural phrase it denotes the future experience of those who are united to Christ by faith; and if, by accommodation, it is applied to a present experience, it should be employed to describe the peace of those, who, in the midst of conflict, have the consciousness of a Saviour's presence and confidence in his unfailing power.

Such is " the rest of faith ", as suggested by the teachers of the Keswick platform. They have never held the theory that sin is dead, or that it has been eradicated. They have ever warned their hearers against the seductions of the " self-life ", and of the power of " the world and the flesh and the Devil "; but they have sounded out the triumphant note; " Thanks be to God who giveth us the victory, through our Lord Jesus Christ ".

There can be peace amidst conflict, yet this thought does not exhaust the meaning which Keswick teachers have intended to embody in the phrase " the rest of faith ". There can be not only peace in the midst of conflict, but restful service for those at toil, and quietness of heart for those beset by the perplexities and disappointments and uncertainties of life. This again is no new doctrine. Such perfect peace has been enjoyed by unnumbered followers of Christ during all the passing centuries, and is known to-day by many who never may have heard of " The Higher Life ", of Keswick, or " the rest of faith ". Yet the church can be glad that the message has been so clearly emphasized in these latter days in which it is peculiarly needed. " Christian Science " and " The New Thought ", and similar movements which have promised peace

·of mind and freedom from worry, might not have attained
their popularity and power, had Christians claimed and enjoyed
and manifested the rest of soul which Christ is ever ready to
give; or had they, in faith, obeyed the exhortation of Paul:
" Rejoice in the Lord always. In nothing be anxious; but in
everything by prayer and supplication with thanksgiving let
your requests be made known unto God; and the peace of God
which passeth all understanding shall guard your hearts and
your thoughts in Christ Jesus ". That such peace and rest
are possible to-day is the message of that beautiful hymn by
Miss Havergal, which, because of its frequent use, is inseparably connected with Keswick Conventions:

> "Like a river glorious
> Is God's perfect peace,
> Over all victorious
> In its bright increase;
> Perfect, yet it floweth
> Fuller every day—
> Perfect, yet it groweth
> Deeper all the way."

> " Stayed upon Jehovah
> Hearts are fully blest;
> Finding, as he promised,
> Perfect peace and rest."

III

POWER FOR SERVICE.

The true end of life is service. It is first of all " to glorify
God " if it is secondly " to enjoy him ". This obvious fact
has been overlooked by many advocates of the higher phases
of Christian life. They have been tempted to reverse the
order, if not to make the subjective experience an end in itself. Yet even these teachers have not failed to call attention
to the indispensible work of the Holy Spirit. All modern
movements for the deepening of the spiritual life devote the
greater portion of their literature to the discussion of the
operations of the Spirit upon the soul and in the life of the

believer. In most cases, however, the purpose has been to so relate the life to the divine will, and to be so endued with divine grace, as to secure what is commonly designated as " power for service ". The phrase itself is objectionable as open to a misinterpretation. It may seem to suggest that spiritual power is a distinct entity, imparted to the believer to be used in Christian service; whereas in reality the believer is only the channel or instrument which the Spirit employs. This would be freely admitted by most exponents of the doctrines which relate to spiritual experience. Many may have been guilty of strange extravagances, and of curious misinterpretations of Scripture, yet all have emphasized anew the divine message, so much needed in these days of multiplied organizations, and complicated religious machinery, and human programmes: " Not by might nor by power but by my Spirit, saith the Lord." The scriptural doctrine concerning the Holy Spirit does not seem to be specially intricate or difficult to understand, however varied may be its form of statement by different exposi- tors. The Christian Church through all the centuries has be- lieved that God, by his Spirit, is present with every follower of Christ; that He grants needed grace for every experience in life; that the essential condition of his fuller manifestation is more complete devotion to Christ.

There is nothing mystical about the doctrine. It suggests no need of sudden crises or mechanical and esoteric processes. Yet a great number of modern movements, seriously intended to secure greater efficiency in Christian service, have been led by those who have intimated that either the presence or the power of the Holy Spirit, is in some way extraordinary, and that his gracious operations can be made possible only by some special method or peculiar plan of action which will result in an experience distinct, separate from and subsequent to conversion.

For instance there are those who teach that " The Gift of the Spirit ", which was promised at Pentecost to all who re- pented and believed, is now granted only to certain Christians, and as a gift separate from regeneration. They urge others to pray for his coming, to seek for " the blessing ", to " re- ceive the Holy Ghost ". The scriptures, however, plainly teach that to speak of a Christian in whom the Holy Spirit is not dwelling, is a contradiction in terms. "If any man have not the Spirit of Christ he is none of his "—he is not a Christian. " No man can say, Jesus is Lord, but in the Holy Spirit." One may have grieved Him by his life, or failed to yield to his gracious bidding; but, in the Bible, Christians are never urged to become holy in order that the Holy Spirit may come to them; even the most impure were urged to cleanse themselves because their bodies were already " temples of the Holy Ghost ". It is at once the encouraging and inspiring doctrine of scripture that the Comforter has come to abide with every Christian forever. The prevalent misconception has been due to the careless interpretation of certain passages.

(a) It is asserted that the Spirit came to the disciples at Pentecost, although their acceptance of Christ and their regeneration were experienced long before. It may be answered that while at Pentecost there was a new manifestation of the Spirit's power, he did not then for the first time, come to the followers of Christ, but had long been with them, as he was with Jesus, and with John and Mary and the saints of old. Nor was the gift granted only to the eleven, but to all the " one hundred and twenty " and to three thousand converts on the day of their accepting Christ.

(b) The delay in the impartation of the Spirit to the Samaritan believers, is adduced as an argument; but it should be remembered that the bestowment of special supernatural gifts at the hands of the apostles is a matter quite distinct from the previous regenerating and sanctifying operations of the Holy Ghost.

(c) Paul is said to have asked the followers of John the Baptist at Ephesus whether they received the Holy Ghost, " when they believed ", thereby implying that such a reception is normally subsequent to the acceptance of Christ. The sufficient answer is that they were followers of John the Baptist, and that, when Paul preached to them Christ, they accepted Christ, and immediately the Holy Spirit came upon them with supernatural power.

The typical case for all believers is that of Cornelius and his household. Even in the midst of the sermon, before any open confession, or baptism, or laying on of hands, the full

Pentecostal blessing was received.   It is not necessary, therefore, that a Christian should agonize in prayer, or by any
peculiar experience or in any particular place seek for "the
gift of the Holy Spirit"; but rather he should be encouraged
so to live as to in no way grieve the divine inhabitant who has
come to abide in every believing heart, and so to seek the
glory of his Lord that he may use him continually for the
doing of his will.

The case of Cornelius may also serve as a helpful corrective
to many others, who, while believing in the presence of the
Holy Spirit with all believers, insist that " the infilling of the
Holy Spirit" is a unique experience, subsequent to regeneration, and only to be attained by some specified and uniform
process.   Certain teachers brought an unnecessary and unfortunate discredit to the Keswick movement by the advocacy
of this theory.   Six " steps " were insisted upon as preparatory to the desired experience: (1) Abandonment of every
known sin; (2) Surrender of the will and the whole being
to Jesus Christ; (3) Appropriation by faith of God's promise
and power for holy living; (4) Voluntary renunciation and
mortification of the self-life; (5) Gracious renewal or transformation of the inmost temper and disposition; (6) Separation unto God for sanctification, consecration and service.
Then would follow the desired blessing, namely (7) Enduement with power and " infilling with the Holy Spirit ".

Now it should be remarked that these seven acts or states,
at some time or in enlarging measure, should be those of
every Christian; but the first three should be regarded as inseparable from conversion; the second three should be continuous processes; and the last, the goal of all, should be regarded as an experience often to be repeated.   As to the first
three, they are involved in a true acceptance of Christ; and
one who has taken those steps has been born of the Spirit who
has come to abide with him forever.   The fourth is equivalent
to " taking up the cross " and must be done " daily ".   The
fifth and sixth are descriptive of the progressive sanctifying
work of the Holy Spirit.   The seventh is the normal state of
all Christians; to be " filled with the Spirit " is as natural as
" not to be filled with wine ".   Those who daily devote them-

selves to Christ should expect to be led and empowered and controlled by his Spirit. Yet this ideal state is not the usual state of professed followers of Christ. There may be an interval between conversion and the fuller manifestation of the Spirit's power; there need be none; but there may have been some lack of knowledge or imperfect obedience, or unconscious disloyalty to the Master, and then gradually, or possibly by a sudden crisis, a more complete knowledge and appropriation of Christ results in a new experience of peace or holiness or power. In such a case, however, this " second blessing " is only, what has been well called, " the missing half of the first blessing."

This experience of being " filled with the Spirit " may be repeated; the early disciples were filled again and again; sin may have grieved the Spirit; or there may be need of some new manifestation of his power; then repentance and renewed consecration result in new blessing. The " second blessing " may be less notable than the twenty-second. By insisting on a process of six steps resulting in a " crisis " called " the infilling of the Spirit ", the false implication is given that to have been " filled with the Spirit ", is to have attained a level which never can be lost, to have been granted a gift which never need be renewed, whereas we need daily fillings, and continual bestowments, and " grace for grace ".

This " filling of the Spirit " may not be attended by the manifestations which have been expected. Many Christians torment themselves by the fear that they are not " Spirit-filled " because they are judging themselves by some fictitious or arbitrary standard. They are looking for some power of utterance, some specific result in service, some particular emotion which the Lord may deny. It is not for us to dictate the mode of his operation but to yield to his sovereign will.

The " fulness of the Spirit " may be an unconscious experience. One most truly under his power will not at the time be much concerned about himself, but will be conscious anew of the love of God, or the glory of Christ. There is no suggestion in scripture that the Spirit glorifies himself or manifests himself; he " sheds abroad in our hearts the love of God ", he has come to " glorify Christ ". The Christian should not be pausing to continually test his spiritual condition by self-imposed standards, but should ever be asking whether he is wholly devoted to his Lord. Such devotion will be inseparable from all that is meant by being " filled with the Spirit ".

In most cases the experience will be gradual. It is true that in the early chapters of the Acts there were recorded sudden and unusual manifestations of the Spirit's power; but, through the entire course of the Epistles, only one such reference is made. Wherever, in the Bible, such experiences are mentioned, nothing is said of uniform " steps " or " processes ". Repentance and faith and identification with Christ are mentioned, and each one of these may involve a crisis; and then the faithful following of Christ may involve a series of crises. But normally the usual " means of grace " may be expected to result in a gradual increase of power, enabling us to serve or to suffer, or to grow into the likeness of our Lord.

Closely connected with these theories as to " the infilling of the Spirit ", is the doctrine concerning, " The Baptism of the Spirit ". This is defined as " a conscious experience, distinct from and additional to regeneration, designed to give power for testimony or service." It is also designated as " the enduement for power ", or " the baptism for service ". It is obviously, therefore, the claim of a similar experience more clearly defined in character than " the infilling ", or is a specific application of the previous theories. It is supposed to be proved by the same passages of scripture, and demands a similar series of prescribed " steps ". The latter are as follows: (1) Acceptance of Jesus Christ as Saviour and Lord; (2) Renunciation of sin; (3) An open confession of this renunciation of sin and acceptance of Jesus Christ; (4) Absolute surrender to God; (5) An intense desire for the baptism with the Spirit; (6) Definite prayer for this baptism; (7) Faith that the baptism has been given.

It is even more clear in the case of these steps, than in those once insisted upon at Keswick, that the four which are preliminary and preparatory to " the experience " are absolutely identical with those in conversion; if one has not " accepted Christ ", " renounced sin ", " confessed Christ ", and " surrendered to God ", he is not a Christian; if he has taken these steps he is a Christian, and as such has been baptized by the Spirit into the one body of Christ. Special work may be given to do, native talents may be developed, special gifts may be received, but this will be as occasions may arise and by the normal guidance and influence of the Spirit which animates this " one body ".

The phrase " baptism with the spirit " is never applied in the New Testament to an experience subsequent to conversion, except in the case of the unique Pentecostal manifestation; and if it is there applied to the little group of believers it is also applied to the three thousand souls who were not previously converted but on that day were united to the Christian church. The impossibility of limiting the use of the term as suggested by this theory appears at once on reading the account of the conversion of Cornelius and his household. Here the experience is described by such phrases as " poured out ", " fell upon ", " received ", " baptized ", " gave "; and it was said by Peter to be identical with the experience at Pentecost which was also described as either a " baptism " or a " filling " or a " gift ". The scriptural usage is to apply the word " baptism " to the initial operation of the Spirit by which a believer is regenerated and incorporated with the body of Christ, while successive " fillings " describe subsequent special manifestations of the Spirit's power. " One baptism but many fillings " seems to be the teaching and the terminology of scripture.

But we are not so much intent upon the name as upon the nature of the alleged " enduement for service". There seems to be no reason for believing that the New Testament describes an operation of the Spirit distinct from regeneration, from the miraculous gifts of the early church and from the continual supply of grace for the various necessities of the Christian life; nor does it in any place suggest that power for service can be obtained by any prescribed spiritual process, or *tour de force* of faith. The conditions of spiritual power are the same for all the experiences of the believer. Nor again does Christian testimony confirm such a theory of a special baptism given once and for all. Dr. Finney declared that he received " an overwhelming baptism of the Holy Spirit " on the day of his conversion, but that he needed to have this same experience repeated again and again. The Spirit is an abiding presence; of course he grants power for service, but so too does he impart patience in suffering, and growth in grace. It is laudable to desire an enduement of power; but we should no more expect this to be secured by a mystical crisis, than we should claim an instantaneous transformation into the likeness of Christ by a sudden exercise of will. Why not as properly expect a sudden "baptism for purity", or "baptism for love", as a "baptism for power"? And why are we to suppose the supply of "power" is given once for all, and not as frequently repeated as occasions may demand? Or, admitting such bestowals to be repeated, why distinguish the first from all the rest, and designate it by the special name of "the baptism"? It is the duty of the Christian to devote himself to the service of his Master, believing that by his Spirit, he will equip him with all needed power for the accomplishment of his perfect will. Crises will come and special difficulties will arise, and particular manifestations will be given; but, for all the experiences of life, the abiding Comforter will supply every need.

The essential fallacy in the theory of "the baptism with the Spirit", is the arbitrary selection of one manifestation of his indwelling, namely, "power for service", and of regarding it as differently conditioned from his other operations, or as a proof that the believer is truly under his control. This fallacy is emphasized by the extraordinary developments of the recent "Pentecostal movement" which has caused so much of excitement and unrest among many faithful Christian workers in America, and England, and India, and China. It is taught that one who is truly "filled with the Spirit" will be granted the miraculous "gift of tongues". This gift is coveted not as an instrument for service, so much as a demonstration of "the fullness of the Spirit". Whether the whole movement is an outburst of fanaticism, and whether the supposed gift is in every case a pitiful delusion, are questions of fact to be determined upon the investigation of evidence; but it is beyond all question that the movement is inspired by a false conception and involves a mistaken theory. No one manifestation can be selected as proof of the indwelling and the operation of the Holy Spirit, least of all some extraordinary gift which tends to draw attention to the possessor rather than to Christ the giver.

Such a movement is manifestly strongly contrasted, in its unscriptural doctrines, with the teachings of those sane and devoted Christians who have held their special theories as to the " filling " or " baptism " of the Spirit. The influence of the latter has been salutary; it has suggested the unquestioned truth that the lives of many Christians are so worldly and selfish that a " crisis " is truly needed,—a new consecration to Christ,—to be followed by a " process " of increasing transformation into his likeness and of larger achievement in his service. Much of the apparent divergence of views, among those who have been discussing the biblical doctrine of the Holy Spirit, is due to a difference in phraseology. All are united in declaring that he is the source of all life and grace and power:

> " And every virtue we possess
> And every victory won
> And every thought of holiness
> Are his alone."

IV

Confidence in Prayer.

Prayer is the vital breath of the Christian church, it is at once the source and expression of its spiritual life; it, alone, makes possible the inception and renders permanent its various forms of service. The " secrets " of prayer have been " open " during the whole history of the race; no recent discoveries have been made as to its nature or conditions or power; yet God has granted, during the past century certain definite messages which have inspired the church to a new confidence in prayer. There has been a new appreciation of the blessed " ministry of intercession ". Many " hidden servants of the King " have learned how to wield in secret an omnipotent power which has achieved marvellous results in distant lands; while certain forms of public service have been so identified with prayer as to stimulate others to depend more definitely upon the willingness of God to honor the believing petitions of his people. Of the latter two examples may be cited as illus-

trations of the many forms of testimony embodied in the
Christian history of the past century. George Müller, the
founder of the great orphanages at Bristol, England, felt specially called to a service which would prove that prayer is a
reality, and that definite petitions receive specific answers from
God. He undertook his great charity on a faith-basis, determining to solicit no funds, and to mention no needs save to
God alone; and to do this, not to suggest a method which all
Christian workers should adopt, but to demonstrate a power
which all believers might wield. He conducted his work, not
only to save orphans from distress and to bring them to Christ,
but primarily to prove the efficacy of prayer. During all
the decades of his prolonged life he made no appeal for aid; in
times of special scarcity he even delayed the publication of his
annual report, lest it might suggest to his friends the need of
relief. He went directly to God. The record of that life, so
thrilling in interest, presents facts as to answered prayer which
can be explained away by no theory of coincidences, and by
no reasoning of naturalism. More than seven and a half mil-
lions of dollars came to this one Christian worker in answer
to believing prayer.

A second familiar figure, which had a definite and inspiring
message to this century of Christians, was that of Hudson
Taylor. He never insisted that all Christian enterprises, nor
even that all Christian missions, should be conducted upon exactly the principles he followed in his work. He held that
other forms of organization might be quite as compatible with
a life of faith; yet he felt called to a peculiar work and for
its accomplishment his sole reliance was upon the power of
prayer. At the time the eleven great interior provinces of
China were wholly unevangelized. That was a memorable day,
when, at Brighton, Hudson Taylor wrote on the margin
of his Bible: " Prayed for twenty-four willing, skillful workers, June 25, 1865." It was the actual record of the founding
of the China Inland Mission. How speedily the prayer was
answered is well known; also how subsequently the specific petition for " seventy new workers within three years " was hon-
ored; and most remarkable of all, how, in 1886, the definite
request for "one hundred missionaries and money for their

equipment" was offered at the opening of the year with such confidence that a meeting for praise was held to return thanks for the blessed reply which the months would and did bring. It all reads like the veritable romance of missions, and yet it was designed of God, not only to open Inland China to the Gospel, but to incline the hearts of all observing believers to a new confidence in prayer.

Such are among the many examples which might be cited of a renewed manifestation of the spirit of prayer, and to that spirit are to be traced, in largest measure, all the great missionary and benevolent activities of the church, during the century just ending.

Such a prayer movement, as is not unnatural, has been marked by certain occasional extravagances, and by partial misinterpretations of the marvellous promises of God upon which confidence in prayer is based. In this connection might be mentioned, as illustrative, the movement which has been known as " faith healing ", or " spiritual healing ", which has relied upon the efficacy of " the prayer of faith." Such reference should be made if only to state again the impropriety of confusing such a movement with " Christian Science " or " mental therapy ". " Christian Science " is anti-Christian, involving a false philosophy and a false religion. It denies the existence of matter, the personality of God, the guilt of sin, the deity and work of Christ. " Psycho-therapy " has no necessary connection with religion, but is based on the scientific principle of the effect of " mind upon matter "; it endeavors to influence physical conditions by mental states and processes. It is at times allied with certain religious doctrines; and at others with the usual practice of therapeutics.

" Faith healing ", however, is wholly a religious movement. Its followers normally hold all the doctrines of Christianity; only their understanding of the promises relative to prayer are such as to lead them to abandon, in cases of bodily sickness, all suggested means, and rely wholly upon " the prayer of faith ". In meeting this theory, or in opposing this practice, one should be careful to admit that God can and may effect cures without the use of known means, but should maintain that it is not of faith to dictate either what God is to do, or

how he is to do it. Submission is of the very essence of prayer.
Nor are we to insist upon the use of some particular means;
scientists still differ as to methods of treatment. Above all we
should remember that there is a greater temptation among
Christians to resort to means without prayer than to depend
upon prayer without means.

Even such side currents as " faith-healing " suggest what
the direction of the stream has been. There are similar suggestions to be found in the appointment of special seasons for
prayer. Among these, the most notable is that at the opening
of the year, when according to the request of missionaries
in India, half a century ago, a special week has been observed
annually as a period of prayer " for the evangelization of the
world ". Such too are the days of " prayer for colleges ", and
the days of " prayer for young men ". In later years these
have been observed too much as days of preaching rather than
as days of prayer. In most churches, also, the weekly prayer
meeting is being displaced by a lecture, or maintained as a mere
formal service. The time has come for a new and definite
movement. There must be a new resort to prayer. The encouragement has been given by providential examples and
credible witnesses. If the church is to succeed in accomplishing the great activities now projected, if she is to enter the
doors open before her, it can only be possible by a revival of
the spirit and practice of believing prayer.

V

Fellowship.

Prayer is not only petition but also communion; it suggests not merely intercession but fellowship; and many modern writers and speakers express a definite longing for a more
real and conscious and direct communion with the Divine.
Such a desire and such a professed experience is characterized
as " modern mysticism ". There are and ever have been forms
of mysticism which are perilous, fanatical, and unscriptural;
but, in a certain sense, all Christians are mystics, although
not all mystics are Christians. The Bible is ever emphasizing
the privilege of divine fellowship, and suggesting the possi-

bility of meeting with God " face to face ". Paul has not been improperly characterized as a " practical mystic "; and it is not difficult to discern the mystical elements in the teachings of St. Augustine; nor can one deny a certain reality in the experiences of a St. Francis; while St. Bernard, the mystic, speaks for the hearts of uncounted believers as he sings:

> " Jesus, the very thought of thee
> With sweetness fills my breast;
> But sweeter far thy face to see
> And in thy presence rest."

As a modern writer has suggested: " As soon as there comes a consciousness of a divine response, in prayer or sacrament, a sense of providential guidance, and faith begins to be confirmed by experience, the resulting state may be called mystical, since it involves a conviction of personal communion with God, of contact, in one degree or another, with divine reality. All Christian life, therefore, which is sustained by this conviction is mystical at heart." This state has been common to the greater number of Christians in all ages, but it has been especially emphasized by certain modern teachers.

It may be noted that, in many minds, confusion has been caused by the contrasted phrases used in describing this state. Some today are speaking continually, as did Jeremy Taylor and " Brother " Lawrence, of " The Practice of the Presence of God ", others, as has been already suggested, dwell upon " The Spirit-Filled Life ", while others emphasize the truth of " The Indwelling Christ ". To many, a totally different experience is suggested by each different phrase; and the question is being asked, most earnestly: " Should we seek for the conscious presence of the Father, the Spirit or the Son." It suggests another familiar question: " In prayer, should we address the Father or the Son or the Holy Spirit?" To the second question, it may be safe to reply, that there can be no impropriety in addressing any one of the three persons of the adorable trinity; but the more common scriptural usage suggests prayer to the Father, in the name of the Son, by the power of the Spirit. So to the question occasioned by the varying phrases of the modern exponents of a true Christian mysticism, it may be replied, that the experiences indicated are all identical, in so far as they express the presence and indwelling of God. We have not three Gods, and where one person of the Trinity is present, the others are present also. The Holy Spirit has not come to take the place of an absent Christ, but to make manifest a Christ who is present. It was the Son who said, in conection with the work of the Spirit: "If a man love me, he will keep my word; and my Father will love him, and *we* will come unto him and make *our* abode with him." It may, however, be suggested that the more frequent expressions in the New Testament would indicate that in the matter of this divine fellowship it is well to emphasize the relation of the soul to God as Father. Christ declared himself to be the way: "No man cometh unto the Father but by me." "Through him," writes Paul, "we have our access in one Spirit unto the Father."

A still more important question has been raised by the modern mystics who have brought their helpful message to an age of materialism and naturalism: "How is the consciousness of a divine presence to be secured?" In spite of much that has been written to the contrary, in spite of many misleading but popular figurative expressions, it should be maintained that the human soul does not have an immediate and direct consciousness of God. There is merely an acceptance of what God has revealed of himself as recorded in the Scriptures; faith accepts what is said of his presence and of the possibility of communion with him; acting upon this belief there comes to the soul a validating, by experience, of the truth believed, and so an assurance of "the presence of God", "the power of the Spirit", or "the indwelling Christ". Many a heart is sorely distressed by the feeling that God is very far off; even in the moment of prayer there is no sense of His presence; and so doubts arise as to the state of the soul, self-condemnation is felt because an experience is lacking which is supposed to be common and necessary to all Christians; and thus discouragement issues in despair. It would not be just to attribute such frequent and painful experiences to the influence of the modern teachers under consideration; only it does seem at times, that they should show more clearly that the state they are describing is not due merely to nature or a " new-birth ", but to the simple acceptance, by faith, of revealed truth. The recorded words of our Lord and his apostles thus form the ground of our belief in the presence of God. As Lord Tennyson once remarked to a friend: " God is with us on this down, as we two are talking together, just as truly as Christ was with the two disciples on the way to Emmaus. We cannot see him, but he, the Father and the Saviour and the Spirit, is nearer, perhaps, now than then, to those who are not afraid to hear the words of the apostles about the actual and real presence of God and His Christ with all who yearn for it."

It should also be noted that the modern Christian mystic has not wholly escaped the peril which has beset the mystics of all the ages, namely, of using phrases, if not claiming experiences, which suggest the loss of human personality by an absorption into the divine. This has been particularly the peril of those who have dealt with the inspiring and blessed truth of " the Indwelling Christ." Some have accepted with too great literalness the words of the Revised Version: "I have been crucified with Christ, and it is no longer I that live, but Christ liveth in me "; or that other fruitful phrase; " For to me to live is Christ." They have asserted or suggested that their being has been lost in Christ, so that their actions and emotions are those of Christ; as a Christian worker of world-wide notoriety recently declared in public: " I died with Christ, and now my thoughts are the thoughts of Christ, my resolutions are those of Christ; yes, I have the actual blood of Christ flowing in my veins." The perilous implications of such pantheistic utterances are at once apparent. One cannot insist too strongly today upon the eternal persistence of personality. The most blessed conceivable experience of the soul will ever be that of a personal relation to a personal God. The mistake, in connection with the passage from Galatians, is in forgetting that the apostle at once adds: " And that life which I now live in the flesh I live in faith, the faith which is in the Son of God "; so that " The Indwelling Christ " should never suggest a mere subjective experience but a conscious and continued dependence upon an objective Christ. So too the phrase " For to me to live is

Christ " should be read in the context of the chapter, and it will probably be found to mean that the service of Christ was the ideal and sum of the apostle's life, and certainly was never intended to even suggest the absorption of personality or the loss of personal identity.

It should, however, be remarked at once, and with great emphasis, that the truth suggested by the phrase, " The Indwelling Christ ", has come into many lives, in recent years, with a transforming and transfiguring power. There has been no thought of a transfusion of natures, or of a loss of conscious responsibility, or the absorption of personality; yet the consciousness that the divine Christ was really present, at every hour, to strengthen, to guide, to control, and to effect through the surrendered life his own gracious purposes, has effected a spiritual revolution, resulting in holiness and power and peace. However wise it may be to carefully safeguard the sacred boundaries of personality, the Church needs to be reminded of all the inspiring implications of the Master's promise: " Lo, I am with you always," and to believe more in the reality of the experience embodied in the hymn of the Huguenot:

> " I have a Friend so precious,
>   So very dear to me;
> He loves me with such tender love,
>   He loves so faithfully,
> I could not live apart from him,
>   I love to feel him nigh,
> And so we dwell together,
>   My Lord and I."

But Christian fellowship denotes not only a divine communion, but a human fellowship which the divine makes possible and by which it can be strengthened. Not the least helpful of modern movements therefore, have been those designed to unite believers in a common effort to increase the knowledge of spiritual realities and to attain the higher spiritual possibilities. The reference is not to the movement for church union and Christian coöperation, significant as these may be; but rather to those voluntary gatherings of

Christians intended to cultivate that life which may be expressed in such ecclesiastical movements or in the various forms of modern Christian activity.

A single recent issue of an English weekly contained the announcements of twenty-two conventions to be held for the specified purpose of " deepening the spiritual life ". These are indicative of the large number of similar gatherings being held in all parts of the world. The attendance varies from the little groups of intimate friends to the vast assemblies of many thousands. The exercises consist commonly in praise and prayer, in Bible study, and in conference upon various phases of Christian life and service.

Such gatherings are obviously beset by their peculiar perils. They minister in part to some who prefer the delights of religious excitement to the dull monotony of active service, and to others who mistake their growing admiration for popular speakers as increased devotion to Christ. They seem to strengthen the belief of still others in the fallacy that spiritual growth is necessarilly conditioned upon special places and times. However, when the largest possible deductions have been made, the net result of these gatherings has been of incalculable benefit to the church of Christ. Multitudes of Christians have been strengthened in their faith, and quickened in their zeal, and prepared for larger and more fruitful service.

Possibly the best known of the summer Conferences have been those of Keswick, and Mildmay and Northfield. Whatever in other days may have been found to criticize in " Keswick teaching ", it is now most careful and conservative and scriptural. The inspiration and authority of the Bible, the regenerating and sanctifying power of the Holy Spirit, the obligation of world-wide missionary enterprise, and the personal return of Christ, are among the doctrines assumed as fundamental. Stress is laid upon the privileges and possibilities of the Christian life, in truer holiness and in more complete consecration.

The Northfield Conference, established by Mr. D. L. Moody in 1880, at his own home in Massachusetts, has attained a world-wide celebrity and influence. According to the opinion of many who are unfamiliar with its history and character, it is supposed to teach some peculiar type of doctrine or to advocate some particular form of experience. On the contrary it stands for the doctrines universally accepted as evangelical, and maintains as its platform the truth of the divine person and redeeming work of Christ and the authority of Scripture as the word of God. In different years special stress has been laid upon particular phases of truth and life; the widest variety of character and talent and ecclesiastical connection has been represented by the teachers; but the outstanding feature of all the conferences has been the manifest aim to prepare believers for active Christian service.

It was also under the guidance of Mr. Moody, and at Mount Hermon, across the river from Northfield, that the first great summer conference for students was held, in 1886. Among the two hundred and fifty college men present, some twenty-three were already pledged to service in the foreign field; but before the conference closed the number had increased to one hundred. Two of these were chosen to visit the American colleges and to present the claim of the world-wide work. Such was the origin of " The Student Volunteer Movement for Foreign Missions ", which has furnished recruits for every evangelical missionary society and has made its impress felt in all the quarters of the globe.

These conventions are named simply to suggest the wide and stimulating influence of these summer gatherings. Yet it would be unfortunate to pass without notice the large number of smaller conferences held in various places and at different seasons of the year. " Quiet Days " and " Retreats " and " Meetings for Fellowship " have been observed in increasing numbers. They have given new life to the stated services and regular activities of countless churches and mission stations. Such seasons of communion and prayer and recollection and exchange of views and experiences, are not possible for all, but are to be prized and cherished and sought. They nurture and express the life which is found in all sections of the Christian church, and bring to mind the words of the prophet: " Then they that feared the Lord spake often one to another; and the Lord hearkened and heard it, and a book of remem-

brance was written before him, for them that feared the Lord
and that thought upon his name."

VI

KNOWLEDGE.

The Niagara Conference antedated by a few years the Conference at Northfield, and continued its meetings for more than twenty-five years. It exercised a wide influence in establishing and determining the nature of other summer conventions; yet it maintained a character absolutely unique, in that its sessions were devoted exclusively to " Bible Study." Few inspirational or devotional addresses were delivered, and the time was wholly occupied by the exposition of Scripture. That which was essential at Niagara became a feature of all subsequent conferences, and naturally suggests a phase of spiritual life which has been strengthened by many modern movements; namely, the effort to secure a fuller knowledge of the revealed truth of God.

The past century has been an era of Bible Study. It has produced a notable and numerous company of scholars who have attained distinction in various fields of Biblical science,—in exegesis, in historical and literary and textual criticism, in archaeology and Biblical philology, in systematic and Biblical theology. It has been marked by the appearance of new versions and translations and editions of the Bible, copies or which, in most attractive form and furnished with marginal references and with notes and other helps for the reader, have been supplied at low prices, in every language, and scattered in almost countless numbers among all the nations of the world. New methods of Bible study have been introduced, commentaries have been published adapted to every class of readers and an unprecedented interest has been awakened and maintained.

However, the most notable movement of the century, in this connection, has been the establishment of theological seminaries. Of the nearly one hundred and fifty Protestant theological institutions in America, all except the (Dutch) Reformed at New Brunswick (1784) and the United Presbyterian at Xenia (1794) were founded in the nineteenth century. Those under the control of the Presbyterian Church were established as follows: Princeton 1811, Auburn 1819, Western 1825, Lane 1829, McCormick, 1830, Dubuque 1852, Danville 1853, Biddle 1867, Newark 1869, San Francisco 1871, Lincoln (Theological Department) 1871, Omaha 1891. Contrary to a popular misconception these are all schools for Bible study; all of their curricula are designed to produce "able ministers of the word". An opposite impression has been prevalent and a different tendency has been noted, due in part to the nomenclature of the departments, to the enforced stress laid upon the discussion of critical theories, to the consideration of changing conditions in the church and in society, to the study of the vast and complicated activities of modern Christianity. Nevertheless, there is manifest on every hand an earnest desire to maintain the original purpose and to produce, as leaders for the church at home and abroad, ministers who are "mighty in the Scriptures".

In additions to these institutions there have recently arisen a number of Bible Schools and Institutes, designed more particularly for those who have not had the collegiate training expected of students in the seminaries, and intended to train layworkers who are to serve in churches at home and in various spheres of usefulness on the foreign field.

Then, too, the Young Men's Christian Association, since its first inception in 1844 has sought to fulfill the original aim of its founder and to "develop the spiritual well-fare of young men" by religious services and Bible study. One of the interesting developments of recent years has been the work among the colleges and universities of the world. In America alone nearly thirty thousand college students are enrolled in voluntary study classes.

The agency for promoting Bible study, in which the church should feel the deepest interest and concern at the present time, is unquestionably, the Sabbath School. In its present form it is a modern institution. Founded by Robert Raikes of Gloucester, England, in 1780, it did not exist as a church institution nor was it organized as an association until early in the last century; and it is since then that it has attained its marvellous growth, until it now numbers some twenty-five million scholars. It has now become practically the sole agency for the religious education of the young. It is to be deprecated that, neither in "day-school" nor at home, attention is given, to any appreciable extent, to Christian instruction. The existing conditions only emphasize the duty of the church to provide for the Sunday-School even better methods and to furnish more careful instruction, that the coming generation may from childhood "know the holy Scriptures which are able to make them wise unto salvation."

An increase of biblical knowledge is absolutely essential for the life of the church. Revealed truth is the instrument used by the Spirit in His renewing and sanctifying work. The study of the word without the guidance of the Spirit results in rationalism; but dependence upon the guidance of the Spirit without the study of the word results in fanaticism. If the church is to continue to manifest a divine life by her evangelistic and missionary and beneficient activities, that life must be controlled by the Spirit of God, but nourished and supported by a continual appropriation of the word of God.

VII

HOPE.

One portion of biblical teaching which has received special attention during the past century is that which is related to the Return of our Lord. 'This "blessed hope" has ever been an essential feature of Christian experience, and its quickening forms an essential factor in those movments which have been making for the maintenance and deepening of the spiritual life of the church.

It is a truth which the New Testament brings into vital connection with every Christian virtue. When the Master inculcated faithfulness in service it was to servants who were told to look for the Lord's return: "Occupy till I come." When he suggested the need of spiritual life and vigilance he speaks the parable of the Bridegroom's Return. When John wishes to impress the need of purity in life, he is saying: "Abide in Him, that ye may have confidence and not be ashamed before Him at His coming;....and when He shall appear we shall be like Him;......and every one that hath this hope in Him, purifieth himself even as He is pure." When James suggests patience under provocation and in spite of delay, it is with the words: " Be ye also patient for the coming of the Lord draweth nigh." When Paul brings comfort to those in bereavement it is with the blessed assurance that " the Lord Himself shall descend from Heaven ".

By this hope the church has been sustained and purified in all ages. It has embodied the belief in her hymns and her creeds; and our own Westminster Confession of Faith closes with these significant words: " So will He have that day unknown to men, that they may shake off all carnal security, and be always watchful, because they know not at what hour the Lord will come; and may be ever prepared to say, Come, Lord Jesus, come quickly."

Attention has been called to this doctrine by scholars like Dean Alford and Tregelles and Meyer, by preachers like Spurgeon and the brothers Bonar, and McCheyne, by Moody and many living evangelists, by the " Plymouth Brethren " by conventions like Mildmay and Northfield, by special " prophetic conferences" and by an increasing prophetic literature. Like most important truths it has been earnestly debated by those who differ as to its details and particulars, and it has been piti- fully distorted and brought into disrepute by those who have borrowed its phrases and denied its realities. Of these mod- ern perversions possibly the most dangerous and distressing is that which has been konwn as " Millenial Dawn ". This is a strange conglomerate of heresies. It declares Christ to have been a mere creature, asserts that in the incarnation he had but one nature, that his death was that of a mere man, that his body was not raised from the dead, but that Christ became di- vine after his death. And, as to the Return of the Lord, in which the interest of the system centers, it is taught that " Christ came to earth in October 1874 ", and has been here in actual person ever since; in 1878 all " the saints " were raised and are now also upon earth at this present time; in 1881 all the professing Christian systems, the " denominations ", were repudiated of God and he has given no recognition to them since; the end of the present order of things takes place in 1914. Such are the teachings received by great throngs of hearers not only in London and New York but in cities and towns throughout England and America. Such are the vagaries contained in volumes which are circulated, not by tens of thousands, but by hundreds of thousands, three editions containing the following figures: 3,358,000; 1,132,000; 909,000.

Such instances of perverted doctrine should only awaken the church to a more careful study of the Scriptures, and to a more earnest proclamation of the truth as it is contained in the word of God. Such faithful testimony could not fail to be used of the Lord in deepening the spiritual life and increasing the devotion of the Church; " for the grace of God that bringeth salvation hath appeared, teaching us that denying ungodliness and worldly lusts, we should live soberly, righteously and godly in this present world, looking for that blessed hope and the glorious appearing of the great God and our Saviour Jesus Christ."

Conclusion

Such are some of the elements in Christian experience which modern spiritual movements have emphasized and developed. They present inspiring possibilities to every follower of Christ, and indicate lines of progress which each can hopefully pursue. As, at the very first, it was pointed out that the external activities of the church are wholly dependent upon the spiritual life of the church for their continuance and growth, so, in conclusion, it should be noted that this corporate life is absolutely conditioned by the spiritual strength and vigor of its component members. Reference has been made to certain general movements, not with the purpose of presenting an historical review, but of securing a practical result in the encouragement of individual believers to advance in spiritual attainment, to experience what is real and vital in all the phases of life to which allusion has been made, to strive more consciously to attain the goal towards which, in all centuries the followers of Christ have been pressing,—the goal of likeness to their Lord, of transformation into His image,—" the prize of the high calling of God in Christ Jesus ". All may not adopt the same methods, all may not choose the same paths, but each should seek for definite progress. The ways are not so divergent as is sometimes supposed. Experiences often differ more in name than in reality. " The means of grace " are not secret; they are common to all believers; but by more faithfully following most familiar paths, new experiences will be known, more glorious possibilities will burst upon the view, more perfectly will be realized the fullness of life in Christ Jesus. In many cases the advance will be marked by definite spiritual crises; unsuspected aspects of " self " will assert themselves to be conquered and subdued; " weights " hindering the progress, but long regarded as innocent, will be laid aside with definite resolve; sudden temptation will rise in ever more subtle and surprising forms, to be withstood and overcome; and all this may mean fierce struggles and sudden advances; but, for most Christians, the progress will be more gradual, step by step, hour by hour, day by day; clouds will rise, conflicts be met, only in their case, light and darkness, peace and struggle will seem less sharply contrasted. Uniformity of Christian experience is not essential; what is necessary is the continual effort and resolution and courage which make possible individual progress. By the faithful use of proffered means, by appropriating promised grace, each one can advance, can inspire others to higher experiences, can encourage the church to larger attainments in life and service, can

> " Strengthen the wavering line,
> Stablish, continue our march
> On, to the bound of the waste,
> On, to the city of God."

HOMILETICS AS A THEOLOGICAL DISCIPLINE

FREDERICK WILLIAM LOETSCHER

Introduction. The practical theological disciplines; their relation to the theoretical theological sciences.

The practical theological disciplines as sciences and as arts.

Discussion.

I. Homiletics as a science.

    1. Etymology and history of the word " homiletics ".

    2. The task of scientific homiletics: the true idea of preaching.

      a. Homiletics and the Scriptures.

      b. Homiletics and the church.

      c. Homiletics and the personality of the preacher.

    3. The independence of homiletics as a science: the relation of homiletics and rhetoric, historically and philosophically considered.

II. Homiletics as an art.

    1. Objections to the use of " art " in preaching.

    2. Homiletic art as a synthetic product.

      a. The results of theological science.

      b. General culture.

      c. Moral and spiritual influences.

    3. Homiletic art as a technique.

      a. Making the theory of preaching practical.

      b. The study of representative preachers.

      c. The practice of the art.

Conclusion.

HOMILETICS AS A THEOLOGICAL DISCI-PLINE[1]

Among the many principles which either philosophic or utilitarian interests have employed in organizing the various branches of theological study into a curriculum, there is none more natural or useful than that which divides the disciplines into two classes, the theoretical and the practical. It was Schleiermacher who gave the first adequate treatment of this principle in his discussion of the subjects belonging to this second group, the so-called practical theology. He unfolded their distinctive genius and showed their peculiar function in the service of the church, and vindicated for them a place of equal honor and dignity by the side of the other disciplines. His theological encyclopaedia is, of course, open to the objection from the dogmatic standpoint that it undermines the Protestant principle that the Bible is the only rule of faith. Nor in technical respects does his work in the several fields of practical theology equal the creative impulse which he gave for the scientific cultivation of the whole domain. But since his time it is an established view in the world of theological education that the very existence of the church as a self-propagating institution calls for a science of its living functions.

Into how many distinct divisions this knowledge is to be distributed must be determined in the light of concrete ecclesiastical developments. Besides homiletics, which we may provisionally regard as a part of the necessary service of the Word, there have thus far been erected, in the ever-expanding circle of practical theological sciences, the following: liturgics, or the science of public worship; catechetics, or the science of the religious training of the young and the spiritually immature;

[1] This discussion contains the substance of an Inaugural Address delivered in Miller Chapel, September 24, 1911.

poimenics, or the science of pastoral care; halieutics, or the science of evangelistic and missionary endeavor; archagics, or the science of organized Christian work in the congregation. We do not mention ecclesiology or sociology in this connection, for these subjects ought rather to be treated as belonging to the theoretical sciences.

Now, all these so-called practical theological sciences have this as their essential characteristic: they are, alike in the etymological and in the common meaning of the words, both theoretical and practical. That is, they are, on the one hand, sciences in the strict sense of the term; on the other hand, they are sciences which have it as the one and only reason of their existence that they transfer into the realm of life and activity all that has been yielded for their special benefit by the other, the purely theoretical theological sciences. These latter deal solely with knowledge, the knowledge, we may say, of the essence and of the historical manifestations of Christianity. They, too, may be, and by their professors in theological seminaries commonly will be called practical. And so, of course, they are; but only in that broader sense that they are capable of being made to serve some end that in the narrower sense of the word is practical. In fine, dogmatics, ethics, the various exegetical and historical sciences, whatever other worth they may have, exist for the sake of the church. And just because, when rightly cultivated they do not commonly carry upon their faces the indications of their ecclesiastical value, it becomes necessary to have another science, or rather group of sciences, that will deal with this very problem of the inner and necessary relation of the theoretical disciplines to the varied functions of the church.

It must at once be added, however, that these practical sciences may never rest in the domain of mere knowledge. The ἐπιστήμη must become a τέχνη. Practical theology as a science will have its theoretical elements; but these will always have reference to an efficient ecclesiastical practice. Presupposing as a historic and present necessity the distinction between the clergy and the laity, practical theology labors to train, by every means within its power—the theoretical theological sciences being one of the most important—a succession of ministers of the gospel who will be "thoroughly furnished unto every good work"; and this task will continue until by its performance the entire λαός will have become the real κλῆρος of the Lord. Meanwhile, Vinet's pointed characterization of practical theology as a whole is true of every one of its branches: "It is the art after the science, or the science resolving itself into an art."

In the light of these general principles we may now dispose of the preliminary question touching the mode in which homiletics, one of these practical theological disciplines, is to be taught. Historically, the two possible extremes in method have presented themselves, the purely scientific and the merely empirical. The former is interested only in the determination of the idea of preaching. The latter, looking solely at the actual exercise of his powers by the young homilete deals only with the most practical suggestions that can add to his immediate efficiency and skill. Neither of these views alone is justifiable. The claims of both must be united. A course in homiletics that does not teach the student how to preach would not be entitled to any place in the schedule of seminary studies. But this does not mean, on the other hand, that the work of the future preacher is to be treated as a mere handicraft. Considered, then, as a theological discipline, that is as one of the studies incorporated into every good training school for the ministry, homiletics must be treated both as a science and as an art; in other words, as an applied science, or as a science that resolves itself into an art.

In the development of my theme, therefore, I shall proceed, in the first place, to set forth the idea or task of homiletics as an independent theological science, and in the second place, to indicate the method by which I shall try to teach homiletics as a practical theological art.

The very name "homiletics" points us to the distinctive subject-matter of this science and the essential nature of its task. Etymology, here as so often in the case of our theological disciplines, is a safer guide than any à priori constructions can be. The term is derived from the Greek ὁμιλία, which, alike in classical and in New Testament usage, preserves more or less of its original along with the derived meanings—

a meeting in one place, an assemblage, mutual intercourse, friendly conversation upon the basis of common interests. In the four or five instances in which the noun or verb is found in the New Testament, the word denotes a converse that presupposes a kinship in disposition, a sympathetic communion. In the early church the term became somewhat technical, signifying the brotherly, familiar, edifying address made in connection with the Scripture lesson at the private assemblies of the Christians for worship. Out of this address, quite colloquial in its simplicity, grew the more formal religious discourse which became in time, next to the celebration of the eucharist, the principal feature of the church service. Presently, the conception of the ὁμιλία was in a double fashion restricted. On the one hand, the word was limited to the religious address made to the community of believers, the truly Christian congregation, while the term κήρυγμα, the herald's proclamation of the good tidings, was used to denote evangelistic or missionary preaching. On the other hand, as the preaching of the church came more and more under the influence of the classical traditions of eloquence, the word ὁμιλία came to mean what we ordinarily understand by our " homily ", a discourse preserving in large measure the simpler structure and style of the primitive religious address, which was often nothing but a quite artless series of comments on the chosen Scriptural passage, while the more pretentious and elaborate synthetic discourses were called λόγοι, orationes, tractatus, sermones. Throughout its history, however, even in the golden age of expository preaching, when the homily itself became a more artistic production, the root idea of the word was never lost sight of. Whatever its form may have been, the sermon was essentially a necessary manifestation of the life of the church striving to realize its true aim in self-propagation, a unique expression of that vital principle that everywhere organized congregations of those feeling themselves a community of believers in Christ Jesus.

Here, then, in the very philosophy of Christianity as a spiritual force in human history do we find the basis of homiletics as an independent science. In the beginning was the Word. In time, the Word, becoming incarnate, achieved a gospel. It wrought a work, it performed an act, so full of divine power, that scarcely had its redeeming efficacy become manifest to men, when there sprang into being under the creative influence of this deed of grace, the three distinctive elements of the characteristically Christian institution of preaching: the Bible, or the completed inspired record and interpretation of the redemptive work itself; the church or the society of believers regenerated by the Holy Spirit; and the ministry, or the succession of officers qualified and called of God to herald or teach the glad tidings of salvation. Scientific homiletics, having as its task the development of the true idea of preaching, will therefore deal chiefly with these three closely connected problems: the sermon in its relation to Holy Scripture; the sermon in its relation to the church; and the sermon in its relation to the personality of the preacher.

I can only allude to some of the more important questions that must be discussed in this domain, if the homilete is to have an adequate theory of his art.

So far as the Bible is concerned, history has abundantly showed that Christianity lives in and through its Word; that is, by the faithful reproduction of the apostolic message in the form of a personal testimony to its content. It is in no sense an accident, but on the contrary a necessary consequence of the different ecclesiastical principles involved, that the Roman Catholic Church does not give the Word the place of honor it has normally held in Protestantism. The *sacerdotium* there eclipses the *ministerium verbi.* Doubless, in evangelical churches the sermon has often received a one-sided emphasis to the serious detriment of other parts of the service. Still, it cannot be too often repeated that by as much as the pulpit is thrust back, the altar comes forward. Spiritual religion must magnify the Word, the Word of God and the word of the man who truly preaches the Word of God.

It goes without saying, therefore, that the evangelical homilete, when he inquires as to the relation of the Bible to the right idea of preaching, will find all manner of questions presenting themselves. I can only mention a few of the more important by way of illustration. I say nothing here of such matters as the lower and the higher criticism of the Biblical

documents, though it is at once apparent that these controversies have their part to play in fashioning the minister's
notions concerning his authority as a spokesman of the
Lord.   Indeed, this whole question of the authority of
the preacher calls for a clear understanding of his pre-
rogatives and duties.   In what sense is he an ambassador
of Jesus Christ?   To what extent does he belong to the succession of the Hebrew prophets and the Apostles?   Again,
what does preaching Christ mean?   How much does the word
of the cross include?   What, if anything, has the message of
the modern pulpit to do with social and political affairs?   How
is the Old Testament to be made homiletically available?
What is the homiletic accent of the Bible in theology?   Or
perchance, can and may theology, as some aver, be kept out
of the pulpit?   What is the office of the Holy Spirit in connection with the preaching of the gospel?   In what respects
is Jesus to be taken as the model preacher?

These and kindred questions are so intimately related to the
very idea of the sermon that no homiletics, worthy of the
name of science, can afford to ignore them.   But this is not
the place to attempt a detailed answer for any of them.   Suffice
it to say that the main task here will be the inductive presentation from the Bible itself of the apostolic as the original and
normative type of preaching.   For the Scriptures are to the
preacher something more than a mere collection of suggestive
and inspiring motto-texts.   They are themselves the great
sermon—not merely the inexhaustibly fertile but the supremely
authoritative homiletic treatment of the redemptive facts that
form the historic basis of our faith.   The homilete's relation
to the Bible is always essentially expository.   He is not to
read his thoughts into the sacred words that give him his
message, but on the contrary he is to make their meaning his
own.

In order, therefore, to ascertain the right idea of the sermon, scientific homiletics must, in the first instance, go to the
Scriptures themselves to learn what preaching was under the
most favorable conditions, and at its highest and therefore
normative development, in the apostolic age.   Indeed, few
studies preliminary to practical work in homiletics will be

more fruitful than those devoted to the consideration of the various terms used in the New Testament to set forth the work of the minister as a preacher; such as herald, ambassador, evangelist, teacher, steward, nurse, shepherd, messenger, and, above all, witness. This last has been especially exploited by Christlieb in his *Homiletics*. It is by far the richest and most comprehensive designation of the preacher's function, and the extreme frequency of its occurrence, in the simple and compound forms of the word, has led this author to the serious proposal of substituting the name martyretics for homiletics. And undoubtedly it gives the most vital conception of this whole art. It is elastic enough to embrace both pastoral and missionary preaching. It does a more ample justice than any other to the personality of the preacher, emphasizing the personal security he feels for the reality of that which he proclaims. But, not to dwell upon such a detail, the idea of preaching must be further determined in the light which these characteristic terms cast upon its aim or purpose. Historically, two views have vied with each other. Many would limit homiletic theory strictly to congregational, that is pastoral or " edifying " preaching. Others, paying more attention to the actual conditions of our churches, in which it is by no means safe to treat all members, much less all worshippers at a given service, as genuine believers, insist that homiletics must expand its scope to include evangelism. Sickel has therefore suggested a new name for our science, halieutics, a noun derived from the Greek verb to catch fish, the allusion being to Christ's promise to make his apostles fishers of men. And Stier has similarly proposed the name Ceryctics, from κῆρυξ, the herald who proclaims the gospel in its newness to the unconverted, and the problem of the subject-matter of preaching is inseparably connected with these. Here the student will need to consider the validity of what have been called the material and the formal principles of all evangelical homiletics: Christ is to be preached; and the Christ to be preached is the Christ of the Scriptures. This will secure for the cross of Christ the same central significance in the sermon that it has in the gospel itself. Once more, the ruling spirit in which the preacher is to discharge his task enters as an essential element into the idea of preaching as set forth in the Bible. This can be no other than the consummate Christian grace, the love which will reflect in some worthy measure the love by which God glorified himself in the salvation of men. And not least will this part of scientific homiletics have to wrestle with the final question, How can a modern preacher secure for his message the note that is so conspicuously lacking in the pulpit of our day, the note of authority?

An adequate view of the task of homiletics must further, as we have said, take account of the fact that preaching presupposes not only a public but a church. The pulpit is not a mere platform. The society of believers is not a mere natural brotherhood. It is a spiritual φιλαδελφία. The proclamation of the message of faith becomes normally, therefore, an essential part of the church service. And this fact in turn directly and powerfully influences the very idea of preaching. It restricts the message to its true sphere, that of religion. It tends to make and keep the speaker devout and reverent and earnest. It stimulates him to make his discourse in the unobjectionable sense of the term artistic; as worthy a production as he can make it for the honor of God and his holy house, and for the delight of the people assembled to celebrate their priceless possessions in Christ Jesus. It inspires him to enter that joy of the Lord which is itself a source of strength for him and his hearers. Wherever, therefore, the idea of the church and of its corporate life fades, there preaching declines. As another has said, " It does not lose in interest, or in the sympathetic note, but it loses in power, which is the first thing in a Gospel. If the preacher but hold the mirror up to our finer nature the people soon forget what manner of men they are ".[2]

And this becomes the more apparent when we remember that even congregational preaching does not exhaust itself in the mere elevation or improvement of the worship as such. For while the latter is intended only to express, for the glory of God, the existing faith of the people, the sermon is an effective work in which the expression of the common or ideal faith

[2] Forsythe, *Positive Preaching and the Modern Mind,* p. 86.

aims at an ever-deepening influence upon the church members and through them upon the world without. The preacher represents the progressive and dynamic, as against the fixed and static elements of the ecclesiastical life. In preaching, the minister is engaged in an individual action; in the liturgy he merely leads the devotions in the name of the people. In the one case he tries to bring forth the new as well as the old from the treasure-house of the ideal church; in the other, he is content to commemorate what has already been attained. In the former function, he is free to give the fullest expression to his own personality, consistently with the limitations imposed upon him by the common faith and the sanctities that encompass his pulpit; in the latter, he feels himself bound by the appointments that have been prescribed for him by external authority. As a matter of fact, therefore, it is through the free homiletic treatment of its common faith by the pastor that the church works most directly upon its own inner life, and receives the inspiration and leadership that it needs for aggressive, efficient missionary and philanthropic service in the community. It is from this point of view that Baur defines homiletics as that theological discipline that deals with the essence of the sermon as a necessary expression of the church's life.

In the course of the last five or six decades, however, homiletic theory, following as usual closely upon homiletic practice, has made most advance by making relatively more of that third factor that enters into the idea of all true preaching, the personality of the preacher. It was largely because Palmer, anticipating even Vinet in this, again conceived the sermon as determined on the one hand by the peculiarity of the Christian principle itself, and on the other by the individuality of the preacher, that his manual became the most influential of the last century. The common treatises had offered little more than abstract rules borrowed from books of logic and rhetoric; and these were either so general in character that the gulf between theoretical precept and practical performance was quite impassible, or so detailed and minute that they imposed intolerable fetters upon the speaker. To-day the conviction is wide-spread that the only cure for dulness and inefficiency in the pulpit is not more brilliance of diction or polish of style but a larger measure of moral and spiritual reality in the preacher. Preaching of late may indeed have become poorer in theological learning, but as a whole it is richer in religious and ethical earnestness. The sermon, according to the best homiletic ideals, is more what Luther said it ought to be, something done rather than something merely said. It is not only an intellectual but also an emotional and a volitional communication. The preacher not only thinks but also feels and wills. He puts his personality into an act. He works energetically through words to reach the conscience as well as to inform the mind, to stir the feelings as well as to engage the understanding; in a word, to kindle all the faculties that may in any wise aid in the attainment of his object, the moving of the hearer's will. He desires, in his own measure to become " a prophet mighty in deed and word before God and all the people ".

True, this whole modern emphasis upon the subjective rights of the Christian worker, as of the believer, has its dangers. There are those who go the length of declaring that the preacher must say nothing that transcends the reach of his own experience, lest his words become of none effect through their sheer emptiness. They quite forget that even the apostles were more concerned to give us the Christ of their experience than their experience of the Christ, and that in the nature of the case many of the teachings of the Bible admit of no experience in this world. Nevertheless, as Dr. Stalker has well said: " What an audience looks for, before everything else, in the texture of the sermon is the blood-streak of experience; and truth is doubly and trebly true when it comes from a man who speaks as if he had learned it by his own work and suffering." [3] The preacher must, after his own fashion, be a reproduction of the truth in a personal form. The Word must become incarnate in him. If the orator is born and not made, the prophet of God must be born and re-born. And just in proportion as the truth becomes a living reality to him and in him, does his message, like the historic

---

[3] Stalker, *The Preacher and his Models*, p. 166.

revelation of God that grew organically into the perfect gospel, assume a marvelous multiformity in his sermons. Christ never dwarfs, he always heightens and enriches the individuality of him whom he indwells. The greatest preachers will be the most original, not because they have any creative power— that is a divine prerogative—but because being most receptive they are most reproductive, in giving forth the truth and grace and life which they have themselves received. They need not, and indeed they cannot, preach themselves; yet will their personalities dominate their messages throughout. After all, the greatest problem for homiletics is not the making of the sermon, but the making of the preacher.

From one quarter only has the independence, not to say the very existence of homiletics as a science been challenged. It has often been treated as a mere branch of rhetoric; a misfortune which some of our theological seminaries have done their part to perpetuate in their chairs of so-called " sacred rhetoric ", and from which they have suffered great harm.

The relation between these two sciences merits a much fuller treatment than it commonly receives in our English homiletic manuals. Indeed, the whole history of our discipline could conveniently and most instructively be written from this point of view. Significant, for example, is the fact that the father of modern scientific homiletics, the Reformed professor of Marburg, Hyperius, gave his epoch-making treatise of the year 1553 the sub-title, *De interpretatione scripturarum sacrarum populari*. True to the spirit of his Church, he conceived the sermon as essentially an exposition of the Bible, whereas the Lutheran practice, confirmed by the attempt of Melanchthon to model the sermon upon Greek classical traditions, gave the first place to the idea of oratory. Hyperius, while freely acknowledging the necessity of rhetoric in general, and its great value for preaching, nevertheless began that long process by which finally homiletics could free itself from the bondage of the pagan ideals. It was not, however, till toward the close of the seventeenth century that the name " homiletics " was coined, having been first used by Göbel in the title of his manual *Methodologia Homiletica* (1672), and then by Baier in his *Compendium Theologiae*

Homileticae (1677), and Krumholz in his *Compendium Homileticum* (1699). The new name betokened a further emancipation from rhetoric. Nor does it occasion surprise that to this day, where rationalistic influences are predominant, or where, as in the Romish Church, the pulpit is made subordinate, preaching is still spoken of merely as " ecclesiastical eloquence ", " the eloquence of the clerical profession ", or " pulpit eloquence ". Even Vinet, brilliant as his work is in its philosophic penetration, was too strongly influenced by Schott's devotion to the ancient rhetoric. Phelps, Broadus, Shedd, and Hoppin begin with Vinet's dictum: " Rhetoric is the genus, homiletics is the species." But following the impulse given by Schleiermacher, such writers as Palmer, Stier, Baur, Gaupp, Harnack, Kleinert, van Oosterzee, Schweizer and Christlieb have vindicated for homiletics an independent place in the circle of the sciences.

The solution of this much discussed problem is possible only upon a philosophic basis. For historically every conceivable position has been taken, from the one extreme of a perfect identification of the sciences to the other extreme of an absolute mutual exclusiveness. At the outset, it is plain that the term rhetoric has been used in two different senses; the one presenting only the formal, the other dealing also with the substantial or ethical considerations involved in discourse. The former was exceedingly common among the ancients. Rhetoric was often treated as the mere knowledge of means, natural or artificial, worthy or unworthy, by which an orator, quite regardless of his subject, could win the good will of his hearers. This was the conception of the Sophists, which was so severely condemned by Plato as a mere art of shamming, and later by Kant, who described it as an art " which utilizes the weakness of men for its own purposes " and " deceives by means of a fair show ". But even in the earliest classical rhetoric the more serious and elevated conception of public speaking, as an ethical transaction, was emphasized. Stress was laid upon the content of the discourse and upon the personality of the speaker. It was maintained that true eloquence was based upon the self-evidencing and convincing power of the truth, when rightly unveiled, and upon the character of the orator as a man worthy of confidence in the double sense of his being a master of his subject and a sincere and veracious exponent of it. Here, then, we have a conception of rhetoric that begins to level up to the heights of homiletic theory as we have sought to unfold it from the New Testament itself. That the two sciences may have much in common is at once apparent. Eloquence in the pulpit or out of it becomes primarily a moral virtue. And in regard to the formal structure of discourse and many stylistic peculiarities, it is evident that there can be only one set of principles by which to arrange the matter of an address in an orderly, attractive and persuasive way. From this point of view there cannot be two rhetorics: there can be only a sacred or a secular use of the same rhetorical principles.

Nevertheless, the elements of difference between the two sciences are more important than those which they necessarily have in common, even after the utmost concessions have been made in favor of the higher ethical conception of discourse which the heathen rhetoric at its best developed. As we have seen, the sermon deals with the gospel; it has a distinctively religious aim, one which transcends the merely human sphere; and it depends for success primarily upon spiritual methods. In these three principles is grounded the distinction between homiletics and rhetoric, a distinction that is essential though it is not absolute. In the nature of the case rhetoric in laying down rules suitable for all possible discourses, the sermon included, can serve only a formal purpose. As Christlieb has well said: " It is only if, instead of finding the subject of Christian preaching in Christ and His salvation, we find it in the general ideas of duty, virtue, and happiness . . . . which also ultimately formed the chief subjects of the best heathen rhetoric, that the distinction in scope and aim between the two sciences, and therefore any difference at all between them, vanishes." [4] If, according to the ethical idea of public address, the very form becomes inseparable from the subject-matter, how can maxims that may have fitted the Greek stage or the Roman forum suit the facts in that field of discourse in

[4] Christlieb, *Homiletics,* p. 17.

which by common consent the subject-matter, the aim, and the method of the address are unique? Only when we define rhetoric in such general terms as to embrace all expression of thought in language, without any distinction as to the matter and the form, can the independence of homiletics as a science be questioned; but such a conception of rhetoric would likewise leave room for no other science whatsoever.

As a mere matter of fact, homiletics has only then flourished when it has been cultivated in its own congenial soil, the field of the theological sciences. Indeed, the influence of rhetoric, in more than one period of the pulpit's history, has been baneful in the extreme. It cannot be too often repeated that the preacher is not the successor of the Greek orator but of the Hebrew prophet. In religious and spiritual matters, the hearer is not convinced by human art but by the demonstration and power of the Holy Spirit. Unction is more than diction.

Meanwhile, however, the homilete, having put first things first, dares to appropriate for his professional labor, as for his personal religious needs, Paul's assurance, " All things are yours." In particular as regards rhetoric, he will act upon Herder's precept: " First till our field as if there were no ancients; then use the art of the ancients, not in order to build our own anew, but to improve and perfect it." Only let homiletics, true to its best developments in the past, grow out of its own independent root, and all the other theological sciences and the church they serve will have reason to rejoice in the goodly fruitage of this tree.

Such, then, is the task of homiletics as the science of preaching; and such are the principles that secure for this branch of theoretical knowledge a place of honorable independence in the circle of the sciences.

But, as we have already said, homiletics must be something more than a science. It belongs to the practical theological disciplines, all of which have this as their distinctive function, that besides giving the minister of the gospel the true conception of his work they aid him by practical counsels to perform that work in the most effective way. Homiletics, then, must itself reduce its scientific principles to a technique. It cannot rest content with its conclusions in the domain of pure knowledge. It has a further duty than the development of the mere idea of the sermon. It must show how this idea may best be realized. The science must resolve itself into an art.

But at the very threshold of this task, homiletics is confronted by the allegation that preaching cannot be taught as an art, and that, even were this possible, it would not be desirable. Thus even so great a preacher and so noble an expositor of preaching as Phillips Brooks declares that " the definite and immediate purpose which a sermon has set before it makes it impossible to consider it as a work of art, and every attempt to consider it so works injury to the purpose for which the sermon was created ". [5]   And he continues: the sermon " knows no essential and eternal type, but its law for what it ought to be comes from the needs and fickle changes of the men for whom it lives. Now this is thoroughly inartistic. Art contemplates the absolute beauty. The simple work of art is the pure utterance of beautiful thought in beautiful form without further purpose than simply that it should be uttered . . . Art knows nothing of the tumultuous eagerness of earnest purpose." There is some truth in this characterization of art; and Brooks is justified in speaking as he does against the vice of " sermonizing ". But he is using the word " art " in an extremely limited sense; and even then it may fairly be questioned whether, for example, the world's great poems could properly be embraced in this sweeping verdict. Be that as it may, the fact remains that, so far as preaching is concerned, art, considered in the first instance as the use of appropriate means to gain chosen ends, is absolutely indispensable. Art thus understood need have nothing to do with mere artifice or artificiality. It is the deliberate, reasoned use of suitable means. But even in the more ideal sense of the term, does not the very glory of the preacher's work lie in his capacity to express " beautiful thought in beautiful form ", and does not such utterance inevitably give a certain expansion and delight, as well as moral impulse, to the mind of the hearer? Indeed, is there any art in which the ideal and the practical are so harmoniously blended? The best answer to Brooks is

[5] Brooks, *Lectures on Preaching,* p. 109.

Brooks himself—the grace and skill of his sermonic art. Far truer is the remark of Vinet: "What, in truth, is art but nature still? Art, from the first moment is present in every creation; if, then, you would exclude art, where will you begin the exclusion? You see at once that you can never ascend high enough. What we call nature, or talent, is, unconsciously to itself, only a more consummate, more spontaneous art. What we call art is but prolonged or perfected instinct, which in all cases is only a more elementary and more rapid process of reasoning. If instinct removes the first difficulties that present themselves, will it also remove the next? That is the question. And it presents itself again under another form. Does looking hinder us from seeing? Does not looking aid us in seeing?"[6] We may add that as a matter of history, the most gifted preachers, like the greatest poets, have cultivated their art with laborious assiduity.

Then again, there have not been wanting those who have condemned homiletic art on what they conceive to be the lofty grounds of religion. They are fond of quoting such texts as this: "But when they deliver you up, be not anxious how or what ye shall speak; for it shall be given you in that hour what ye shall speak." But dare any one apply this promise of extraordinary help made to the apostles for an extraordinary need to the case of a pastor drawing his salary in regular installments from a congregation he has vowed to serve with the best use of all his talents? Just as far-fetched is the exegesis that invokes Paul's statements about "wisdom of words" and the "philosophy" of some Greeks at Colossae as an excuse for the systematic neglect of the study of Hebrew or dogmatic theology. Nor is it safe for any young minister on purely à priori grounds to number himself among those exceptional servants of God with whom art has all the spontaneity of instinct in a genius. For nothing is more fatal to talent than to mistake itself for genius. Meanwhile, the rank and file of our preachers must remember that God helps them who help themselves through the best use of the gifts he has given them. Here, too, the saying applies in all its scope:

[6] Vinet, *Homiletics*, p. 33.

" If a man strive, yet is he not crowned except he strive lawfully."

On the other hand, however, it behooves alike the student and the teacher of any practical art to cherish a sober estimate of what may be accomplished. No homiletic training can ever be a substitute for native endowment. It can give no new powers of speech. It may do much to kindle and intensify, but it can never impart, the divine spark of true eloquence. It can furnish correct principles and helpful precepts; but the application of these is always a personal matter for the student himself. As Phelps tersely puts it: "In brief, it can make the business practicable, but it can never create the doing of it. A man must work the theory into his own culture, so that he shall execute it unconsciously. This he can do only by his own experience of the theory in his own practice till it becomes a second nature."

With this conception of homiletics as a theological art, how can the discipline best be taught under the concrete conditions under which the work must be done in our theological seminaries? This, then, is the remaining question before us.

In attempting a solution of this problem, I have tried to do full justice to the two principles which, I take it, are fundamental in this task: that the distinctive trait of all art is its synthetic quality, and that efficiency in the exercise of any practical art depends upon the thoroughness with which its theories are converted into an adequate technique.

I have time only to indicate in a general way the method by which I hope to give effect to these two principles in my conduct of the work in homiletics. I must be brief, for I am well aware that at this late hour there is nothing, among the many things that may be said of homiletic or of any other art, that is more to the point than Longfellow's line, " Art is long, and time is fleeting".

On the one hand, then, the instruction must be vitally and constantly related to all the elements which in their combination make the sermon. Preaching as an art is the harmonious synthesis of the three factors which the science of homiletics has taught us enter into the very idea of preaching; the subject, the congregation, and the speaker, or the content of the message, its adaptation to the hearer and the personality of the preacher.

As regards the first, the subject-matter of preaching, homiletics can render an invaluable service to the theological student by relating all his work in the seminary to the needs of the pulpit. Some one has said that every university ought in these days to have a professorship of things in general, because owing to the extreme specialization of the sciences many a man after four years of college work is sadly puzzled in trying to organize his intellectual world into an orderly, unified system. And this difficulty is likely to be increased, rather than diminished, when the student enters upon his seminary course. Certain it is that he frequently has no proper notion of the relations which his highly diversified studies bear to one another and to the work of the ministry. He not seldom comes to the close of the day's exercises feeling that what he has heard in the several class-rooms may fill note-books with a variegated lore, but not satisfy the mind of a prospective homilete or the heart of a would-be pastor. He begins to think that he is in real danger of being over-educated, and that he can become more efficient as a minister of the gospel, if he will not burden himself with any excess of scientific knowledge.

It is, indeed, a difficult problem to bridge this gulf for the student. But I am convinced that more can be done by the practical chairs than commonly is attempted in our American institutions of sacred learning. The method employed in some of the Scotch seminaries is highly to be commended. The professors in the practical department devote a substantial part of their courses to this specific task of showing how the whole body of instruction bears on the equipment of the preacher and pastor. And I do not know of a more useful service that I ought to try to render than to pass in review the courses of our curriculum in order to emphasize not only the practical character of their results but also the homiletic benefits of the peculiar discipline imparted in each case.

But there is still another and more practical expedient. I refer to that used in the homiletic seminars of the German universities, a method for the introduction of which into this

Seminary the marked development and popularity of our extra-curriculum classes paves the way. With smaller groups of students thus banded together the problem can be quite satisfactorily solved by having the scientific and the practical work done under the guidance of the same professor. Of course, his limitations are here the serious concern. He can in no sense vie with the specialists in their particular fields. But if he is not utterly disqualified for his position, he can, at least in some of the departments, be both scientific and practical in his methods, and that, after all, is here the main consideration. At any rate, he can encourage the students to use in their own independent work in such classes the most thorough scientific methods they have learned in the prosecution of the theoretical disciplines, in order that under his guidance they may then utilize their results in the actual production of apologetic, expository, doctrinal, ethical, sociological, or historical sermons. To what extent the scientific end of such work may be emphasized it scarcely becomes me to intimate. But I may be pardoned for adding that I certainly should never have accepted the invitation to this chair, had I not felt convinced that one of its richest opportunities lies in the possibility it offers in such classes for combining, at first hand, scholarly work in favorite departments with practical exercises in the formal statement of results for the pulpit.

And there is still a third way by which a professor of homiletics can show the students the practical significance of the other work done in the curriculum. The sermons submitted in writing or delivered by them may be made the basis for this instruction. Now and then, for instance, a man will need to be told with great plainness that if the pulpit is his objective point, then for him the course in voice culture is the most important of all. Another, perchance, must learn how to bring his dogmatic and ethical wings together for a truly homiletic flight; preaching his doctrines with ethical applications in view and his ethics in their doctrinal origins. Still a third may need the reminder that he is supposed to preach only the whole counsel of God, not also all the results of the latest scholarship on some point of merely antiquarian interest, to say nothing of the latest guesses of some rationalistic critic who in any event would not leave the pastor a preachable Bible. And here, no less than in the constructive part of the course, there need not fail the word of guidance that shall make the cross of Christ borrow radiance from every page of text-book and from every course of study in the school of sacred learning.

But homiletic art, as we have intimated, demands a still richer synthesis. There is a second factor that enters into the construction of every truly successful sermon,—its adaptation to the hearer. Indeed, this is a consideration of scarcely less importance than the subject-matter itself. And yet many a preacher fails at this very point. As a student in the seminary he may even have distinguished himself by his scholarly attainments; but as a pastor trying to minister to a particular congregation he at once shows that he is hopelessly out of touch with the concrete environment in which he finds himself. More pathetic still are the chapters that sometimes follow this mournful introduction to the story of his professional life: the older he grows the more obvious is his aloofness from the age of which he is supposed to be a part. He simply does not understand the great law of adaptation by which the sermonic material is made not only intelligible but also interesting, attractive and impressive. With all his learning he is the victim of a defective culture, in consequence of which he may have to labor under a contracted usefulness to the end of his days.

What, then, can a professor of homiletics do to prevent or to remedy such an evil? In general it may be said, he can give both inspiration and practical guidance for the attainment of the more adequate culture that is needed. He can project the scope of his task beyond the narrow confines of the student's academic years and emphasize the principles by which alone the pastor can secure and maintain a high intellectual efficiency in the pulpit.

For one thing, he can expedite the experience of the future preacher by helping him in advance to understand the signs of the times in which his ministry will lie. Here, I take it, is the secret of that deep and wide influence which the " Lyman Beecher Lectureship on Preaching " at Yale University has exerted. The incumbents have been men of distinguished usefulness in the active pastorate, and as such they have commonly dealt, not with the details of homiletic technique, but with the large questions that pertain to ministerial efficiency in the modern world.   As Dr. James Stalker, one of the most helpful of these Lecturers, said to the students, " there is room amidst your studies, and without the slightest disparagement to them, for a message more directly from life, to hint to you, that more may be needed in the career to which you are looking forward than a college can give, and that the powers on which success in practical life depends may be somewhat different from those which avail most at your present stage ".[7] And throughout his lectures he, like most of his predecessors and successors on that foundation, lays great stress upon the point I am now emphasizing, the necessity of a thorough understanding of the peculiar and distinctive features of our age. And as I conceive the work of this chair, one of its most useful services is that of aiding young men to a secure homiletic platform as they stand with the ancient gospel on their lips before the marvelous complexities and difficulties of our modern life. No young man ought to be left altogether to the tender mercies of his own experience in grappling, as many a one must do with the very instinct of intellectual self-preservation, with the problem of interpreting the conditions under which he will have to exercise his ministry. He ought to be told in advance something about the absorbing interest of this generation in its material welfare and of the influence that this is likely to exert upon the content and form of his message. He must know the significance of the inductive process of investigation as employed in the natural sciences, and the bearings of this fact upon men's conceptions of the Supernatural in history. He must realize what changes psychology has wrought in the valuation of many religious phenomena, as well as in the province of pedagogical and therefore also of homiletic methods. He must understand the shifting of the centre of gravity in our ecclesiastical life from narrow partisan polemics to the broader statesmanship found, for example,

[7] Stalker, *The Preacher and His Models,* p. 5.

in the aggressive leadership of our denominational Boards for harmonious and effective coöperation in spiritual and philanthropic labors at home and abroad. He must know the meaning of the profound social unrest of these days, and of the insistent and universal demand that our ministers shall give intelligent and courageous direction to the work of making social applications of the principles of the gospel. And in this connection he may need the reminder that our Biblical commentaries have too often been written by scholarly recluses who may have tried hard enough to see the social message of Christianity in the right perspective, but who have failed because they have lacked the sympathy, the insight, the wisdom begotten of a personal experience of the world's need of such a message. In fine, the student must be encouraged and fitted to live the homiletic life of the twentieth century, lest the church, as well as the Christian agencies outside of the church, pass him by to take up the legitimate order of the day. He cannot possibly have too much scholarship, but at every cost he must learn to focus his scholarship upon the real issues of life and make his knowledge fruitful of good. He must understand the age, if for no other reason than to be able to talk to it in the intelligible forms of a living faith. He must put upon the pure gold of his gospel a stamp and superscription that will make his homiletic coinage current throughout the whole realm of his ministerial influence.

And here the beneficent ministry of general literature may well be invoked to aid the future preacher in his necessary self-cultivation. It is by no means an accident that the three most gifted and influential teachers of homiletics whom this country has produced, Dr. Broadus, Dr. Shedd and Dr. Phelps, have written so extensively and so forcibly upon this subject of the importance to the pastor of a growing knowledge of the world's best literature. These writers have not deemed it beneath their dignity to show how even in these days of intellectual scraps and mental dissipation through ephemeral reading, it is possible for one who would resolutely go upon the nobler errands of the mind, to secure a choice culture through converse with the sceptred immortals in the literary history of the race. To inspire men who are rightly to re-

gard themselves as the servants of one Book to become nevertheless the masters of many other books that are worthy of
a life-long study, is about as useful a service as a seminary
professor can render.   Nothing is more practical or valuable
than the giving to a fellow-man of a higher ideal by which
he may come into the fuller possession of himself.   And in
the department of homiletics this is the truly apostolic way of
overcoming evil with good in the case of those who are tempted
to use the meretricious hints and helps, the elaborate cabinets
of sermonic skeletons and the well indexed collections of
ready-made illustrations and quotations which avarice is so
quick to place into the hands of ignorance and indolence.

But the most subtle element of the three which in their synthesis make the sermon is the personality of the preacher.   It
has well been said: " The effect of a sermon depends, first
of all, on what is said, and next, on how it is said; but hardly
less, on who says it."   And if we are justified in regarding
the spokesman of God as a personal witness to the truth he
proclaims, and in making goodness, therefore, a prime qualification for the ministry of the gospel, then our seminaries must
ever be schools in which men will grow in the grace as well as
in the knowledge of the Lord.   For homiletics, accordingly,
the fundamental problem is the problem of the spiritual life
of the minister.   He must not only know about Christ, he
must know Christ; nay, he must have Christ and Christ must
have him.

Now, of course, all teachers in a seminary have this burden
of responsibility resting upon their hearts and consciences.
They are all, first of all, ministers of grace to those whom they
instruct.   They are all concerned with this task of making the
student, like that disciple whom Jesus loved, a true divine.
But here, too, the teacher of homiletics has a special duty and
a unique privilege.   Not only is he led by the very nature of
his course to speak heart-searching words on such subjects as
the call to the ministry, the personal requisites for the office,
and the conditions for the realization of spiritual power in
preaching.   But before him and in the presence of their
classmates the students, many of them for the first time in
their lives, give expression in public to their most sacred re-

ligious convictions, and in this atmosphere of prayer and devout meditation a personal word from the professor will often mean more than lengthy general counsels, however appropriate, given under less favorable circumstances to a whole class or the entire student body. By as much as these matters are more intimately related to the personality of the man, by so much the more readily may the class-room in homiletics become, next to the stated services of the sanctuary, the assembly-place for the focusing upon the hearts and minds of the prospective preachers the constraining and sanctifying power of the motives which they have themselves avowed in seeking the gospel ministry. Nor ought these services to fail to do their part in bringing the highest principles of duty to bear upon the daily routine of study. Moreover, as in dealing with the question of the minister's future intellectual life many helpful counsels may be given, so in connection with this problem of his spiritual development after his entrance upon his profession, much can and should be done in the way of making practical suggestions as to books of devotion, habits of reading and meditation, methods of work, and the best ways of cultivating personal piety amid the engrossing duties of the pastoral office.

Such, then, in broad outline, is my conception of the way in which the synthetic nature of homiletics as a theological art may be most advantageously realized. But this, as we have remarked, is only one half of the task. The second of the two questions remains. How can this art be most effectively taught as a technique?

Measured by the amount of time it will require, this part of the work in homiletics is, of course, the most important. But concerned as we now are solely with the method of instruction, we may dispose of this problem with a few brief remarks.

In the first place, the whole mass of homiletic theory must constantly be related to the final purpose which this discipline has in view, the securing of an adequate technique. All the instruction must be practical. The lectures or the text-books used must abound in concrete examples and illustrations. Much will have to be said that will be speedily outgrown in the experience of the preacher, but which may serve a most useful purpose in moulding his tastes and fashioning his sermonic methods for the future. The directions and counsels must always be sufficiently minute and detailed to be really practicable, while on the other hand those rules will be most serviceable which are presented as the results of sound basal principles. Here, as in the teaching of every art, the best guidance is that which helps the beginner to help himself and thus outgrow his need of a teacher.

Again, training in sermonic technique may be conveniently given upon the basis of an inductive study of worthy representatives of the homiletic art. In this connection I cannot forbear alluding to the provision which the governing Boards of the Seminary have in their wisdom made for the benefit of our students by securing for them the opportunity of making a limited number of visits to some of our great metropolitan churches. I am not one of those who believe that the chief desideratum for the theological student of to-day is that he shall spend a considerable fraction of the brief academic year in so-called practical work, whether it be in the neighborhood of his seminary, or in the slums or the mission Sunday Schools or the highly organized parish activities in our great cities. But having during the past year received the written and oral reports of the students who availed themselves of this privilege of hearing some of our ablest preachers of the gospel, I cannot but express my opinion that this policy, under the restrictions that have been imposed by the Faculty, is amply justified by its results. To the best of my knowledge and judgment, it is a distinct aid to the work of the entire practical department; an aid, too, which the student may secure without entailing a disproportionate cost in time or strength.

But I would here particularly emphasize the critical study of the published sermons of the acknowledged masters of the homiletic art. This is a method that merits a much more thorough application than is commonly made either by the student or the minister himself. True, an adequate history of preaching is still to be written; but special periods have been fairly well treated in our own as in other tongues. At any

rate, the material itself in our English and American literature
is exceptionally rich.   The cultivated minister will not ignore
the works of men like Hooker, South, Barrows, Taylor, Til-
lotson, Howe, Bunyan, Whitefield, Hall, Chalmers, Robertson,
Maclaren, Jonathan Edwards, Bushnell, Beecher, and Brooks.
Nor will he fail to study sympathetically and critically the
sermons of the living preachers who best understand the art
of putting the evangel into the forms that win and hold the
modern mind.   By means of such a study the young homilete
comes to a more objective understanding of himself.   He
discovers his native bent, the limitations of his gifts and
methods, and the conditions of his future growth.   He learns
also what is of perennial worth in the substance of the message itself, so that he may the more boldly proclaim, not
what he guesses the people may want, but what he knows they
must need.   Care has to be exercised in securing proper
variety in the representatives chosen for special consideration.
There will then be no danger of a servile imitation or of a
one-sided and eccentric development.   The aim throughout is
something more than a mechanical transfer of ideas or peculiarities of form.   There ought to be a real transfusion of
spirit from the master to his reader.   And for this purpose the
biographies of the celebrated preachers are an invaluable aid.
They admit us into the secret of those vital processes that
find their consummate expression in the finished sermon.   They
disclose the tools and methods of the master's workshop; but
more than that, they put us under the spell of his nobler
ideals.   In such an atmosphere we feel the truth of Wordsworth's lines:

> We live by Admiration, Hope and Love,
> And, even as these are well and wisely fixed,
> In dignity of being we ascend.

And most of all, technical training must be perfected by
the actual practice of the art.   *Fabricando fabri fimus.*   The
important question here is that concerning the amount of
actual pulpit work that a seminary student may undertake
during his course.   Obviously, no uniform answer can be
given.   Few members of theological faculties would approve
the suggestion of President Faunce of Brown University,

when he says: the department of homiletics " should keep every student preaching or teaching on every Sunday during his three years in the seminary, and so make sure that, whether he have ten talents or one, that which he does possess is not hidden in a napkin, but ready at any instant for the service of man ". Certainly, this is an extreme which, to say the least, can be justified only in extraordinary cases. From the standpoint of good work in homiletics alone, to say nothing of the just claims of the other courses, it will be far better, in this formative period of the preacher's development to put the emphasis upon quality rather than quantity. Many a tragedy in the early and later years of ministerial life may be traced directly back to those misspent years of preparation when the young preacher, quite unconsciously, his judgment warped by the deceptive breezes of a momentary popular favor, irretrievably sacrificed his worthiest sermonic ideals. Far more fortunate will be the student who, discouraging all excessive demands upon his time and strength, will never allow himself to become accustomed to, much less satisfied with, any inferior work, but will resolutely and persistently, by dint of the utmost care in the planning and writing of his first sermons secure the best results of which he is at the time capable. This being conceded, there ought to be abundant classroom exercises in homiletic technique. The custom of having students preach to their classmates in the presence of the teachers who are to criticize the sermons as to their matter, form and delivery, is often made a subject of unfavorable comment, not to say of cheap ridicule. No doubt, it would be far better if the same audience could transfer itself to the more congenial atmosphere of some regular church or chapel service, the criticism being left for another occasion. But this is seldom possible, and meanwhile the best must be made of a difficult situation. Even under these circumstances, however, great good can be done. Where the criticism is what it should be, incisive yet kindly, thorough but sympathetic, constructive rather than negative, giving new and better points of view, supplementing deficiencies, making the most of the strong qualities of the preacher, and aiming throughout at a positive enrichment of his homiletic personality, there, as my experience leads me to testify, some of the most useful and therefore by the students most highly appreciated work of the department may be accomplished. Here as perhaps nowhere else the instruction of the seminary may be made vital, personal, and in the deepest sense of the word practical.

I have done. In this general discussion of principles and methods I have contented myself with the simple purpose of unfolding my conception of the work to which I have been summoned. But believing as I do, that our evangelical churches owe their very life to the faithful preaching of the Word of God and that the prime object of this school of sacred learning can be no other than the training of able and efficient ministers of the gospel who may continue to be what their predecessors from apostolic days have ever been, the most useful men of their day and generation, I must utterly have missed my aim in this address, if I have not succeeded in making clear my sincere conviction, that in the modern theological seminary, the department of homiletics, as the cutting edge of the whole curriculum and the meeting-place in which the best cultural influences and the strongest spiritual forces of the institution are most directly and fully converted into power for service in the kingdom of God, is second in dignity and importance to no other. Alas! that here, too, however, it is far easier to form than to realize one's ideal. But taking encouragement from the call which has been given me, and from the cordial welcome of my colleagues in the Faculty and the student body as a whole, as well as from the year's work I have already been permitted to do, I shall continue to find my chief comfort and support in him from whom cometh all our help. May his strength perfect itself in my weakness, and his grace glorify itself in filling up the measure of my varied need, that my labor in this chair may be for the good of his church and to the praise of his name.

SIN AND GRACE IN THE BIBLICAL NARRATIVES REHEARSED IN THE KORAN

James Oscar Boyd

Introduction: Explanation of the subject; summary of the material; peculiarities of the Koran affecting this material:

All uttered by Allah; all addressed to an individual; all cast in the oratorical mold.

Sin and Grace:

1) In the narrative of the fall:

Sin of Adam and Eve: its nature and consequences; its explanation in the fall of Satan and his tempting of them.

Grace of God to sinful man: central grace is revelation; its mediation to Adam left vague; other gracious gifts to mankind.

2) In the progress of individual wickedness and of divine direction:

Conception of progressive revelation: soundness of its framework; in what sense it is an evangel; its universality and perspicuity; the relation of these qualities to a limited election.

Conception of sin in the individual: root religious rather than ethical; sins against God, apostle and gospel; transgression of the moral law.

Conclusion: Suitability of kindred themes for further comparison.

(NOTE.—Quotations from the Koran are rendered from the Arabic edition of Fluegel, Leipsic, 1841.)

SIN AND GRACE IN THE BIBLICAL NARRATIVES REHEARSED IN THE KORAN

Much has been written by many scholars on the subject of Mohammed's indebtedness to the Scriptures. In particular his use of the Biblical narratives as the basis of much of his preachment in the Koran has awakened a variety of comment, and from authors varying all the way from the professional Arabist to the missionary apologist. Moreover, since 1833, when Abraham Geiger published his study[1] entitled *What Did Mohammed Adopt from Judaism?* there has been a growing literature on the genetic relation sustained by Judaism to Islâm, including on the one side an investigation of the Moslem commentators, and on the other side a comparison of all the cognate material in the Jewish midrash-literature. That this last-named comparison, however, is not even yet felt to be fairly completed, is indicated by the present appearance of a new work[2] on *The Haggadic Elements in the Narrative Portion of the Koran.*

Similarly, it may be felt that, with all that has hitherto been said, and well said, concerning Mohammed's use of the Old Testament characters and events, the last word has not yet been written on even this familiar subject. There is yet lacking, for example, a systematic grouping of the material, the usual arrangement of which has been the chronological order—surely a principle as foreign as possible to Mohammed's unchronological mind! Let what has been said, then, suffice as an apology for the choice of the subject of this paper, which will not pretend to say that "last word", but will

[1] *Was hat Mohammed aus dem Judenthume aufgenommen?* by Abraham Geiger, Bonn, 1833.

[2] *Die haggadischen Elemente im erzählenden Teil des Koran,* by Dr. Israel Schapiro; Heft I covers the life of Joseph.

seek, within well-defined limits, to contribute something to this comparison, which is so fruitful for the correct understanding of Mohammed and his mission.

What those limits are, is indicated in the title. By it the inquiry is limited, first, to those parts of the Koran which are indebted to the Bible for their subject-matter; second, within these, to that which deals with persons, places and events,—the narrative-material; and third, within this again, to the treatment of the themes of sin and grace, which play so large a part in the purpose of the story-teller both in the Bible and in the Koran.

In order to have the facts before us, in their broad outlines, it will be necessary, first, to state as briefly as possible what Biblical narratives are reflected in the Koran.

Of the first eleven chapters of Genesis much is represented: the stories of creation, including matter from both the first and the second chapters; the fall; the brothers' quarrel; Enoch (?); Noah and the flood; the dispersion of the nations; and the family of Terah.

With Abraham we reach a character whose career is expanded in both the Old Testament and the Koran. His separation from Terah, the ratification of the covenant in chapter xv., the birth of Ishmael and of Isaac, the episode of Lot, and the sacrifice of Isaac,—to all these portions of Abraham's biography reference is made by Mohammed with greater or less fullness.

As Isaac appears only in connection with Abraham, so Jacob, apart from a couple of bare allusions to him, appears only as a character in the story of Joseph. But there is a wealth of detail in the treatment of Joseph's life, most of which is covered in the long Sûra devoted thereto.

With Exodus Moses is reached, and there is no other Biblical character so thoroughly appropriated by the Koran as is Moses. The story begins with the oppression by Pharaoh and the slaying of the male children. Moses' rescue from the water by the wife (*sic*) of Pharaoh, his adoption, and the part his own mother and sister play in the drama, are all reflected in the Koranic story. The two attempts to help his Hebrew brethren, the consequent flight to Midian, the meeting with

Jethro's daughters, and his marriage with one of them and service of their father as shepherd, the account of the burning bush with the divine call, the accrediting miracles and the commission of Aaron as spokesman:—all this leads up, in Mohammed's account as in Exodus, to the narrative of the plagues. From the contest with the Egyptian magicians to the departure from Egypt by night, most of the story of the plagues is recorded or alluded to. The Egyptian pursuit, the crossing of the sea dry-shod and drowning of the enemy, the manna and quails, the arrival and covenant at Sinai, God's rendezvous with Moses on the mount, Aaron's lieutenancy together with the whole episode of the golden calf, Moses' wrath, intercession and publication of the tables of the Law— this fills in with tolerable completeness the outline of the historical portions of Exodus. The remainder of Moses' career, as depicted in portions of Numbers and Deuteronomy, is represented in the Koran by allusions to the smitten rock, the murmuring of the Israelites, their refusal and consequent prohibition to enter the " holy land ", the revolt of Korah, and— what is purely legal in the Old Testament, but is transformed into a story by Mohammed,—the red heifer of Numbers xix., combined with the heifer mentioned in Deuteronomy xxi.

There is no indication that the contents of the books of Joshua and Judges were known to Mohammed, save one reference to Gideon's odd test of his followers by drinking, and this is erroneously ascribed to Saul. But with Samuel and the choice of Saul we again reach stories for which the Koran finds a place. The earlier part of the struggle with the Philistines is probably represented by an allusion to the ark as " coming " to Israel. David's victory over Goliath is expressly mentioned. David's skill in music and his authorship of the Psalms, his sin and repentance, together with the substance of Nathan's parable and the restoration of David to divine favor:—these constitute all of the remainder of Samuel that finds a place in the Moslem Scriptures.

Solomon plays a larger rôle. In the Koran, as in other oriental literature, his judgments, his splendor, his buildings, his wisdom and knowledge of nature, and the visit to him of the Queen of Sheba, have appealed to the author's imagination. Elijah's contest with the Baal-worshippers is the only other incident in the books of Kings to receive Mohammed's attention. Elisha is barely named. Ezra is mentioned, merely to rebuke the Jews for saying of him that he is the Son of God.

Among the narratives embedded in the poetical and prophetical books of the Old Testament, those which have appealed to Mohammed are the story of Job and the story of Jonah. Job's afflictions, prayers, patience, deliverance, and acceptance with God, all find a place in the few verses that refer to him. And of Jonah we learn from the Koran that he was a prophet, how he withdrew from God's mission, of the casting of the lots on the ship, his being swallowed by the fish (he is known to Mohammed as " He of the fish "), his prayer from its belly, his deliverance, the growth of the gourd, Jonah's preaching and its success.

Turning now to the New Testament, we find none of its narratives reproduced, save a perverted version of the angelic announcement to Zacharias, his dumbness for a season, and the birth and naming of John; and, mingled with the events in this family, the similar events in the kindred family of Jesus: the annunciation, the miraculous conception and the birth of our Lord. But through the crassest anachronism this cycle of sacred story is united with the cycles of Moses-stories and Samuel-stories, by the confusion of Mary (Maryam) with Miriam the sister of Moses and Aaron, and the confusion of Anna the (traditional) mother of Mary with Hannah the mother of Samuel. So that it is hardly too much to say that for Mohammed there are no New Testament narratives; such as he knows are amalgamated with those of the Old Testament. For references to Jesus' life and death amount to little more than allusions; as, for instance, to his miracles, his mission to Israel, his institution of the Supper, his promise of the Paraclete (Ahmed, i. e. Mohammed), his attitude toward the Law, and the Jews' hostility to him resulting in their crucifying—not Jesus but a man who resembled him, Jesus himself being translated without tasting of death. Our Lord's Apostles are barely mentioned, under the style Ḥawârî,—a word borrowed from the language of the Abyssinian Church, since the Arabic equivalent Rasûl is Mohammed's favorite appellation of himself and his predecessors as the " Sent " of God.

Such being the material available for our inquiry, we proceed first to note certain characteristic formal differences, that have had the effect of molding this material, taken as a whole, into different forms from those it exhibits in the Bible.

The first of these formal peculiarities of the Koran is that every word of it is supposed to be uttered by Allâh himself. This oracular style is not foreign to the Bible, but it is there confined for the most part to limited portions of the prophetic discourse and to the laws. By no means all of the matter introduced or completed with a " saith Jehovah " is so molded by the prophets as to read like a divine utterance to them or, through their lips, to the people. In fact there is so constant a variation between the first and the third persons in such passages, when referring to the revealing deity, that it amounts to what may be termed a consistent inconsistency, and only logical analysis can resolve the blended personality of the revelatory subject. We should err in using of an Isaiah so harsh an expression as has been used of Mohammed,[3] that " he falls out of his rôle ". Mohammed's claims are quite different from those of the Hebrew prophets. The dictation, or rather recitation (Koran = reading aloud) of a portion (âya) from a heavenly book by the archangel Gabriel to the listening Mohammed, is quite unlike what the prophets of Israel have to say of their revelations, even when they insist most strongly upon their objectivity, certainty and divinity.

If this is true of the Biblical prophecies, how much greater still is the contrast between the utter freedom of the Biblical narratives and the stiffness of the Koran! It is obvious that these must undergo a great change in being recast in accordance with the conception that God is the speaker. The facts and actors must be viewed as from the seventh heaven. History must be conceived *sub specie aeternitatis*.

And it must be said to the credit of Mohammed that this exalted level is remarkably well maintained. The hold of this

[3] E. g. by H. P. Smith in *The Bible and Islam,* p. 66, in referring specially to *Sûra* xi. 37.

book upon Islâm through all the centuries and lands is undoubtedly due to its power to appeal to the religious imagination, to transport its readers into the same frame of mind, to
enable men of narrow views to see themselves and one another
as transient, trivial and helpless creatures of an eternal, almighty, self-sufficient Lord.   Even the woeful lapses from
this high God-centered ideal of the Koran have not been able
to destroy its power of lofty appeal, because Mohammed
succeeded in so interweaving his own personality and interests with those of deity, that even selfish ends, the temporary
makeshifts of a time-server, and the weaknesses of a sinful
man are made to appear in the rosy light of a divine interest
and commendation.

Yet Allâh in the rôle of a story-teller has necessarily something absurd about it.   " We are going to relate to thee the
best of stories in our revealing to thee this recital ",[4]—such
is the introduction to the long narrative of Joseph's life; and at
its close the divine story-teller warns his human *râwî* that
he is "not to demand pay for "[5] reciting the story.   And at
the conclusion of the story of Moses in Sûra xxviii.   Allâh is
actually made to boast of his superior facilities in obtaining
the information implied in the teller of these tales, seeing that
he was present and active in those scenes: "Thou wast not
present on the Westward Side[6] when we communicated the
Commandment unto Moses, nor wast thou among the witnesses   .   .   .   nor wast thou dwelling among the people of
Midian rehearsing our revelations unto them; yet we have
sent (thee) as (our) messenger ".[7]

The second pervasive difference in the form of these narratives arises from their being addressed primarily to an individual.   Like all the rest of the Koran, they are intended
for the ears of many—for Mohammed's own tribe of Koreish
in the earlier Sûras, later for various groups of men, Jews,
Christians, " Helpers ", " Emigrants ", all men of Arabian
speech, or even all the " sons of Adam ";—but only through
Mohammed's mediation.   Whenever there is a " ye " of direct

---

[4] *Sûra* xii. 3.   [5] *Ibid.,* 104.
[6] Viz., of Sinai.   [7] *Sûra* xxviii. 44 f.

address, there is an actual or an implied " say thou " preceding it, and much of the Koran would have to be printed between quotation-marks, if the devices of modern printing were employed. Often also Allâh talks to Mohammed about those who are to be influenced by the revelation, referring to them in the third person.

When this peculiarity of the Mohammedan revelation in general is considered in connection with the narratives in particular, its effect upon them is seen to be striking. There is such a complication in the machinery of expression as to cumber the whole, and the machinery threatens at any moment to break down. There are wheels within wheels. The actual human author (Mohammed) has to represent the supposed author (Allâh) as telling the real author to tell others about how somebody else did this or that, or—worse still—said this or that. When these characters in the story are to answer their interlocutor, or when former words of Allâh addressed to any of the parties in the story are to be rehearsed, the confusion becomes unparalleled. It is no wonder then that Mohammed occasionally " falls out of his rôle ", particularly when we consider that to his lively imagination he is but painting himself in the character of the ancient " prophet " of his story, and his own hearers in the character of those ancient auditors. Even when the author cannot be charged with so serious a fault, it is often difficult or impossible to say of this or that sentence whether it was meant to be a part of the story, or to interrupt it with an appropriate comment (addressed to Mohammed).[8]

A third formal peculiarity that differentiates the Koran, even in its narrative-portions, from the Bible, is the exclusively oral or oratorical mold of the Koran. Whatever may be thought of the origin of the Old Testament stories, they are not clothed, as we read them, in a literary style that can be described as oratorical. How they would sound if they were so constructed, may be seen from such passages as the first four chapters of Deuteronomy, or the last chapter of Joshua. Comparison of these and similar passages with the Koran

[8] So, e. g., *Sûra* xl. 37.

affords an instructive parallel; for it reveals how, to the orator, his rôle affects not only the manner of his narration, but
his selection of material. He is always a man of his day.
To convince and move his audience is his one aim. What
therefore he draws from the past in narrative must be so
obviously instructive and decisive for the hearers, that they
cannot fail to recognize the lesson for the present conveyed by
that past. It is this, more than any other consideration, that
has determined Mohammed's attitude towards the Biblical narratives, in selecting, recasting and applying them.

With these preliminary observations upon the general character of the Koranic narratives we are ready to pass to the
examination of that specific phase of them which has to do
with their treatment, first, of human sin, and secondly, of
divine grace. No doubt these two subjects, sin and grace, are
important chapters in any theology of the Koran in general.
But we are to be concerned, not with sin and grace in the
Moslem theology which has been developed out of the Koran
supplemented by traditions, but with sin and grace as they
appear in the narratives drawn from the Bible.[9] We accordingly observe, first, Mohammed's treatment of the narrative of
the fall.[10]

The sin of the protoplasts consisted in their eating of the
fruit of a tree in paradise that is described as a "tree of
eternity".[11] To this act they are led by Satan. He uses

[9] To attempt an historical treatment of Mohammed's teaching, within
these limits, would no doubt be theoretically desirable; but it is rendered
impracticable by the obscurity which veils the order of its delivery, and the
consequent disagreement of scholars in constructing historical schemes of
doctrinal development.

[10] This is told in *Sûras* ii., vii., xv., xvii., xx. and xxxviii., and alluded to
in *Sûras* xviii. and xxxiv.

[11] xx. 118. With this phrase is combined the parallel expression, "and
a kingdom that fadeth not away". Moreover, Satan declares the reason
for the divine prohibition to be, to prevent Adam and his wife from "becoming angels or becoming of the immortals". Yet though the tree is elsewhere indicated only by the pronoun "this", its character is assimilated
to the "tree of the knowledge of good and evil" in *Sûra* vii., where both
Satan's "whispering" to the human pair and their consequent partaking
of the fruit are connected with the discovery to them of their nakedness.

deceit to accomplish his purpose. The deceit consists in awakening in them ambition to " become angels or of the immortals ", in suggesting a hostile purpose in God, who prevents them by his prohibition from attaining this, in denying with an oath that he is the enemy to them that God has represented him to be, and of whom he has warned them, and in asserting his own benevolent intentions.[12]

The immediate consequences of this act of " forgetfulness ", " irresoluteness " and " disobedience " [13] are the " discovery " of what had been " hidden " from them, namely their " nakedness ",[14] so that they " set about sewing leaves of the garden to put upon themselves "; the divine " summons " and reminder of his prohibition and warning; the recognition of their having " done a wrong to themselves ", which would involve their " destruction " or " loss "; and their banishment from the garden.[15]

The more general and remote consequences of the transgression embrace the " Benî Âdam " as well as the transgressors themselves in a state that is characterized by mutual hostility,[16] by misery,[17] and by constant exposure to the moral assaults of Satan,[18] with their inevitable issue for all those who succumb,—" the Fire " of " Gehannem " forever.[19]

The terms used in the compass of these narratives to describe the operations of Satan upon mankind are: to cause to slip or stumble,[20] to delude[21] (literally, to let down by delusion), to allure (apparently by making evil appear attractive), to seduce or cause to err[22] (the same act as Satan at-

[12] vii. 19, 21, xx. 115, 118.

[13] xx. 114, 119. " Revolt " is perhaps better than " disobedience ".

[14] Apparently by stripping off something that could be called *libâs,* vii. 26. Cf. Ginzberg, *The Legends of the Jews,* vol. i, p. 74.

[15] It is difficult to harmonize *Sûra* ii. 28 with other indications of the original home of the race. We read there that God said to the angels, before the creation of man, " Behold, we are about to place on the earth a representative (*chalîfa*)". But in the account of the fall we read repeatedly, " Get you down " (viz. from paradise to earth), and the humorous remark is often made that Mohammed believed in a literal fall.

[16] ii. 34, vii. 23, xx. 121.   [17] xx. 115, 122 f.

[18] vii. 26, cf. 15 f.   [19] ii. 37, vii. 17, xv. 43, xvii. 64, etc.

[20] ii. 34.   [21] vii. 21.   [22] xv. 39, xxxviii. 83.

tributes to God as the cause of his own fall), to take complete mastery over,[28] to affright,[24] to attack as with an army.[25]

The story of Satan's fall does not belong to the Biblical narrative itself, but it has been brought by Mohammed, following his Jewish teachers, into such close connection with the story of the fall of man, that the one cannot be studied without reference to the other. In the Koran the beginning of evil is coincident with the creation of man and associated therewith. A great drama is unfolded in which God, the angels and Adam play their respective parts, with the result of introducing a moral distinction among the angels. For the angels are represented at first as acquiescing reverently in the divine wisdom, though inscrutable to them, when God proposes to make man, and in the divine ordinance in giving knowledge to his creatures or withholding it from them, when God endows man with ability to name the animals—an ability which the angels do not possess. But there arises subsequently the first moral schism, when God commands them to prostrate themselves before Adam. Iblîs (Διάβολος) refuses.[26] The evil phases of this refusal are not left to the reader's imagination. " Pride " is repeatedly specified as its inward accompaniment and cause. " Denial ", that is to say, refusal to recognize the right of God to his creatures' faith, gratitude and fealty, is ascribed to Iblîs; he becomes the first "kâfir ". His hostility to men is explicitly traced to his purpose thereby to revenge himself on God for having " seduced " him. This malignity of purpose is matched by a confidence in the power of evil (or, self-confidence), which enables him to predict that most of mankind will become his followers, " unthankful " to God,[27]—an opinion, by the way, that seems to coincide with

---

[23] xvii. 64. [24] xvii. 66. [25] Ibid.

[26] In Sûra xviii. 48 Iblîs is called " one of the Ginn ". Sale (The Koran with Explanatory Notes) has this note on the passage (p. 243) : " Hence some [Arabic commentators] imagine the genii are a species of angels: others suppose the devil to have been originally a genius, which was the occasion of his rebellion, and call him the father of the genii, whom he begat after his fall; it being a constant opinion among the Mohammedans, that the angels are impeccable, and do not propagate their species."

[27] vii. 16.

the preconceived opinion of man entertained by the angels before his creation.[28]

Such being the idea entertained by Mohammed concerning the introduction of evil, into the human race and into the created universe, respectively, as derived from his stories of creation and the fall, the attitude of God towards this revolt of his creatures becomes the subject of primary interest. What degree of grace is ascribed to Allâh in determining the penal consequences of their sin? How is that grace to be mediated to man? What is to determine its application?

The great, central grace of God revealed in these narratives consists in guidance through revelation. Consistently with the metaphor of life as a path, the Koran extols the divine grace in providing for those who have erred from the true path a " direction " from heaven, that enables them to follow the right and safe course to a fortunate goal. Just as the Koran itself is the one great miracle of Islâm, so its conception of the redemption of fallen man resolves itself ultimately into revelation to him: a revelation that is not only a discriminating test, exculpating those who receive it and irremediably incriminating those who refuse it, but also in itself a grace, an unmerited proof and product of the divine *rahma,* or pitying love.[29] The first token of God's mercy upon Adam is that Adam " found words from his Lord ":[30] evidently, words by means of which he could approach God in penitence and petition. For the consequence of this gift is said to be that " God turned unto him ", that is, forgave him; " for ," adds Mohammed, " he is inclined to turn (forgiving) and merciful. "[31]

The mediation of this divine revelation is no uncertain matter in the case of mankind in its later generations, as will appear subsequently. But in the case of Adam and Eve it is a subject that is left vague, perhaps intentionally vague. The verb " found ", by which Mohammed expresses the way Adam

---

[28] ii. 28.   [29] ii. 36, xx. 121.   [30] ii. 35.

[31] It should be noted that the Arabic uses the same word for man's repentance and God's forgiveness: each party " turns " or " returns " to the other; cf. with such passages as Joel ii. 12-14.

got those " words from his Lord ", is the vaguest possible word
for getting: it is getting in the sense of lighting upon something that one meets in his path. It may be that Mohammed
intended thereby to avoid the confusion of these " words "
with the " direction " promised in response to that penitence
of Adam which he voiced in those very " words ". Yet the
whole subject of an Adamic revelation remains obscure in the
Koran, and the ideas of its author can only be inferred from
the kindred notions of his predecessors and successors in the
genealogy of haggadic speculation.

But besides this central act of divine grace in the " direction " of erring man, the narrative of the fall exhibits other
manifestations of God's grace to his sinful creatures. Even
Satan, for the mere asking and without so much as a hint of
penitence, obtains reprieve till the day of resurrection. Adam
himself, though banished from the garden, has a settled
abiding-place and sufficient provision assigned him and his
progeny. This gift is not granted, however, without repentance and supplication on the part of Adam and Eve. When
they have acknowledged their offence and begged for forgiveness and mercy, they obtain these tokens of the divine
clemency. At the same time it should be observed that all
these gracious gifts, of which a habitation, food, drink, shade,
clothing and adornments are enumerated, are called by the
same word, âyât, by which Mohammed designates all God's
signs and revelations, including the Koran itself. The central
grace is thus never lost sight of in the details, which derive
their worth, it appears, from their power to reveal to man the
knowledge of God and his will.

We may best discuss the relation which the grace of God
thus manifested to Adam and his posterity taken as a whole
sustains to the salvation of the individual man, when we have
passed—as we shall at once pass—to those later stages of
revelation in which individuals, other than the first pair, are
concerned. Of that first pair we can only say that it is evidently the belief of the author of the Koran that in their case
the grace of God was " not in vain ", but that they became
sharers in eternal felicity.

The second section of our inquiry will therefore be an attempt to trace the grace of God in his progressive revelations to mankind through the apostles he has raised up in historical succession, and, together with this, the relation of the individual man to the revelation of his day, the sin of man which necessitated a revelation, and the sin which was involved in its rejection.

However ill we may think of Mohammed's notions of history, chronology and geography, we cannot withhold a certain measure of admiration for a man of his opportunities and attainments who has succeeded in so grasping the essential facts in the progress of divine revelation as to be able to write: "Verily God has chosen Adam and Noah and the people of Abraham and the people of Imrân above all creatures, a genealogical succession one from another." The context of this verse shows that by Imrân is here meant the father of the Virgin Mary, so that, even if Mohammed is to be charged with a confusion of Mary with Miriam the sister of Moses, he can at the worst be understood to include Moses as well as Jesus in the expression "the people of Imrân ".[32] Adam, Noah, Abraham and Jesus, with Moses perhaps included,—this is surely a list that shows in its author the ability to construct a sound framework for his philosophy of religious history.

In confirmation of this conclusion we observe that it is precisely these figures that possess the chief interest for Mohammed among the personages of the past. Joseph and Solomon, no doubt, are dignified by considerable space in the Koran devoted to their careers: yet these are not treated in the same way. And as a matter of fact it is precisely those five names of the above list, that, with Mohammed's name, make up for Moslem writers the series of the innovating or abrogating apostles of God. Among the very numerous " prophets " of history there have been some hundreds of " apostles "; and among these latter, Adam, Noah, Abraham, Moses, Jesus and Mohammed have received revelations that mark the beginning of a new era in the progress of religion,

---

[32] vi. 30. Imrân really represents Amram,. Ex. vi. 20, &c.

by substituting for the revelation that sufficed for the previous age a fuller and better knowledge of God, while each in turn, save the last, pointed forward to that better revealer who should follow him.

This ladder of revelation, with Mohammed as its topmost rung, is at the same time the only history of redemption that Mohammed knows. This explains what is otherwise incomprehensible,—why these apostles of God can be called bearers of good tidings and their message a gospel.[33] What they say to their contemporaries is a condemnation of idolatry and immorality: such is God's message through them to their age. Yet the fact of what they are—God's representatives and spokesmen—and the fact of the message, fearful as is its content, constitute them evangelists. If this seems a gloomy conception of divine grace, it must be remembered that at least it is consonant with the general tenor of Islâm. Prophecy without the Promise is no more of a travesty of the Biblical revelation, than is Salvation without Saviour or Holy Spirit a travesty of the Biblical redemption.

Beside these great epoch-making apostles of history there is assumed a crowd of lesser lights, as already remarked, each of whom is sent to illumine his own restricted area of space and time. In fact, it is an essential part of this Mohammedan conception of the grace of God, that no single homogeneous portion of the human race has lacked its own peculiar spokesman for God. This is reiterated with emphasis in the Koran. So for example Sûra xxxv, verse 22: "Verily we have sent thee with the truth as an evangelist and a warner; and there is no people among whom there has not been a warner."[34] The principle on which mankind is distributed into these chronological and geographical divisions for the purposes of revelation is the principle of language. Just as Mohammed insists that the perspicuity of his Koran for all men of Arabic speech has an accrediting power superior to any hypothetical revelation in an unknown, ancient or heavenly tongue, so also the Koran attributes to each divine messenger a perspicuous

[33] *Bashîr,* and *bushrâ.*

[34] Grimme (*Mohammed,* vol. ii. p. 76, note 1) compares also xiii. 8 and x. 48.

revelation, so that his contemporaries who speak his own language may understand his message, and be "without excuse". Mohammed regards his own mission as the antitype of the missions of all his predecessors, as where he makes God say: "(Thou art) mercy[35] from thy Lord, to warn a people unto whom before thee no warner has come; that perchance they may be admonished, and, when misfortune befalls them for what their hands have already wrought, they may not say, 'O our Lord, if thou hadst sent an apostle unto us, we would have followed thy revelations and come to be of the number of the believers'".[36]

The attitude of the individual man toward this general gracious guidance from God is also represented as decisive for his own sharing in the blessings of divine grace. "Upon them that follow my direction there shall come no fear, neither shall they come to grief; but such as deny and dispute our revelations, these shall be inmates of the Fire,—they shall abide forever therein."[37] This would seem to suggest a classification of grace into "common grace" and "efficacious grace", at least analogous to the familiar classification of Christian theology. But the matter is not so simple as it appears. Whatever may be averred of Moslem theology, it is impossible to say of the Koran, still more of these portions that we are considering, that Mohammed ever gives a decisive and final answer to the question, Does the ultimate ground of salvation lie in God or in man? His utterances vary with his point of view at the moment.

The Koran has its Romans ix. 18 in Sûra xxix, verse 20: "He punishes whom he will, and upon whom he will he has mercy." It has its Jno. x. 28 in Sûra xv, verse 42, where Allâh says to Iblîs: "As for my servants, thou shalt have no power over them, but only over him that follows thee, of those who are seduced." Yet the Koran has too its repeated iterations of the principle that man's faith or unbelief in God's revelation is the decisive element in salvation. When Mohammed asks himself, Whence comes this faith? he does not

---

[35] A *rahma*, that is, an evidence and gift of the divine *rahma*.
[36] xxviii. 46 f.   [37] ii. 36 f.

hesitate to answer, From God. But when he asks again, Why
does God give faith to this one and withhold it from that one?
he answers, Because God sees that this one possesses and that
one lacks a certain disposition toward God's revelation, which
he terms a "turning" or "inclining"[38] towards God, or,
more commonly, a "resignation" or "commitment"[39] to
God.   Indeed the latter term, *islâm*, has given its name
to his religion, and we feel that when we have reached it we
must have reached the foundation-fact in Mohammedan soteriology.

Yet even the elephant must have a tortoise on which to
stand.   Once more the question rises, Whence comes this
favorable disposition toward God and his word? and again
Mohammed does not hesitate to reply, From God. God gives
to whom he pleases that disposition which determines that his
guidance shall be efficacious; and conversely, in those "whom
he has produced for Gehannem", God atrophies the organs
for apprehending his revelation, "that they may not understand it".[40]   There seems to be no good reason for supposing
that this chain of questions and answers need stop just here.
Rather we feel confident that if Mohammed were to be asked,
Why then does God thus blind and deafen these, while inclining those to observe and hearken? he would again point us
to some subtle differences in the creatures themselves, yet
would acknowledge that those differences in turn could only
be ascribed to God's sovereign act.   The fact is, as above
stated, that his attitude towards grace and merit varies with
his changing point of view.[41]

What now, finally, is the nature of that sin in man, which

[38] *nâba*, ivth stem.   [39] *salama,* ivth stem.   [40] vii. 178, xvii. 48.

[41] Every attempt to formulate Mohammed's notion of the relation of
individual responsibility to original sin, of a universal revelation to a
limited election, must reckon with the view adopted in *Sûra* vii. 171 f,
—a silly rabbinical fiction designed to show how men "are without excuse, because that, knowing God, they glorified him not as God, neither
gave thanks". (Rom. i. 20 f). For in that passage Mohammed makes
God say to him, "When thy Lord took from the sons of Adam out of
their backs their posterity, and made them testify concerning themselves,
(saying) 'Am I not your Lord?' they said, 'Yea, we testify:' lest ye
should say on the resurrection-day, 'We have only been indifferent about

at once necessitates the sending of these "warners" to condemn it, and finds its culmination in the rejection of their ministry?

A writer who has attempted to formulate an answer to this question[42] states it thus: "Man's injustice to man (*azlama*) and idolatry (*atgâ*) are the names of those by-paths on which ere long the whole race came to walk; the former was the root, the latter the fruit that it produced." For proof he offers this passage in evidence: "Verily man practises idolatry,—because he sees that he (by injustice) has become rich".[43] But apart from the question of whether the words and the idea of the original are correctly rendered by this translation, it is doubtful how stringent a proof it affords of the assertion that injustice is the root and idolatry the fruit. For whatever may be true of the Koran as a whole,[44]—not to say, of Moslem theology,—the impression made upon the reader of those narratives of the Koran with which we are concerned, is rather that if either one or the other is fundamental, it is the sins against religion that are fundamental and the offences against ethical standards that are attributable thereto. Just as in Romans Paul exhibits the ethical consequences of religious degeneration, instead of the perverting effect of unrighteousness upon the saving knowledge of God, so also in these portions of the Koran which represent Mohammed's philosophy of religious history, the Arabian prophet gives prominence and apparently causal priority to the sins that represent perversions of true religion rather than of sound ethics.

In the catalogue of offences against God charged against the men of the Bible to whom the prophets of the Bible are said to have brought divine reprehension and warning, we find the following specifications.

this matter,' or lest ye should say, 'Our fathers before us did indeed have other gods, and we are their offspring after them; wilt thou then destroy us for what those triflers did?'"

[42] Grimme, *op. cit.*, p. 71.　　[43] xcvi. 6, 7.

[44] In the Koran, however, "believe" is always the *prius* of "perform good works"; and in Moslem theology religion as *îmân*, "faith", precedes religion as *dîn*, "religious observance" (including duties to both God and man).

First, the great sin of sins, which the Koran calls *shirk*, i. e.
" association " or " partnership ",[45] the attribution to other
deities of the glory and worship belonging of right to Allâh
alone. It is the sin that is the antithetic of the divine jealousy.
With this sin are charged specifically the contemporaries of
Noah, the nation of Israel, and in particular the Israelites of
Elijah's day in worshipping Baal.[46] Akin to this in the mind
of Mohammed as in the Decalogue is the sin of idolatry in the
narrower, etymological sense of that word. The worship of
images is especially attributed to the men of Abraham's time
and family; much also is made of the calf-worship at Sinai.
The word *gahiliyya*, " ignorance ", which has become the
technical Moslem term for the pre-Mohammedan era in
Arabia, is a quality ascribed to ancient Israel also,[47] and
clearly as a means of designating their *penchant* for idolatry.
The figurative equivalent for the same sinful state of mind
is " blindness ".[48] To Abraham's folk is even attributed the
service of Satan; the former terms were negative, this one is
positive, and finds its complement in the attitude towards
God that these servants of Satan share with Satan himself.
The same pride, the same " denial " or unbelief and ingratitude,
and the same malignity, which we found ascribed to Satan in
the story of the fall are all explicitly ascribed to these sinners
in his service, notably to the men of Noah's age, to Pharaoh
and to Israel.

This attitude of men towards God determines in the first
place their attitude towards his *chalîfa,* his representative sent
to them. And we find Mohammed attributing to the sinners
of the Bible, from Noah's day to Christ's, not only jealousy
and disdain of their apostles, but outspoken accusations against
them, accusations of lying, sorcery and imposture, with insolence and mockery of them. And, worst of all, like the
wicked husbandmen in our Lord's parable of the vineyard, they
are charged with actual persecution, plotting, and full intent
to murder. It is contrary to Mohammed's conviction and
policy alike, to allow that one of these representatives of God

[45] E. g. vi. 80 f, 88, &c.
[46] xxxvii. 125.   [47] vii. 134.   [48] vii. 62.

was ever actually murdered; God always steps in and, being the better " strategist ", thwarts their plots, disappoints their rage, and vindicates and rescues his servant.[49]

The climax, then, of human sin against a God whose very warnings are mercies and whose messengers are therefore evangelists, is only reached by those to whom have already come these messages and who have turned from them. Indifference or neglect is the least flagrant of these crimes of *lèse-majesté*. Refusal to receive the gospel is for Mohammed, as for Christ himself, the supreme indictment against those who have rejected Christ's message.[50] Other and more overt manifestations of the same inward state of heart—a hard, perverse or impious heart—are covenant-breaking and gainsaying; and finally,—depth of human depravity!—a blatant bravado, such as that of Pharaoh, who would himself mount up to the God of Moses, or that of the enemies of Noah, who said of the threatened flood, " Bring upon us that wherewith thou art threatening us, if thou art speaking the truth! "[51]

Turning now to transgressions of the moral law imposed on his creatures by him who, according to Mohammed as according to the Scriptures, requires men both " to believe and to perform good works ", we find the following sins charged against those to whom the ancient apostles of God brought their warnings.

Murder, which began with Cain, is to be imputed to such as have the inward intent as well as those who do the actual deed. And even when Moses kills the Egyptian to help his Hebrew kinsman, Mohammed feels it necessary to attribute to Moses the intention merely to strike and not to kill, but to Satan the fatal result of the blow; even so Moses must be represented as acknowledging immediately the wrong he has

---

[49] Mohammed's adoption of the Docetic expedient of rescuing Jesus from an actual death upon the cross is well known; it is in connection with his exposition of this view that he uses the remarkable language referred to in the text: *Sûra* iii. 47, " They (the Jews) played a trick (upon Jesus), and Allâh played a trick; and Allâh—he is the best of tricksters."

[50] Cf. Jno. xv. 22, xvi. 9, with *Sûra* v. 115.

[51] xi. 34.

thereby done to his own soul and craving the divine forgiveness.[52]

Offences against chastity are particularly associated in these narratives with the stories of Lot and of Joseph. It is significant that not only the grosser forms of this sin are condemned, but even those violations of the divine law which are inward and latent, quite in the spirit of Matthew v. 28; for after Joseph has been cleared of all suspicion through the confession of his mistress, he adds: "I do not wholly clear myself; verily the soul is imperious in demanding what is foul, unless my Lord grant grace." [53]

Theft is of course reprehended; but also injustice, oppression, threats, persecution, and even the greed that begets these.

Just as that counterpart of the Decalogue in Sûra xvii.[54] includes among the prohibitions given at Sinai a further command to " perform the covenant; verily the covenant is an object of (divine) inquisition ",[55] so also we find the sins of faithlessness and ingratitude among the sins specified as having brought down the just judgment of God upon those who of old were guilty of them. And other phases also of man's failure in his duty to man that might easily be passed over by even a strict moralist are not forgotten, in the sketching of these classical examples for the world of Islâm of human wickedness and its repudiation by God: namely, pride, insolence, contempt, scorn, and—a right Puritan touch!—" light behaviour ".[56]

Such an inquiry as the one we have thus pursued naturally suggests the methodical treatment of all the other subjects which, like sin and grace, are handled in this material common to Bible and Koran. The mutual relations of God and the believer and of God and the apostle, the ideal of the ancient " Moslem ",—for in spite of Mohammed's repeated claim to the title of the " first Moslem ", he represents Islâm as older

[52] xxviii. 14 f.   [53] xii. 53.
[54] Verses 23-39; in shorter form also in *Sûra* vi. 152 f.
[55] Verse 36.
[56] xliii. 54, of Pharaoh and his people.

than Israel, as old as the race,—worship, prayer, providence, theophany and angelic mediation;—all these themes might well furnish the basis for further comparison of this interesting material common to the sacred books of three religions. Such comparison can only aid in our comprehension of both the power and the limitations of the Koran and of that strange person who produced it.

THE FINALITY OF THE CHRISTIAN RELIGION

Caspar Wistar Hodge, Jr.

I.—Nature and Importance of the question.

II.—The nature of Christianity and what is meant by the term "finality" as applied to Christianity.

III.—Finality of Christianity ultimately dependent upon the supernatural character and claims of Christianity.

IV.—Statement and Criticism of the various attempts to vindicate the finality of the Christian Religion.

a) The Hegelian. b) The Ritschlian, as represented by Kaftan, Wobbermin, and Traub. c) The "experiential school" as represented by Ihmels and Hunzinger.

V.—Statement and Criticism of the position of Troeltsch representing the school of Comparative Religion, and denying the finality of Christianity over against the Ritschlian theologians.

VI.—Concluding statement showing that the finality of Christianity depends on the supernatural character of Christianity, especially of the Christian Revelation; that this depends on a truly supernaturalistic view of God's relation to the world; that this is possible upon a truly theistic world-view; and that the denial of the possibility of the supernaturalism of New Testament Christianity must ultimately rest upon an anti-theistic philosophy.

THE FINALITY OF THE CHRISTIAN RELIGION

The continued and sustained interest in the question of the finality or " absoluteness " of the Christian Religion is shown by the recent renewed discussion of the subject by Professors Hunzinger of Erlangen, and Ihmels of Leipzig,[1] carrying on the well known controversy in the *Zeitschrift für Theologie und Kirche* between Troeltsch on the one side and Kaftan, Wobbermin, Reischle, and Traub on the other.[2] The continued interest and renewed discussion of this subject, however, is not surprising when once we realize that it is not a new problem, but one that is as old as Christianity, and that the question raised is an absolutely vital one for the Christian religion.

The interest which Christianity has in this question is both scientific and religious. As regards the former, the truth of the Christian religion is involved in the question of its finality. We shall see that this claim is essential to Christianity, and that it is really the truth of the Christian religion which is involved in the discussion. Modern historical investigation is being applied to the sphere of religion and especially to the question of the relation of Christianity to the other religions, and the question necessarily arises whether Christianity is historically conditioned in such a way as to be only of relative value, or whether it is, as it claims to be, the one final religion.

[1] Hunzinger, Die Absolutheit des Christentums, *Probleme und Aufgaben der gegenwärtigen systematischen Theologie*, 1909, pp. 63-88; Ihmels, Das Christentum, sein Wesen und seine Absolutheit, *Centralfragen der Dogmatik in der Gegenwart*, 1911, pp. 31-54.

[2] Troeltsch, Die Selbständigkeit der Religion, *Zeitschrift für Theologie und Kirche*, V. 1895, pp. 361 sq., VI. 1896, pp. 71 sq., 167 sq., VIII. 1898, Geschichte und Metaphysik, pp. 1 sq.; Kaftan, Die Selbständigkeit des Christentums, *ibid.* VI. pp. 373 sq.; Erwiederung, 1. Die Methode; 2. der

The interest which Christianity has in this question is also deeply religious and practical. This can be seen in a twofold way. The type of religious consciousness and life represented by Christianity is closely related to this question. Whoever thinks that there is in the natural man a power to save himself if only he have instruction or incentive, and whoever therefore sees in Jesus only a human teacher of the love of God, will not be able to see in him the only Saviour, and hence will not be able to regard Christianity as in a true sense the only and final religion. On the other hand, whoever recognizes in the natural and sinful man no power of self-salvation, will be in a position to see in Christ the only Saviour of man and the object of religious faith. And not only is this a question thus closely related to religious life, the way in which it is answered will likewise have a far reaching effect on the nature and value of foreign missions, as can be clearly seen from the recent discussions on this subject.[8]

Before discussing the finality of Christianity, it is necessary to state as briefly as possible what is meant by Christianity and what is meant by the term " finality " as applied to the Christian religion.

The question, What is Christianity? is a historical one. It is, accordingly, absolutely essential to answer this question in a

Supernaturalismus, *ibid.*, 1898, pp. 70 sq. (a reply to Troeltsch's Article on History and Metaphysics) ; Wobbermin, Das Verhältnis der Theologie zur modernen Wissenschaft und ihre Stellung im Gesammtrahmen der Wissenschaften, *ZTuK*. pp. 375 sq.; Traub, Die religionsgeschichtliche Methode und die systematische Theologie, *ibid.*, XI. 1901, pp. 301 sq.; Reischle, Historische und dogmatische Methode der Theologie, *Theologische Rundschau*, IV. 261 sq., 305 sq. Troeltsch replied by developing more fully his views in his work *Die Absolutheit des Christentums und die Religionsgeschichte* 1902. For a comparison of the views of Troeltsch and Kaftan *vid.* Niebergall, Ueber die Absolutheit des Christentums, *Theologische Arbeiten aus dem Rheinischen Wissenschaftlichen Prediger-Verein*, N. F. Heft 4, 1900, pp. 46-86; to which Troeltsch replied in an Article Ueber historische und dogmatische Methode der Theologie, *ibid.*, pp. 87-108.

[8] *Christliche Welt*, 1904, Nr. 52, 1906, Nrs. 1-3, for the discussion of Missions between Troeltsch, from the standpoint which denies the finality of Christianity, and his opponents. Cf. also von Walter, Die Absolutheit des Christentums und die Mission, *Neue Kirchliche Zeitschrift*, 1906, pp. 817 sq.

historical way, and to keep it entirely distinct from the question as to the truth and finality of Christianity. Moreover the identification of Christianity with primitive Christianity, *i. e.* the Christianity of Christ and his Apostles, though it may ultimately depend upon the apologetic and dogmatic basis of their authority, yet quite apart from the settlement of the authority of Christ and his Apostles as teachers, does not depend upon any dogmatic judgment, but follows from the historical character of the Christian religion. In emphasizing this point Wendt[4] is right against such a view as that of Foster[5] who asserts that the question of the nature of Christianity is not a historical one, but that we have to " construct " Christianity, and that in doing this the constructive imagination plays a part. The issue involved in this question is not between " primitive Christianity " and some supposedly higher form of the Christian religion, but between Christianity and the natural religious sentiment of man. When, for example, Foster[6] says that Jesus held the popular and erroneous view of the world, of miracles, of angels; that even his ethical views are temporally conditioned and not universally valid; in a word, that " what the Gospel that saves requires is that I confess, not Jesus' confession, but my own—with Jesus-like pains, courage, sincerity, and in the use of all the means at my disposal ",[7] it is quite evident that the " Gospel " as conceived by Foster is not Christianity, but the ethical spirit which we all naturally approve and which was manifested by Jesus. There is no justification whatever for the identification of Christianity with the natural moral or religious sentiment of man.

Approaching the question historically and putting the matter in a few words, Christianity involves the idea of a divine Saviour from sin. Christianity, therefore, as Drews has said in his *Christusmythe,* originated in the idea of a God who has become man; not in the idea of a man who was deified in the thought of his first disciples. Whether, with Drews, we

[4] Wendt, *System der Christlichen Lehre,* 1906, pp. 23-25.
[5] G. B. Foster, *The Finality of the Christian Religion,*[2] 1909, pp. 279 sq.
[6] Foster, op. cit., pp. 407 sq.
[7] Foster, op. cit., p. 418.

hold this to be a myth or whether with Paul we believe in
this "mystery of godliness", this is the only Christ and
the only Christianity that we can discover. It is, as such men
as Kalthoff, Drews and von Schnehen have shown over against
the modern liberal Jesus-theologians, not only the Christ of
Paul and John, not only the Christ of our Synoptic Gospels,
but the Christ and the Christianity of the sources which are
supposed to underlie the Synoptic Gospels. The attempt to
get behind the earliest sources and to separate the so called
historical Jesus from the Christ of faith, rests upon such arbitrary and subjective methods of criticism as to be without
historical and scientific validity or justification, and to leave
us without basis for belief in the existence of the human
Jesus of the liberal theology. Furthermore this divine Christ,
according to Christianity, is the Saviour of sinners. Jesus is,
therefore, not only according to the Apostolic teaching, but
according to his own (Mt. xi. 25-30; Lk. x. 21, 22), the only
Revealer of God and the only Mediator between God and men.
In a word, he is not simply the first and greatest example of
saving faith, but its object.

In consequence of this, " finality " belongs to the essence of
Christianity. If we start from the presupposition that man
is, in his present state and by means of his own native powers,
capable of attaining perfection and peace and fellowship with
God; that he needs no new birth and no Saviour; then all
that he needs is instruction and moral incentive. And man
can derive this from other sources as well as from Jesus.
Having thus started out from the presuppositions of the
rationalistic and naturalistic Illumination, we have precluded
the possibility of recognizing any " finality " in Christianity;
for the very reason that our presuppositions are the opposite
of those of Christianity. If, on the other hand, we are convinced that man is fallen and incapable of saving himself or
of attaining communion with God, then we are able to see
Jesus as he is portrayed in the Gospel as the Saviour from sin.
And since fellowship with God is attainable only through this
salvation, the finality of Christianity follows from the idea of
the Mediatorship of Christ, and thus is seen to belong to the
essence of the Christian religion. Von Walter is right in

affirming that we can really be Christians only by asserting the
" absoluteness " of Christianity,[8] by which statement he means
simply that it is not only essential to historical Christianity,
but is also an essential element in the Christian consciousness.

In view of what has been said, we can state very briefly
what is meant by ascribing " finality " or " absoluteness " to
Christianity. It is not intended in the Hegelian sense which
would regard Christianity as the culmination of the process
by which God is realizing himself in the world and history, so
that it is ' absolute ' as the final form of God's self-consciousness. Nor does it mean that in Christ the idea of the essential unity of God and man is fully realized. Nor does it mean
that in the Christian revelation we have an exhaustive and
fully adequate knowledge of God. Neither does it signify
that the fellowship with God which the Christian has in Christ
is incapable of growth and of a higher realization in the future
life. When finality is predicated of Christianity, it is intended
that Jesus Christ is the only revealer of God because he has
such an exhaustive and adequate knowledge of God, and it is
intended that though the Christian's communion with God is
capable of a future perfection, the eternal life which is thus
to be completed is absolutely bound to Jesus Christ and his
saving work. The three ideas which seem to be implied in
the term " finality " when applied to Christianity are, ab-
stractly put, first that the Christian religion as the product of a
special supernatural revelation is independent of and unde-
rivable from other religions; secondly, that it is unsurpassable
i. e. that no more perfect religion will be attained by any
conceivable evolution of religion; and thirdly, that it is exclusive. This last idea does not mean that other religions
contain no truth, but that since Christ is the only Saviour,
Christianity is the only religion in which we can truly find
communion with God. Applying these ideas to Christianity,
it is at once clear that the finality of Christianity is essentially
bound up with the distinctively supernatural character of the
Christian religion. It claims in contradistinction to other religions, an exclusive supernaturalism. Its revelation claims to

[8] von Walter, op. cit., p. 824.

be supernatural in this distinctive sense. While Christianity does not deny that God has revealed himself outside of its sphere, it nevertheless maintains that in Christianity God has directly communicated to man, in a supernatural manner, truth concerning himself. This is quite different from the pantheizing idea which obliterates the distinction between the natural and the supernatural in this high sense, and which asserts that all revelation is supernatural from the point of view of its source in God, and that all revelation is natural from the standpoint of its mode of occurrence. According to this latter view there can be nothing distinctive about the Christian revelation which distinguishes its revelation from that in other religions. In contradistinction to this view Christianity claims that, while all other religions are products of man's natural religious consciousness in direct contact with God, as Troeltsch asserts, in the Christian revelation God has directly spoken to man, giving him the final and authoritative interpretation of the great supernatural facts of the Christian religion. Christianity, moreover, claims finality because in the historical person and work of Christ, it has an exclusive and unsurpassable, because supernatural, Redeemer and redemption. It does not assert merely that Christ is the perfect revealer of God; it claims that he is the only Mediator between God and man, and that fellowship with God and eternal life are forever indissolubly connected with his person and work. Here again the finality of Christianity rests upon its supernatural character. It is, as was said, because of the inability of man to save himself, that this direct intervention of God for man's salvation is the only and final way by which he can have fellowship with God. This is not only the teaching of the Apostles (Acts iv. 12; 1 Cor. iii. 11; 1 Tim. ii. 5); it is the teaching of Jesus himself (Mt. xi. 25 sq). It is thus that finality is of the essence of Christianity, and any abatement of the claim of finality for Christianity is a denial of the exclusive Mediatorship of Christ.[9]

When we inquire into the presuppositions and grounds of this view, and ask whether it is still to be maintained, it is

[9] Cf. Hunzinger, Die Absolutheit des Christentums, *Probleme* usw. p. 74.

evident at once that a definite world-view, i. e. a definite conception of God and his relation to the world, underlies this idea of the finality of Christianity. It is the high supernaturalism which is characteristic of the Scripture doctrine of God and which is based upon a thoroughly consistent theism. It is the idea of God as an extramundane and infinite Person, infinitely exalted above the works of his hands, who preserves the universe and governs it in accordance with his will. This infinitely transcendent God, therefore, acts not only through and by second causes i. e. in his providential control of all things, but also is free to act directly upon or in the universe without and apart from the action of second causes. In other words, this view of God asserts the possibility of two different kinds or modes of activity in God, one through and concurring with natural causes, and one independent of these and immediate. This world-view, accordingly, asserts the possibility of events in the world of psychic life and in the world of external Nature which are due to the immediate efficiency of God. This view is called "dualistic" by its opponents. It is dualistic in the sense that God is not identified with the world, that some efficiency in second causes is recognized, and that in addition to God's providential action, his capacity for this directly supernatural mode of activity is asserted. It is not "dualistic", however, in any naïve or "mechanical" sense. Such a naïvely dualistic view is illustrated by a passage from Herodotus which Dr. McCosh has cited in his work *The Supernatural in Relation to the Natural*.[10] According to this view the action of God is recognized only in events which supposedly interrupt the course of Nature. Thus the Egyptians told Herodotus that, since their fields were watered by the Nile, they were less dependent upon their God than the Greeks, whose lands were watered by showers which they thought were sent directly by Jupiter. This view sees God only in events which are inexplicable by natural causes. It therefore loses God in so far as science traces one series of events after another to their proximate natural causes. Hence

[10] Herodotus, ii. 13; cf. McCosh, *The Supernatural in Relation to the Natural*, 1862, p. 8.

the progress of scientific knowledge becomes a progressive banishment of God from the world, the goal of such a process being atheism. In reaction from this mechanical and deistic conception, the recognition of God's providential control in all events has led so far in the opposite direction as to result in the denial of any action of God apart from his providential control through second causes.

This denial of direct supernaturalism is not only seen in pantheism which denies any efficiency to second causes, it is seen also in theistic writers who recognize both the efficiency of second causes and God's providential control of them. Such writers are accustomed to identify the high supernaturalism we have described with the näive and mechanical view, and hence to pronounce it " unscientific " and directly opposed to the "modern consciousness ". Some of these theologians, moreover, assert that their view of the world is supernaturalistic, so that it becomes necessary to have a clear understanding of the differences in the use of the terms supernatural and natural. Thus " naturalism " is often used to denote either materialism which seeks to derive all mental phenomena from matter and force, or the view which asserts that the mathematico-mechanical explanation of the universe is the ultimate one. It is this latter view which Ward opposes in his *Naturalism and Agnosticism*.[11] Over against such forms of naturalism, an idealistic pantheism might be called supernaturalistic in asserting a reality other than physical nature. Others would call any pantheistic view " naturalistic " because it recognizes no God above and distinct from Nature. Hence the recognition of the transcendence of God, of his providence, of teleology and of ethical and religious values is sometimes called supernaturalism and usually regarded as anti-naturalistic. Such a view recognizes the transcendence of God, but only his immanent and providential mode of action. Such, for example, is the view of Troeltsch who asserts what he calls a direct action of God on the human heart in all religions, but who clearly distinguishes his view from the direct supernaturalism of the older evangelical theology, and who

---

[11] James Ward, *Naturalism and Agnosticism*,[2] 1903.

recognizes fully that it is just this high supernaturalism alone which can justify the idea of the finality of Christianity.[12] Such also is the view of Pfleiderer who believes in the supernatural basis of the world, i. e. God; in a supernatural government of the world, i. e. divine providence; in a revelation which is supernatural simply as coming from God, but which is only the natural development of the religious nature of man; and yet will not admit anything miraculous or supernatural in the sense which implies an immediate activity of God apart from second causes.[13] Foster's view is essentially the same, though his terminology is slightly different. He would not call his view of the world either naturalism or supernaturalism. The former he identifies with the assertion that the mechanical causal explanation of the world is final; the latter with immediate or direct supernaturalism. Both these views he explicitly rejects. He says that we may not suppose that there is a " twofold activity of God, a natural and a supernatural "; and that there is nothing which happens which is not in accordance with natural law.[14] Here, then, are views which their authors call anti-naturalistic, but which definitely and consciously oppose the high supernaturalism of the Christianity of the New Testament and the whole Scripture idea of God; and which recognize in this high supernaturalism a view of the world diametrically opposite to their own.

Accordingly the view of God and the world which underlies the claim of Christianity to be the final religion is not merely in contradiction to " naturalism " in the philosophical sense of the term, but also to the " anti-supernaturalism " just described.

[12] Troeltsch, Ueber historische u. dogmatische Methode usw. in *Theologische Arbeiten aus dem Rheinischen wissenschaftlichen Prediger-Verein*, N. F. Heft 4, p. 100.

[13] Pfleiderer, *The Philosophy and Development of Religion*, Gifford Lectures, 1894; and for his denial of direct supernaturalism *vid*. his Essay entitled Evolution and Theology, in *Evolution and Theology and Other Essays*, 1900, p. 1-26. For a criticism of Pfleiderer, cf. James Orr, Can Prof. Pfleiderer's View Justify Itself, *The Supernatural in Christianity*, 1894, pp. 35-67.

[14] Foster, op. cit., p. 132.

This high supernaturalism was rejected through the influence of the English Deism of the 18th Century and the illumination rationalism in Germany. The reaction moreover from the näive dualism of deistic types of thought led to an overemphasis of the immanence of God which also contributed to the rejection of this supernaturalism. This having taken place, it became no longer possible to distinguish the natural and the supernatural in this way, and the supernatural is reduced, as we have just seen, to the spiritual in contrast to the material, or the doctrine of Providence over against deism and pantheism, or teleology as against mechanical causation.

But the so-called principle of a wholly "immanent causality" which lies at the root of the abandonment of the Scriptural supernaturalism, necessarily and logically gives rise to the thoroughgoing type of Naturalism which will explain the entire universe by causes wholly immanent or within the developing series of second causes. It is this "naturalistic" philosophy which lies at the basis of what is called "historical relativism". This philosophy applies the idea of evolution through wholly immanent causes to the sphere of history as well as to that of Nature. Everything is in a continuous state of change or "becoming", and between all phenomena in Nature and history there is a genetic connection of a purely mechanical character. Hence there can be no absolute values of any kind in history, and no norms whether of truth, religion, or ethics. Since, therefore, everything in history is thus reducible to lower terms and likely to be surpassed in the process of evolution, and since Christianity is a historical phenomenon, it too, it would seem, must be of only relative and temporal significance and value. The finality of Christianity would appear to be lost.

It was out of this situation that the main attempts to vindicate the finality of the Christian religion arose. All of these attempts, generally speaking, have two things in common. They all point out the limitations and errors of thorough going naturalism, and they all abandon the high supernaturalism which we have seen to be inseparably connected with the Christianity of the New Testament.

The first of these attempts may be loosely designated as the

Hegelian. This view will abandon to the sphere of relativity the entire historical element in Christianity, maintaining the finality of the " religious consciousness " which is expressed in these historically conditioned forms. This religious consciousness and its ideas are absolute and final because they realize the ideal of religion as the unity of God and man. Hence the evolution of religion reaches its climax in Christianity. The determining idea of this view, however, is not so much that of an evolution toward a goal, as it is the old rationalistic one of the distinction between the " kernel " and the " husk " in Christianity, the historical element being relegated to the latter category. The way for this was prepared by Lessing and Kant. The difficulty which was felt in regard to historical facts was not the modern one of attaining certitude of belief. The most undisputed fact, it was held, could neither support nor form the content of religious belief. Hence all positive religions were regarded as but the outward expression of the pure religion of reason. Lessing expressed this in his famous utterance that " accidental historical truths " can never be the ground of " eternal rational truths ", the whole of historical Christianity being considered as " accidental ". In the same manner Kant[15] regarded moral truths as the kernel of all historical religions. This idea was taken up by Hegel and his followers, though they sought to do more justice to history. History, however, they regard not as an " outer " or "empirical " history, but as the history of the development of God's life in man. In the historical facts and truths of Christianity are found only symbols of eternal truths in a relative form. Hence Christianity is not separated from other religions as the product of a supernatural revelation, but its symbols are regarded as the most adequate expression of eternal religious truths.[16]

---

[15] Kant, *Die Religion innerhalb der Grenzen der blossen Vernunft.*

[16] Modern examples of this view are seen in E. Caird, *The Evolution of Religion,* 1894, and O. Pfleiderer, *Religionsphilosophie auf geschichtlicher Grundlage,*[3] 1896, though Pfleiderer does not adopt the pantheistic conception of God which is characteristic of Hegelianism. This is also the view taken in a more recent Article on the " Absoluteness " of Christianity, *vid.* E. Sulze, Die Absolutheit des Christentums, *Protestantische*

This whole conception has been subjected to a searching criticism by Troeltsch.[17] He points out that three ideas underlie it, each of which he thinks unwarranted. It first abstracts from all religions the universal element. This is not possible because religious ideas are always inseparably connected with their historically conditioned form, so that the " kernel " and " husk " or the " form " and " content " cannot be separated. Secondly, this universal idea of religion is regarded as a normative ideal of religion as it ought to be. This involves a fallacy, since a universal idea abstracted from all religions is too abstract to be the ideal of religion. Thirdly, this ideal is supposed to be realized in Christianity. This Troeltsch regards as impossible because no ideal is ever fully attained in history, and because the " kernel " of religious truth is inseparable from its historical " husk " or clothing. Whether or not any historical religion can be final, is just the question at issue, and one upon which we shall take issue with Troeltsch. For the rest, he has uncovered some of the fallacies which underlie this method of maintaining the finality of Christianity. The fundamental mistake of this view, however, is that it is not the Christian religion for which finality is asserted. Having separated this so called Christianity from all historical events and also from the teaching of Christ and his Apostles, this view has not liberated true Christianity from its " husk ", but has reduced it to the ideas of natural religion or of the natural religious sentiment. But Christianity is not the product of the natural human reason nor of the natural religious sentiment. Whatever, therefore, may be said as to the truth and finality of the Christian religion, it should be recognized that it is not the finality of Christianity which is here maintained.

It was out of this situation that the well known dispute

Monatshafte, VI. 1902, pp. 45-56. Sulze believes that evangelical supernaturalism is mistaken in supposing that anything " absolute " can be found in history, and that " historical relativism " is mistaken in supposing that we are chained to history. Christ and historical Christianity are simply a crutch to bring us to God, and then to be laid aside.

[17] Troeltsch, *Die Absolutheit des Christentums und die Religiongeschichte*, 1902, pp. 9 sq., 23 sq.

on this subject between Kaftan and Troeltsch grew; and the second attempt to maintain the finality of Christianity may be called the Ritschlian. Kaftan wishes to show that Christianity is the final religion and at the same time to do justice to the historical element in Christianity. He will isolate the Christian religion from the application of the so called historical method which would reduce Christianity to the level of other religions. He maintains that there is something specifically different in Christianity; it is a " supernatural " religion in a unique sense.[18] He opposes, therefore, the Hegelian conception which recognizes finality only in the ideas which historical Christianity is supposed to symbolize. He opposes also Troeltsch, the representative of the school of comparative religions, with whom Kaftan carried on this debate.[19] Troeltsch starts from the entire phenomenon of human religion. In all religion there is a revelation from God, and to all religions alike must be applied the historical method. The history of religions shows a teleological movement, so that while the historical method forbids us to regard any religion as final, Christianity appears as the highest point in the evolution of religion. But this, according to Kaftan, is to push the historical method beyond its limits in two respects—both in affirming that Christianity is the highest or best religion, and in denying that it is anything more than this. From the historical point of view, Kaftan says, all different forms of religion are simply phenomena to be described and determined. The differences between different religions are simply facts to be recorded. On the basis of a strictly historical investigation there can be no absolute or final religion, but only different religions making this claim. The question as to the validity of this claim transcends the historical point of view altogether. It is a dogmatic and apologetic question, depending on other than historical considerations.[20] Hence historical science can

[18] Kaftan, *ZTuK*. VII pp. 82 sq.

[19] For a comparison of the views of Kaftan and Troeltsch *vid*. the Article of Niebergall already mentioned, Ueber die Absolutheit des Christentums, *Theologische Arbeiten aus dem Rheinischen wissenschaftlichen Prediger-Verein*, N. F. Heft 4, pp. 46-86.

[20] Kaftan, *ZTuK*. XIII. 1903, pp. 257 sq.

say nothing against the standpoint and method of Christian Dogmatics, in which the theologian takes his standpoint within Christianity and presupposes its final character which rests on other than historical grounds. In so far as historical method is supposed to contradict this, it rests upon the erroneous supposition that the judgment affirming the finality of Christianity is the more valid, the greater the amount of historical phenomena upon which it can be based. The mistake, Kaftan thinks, lies in overlooking the fact that the question as to the truth and finality of a religion is a question of an ideal, and one which, therefore, cannot be settled by the historical study of religions. We must, accordingly, take our starting point within Christianity, and recognize in it the final revelation of God. Kaftan does not deny that there is a revelation from God in other religions.[21] He affirms, however, that Christ is in such a special sense the revealer of God, as that Christianity is to be recognized as the final religion. The claim that such a revelation is found in Christ does not require to be based on a philosophy of religion, because revelation does not consist in the supernatural communication of truth. Kant, he says, has shown the limits of theoretic reason, so that the judgment which affirms the finality of Christianity rests on the fact that in Christ we experience the satisfaction of our ethical and religious needs. It is true that, in stating the difference between himself and Troeltsch, Kaftan asserts that it lies in the fact that he recognizes a specifically supernatural revelation in Christianity not found in other religions, while "supernaturalism" for Troeltsch denotes only the relation of all religious life and thought to a transcendent God. This supernaturalness, moreover, Kaftan describes by saying that in Christianity God has entered the world in a way which has occurred only once and which is distinct from the ordinary course of events.[22] But Kaftan explicitly repudiates the older or evangelical supernaturalism, and when one asks in what this supernaturalism which is ascribed to the Christian revelation consists, we are told that we meet God in Christ as we do nowhere else. Christianity is not super-

[21] *ZTuK*. XIII. 1903, pp. 257 sq.   [22] Kaftan, *ZTuK*. VI. p. 392.

natural because more immediately the product of the divine causality than other religions, but because there is experienced in Christ a satisfaction of our ethical needs such as is nowhere else to be found. Hence in seeking to show that Christianity is the absolute or final religion Kaftan says that we start with the heart and conscience, and recognizing in Christ the complete satisfaction of our ethical and religious needs, we see in him the only revelation of God, and hence can assert the finality of Christianity. Having thus from the standpoint of faith reached this decision, the science and philosophy of religion can confirm us in it, inasmuch as the ideals by which we reach this judgment are found to be those towards which the religious development of man is striving.

Wobbermin's position in his article in criticism of Troeltsch[23] is similar to that of Kaftan. Like Kaftan he asserts that Christianity claims to be the final religion, and like Kaftan he says that there is no " exact proof " of this. He asserts, however, that " scientific reflection " upon historical and psychological data of a religious character enable us to claim finality for Christianity, and that Troeltsch is mistaken in saying that from the scientific point of view nothing in support of this can be urged.[24] The " absolute values " of religion, which are matters of inner life, are found to be satisfied in Christianity, so that it appears not merely " absolute " in a negative sense that no higher or better religion is conceivable, but in the positive sense of the only and perfect religion.

Neither Kaftan nor Wobbermin have successfully defended the finality of Christianity against Troeltsch. The question is not whether they and Troeltsch use the word " scientific proof " in different senses. The question is whether the finality of Christianity in its full sense can be maintained on their premises. Troeltsch is right in denying this, because entirely apart from the question whether this is a " scientific " or a " practical " proof, the religious and ethical consciousness may itself conceivably be subject to a development or evolution

[23] Wobbermin, Das Verhältnis der Theologie zur modernen Wissenschaft und ihre Stellung im Gesammtrahmen der Wissenschaften, *ZTuK.* 1900, X. 375 sq.

[24] Wobbermin, *ibid.,* p. 392.

which will carry it so high that Christianity will no longer satisfy it. Christianity may appear to our thinking as the perfect fulfilment of our religious and moral ideals, but according to the principles of a naturalistic evolutionary philosophy which denies the high supernaturalism of the old evangelical theology, these ideals are in a process of development, so that the moral and religious ideals of the Christian religion will be surpassed. Nor can the naturalistic philosophy be refuted by pointing out the limits of the "historical method" and its inability to pronounce upon these questions; it must be shown to be an inadequate view of the world, and Christian supernaturalism in the high sense of the old theology must be defended, if Christianity's claim is to be validated.

Wobbermin feels the force of this objection, but his reply is unsatisfactory. He seeks to show that religious and ethical life is distinct from other forms of human culture and life. Hence he concludes that while higher forms of mental life in other than the religious and moral sphere are conceivable, any attempt to conceive a form of religious life higher than that of Christianity ends by destroying the idea of religion and ethics altogether. Moreover, he says, that since religion involves the relation of the finite to the Infinite, no conclusion as to the development or perfectibility of the religious consciousness can be drawn.[25] This latter consideration may be true, but is purely negative and proves nothing in support of the claim of the finality of Christianity. As regards the first point, it must be said that the religious and ethical consciousness is not distinctive in this sense. There is no finality about our religious or ethical ideals which does not attach to other norms of human thought. A philosophy which makes no room for the direct supernaturalism of New Testament Christianity, will not be able to stand against one that is antisupernaturalistic in this sense, and which renders impossible a belief in the finality of the Christian religion.

Furthermore no such sharp distinction, as Kaftan appears to make, can be held to exist between the so called theoretic

---

[25] Wobbermin, *ibid.*, p. 393.

and practical reason. It is one reason which deals with data of various sorts, some of which are of a practical and religious character. The judgment which affirms the finality of Christianity must therefore be rationally, theoretically if you will, grounded. These grounds may be in part or to a large extent religious or ethical, they must nevertheless be grounds which are rationally valid. They may well be wider than any which a merely comparative study of religion will yield, but they must be reasonably and rationally, or theoretically sufficient grounds of belief.

There is another difficulty inherent in the Ritschlian position. If, as those who deny all " natural theology " suppose, the whole course of Providence does not reveal God, how can Christ, regarded simply as one fact or event in God's providence, reveal him, if Christ's deity in the sense of the metaphysical supernaturalism of Christian theology be abandoned? On the other hand, if God is revealed in history and providence, as Kaftan would seem to affirm,[26] then the question arises upon what ground the Christian revelation is separated from and held superior to the revelation of God in other religions. Kaftan would reply that the Christian revelation with its ideas of the kingdom of God and reconciliation through Christ perfectly satisfies our religious ideals and needs. But the selection of certain ideas from the religious consciousness, which Christianity is supposed to satisfy, will depend either upon a religious philosophy or upon the Christian revelation itself. In the former case the question of the absolute finality of this philosophy rather than of Christianity is the result whereas in the latter case no proof of the finality of Christianity is given unless these ideals are the product of a directly supernatural revelation. Only the supernaturalism of the old theology, which Kaftan abandons, can ground adequately the finality of Christianity.

When we turn from these religious " norms " or " values " to the historical Christ who is supposed to satisfy them, we meet with new difficulties. Traub,[27] in an article on the

[26] Kaftan, *ZTuK*. VI. p. 392.

[27] Traub, Die religionsgeschichtliche Methode und die systematische Theologie, *ZTuK*. XI. 1901, pp. 301-340.

method of comparative religions in its application to theology, took issue with Troeltsch on the question of the finality of the Christian religion. Traub's contention is that the ground of certitude as to the finality of Christianity is one with the ground of certitude as to its truth, and is given with this through the revelation of God in Christ. But since Christ is a historical person, Traub is compelled to ask whether historical criticism does not render uncertain this basis of certitude. Traub asserts that historical criticism cannot touch this ground of Christian certitude because the question does not concern " the details of the external events, but the life-content of the entire person ".[28] Historical criticism, therefore, can say nothing against the historicity of Jesus, because of the originality of his personality. To deny the historicity of such a personality, according to Traub, is pure dogmatism. This follows, he thinks, from the nature of the historical method which cannot speak either affirmatively or negatively on such a point. The ground of certitude that there is in Christ the final revelation of God is a matter of faith, and is quite independent of historical criticism and of the historical method.

In reply to Traub, however, it must be said that this separation of the question of the ground of belief in Christianity as a divine revelation and the final religion, from the questions of historical criticism, is impossible. This follows from the simple fact that Christianity is a historical religion. The question whether in Christ is found the final revelation of God is one that is inseparably connected with questions of a historical nature. It is quite impossible, moreover, to regard the " external details " of Christ's life as matters for historical criticism to pronounce upon, and to suppose that Jesus' inner life is quite independent of historical questions. Traub asks us to let the inner life of Christ " work upon us ". This may of course be done, but not if historical questions are simply brushed to one side. All difficulties, Traub says, are overcome by " faith ". But the question necessarily arises as to the content of such faith. If an historical person, or his-

[28] Traub, *ibid,*, p. 323.

torical events, or an " inner life " which is inseparably connected with historical matters and is itself a historical phenomenon, be the content or object of such faith, then the
question of its grounds of certitude cannot be independent of
considerations of a historical kind. Notwithstanding Traub's
assertion to the contrary, historical criticism can conceivably
reach negative results on points which are absolutely essential
to Christianity, even to the extent of denying the historicity of
Jesus himself. Christian faith, therefore, cannot simply
" demand " that historical criticism shall not discuss the realities of such faith. Traub admits[29] that it would make an end
to the Christian faith if Christ should be shown not to be a
historical figure; but this is just the logical result of a historical criticism determined by anti-supernaturalistic principles,
as Kalthoff and Drews have pointed out against Bousset and
J. Weiss. Traub's criticism of Troeltsch, therefore, would
have been more to the point, had he driven to its logical conclusion the naturalism which determines Troeltsch's so-called
historical method, rather than have resorted to a vain attempt to prove the independence of the Christian faith in this
respect.

To make this perfectly clear it is only necessary to notice
two facts which are evident from the earliest historical sources
of the life of Jesus. One is that in Christ's inner life we find
a distinctly supernatural element, and the other is that his
entire Messianic consciousness is inseparably and essentially
related to the miracles which he performed and to the great
miraculous events of his life. Accordingly we cannot escape
from a supernatural Christ by turning to his inner life. In
order to separate Christ's life from all that is supernatural, it
is necessary to proceed by a process of elimination which must
deny the historicity of certain elements in the Gospel portrait
of Jesus, elements which on purely objective historical grounds
are on the same footing with those parts of the Gospels from
which a merely natural Christ is to be reconstructed. This
means that the Christ which remains after such a criticism
has done its work is a Christ of whose historicity there is no

[29] Traub, *ibid.*, p. 324.

evidence. This means that Traub and the other Ritschlian theologians, no less than Troeltsch, must face the question of the direct supernaturalism of the evangelical theology. If such a supernatural revelation and such a supernatural Christ be impossible, the finality of the Christian religion cannot be maintained, since even the historicity of the Christ on which the claim is based, is rendered uncertain. The conclusion of all this is simply that Christianity in its essence is a supernatural religion in the high sense of the old theology, and therefore that the question of its truth and finality depends upon the reality of such a supernatural action of God in the world. If one abandons this high supernaturalism, one cannot maintain the truth or finality of Christianity, just because historically it is through and through a supernatural religion in this high sense. Even the religious value of a so called " natural Christianity " is being rightly questioned. Upon such grounds the affirmation that it is unsurpassable is entirely without warrant.

This is fully recognized and emphasized by Troeltsch who, in abandoning this high supernaturalism, frankly gives up the finality of Christianity, so that the issue really lies between a naturalism which denies the supernatural in the sense of the direct action of God in the world apart from second causes, and the supernaturalism of the Christianity of the New Testament which affirms the supernatural nature and origin of Christianity in this sense.

Before, however, considering the view which Troeltsch maintains over against that of Kaftan, something must be said concerning the recent attempt to maintain the finality of Christianity on the basis óf Christian experience. This attempt has recently been made by Professors Hunzinger and Ihmels.[30] In some respects their way of approaching the question is like that of the Ritschlian theologians whose views have

[30] Hunzinger, Die Absolutheit des Christentums, *Probleme und Aufgaben der gegenwärtigen systematischen Theologie*, 1909, pp. 63-88; also Die religionsgeschichtliche Methode, *Biblische Zeit- und Streitfragen*, 1908, Serie IV. Heft 11; Ihmels, *Centralfragen der Dogmatik in der Gegenwart*, 1911, pp. 44-54, on Die Absolutheit des Christentums im Licht moderner Fragestellung; and pp. 54-80 on Das Wesen der Offenbarung.

just been discussed. The Essays of Hunzinger and Ihmels are written in direct opposition to Troeltsch. And, like the Ritschlians, Hunzinger and Ihmels wish to rest the finality of Christianity in the fullest sense upon the Christian's experience of Christ, denying the right of the historical comparison of religions to speak either positively or negatively upon the question. The difference between these theologians and those of the Ritschlian school in regard to this subject consists chiefly in two points,—first, in the fuller recognition of the directly supernatural influence of the Spirit of God on the heart in the production of Christian experience, and secondly in the circumstance that in resting the claim of the truth and finality of Christianity on the inner experience of the soul, these theologians do not suppose that the " essence of Christianity " is independent of the supernatural events of the historic Christianity of the New Testament.

Hunzinger is more typical of the " experiential theology " in regard to this question than is Ihmels. For while the latter asserts a twofold basis of the finality of Christianity—the immediate experience of communion with God through Christ, and the objective revelation in Christ—the former bases the claim of Christianity to be the final religion upon experience alone. In addition to this, Hunzinger draws a sharp distinction between the revelation which gives us Christianity, which he calls a purely " formal " matter, and the " content " of Christianity, insisting that the nature as well as the ground of the finality of Christianity lies in the final character of its truths as experienced by us, rather than in the fact that Christianity rests upon a supernatural revelation, though this latter truth is apparently accepted. The finality of Christianity, then, attaches to its centre,—Jesus Christ. And not simply to Christ as the perfect revelation of God, but in the sense that in Christ's Person and Work is found the only means of communion with God.[31] The basis of such a claim, therefore, cannot be determined by asking in what sense Christianity rests on a special revelation, but rather depends upon the fact that a critical analysis of Christian experience shows that " abso-

[31] Hunzinger, *Probleme u. Aufgaben* usw. pp. 68, 69.

luteness " or finality is a " constitutive factor " of it. Hence the method of proof is simply to show that the finality of Christianity is necessarily involved in the experience of fellowship with God through Christ.[32]

This separation of the question of the nature and grounds of the finality of the Christian religion, from the question of Christian supernaturalism and especially of supernatural revelation, cannot be carried out. It is not necessary to dwell on the reason which Hunzinger gives for taking his position. The alleged fact that all other religions claim finality only in respect to resting on a divine revelation, besides being questionable, affords no valid reason for seeking the finality of Christianity only where it might not be a claim of other religions. Hunzinger's position, however, is impossible because of the nature of Christian experience. No doubt the experience of reconciliation and communion with God which is given in Christian experience, is in its nature final and absolute in the fullest sense. But still it is not possible to avoid the question of the supernatural character of the Christian revelation, just because of the nature and presuppositions of Christian experience. Its nature is determined by the opposition of sin and grace, the natural consciousness and the regenerate consciousness. That sin has obscured our natural knowledge of God and destroyed communion with God, is a fact of experience no less than a truth of Scripture. It is for this reason that the change from the natural religious consciousness to the regenerate or Christian religious consciousness, cannot be explained as a natural evolution, as Hunzinger would fully admit. It is, however, on the full recognition of this fact, that the argument from Christian experience must proceed. But this shows that the validity of the argument depends upon presuppositions. The efficient cause of Christian experience, on this view, is the Holy Spirit. But from the human side Christian experience springs from faith, the doctrinal content of which faith is determined by the special Christian revelation. For just as the general religious consciousness of man is determined by a conception of God, so the Christian consciousness and exper-

[32] Hunzinger, ibid., p. 79.

ience is determined by the conception of God given in the Christian revelation. From this it follows that the question of the nature of this Christian revelation is fundamental for the determination of the question of the truth and finality of the Christian religion. This is a presupposition of the argument from Christian experience, which is a strong argument in connection with the " external " arguments for Christianity, but which cannot be independent of them. Troeltsch is right in asserting that the claim of the finality of Christianity rests ultimately upon this basis of supernatural revelation, and Hunzinger·cannot escape this by resorting to the argument from Christian experience, for the reasons just given. Nor is it easy to see why he does so, since he apparently admits the claims of the old theology as to the supernatural character of the Christian religion. It only weakens his position, then, to turn from this and to seek in Christian experience alone the ground of Christianity's claim to be the final religion. Moreover, his idea that the question as to the finality of Christianity has to do with the " content " of Christian truth rather than with the " formal " question of revelation, erects too sharp and artificial a distinction between the truths of Christianity and the revelation of which they are the product. The claim that these religious truths are absolute and final, rests upon the supernatural character of the revelation which gives them to man. They determine Christian experience and are implicated in it, and therefore this experience witnesses to the finality of this revelation, but this is ultimately dependent on the supernatural and hence final character of the revelation which gives us Christianity rather than on the experience which Christianity produces.

In this respect the position of Ihmels is more adequate. After affirming against Troeltsch, that the finality of Christianity is a matter of faith and that it depends on the experience of the satisfaction of our religious needs by Christ, Ihmels goes on to show[33] that this subjective ground of belief in the finality of Christianity, must be supplemented by an objective ground, which he finds in the final character of the Christian

[33] Ihmels, *op. cit.*, p. 54.

revelation. The weakness of Ihmel's position, however, lies in the inadequacy of his discussion of the whole subject of revelation.[34] He gives no clear distinguishing mark between the special revelation which he claims for Christianity and the general revelation which he recognizes in other religions. His conception of the " special " and final character of the Christian revelation is not clearly thought out nor adequately grounded over against the school of comparative religions. In the section on the idea of revelation,[35] after rejecting explicitly the idea of the " old Dogmatics " which conceived of Revelation as " the communication of supernatural truth ", (the supernatural communication of truth would express the idea more accurately), and after asserting that the Christian revelation consists chiefly in the " facts " of the Gospel, Ihmels goes on to point out the necessity of what he calls a " word-revelation " in order that the " fact-revelation " may be understood. And in speaking of the way in which this comes to man, he speaks of it, in some undefined way, as from God's Spirit and as " created by God in the sphere of history ", thus apparently recognizing its supernatural character. In all this it is difficult to see the point which discriminates Ihmels' view from the older evangelical view which he rejects, and which would have afforded a basis for his claim of the finality of Christianity. But in the immediately following section of this chapter, in which he discusses the claim of Christianity to be the religion of a special revelation,[36] Ihmels apparently changes his view. He raises the question whether the fact of the historically conditioned character of Christianity is compatible with its claim to a specifically supernatural origin. He asserts that it is, but bases this upon what he calls a " universal supernaturalism " which maintains that in all historical events, notwithstanding their historical relations and conditions, God is directly operative. But if all history and all revelation is thus immediately or directly from God, the question arises whether, in view of this, and especially in view of the analogies between Christian ideas and those of other religions, the specific and

---

[34] Ihmels, *ibid.*, pp. 55-80. [35] Ihmels, *ibid.*, pp. 55-72.
[36] Ihmels, *ibid.*, pp. 72-80.

final character of the Christian revelation can be maintained. This so called "universal supernaturalism" or the idea that God is providentially back of all history is just what Troeltsch would assert. Indeed Ihmels is compelled to fall back on Christian experience after all, for he says that the specifically supernatural character of Christianity rests on the supernatural character of Christ, and belief in this is based ultimately on Christian experience.

In this Ihmels appears to be moving in a circle in affirming that the experience of the finality of Christianity depends on the supernatural character of the Christian revelation, and in conceiving that this depends on the Christian's experience of the power of Christ. Moreover in affirming that all revelation is supernatural and that all revelation, including the Christian, is "psychologically mediated", he removes all basis for maintaining the specifically supernatural character of Christianity, and all essential distinction between his view and that of Troeltsch who asserts a direct mystical revelation of God in all religions. This leaves Ihmels no basis upon which to defend his view of the final character of Christianity against Troeltsch who maintains that Christianity is simply the highest point yet attained in the evolution of religion, and only relatively higher than other religions. In attempting to find any point of discrimination, therefore, between Christianity and other religions, Ihmels falls back on Christian experience, so that we never escape from the circular reasoning to which attention was called. If all revelation in all religions is "supernatural" as resulting from a general mystical contact of God with the soul, and if the Christian revelation is "psychologically mediated" i. e. natural as regards its mode of occurrence, there is no basis for belief in the specifically supernatural character of Christianity, and no essential difference between Ihmels and his opponent Troeltsch, for this is just what Troeltsch would assert. The conclusion which Troeltsch draws in regard to the relation of Christianity to other religions must logically result.

Accordingly the question of the finality of the Christian religion depends upon that of the validity of the claim of Christianity to rest upon a specifically supernatural revelation, and that not merely in regard to the great supernatural facts of Christianity, but also in regard to the doctrinal interpretation of these facts in the Scripture. This revelation claims to differ from the general revelation of God in human religious thought in this respect, that while other revelation is natural in its mode of occurrence, this special revelation is given in a supernatural manner, coming directly from God.

This, as has been said, is fully recognized by Troeltsch, the spokesman on this question for the school of comparative religion. He denies the finality of Christianity in the fullest sense, just because he denies the supernaturalism upon which it rests. This, indeed, is the main point of his criticism of the Ritschlian school, that they make claims as regards the finality of Christianity, after they have abandoned the only possible basis of these claims. Troeltsch affirms that the " old supernaturalism " affords the only basis for the claim that Christianity is the final religion. The old theology can, he says, logically escape the results of the application of the " historical method " because its view of the nature of the Christian history is thoroughly supernaturalistic. The finality of Christianity cannot be based upon a " value judging " interpretation of certain historical facts, but requires historical facts which, by reason of the " concentration " in them of " absolute " values, are separate and distinct from all other history. It requires, moreover, a separation of Christianity from any causal connection with the general evolution of religion. Troeltsch says that " in all these respects the traditional dogmatic method has an absolutely consequent and correct sense. Everything, therefore, depends upon the proof of the supernaturalism which shall ground this claim, and abolish the relativity of the historical method ".[37] He also asserts that " it is only by this proof that the dogmatic method wins a secure basis and the character of a methodical principle ".[38] In this respect it resembles the historical method, for just as " the historical method starts with a metaphysical assumption of an immanent causal interconnection of all human pheno-

[37] Troeltsch, Ueber historische und dogmatische Methode der Theologie, *Theologische Arbeiten aus dem Rheinischen wissenschaftlichen Prediger-Verein*, N. F. Heft 4, 1900, p. 98.   [38] Troeltsch, *ibid.*, p. 99.

mena ", so the dogmatic method starts with a metaphysical principle which lies at its basis. This is the high supernaturalism of the old evangelical theology, without which the claim of the finality of Christianity, is, according to Troeltsch, no better than " a knife without handle and without blade ".

This supernaturalism, moreover, as Troeltsch correctly perceives, must find its ground in a conception of God, of man, and of the world. Upon this view, Troeltsch says, God is not confined to the merely immanent mode of action through second causes, but in addition to this is conceived " as capable also of an extraordinary mode of action which interrupts and breaks through this plexus of second causes "; and man is conceived of as fallen and sinful, and in need of such a supernatural salvation.[39] This is what Troeltsch calls the " dualistic " idea of God and the world: and he is right in regarding it as the indispensable foundation of the finality of Christianity. He finds it strange that the Ritschlians should maintain the finality of the Christian religion, having abandoned this view of the world.

Since therefore, according to Troeltsch, this supernaturalistic view of the world must be abandoned, the demand of the " scientific situation " at the present time is that the " historical method " be stringently applied to theology. And since the standards or " values " by means of which the Ritschlians separate Christianity as the final religion from all other religions are subjective, we must start, not from a position within Christianity, but from the entire phenomenon of human religion. All religion rests on divine revelation, and in all is found a similar religious consciousness.[40] The separation of Christianity from the evolution of religion is a remnant of the old dualistic view of the world. Troeltsch, however, is fully aware that the so called historical method rests on philosophical presuppositions. His idea is that the Illumination of the 18th Century rendered necessary a new idea of scientific method and a new view of God and the world. Its essential nature is expressed by the words " immanence " and " anti-

[39] Troeltsch, *ibid.*, p. 100.

[40] Troeltsch, *Die wissenschaftliche Lage und ihre Anforderungen an die Theologie,* 1900, p. 37.

supernaturalism ", or a world-view which explains everything by a causuality which acts only through and within the evolving world.   This view is to take the place of the idea of a transcendent and supernatural causality, which acts upon and independently of the evolving series of phenomena.   This renders impossible belief in the supernatural origin of Christianity, which must be regarded as a natural phenomenon and as absolutely conditioned by the complex of causes in the midst of which it arose.

This " modern view " of the world, as Hunzinger says,[41] has as its watchwords, immanence, evolution, and relativity.   The principle of " immanence " calls for the explanation of every event and every thought in the world's history by causes solely within the world.   Everything supernatural is excluded.   The means by which such a naturalistic explanation of Christianity is made, is the idea of an evolution which would show that Christianity is the product of the general evolutionary process which operates by purely immanent causes, so that the limits which separate Christianity from other religions are done away with.   The resulting principle of " relativity " will recognize no absolute or fixed religious values in this religious evolution, so that Christianity cannot be regarded as the final religion in the sense of being unsurpassable.   This philosophy really determines the so called historical method which accordingly makes use of three principles,—[42]" criticism ", " analogy ", and " correlation " or the mutual interdependence of all phenomena. " Criticism " renders uncertain all historical events.   It operates by " analogy " which lays it down as a rule of historical criticism that all past history is to be judged as to its possibility by its analogy with our present experience.   The principle of "correlation", being likewise predetermined by the naturalistic philosophy, asserts that all historical events form one unbroken stream to the exclusion of everything supernatural in the sense of being immediately produced by God.

The " scientific situation " calls for the stringent application of this method to the study of Christianity, and makes three

[41] Hunzinger, *Die religionsgeschichtliche Methode* usw. p. 7.

[42] Troeltsch, Ueber historische u. dogmatische Methode usw. cf. *Theol. Arbeiten* usw. N. F. Heft 4, pp. 89 sq.

demands—:[43] First, that Christianity be studied in its relation to other religions. Secondly, that this historical study of religion must proceed to a philosophy of religion which shall interpret the meaning of this religious evolution. This religious development is not a chaotic affair, [44] but exhibits a scale of values which are not merely subjective nor yet mere abstractions from the different religions, but which are the guiding ideals towards which the development of religions is tending. Christianity will thus appear as the highest of all religions because most fully realizing these ideals. Thirdly, the Christian faith must be stated in the light of modern science, so that the old doctrines will disappear, and Christianity will assume a form determined by the scientific culture of the present age.[45] Applied concretely to Christianity these so called historical principles do away with the supernatural Christianity of the New Testament. They forbid belief in a supernatural revelation, a supernatural Redeemer, and a supernatural salvation. They demand a purely " natural " explanation of Christianity, which must reduce its truths to the basis of natural religion.

The result of the application of these principles to the question of the finality or " absoluteness " of Christianity is obvious. In earlier writings Troeltsch asserted that Christianity is the " absolute " religion since it is the highest and best of all religions. Later, however, he published an elaborate discussion of the whole idea of " absoluteness " or finality, in which he abandons the claim that Christianity is the " absolute " religion, except in what he calls a " näive " sense,[46] which is only expressive of the feeling of satisfaction in Christ which the Christian possesses. This becomes " artificial " and invalid when the attempt is made to rationalize it, either after the manner of the " old theology ", of Hegelianism, or of Ritschlianism.

The result, of course, is that every element in Christianity is of relative significance only. This is not intended in the " un-

[43] Troeltsch, *Die wissenschaftliche Lage* usw. pp. 47 sq.

[44] Troeltsch, *ibid.*, p. 102.   [45] Troeltsch, *ibid.*, pp. 47-56.

[46] Troeltsch, *Die Absolutheit des Christentums und die Religionsgeschichte,* 1902, pp. 100 sq.

limited " sense that all religious values and ideas are illusions, nor that Christianity is genetically derivable from the other religions, which Troeltsch roundly denies.[47] He means simply that everything in history, including Christ and Christianity, can only be understood in connection with its historical environment; that Christianity and every other religion, is the product of the mystical contact between God and the human soul, the specific differences between them being determined by the religious receptivity of the bearers of the divine revelation. The philosophy of religion, however, can show, that, while the primitive Christian doctrines were stated in the forms of thought of the past, Christianity is nevertheless the highest level of man's religious development because most nearly approaching the realization of the religious ideals which are guiding the historical evolution, but which can never be fully realized by it.[48] Troeltsch means what Bousset does when he affirms that history shows the " absolute superiority " of Christianity over other religions.[49]

The inconsistency and defects of this view are apparent. In the first place, the question of the validity of the religious view of the world and the question whether Christianity is the highest and best religion, are questions which transcend the limits of purely historical investigation and of the historical method.   The demand for the application of a comparative and historical method to the study of religion and Christianity may intend either the study of religion as a psychological phenomenon, or the question of the objective validity of religious knowledge.   From the former point of view the question as to whether or not the religious consciousness is illusory cannot be raised.   On the other hand, if this latter question is raised, then the so called historical method proceeds upon certain metaphysical assumptions which transcend the sphere of " historical science " altogether.   The application of the principle of " immanent causality ", therefore, may only denote the limitation of the investigation to the study of religious phenomena from this standpoint of their human con-

---

[47] Troeltsch, ibid., p. 50 sq.   [48] Troeltsch, ibid.,. p. 62.
[49] Bousset, Wesen der Religion, p. 237.

ditions, in which case the question of the objective validity of
the religious consciousness cannot be raised—much less the
question of the supernatural claims and nature of Christianity;
or, on the other hand, if this principle of " immanent causality " is to deny the possibility of the supernatural modes of
God's activity, then it must proceed upon a metaphysical basis
which will cut so deeply as to do away with Religion in so far
as it involves a relation of man to God. In other words, the
consequent carrying out of this anti-supernaturalism is to be
found, as Hunzinger says,[59] in Monism whether materialistic
or idealistic, and in positivism. The latter philosophy asserts
that the purely phenomenalistic point of view, which science
may take, is the only possible and ultimate one. Since it recognizes only phenomena and their relations, no affirmations about
religion, considered as a relation of man to God, are possible.
Monism in both its forms is also destructive of religion.
Materialism resolves religious life into a " mechanism of the
atoms ", and idealistic monism makes no adequate distinction
between man and God. Its God is simply a name for the sum
total of spiritual life in the world. However vigorously, therefore, this philosophy may protest against what it calls the
" naturalism " of materialistic monism, it itself not merely sets
aside the supernaturalism of the New Testament Christianity,
but is destructive of religion itself considered as a relation of
man to God. To follow a method which will really know of
nothing but immanent causes, must result in the destruction of
the basis of religion, or in a merely phenomenalistic study of
religious phenomena, which makes no assertions in regard to
the ultimate religious problems. In attempting to answer these
questions Troeltsch transcends the limits of his method
altogether.

In the second place, it is, therefore, only a necessary result
of this that Troeltsch is quite inconsistent in the application of
his so called historical method. He uses this method only so
far as to enable him to do away with the claim of Christianity
to rest upon a supernatural revelation and to come more
directly from God than do other religions, and to be the final

[59] Hunzinger, *Die religionsgeschichtliche Methode* usw. p. 9.

religion. He abandons the application of his method in order to affirm the independence of religion and its underivability from other forms of life, the objective validity of our religious knowledge as resting on divine revelation, and the superiority of Christianity to all other religions. This inconsistency can be illustrated by the way in which Troeltsch arbitrarily limits the application of each of his principles of method. Thus, the principle of " correlation " demands the derivation of all religious phenomena from causes wholly within the Universe. This would do away with the underivability or " independence " of religion in human life. It would demand its explanation from lower and simpler elements in human nature. But Troeltsch asserts over and over again in his Article on ¹ᵘ The Independence of Religion " and in his more recent work on " Psychology and Epistemology ",[51] that religion cannot be reduced to lower terms and that it is the result of a revealing act of God which " breaks through " the natural phenomena of our psychic life. The " principle of method ", therefore, which is applied in order to reduce Christianity to the level of other religions, is not applied to the explanation of religion in general. In the same way the principle of a wholly immanent causality is not consistently applied in reference to the evolution of religion. Perceiving the impossibility of a genetic derivation of all religions, one from the other, Troeltsch affirms that each religion springs independently from the direct contact of God with the soul of man. This is not equivalent to the universalizing of the principle of Christian supernaturalism, but it is a conception which evidently far transcends the limits of Troeltsch's method.

The same inconsistent limiting of his method is seen in his assertion that Christianity is the highest religion. Troeltsch does not, as some of his critics have affirmed, proceed by a standard which is wholly subjective. The ideal by which he ascribes this place to Christianity is supposedly determined by the historical and comparative study of religion. It is not a general abstraction from all religions, but rather the ideal

[51] Troeltsch, *Psychologie und Erkenntnistheorie in der Religionswissenschaft*, p. 38.

toward which they all strive, and which Christianity most fully realizes. But the religious value and the validity of this ideal is dependent on the fact that it is supposed to transcend the whole historical evolution of religion and every historical religion. It is only, therefore, because Troeltsch's religious consciousness is under the influence of historical Christianity, that he recognizes this ideal as most fully realized in it. The comparative study of religions could never yield this result, as Troeltsch fully realizes and explicitly affirms. The question of the place of Christianity among the world's religions is one that cannot be answered by such a method.

This method, moreover, if it is to observe its limits as a method which seeks to explain historical phenomena from purely immanent causes, may explain that which may be explained in this way; it cannot affirm that supernatural events, which cannot be thus explained, are impossible, without going beyond its limits and becoming dogmatically anti-supernaturalistic.

In the third place, therefore, it should be noted that this is precisely what Troeltsch has done. This so-called historical method is not historical; it is dogmatic, that is, determined by naturalistic metaphysical presuppositions. In this lies the fundamental inconsistency of Troeltsch's position. At times it is made to appear as if the denial of any direct supernaturalism were the result of the application of a purely unbiased historical method to the investigation of the different religions. But in point of fact this naturalistic philosophy underlies and pre-determines the rules of the so-called historical method. It is, therefore, a foregone conclusion that only naturalism will be read out of any study of the history of religions, which is prosecuted under the control of these rules. Thus, to take but one example, the principle of "analogy" affirms that nothing can have happened in the past that we do not experience to happen in the present. But this is a pure assumption begging the question and involving the very point at issue. It is conceivable that there might be historical evidence which would lead us to the opposite conclusion, unless we have pre-judged the whole question. In other words, if we base our conclusions on a study of the

entire experience of the human race instead of on a mere
section of that experience, we may find that it is fallacious to
erect one section of that experience into a norm for the determination of the character of the whole. It is no historical
judgment to assert that Jesus never rose from the dead because we now do not see dead men rising again. In a word,
the method which is supposed to yield a naturalistic result,
is itself the product of an anti-supernaturalistic metaphysics
which must justify itself as a view of the world, and cannot
rest upon any so-called historical study which it itself pre-
determines.

At times Troeltsch recognizes this. We have seen how, in
comparing what he calls the " dogmatic method " with what he
calls the " historical method ", he asserts that just as the former proceeds upon the metaphysical basis of supernaturalism,
so the latter is based upon the metaphyicsal idea of an " immanent causation " which he says is the precise opposite of
supernaturalism.[52]

It is the great defect of Troeltsch's whole mode of procedure that he gives no adequate defense of this metaphysics
over against the supernaturalism of evangelical Christianity.
He simply asserts that the Illumination of the 18th Century
has rendered belief in it impossible; or that " historical
science " has rendered it untenable. But he gives no adequate
refutation of it, and in every case his anti-supernaturalism appears as an unwarranted assumption which pre-determines the
so-called scientific investigation, which is in turn called upon
to serve as its support.

This is true not only of Troeltsch, it is true of all naturalism which is not based upon materialism or pantheism.
Bousset affirms[53] that it is a fundamental characteristic of
modern thought to explain everything in the world by purely
immanent causes (von innen heraus), and that the modern
view of the world postulates the universal reign of law in
nature and also in spiritual life.[54] No really adequate reason

[52] Troeltsch, Ueber historische und dogmatische Methode der Theol.,
Theol. Arbeiten usw. p. 99.

[53] Bousset, Das Wesen der Religion, 1903, p. 243.

[54] Ibid., p. 257.

however, is given to justify this postulate or to show why a transcendent and personal God may not act in a supernatural manner in the Universe which he created. The same thing is illustrated in the case of the late Prof. Pfleiderer. He differs from Troeltsch in that he asserts the finality of Christianity somewhat after the Hegelian fashion. But his method of getting rid of historical and supernatural Christianity is similar to that of Troeltsch. It is in the name of "history", of "science", and of "method", that Pfleiderer would do away with supernatural Christianity,[55] and yet it is perfectly evident that an anti-supernaturalistic philosophy is at the bottom of the so-called "scientific method". For it is said to be a method of "causal thinking", according to which "every event is the necessary effect of causes whose operation is determined by their connection with other causes, or by their place in the totality of a reciprocal action of forces in accordance with law ".[56] This method is to be applied to Christian theology and renders impossible miracles in nature and such supernatural events as regeneration. These are declared to be "unscientific" and "impossible ".[57] Pfleiderer is too clear a thinker not to see that this view is the precise opposite of that of the Christianity of the New Testament and of the "old theology" which recognizes the direct or supernatural activity of God apart from all natural or second causes, and which regards the great Christian facts as "effected by causes which are outside the causal connections of finite forces ". It is clear, then, that it is not "science", but this naturalistic philosophy which is at the bottom of Pfleiderer's rejection of the supernatural Christianity of the New Testament.

Accordingly the real issue in reference to the truth and finality of Christianity is whether the high supernaturalism of the Christianity of the New Testament can be maintained, or whether a naturalistic philosophy expresses the ultimate truth concerning God's relation to the world. Troeltsch, moreover, is right in affirming that this supernaturalism presupposes a

[55] Pfleiderer, *Evolution and Theology and Other Essays*, 1900, pp. 1-26.
[56] *Ibid.*, p. 2.   [57] *Ibid.*, p. 9.

definite conception of God and of his relation to the world;
and Troeltsch states this conception correctly when he says
that according to this view God is not confined to his action
through second causes, but is capable of " breaking through "
these causes and " intruding " directly in the world to produce effects which the whole course of Nature and history
could not produce even under God's providential control.[58]
Can God thus " intrude "? Can he intervene in the world to
save man from sin? This is the question upon which the very
life of Christianity depends, for Christianity is through and
through a supernatural religion in just this sense.

That this question of the possibility of such a supernatural
mode of God's activity is the fundamental question, can be
seen from the fact that most of the denials of the supernatural character and origin of Christianity rest ultimately on
the assumption of the impossibility of the supernatural in this
sense. We have seen, for example, that this assumption is
supposed to be a rule of method of " modern historical
science ". That it is a mere assumption follows from the fact
that no valid objection to events supernatural in this sense,
can be made if their possibility be granted. A miracle, to take
one instance of such a supernatural event, can be said to be
incredible only if incapable of proof, or if impossible. It can
be held to be incapable of proof, however, only if it is supposed to be impossible. Two arguments have been advanced
to show that a miracle, though possible, is nevertheless incapable of proof, neither of which is valid. One of these is
that which Hume advanced in his famous Essay on Miracles.[59]
It is, in a word, that there is always a uniform experience

---

[58] Ueber historische u. dogmatische Methode, usw., *Theol. Arbeiten* usw.
p. 100. Troeltsch here gives a clear description of the old evangelical supernaturalism when he says that God is not confined to an action through
second causes, but can directly intrude into the complex of such causes.
His words are that, according to this view, " Gott ist nicht in den Zusammenhang eines correlativen, sich überall gegenseitig bedingenden Wirkens
und eines jede lebendige Bewegung nur als Bewegung des Gesammtzu-
sammenhangs schaffenden Zweckwollens eingeschlossen, sondern seiner
regelmässigen Wirkungsweise gegenüber auch zu ausserordentlichen, die-
sen Zusammenhang aufhebenden und durchbrechenden Wirkungen fähig."

[59] Hume, *Works*, vol. IV. pp. 124 sq.

against the occurrence of any such event which amounts to a proof of its non-occurrence. The nerve of this argument is expressed in Hume's statement " that no testimony is sufficient to establish a miracle unless the testimony be of such a kind that its falsehood would be more miraculous than the fact which it endeavors to establish." The fallacy here is obvious. The question at issue is precisely whether human experience as a whole has or has not included such events. Huxley criticised Hume's argument, pointing out how it amounts to a denial of the possibility of miraculous events and giving it a more plausible form of statement.[60] Regarding simply the concrete question of the grounds of belief in such events, Huxley asserted that " the more a statement of fact conflicts with previous experience, the more complete must be the evidence which is to justify us in believing it." This demands that we require an amount of evidence equal to the improbability of the event, which is just a " miraculous " amount of evidence. Hence a miracle is in the nature of the case incapable of proof. But this argument is not valid. Notice what one must prove. Is it simply the occurrence of the event, or the supernatural character of the cause? Obviously it is primarily the former. Rothe[61] insisted on this distinction, and Warfield has called attention to it very pointedly.[62] We are not required to give evidence to show that an event which has occurred is due to a supernatural cause, but simply that an event which must be due to a supernatural cause has taken place. But if the evidence is only to establish the fact of the occurrence of the event, there is no reason to demand any miraculous amount of evidence, unless we have some a priori notion regarding its causality which really makes us regard it as impossible. And even granting that the evidence must not only establish the occurrence of the event, but also show that its cause is supernatural, no argument from a uniform past experience can be sufficient to render the event incapable of having sufficient evidence for it presented, unless the impossibility of such an event be presupposed. This whole line of argument amounts simply

[60] Huxley, *Hume,* pp. 131, 132.
[61] Rothe, *Zur Dogmatik,* pp. 88 sq.
[62] B. B. Warfield, On Miracles; *Bible Student,* VII. pp. 121-126.

to this—that while in the abstract the possibility of supernatural events is admitted, one is nevertheless so convinced by his own small section of experience that such events cannot happen that no amount of evidence can convince him.

The other main argument to show that while miracles are possible, they are nevertheless incapable of proof, is that there is always the possibility that they are due to some unknown higher natural laws. This argument has plausibility only upon the supposition of the impossibility of the direct action of God within the sphere of and apart from second causes. Once grant the occurrence of the Resurrection of Christ; it is more reasonable to refer it to the immediate power of God than to any unknown natural laws, unless we presuppose the impossibility of such action by God. And if we do, we will scarcely be convinced of the Resurrection of Christ by any amount of evidence.

The question, therefore, as was said, is whether God can act in this directly supernatural manner; or whether events due to this direct Divine power are possible. The answer to the question may be briefly put as follows—that the impossibility of the supernatural in this sense, can be maintained only upon grounds that transcend not only actual and possible experience, but also any supposed necessity arising from the causal judgment or the idea of natural law; in a word only on the basis of some antitheistic view of the world.

It goes without saying that there can be no question of anything supernatural on the basis of the old fashioned materialism. There being no God and no human soul except as a perishable product of the body, it is useless to talk of any religion, not to speak of Christianity.

This view of the world is very largely abandoned, and its place has been taken by what goes by the name of Naturalism. This, in a word, is the view of the world which dogmatically asserts that the mathematico-mechanical description of the world is the only and ultimate explanation of the entire universe. Its principles are, as James Ward says,[63] the mechanical theory of the universe, the evolution theory in a mechanical

---

[63] James Ward, *Naturalism and Agnosticism*, 1903, I. Preface.

form, and the theory that mental states are shadows, "epi-phenomena" of physical phenomena. Though too sceptical to assert the existence of any "substance", and hence reject-ing materialism, naturalism, as Ward says, abandons neither the materialistic standpoint, nor the materialistic attempt to give a purely mechanical explanation of all the facts of life and mind. Its method consists simply in taking the ideas of abstract mathematical mechanics, and applying them to the real world of concrete experience. The mechanical scientist simply leaves all qualitative distinctions unexplained; the naturalist explains them all away by reducing them to merely quantitative and mathematical ones. It is simply mechanical science become dogmatic and offering a final explanation of everything. This view leaves no room for teleology, for re-ligious or any other ideals. It rules out the supernatural in any sense, and is essentially anti-theistic. It has been ably criticised by James Ward in his well known Gifford Lectures. On the other hand, idealistic pantheism, or "spiritualistic monism" as it is sometimes called, is just as much opposed to the directly supernatural action of God and to the dis-tinction between the natural and the supernatural as above set forth, as is materialism and naturalism. It is true that it interprets the world in terms of spirit, but since it identifies God and the world and allows no existence or activity tran-scendent to the universe, any distinction whatever between the natural and the supernatural is impossible. There is really no basis for any religion since the distinction between God and man, and with it the personality of God is denied.

It is not our purpose, however, nor would it be possible within the limits of this essay, to give any criticism or discus-sion of the anti-theistic theories. Those theories, as has been said, leave no room for any religion, if religion is a relation of man to God, since they do away wth any distinction between God and man. It is of course impossible to discuss the ques-tion of the finality of Christianity or of the possibility of the supernatural modes of God's activity with one who does not believe in God. The theological writers whose views we have been discussing, however, are theists. What we wish to do, therefore, is to show that upon a theistic view of the world the possibility of this directly supernatural activity of God, implied in the Christian view of the world, cannot be denied. In saying this, it is a truly theistic view that is meant; a view which is in earnest with the idea of the personality and transcendence of God. But since the main reasons which theists urge against pantheism are just those reasons which lead us to regard God as personal and transcendent, this is the only theism which can maintain itself against pantheism. The evidences of teleology or purpose which mind is called on to explain, are explained only if this finality or purposiveness is intentional. In other words a " pantheistic theism ", to use a phrase of Rashdall's,[64] is untenable. To say that God is a Person, but " God is all ", is not possible. If finite spirits are all parts of God, then theism is abandoned, for, as Rashdall says, upon such a view we could only call God good by maintaining that the deliverences of our moral consciousness have no validity for God, and this Bradley would have us believe. But a God who is " beyond good and evil " is not God and assuredly not an object of worship.[65] Moreover the formula " God is all " is really unmeaning. Such an all inclusive consciousness swallows up all distinctions including its own personality as well as that of man. It is really meaningless to speak of one consciousness as " included in another consciousness ". It is the characteristic of consciousness " to exist for itself ". The finite spirit is not independent of God, but its consciousness cannot be " included " in God's consciousness without losing the personality of both God and man. We agree with Rashdall that McTaggert is right in asserting that if God is to include in himself all other spirits, and if the personality and self consciousness of those spirits is not to be denied, then this absolute or so-called God in which they are to be included, cannot be considered as conscious or self-conscious or have the attributes of God. We thus lose God and fall into " non-theistic idealism " and pluralism. Hence a truly theistic view asserts the personality of God and also that he infinitely transcends the entire universe, the entire sum of

[64] H. Rashdall, *Philosophy and Religion,* 1910, p. 101.
[65] *Ibid.,* p. 104.

whose energies is as nothing compared with the infinite power of God.

Theism, moreover, not only asserts the personality and transcendence of God, it regards him as the Creator of the universe. The world cannot be regarded simply as an " experience " or " thought " of God, as the idealist would have us believe, for then it could not be distinguished from all the thoughts of God which are not actually realized, nor would its relative independence be explained. The world is the created product of God's power, upheld and governed by him. This is the theistic view, and it is our contention that no theist can deny the directly supernatural modes of God's activity, because in the act of Creation itself is given the first instance of such activity, and since God, being the Creator of the world, cannot be entangled in his created product.

We have to ask, then, upon what grounds the transcendence of God is affirmed and the transcendent modes of his action on the world denied; or upon what grounds it is held that God is not only immanent and yet that only his immanent mode of action is possible. This is done usually upon two grounds. In the first place, supernatural events are said to be impossible because they imply a suspension of or interference with natural laws. But what is a natural law? The term is sometimes used simply as an empirical statement or description of the way in which events uniformly happen. If this is the meaning of natural law, it is obvious that it does not render impossible miracles or any other class of supernatural events. A miracle, for example, being *ex hypothesi* an event outside of the natural empirical order of things, cannot be proven either possible or impossible by any experience of this natural order. If experience includes such events, it is no longer an experience based on the purely natural order of things, while on the other hand we cannot infer from any merely uniform experience that events cannot occur which will transcend this hitherto experienced uniformity. Sometimes the term natural law is used to denote a necessary mathematical equation, and is applied in an attempt to describe phenomena from the idea of a number of mass points in motion. But the science of mechanics is fully aware that this mechanical view is not an ultimate explanation of everything. If this latter supposition is made, then the view point of natural science is transcended, and we fall into naturalism which is an anti-theistic speculative theory. Or once more, a natural law is sometimes supposed to be an efficient force which causes the observed phenomena to follow the uniformity which is observed. In this case the uniformity could be predicted, and would be more than an empirical generalization. But even this idea of natural law does not render supernatural events impossible. We may not suppose that God the Creator of the universe is so subjected to the laws of his creation that he cannot act in the world directly. If God is not simply a name for nature, but is the Creator of nature, he cannot be entangled in his creation. Nor can the sum of the energies in the universe in any way express the totality of his power. It was infinite power that brought the world into being, and that world whose laws simply express the providential control of the Creator, cannot constitute a limit to the Omnipotence which gave rise to it. Neither does this providential control exhaust the ways by which God may act upon his creation. The possibility of the directly supernatural mode of God's action follows from the idea of the divine transcendence which is the center of an adequately theistic conception of God. It is not necessary to go with the pantheist and deny all efficiency to second causes, in order to realize that they cannot limit God. If we believe that God is infinite and the universe finite, there is absolutely no basis for the assertion that God's action through second causes is the only way he can act. Moreover the immanent activities of God are rooted in his transcendence. If we resolve his providential control into a mere name for the forces of Nature, we are really giving up the idea of God's providence and falling into a pantheism which does not distinguish God from the world. On the other hand, if the real nature of God's Providence, according to theism, be recognized it will be seen to involve the personality and the transcendence of God. In a word, the reasons for belief in God as against pantheism, are reasons for belief in an infinite Person, infinitely transcending the world. The affirmation that God is infinitely transcendent of the world, and yet can only act through natural causes is one that cannot stand against pantheism.

In the second place, it is sometimes affirmed that supernatural events are impossible because they contradict the causal judgment as a necessary law of thought which presupposes that nature is an absolutely closed and concatenated system of second causes. Any intrusion into this system is supposed to violate a necessary law of thought. This objection, which appears still more serious, is still less plausible than the former. All that the causal judgment asserts is that there is no effect without an adequate cause. There is no possible way by which this can be made to exclude the immediate causality of God, if it be granted that there is a God. It will be replied that the idea of cause is one that applies only to relations between phenomena, and does not apply to the relation of God to the world. But this can only mean that the idea of cause which is valid for natural science cannot be applied to God. If God is the Creator of the world, he can be the efficient agent of effects in the world, call this by what name you will.

The conclusion of all this is that upon no ground other than that offered by an anti-theistic view of the world, can be based a denial of the possibility of the supernatural modes of God's activity.

If this be so, then the question of the supernatural origin and character of Christianity which lies at the basis of its claim to finality, is simply one of evidence. Into the question of Christian evidences we cannot enter. The question ultimately reduces itself to this—is it more reasonable to believe that the divine Christ of the New Testament, who has transformed the world, is a myth or a reality. The idea that Jesus was a mere man who spake no mighty words and wrought no mighty deeds, who was deceived by current Messianic notions, who was killed by his enemies and never rose again;—this idea is that of a Jesus who cannot be found in the historical sources of Christianity, and who, if he could be so found, could never have inspired his followers to deify him, nor be the cause of the rise and progress of historical Christianity. The only Christ of the earliest sources is a supernatural and divine Christ,—the Christ of Peter, of Paul, of John, of the Synoptists, and of the sources which are supposed to underlie the Synoptists—a Christ, in a word, who claimed to be God, who lived like God, and who has wrought effects which only God could, and who is an adequate explanation of the Christian religion in its rise and progress. The question of the truth and consequently of the finality of Christianity, therefore, reduces itself to this—whether in view of the possibility of the supernatural and of a theistic view of the world, and of the evidences for the reality of this Christ, it is more reasonable to suppose that Christianity is a product of the myth building fantasy, or that the Christ of the New Testament is a reality.

THE INTERPRETATION OF THE
SHEPHERD OF HERMAS

KERR DUNCAN MACMILLAN

THE INTERPRETATION OF THE
SHEPHERD OF HERMAS

One need not apologize for choosing what may appear to some an unimportant and petty problem in the history of the church. It is not such. Its solution will affect considerably our estimate of the church of the second century, especially in respect to its literary activity, its dogmatic conceptions, and the part played in it by Christian prophecy. Moreover it has a direct bearing on the question of the origin and growth of the New Testament canon. For there is a number of scholars to-day who affirm that the idea of a New Testament canon as we now have it does not appear in the church until toward the end of the second century; that up to that time the Old Testament (including the Apocrypha and Jewish Apocalypses) had been the " Bible " of the church, and the words of the Lord and the utterances of Christian prophets had been closely associated with it as authoritative; that this condition continued until about the close of the second century, when, out of the struggle with Gnosticism and Montanism the church emerged with a new standard of canonicity namely *apostolicity*.[1] That is to say it is asserted that Christian prophecies even when reduced to writing were regarded as authoritative in the church just because they were prophecies and without any regard to their date or the person of the prophets, and this continued until the exigencies of the church demanded that a new test be erected, at which time those prophecies which had hitherto been regarded as authoritative were deposed from their high dignity unless they could establish a claim to apostolic origin.

[1] E. g. Harnack, *Dogmengeschichte*, 4 Aufl. I, pp. 372-399. Leipoldt, *Entstehung des neutest. Kanons*, I, pp. 33, 37 f., 39 Zusatz 2, 41 ff. B. Weiss, *Einleit. in d. Neue Test.* 3 Aufl. Sec. 5, 4, n. 1; 8, 5; 9, 6.

The *Shepherd* of Hermas has always played a part in the discussion attending this theory for it is one of the so called prophecies which are said to have been degraded, but it has not, I think, played the part it should have or will when its unique position is understood. For not only can its date be approximately fixed in the first half of the second century, but it is the only one of the so called prophecies which does not claim for itself apostolic origin. In connection with its history therefore, can the test of prophecy versus apostolicity in the middle and third quarter of the second century be brought to the clearest issue. If it be found that the book was published and accepted as a prophecy, we shall be able to tell from the nature of the reception accorded it what the opinion of the church then was regarding contemporaneous Christian prophecy. And if on the contrary it turns out that it was not published or accepted as a prophecy, the main problem will be to ascertain how such a work could in the course of say forty years claim equal rank with acknowledged inspired and authoritative books; and we shall incidentally have removed from the discussion the only work, which at present can be pointed to in support of the theory that Christian prophecy *qua* prophecy, was authoritative in the second century. I therefore propose to examine the *Shepherd* of Hermas and its early history with a view to determining the author's intention regarding it, the nature of its reception and treatment by the early church, and how and why it is involved in the history of the canon of the New Testament.

It is strange that this subject has been comparatively neglected. The text of the *Shepherd* has recently received very careful attention, the questions of its origin and unity and date have been, and are still, warmly debated, and the material furnished by it is liberally drawn upon by all students of the early Christian church. But the question of the intention of the author in publishing his work in the form of an apocalypse has been on the whole much neglected. Most writers to-day seem to assume that its author and his contemporaries ingenuously believed that he had been the recipient of real and divine revelations. But little or no discussion is given to the matter. For the sake of completeness I shall enumerate the four hypotheses which to my mind exhaust the possibilities, any one of which might be regarded as satisfactory; and I may add that each of them has its supporters. (1) The work may be regarded as a genuine revelation.[2] (2) It may be regarded as a deliberate though pious fraud.[3] (3) The visions and revelations may be regarded as purely subjective. In this case Hermas may be regarded as a mystic, or a visionary, or epileptic, or be classed in a general way with the " prophets " of the second century, without inquiring particularly about the psychology of such " prophecy ". Some such explanation as this is quite possible, being not infrequently paralleled in history, and we must give it the more consideration as it is the view most generally accepted by scholars to-day.[4] (4) We may regard it as fiction, pure and simple, and the visions and heavenly commands as a literary garb deliberately chosen by the author without any intention of deceit; in other words it may be an allegory.[5] Of these four possibilities

[2] In modern times this has been held by Wake (*Apostolical Fathers*, p. 187), and some Irvingite scholars, e. g. Thiersch, *Die Kirche im apostolischen Zeitalter*, pp. 350 ff.

[3] So apparently Bardenhewer, *Geschichte der altkirchlichen Literatur* (1902), Vol. I. p. 563, " Der Verfasser schreibt auf Grund göttlicher Offenbarungen und infolge göttlichen Auftrags. Er tritt als ein vom Geiste Gottes inspirierter Prophet auf. Ohne Zweifel hat er damit seinen Mahnungen und Mitteilungen eine grössere Kraft, eine höhere Weihe geben wollen. Dass er Anstoss erregen würde, war kaum zu befürchten. Er schrieb zu einer Zeit, wo der Glaube an die Fortdauer des prophetischen Charismas noch allegemein geteilt wurde ". Mosheim, *De rebus Christ. ante Constant.*, pp. 163, 166 inclines to a view of Hermas which makes him " *scientem volentemque fefellisse* ". Salmon, *Dict. Chr. Bio.*, Art. " Hermas ", thinks Hermas " probably cannot be cleared from conscious deceit ".

[4] Bigg, *Origins of Christianity*, p. 73 f. Zahn (*Der Hirt des Hermas* pp. 365 ff.) perceives the importance of the problem and laments the lack of interest shown in it to-day. He regards the visions as real experiences of the author and thinks the Roman Church was right in seeing in them a divine message, but refuses to discuss the question of their permanent worth (pp. 381 f.). Harnack, *Zeitschrift für Kirchengeschichte* III, p. 369, and elsewhere. Leipoldt, *op. cit.*, p. 33, n. 2, and others.

[5] Donaldson, *The Apostolical Fathers*, p. 326 ff. Lightfoot, *Bibl. Essays*, p. 96. Charteris, *Canonicity*, p. xxiv. Behm, *Ueber den Verfasser der Schrift, welche den Titel "Hirt" führt*. J. V. B(artlet), *Encyc. Brit.* 11th ed. Art *Hermas* favors the more symbolic view. How these views

the second should only be made on the basis of far stronger evidence than has yet been adduced, and after all other hypotheses have been shown to be insufficient. Moreover, as the first and third have certain points of contact and in the minds of some cannot be sharply sundered, we may state our problem in the question: *Is the Shepherd of Hermas an apocalypse or an allegory,*—using the word " apocalypse " as significant, not of the real nature of the contents of the work, but of its claims. And should it appear in the course of our examination that the *Shepherd* does indeed claim to be a revelation, then, and not till then, will emerge the question of the justification of such a claim.

There is no difficulty about determining the date of the *Shepherd* in a general way. Most scholars agree that it was written somewhere between 97 and 140 A.D., or thereabouts.[6] But when we seek to define the time more accurately, a difficulty presents itself, for we have, curiously, two excellent pieces of testimony, one internal and one external, which are hard to harmonize. In the early part of his work[7] Hermas refers in quite a natural unforced manner to a certain Clement as one to whom had been committed the duty of corresponding with foreign churches, and apparently as one of the presbyters of the Church at Rome, of which Hermas was a member. Now there is one Clement well known to all antiquity as the author of the epistle of the Church of Rome to that at Corinth, to whom this seems undoubtedly to point. That would give a date somewhere about 100 A.D. The other piece of evidence is that contained in the so-called *Muratori Fragment,* which dates from about the end of the second century. This informs us that the *Shepherd* was written " very recently, in our own times ", during the episcopate of Pius of Rome, by Pius's brother Hermas. This would give a date about 150 A.D.

have received modification and been related to the varying opinions concerning the date and authorship of the *Shepherd* may be seen in the table furnished in Gebhardt und Harnack, *Patrum Apostolicorum Opera,* Fasc. III., p. lxxxiii, n. 2.

[6] For the few who go outside these limits, see the table referred to in note 5.

[7] *Vis.* ii. 1.

Until quite recently scholars have been divided according as the first or the second of these testimonials seemed to them the more weighty, and ingenious conjectures have been proposed for explaining away the rejected evidence.[8] Lately, however, as an outcome of discussion concerning the unity of the work, the opinion has gained ground that the *Shepherd* was not produced at one time but piecemeal throughout a number of years. This and the uncertainty both of the date of Clement's death and of the years of Pius' episcopate have made it possible for Prof. Harnack to propose a compromise.[9] He thinks now that the earlier portion of the work was produced about 110 A.D. (possibly in the 3rd year of Trajan) when Clement may still have been living, and that the book was published in its completed form about 135-140 A.D., when Pius may have been bishop of Rome. For our purposes we need not enter into the details of the argument. We shall assume, that which is denied by very few, that the work was in existence in its finished form about the year 135 or 140—always remembering that it may have been known earlier.

Taking this, then, as the date when the *Shepherd* was given to the church, we ask: how was it received? Remember, it is not a small book; it is about equal in size to our first two gospels together. Nor was it published in a corner, but at the center of the world, in the city of Rome. Such a work as this, if regarded as divinely inspired, and equal to the Old Testament in authority, must have made a considerable stir, and that immediately, and in the whole church. And yet there is not one particle of evidence to show that it was regarded as Scripture or in any sense divine during the 30 or 40 years following its publication. Not until we come down to Irenaeus, the *Muratori Fragment,* Clement of Alexandria, Origen and Tertullian is it quoted and referred to as Scripture or of divine inspiration. Nor can it be objected that this is merely an argument from silence and so of no cogency.

[8] Zahn, in *Der Hirt des Hermas* and elsewhere, has been the strongest defender of the earlier date.

[9] *Geschichte d. altchristlichen Literatur* ii., i. pp. 257 ff., where a brief review of the argument and the more important literature may be found.

For there were events in Rome at this time, and discussion in the church concerning authoritative and non-authoritative writings, of which we are well informed, and into which the *Shepherd* undoubtedly would have been drawn had it occupied the exalted position that is claimed for it. The result is the same wherever we look—not only at Rome but throughout the whole of the Christian literature coming from or dealing with this period, there is not the slightest evidence that the *Shepherd* was regarded as of any special importance.

It was at this time, for instance, that Marcion founded his school at Rome and formed his canon. But in all the discussions about the books he rejected or received, there is no word of the Shepherd, although we are informed by Tertullian[10] that he rejected a work now frequently associated with it in discussions concerning the canon, *viz.*, the Apocalpyse of John. This should be decisive alone. If the Shepherd were regarded by either party as divinely inspired, it is incomprehensible that it should not have been brought into the controversy by one side or the other.[11] The Gnostic Valentinus was also established in Rome at this time. He accepted all the Catholic Scriptures, as we are informed by Tertullian,[12] and turned them to suit his own ends by means of the allegorical method of interpretation. But there is no sign that he accepted, or so used the *Shepherd;* although its form and contents are admirably adapted to his methods and results We know that he so used the Apocalypse of John,[13] but neither Irenaeus, who gives us this information, and who was acquainted with the *Shepherd,* nor Tertullian, who would not have failed to attack the heretic for making use of a work which he himself regarded as apocryphal and false, contains the slightest indication that Valentinus knew anything about the *Shepherd.* Hegesippus was in Rome at this time—during

---

[10] *Adv. Marc.* IV. 5.

[11] Harnack (*Gesch. d. altchrist. Lit.* I. i., p. 51), remarks without comment, and apparently without perceiving the import of his remark: "Bemerkt sei, dass sich bei den Gnostikern und Marcion keine Spur einer Benutzung unseres Buches findet."

[12] *Praescr.* c. 38.   [13] Irenaeus, *Haer.* i. 15.

the episcopate of Anicetus.[14]   Unfortunately, the only piece
of evidence we have from his pen is the statement preserved
by Eusebius to the effect that some of the so-called apocrypha
were composed in his (i. e. Hegesippus') day by heretics.
And yet even this is important coming as it does through
Eusebius, who used all diligence to discover the origin of the
books disputed or rejected in his own time—one of which was
the *Shepherd* of Hermas.   For, on the one hand, as the
Shepherd was certainly not regarded as heretical or apocryphal
in the days of Anicetus, it cannot be assumed among those
referred to by Hegesippus in this passage; and, on the other
hand, as Eusebius records nothing from Hegesippus' writings
concerning the *Shepherd,* the probable inference is that he
found nothing worthy of record; certainly it was not one of
the authoritative books of the Church.   Justin Martyr, too,
was acquainted with the Rome of this period, and speaks in a
general way of prophets being still known in the church,[15]
but in all his writings there is no mention of Hermas or any
reference to his book.   The answer is the same when we inquire of Celsus, the opponent of Christianity, who probably
wrote during the period under review.   He shows considerable
acquaintance with Christianity and the Christian writings, but
there is no sign of Hermas or his *Shepherd.*[16]   Nor does the
early history of Montanism, although concerned with prophecy,
afford any evidence.   It is not until the time of Tertullian that
it is brought into the discussion.[17]   It is true that a relationship
has been found or fancied between the *Shepherd* and the letters of Ignatius,[18] that of Polycarp,[19] the so-called Second

---

[14] Eusebius, *HE.* iv. 22.   [15] *Trypho,* c. 82.

[16] A definite reference could hardly be expected.   Celsus knows of Christian prophecy in his own time, but the description he gives of it does not
tally with the contents of the *Shepherd.*   See Origen, *contra Cels.* vi. 34 f.,
vii. 11.

[17] The Anti-montanist of Eusebius (*HE.* v. 17), gives a list of those who
prophesied under the new covenant.   Two names are added to those known
in Scripture, but Hermas is not one of them.   This writer is later however than the period we are discussing; Bonwetsch (Art. Montanismus in
Herzog, *Realencycl.,* third ed.) and McGiffert (*Nicene and Post Nicene
Fathers,* Vol. I., p. 233, n. 32), put him about 192 A. D.

[18] Zahn, *Ignatius von Antioch,* pp. 618 f.   [19] *Ibid.,* p. 620.

Epistle of Clement,[20] the Preaching of Peter,[21] Theophilus of Antioch[22] and Melito of Sardis,[23] but these are mere resemblances[24] and prove at most only acquaintance with it. None of them rises to the rank of citation, much less is there anything to show that the *Shepherd* was regarded as on an equality with the Old Testament or divinely inspired. In short, there is nothing in the literature of this period to show that the *Shepherd* of Hermas commanded any more respect than might be given to any work suitable for edification.[25]

In and after the last quarter of the second century we find a change of attitude toward the *Shepherd*. In Gaul Irenaeus quotes it as " Scripture ",[26] thus apparently putting it on a par with the other canonical works. And yet scholars are by no means agreed that this is his intention. It is difficult to reconcile Irenaeus' usage elsewhere, and his emphasis upon apostolicity as a prerequisite of canonicity, with such an explanation. It is noted that the *Shepherd* is not named in this quotation,[27] nor is it quoted anywhere else in Irenaeus' works as far as we know them, although some resemblances are found;[28] moreover, when he is confessedly marshalling the

[20] Harnack, *Theol. Literaturzeitung*, 1876, Col. 104. Cf. Overbeck, *ibid.*, 1877, Col. 287 f.

[21] Hilgenfeld, *Hermae Pastor*, p. 1 f., 35.

[22] Harnack, *Patr. Apostol. Op.*, Fasc. iii., note to *Vis.* 1, 6.

[23] Harnack, *Sitzungsbericht d. Berliner Akademie d. Wissenschaft*, 1898, p. 517 ff.

[24] For still more doubtful resemblances to other works, see Gebhardt und Harnack, *Patr. Apostol. Op.* Fasc. iii., p. xliv f., n. 2.

[25] Leipoldt, *op. cit.*, pp. 33 ff., p. 38, Zusatz 1, gives the earliest references to the Apocalypses. A convenient list of early citations of the *Shepherd* may be found in Harnack's *Geschichte d. altchristl. Literatur*, I. i., pp. 51 ff., and a fuller discussion of them in the various editions of the text, particularly that of Gebhardt and Harnack.

[26] *Haer.* IV. 20, 2, quoting *Mand.* I., 1.

[27] It is a possible but not necessary inference that Harnack (*Patr. Apostol, Op.*, Fasc. iii. p. xlv, n. 1, c.) draws from this fact, viz. that the book was so well known that its name might be omitted.

[28] Harnack, *Geschichte d. altchr. Lit.*, I, i., p. 52, gives the following passages: *Haer.* I, 13, 3 = *Mand.* xi. 3; I, 21, 1 = *Mand.* I, 1; II, 30, 9 = *Sim.* IX, 12, 8; *Frag. Gr.* 29 (Harvey II, p. 494) = *Sim.* VIII, 3, 2, and perhaps *Haer.* IV, 30, 1 = *Sim.* 1. Cf. Zahn, *Der Hirt des Hermas*, p. 267, n. 2. None of these are more than resemblances.

scriptural arguments against the Valentinians,[29] though he quotes freely from most of the books of the New Testament (as we know it), he has no reference to, or proof drawn from, the *Shepherd*. In view of these facts some scholars have thought that Irenaeus regarded the book as of apostolic origin;[30] others have supposed that he may have used the term " Scripture " in this place in the general sense of " writing ", or that he made a mistake, fancying that the passage he quoted was Scripture;[31] others again are of the opinion that Irenaeus, while not ascribing the same honor to the *Shepherd* as to the prophetical and apostolical writings, regarded it nevertheless as authoritative.[32] It is not necessary for the purposes of this investigation to decide between the merits of these differing views, but I may be allowed to say in passing that neither the view that Irenaeus regarded the *Shepherd* as fully canonical and of apostolic origin, nor that which asserts that he regarded it as authoritative, but not canonical in the strict sense of the word, accounts for the fact that he quotes the *Shepherd* only once when he might have used it many times to his advantage, unless it be assumed that he was not well acquainted with the contents of the work. Again to say that he was mistakenly of the impression that he was quoting from some canonical book is to take refuge in a conjecture which is incapable of proof; and to take " Scripture " in any other than its usual technical sense, while permitted by the usage of this author in a few places,[33] is contrary to the general custom of the time, and unsuitable in the passage before us, where the section from Hermas is used for the purpose of proving a doctrine and inserted between two passages from

[29] *Haer.* Book III.

[30] Hilgenfeld, *Apostolische Väter,* p. 180. Zahn, *Geschichte des neutest. Kanons,* i., p. 335.

[31] Donaldson, *The Apostolical Fathers,* p. 319, though not committing himself to this view. Gregory, *Canon and Text of NT.,* p. 241 f. But he treats the evidence too cavalierly.

[32] Harnack, *Geschichte d. altchristl. Literatur,* I, i., p. 52; *Patr. Apostol. Op.,* Fasc. III, p. xlvi. A fuller discussion of the matter may be found in this latter place, or, where a different conclusion is reached, in Zahn, *Geschichte d. neutest. Kanons,* I, p. 333 f.

[33] *Haer.* III, 6, 4; III, 17, 4; V, Preface.

the Old Testament. All the facts of the case would be accounted for if we might assume that the *Shepherd* had only lately come into Irenaeus' hands, that he regarded it as canonical and of apostolic origin, but had not been able to acquaint himself intimately with it.

In North Africa, Tertullian, in his treatise *De oratione*, not only shows acquaintance with the *Shepherd,* but also informs us indirectly that the book was well known in the church[34] and that some Christians regarded it as normative in matters of devotional conduct. Whether or not he shared their views may not be clear; but certainly he was not concerned to argue the matter at this time.[35] In another work, however, after he had been converted to Montanism, and found the *Shepherd* in conflict with his rigoristic views, he calls it " that apocryphal *Shepherd* of adulterers ",[36] and reminds his opponents that it had been condemned as " apocryphal and false by every council of the churches, even your own ",[37] and that the Epistle of Barnabas (the canonical Hebrews) was more received among the churches than it was.[38] It is sometimes said that in the period which elapsed between these two references to the *Shepherd* the attitude of the church generally toward the work had undergone a change; the first coming from a time when it was universally regarded as authoritative and inspired, the second from a later time when the apocalypses were being excluded from the canon. Such a sweeping inference is, of course, unjustifiable; we cannot say that Tertullian speaks for a larger section of the church than

---

[34] Harnack, in *Patr. Apostol. Op.,* Fasc. iii. p. xlviii, n. 1, a. e. agreeing with Zahn (*Gött. Gel. Anz.* 1873, st. 29, s. 1155), concludes that in Tertullian's time the Shepherd was known to the North Africans in a Latin Translation. Since then Zahn has changed his opinion and affirms that it was not translated until later, (*Gesch. d. neutest. Kanons,* I, 345). Cf. also Harnack, *Das Neue Testament um* 200, p. 87.

[35] Tertullian, *de orat.* 16.

[36] *De pudic.* 20.   [37] *Ibid.,* 10.

[38] Utique receptior apud ecclesias epistola Barnabae illo apocrypho Pastore moechorum, *ibid.,* 20. I cannot find any justification for Gregory's translation, " Would that the letter of Barnabas were rather received among the churches than that apocryphal *Shepherd* of adulterers " *Canon and Text of the NT.,* p. 223.

that with which he was familiar.   But we are bound to ascertain, if we can, Tertullian's attitude toward the *Shepherd,* and whether he changed it, and, if so, why.   There can be no doubt of his later attitude.   He then considered the work " apocryphal and false " and so unworthy of a place in the " divine instrument ".   We cannot be altogether sure what he meant by " apocryphal " here.   The word has been variously understood in different periods.   The earliest meaning[39] appears to have been " excluded from public use in the Church ", without reference either to origin or contents of the book excluded.   Soon, however, it came to denote not the fact but the grounds for such exclusion; that is to say, it stigmatized a work as untrue with respect either to its contents or to its origin[40] or both.   But though we know that these several connotations existed in the early centuries, we cannot always be sure in which of them a writer uses the word.   It is indeed sufficiently clear, from the opprobrious terms Tertullian heaps up, that he condemns the teaching of the *Shepherd* out and out, but we should like to know whether by " apocryphal " he means to imply that the work is also not what it claims to be with respect to origin; and of this we cannot be certain.

Let us now turn to an examination of the earlier reference. Some of the North Africans apparently regarded it as important to lay aside their cloaks during prayer and to seat themselves afterwards.   In justification of the first of these they appealed to 2 Tim. iv. 13, and for the second to the fifth vision of the *Shepherd.*   Tertullian treats both customs and both passages appealed to in the same way.   Such customs he says are irrational, superstitious, and savor of idolatry, and such an interpretation of Scripture childish, and leads to the foolishest consequences if consistently applied.   Now while it is true that this argument says nothing either of the canonicity of Paul's letter or the uncanonicity of the *Shepherd,* still as

[39] See Zahn, *Geschichte des Neutestamentl. Kanons,* I, p. 125 ff.   E. Schürer in *Herzog, Realencyclopaedie,* ed. 3, vol. I, p. 622 ff.

[40] To Augustine " apocryphal " meant that the origin of a book was " hidden " or unknown, *De civit. Dei.* xv. 23, 4.   Harnack, *Patr. Apostol. Op.,* III, p. xlix., n. 1, b., thinks Tertullian uses it with reference to authorship.

Tertullian did regard Paul's epistles as canonical, and as the North Africans to whom he was writing seemingly regarded the *Shepherd* as equally authoritative in matters of conduct, it is often affirmed that the African father would not have lost this opportunity to correct the erroneous estimation placed upon the latter, had he been at the time of this writing of the same opinion that he was when he wrote *De pudicitia*. Moreover, it is noted that he here calls the *Shepherd* " *Scriptura* ". It is true that he does this also in the later reference, but in that case it is obvious that he does so sarcastically with reference to the attitude of those who would appeal to it, and that he may contrast it with the true Scriptures.[41]   But in the former case there is, it is said, no sign of sarcasm, nor anything to show that he differed from his correspondents in his estimate of the *Shepherd,* or that he regarded it as less binding than the writings of Paul.[42]

[41] At ego eius pastoris scripturas haurio qui non potest frangi."

[42] Harnack (*Patr. Apost. Op.,* Fasc. iii., p. xlix) thinks that Tertullian at this time regarded the *Shepherd* as " Scripture" but as inferior to the prophets and the apostles ("sed minime audeo dicere Carthaginienses tum temporis Pastorem inter scripturas prophetarum et apostolorum recensuisse"). He refers to Tertullian's treatment of the Book of Enoch and suggests that the *Shepherd* may have had a place at the close of the New Testament after the Epistle to the Hebrews. But, in Tertullian's treatment of the Book of Enoch (*de cult. fem.* I, 3; II, 10, *de idol.* 15), there is every sign that he himself regarded this work as of equal authority with other Old Testament Scriptures; he calls it "*Scriptura*", cites it by way of proof, answers criticisms of its authorship and transmission, says it is vouched for by the Apostle Jude, and tries to explain why it was unjustly rejected by the Jews. Nor can the statement " et legimus omnem scripturam aedificationi habilem divinitus inspirari" (*de cult. fem.* I, 3, 2 Tim. iii. 16), be taken to explain Tertullian's attitude toward the *Shepherd*, for Tertullian is speaking here only of the Old Testament Scriptures, as was St. Paul before him—a thing that is often overlooked in discussing this passage (on the importance of this interpretation of Paul's words for the history of the New Testament canon, see Harnack, *Das Neue Test. um das Jahr* 200, pp. 25, 39 f., and opposed to him Leipoldt, *op. cit.,* p. 40).

With regard to the relative value of the *Shepherd* and the Epistle to the Hebrews the matter is somewhat different. Harnack is here following Credner (*Geschichte d. neutest. Kanons*) and Rönsch (*Das neue Testament Tertullians*), in the view that Tertullian had in his New Testament as a kind of appendix, some works which were to some degree

If this be the correct explanation of this passage we have to ask further on what grounds Tertullian granted such a high inspired and authoritative but on a lower plane than others. Rönsch gives as the names of these the Epistle of Peter *ad Ponticos* (1 Peter), the Epistle of Barnabas to the Hebrews (Hebrews), the Epistle of Jude, and the Epistle of the Presbyter (2 John). But, without going into details, it is hard to believe, after reading *Scorp.* 12 and 14, and *de orat.* 20, that Tertullian set the known writings of Peter in any respect below those of Paul; the Epistle of Jude is referred to only once (*de cult. fem.* I, 3), but then as a work of an Apostle and as authoritative; and 2 John is neither mentioned nor used by the North African Father (*Rönsch*, p. 572, see Zahn, *Gesch. d. NT. Kanons,* Vol. I, p. 111, n. 1, pp. 304 ff., pp. 320 f.).

Tertullian's attitude toward the Epistle to the Hebrews requires closer examination. In his treatise *de pudic.*, after he had passed in review the teaching of the Evangelists, the Acts of the Apostles, Paul and the other Apostles, concluding with the Revelation and First Epistle of St. John, Tertullian draws the argument to a close (*de pud.* 20), and then adds, " I wish however to subjoin in addition, redundantly, the testimony also of a certain companion of the Apostles, which is well adapted for confirming, by nearest right, the teaching of the masters " (volo tamen ex redundantia alicuius etiam comitis apostolorum testimonium superducere idoneum confirmandi de proximo jure disciplinam magistrorum (Ed. Oehler). He then introduces the Epistle to the Hebrews as the work of Barnabas for whom Paul vouched, and adds, " and at all events the Epistle of Barnabas is more received among the churches than that apocryphal *Shepherd* of adulterers " (et utique receptior apud ecclesias epistola Barnabae illo apocrypho Pastore moechorum). He then quotes Heb. vi., 4-8. There are two questions raised by this passage: the first concerns Tertullian's estimate of Hebrews, the second the comparative value of the *Shepherd* and Hebrews. With regard to the first of these it is evident that the Epistle to the Hebrews, according to Tertullian, was not in itself possessed of divine authority. This appears from the formal conclusion of his argument based on the Apostolic teaching (*disciplina apostolorum proprie*) before he turns to it, from the express statements that he uses it only to *confirm* the teaching of the Apostles and that it is excessive (*ex redundantia*), from the fact that he does not ascribe but rather denies apostolicity to it, and that he never calls it " Scripture " (he uses *titulus* instead or refers to it by name). The view, which Zahn thinks possible, (*Gesch. d. Neutest. Kanons,* Vol. I, p. 291) that Tertullian himself placed a higher estimate on the work than is here apparent, and did not cite it among the writings of the New Testament only because it was not universally received, and therefore any argument drawn from it not universally valid, while commending itself for several reasons is incapable of proof. According to the evidence before us the Epistle to the Hebrews was outside of Tertullian's canon, and enjoyed only that amount of favor which was

place to the *Shepherd*. In the first place it cannot be thought
that he accepted it without having some opinion of its authorship; for he denounces strongly all works that do not "bind

due to the writings of a man who was approved of St. Paul and God. But
what does Tertullian mean by saying that the Epistle to the Hebrews was
"more received among the churches" than was the *Shepherd?* Does
"*receptior apud ecclesias*" mean that it was more highly esteemed, or that
it was received as canonical by more churches? Rönsch understands it
to mean both (*Op. cit.,* p. 565); Harnack to mean one or the other, he
does not say which (*Patr. Apost. Op.* III, p. xlix f., n. 1, c), but in
stating that the *Shepherd* seems to have had a place at the end of the New
Testament *after* the Epistle to the Hebrews (*ibid.,* p. xlviii. f., n. 1 e)
he favors the former, and in another place (*Texte und Untersuchungen*
V, i., p. 59), the latter. Zahn holds firmly to the latter interpretation (*Gesch.
d. neutest. Kanons,* I, pp. 121, n. 292 f.) on the ground that "*receptus*"
is not capable of degrees, and of the presence of the plural "*ecclesias*".
So also Credner, *Gesch. d. neutest. Kanons,* p. 117. But neither of these
explanations is free from difficulty. By the first Tertullian is made to dis-
agree with his other statement in this same treatise, that all the councils of
the church had declared the *Shepherd* "apocryphal and false". To accuse
him of exaggerating in the latter remark (Harnack, *Texte u. Untersuchungen,* V, i., p. 59, Weiss, *Einleitung in d. NT.,* 3rd ed. p. 74) is unwarranted,
and, as we shall see later these words may express literally a natural
interpretation of a Roman statement concerning the *Shepherd*. Zahn's
argument is unsatisfactory because it does violence to the Latin. Had
Tertullian wished to say that the Epistle to the Hebrews was received
by more churches than the *Shepherd* we should expect "*receptus apud
plures ecclesias*". It seems to be true that "*receptus*" was used as
terminus technicus to denote the inclusion of a work among the canonical
books, and that in this sense it was incapable of degree. But the word
was not used exclusively in this connection, and when not it could be
compared (see instances in Zahn *loc. cit.*). It is in this latter sense that
the word is used in the passage before us. The discussion is not about
canonical works, but about two, both of which Tertullian definitely excludes from the Scriptures. With this in mind the argument in this
chapter of *de pudicitia* is both clear and consistent with other parts of the
treatise. I have now, says Tertullian in effect, concluded my argument
from the New Testament Scriptures, but I wish to add the testimony of
one other, which may not be used in the argument proper but is of value
in confirming the teaching of the Apostles, for its author was their com-
rade. I refer to an Epistle of Barnabas, a man commended by God and the
Apostle Paul. And though he is not an authority, you must at least acknowledge that his Epistle is recognized as of more value by the churches
than that apocryphal *Shepherd* of adulterers which has been condemned
by all the councils of the churches.

themselves by full title and due profession of author ",[43]   And
it is equally clear that he received only such works as were of
apostolic origin, that is to say, composed either by Apostles or
apostolic men.[44]   We would therefore conclude that Tertullian
regarded Hermas as a disciple of the Apostles.   But if this be
so the question immediately thrusts itself upon us, why does he
not use the *Shepherd* more frequently in his writings?   To this
no certain answer can be given, though it may be pointed out
that Paul's Epistles to Titus and Philemon, the First Epistle of
Peter and that of Jude, although undoubtedly belonging to
Tertullian's canon, are referred to no more frequently or
hardly so than is the *Shepherd*.

But this view, although held in slightly differing forms by
many scholars, appears to me to be wrong from beginning to
end.   When the Christians of North Africa, in defence of
their superstitious practices of laying aside their cloaks before
prayer and of sitting down after it, appealed to the statements that Paul had left his cloak behind him at Troas (presumably having laid it aside at prayer) and that Hermas had
sat down on his bed after prayer, the answer that sprang to
Tertullian's lips, as it would to those of any other sensible
Christian, was that such a use of Scripture was childish, silly,
superstitious, and incapable of being indulged without entailing ridiculous results.   More was unnecessary.   To argue
the question of the authority or canonicity of the *Shepherd*
would not have been to the point.   On the contrary it would
have weakened the argument, as it might be taken to imply
that had the *Shepherd* been authoritative, such a use of it
would have been justified.   Tertullian here as elsewhere sees
the main issue clearly and sticks to it.   And yet he has not
left us without at least a hint of his estimate of Hermas and
his book.   He introduces them with the words " that Hermas
whose scripture is generally called the *Shepherd* ".[45]   This is

---

[43] *Marc.* IV, 2.

[44] To Tertullian apostolic men (*apostolici*) were those who had associated
with and learned from the Apostles, *Marc.* IV, 2; *Praescr.* 32. Cf. also
Praescr. 21 ff.; 30; 44; and what he says against works of post-apostolic
date, *Praescr.* 30.

[45] Quid enim, si Hermas ille cuius scriptura fere Pastor inscribitur, etc.
De orat. 16.

not the way one introduces a well known and acknowledgedly canonical book. The demonstrative "that" pointing to Hermas with quite particular emphasis is hard to account for unless we find in it, as several scholars do,[46] the note of contempt. The words "that Hermas" find their parallel in "that *Shepherd* of adulterers", and the delicate sarcasm of the words "whose (i. e., Hermas') scripture" is perceived at once when they are put beside those others, which we have heard Tertullian using elsewhere in discussing the *Shepherd,* "but I quaff the scriptures of that Shepherd who cannot be broken".[47] We are compelled therefore to the conclusion that, though some of his countrymen estimated the *Shepherd* very highly,— exactly how highly we cannot say for lack of evidence,—Tertullian at no period of his life of which we have any knowledge shared their views. He despised it.

In Alexandria Clement knew the *Shepherd* and was fond of it. He quotes it freely and shows beyond possibility of doubt that he believed it to contain a genuine revelation. He speaks of "the Shepherd, the Angel of Repentance" that spoke to Hermas,[48] of the "Power that spoke divinely to Hermas by revelation"[49] or "the Power that appeared to Hermas in the vision in the form of the Church";[50] more frequently he cites it simply as the "*Shepherd*".[51] He appeals to it as proof of Christian teaching associating it with the books of our Bible, he even interprets one passage allegorically.[52] And yet in spite of all this there are few who venture to affirm that Clement puts the *Shepherd* on a par with the Gospels and writings of the Apostles. It is noted that he never calls Hermas an Apostle as he does Barnabas and Clem-

---

[46] So Credner, *Gesch. d. neutest. Kanons,* p. 117; Oehler, *Tertull. op.* Vol. I, p. 567, *not.* c; Gregory, *Canon and Text of the NT.,* p. 242.

[47] See note 41.   [48] *Strom.* i., 17, 85.   [49] *Strom.* i., 29, 181.

[50] *Strom.* vi., 15, 131, cf. *Strom.* ii., 1, 3.

[51] The passages have been gathered by Harnack, *Gesch. d. altchristl. Lit.,* I. i., p. 53.

[52] Harnack (*Gesch. d. altchristl. Lit.,* I. i., p. 53). Kutter, (*Clemens Alexandrinus und das Neue Testament,* p. 86) would weaken the force of this, by showing what Clement does is to interpret allegorically an *act* of Hermas. But in any case Clement is dealing with a passage out of the *Shepherd.*

ent of Rome, that he does not cite his book as " Scripture " as
he does for example the Teaching of the Twelve Apostles.[53]
It is pointed out that he regarded Greek Philosophy and the
oracles of the Sybil as in a sense divine.[54] And the testimony
of Eusebius is called to show that in the *Hypotyposes* in which
he commented upon all the books of the canonical Scriptures
not omitting the disputed books, which are more nearly defined as Jude, the other Catholic Epistles, Barnabas and the
Apocalpse of Peter, the *Shepherd* of Hermas is not included.[55] It has been argued too that, as the final authority
for Clement was the Lord and his Apostles[56] and as the
apostolic time ended for him in the days of Nero,[57] he could
not have regarded a work, which he must have known to be of
later origin, as on a par with the writings of the Apostles.[58]
It does not come within the scope of our investigation to inquire more definitely into the merits of these views. Our purpose is accomplished when we have ascertained that Clement
as a matter of fact did regard the *Shepherd* as at least containing a divine revelation; though it is not unimportant to note
that of all the Christian writings appealed to by Clement as

[53] Kutter, *Clemens Alex. u. d. Neue Test.*, p. 139 f. On the use of γραφή
in a broad sense and the extension of the term apostolic to include the
later years of John's life and also Clement of Rome and Barnabas, *ibid.*,
pp. 130, 136.

[54] *Strom*, vi., 5, 43. *cf. Protr.* vi. 72; viii, 77, *et al.* See Eickhoff, *Das
Neue Testament des Clem. Alex.* p. 7. Kutter, *op. cit.* 140 f.

[55] Eusebius, *HE.* vi., 14. Photius' statement (*Bibl. cod.* 109) that the
Hypotyposes covered only Genesis, Exodus, the Psalms, the Pauline Epistles, the Catholic Epistles and Ecclesiastes, cannot stand in the face of
Eusebius' explicit reference to the Apocalypse of Peter. Nor is the omission of the *Shepherd* acounted for by saying that Eusebius has probably
omitted it through accident (Harnack, *Gesch. d. altchristl. Lit.* I. i., p. 53)
or that Clement did not comment on it because of its length (Zahn, *Gesch.
d. neutest. Kanons*, i., p. 330). Nor does Eusebius' failure to mention the
Shepherd among the works used by Clement (*HE.* vi., 13) destroy the
argument.

[56] *Strom.* i., 1, 11.   [57] *Strom.* vii., 17, 106.

[58] Kutter, *op. cit.*, pp. 108, 128 ff., 139 f., cf. Kunze, *Glaubensregel* etc.,
pp. 40, 138. But it is by no means sure that Clement was as well informed
of the origin of the *Shepherd* as was the author of the Muratori Fragment,
as Kutter assumes.

authoritative, this is the only one for which apostolical origin was not claimed in one way or another; and the difficulties which arise in connection with his use of the *Shepherd* would be to a large extent removed, and his procedure shown to be consistent with his own principles, if we might assume that for which there is nothing *pro* or *contra* in his writings, namely, that he thought this book to be the product of the golden age of the Apostles.

Origen, the successor of Clement in Alexandria, regards the *Shepherd* as " very useful and divinely inspired ",[59] and frequently adduced proof from it as from any other Scripture.   But he also informs us that the book was not universally received but even despised by some.[60]   From him also we have a definite statement concerning the authorship and date of the *Shepherd,* namely that it was written by the Hermas to whom the Apostle Paul sends greetings in his Epistle to the Romans;[61] that is to say he refers it to apostolic times, the period which produced all the other canonical books.[62]   Nor can we doubt that the opinion of Origen with respect to the authorship of the *Shepherd* was shared by a large proportion of the Alexandrian church.[63]

Among the Roman writers of this period we find no such high respect for the *Shepherd* as we have found in Alexandria.   Hippolytus especially, than whom none was better ac-

[59] Valde mihi utilis videtur et ut puto divinitus inspirata. *In Rom.* (xvi. 14), com. x. 31.

[60] καταφρονούμενος, *De princip.* iv. 11; cf. *In Psalm. Selecta, hom.* i. *in Psalm.* 37; *In Ezech.* xxviii. 13, *hom.* xiii. These and other references in Harnack, *Gesch. d. altchristl. Lit.,* I. i., pp. 53 ff.

[61] *In Rom.* xvi. 14, *com.* x. 31, " Puto tamen, quod Hermas iste sit scriptor libelli illius qui Pastor appellatur ".

[62] Cf. Origen in *Euseb. HE.* vi., 25, 12 f.

[63] See Zahn, *Gesch. d. neutest. Kanons,* i., pp. 330 ff, where he retracts his earlier statements. Harnack (*Patr. apost. op.* iii., p. lvii) would have us believe that Origen is expressing only his own opinion when he ascribes the *Shepherd* to the Hermas of Rom. xvi. 14. It may be true, as he asserts, that Origen does not claim to have any traditional basis for this opinion and never calls Hermas *virum apostolicum,* but it is hard to believe that a man of such scholarly methods as Origen was should make such a statement without basis for it.

quainted with the affairs of the Roman Church, and who had
plenty of opportunities to use it, does not once mention by
name, or quote from, the work.[64]   And yet there is asserted
to be reason for believing that here too the book was regarded
as inspired and authoritative and on a par with other canonical
writings.   I shall briefly review what evidence there is.   (1)
Tertullian, in a passage already referred to, has in mind that
the *Shepherd* is opposed to his montanistic views and defends
himself against its teachings.   "But I would yield to you",
he says, "if the Scripture called the *Shepherd,* which alone
loves adulterers, were worthy of a place in the divine instrument,—if it had not been adjudged among the apocryphal and
false writings by every council of the churches even your
own ".[65]   As Tertullian throughout this treatise has the bishop
of Rome in mind, the *Pontifex Maximus* as he sarcastically
calls him in the initial chapter, it has been inferred that the
Roman had appealed to the *Shepherd* in defence of his laxer
administration of discipline.[66]   The inference is possible but
but by no means necessary.   Tertullian had to defend himself
not only from the actual arguments of the past but also from
the possible ones of the future, against attacks not only from
Rome but also from nearer home, where as we have seen the
Shepherd was in high repute.   The words "your churches"
refer of course to the Catholic churches, not to those of any
particular locality.[67]   (2)   The next witness is the so-called
Liberian Catalogue of the bishops of Rome, which has the following note under the name Pius: "During his episcopate his
brother Hermes wrote the book in which is contained the command which the angel enjoined upon him when he came to him
in the garb of a shepherd ".[68]   This catalogue in its completed

[64] Bonwetsch, *Zu den Komm. Hippolyts. Texte u. Untersuchungen*
N. F. Vol. i., 2, p. 26, finds a couple of resemblances.

[65] *De pudic.* 10. "Sed cederem tibi si scriptura Pastoris qui sola moechos
amat divino instrumento meruisset incidi, si non ab omni concilio eccle-
siarum etiam vestrarum inter apocrypha et falsa iudicaretur".

[66] So Harnack, *Gesch. d. altchristl. Lit.,* I. i, 52, and others.

[67] According to Harnack, Tertullian could not be referring to Roman or
Italian councils (*Texte u. Untersuch.* V. i., p. 59).

[68] "Sub hujus episcopatu frater ejus Hermes librum scripsit in quo

form belongs to the middle of the fourth century and therefore lies outside the period of our investigation; but there is good reason for supposing that the earlier part of it, down to 231 A.D., was composed a century or more earlier and is from the pen of Hippolytus himself.[69]   But even the earlier part did not leave the hand of Hippolytus in its present form.   Some later editor or continuator added chronological synchronisms at least (the names of contemporary consuls, Emperors, &c.), and perhaps also this and one other note (concerning the death of the Apostle Peter).   According to the table of contents appended to one of the recensions of Hippolytus' *Chronica* we should find in it *Nomina episcoporum Romae et quis quot annis praefuit*.[70]   The natural inference is that all except the names and the number of years was added later.   Still, while expressing doubt on the matter both Lightfoot and Harnack think it probable that the notice concerning Hermas was in the original work, the former because it " seems intended to discredit the pretensions of that work to a place in the canon and therefore would probably be written at a time when such pretensions were still more or less seriously entertained ", the motive being " the same as with the author of the *Muratorian Canon* who has a precisely similar note ",[71] the latter because " just at Hippolytus' time the *Shepherd* was excluded from the sacred collection in many churches and this notice apparently has reference to the controversy [involved]".[72]   It is true that the *Liberian Catalogue* agrees with the *Muratori Fragment* in ascribing the *Shepherd* to a certain Hermas (or Hermes), the brother of Pius, but it is equally important to note that it definitely asserts that it is a genuine revelation, which the Muratori Fragment does not; and it is highly improbable that Hippoltyus, had he entertained this view of the work, would have made no mention of, or citation from, it in his other works.

mandatum continetur quod ei praecepit angelus cum venit ad illum in habitu pastoris."

[69] See discussion in Lightfoot, *Apostol. Fathers*, I. i., pp. 253 ff. and a summary of results in Harnack, *Gesch. d. altchristl. Lit.*, II. i., pp. 144 ff.

[70] Lightfoot, *Loc. cit.*, p. 260.   [71] *Ibid.*, p. 261 f.

[72] Harnack, *Loc. cit.*, p. 150.

Moreover, if the purpose of the author of this notice was to contribute something toward the settlement of the controversy concerning the canonicity of the book, he chose a very inappropriate method. The statement that the book dates from the days of Pius does indeed implicitly deny apostolicity to the work, but the affirmation of its prophetic character definitely asserts its inspiration.[73] [74]

[73] The singular *mandatum* also is suspicious. *Mandata* (pl.) might by a stretch be made to cover the whole book, but not its singular. The question rises what is meant thereby. The explanation of Zahn (*Hirt des Hermas*, p. 25 f.) would solve the problem. In a letter of Pseudo-Pius dealing with the Quarto-decimanian controversy and therefore dating probably from early in the 4th cent., the writer appeals to a command given to Hermas by the angel that appeared to him in the garb of a shepherd, to the effect that the *Pascha* should be celebrated on the Lord's day ("eidem Hermae angelus domini in habitu pastoris apparuit et praecepit ei ut pascha die dominica ab omnibus celebaretur"). Zahn thinks this is the command referred to in the *Liberian Cat.* in which case the notice there contained must not only be from the fourth cent., but also have no reference to our work for it contains no such command. See also Harnack, *Gesch. d. altchristl. Lit.* I, i., p. 56, who finds Zahn's explanation "very improbable".

[74] For the sake of completeness we must say a word about the puzzling Pseudocyprianic tract known as *de aleatoribus*. This work might be ignored here were it not that Prof. Harnack (*Texte und Untersuchungen*, Vol. v.) some years ago endeavored to show that it is from the pen of the Bishop Victor of Rome. This view has not found much favor with scholars and recently Prof. Harnack himself does not seem so desirous of maintaining it (*Gesch. d. altchristl. Lit.*, i. 52, 719. Cf. Herzog, *Realencycl.* 3rd ed. vol. iv., p. 347; xx., p. 602). It has, however, been taken up by Leipoldt in his *Entstehung des neutestamentlichen Kanons*, and part of Harnack's argument made the basis of much of this work. In this tract the *Shepherd* is quoted once fairly literally, once loosely, and several passages seem to reflect the words and thoughts of Hermas. In no case is the *Shepherd* or its author mentioned by name. In the case of the first quotation (cap. 2) the introductory words are *dicit enim scriptura divina* and the quotation is coupled with a passage from Sirach and one from an unknown source ["dicit enim scriptura divina (quotation from *Sim.* ix. 13, 5), et alia scriptura dicit (Sirach xxxii., (xxxv. 1), et iterum (an unknown passage)"]. In the second case (cap. 4) the author evidently thinks he is quoting St. Paul, ["apostulus idem Paulus commemorat ... dicens (several passages from the Epp. to Timothy being combined), iterum (1 Cor. v. 11), et alio loco (apparently from *Mand.* iv. 1, 9) in doctrinis apostolorum est (a quotation from an unknown source, possibly

We may pause here for a moment to review our examination to this point.   There is no evidence that, during the first thirty or forty years of its existence, the *Shepherd* occupied any preëminent position in the church.   There are signs that it was known and used, but there is not the slightest reason for thinking that it was regarded as an apocalypse, as authoritative, or in any sense on a par with the Scriptures of the Old Testament.   On the contrary, there is good reason for the opinion that no one, orthodox or heretical, was concerned to make or maintain any such claims for it.   After that period a higher estimate of it appears in some sections.   In Gaul it is quoted by one great teacher as " Scripture ", but in such a way as to

dependent on the *Didache*)"].   Our hesitancy, in the face of this, to receive this author as a first-class witness to the canonical authority of the *Shepherd* is increased when we take into account his very loose manner of quoting, the fact that several of his quotations cannot be identified, and also that all the Old Testament passages he cites are to be found in Cyprian's *de Lapsis* or *Testimonia*.

We are not concerned except indirectly with the general question of his forms of citation and the argument that is built upon them in the discussion of the history of the canon of the New Testament; but I cannot refrain from remarking that when Prof. Harnack lays down, as the basis of further argument, the *dictum* that the author (of *de aleatoribus*) "follows a quite definite and strongly consistent method of citation" ("*eine ganz bestimmte und streng festgehaltene Citationsweise befolgt*," loc. cit., p. 56) he seriously weakens his own argument by assuming that the author had two forms of citation, *dicit scriptura divina* and *dicit dominus*, that were apparently of equal value (*augenscheinlich gleichwerthig*).   Nor should he say in another place (*Das neue Testament um 200*, p. 36) that according to *de aleatoribus* "the Old Testament and the Apocalypses of Hermas and John belong to the *scripturae divinae* but not so the Gospels and Epistles."   Nor should Leipoldt follow him by saying (*loc. cit.*, p. 37) that "this writing (*de aleatoribus*) regards apparently only two books outside of the Old Testament as Holy Scripture in this strict sense of the term".   As a matter of fact the Old Testament is never cited as *scriptura divina* in *de aleatoribus*, the passage from Sirach alone excepted, nor is the Apocalypse of John, which is introduced by the words *dominus occurrit et dicit* (cap. 8).   To say, as Leipoldt does (*loc. cit.*) that this is apparently accidental is to confess that the whole argument is unfounded.   It has escaped the notice of these writers that another and simpler, and consistent principle may be found for the author's method of citation, namely, that in all passages, whether from the Old or the New Testament, from the Gospels or Apocalypse, in which, *in the Scriptures*, the Lord is repre-

leave us in doubt whether he really regarded it as Scripture in the strict sense of the word.   In Africa the common people esteemed it highly, but their scholarly leader Tertullian despised it.   In Alexandria it fared better.   Both Clement and Origen regarded it as a real revelation, the former for reasons not clear to us, the latter ascribing it to the Apostolic age. From Rome, where it was produced and where it presumably was best known, comes exceedingly little evidence.   Not a single author can be proved to have regarded it as divine or authoritative, but neither do we find any condemnation of it. This cannot be the record of a work which was originally published as a divine revelation, accepted as such by the leaders of the church, and drawn upon by them in matters of faith and practice.   It is rather the story of a book that began its career in a humbler fashion, that found its way to the hearts of the common people first, that was then occasionally dimly reflected in the words of some writer or other, and that then here and there, especially far from its native place, and where a wrong opinion of its origin was current, came to be regarded as divine. But we have still one piece of evidence to consider, perhaps the most important of all, and we shall turn to it now.

The so-called *Muratori Fragment*,[75] it is generally conceded,

sented as speaking the introductory formula is *dominus dicit*.   In the one occasion where the words quoted are not immediately ascribed to God in the Scriptures, the introductory phrase is enlarged by the addition of *per prophetam* (cap. 10, quoting Eli's words in 1 Sam. ii. 25).   When the quotation is from the Gospels the addition *in evangelio* is found three times (cap. 3, 10) and in the only other formal quotation from them, both *dominus* and *in evangelio* are lacking (cap 2).   The subject could be mentally supplied; and *in evangelio* was apparently not regarded as necessary.   When the quotation is from the Epistles either the name of the apostle (Paul, cap. 3, 4, John, cap. 10), or the title *apostolus* without name (cap. 4, 10) is found with *dicit* (*dicens*).   When the authority of the apostolic college is cited the formula is *in doctrinis Apostolorum* (cap. 4).   In all other cases the general term *Scriptura* is used (cap. 2).   The author has given us no passage from the Acts of the Apostles or from narrative portions of the Bible, and so we cannot say how he would have introduced them.

[75] The text may be found in an appendix to Westcott's *Canon of the New Testament*, also in Zahn, *Grundriss der Gesch. d. neutest. Kanons*, p. 75, Harnack, *Zeitschrift für Kirchengeschichte*, Vol. v., p. 595, and elsewhere. An English translation is given in *The Ante-Nicene Fathers*, Vol. v., p.

comes from about the end of the second century and reflects the opinion of the Roman or Italian church. It contains an incomplete list of the books received into or rejected from the New Testament Scriptures, with notes on the same. Toward the end of the list is found the following paragraph: " Of apocalypses also we receive only those of John and Peter which (latter) some among us will not have read in the church. But the *Shepherd* was written by Hermas, very recently, in our own times, when his brother Pius the bishop was sitting in the episcopal chair of the church of the city of Rome, and therefore it ought indeed to be read, but it cannot be publicly read to the people in church, either among the Prophets whose number is complete, or among the Apostles to the end of time." [76] Such a statement as this would not be found in this place unless canonicity had been claimed for the *Shepherd*. It is natural too to infer that such claims had been made within that particular church from which the *Fragment* emanates. But this is not necessary. The writers had in mind not their own community only, but also the whole Catholic Church,[77] and therefore had to take cognizance of works for which claims were made by outsiders. From whatever quarter these claims may have come, however, the *Fragment* leaves us in no doubt about certain pretensions which were made for the *Shepherd,* and which were doubtless urged in favor of its canonicity. These were two in

603. This is not the place to discuss the date and source of this unique document. I shall assume that it comes from Rome or at least represents the Roman tradition. Also when the plural number is used to denote the authors, I am only following a hint contained in the *Fragment* itself, (" *recipimus* "), without affirming anything of the authorship.

[76] Ll. 71-79. " Apocalypse etiam iohanis et pe|tri tantum recipimus quam quidam ex nos|tris legi in eclesia nolunt pastorem uero | nuperrim e temporibus nostris in urbe | roma herma conscripsit sedente cathe|tra urbis romae aeclesiae pio $\overline{eps}$ fratre | eius et ideo legi eum quidē oportet se pu|plicare vero in eclesia populo neque inter | profetas completum numero neque inter | apostolos in finē temporum potest ". In corrected Latin: " Apocalypses etiam Johannis et Petri tantum recipimus, quam quidam ex nostris in urbe Roma Hermas conscripsit sedente cathedra urbis Romae ecclesiae Pio episcopo fratre ejus; et ideo legi eum quidem oportet, se publicare vero in ecclesia populo, neque inter prophetas completo numero, neque inter apostolos in finem temporum potest ".

[77] *Frag.,* l. 66, cf. 69.

number. The first was that the *Shepherd* dates from apostolic times. This is evident from the way the *Fragment* heaps up clauses to disprove such an early origin.[78] It was written, it says, " very recently ", " in our own times ", " when Pius was bishop of Rome ", by the brother of this same Pius and this is given as the ground (*et ideo*) for its exclusion from the Canon.

The second argument was that the *Shepherd* was an apocalypse. This is evident enough from its being classed with the Apocalypses of John and Peter. What is the attitude of the *Fragment* toward this? In the first place, it cannot be urged that the parallelism " we receive only . . . . but " shows the writers' own view *viz.* that the *Shepherd* too is in an apocalypse. The only necessary inference is that the work was commonly or sometimes ranked as an apocalypse. Again, it may be asked, whether in asserting the late date of the book the *Fragment* does not mean to imply that it is not apocalyptic. No definite answer can be given to this, but the indications are that it does. Elsewhere[79] the *Fragment* is pronouncedly anti-montanistic, and it is hard to believe that its authors could have thought of revelations as late as the time of Pius.[80] But there is still another indication that this is really the view of the *Fragment*. The last lines of our paragraph read, " it cannot be publicly read . . . . either among the Prophets whose number is complete or among the Apostles till the end of time." " Prophets " and " Apostles " here, as elsewhere in the literature of this period, are doubtless equivalent to the Old and New Testaments. But there seems to be an especial appropriateness in the use of the terms here. Out of several designations of the Scriptures at their disposal, all current at the time, the authors of the *Fragment* have chosen two which had reference to the two arguments advanced in favor of the *Shepherd* by their opponents. That this is so, that the use of these words is not perfunctory, is shown too by the insertion of the phrase "whose number is complete " after " prophets ". This phrase indeed

[78] So too Zahn (*Gesch. d. neutest. Kanons*, i., p. 340) who however does not regard the *Fragment* as well informed concerning the date of the *Shepherd*, but thinks its author was driven to exaggeration by the zeal of the advocates of an early date.

[79] L. 84.   [80] Zahn, *op. cit.*, ii., p. 116.

amplifies and completes the argument against the reception of the *Shepherd,* begun in the assertion of its late date. The *Fragment* therefore says in effect, that the *Shepherd* cannot be classed with the Apostles for it is of later date, nor with the Prophets for their number is complete, that is Hermas was not a prophet nor his work a revelation.[81]

Taking this then as the view of the authors, and remembering the historical situation, this little section of the *Muratori Fragment,* so puzzling to commentators, becomes a well conceived and carefully guarded statement. The problem was this: Here was a work forty or fifty years old, which had been popular and useful in the church. On account of its apocalyptic form and the apostolic name of its author it was held by some to be divinely inspired and equal to the canonical Scriptures. The authors of the *Fragment* knew better. They knew by whom it was written and when, and that it was not a revelation. They had to remove the misunderstanding that was abroad concerning the work, but they had to do so warily or create an opinion of the *Shepherd* as incorrect as the one they would destroy. They dared not say for instance " we do not receive it", a phrase which is used of other books.[82] Of course in one sense the *Shepherd* is rejected.[83] It is not recognized as part of the canonical Scriptures. But all the works of which " not received " is said (apocryphal letters of Paul and the writings of Arsinous and others), are not only rejected from the Canon but positively stigmatized as evil; as the *Fragment* says, " gall should not be mixed with honey. "[84] This phrase could not therefore be used of the *Shepherd* without giving rise to the impression that it was " gall ", and so the authors avoid it. Again, let us put ourselves for a moment mentally in the position of those who believed Hermas to be the friend of Paul to whom he sent greetings, and the *Shepherd* to be the record of

---

[81] Similarly, Leipoldt, *op. cit.,* p. 48; Hesse, *Das muratorische Fragment* p. 270 f.; Credner, *Gesch. d. neutest. Kanons,* p. 117, whose statements however are not in full harmony, cf. p. 165; Overbeck, *Zur Gesch. des Kanons,* pp. 100, 105, and others.

[82] Ll. 63 ff.; 81 ff.

[83] This is involved in " *tantum* . . . *vero* ".

[84] L. 67.

divine revelations which had been vouchsafed to him. What would be our first thought, were we informed that the book was written a hundred years after we had supposed, and was not a revelation? We would say at once: then the book lies about its origin and its contents, it is apocryphal and false. These are exactly the words Tertullian, as we have seen, used to describe the declaration of some councils of the churches concerning the Shepherd, and it seems more than probable that just such a statement as the one before us was in his mind.[85] Whether, however, Tertullian is guilty of this or not, such a false inference had to be guarded against, and it is for this purpose that the authors of the *Fragment* after the assertion of the *Shepherd's* late date hasten to add " therefore it ought to be read. " Commentators have been puzzled by the " therefore " here. One, who otherwise has excellently understood the situation, is driven to the extremity of saying that the work was ordered to be read because it was written by the brother of a bishop.[86] But the matter is clear when seen in its proper setting. The writers have in view those who would be inclined to go from the extreme of admiration to that of denunciation. To these they say: " the *Shepherd* is not what you think it is, but you must not condemn *it* because *you* have made a mistake; it is a good book and therefore it ought to be read." But after all the main thing in the writers' minds is to ensure the exclusion of the *Shepherd* from the Scriptures, and so, after having qualified its rejection in this way, they conclude strongly (the " therefore " being still in force): " but it cannot be read publicly in the church to the people either among the Prophets whose number is complete or among the Apostles to the end of time; " that is to say, it is to be ranked with neither the Old nor the New Testament.

The correctness of this interpretation will be more apparent

---

[85] Similarly Credner, *Gesch. d. neutest. Kanons*, p. 117. An interesting parallel to Tertullian's statement is found in Zahn, *Gesch. d. neutest. Kanons*, ii., p. 113, " wer das Buch trotz des Namens Clemens (vis. ii. 4) und vieler anderer Anzeichen für ein Werk aus der Zeit um 145 hielt, musste es für eine pseudepigraphe Fiction halten ". Cf. also p. 118 and vol. i., p. 342.

[86] Hesse, *op. cit.*, pp. 268 ff.

when we see how others are involved with difficulties. I will take for examples those of Professors Zahn and Harnack, who approach the matter from different standpoints.   Professor Zahn,[87] who has little respect for the judgment of the author of the *Fragment*, explains the injunction to read the *Shepherd* as follows. The Fragmentist believed that the *Shepherd* had been published as an apocalypse but was himself of the opinion that it was not 'such, and was not kindly disposed toward it.   But because it could not be charged with heresy, or intentional falsehood, or because it had been found valuable in the church, or perhaps by way of concession to the opposite party,—we cannot be sure of his motives,—he retained the work in a minor position, as a sort of deutero-canonical work, and ordered it to be read, only providing that it shall not be read in the public services of the church along with the Old and New Testament. But such an interpretation is possible only to one who holds as low an opinion of the author or authors of the *Fragment* as Prof. Zahn does.   In several respects it is out of accord with the statements of the *Fragment,* and what we know from other sources about this time.   Elsewhere the *Fragment* is straight-forward, honest, and, we may add, definite in its statements concerning the rejection or acceptance of writings.   When there is a difference of opinion in the church regarding a work, as in the case of the Apocalypse of Peter, the fact is recorded without comment or attempted compromise.   It is hardly think-able therefore that the author or authors would admit even to a secondary place a work which they believed laid claim to in-spiration falsely.   Moreover, there is no sign in the *Fragment* or in the other literature of this time of any deutero-canonical books,[88] and later when there were, only such works were in-volved as were of obscure origin.   For the authors of the *Fragment* the origin of the *Shepherd* was not doubtful.

Professor Harnack[89] thinks that the author of the *Fragment,* in agreement with the church generally, regarded the Shepherd as a genuine prophecy; that the eloquent silence of the author

---

[87] *Gesch. d. neutest. Kanons,* vol. i., pp. 342 ff., vol. ii., pp. 111-118; in Herzog, *Realencycl.* 3rd ed. vol. ix., pp. 778 f.

[88] Harnack emphasizes this, *Zeitschrift für Kirchengeschichte,* iii. p. 399.

[89] *Ibid.,* pp. 369 ff.

concerning Christian prophetic writings in their relation to the authoritative church collection is very significant; that the time was past when prophecy just because it was prophecy could be accounted canonical; other conditions were now prerequisite to reception into the sacred collection; that it was necessary therefore for the Fragmentist to create a new category for Christian prophetical books, and that he did this by making it the *duty* of Christians to read them *privately,* that is, not in the public church services. But how inconsistent that is with itself and with what Prof. Harnack says elsewhere in the same article! How can the *Fragment* be " eloquently silent concerning the relation of the prophetical writings to the authoritative church collection " and at the same time " create for them a special category "? And how does the creation of a special category differ from the erection of a deutero-canon, of which Prof. Harnack tells us there is no sign at this time in the *Fragment* or elsewhere? Or, looking at the larger question, is it possible that works which a few years before had occupied a position second to none among the Christian writings, should within one generation be relegated to at least comparative obscurity?[90] But quite apart from these considerations Harnack's interpretation is wrecked on the fact that the *Muratori Fragment* has not one word to say about Christian prophetical writings as a class being read. All other so-called Apocalypses are definitely excluded by the " only " of line 72; the *Shepherd* alone is separated from them and made the subject of special remark. There is not a shadow of justification for the statement that the contents of this remark were applicable to any other writings or class of writings.

When, therefore, we find these scholars, differing as they do in their attitude toward the history of the Canon and in their estimate and interpretation of the *Muratori Fragment,* both alike involved in difficulties and inconsistencies through the assumption that the *Shepherd* was published, and for long regarded, as an apocalypse, we come back with the more con-

[90] Harnack himself (*ibid.,* p. 405) acknowledges the "ausserordentlich raschen Verlauf des Prozesses. Cf. the criticism by Overbeck, *op. cit.,* p. 75 f.

fidence to the interpretation of this passage to which we were led by our investigation of the historical background. What the authors of *Muratori Fragment* say here is in effect: "We know in detail the history of the origin of the *Shepherd* of Hermas and can assure the church that it never was intended to be taken as an apocalypse; those who have so regarded it have been mistaken; it is a good book and ought to be read, but it is not part of the Scriptures." In other words, what the *Muratori Fragment* does, is not to take away the authority which had universally been conceded to the *Shepherd* at one time, but to check a growing tendency to regard it as canonical.

When we turn to the *Shepherd* of Hermas itself, the first thing that engages our attention is that the work is in the form of a revelation, then that there is a certain correspondence between it and the other apocalyptic and cryptic literature of the time. Divine messengers as mediators, visions as the mediums of the revelations, prayer and fasting as suitable means of preparation, the dialogue form, are common features. Moreover, some of the incidents in the *Shepherd* are strikingly similar to those in the apocalypses, for instance, the command to write down the revelations, the appearance of the saints of God in the form of sheep, the mention of angels' names, the church in the form of a woman; and finally as Hermas quotes from one of the apocalypses—the lost book of Eldad and Modat—there can be no reasonable doubt that he was acquainted with, and influenced by this sort of literature in the production of his own work.

More recently the attempt has been made to connect the *Shepherd* of Hermas with the Hermetic literature of Egypt. Reitzenstein[91] would have us believe that not only is the name

[91] Reitzenstein, *Poimandres*, pp. 11 ff., 32 f. C. Taylor (*Jour. of Philology*, xxviii., p. 37) finds "an intricate and artificial correspondence" between the *Shepherd* and the *Tabula Cebetis* which he can account for only "on the hypothesis that Hermas used the *Tabula* with necessary variations as material for his Christian allegory." Taylor has done good service in pointing out the intentional enigmatic character of the *Shepherd*, but his conclusions, both in the article referred to and in his *Hermas and the Four Gospels* are too far fetched always to command respect. See the criticism by St. John Stock in *Journ. of Phil.*, xxviii.

" Hermas " connected with Hermes Trismegistus and the title
" Shepherd " with Poimander, and the Arcadia in the *Shepherd*
with the belief that this was the home of Hermes, but also,
from a striking parallel between the fourth vision of Hermas
and the introduction to the *Poimander*, concludes that the
author of the former had the other work before him, though
in a form somewhat different from that which has come down
to us.

But if the *Shepherd* is undoubtedly similar to the apocalypses in form, it is just as certainly different from them in
every other respect.[92] The best proof of this is a perusal of
the works themselves.   The other Jewish and Christian so-
called apocalypses belong to an entirely different world of
ideas.   The intellectual background, the purpose of writing, the
attitude toward the past, the present, the future, the object
of writing, the centre of interest—in all these matters the
Shepherd goes its own way.   The eschatological interest which
dominates the other apocalypses is almost entirely lacking.   We
learn that the future world is summer to the righteous and
winter to sinners,[93] that for some there is no hope but even a
double penalty, even eternal death,[94] that the Church at last
shall be utterly pure from spot and blemish,[95] that the building of the tower has been stopped for a little to allow some to
repent,[96] that the Master is now away but may return at any
moment,[97] but beyond such general statements the writer does
not go.   Not that the church and present conditions are isolated from the past and present—the *Shepherd* knows that
God who made all things of nothing has created the heaven
and the earth, and all things for his Church.[98] But he does
not pry into these matters nor do they ever occupy the central place in his thought.   In general he is content with the
knowledge that God is back of all.   Nor of the secrecy which
is such a prominent feature of the Jewish apocalypses is there

---

[92] See Zahn, *Der Hirt des Hermas*, p. 366 ff. where earlier literature is
noted. Hilgenfeld, *Die apostolischen Väter*, p. 158. Hennecke, *Neutestamentliche Apokryphen*, pp. 16,* 208. Donaldson, *The Apostolical Fathers*,
p. 336 f. Krüger, *Hist. of early Christian Literature*, Engl. trans., p. 42.

[93] *Sim.* iv.   [94] *Sim.* ix. 18.   [95] *Ibid.*

[96] *Sim.* ix. 14.   [97] *Sim.* v. 5, ix. 5, 7.   [98] *Vis.* i. 3.

any trace. On the contrary there is hardly a paragraph, certainly not a section, which does not contain an injunction to Hermas to publish what he has heard to all the saints or a statement that the promises made to him hold good for all others as well. The *Shepherd* is the only so-called apocalypse which does not take refuge in a fictitious claim to antiquity, and put forward one of the prophets or heroes of the past as author. The writer " comes forward unabashed as the bearer of a presently given message for his contemporaries ". Some writers have thought the contrary but their evidence is not drawn from the work itself.[90] As little is there any wish to pry into the mysteries of the other world. Angels and other heavenly beings are mentioned, but only as part of the necessary machinery,[100] and occupy a small place. They are interesting to the writer only in so far as they are subservient to the building of the church. Of heavens piled upon heavens, of the entrances and the exits of the greater and lesser luminaries, of the myriads of angels and their glory, of the mysteries of the spiritual world, there is no word. And finally, of the sadness which beclouds every page of the apocalyptic literature, the sorrowful review of the past and its many sins, the sense of present tyrannical oppression, the terrible questions concerning sin and retribution, the old promises and their apparent lack of fulfilment—of all this there is no trace. The *Shepherd* is as little concerned with the past as with the future. The present is his sole concern. The tower of the church of God is abuilding, white and shapely stones are needed and

[90] Such an hypothesis was thought necessary to account for the conflicting views of the early church, viz. that the *Shepherd* was written by a brother of Pius (cir. 150), that the author was a contemporary of Clement, and that the author was identical with Paul's contemporary. The various forms of the hypothesis are tabulated by Harnack (cf. note 5).

[100] This is a noteworthy fact. There is scarcely anything mentioned in the *Shepherd* that has not an allegorical import and of which the interpretation is not given. So consistent is the author in this respect, that we must assume that those things which obviously were intended to be taken as symbols and whose explanation is obscure to us (e. g. the roots of the white mountain, *Sim.* ix. 30; the four legs of the bench, *Vis.* iii. 13) were quite intelligible to the early readers.

it is his concern to provide them; and he sets himself joy-
fully to this task.

The Jewish apocalypses regarded the future kingdom of the
Messiah as a transformed material world. The *Shepherd* regards the church of God as something drawn out from the
world both now and hereafter. He can therefore contemplate
with equanimity the horrors and signs of evil that so oppressed the Jewish and Judaistic apocalypses, and confine his
view to the beauty of the tower which shall surely be completed according to the plan of the Master.[101]   There is a
great calm over the *Shepherd*.   This is the more remarkable
as the work was produced in the midst of persecutions, when
the church might be called on at any time to suffer stripes,
imprisonments, great tribulations, crosses and wild beasts for
the Name's sake;[102] when friend might betray friend, and
even children their parents.[103]   No one can read the vision of
the beast,[104] or the parable of the willow tree,[105] or of the
stones cut out of the mountains of Arcadia,[106] without perceiving that the writer was familiar with scenes like those
pictured in the story of the martyrdom of Polycarp, of Per-
petua and Felicitas, or of those of Vienne.   The *Shepherd* of
Hermas too was written in the blood of the martyrs; and it
would not have surprised us if the author had been goaded into picturing the judgment about to fall on persecutors, or the
sufferings of the blessed martyrs, or had caught at the current
ideas of the coming antichrist, or pictured in glowing visions

---

[101] The keynote of the *Shepherd* is struck in the passage (*Vis.* i. 3):
"Behold the God of hosts, who by his invisible and mighty power and by
his great wisdom created the world, and by his glorious purpose clothed his
creation with comeliness, and his strong word fixed the heaven and
founded the earth upon the waters and by his own wisdom and providence
formed his holy church which also he blessed—behold, he removeth the
heavens and the mountains and the hills and the seas, and all things are
made level for his elect, that he may fulfil to them the promise which he
promised with great glory and rejoicing, if so be that they shall keep the
ordinances of God, which they received with great faith." I have availed
myself here and elsewhere of Dr. Harmer's excellent translation. Cf. the
description of the finished tower, *Sim.* ix. 9 f., ix. 18.

[102] *Vis.* iii. 2.   [103] *Vis.* ii. 2.   [104] *Vis.* iv.

[105] *Sim.* viii.   [106] *Sim.* ix. 19 f.

the brightness of the heavenly home. Nor would it be strange
under such oppression and with the view of families divided
against themselves—of many being eaten up with the cares of
riches[107] or preferring the life of the Gentiles,[108] if he had
allowed doubts to arise and pessimism to dominate. Compared with the over-wrought dreams of the apocalypses the
Shepherd of Hermas is a sane and wholesome work. Instead
of their fatalistic lamentation it is a song of hope; instead of
the swan-song of a despairing nation, the battle-cry of a
vigorous community,—a community so young that it is not
yet clear as to its beliefs or its rules of conduct,[109] but old
enough to have pride in its witnesses, confidence in its divine
Lord, assurance of ultimate victory and peace amid turmoil.

All this is not without bearing on the meaning and purpose
of the author. For knowing as he did these other movements
in the church, feeling as he must have the perils that threatened, and having in mind, as we know, the other apocalypses,
he has deliberately turned his back upon them, and sharply
condemned the prevalent desire to penetrate the mysteries of
the unseen future. For when Hermas after watching the
building of the tower of the church ventured to ask his
heavenly guide whether the consummation should be even
now, " She cried out with a great voice saying, ' Senseless man,
dost thou not see that the tower is still building? Whenso-
ever therefore the tower shall be finished building the end
cometh; but it shall be built up quickly. Ask me no more
questions: this reminder is sufficient for you and for the
saints and to the renewal of your spirits.' " [110]   On only one
other occasion was Hermas so sharply reproved by his guide.
It is not without meaning that the terrible words which were
for the heathen and apostates are omitted, and only those
recorded which were " suitable for us and gentle ".[111]

Of the relation of the *Shepherd* to the Hermetic literature
it is more difficult to speak. Reitzenstein's recent critics have
shown that its dependence upon the *Poimander* is at least not

---

[107] *Sim.* i., ii.   [108] *Mand.* x. 1.

[109] This is fundamental and cannot be harmonized with a theory of Jewish
origin of the *Shepherd*.

[110] *Vis.* iii. 8.   [111] *Vis.* i. 3.

yet proven, but there is a general agreement that both works, in form at least, have much in common.[112]   And indeed, Reitzenstein claims little more.   For although he points out resemblances between Hermas' conception of prophecy and that of the Hermetic literature,[113] between the lists of good and evil powers,[114] these are things common to a larger literature, and he is too well acquainted with both the *Shepherd* and the Hermetic literature to affirm more than a literary relationship.   In discussing what he considers the clearest case of borrowing he says that the appearance of the divine messenger in the form of a shepherd is a "perfectly meaningless mask" in the Christian work and that "his (Hermas') conception of the shepherd is blurred and confused, so that everything indicates that here we have to do with a foreign type which has been clumsily introduced into the Christian apocalyptic literature".[115]   And again, "I do not venture just now to say how far these heathen ideas have influenced the theology of the Christian author, that is to so say, how far the phenomenon of the shepherd was a matter of belief or only literary fiction; the writing (the *Shepherd*) is too unique for us to determine whether the lack of prominence given to Christ and of clearness in picturing him is to be explained by the assumption that his heathen counterpart has been taken over along with the literary form."   After saying that "the whole fiction of these progressive revelations and visions is quite consonant with such an assumption", he continues, "But even if we admit only a purely literary influence we have a result both peculiar and well worthy of notice. The Christian author uses heathen models quite as unconcernedly as did the author of the Christian Clementine romance or the inventor of the apocryphal Acts of an Apostle at a

---

[112] Krebs, *Der Logos als Heiland im ersten Jahrhundert*, pp. 136 ff. Bardy, *Le Pasteur d'Hermas et les livres hermétiques*, Rev. Biblique, 1911, pp. 391 ff. Lietzmann, *Theol. Literaturz.*, 1905, sp. 202. *Cf.* Cumont, *Les religions orientales dans le paganisme romain*, p. 340, n. 41; Dibellius *Zeit. f. Kirchengesch.*, 1905, pp. 169 ff. who will not go so far.

[113] *Op. cit.*, p. 203 f.   [114] *Ibid.*, p. 231 f.

[115] *Ibid.*, p. 13. But see the severe criticism by Krebs (*op. cit.*, p. 138 f.), who however has to assume that the Angel of Repentance in the *Shepherd* is identical with the youth in the previous visions.

later time. This indeed contradicts such conceptions (of Hermas) as for instance that of Zahn, who makes of him a 'man of the people' to whom literary influences could not come, and who on account of his lack of culture must have really seen his visions as he reported. I will not speak of the biased exaggeration that underlies the expression 'man of the people'. . . . It does not follow from the author's lack of culture that he was fully independent of literary models; the only immediate inference is that we have to seek these models among the lower strata of literature and as a rule must assume a more independent attitude toward them on the part of the author." [116] In these sentences Reitzenstein shows that he has a keener appreciation of the problem of the interpretation of the *Shepherd* than some theological writers. For if the *Shepherd* of Hermas is " quite unique ", if only a formal relation to the apocalyptic and Hermetic literature can be asserted and the whole intellectual and religious background is different, and this in spite of the presence of some heathen and perhaps Hermetic ideas, is it not difficult to conceive of it as the naïve record of the real or fancied experiences of a Christian prophet? Much more likely is it the conscious, and in some respects clumsy imitation that Reitzenstein supposes it to be.

That Hermas was one of the " prophets " occasionally mentioned in early Christian literature has now become so firmly fixed an opinion that it is more often asserted than examined. And yet both the " prophets " and Hermas are sufficiently described in the *Shepherd,* for us to institute a comparison, which will show that Hermas could not have regarded himself as one of this order, in spite of Harnack's contention that the appearance of " apostles and teachers " in the *Shepherd* instead of the usual " apostles, prophets and teachers " indicates the contrary.[117] In the eleventh mandate after a description of the false prophet, who with other criticisms is described as " not having the power of a divine Spirit in him ", as being " empty ", or, because he sometimes speaks truth, as one whom " the devil fills with his own spirit ", Hermas describes true prophecy. " No Spirit given by God needeth to

[116] *Op. cit.,* p. 33.
[117] *Mission and Expansion of Christianity,* 2nd ed. Engl. trans., I, p. 339f.

be asked: but such a Spirit having the power of divinity speaketh all things of itself for it proceedeth from above, from the power of the divine Spirit." The true prophet may be recognized by the following signs: "By his life test the man that hath the divine Spirit. In the first place he that hath the divine Spirit which is from above, is gentle and tranquil and humble minded, and abstaineth from all wickedness and vain desire of this present world, and holdeth himself inferior to all men, and giveth no answer to any man when inquired of, nor speaketh in solitude, for neither doth the Holy Spirit speak when a man wisheth him to speak; but then he speaketh when God wisheth him to speak. When therefore a man having the divine Spirit comes into an assembly of righteous men who have faith in a divine Spirit and this assembly of men offers up prayer to God, then the angel of the prophetic Spirit who is attached to him filleth the man, and the man, being filled with the Holy Spirit, speaketh to the multitude as the Lord willeth.[118] In this way therefore the divine Spirit shall be evident. As touching the divine Spirit therefore whatever power there is, is of the Lord." If the test of the true prophet is his life, Hermas, according to his own statements, could not have passed examination. There are indeed good things said of him. He is temperate, he abstains from every evil desire and is full of all simplicity and guilelessness,[119] but he also is over indulgent toward his family, corrupted by the sins of the world,[120] covets a place of honor higher than he is entitled to,[121] is doubtful minded in religious matters,[122] and even says weeping of himself and without contradiction " Never in my life spake I a true word but I always lived deceitfully with all men and dressed up my falsehood as truth before all men," [123] and in another place, " I know not what deeds I must do that I may live, for my sins are many and various." [124] Examples might be multiplied but it is not necessary for the Angel of Repentance himself in

---

[118] τότε ὁ ἄγγελος τοῦ προφητικοῦ πνεύματος ὁ κείμενος πρὸς αὐτὸν πληροῖ τὸν ἄνθρωπον, καὶ πληρωθεὶς ὁ ἄνθρωπος τῷ πνεύματι τῷ ἁγίῳ λαλεῖ εἰς τὸ πλῆθος καθὼς ὁ κύριος βούλεται.

[119] *Vis.* i. 2. [120] *Vis.* i. 3. [121] *Vis.* iii. 1.

[122] *Vis.* iv. 1. [123] *Mand.* iii. [124] *Mand.* iv. 2.

reminding him that " there are others before thee and better than thou art unto whom these visions ought to have been revealed " [125] informs us that Hermas did not measure up to the standard required of a " prophet ".

But even though Hermas were able to stand the moral test, or be regarded as an exception, as the words of the Angel of Repentance might imply, the manner in which he received the revelations does not accord with his description of prophecy. According to the passages we have quoted the prophet is filled with the prophetic spirit, he does not speak when he will or where he will but only at the instance of the divine spirit that descends upon him *ab extra,* and the words that he speaks are wholly divine. That is to say Hermas conceives of a prophet as a mere tool in the hands of the prophetic spirit and as contributing nothing of his own but the voice. Such is not the case with Hermas. The " prophetic spirit " is never mentioned as the source of his revelations. The divine messengers do not speak through him but to him. He fails to comprehend, is reproved for his curiosity, argues with his guide, and always maintains his own personality and the human point of view. He is throughout not a passive instrument but an active and fallible reporter. " Canst thou carry a report of these things to the elect of God ? " asks the Church appearing as an old woman. " Lady, I say to her, I cannot retain as much in my memory but give me the book and I shall transcribe it." [126]   The angel of Repentence commands him " to write down the commandments and parables . . . . that thou mayest read them off-hand, and mayest be able to keep them ".[127]   And the possibility of neglect of duty is implied in the repeated injunction " Continue in this ministry and complete it unto the end ".[128]   " Quit you like a man in this ministry, declare to every man the mighty works of the Lord and thou shalt have favor in this ministry." [129]   Such words would be inappropriate to the prophets the Angel describes.[130]   We are not surprised therefore that Hermas never

[125] *Vis.* iii. 4.   [126] *Vis.* ii. 1.   [127] *Vis.* v.
[128] *Sim.* x. 2.   [129] *Sim.* x. 4.
[130] The *Shepherd's* conception of a prophet as one completely dominated by the divine Spirit, suggests a simpler reason for the omission of the

calls himself, nor does any other early writer give him the title of prophet. Neither is his work called a prophecy, nor after the name of the reputed author as was customary with prophecies and apocalypses but after the chief mediator of the revelations, the *Shepherd.* Clement of Alexandria, though he occasionally when quoting loosely, uses *Shepherd* as the title of the book,[131] generally nicely distinguishes by his method of citation those parts which were revealed by the *Shepherd,* the Angel of Repentance[132] from the revelations given by others whom he calls " the power that spoke to Hermas ",[133] or " the power that appeared to Hermas in the vision ",[134] or " the power that appeared to Hermas in the form of the Church ".[135] We must conclude that Hermas was not the spirit-filled passive being such as is meant by " prophet ", and, if the *Shepherd's* statements are to be taken literally, had the gift of seeing visions, which Irenaeus also distinguishes from that of prophecy.[136]

This latter hypothesis necessitates that the statements of the *Shepherd* concerning Hermas' life and character be true, and to test it we must examine them with a view to determining their consistency and probability. Of the outward circumstances of his life we learn very little. The first *Vision* be-

"prophets" from their usual place between "apostles" and "teachers" than that proposed by Prof. Harnack. The apostles and teachers, as well as others, are introduced by the *Shepherd* only for commendation or blame, —in order to relate their rewards or punishments (*Vis.* iii. 5; *Sim.* ix. 15, 16, 25). But the prophet *qua* prophet was irresponsible and consequently above praise or blame. In omitting them the author is simply obeying the injunction of the *Didache* (chap. x. f.) " the prophet that speaketh in the Spirit is not to be tried or judged."

[131] *Strom.* ii, 12, 55 (13, 56); iv, 9, 74.

[132] *Strom.* i, 17, 85; cf. vi. 6, 46; ii, 9, 43.

[133] *Strom.* i, 29, 181.   [134] *Strom.* ii, 1, 3.

[135] *Strom.* vi, 15, 131. With Origen this is reversed. He generally cites the book by its title (ποιμήν), only rarely speaking of the Angel of Repentance as the source of the revelation, e. g. *De princip.* i, 3, 3; *In Joann,* i, 1 comm. t. I, 18. The references are from Harnack, *Gesch. d. altchr. Lit.* I, i, pp. 53 f.

[136] *Haer,* ii. 32, 4; v, 6, 1. Cf. Euseb. *Hist. Eccl.* v, 7. Hermas uses the terms vision (ὅρασις) and revelation (ἀποκάλυψις) of his experiences, e. g. *Vis.* iii, 10.

gins: " He who reared me sold me to a certain Rhoda in
Rome. After many years I met her again and began to love
her as a sister. After a certain time I saw her bathing in the
river Tiber and I gave her my hand and led her out of the
river. So, seeing her beauty, I reasoned in my heart, saying,
' Happy were I if I had such an one to wife, both in beauty
and in character ' ". Later in the same vision we gather that
he already has a wife and grown children, who are fearfully
corrupt and through whose sins Hermas has lost his possessions. The second *Vision,* which is said to have occurred a
year after the first, mentions the children as being still evil,
this time as having betrayed their parents, and still further added to their sins wanton deeds and reckless wickedness. Of
his wife too it is added that she does " not refrain from using
her tongue, wherewith she doeth evil ". From the third *Vision*
we learn that a little distance from the city he had a field in
which he cultivated grain,[137] and also that " when thou (Hermas) hadst riches thou wast useless but now thou art useful
and profitable unto life ".[138] Several later passages imply that
he was engaged in business,[139] and on one occasion he is addressed as " thou who hast fields and dwellings and many other
possessions ".[140] Toward the end we are informed that his
family repented and was reunited.[141] There is nothing necessarily inconsistent about these statements. Harnack indeed
doubts the historicity of the first *Vision* on chronological
grounds,[142] Donaldson points out the improbability of anyone,
however naïve, speaking of his wife and children as Hermas
does,[143] and the statement that Hermas had fields, dwellings
and other possessions is certainly surprising, coming where it
does, and especially as it is coupled with a warning against
seeking wealth. Still it is quite possible to weave the incidents, as Zahn has done,[144] into a self-consistent and touching

---

[137] χονδρίζεις. Cf. Zahn, *Der Hirt. des Hermas,* p. 83 f.

[138] The loss of wealth is mentioned also in *Vis.* i, 3, if we accept Zahn's
interpretation of ἀπό as a privative, *op. cit.,* p. 490 f.

[139] *Vis.* ii, 3; *Mand.* iii; x; *Sim.* iv.

[140] *Sim.* i.   [141] *Sim.* vii.

[142] *Patr. Apost. Op.,* not. ad loc.   [143] *Apostolical Fathers,* p. 327.

[144] *Op. cit.,* pp. 70 ff. But he omits the reference to wealth in *Sim.* i.

picture of wealth, early sins, persecution, loss of possessions, repentance and restoration.

We turn to Hermas' intellectual and moral qualities. We learn that he was habitually patient, good-tempered and always smiling,[145] that he abstained from every evil desire and was full of all simplicity and great guilelessness,[146] that he is saved by his simplicity, great continence and guilelessness,[147] that he is useful and profitable unto life since he has lost his wealth,[148] and has great zeal for doing good.[149] That is one side. On the other, we have the statement that he was an over-indulgent and careless husband and father,[150] that his double-mindedness made him of no understanding, and his heart was not set on the Lord,[151] that his spirit was aged and already decayed and had no power by reason of his infirmities and acts of double-mindedness.[152] Indeed, double-mindedness, one of the worst of faults, is frequently ascribed to him.[153] He says of himself with tears, " Never in my life spake I a true word, but I always lived deceitfully with all men and dressed up my falsehood as truth before all men." [154] He is ignorant concerning repentance because his heart was made dense by his former deeds.[155] He is included among those who " have never investigated concerning the truth, nor inquired concerning the Deity, but have merely believed and have been mixed up in business affairs, and riches and heathen friendships, and many other affairs of this world ".[156] He will not cleanse his heart and serve God, and has to be warned lest haply the time be fulfilled and he be found in his foolishness.[157] And yet in spite of all this he is commended for having done nothing out of order since the Angel of Repentance came to him.[158]

All attempts to refer Hermas' sins to an earlier period[159] in his life must fail. In most cases at least the sins referred to are stated to be present ones, as is shown by his tears, his

---

[145] *Vis.* i, 2.   [146] *Ibid.*   [147] *Vis.* ii, 2; iii. 1.
[148] *Vis.* iii, 6.   [149] *Sim.* v, 3.   [150] *Vis.* i, 3; ii, 2.
[151] *Vis.* iii, 10.   [152] *Vis.* iii, 11.
[153] *Vis,* iv, 1; vi, 1; *Mand.* ix; xii, 3 f.
[154] *Mand.* iii.   [155] *Mand.* iv, 2.   [156] *Mand.* x, 1.
[157] *Sim.* vi, 5.   [158] *Sim.* x, 2.   [159] As Zahn does.

ignorance of the sinfulness of certain actions, his prayers for forgiveness, and his joy at the possibility of repentance.[160] The simple fact is that the statements regarding Hermas' moral character are difficult if not impossible of union in a self-consistent picture. Moreover, what are we to think of a Christian who has penetrated so far into the principles of Christian morality that he can put nice questions concerning the treatment of an adulterous wife, or the rightfulness of second marriage,[161] or the possibility of repentance after baptism,[162] and yet is not aware that evil thoughts are sinful,[163] thinks the Church appearing in the form of a woman is the Sybil,[164] is unaware that business lies are wrong;[165] and can we conceive of a Christian, however low his station, who did not know that the Church was built upon the Son of God,[166] or was ignorant of what the martyrs had suffered?[167]   In the light of such inconsistencies it is easier to regard Hermas as a composite and fictitious figure, which could and did vary to suit the requirements of the author, who at times must address even the very ignorant. Only such an assumption will explain Hermas' repeated estimate of himself: " I am absolutely unable to comprehend anything at all." [168]

· But even though we were to admit the possibility of these mutually exclusive elements existing in one person, and should accept the resultant picture of a " man of the people " somewhat as Zahn has so sympathetically drawn it, we should only involve ourselves in a greater difficulty. For whether we agree with this same writer in saying that one of such little culture was incapable of producing a romance, we can most decidedly affirm that such a Hermas as is pictured in the *Shepherd* was not the author of the work that bears his name. This is a matter so obvious that it is surprising it has not been more clearly perceived. For, if Hermas be ignorant it is another than he that informs his ignorance, that is to say that provides the major portion of the *Shepherd*. In other words, either Hermas as author gives answers to his own

---

[160] E. g. *Vis.* i, 1 f.; *Mand.* iii; iv, 2 f.

[161] *Mand.* iv, 1.   [162] *Mand.* iv, 3.   [163] *Vis.* i, 1 f.

[164] *Vis.* ii, 4.   [165] *Mand.* iii.   [166] *Sim.* ix, 4.

[167] *Vis.* iii, 2.   [168] *Mand.* iv, 2; *Sim.* ix, 14.

questions, and corrects his own faults, or else he was the recipient of real external revelations. Wake, Thiersch, and others who hold to the reality of these revelations, were consistent. Prof. Zahn too feels the logical necessity of making Hermas a man of the people, and regards them as real, though refusing to estimate their present value. But there is no excuse for those who describe Hermas as he describes himself and still make him the author of the *Shepherd*. The author of the *Shepherd*, whether he wrote in ecstasy or with deliberation, was somehow or other competent both to picture his shortcomings and correct them. Von Dobschütz, although dominated by the current theory of Hermas' prophecy, feels the necessity of accounting for the didactic portion of the work in some tangible way when he says: " All this is said to Hermas by the Church. To be sure she appears to the prophet as a heavenly figure. But we do not err when we transfer the vision to earth." [169] Why not then boldly transfer it, as our evidence requires, and recognize in Hermas not the naïve prophet, not the unconscious type of the Roman Christian of his day, not the " strange, solitary, weak, ignorant, ecstatic, inspired perhaps but not inspiring " teacher, who " if he was really brother to a bishop must have been a trial to his relative ",[170] but the intentional, variable type, drawn indeed from life, but from more lives than one, the result of the experience of the author, who, as the apparently reliable *Muratori Fragment* reports, was brother to Bishop Pius. A book that imposed upon Clement and Origen and was regarded as most useful by Athanasius,[171] was not written by a fool, however ecstatic.

The silly, well-meaning Hermas in the *Shepherd*, with his hopes and fears, his delight in all he sees and hears, his changing moods of doubt and confidence, and especially his ques-

---

[169] *Christian Life in the Primitive Church,* Engl. trans. p. 315. Leipoldt, (*op. cit.,* p. 33 n. 2) says: " Die Apokalyptik als literarische Form zu benutzen, dazu was Hermas zu ungeschickt." Of course he was—and too ignorant to instruct himself or others. He says so himself. Then who did it?

[170] Bigg, *Origins of Christianity,* p. 73.

[171] *De incarn. verb. Dei,* iii, 1.

tions, frequently stupid, as the Angel tells him, very often
quite unnecessary and sometimes to our mind (and we doubt
not to the minds of the early Christians) amusing in their
naïveté, is merely a foil for the writer. Through him he
addresses directly any and every member of the community.
For the Hermas so pictured is guilty, or in danger of falling
into practically every venial sin mentioned in the book, evil
thoughts, morbid introspection, a wrong estimate of fasting,
curiosity, doubt, business lies, heathen friendships, pride, sadness, anger, the love of wealth, lack of faith, seeking revelations, double-mindedness, unchastity, indulging his wife and
children. This is the reason that he appears suddenly in the
middle of the work as possessed of lands, dwellings and other
possessions, and it is probably because he is here so plainly a
type that Zahn has passed over this passage in picturing his
life and character. By this device, too, the author has a simple
means of breaking up the otherwise wearisome (or more
wearisome) mandates and similitudes, and of introducing ex-
positions of his visions. In his Pilgrim's Progress, John Bunyan on only one occasion steps over the frame of the picture,
namely when he asks Hope concerning the Slough of Despond.
The incident undoubtedly mars the picture, and we feel that he
would have done better to allow the explanation to be given
to someone within the picture as he invariably does elsewhere.
The author of the *Shepherd* has adopted as his usual method
that which was exceptional with Bunyan, but with the same
results, save that he partly defeated his own purpose, for his
fiction, like so many others, was mistaken by some for literal
truth. Such is the most natural conclusion to draw from what
we have seen of the history and contents of the *Shepherd* and
there are still other indications that it is the right one.

Contrary to the manner of Apocalyptic books, the *Shepherd*
despises secrecy. Its teachings are to be flung broadcast over
the earth. What is said to Hermas is intended for all, and
there is scarcely a paragraph in which he is not charged with
the duty of publishing it to his fellow-Christians either orally
or by writing. But this is not all. Not infrequently the
writer (through the Angel) addresses the many directly. The

first instance of this[172] is introduced by a command to Hermas to bear the message to the leaders and others, but such direction is so frequently omitted and the singular and plural alternate without reason or excuse, that the most natural explanation is that the writer was not always true to his fiction of one interlocutor but unconsciously addressed the many whom he really had in mind.[173] One who reads these passages with attention to the alternation of the singular and plural cannot but mark how the person of Hermas is dimmed and merged in the crowd back of him. One example must suffice here. " ' Sir, this one thing alone *I* ask concerning the three forms of the aged woman, that a complete revelation may be vouchsafed to *me* '. He saith to *me* in answer, ' How long are *ye* without understanding? It is *your* double-mindedness that maketh *you* of no understanding, and because *your* heart is not set towards the Lord.' I answered and said unto him again, ' From thee, Sir, *we* shall learn the matters more accurately.' ' Listen ', saith he, ' concerning the three forms of which *thou* inquirest. In the first vision wherefore did she appear to *thee* an aged woman and seated on a chair? Because *your* spirit was aged, and already decayed, and had no power, by reason of *your* infirmities and acts of double-mindedness. For as aged people, having no longer hope of renewing their youth, expect nothing else but to fall asleep, so *ye* also, being weakened with the affairs of this world, gave *yourselves* over to repining and cast not *your* cares on the Lord ; but *your* spirit was broken, and *ye* were aged by *your* sorrows. . . .   But in the second vision *thou* sawest her standing and with her countenance more youthful and more gladsome than before, but her flesh and her hair aged. . . .   For he (the Lord) had compassion on *you* and renewed *your* spirits and *ye* laid aside *your* maladies. . . .   And therefore he showed *you* the building of the tower. . . .   But in the third vision *thou* sawest her younger and fair and gladsome and her form fair. . . .   So *ye* have received a renewal of *your* spirits by seeing these good things. And whereas *thou* sawest her

[172] *Vis.* ii, 2.

[173] E. g. *Vis.* ii, 6; iii, 10; iii, 11; *Sim.* i; *Sim.* vi, 1; vii; ix, 24, 28, 29, 31, 32, 33; x, 1, 4; et. al.

seated upon a couch, the position is a firm one.' " [174]   The real mind of the writer is expressed in the words of the Angel of Repentance: " All these things which are written above, I, the Shepherd, the Angel of Repentance, have declared and spoken to the servants of God."[175]   These servants of God with their virtue and weakness, their steadfastness and doubt, their simplicity and double-mindedness, their hope and their fear, are all to be found within the figure of Hermas.

Some striking omissions in the *Shepherd* have been frequently pointed out, and occasionally used to draw unwarranted conclusions regarding the church of the time.   There is not a single quotation from the Old or the New Testament. There is no direct reference to any of the events of our Lord's life, or to any of his teachings.   The words " Jesus ", " Christ ", " Jew ", " Israel ", " Christian ", " Gospel ", " baptism ", " Eucharist ", " resurrection ", are all absent, and the word " grace " though found is not used in the Christian sense.[176] Had these omissions been fewer or less striking, it might be possible to refer them to accident or ignorance, but the matter is important enough to demand an explanation which will account for them all.   Is it possible to conceive of a Christian work, written as late as the middle of the second century, intended, not for outsiders, but for the Christians themselves, from which all these words—some of them catch-words of universal familiarity—are excluded?   To say that the author was ignorant of them would be absurd.   To say he was not interested in them is scarcely less tenable.   In most cases the idea is present and only the familiar designation absent.   There can be no doubt of his knowledge both of the Old Testament and

---

[174] *Vis.* iii, 10 f.   [175] *Sim.* ix, 33.

[176] To say that the absence of quotations from the New Testament proves that this was not yet on a par with the Old (e. g. Holtzmann, *Einleitung in d. NT.* p. 110) is merely frivolous.   To explain the absence of any citation (except that from the book of Eldad and Modat) on the theory that revelation needs no other authority to support it (Weinel in Hennecke, *Neutest. Apokr.*, pp. 228 f.) or that Hermas was commanded to tell what he had seen not what he had read (Zahn, *Hirt. d. Hermas*, p. p. 393), might suffice if this were the only striking omission.   And yet may not the *Shepherd* have appealed to Scripture quite as really by suggestion (see even Holtzmann's view, note 178) as if he had formally cited it?

of part of the New.[177] The idea of grace is found in his frequent references to the mercy of God in forgiving sins, and sending repentance. Jesus Christ moves all through the work under the title of " Son of God ". Baptism appears frequently, only without the name. We are forced to the conclusion that these omissions were deliberate and intentional—a thing practically impossible if the *Shepherd* be the naïve record of the experience of a vacillating though devout prophet, but which finds a simple and natural explanation if it is an allegory. For an allegory is of the same nature as a puzzle and has the same sort of charm. The truth is concealed behind unusual words and images, and the reader has the same satisfaction in searching for it, as in solving a rebus or an acrostic. It appeals to one of the strongest of human passions—curiosity, and it has the merit of presenting truth in a new and interesting guise. Of course the puzzle may be easy or difficult to solve, the veil of the allegory easy to lift or almost impenetrable. This will depend upon the author and his estimate of his readers. John Bunyan frequently quotes the Bible verbatim. The *Shepherd* never does, but he frequently suggests passages in such a manner that we wonder how he escaped doing so.[178] But whether easy of solution or heavily veiled, an allegory to be an allegory must make some pretense of being an enigma, and this we think is the most natural explanation of these remarkable omissions.

It is not our purpose here to discuss the merits of the *Shepherd* either as a Christian book of instruction or as an allegory. The part it played in the early church is sufficient proof that the author understood his contemporaries. What we do wish to point out afresh is that in interpreting it we must begin, not with the exceedingly human Hermas who lives so delightfully on every page, but with the author who could delineate such a character, and use it in correcting the

---

[177] See *The New Testament in the Apostolic Fathers*, pp. 105 ff. Zahn, *op. cit.*, pp. 391 ff. and notes to critical editions.

[178] " Wenn er fast ermüdende Umschreibungen von Jac. i, 6-8 (*Mand.* ix) und Jac. iv, 7-12 (*Mand.* xii, 2-6) gibt, ohne dass es ihm in den Sinn käme die betreffenden Stellen selbst zu citeren." Holtzmann, *Einl. in d. NT.* p. 110.

faults and failings of his own times. The *Shepherd* was
written from above down, and not the reverse.[179]   This is
supported by the testimony of the *Muratori Fragment* as to
its authorship, and by the fact—fact at least so far as we can
judge—that it was always regarded by the Roman church as
suitable for edification. On the other hand, we must remember its undoubted resemblance to the popular pseudo-apocalyp-
ses of the time, and its possible relation to the Hermetic literature. This coupled with its lack of prominence in the literature of the Roman church for some decades after its publication suggests that it was intended for the lower classes. In
it they received more wholesome teaching in the style of the
popular religious literature of the day. It is in the form of
a revelation but it roundly condemns those that seek revelations.[180]   It is an imitation of apocalypses, but it cries out in
horror at anyone wishing to pierce the mystery to whose solution the other apocalypses were devoted.[181]   It reminds us
of the Hermetic literature but it prohibits all attempts to understand the mysteries which called this class of literature into
being.[182]   This consideration immediately brings into prominence the word-bandying that forms no inconsiderable portion
of the work, and the many accusations of foolishness and
stupidity take on real meaning. Rome already was requiring
implicit obedience of her humbler members. The Hermas
that wishes to solve mysteries, asks questions, has his opinions,
dares to dispute with his guide, is cried down, snubbed and
held up to ridicule. When he timorously doubted his ability to
keep the commandments the Church could swell with anger and
forbid such impious thoughts,[183] when he was troubled over
his unknown sin of evil desire, she could smile—it was a little
sin—and assure him that God was not angry with him for
that.[184]   Just so we treat little children.

We may venture now to state positively what seems to be
the theory of the origin and early fortunes of the *Shepherd*

---

[179] This is the unexpressed assumption back of Prof. Lake's article in the
Harvard Theological Review, Jan. 1911, pp. 25 ff.

[180] *Vis.* iii, 3, 10, 13; *Sim.* v, 4 f.

[181] *Vis.* iii, 8.

[182] *Sim.* ix, 1 f.

[183] *Mand.* xii, 3 f.

[184] *Vis.* i, 1 ff.

most consonant with the available evidence. It was written by a certain Hermas, who was the brother of Pius, bishop of Rome, and so presumably close to the leaders of the church. In the words of the Church and the Shepherd and the other heavenly messengers we are to see the official teaching of the church of Rome. It was intended chiefly for the edification of the lower class of church members, who are typified in the figure of Hermas within the story. It is in the form of a revelation in order to compete with the popular apocalyptic and cryptic literature of the time, to the teachings and attitude of which it is opposed. There is no evidence that the author intended it to be taken for revelation, nor that the Roman church did so mistake it. Its immediate popularity is indubitable for it soon was known far beyond the place of its origin. In the West it circulated chiefly among the common people, for it appears very rarely in the better literature, and in Africa anyway was regarded with superstitious reverence by the masses, who were sharply rebuked by their leader. The correspondence of the author's name with that of a contemporary of St. Paul, and the literary form of the work, easily suggested an erroneous view of its origin and nature. In Alexandria even the church leaders accepted it as a genuine revelation, one of them definitely ascribing it to St. Paul's friend. The real usefulness of the book was imperilled by such extravagant claims, and the Roman authorities, as represented in the *Muratori Fragment,* speaking out of full knowledge of the matter, attempted to restore it to its original place and function in the church.

JESUS AND PAUL

John Gresham Machen

Importance of the problem.—It is better to begin the discussion with Paul, because Paul is more easily known than Jesus, and because there is direct testimony as to Paul's relation to Jesus.—The original apostles regarded Paul as an innovator neither with respect to freedom from the law nor with respect to the person of Christ.—Paul does not deny dependence on tradition for the facts of the life of Jesus.—The paucity of references in the epistles to words and deeds of Jesus has been exaggerated and misinterpreted.—Both by his contemporaries, therefore, and by Paul himself, Paul is represented as a true disciple of Jesus.—This conclusion is not overthrown by comparison with the Gospels.—Such comparison is valuable, because the exalted Christology of the Gospels is not due to Pauline influence.—The formation of this Christology is inexplicable upon naturalistic principles.—The harmony between Jesus and Paul extends even to what is regarded by modern criticism as characteristic of Jesus—for example, the fatherhood of God, and love as the fulfilling of the law.—But the essence of Paulinism is communion with the risen Christ, not imitation of the earthly Jesus.—Paul was a disciple of Jesus only if Jesus was a supernatural person.

JESUS AND PAUL[1]

The Apostle Paul is the greatest teacher of the Christian
Church. True, he has not always been fully understood. The
legalism that he combatted during his lifetime soon established
itself among his converts, and finally celebrated a triumph in
the formation of the Catholic Church. The keen edge of his
dialectic was soon blunted. But however his ideas may have
been injured in transmission, they were never altogether destroyed. Much was forgotten; but what remained was the
life of the Church. And the great revivals were revivals of
Paulinism. Protestantism—in its practical piety as well as
in its theology—was simply a rediscovery of Paul.

Yet Paul has never been accepted for his own sake. Men
have never come to him for an independent solution of the
riddle of the universe. Simply as a religious philosopher,
he is unsatisfactory; for his philosophy is rooted in one definite
fact. He has been listened to not as a philosopher, but as a
witness—a witness to Jesus Christ. His teaching has been
accepted only on one condition—that he speak as a faithful
disciple of Jesus of Nazareth.

The question of the relation between Jesus and Paul is therefore absolutely fundamental. Paul has always been regarded
as the greatest disciple of Jesus. If so, well and good. The
Christian Church may then go forward as it has done be-

[1] The following paper is merely a sketch. It raises many questions which
it does not answer. It attempts no exposition of recent discussion. Suggestions have been received from many sources, but it is hoped that a
general acknowledgment of indebtedness will render a series of footnotes
unnecessary. The following list of monographs, pamphlets and articles
is far from exhaustive:—Paret, Paulus und Jesus, in *Jahrbücher für
deutsche Theologie*, iii (1859), pp. 1-85; Wendt, Die Lehre des Paulus
verglichen mit der Lehre Jesu, in *Zeitschrift für Theologie und Kirche*,
iii (1894), pp. 1-78; Hilgenfeld, Jesus und Paulus, in *Zeitschrift für wissen-*

fore. But in recent years there is a tendency to dissociate Paul from Jesus. A recent historian has entitled Paul "the second founder of Christianity". If that be correct, then Christianity is facing the greatest crisis in its history. For—let us not deceive ourselves—if Paul is independent of Jesus, he can no longer be a teacher of the Church. Christianity is founded upon Christ and only Christ. Paulinism has never been accepted upon any other supposition than that it reproduces the mind of Christ. If that supposition is incorrect—if Paulinism is derived not from Jesus Christ, but from other sources—then it must be uprooted from the life of the Church. But that is more than reform—it is revolution. Compared with that upheaval, the reformation of the sixteenth century is as nothing.

schaftliche Theologie, xxxvii (1894), pp. 481-541; Feine, Jesus Christus und Paulus, 1902; Brückner, Die Entstehung der paulinischen Christologie, 1903, Zum Thema Jesus und Paulus, in Zeitschrift für die neutestamentliche Wissenschaft, vii (1906), pp. 112-119, Der Apostel Paulus als Zeuge wider das Christusbild der Evangelien, in Protestantische Monatshefte, x (1906), pp. 352-364; Wrede, Paulus, 1905; Vischer, Jesus und Paulus, in Theologische Rundschau, viii (1905), pp. 129-143, 173-188; Kölbing, Die geistige Einwirkung der Person Jesu auf Paulus, 1906; Kaftan, Jesus und Paulus, 1906; Ihmels, Jesus und Paulus, in Neue kirchliche Zeitschrift, xvii (1906), pp. 452-516; Pfleiderer, Der moderne Jesuskultus, in Protestantische Monatshefte, x (1906), pp. 169-182; Johnson, Was Paul the Founder of Christianity?, in Princeton Theological Review, v (1907), pp. 398-422; Jülicher, Paulus und Jesus, 1907; Meyer, Wer hat das Christentum begründet, Jesus oder Paulus?, 1907; Sanday, art. "Paul", in Hastings' Dictionary of Christ and the Gospels, ii (1908), Appendix, pp. 886-892; Dunkmann, "Bedeutet die Paulinische Predigt vom Kreuz eine Veränderung des einfachen Evangeliums Jesu?", in Evangelische Kirchen-Zeitung, 82 (1908), columns 61-67, 81-86, 101-104, 121-127; W. Morgan, The Jesus-Paul Controversy, in Expository Times, xx (1908-1909), pp. 9-12, 55-58; Weiss, Paulus und Jesus, 1909; Olschewski, Die Wurzeln der paulinischen Christologie, 1909; G. Milligan, Paulinism and the Religion of Jesus, in Expositor, 1909 (i), pp. 534-546; Scott, Jesus and Paul, in Cambridge Biblical Essays, 1909; Holtzmann, Zum Thema "Jesus und Paulus", in Protestantische Monatshefte, iv (1900), pp. 463-468, xi (1907), pp. 313-323, Paulus als Zeuge wider die Christusmythe von Arthur Drews, in Christliche Welt, xxiv (1910), columns 151-160. Compare also Warfield, The "Two Natures" and Recent Christological Speculation, in American Journal of Theology, xv (1911), pp. 337-361, 546-568.

At first sight, the danger appears to be trifling. The voices that would separate Paul from Jesus have been drowned by a chorus of protest. In making Paul and not Jesus the true founder of Christianity, Wrede is as little representative of the main trend of modern investigation as he is when he eliminates the Messianic element from the consciousness of Jesus. Measured by the direct assent which he has received, Wrede is a negligeable quantity. But that is but a poor measure of his importance. The true significance of Wrede's " Paul " is that it has merely made explicit what was implicit before. The entire modern reconstruction of primitive Christianity leads logically to Wrede's startling pronouncement. Modern liberalism has produced a Jesus who has really but little in common with Paul. Wrede has but drawn the conclusion. Paul was no disciple of the liberal Jesus. Wrede has merely had the courage to say so.

This essential harmony between Wrede and his opponents appears even in some of the criticisms to which he has been subjected. No doubt these criticisms are salutary. They fill out omissions, and correct exaggerations. But they obscure the issue. In general, their refutation of Wrede amounts to little more than this—Paul's theology is abandoned, in order to save his religion. His theology, it is admitted, was derived from extra-Christian sources; but in his practical piety he was a true disciple of Jesus. Such a distinction is thoroughly vicious; it is contradicted in no uncertain tones by the Pauline Epistles. Where is it that the current of Paul's religious experience becomes overpowering, so that even after the lapse of centuries, even through the dull medium of the printed page, it sweeps the heart of the sympathetic reader on with it in a mighty flood? It is not in the ethical admonitions. It is not in the discussions of the practical problems of the Christian life. It is not even in the inspired encomium of Christian love. But it is in the great *theological* passages of the epistles—the second chapter of Galatians, the fifth chapter of Second Corinthians, the fifth to the eighth chapters of Romans. In these passages, the religious experience and the theology of Paul are blended in a union which no critical analysis can dissolve. Furthermore, if it is impossi-

ble to separate Pauline piety and Pauline theology in the life
of Paul himself, it is just as impossible to separate them in
the life of the Church of to-day. Thus far, at least, all attempts at accomplishing it have resulted in failure. Liberal
Christianity has sometimes tried to reproduce Paul's religion
apart from his theology. But thus far it has produced nothing which in the remotest degree resembles the model.

In determining whether Paul was a disciple of Jesus, the
whole Paul must be kept in view—not the theology apart from
the warm religious life that pulses through it, and not the
religious emotion apart from its basis in theology. Theology
apart from religion, or religion apart from theology—either
is an empty abstraction. The religion and the theology of
Paul stand or fall together. If one is derived from Jesus,
probably the other is also.

In discussing the relation between Jesus and Paul, it is
better to begin with Paul. For, in the first place, Paul is more
easily known than Jesus. That will be admitted on all sides.
Jesus wrote nothing; all the extant records of his words are
the reports of others. The trustworthiness of the records of
his life is at present a matter of dispute. Yet even if the most
favorable estimate of the Gospel narratives be adopted, Jesus
remains far more incomprehensible than Paul. Indeed it is
just when the Gospel picture is accepted in its entirety that
the sense of mystery in the presence of Jesus becomes most
overpowering.

For the life of Paul, on the other hand, the historian is in
possession of sources which are not only trustworthy, but universally admitted to be trustworthy. At least seven of the
Pauline Epistles—1 Thessalonians, Galatians, 1 and 2 Corinthians, Romans, Philippians, and Philemon—are now assigned
by all except a few extremists to Paul himself; and the critical
doubts with regard to three of the others are gradually being
dispelled. In general, the disputed epistles are not of fundamental importance for determining the relation of Paul to
Jesus. Colossians, perhaps, forms the only exception, and it is
just Colossians that is most commonly accepted as Pauline. All
the characteristic features of Paul's thinking appear within the
homologoumena; and it is the characteristic features alone

which can determine the general question whether Paul was a disciple of Jesus.

With regard to the book of Acts as a source for the study of Paul, there is more difference of opinion; and the difference is of more importance for the question now in hand. But three remarks can be made. In the first place, those sections of Acts where the first person plural is used are universally regarded as the work of an eye-witness. In the second place, the framework—the account of external events in the life of Paul—is for the most part accepted. In the third place, the tendency of recent criticism is decidedly towards a higher estimate of the general representation of Paul. The conciliatory attitude toward the Jews, which the book of Acts attributes to Paul, is no longer regarded as due altogether to an " irenic " purpose on the part of the historian.

The sources for the life of Paul are insufficient, indeed, for a complete biography. For the period up to the conversion, the extant information is of the most general kind, and after the conversion some fifteen years elapse before anything like a connected narrative can be constructed. Even from the years of the so-called missionary journeys, only a bare summary has been preserved, with vivid, detailed narratives only here and there. Finally, the close of Paul's life is shrouded in obscurity. But what the sources lack in quantity they make up in quality. Paul was gifted with a remarkable power of self-revelation, which has been exercised in his epistles to the fullest extent. Free from self-centred vanity, without the slightest indelicacy, without a touch of morbid introspection, he has yet revealed the very secrets of his heart. Not only the exquisite delicacy of feeling, the fine play of affection, the consecrated anger, the keen practical judgment are open before us, but also the deepest springs of the tremendous religious experience. The Pauline Epistles make Paul one of the best-known men of history. We might be able to account, in an external way, for every day and hour of his life, and yet not know him half so well.

As thus revealed, Paul is comprehensible. With all his greatness, almost immeasurably exalted as he is above the generality of mankind, he yet possesses nothing which any man might not conceivably possess. Starting from the common misery of sin, he attained to a peace with God, which, again, has been shared by humble Christians of all ages. His commission as apostle exceeds in dignity and importance that of other disciples of Christ, but does not free him from human limitations. It was Christ's strength which was made perfect in weakness. In all essential features, the religious experience of Paul may be imitated by every Christian. Jesus, on the other hand, is full of mystery. Of course the mystery may be ignored. It is ignored by Wrede, when he denies to Jesus the consciousness of his Messiahship. But even by the most thorough-going modern naturalism, that is felt to be a desperate measure. The Messianic consciousness is rooted too deep in the sources ever to be removed by historical criticism. That Jesus lived at all is hardly more certain than that he thought himself to be the Messiah. But the Messianic consciousness of Jesus is a profound mystery. It would be no mystery if Jesus were an ordinary fanatic or unbalanced visionary. Among the many false Messiahs who championed their claims in the first century, there may well have been some who deceived themselves as well as others. But Jesus was no ordinary fanatic—no megalomaniac. On the contrary, he is the moral ideal of the race. His calmness, unselfishness, and strength have produced an impression which the lapse of time has done nothing to obliterate. It was such a man who supposed himself to be the Son of Man who was to come with the clouds of heaven! Considered in the light of the character of Jesus, the Messianic consciousness of Jesus is the profoundest of problems. It is true, the problem can be solved. It can be solved by supposing that Jesus' own estimate of his person was true—by recognizing in Jesus a supernatural person. But the acceptance of the supernatural is not easy. For the modern mind it involves nothing short of a Copernican revolution. And until that step is taken, the person of Jesus cannot be understood. Paul, on the other hand, is more easily comprehended. To a certain extent, his religious experience can be understood, at least in an external way, even by one who supposes it to be founded not on truth but on error. Paul, therefore, may perhaps be a stepping-stone on the way to a comprehension of Jesus.

In the first place, then, the investigation of the relation between Jesus and Paul should begin with Paul rather than with Jesus, because Paul is, if not better known than Jesus, at least more easily known. In the second place, Paul should be studied before Jesus just because he lived after Jesus. If the object of the investigation were Jesus and Paul, taken separately, then it would be better to begin with the earlier rather than with the later of the two; but since it is the relation between Jesus and Paul that is to be studied, it is better method to begin with Paul. For the investigator need not rely merely on a comparison of Jesus and Paul. If Paul was dependent upon Jesus, the fact may be expected to appear in direct statements of Paul himself, and in the attitude of his contemporaries toward him. Did Paul feel himself to be an innovator with respect to Jesus; and was he regarded as an innovator by the earlier disciples of Jesus?

The latter question, at any rate, cannot be answered offhand. There were undoubtedly some men in the primitive church who combatted Paul in the name of conservatism. These were the Judaizers, who regarded Paul's doctrine of Christian freedom as a dangerous innovation. The Jewish law, they said, must be maintained even among Gentile Christians. Faith in Christ is supplementary to it, not subversive of it. Were the Judaizers justified in their conservatism? Were they right in regarding Paul as an innovator? What was the relation between these Judaizers and the original apostles, who had been disciples of Jesus in Galilee? These are among the most important questions in apostolic history. They have divided students of the New Testament into hostile camps. F. C. Baur supposed that the relation between Judaizers and original apostles was in the main friendly. The original apostles, though they could not quite close their eyes to the hand of God as manifested in the successes of Paul, belong nevertheless inwardly with the Judaizers rather than with Paul. The fundamental fact of apostolic history is a conflict between Paul and the original apostles, between Gentile Christianity and Jewish Christianity. The history of early Christianity is the history of the development and final adjustment of that conflict. The Catholic Church of the close of the second century is the result

of a compromise between Pauline Christianity and the Christianity of the original apostles. This reconstruction of early
Christian history was opposed by Albrecht Ritschl. According
to Ritschl, the conflict in the apostolic age was not between
Paul and the original apostles, but between apostolic Christianity—including both Paul and the original apostles—on the one
side, and Judaistic Christianity—the Christianity of the Judaistic opponents of Paul—on the other. Specifically Jewish
Christianity exerted no considerable influence upon the development of the Church. The Old Catholic Church of the close of
the second century was the result not of a compromise between
Jewish Christianity and Gentile Christianity, but of a natural
process of degeneration from Pauline Christianity on purely
Gentile Christian ground. The Gentile Christian world was
unable to understand the Pauline doctrine of grace. Christianity came to be regarded as a new law—but that was due, not to
the rehabilitation of the Mosaic law as a concession to Jewish
Christianity, but to the tendency of the average man toward
legalism in religion. As against Baur, Harnack belongs with
Ritschl. Like Ritschl, he denies to Jewish Christianity any
considerable influence upon the development of the Catholic
Church. The Church of 200 A. D. owes its difference from
Paul, not to a compromise with Jewish Christianity, but to the
intrusion of Greek habits of thought.

If Baur was correct, then Paul was probably no true disciple
of Jesus. For Baur brought Paul into fundamental conflict
with the men who had stood nearest to Jesus. But Baur was
not correct. His reconstruction of apostolic history was arrived at by neglecting all sources except the epistles to the
Galatians and Corinthians and then misinterpreting these. He
failed to do justice to the " right hand of fellowship " (Gal. ii.
9) which the pillars of the Jerusalem Church gave to Paul.
And the account of Paul's rebuke of Peter in Antioch, apparently the strongest evidence of a conflict between Paul and
the original apostles, is rather to be regarded as evidence to the
contrary. For Paul rebukes Peter for hypocrisy—not for false
opinions, but for concealing his correct opinions for fear of
men. In condemning his practice, Paul approves his principles.
Peter had therefore been in fundamental agreement with Paul.

As for the Judaizers in Corinth, their opinions are as uncertain as their relation to the original apostles. It is not certain that they combatted Paul's doctrine of justification by faith, and it is not certain that they had any kind of endorsement from the original apostles. Surely the apostles were not the only ones who could have given them " letters of recommendation " (2 Cor. iii. 1).

Baur's thesis, then, was insufficiently grounded. One fact, however, still requires explanation—the appeal of the Judaizers to the original apostles against Paul. It is not enough to say simply that the appeal of the Judaizers was a false appeal. For if the original apostles were as Pauline as Paul himself, it is difficult to see why they should have been preferred to Paul by the anti-Pauline party. Surely the original apostles must have given the Judaizers at least some color of support; otherwise the Judaizers could never have appealed to them. Until this appeal is explained, Baur remains unrefuted. But the explanation is not difficult to find. It was the life, not the teaching, of the original apostles which appeared to support the contentions of the Judaizers. The early Christians in Jerusalem continued to observe the Jewish law. They continued in diligent attendance upon the Temple services. They observed the feasts, they obeyed the regulations about food. To a superficial observer, they were simply pious Jews. Now, as a matter of fact, they were not simply pious Jews. They were relying for salvation not really upon their observance of the law, but solely upon their faith in the crucified and risen Christ. Inwardly, Christianity was from the very beginning no mere continuation of Judaism, but a new religion. Outwardly, however, the early church was nothing more than a Jewish sect. And the Judaizers failed to penetrate beneath the outward appearance. Because the original apostles continued to observe the Jewish law, the Judaizers supposed that legalism was of the essence of their religion. The Judaizers appealed to the outward practice of the apostles; Paul, to the deepest springs of their religious life. So long as Christianity was preached only among Jews, there was no acute conflict. True Christians and mere Jewish believers in the Messiahship of Jesus were united by a common observance of the Mosaic law. But when Christianity began to transcend the bounds of Judaism, the division became apparent. The apostles, true disciples of Jesus, attested their own inward freedom by accepting the outward freedom of the Gentiles; the Judaizers, false brethren privily brought in, insisted upon the observance of the law as necessary to salvation.

Paul, then, was not the founder of universalistic Christianity. In principle, Christianity was universalistic from the very beginning. In principle, the first Christians in Jerusalem were entirely free from the Judaism with which they were united outwardly by observance of the Temple ritual. If Paul was not the founder of universalistic Christianity, what was he? What was his peculiar service to the Church? It was not the mere geographical extension of the frontiers of the Kingdom. That achievement he shares with others. Paul was perhaps not even the first to preach the Gospel systematically to Gentiles. That honor belongs apparently to certain unnamed Jews of Cyprus and Cyrene. The true achievement of Paul lies in another sphere—in the hidden realm of thought. When Christianity began to be offered directly to Gentiles in Antioch, the principles of the Gentile mission had to be established once for all. Conceivably, of course, the Gentile mission might have got along without principles. The leaders of the church at Antioch might have pointed simply to the practical necessities of the case. Obviously, the Gentile world, as a matter of fact, would never accept circumcision, and would never submit to the Mosaic law. Consequently, if Christianity was ever to be anything more than a Jewish sect, the requirements of the law must quietly be held in abeyance. Conceivably, the leaders of the church at Antioch might have reasoned thus; conceivably they might have been " practical Christian workers " in the modern sense. But as a matter of fact, the leader of the church at Antioch was the Apostle Paul. Paul was not a man to sacrifice principle to practical necessity.

What was standing in the way of the Gentile mission was no mere Jewish racial prejudice, but a genuine religious principle. Jewish particularism was part of the very essence of the Jews' religion. The idea of the covenant between God and his chosen people was fundamental in all periods of Judaism. To have offered the Gospel to uncircumcised Gentiles simply because that was demanded by the practical necessities of the case, would have meant to a Jew nothing less than disobedience to the revealed will of God. It would have been an irreparable injury to the religious conscience. Particularism was not a prejudice, but a religious principle. Therefore it could be overcome only by a higher principle. Its abrogation needed to be demonstrated, not merely assumed. And that was the work of Paul.

The original apostles, through their intercourse with Jesus upon earth, and their experience of the risen Lord, had in principle transcended Jewish particularism. Inwardly they were free from the law. But they did not know that they were free. Certainly they did not know why they were free. Such freedom could not be permanent. It sufficed for the Jewish Church, so long as the issue was not clearly drawn. But it was open to argumentative attack. It could never have conquered the world. Christian freedom was held by but a precarious tenure, until its underlying principles were established. Christianity could not exist without theology. And the first great Christian theologian was Paul.

In championing Gentile freedom, then, in emphasizing the doctrine of salvation by faith alone, Paul was not an innovator. He was merely making explicit what had been implicit before. He was in fundamental harmony with the original apostles. And if he was in harmony with the most intimate disciples of Jesus, the presumption is that he was in harmony with Jesus himself.

If the harmony between Paul and the original apostles was preserved by Paul's conception of Christian freedom, it was preserved even more clearly by his view of the person of Christ. Just where modern radicalism is most confident that Paul was an innovator, Paul's contemporaries were most confident of his faithfulness to tradition. Even the Judaizers had no quarrel with Paul's conception of Christ as a heavenly being. In the Epistle to the Galatians, where Paul insists that he received his apostleship not from men but directly from Christ, he does so in sharp opposition to the Judaizers. Paul says, " not by man, but by Christ "; the Judaizers said, " not by Christ but by man ". But if so, then the Judaizers, no less than Paul, distinguished Christ sharply from men, and placed him clearly on the side of God. If Paul can prove that he received his apostleship directly from Christ, then he has already proved that he received it directly from God. Apparently, it never occurred to him that his opponents might accept the former proposition and deny the latter. For the Judaizers as well as for Paul, God and Christ belong together. In 2 Cor. xi. 4, it is true, Paul hints that his opponents are preaching another Jesus. If that passage stood alone, it might mean that the Judaizers differed from Paul in their conception of the person of Christ. But if there had been such a difference, it would surely have appeared more clearly in the rest of the Corinthian epistles. If the Judaizers had taught that Jesus was a mere man, son of David and nothing else, surely Paul would have taken occasion to contradict them. So dangerous an error—an error so completely subversive of Paul's deepest convictions—could not possibly have been left unrefuted. The meaning of the passage is quite different. It was the Judaizers themselves, and not Paul, who said that their Jesus was another Jesus. " Paul ", they said to the Corinthians, " has not revealed the Gospel to you in its fulness (2 Cor. iv. 3, xi. 5). Paul has had no close contact either with Jesus himself, or with the immediate disciples of Jesus. Paul has preached but an imperfect gospel. We, on the other hand, can offer you the true Jesus, the true Spirit, and the true gospel. Do not listen to Paul. We alone can give you fully authentic information. " In reality, however, the Judaizers had nothing new to offer. Paul had been no whit behind " the preëminent apostles ". He had made the full gospel plain and open before them (2 Cor. xi. 5, 6). If Paul's gospel was hidden, it was hidden only from those who had been blinded by the god of this world (2 Cor. iv. 4). The " other Jesus " of the Judaizers existed only in their own inordinate claims. They preached the same Jesus as did Paul—only their preaching was marred by quarrelsomeness and pride. They preached the same Jesus; but they had not themselves come into vital communion with him. In that they differed from Paul.

It is not until the Epistle to the Colossians that Paul is compelled to defend his conception of the person of Christ. And there he defends it not against a conservative, naturalistic view of Jesus as a merely human Messiah, but against Gnostic speculation. With regard to the person of Christ, Paul appears everywhere in perfect harmony with all Palestinian Christians. In the whole New Testament there is not a trace of a conflict. That is a fact of tremendous significance. For Paul's conception of the supernatural Christ was formed not later than five years after the crucifixion of Jesus. There is every reason to believe that it was formed at the conversion. With regard to this matter, there is no evidence of a development in Paul's thinking. One passage, 2 Cor. v. 16, has occasionaly been regarded as such evidence. But only by palpable disregard of the context. When Paul says, " Even if we have known Christ according to the flesh, yet now we know him so no longer ", he cannot possibly mean that for a time after his conversion he regarded Christ simply as a human, Jewish Messiah. For the point of the whole passage is the revolutionary change wrought in every Christian's life by the death of Christ. It is clearly the appropriation of that death—that is, conversion—and not some subsequent development of the Christian life which brings the transition from the knowledge of Christ after the flesh (whatever that may be) to the higher knowledge of which Paul is now in possession. The revelation of God's Son (Gal. i. 16) on the road to Damascus clearly gave to Paul the essential elements of his Christology. What is more, that Christology must have formed from the very beginning the essence of his preaching. The " Jesus " whom he preached in the Damascan synagogues was also Christ—his Christ. That he preached in Damascus is directly attested only by the book of Acts, but, as has been observed by some who entertain rather a low estimate of Acts, it is implied in 2 Cor. xi. 32, 33. What could have caused the persecution of Paul except Christian activity on his part? If the book of Acts is correct, Paul preached also in Jerusalem only three years after his conversion. Yet the churches of Judea glorified God in him. If there was opposition to his heavenly Christ, such opposition has left no trace. Yet Paul had been in direct consultation with Peter. There is every reason to believe, therefore, that from the very beginning, the exalted Christology of Paul was accepted by the

Jerusalem Church. The heavenly Christ of Paul was also the Christ of those who had walked and talked with Jesus of Nazareth.

By his contemporaries, then, Paul was regarded not as the founder of a new religion, but as a disciple of Jesus. That testimony may be overthrown by contrary evidence. But there is a strong presumption that it is correct. For among those who passed judgment upon Paul were included the most intimate friends and disciples of Jesus. Their estimate of Paul's relationship to Jesus can be rejected only under the compulsion of positive evidence. Those who knew Jesus best accepted Paul as a disciple of Jesus like themselves.

Thus, by his contemporaries, Paul was not regarded as an innovator with respect to Jesus. Did he regard himself as such?

Put in this form, the question admits of but one answer. " It is no longer I that live ", says Paul, " but Christ that liveth in me. " Christ, for Paul, was absolute Lord and Master. But this " Christ " whom Paul served was identified by Paul with Jesus of Nazareth. Of that there can be no manner of doubt. Moreover, even in his estate of humiliation, Christ was regarded by Paul as Lord. It was " the Lord of glory " (1 Cor. ii. 8) who was crucified. The right of the earthly Jesus to issue commands was for Paul a matter of course. That is proved beyond question even by the few direct references which Paul makes to words of Jesus. So much is almost universally admitted. That Paul regarded himself as a disciple of Jesus can be denied by no one. The difference of opinion appears when the question is formulated in somewhat broader terms. Do the Pauline Epistles themselves, even apart from a comparison with the words of Jesus, furnish evidence that Paul was not, as he supposed, a disciple of Jesus, but the founder of a new religion?

In favor of the affirmative, two considerations have been adduced.

In the first place, in the Epistle to the Galatians Paul himself insists upon his independence of tradition. He received his gospel directly from Christ, not through any human agency. Even after he had received his gospel, he avoided all contact with those who had been apostles before him. He conferred not with flesh and blood. Paul received his gospel, then, by revelation from the risen Christ, not by tradition from the earthly Jesus. But the earthly Jesus was the historical Jesus. In exalting his direct commission from the heavenly Christ, Paul has himself betrayed the slenderness of his connection with Jesus of Nazareth.

In the second place, the same low estimate of historical tradition appears throughout the epistles, in the paucity of references to the words and deeds of Jesus. Apparently Paul is interested almost exclusively in the birth and death and resurrection. He is interested in the birth as the incarnation of a heavenly being, come for the salvation of men; and in the death and resurrection as the great cosmic events by which salvation was obtained. But for the details of the life of Jesus he displays but little interest. His mind and fancy are dominated by a vague, mysterious, cosmic personification, not by a definite historical person—by the heavenly Christ, not by Jesus of Nazareth.

The latter of these two arguments can be established only by exaggeration and by misinterpretation—by exaggeration of the paucity of references in Paul to the life of Jesus, and by misinterpretation of the paucity that really exists. In the first place, Paul displays far greater knowledge than is sometimes supposed, and in the second place, he possesses far greater knowledge than he displays. The testimony of Paul to Jesus has been examined many times—it will not be necessary to traverse the ground again. The assertion that the details of the life of Jesus were of little value for Paul is contradicted in no uncertain terms by such passages as 2 Cor. x. 1 and Rom. xv. 3. When Paul urges as an example to his readers the meekness and gentleness of Christ, or his faithfulness in bearing reproaches in the service of God, he is evidently thinking not primarily of the gracious acts of the incarnation and passion, as in Phil. ii. 5 ff., and 2 Cor. viii. 9, but of the character of Jesus as it was exhibited in his daily life on earth. Such expressions as these attest not merely knowledge of Jesus but also warm appreciation of his character. The imitation of Jesus (1 Cor. xi. 1) had its due place in the ethical life of Paul. Direct commands of Jesus are occasionally quoted, and Paul is fully conscious of the significance of such commands (1 Cor. vii. 10, 12, 25). In 1 Cor. xi. 23 ff., he quotes in full the words of Jesus instituting the Lord's Supper, and incidentally shows that he is acquainted with the exact circumstances under which the words were spoken ("the night in which he was betrayed").

The incidental character of Paul's references to the life of Jesus itself suggests that he knew far more than he chooses to tell. The account of the institution of the Lord's Supper, for example, would never have found a place in the epistles except for certain abuses which had sprung up in Corinth. Yet Paul says that he had already "delivered over" that account to the Corinthians. It had formed part of his elementary preaching. And it displays intimate knowledge of detail. That one example is sufficient to prove not only that Paul knew more than he tells in the epistles, but also that what is omitted from the epistles formed part of the essential elements of his preaching. It is omitted not because it is unimportant, but on the contrary because it is fundamental. Instruction about it had to be given at the very beginning, and did not often have to be repeated. The hint supplied by such passages as the account of the Lord's Supper in 1 Cor. xi. 23 ff. is only supplementary to weighty *a priori* considerations. A missionary preaching that included no concrete account of the life of Jesus would have been preposterous. The claim that a crucified Jew was to be obeyed as Lord and trusted as Saviour must surely have provoked the question as to what manner of man this was. It is true that the gods of other religions needed to be described only in general terms. But Christianity had dispensed with the advantages of such vagueness. It had identified its God with a Jew who had lived but a few years before. Surely the tremendous prejudice against accepting a crucified criminal as Lord and Master could be overcome only by an account of the wonderful character of Jesus. The only other resource is an extreme supernaturalism. If the concrete figure of the crucified one had no part in winning the hearts of men, then the work must have been accomplished by a magical exercise of divine power—working out of all connection with the mind and heart. That is not the supernaturalism of Paul. When Paul writes to the

Galatians that Jesus Christ crucified was placarded before their eyes, he refers to something more than a dogmatic exposition of the atonement. The picture of the crucified one owed part of its compelling power to the conviction that the death there portrayed was the supreme act of a life of love.

It is already pretty clear that the first chapter of Galatians cannot mean that Paul had a contempt for Christian tradition. When Paul says that he received his gospel by direct revelation from Jesus Christ, he cannot mean that he excluded from his preaching what he had received by ordinary word of mouth from the eye-witnesses of the life of Jesus. He cannot mean even that his proof of the resurrection of Jesus was based solely upon his own testimony. That inference, at least, would be very natural if Gal. i stood alone. But it is refuted in no uncertain terms by 1 Cor. xv. 3-7. In this passage the appearances of the risen Christ to persons other than Paul are reviewed in an extended list, and Paul distinctly says that this formed a part of his first preaching in Corinth. So not even the fact of the resurrection itself was supported solely by the testimony of Paul. On the contrary, Paul was diligent in investigating the testimony of others.

The first chapter of Galatians, therefore, bears a very different aspect when it is interpreted in the light of the other Pauline epistles. Paul does not mean that all his information about Jesus came from the risen Christ. In all probability, Paul knew the essential facts in the life of Jesus even before he became a Christian. Since he was a persecutor of the Church, he must have had at least general information about its founder. The story of the life and death of the Galilean prophet must have been matter of common knowledge in Palestine. And after the conversion, Paul added to his knowledge. It is inconceivable that during the brief intercourse with Peter, for example, the subject of the words and deeds of Jesus was studiously avoided. Such an unnatural supposition is by no means required by the actual phenomena of the epistles. That has been demonstrated above. The true reason why Paul does not mention his knowledge of the life of Jesus as part of the basis of his faith, is that for him such factual knowledge was a matter of course. For us it is not a matter

of course, because many centuries stand between us and the
events. For us, painful investigation of sources is necessary
in order that we may arrive even at the bare facts. Indeed,
it is just the facts that need to be established in the face of
the sharpest criticism. But for Paul, the facts were matter of
common knowledge; it was the interpretation of the facts
which was in dispute. Paul was living in Jerusalem only a
very few years at the latest after the crucifixion of Jesus. The
prophet of Nazareth had certainly created considerable stir in
Jerusalem as well as in Galilee. These things were not done
in a corner. The general outlines of the life of Jesus were
known to friend and foe alike. Even indifference could
hardly have brought forgetfulness. But Paul was not indifferent. Before his conversion, as well as after it, he was interested in Jesus. That was what made him the most relent-
less of the persecutors.

The bare facts of the earthly life of Jesus did not, therefore,
constitute in Paul's mind a " gospel ". Everyone knew the
facts—the Pharisees as well as the disciples. The facts could
be obtained through a thousand channels. Paul did not reflect
as to where he got them. Before the conversion, he heard the
reports of the opponents of Jesus, and the common gossip of
the crowds. After the conversion, there were many eye-witnesses who could be questioned—perhaps in Damascus and
even in Arabia as well as in Jerusalem. It never occurred to
Paul to regard himself as a disciple of the men who merely reported the facts, any more than the modern man feels a deep
gratitude to the newspaper in which he reads useful information. If that particular paper had not printed the news, others
would have done so. The sources of information are so numerous that no one of them can be regarded as of supreme importance. For us, the sources of information about the life
of Jesus are limited. Hence our veneration for the Gospels.
But Paul was a contemporary of Jesus; the sources of his information about Jesus were so numerous that they could not
be counted.

Thus, when Paul says that he received his gospel from the
risen Christ, he does not mean that the risen Christ revealed
to him the facts of the life of Jesus. He had known the facts

before—only they had filled him with hatred. What he received at his conversion was a new interpretation of the facts. Instead of continuing to persecute the disciples of Jesus, he accepted Jesus as living Lord and Master. Conceivably, the change might have been wrought through the preaching of the disciples; Paul might have received his gospel through the ministrations of Peter. But such was not the Lord's will. Suddenly, on the road to Damascus, Jesus called him. Paul had heard, perhaps, of the call of the first disciples; he had heard of those who left home and kindred to follow the new teacher. He had heard only to condemn. But now it was his turn. Jesus called, and he obeyed. Jesus, whom he knew only too well—destroyer of the Temple, accursed by the law, crucified, dead and buried—was living Lord. Jesus called him— called him not merely to revering imitation of the holy martyr, not merely to a new estimate of events that were past, but to present, living communion with himself. Jesus himself, in very presence, called him into communion, and into glorious service. That, and that only, is what Paul means when he says that he received his gospel not from man but by revelation of Jesus Christ.

Neither by Paul himself, therefore, nor by the original apostles was Paul regarded as an innovator with reference to Jesus. On the contrary he regarded himself and was regarded by others as a true disciple. The presumption is that that opinion was correct. For both Paul himself, and the early Christians with whom he came into contact were contemporaries of Jesus, and had every opportunity to know him. If Paul had detected any fundamental divergence between his own teaching and that of Jesus of Nazareth, then he could not have remained Jesus' disciple. Unless, indeed, the conversion was supernatural. But the conversion was not supernatural if it left Paul in disharmony with Jesus. For it purported to be wrought by Jesus himself. If supernatural, the conversion could not have left Paul in disharmony with the historical Jesus, because it was wrought by an appearance of Jesus; if not supernatural, it would have been insufficient to make Paul regard himself as a disciple of one with whom he did not agree. That the original apostles had every opportunity

for knowing the historical Jesus requires no proof. Yet undoubtedly they accepted Paul as a disciple.

The presumption thus established in favor of regarding Paul
as a true disciple of Jesus could be overthrown only by positive divergence, established by an actual comparison of Jesus
with Paul. At the very outset of such comparison, a serious
difficulty is encountered. How is Jesus to be investigated?
Paul we know, but what is the truth about Jesus? It will
not do, it is said, to accept the Gospel picture in its entirety.
For the Gospels were written after Paul, and have been
affected by Pauline thinking. To a certain extent, therefore,
it is no longer the historical Jesus which the Gospels describe,
but the Pauline Christ. To compare Paul with the Gospels,
therefore, is to compare not Paul with Jesus, but Paul with
Paul. Naturally the comparison establishes coincidence, not
divergence; but the result is altogether without value.

This objection was applied first of all to the Fourth Gospel.
The Fourth Gospel was written undoubtedly many years after
the Pauline Epistles. And undoubtedly it exhibits a remarkable harmony with Pauline thinking. The Pauline Christ is
here made to appear even in the earthly life of Jesus. In
this respect, it is said, the Gospel is more Pauline than Paul
himself. Paul had done justice to the human life of Jesus by
distinguishing sharply between the humiliation and the exaltation of Christ. Jesus had become Son of God in power only at
the resurrection. In the Fourth Gospel, on the other hand, the
heavenly Christ appears in all his glory even on earth. Furthermore, the new birth of Jno. iii is identical with the
Pauline conception of the new life which the Christian has by
sharing in the death and resurrection of Christ. Even the
Pauline doctrine of the sacrificial death of Christ, though not
prominent in the Fourth Gospel, appears in such passages as
Jno. i. 29 and iii. 14, 15.

The objection could be overcome only by an examination
of the Fourth Gospel, which would far transcend the limits of
the present discussion. The Fourth Gospel will therefore here
be left out of account. It should be remarked, however, in
passing, that dependence of the Fourth Gospel upon Paul has
by no means been proved. A far-reaching similarity in ideas

may freely be admitted. But in order to prove dependence, it is necessary to establish similarity not only of ideas, but also of expression. And that is conspicuously absent. Even where the underlying ideas are most clearly identical, the terminology is strikingly different—and not only the bare terminology but also the point of view. The entire atmosphere and spirit of the Fourth Gospel is quite distinct from that of the Pauline Epistles. That is sufficient to disprove the hypothesis of dependence of the Gospel upon Paul. The underlying similarity of thought, when taken in connection with the total dissimilarity of expression, can be explained only by dependence upon a common source. And that source can hardly be anything but Jesus Christ.

Provisionally, however, the Fourth Gospel will be left out of account. That can be done with the greater safety, because it is now universally agreed that the contrast between the Fourth Gospel and the Synoptics is not an absolute one. The day is past when the divine Christ of the Gospel of John could be confronted with a human Christ of Mark. Historical students of all shades of opinion have now come to see that Mark as well as John (though, it is believed, in a lesser degree) presents an exalted Christology. The charge of Pauline influence, therefore, has been brought not only against John, but also against the earlier Gospels. Hence, it is maintained that if Paul be compared even with the Jesus of the Synoptics, he is being compared not with the historical Jesus, but with a Paulinized Jesus. Obviously such comparison can prove nothing.

If the Synoptic Gospels were influenced by Paul, then there is extant not a single document which preserves a pre-Pauline conception of Christ. That is a very remarkable state of affairs. The original disciples of Jesus, those who had been intimate with him on earth, those from whom the most authentic information might have been expected, have allowed their account of the life of Jesus to be altered through the influence of one who could speak only from hearsay. Such alteration would certainly fall within the lifetime of many of the eye-witnesses. For the Gospel of Mark is generally admitted to have been written before 70 A.D. It is conceivable that the Pauline conception might thus have gained the ascendancy over the primitive conception. But it is hardly conceivable that it could have done so without a struggle, and of struggle there is not a trace. In the supposed Pauline passages in the Synoptic Gospels, the writers are quite unaware that one conception is being replaced by another. And the Pauline Epistles themselves, as has already been observed, presuppose a substantial agreement between Paul and the Jerusalem Church with regard to the person of Christ. This remarkable absence of struggle between the Pauline conception and the primitive conception can be explained only if the two were essentially the same. Only so could the Pauline conception have been accepted by the Jerusalem Church, and permitted to dominate subsequent Christianity. This conclusion is supported by the positive evidence, which has recently been urged, for example by Harnack, for a pre-Pauline dating of the Synoptic Gospels—that is, for dating them at a time when the Pauline Epistles, even if some of them had already been written, could not have been collected, and could not have begun to dominate the thinking of the Church at large. The affinity between the Christology of Paul and the Jesus of the Synoptic Gospels does not prove the dependence of the Gospels upon Paul. For the Christology of Paul was also, in essentials, the Christology of the primitive Christian community in Jerusalem.

The transition from the human Jesus to the divine Christ must be placed therefore not between the primitive church and Paul, but between Jesus and the primitive church. A man, Jesus, came to be regarded as a divine being, not by later generations, who could have been deceived by the nimbus of distance and mystery, but almost immediately after his death, by his intimate friends, by men who had seen him subject to all the petty limitations of daily life. Even if Paul were the first witness to the deification of Jesus, the process would still be preternaturally rapid. Jesus would still be regarded as a divine being by a contemporary of his intimate friends—and each deification would be no mere official form of flattery, like the apotheosis of the Roman emperors, but would be the expression of serious conviction. The process by which the man Jesus was raised to divine dignity within a few years of his death would be absolutely unique. That has been recognized even by men of the most thorough-going naturalistic principles. The late H. J. Holtzmann,[2] who may be regarded as the typical exponent of modern New Testament criticism, admitted that for the rapid apotheosis of Jesus, as it appears in the thinking of Paul, he was unable to cite any parallel in the religious history of the race. In order to explain the origin of the Pauline Christology, Brückner and Wrede have recourse to the Jewish Apocalypses. The Christology of Paul was formed, it is said, before his conversion. He needed only to identify the heavenly, preëxistent Christ of his Jewish belief with Jesus of Nazareth, and his Christology was complete. But that explanation does not help matters. Even if it be accepted to the fullest extent, it explains only details. It explains why, if Jesus was to be regarded as a divine being, he was regarded as just this particular kind of divine being. But it does not explain how he came to be regarded as a divine being at all. And that is what really requires explanation. One might almost as well say that the deification of a man is explained if only it be shown that those who accomplished such deification already had a conception of God. The apotheosis of Jesus, then, is remarkable, even if it was due to Paul. But it becomes yet a thousand fold more remarkable when it is seen to have been due not to Paul, but to the intimate friends of Jesus of Nazareth. Indeed, the process is so remarkable that the question arises whether there is not something wrong with the starting-point. The end of the process is fixed. It is the super-human Christ of Paul and of the primitive church. If, therefore, the process is inconceivable in its rapidity, it is the starting-point which becomes open to suspicion. The starting-point is the purely human Jesus. A suspicion arises that he never existed. If indeed any early Christian extant document gave a clear, consistent account of a Jesus who was nothing more than a man, then the historian might be forced to regard such a Jesus as the starting-point for an astonish-

---

[2] In *Protestantische Monatshefte,* iv (1900), pp. 465 ff., and in *Christliche Welt,* xxiv (1910), column 153. Holtzmann is careful to observe that it is only apparent uniqueness and not actual uniqueness that he admits. There may be a parallel, but it has not come under his observation. In view of Holtzmann's learning, the significance of the admission remains.

ingly rapid apotheosis.   But as a matter of fact, no such
document is in existence.   Even those writers who represent
Jesus most clearly as a man, represent him as something more
than a man, and are quite unconscious of a conflict between the
two representations.   Indeed the two representations appear as
two ways of regarding one and the same person.   If, therefore,
the purely human Jesus is to be reconstructed, he can be reconstructed only by a critical process.   That critical process, in
view of the indissolubly close connection in which divine and
human appear in the Synoptic representation of Jesus, becomes,
to say the least, exceedingly difficult.   And after criticism has
done its work, after the purely human Jesus has been in some
sort disentangled from the ornamentation which had almost
hopelessly defaced his portrait, the critic faces another problem yet more baffling than the first.   How did this human
Jesus come to be regarded as a super-human Jesus even by
his most intimate friends?   There is absolutely nothing to
explain the transition except the supposed appearances of the
risen Lord.   The disciples had been familiar with a Jesus who
placed himself on the side of man, not of God, who offered
himself as an example of faith, not as the object of faith.
And yet, after his shameful death, this estimate of his person
suddenly gave place to a vastly higher estimate.   That is bare
supernaturalism.   It is supernaturalism stripped of that harmony with the laws of the human mind which has been preserved even by the supernaturalism of the Church.   In its
effort to remove the supernatural from the life of Jesus, modern criticism has been obliged to heap up a double portion of
the supernatural upon the Easter experience of the disciples.
If the disciples had been familiar with a supernatural Jesus—
a Jesus who forgave sin as only God can, a Jesus who offered
himself not as an example of faith but as the object of faith,
a Jesus who substantiated these his lofty claims by wonderful
command over the powers of nature—then conceivably, though
not probably, the impression of such a Jesus might have been
sufficient to produce in the disciples, in a purely natural way,
the experiences which they interpreted as appearances of the
risen Lord.   But by eliminating the supernatural in the life
of the Jesus whom the disciples had known, modern criticism

has closed the way to this its only possible psychological explanation of the Easter experience. In order to explain the facts of primitive Christianity, the supernatural must be retained at least either in the life of Jesus of Nazareth or else in the appearances of the risen Lord. But of course no one will stop with that alternative. If the supernatural be accepted in either place, then of course it will be accepted in both places. If Jesus was really a supernatural person, then his resurrection and appearance to his disciples was only what was to be expected; if the experience of the disciples was really an appearance of Jesus, then of course even in his earthly life he was a supernatural person. The supernaturalism of the Church is a reasonable supernaturalism; the supernaturalism into which modern criticism is forced in its effort to avoid supernaturalism, is a supernaturalism unworthy of a reasonable God. In order to explain the exalted Christology of the primitive church, either the appearance of the risen Christ or the Easter experience of the disciples must be regarded as supernatural. But if either was supernatural then there is no objection against supposing that both were.

The similarity of the exalted Christology of the Synoptic Gospels to the Christology of Paul is therefore no indication of dependence upon Paul. For the Christology of Paul was in essence the Christology of the primitive church; and the Christology of the primitive church must have found its justification in the life of Jesus. Furthermore, comparison of Pauline thinking with the teaching of Jesus in the Synoptic Gospels will demonstrate that the harmony between Jesus and Paul extends even to those elements in the teaching of Jesus which are regarded by modern criticism as most characteristic of him. For example, the fatherhood of God, and love as the fulfilling of the law. The conception of God as father was known, it is true, in pre-Christian Judaism. But Jesus brought an incalculable enrichment of it. And that same enrichment appears in Paul in all its fulness. In the earliest extant epistle (1 Thess. i. 1) and throughout all the epistles, the fatherhood of God appears as a matter of course. It requires no defence or elaboration. It is one of the commonplaces of Christianity. Yet it is not for Paul a mere matter of tradition, but a vital element in his religious life. It has not, through familiarity, lost one whit of its freshness. The cry, " Abba, Father ", comes from the very depths of the heart. Hardly less prominent in Paul is the conception of love as the fulfilling of the law. " The whole law is fulfilled in one word, even in this, ' Thou shalt love thy neighbor as thyself.' " " And if I bestow all my goods to feed the poor, and if I give my body to be burned, but have not love, it profiteth me nothing." In the epistles, it is true, Paul is speaking usually of love for Christian brethren. But simply because of the needs of the churches. The closeness of the relationship with fellow-Christians had sometimes increased rather than diminished the tendency towards strife and selfishness. The epistles are addressed not to missionaries, but to Christians of very imperfect mold, who needed to be admonished to exhibit love even where love might have seemed most natural and easy. On account of the peculiar circumstances, therefore, Paul speaks especially of love for fellow-Christians. But not to the exclusion of love for all men. Never was greater injustice done than when Paul is accused of narrowness in his affections. His whole life is the refutation of such a charge—his life of tactful adaptation to varying conditions, of restless energy, of untold peril and hardship. What was the secret of such a life? Love of Christ, no doubt. But also love of those for whom Christ died—whether Jew or Greek, circumcision or uncircumcision, barbarian, Scythian, bond or free.

The fatherhood of God, it is true, does not mean for Paul that God is pleased with all men, or that all men will receive the children's blessing. And Christian love does not mean obliteration of the dividing line between the Kingdom and the world. But these limitations appear at least as clearly in Jesus as in Paul. The dark background of eternal destruction, and the sharp division between the disciples and the world are described by Jesus in far harsher terms than Paul ever ventured to employ. It was Jesus who spoke of the outer darkness and the everlasting fire, of the sin that shall not be forgiven either in this world or in that which is to come; it was Jesus who said, "If any man cometh unto me, and hateth not his own father, and mother, and wife, and children, and brethren and sisters, yea, and his own life also, he cannot be my disciple."

These examples might be multiplied; and they should be supplemented by what has been said above with regard to Paul's appreciation of the character of Jesus. Jesus of Nazareth, as he is depicted for us in the Gospels, was for Paul the supreme moral ideal. But that does not make Paul a disciple of Jesus. Be it spoken with all plainness. Imitation of Jesus, important as it was in the life of Paul, was overshadowed by something else. All that has been said about Paul's interest in the earthly life of Jesus, about his obedience to Jesus' commands, about his reverence for Jesus' character, cannot disguise the fact that these things for Paul are not supreme. Knowledge of the life of Jesus is not for Paul an end in itself but a means to an end. The essence of Paul's religious life is not imitation of a dead prophet. It is communion with a living Lord. In making the risen Christ, not the earthly Jesus, the supreme object of Paul's thinking, modern radicalism is perfectly correct. Paul cannot be vindicated as a disciple of Jesus simply by correcting exaggeration—simply by showing that the influence upon him of the teaching and example of Jesus was somewhat greater than has been supposed. The true relationships of a man are to be determined not by the periphery of his life, but by what is central—central both in his own estimation and in his influence upon history. But the centre and core of Paulinism is not imitation of the earthly Jesus, but communion with the risen Christ. It was that which Paul himself regarded as the very foundation of his own life. "If any man is in Christ, he is a new creature." " It is no longer I that live, but Christ that liveth in me." It was that which planted the Pauline gospel in the great cities of the Roman Empire; it was that which dominated Christianity, and through Christianity has changed the face of the world.

The tremendous difference between this communion with the risen Christ and mere imitation of the earthly Jesus has sometimes been overlooked. In the eagerness to vindicate Paul as a disciple of Jesus, the essential feature of Paulinism

has been thrust into the background. It is admitted, of course,
that in Paul's own estimation the thought of Christ as a divine
being, now living in glory, was fundamental. But the really
important thing, it is said, is the ethical character that is attributed to this heavenly being. Paul's heavenly Christ is the
personification of self-denying love. But whence was this
attribute derived? Certainly not from the Messiah of the
Jewish Apocalypses. For he is conceived of as enveloped in
mystery, as hidden from the world until the great day of his
revealing. The gracious character of Paul's heavenly Christ
could only have been derived from the historical Jesus. Perhaps directly. The character of the historical Jesus, as it was
known through tradition, was simply attributed by Paul to the
heavenly being with whom Jesus was identified. Or perhaps
indirectly. The heavenly Christ was for Paul the personification of love, because Paul conceived of the death of Christ as
a supreme act of loving self-denial. But how could Paul conceive thus of the death of Christ? Only because of the loving spirit of Jesus which appeared in·the disciples whom Paul
persecuted. It was therefore ultimately the character of the
historical Jesus which enabled Paul to conceive of the crucifixion as a loving act of sacrifice; and it was this conception of
the crucifixion which enabled Paul to conceive of his heavenly
Christ as the supreme ideal of love. Of course, for Paul, owing to his intellectual environment, it was impossible to submit
himself to this ideal of love, so long as it was embodied merely
in a dead teacher. The conception of the risen Christ was
therefore necessary historically in order to preserve the precious ideal which had been introduced into the world by Jesus.
But we of the present day can and must sacrifice the form to
the content. The glorious Christ of Paul derives the real
secret of his power over the hearts of men not from his glory,
but from his love.

Such reasoning ignores the essence of Paulinism. It represents Paulinism as devotion to an ideal. If that were
granted, then perhaps all the rest might follow. If Paulinism
is simply imitation of Christ, then perhaps it makes little difference whether Christ be conceived of as on earth or in heaven,
as a dead prophet or a living Lord. Past or present, the ideal,

as an ideal, remains the same. But Paulinism is not imitation of Christ, but communion with Christ. That fact requires no proof. The epistles are on fire with it. The communion is, on the one hand, intensely personal—it is a relation of love. With Christ Paul can hold colloquies of the most intimate kind. But, on the other hand, the communion with Christ transcends human analogies. The Lord can operate on the heart and life of Paul in a way that is impossible for any human friend. Paul is *in* Christ and Christ is *in* Paul. The relation to the risen Christ is not only personal, but also religious. But if Paulinism is communion with Christ, then quite the fundamental thing about Christ is that he is alive. It is sheer folly to say that this Pauline Christ-religion can be reproduced by one who supposes that Christ is dead. Such a one can envy the poor sinners in the Gospels who received from Jesus healing for body and mind. He can admire the great prophet. When, alas, shall we find another like him? He can envy the faith of others. But he cannot himself believe. He cannot hear Jesus say, " Thy faith hath made thee whole. "

When Paulinism is understood as fellowship with the risen Christ, then the disproportionate emphasis which Paul places upon the death and resurrection of Christ becomes intelligible. For these are the acts by which fellowship has been established. To the modern man, they seem unnecessary. By the modern man fellowship with God is taken as a matter of course. But only because of an imperfect conception of God. If God is all love and kindness, then of course nothing is required in order to bring us into his presence. But Paul would never have been satisfied with such a God. His was the awful, holy God of the Old Testament prophets—and of Jesus. But for Paul the holiness of God was also the holiness of Christ. Communion of sinful man with the holy Christ is a tremendous paradox, a supreme mystery. But the mystery has been illumined. It has been illumined by the cross. Christ forgives sin not because he is complacent towards sin, but because of his own free grace he has paid the dreadful penalty of it. And he has not stopped with that. After the cross came the resurrection. Christ rose from the dead into a life of glory

and power. Into that glory and into that power he invites
the believer. In Christ we receive not only pardon, but new
and glorious life.

Paul's interpretation of the death and resurrection is not
to be found in the words of Jesus. But hints of it appear,
even in the Synoptic discourses. " The Son of man came not
to be ministered unto, but to minister, and to give his life a
ransom for many " (Mk. x. 45). Modern criticism is inclined to question the authenticity of that verse. But if any
saying of Jesus is commended by its form, it is this one. The
exquisite gnomic form vindicates the saying to the great
master of inspired paradox. Even far stronger, however, is
the attestation of the words which were spoken at the last
supper. Indeed these are the most strongly attested of all
the words of Jesus; for the Synoptic tradition is here supplemented by the testimony of Paul; and the testimony of Paul
is also the testimony of the tradition to which he refers. That
tradition must be absolutely primitive. But the words which
Jesus spoke at the last supper designate the death of Jesus as
a sacrifice. And why should the idea of vicarious suffering be
denied to Jesus? It is freely accepted for his disciples and for
Paul. They interpreted the death of Jesus as a sacrifice for
sin, because, it is said, the idea was current in Judaism of that
day. But if the idea was so familiar, surely Jesus was more
susceptible to it than were his disciples. They had an external
conception of the Kingdom, he regarded the Kingdom as
spiritual; they exalted power and worldly position, he insisted
upon self-denial. Was it then the disciples, and not Jesus,
who seized upon the idea of vicarious suffering? Surely if
Jesus anticipated his death at all, he would naturally regard
it as a sacrificial death. And to eliminate altogether Jesus'
foreknowledge of his death involves extreme skepticism.
Aside from the direct predictions, what shall be done with Mk.
ii. 20: " But the days will come when the bridegroom shall be
taken from them, and then will they fast in that day "? If
Jesus expected the Kingdom to be established before his death,
then he was an extreme fanatic, who could not even discern
the signs of the times. The whole spirit of his life is op-

posed to such a view. Even during his life, Jesus was a suffering servant of Jehovah.

Nevertheless, the teaching of Jesus about the significance of his death is not explicit. It resembles the mysterious intimations of prophecy rather than the definite enunciation of fundamental religious truth. That fact must be admitted; indeed, it should be insisted upon. The fundamental Pauline doctrine—the doctrine of the cross—is only hinted at in the words of Jesus. Yet that doctrine was fundamental not only in Paul, but in the primitive church. Certainly it has been fundamental in historic Christianity. The fundamental doctrine of Christianity, then, was not taught definitely by Jesus of Nazareth. As a teacher, therefore, Jesus was not the founder of Christianity. He was the founder of Christianity not because of what he said, but because of what he did. The Church revered him as its founder only because his death was interpreted as an event of cosmic significance. But it had such significance only if Jesus was a divine being, come to earth for the salvation of men. If Jesus was not a supernatural person, then not only Paulinism but also the whole of Christianity is founded not upon the lofty teaching of an inspired prophet, but upon a colossal error.

Paul was a disciple of Jesus, if Jesus was a supernatural person; he was not a disciple of Jesus, if Jesus was a mere man. If Jesus was simply a human teacher, then Paulinism defies explanation. Yet it is powerful and beneficent beyond compare. Judged simply by its effects, the religious experience of Paul is the most tremendous phenomenon in the history of the human spirit. It has transformed the world from darkness into light. But it need be judged not merely by its effects. It lies open before us. In the presence of it, the sympathetic observer is aghast. It is a new world that is opened before him. Freedom, goodness, communion with God, sought by philosophers of all the ages, attained at last! The religious experience of Paul needs no defense. Give it but sympathetic attention and it is irresistible. But it can be shared as well as admired. The relation of Paul to Jesus Christ is essentially the same as our own. The original apostles had one element in their religious life which we cannot share—the memory of their daily intercourse with Jesus. That element, it is true, was not really fundamental, even for them. But it appears to be fundamental; our fears tell us that it was fundamental. But in the experience of Paul there was no such element. Like ourselves he did not know Jesus upon earth—he had no memory of Galilean days. His devotion was directed simply and solely to the risen Saviour. Shall we follow him? We can do so on one condition. That condition is not easy. To fulfil it, we must overcome our most deep-seated convictions. We must recognize in Jesus a supernatural person. But unless we fulfil that condition, we can never share in the religious experience of Paul. When brought face to face with the crisis, we may shrink back. But if we do so, we make the origin of Christianity an insoluble problem. In exalting the methods of scientific history, we involve ourselves hopelessly in historical difficulty. In the relation between Jesus and Paul, we discover a problem, which, through the very processes of mind by which the uniformity of nature has been established, forces us to transcend that doctrine—which pushes us relentlessly off the safe ground of the phenomenal world toward the abyss of supernaturalism—which forces us, despite the resistance of the modern mind, to make the great venture of faith, and found our lives no longer upon what can be procured by human effort or understood as a phase of evolution, but upon him who has linked us with the unseen world, and brought us into communion with the eternal God.

THE TRANSCENDENCE OF JEHOVAH GOD OF ISRAEL

Isaiah xliv: 24-28

Oswald Thompson Allis

THE TRANSCENDENCE OF JEHOVAH GOD OF ISRAEL[1]

It is a fact too generally recognized to require proof, that the Isaianic authorship of the Cyrus Prophecy (Is. xliv. 28-xlv. 7) is regarded as impossible or at any rate as highly improbable by many scholars of widely differing shades of theological opinion. That this should be the contention of antisupernaturalistic thinkers is only to be expected, for as Bredenkamp has well said, " From a critical standpoint which denies prophetic prescience and reduces it to premonition or conjecture the book of Isaiah must *a priori* be regarded as an anthology in which utterances of writers of very different periods have found a place." [2] But it must be recognized that there are scholars who believe in miracle and prophecy and in the pronounced supernaturalism of revealed religion who are yet unable to believe that the Cyrus prophecy of the restoration was uttered at a time when the captivity itself lay yet a century or more in the future, at a time when haughty Babylon had been humbled almost to the dust by her all but invincible Assyrian neighbor, and when the Persians were known to history, if indeed they were known at all, only as one of the many barbaric or semi-barbaric Aryan tribes, some of which yielded an unwilling homage to the warrior king of Assyria.[3] Not

---

[1] The writer wishes to acknowledge indebtedness for valuable suggestions to Dr. John D. Davis; and also to Drs. R. D. Wilson and J. Oscar Boyd.

[2] Bredenkamp, *Der Prophet Jesaia* (1887).

[3] According to Ed. Meyer (*Encycl. Brit.* 11th ed. art. " Persis "), who regards as untenable the view that the Parsua of the inscriptions are to be identified with the Persians, the latter are nowhere mentioned until the time of Cyrus. This statement of the case is not strictly correct even if Prof. Meyer's view regarding the Parsua be accepted—and we will not enter upon a discussion of that point—unless it can be proved that by Paras (פרס) in Ezek. xxvii. 10, Persia is not meant and for such a contention there is in our opinion no adequate basis. ,

merely do they assert that there is practically no parallel in the Old Testament for so remarkable a prophecy as this would necessarily be if regarded as an Isaianic utterance.[4] But they tell us furthermore that the prophecy shows unmistakable indications of exilic composition, that " Cyrus is mentioned as one already well known as a conqueror ",[5] that " unless he had already appeared and was on the point of striking at Babylon with all the prestige of unbroken victory a great part of xl.-xlviii. would be unintelligible ".[6]

It is safe to say that to all students of the Old Testament whose theism is thoroughgoing enough to admit that Isaiah could and did foresee the rise and fall of Babylon and a Babylonian captivity of his own people (xiii.-xvi.23, xxi. 1-10, 39), the strongest evidence which can be advanced in favor of the late date of this prophetic utterance is the " internal evidence ", the evidence that the prophecy itself shows indications of exilic composition. External evidence in support of late date is scarcely to be found.[7] The most that the advocates of late date can do is to seek, as does, for example, G. A. Smith, to find reasons to justify the rejection of the external evidence in favor of Isaianic authorship. Their own case they must prove if it is to be proved at all, on the basis of " internal evidence ".

Owing to the definiteness with which this prophecy speaks of Cyrus and of the restoration it has been cited more frequently perhaps than any other as requiring exilic dating. The admission of this contention involves necessarily the ques-

---

[4] The " Josiah prophecy ", uttered by the unnamed prophet of Judah during the reign of Jeroboam (1 Kings, xiii) is, in respect of definiteness and perspective, strikingly parallel to the " Cyrus prophecy ", regarded as an Isaianic utterance. But the tendency in " critical circles " is to regard the former as largely if not entirely *Deuteronomic* (using the term in the sense given to it by the " critics ") in origin and to empty it of much if not all of its prophetic significance.

[5] Skinner, *Isaiah* in the Cambridge Bible Series.

[6] G. A. Smith, Article " Isaiah " in Hastings' *Bible Dictionary*.

[7] The claim that Isa. xl.-lxvi. shows traces of literary dependence on post-Isaianic writers, e. g. Jeremiah, is very precarious, since in instances of this kind it is rarely possible to show conclusively on which side the alleged dependence lies.

tion of the relation in which this exilic passage stands to the
larger context of which it forms a part. This question has
been answered in two ways. It is argued on the one hand
that it is a later addition to an Isaianic document (Interpolation
Hypothesis) ; on the other hand it is affirmed or rather assumed that it is an integral part of the document and as such
may be regarded as furnishing a legitimate criterion for ascer-
taining the date of the whole, or at least of a large part of
xl-lxvi. (Deutero-Isaianic Hypothesis).

To discuss these two hypotheses as fully as they deserve
would carry us too far afield, since it is impossible to estimate them justly in their bearing upon the Cyrus prophecy
without considering more or less fully their bearing upon the
whole " Book of Consolation " and even upon the entire book
of Isaiah. Suffice it to say that while in the one the question
of the authenticity of the allusion to Cyrus as a part of the
prophecy and of the prophecy itself as a constituent part of the
Latter Part of the Book of Isaiah occupies a very prominent
place, in the other this question is, at the outset at least, scarcely
raised, the acceptance of the integrity of the record, of the
genuineness of the passages which seem most clearly exilic,
making the argument for the late date doubly strong.[8] These
rival hypotheses set forth the two great problems involved in
the investigation of the Cyrus prophecy, viz., its unity and
integrity and the date of its composition.

[8] It should be remarked, of course, at this point that, although the advocates of the latter hypothesis, far from finding any dogmatic objection to
the integrity of the Cyrus prophecy, as part of an exilic document, find in
it a strong argument for the late date of the chapters of which it forms a
part, this hypothesis has at the same time long ceased to stand for the
integrity and unity of chaps. xl.-lxvi. as constituting such an exilic document. Deut.-Isa. is now limited to about one half (chaps. xl.-lv., Duhm,
Marti) or one third (chaps. xl.-xlviii., Cheyne) of the whole, and it is
regarded by Cheyne, Duhm and Marti as very extensively interpolated.
So, although in 1839 Hävernick was able to cite such champions of this
hypothesis as Gesenius, De Wette, Rosenmüller and Hitzig, as affirming
the unity of authorship of the Book of Consolation, in the opinion of
many of the present advocates of this view, this group of prophecies is
rather to be regarded as a " prophetic anthology ". Marti goes so far as
to call the book of Isaiah " a little library of prophetic writings ". And
as we shall see presently, the " Metricists " have not shown any hesitancy in

It is the purpose of this article to ascertain whether the claim that the Cyrus prophecy, either in whole or in part, shows indications of exilic composition is as well grounded as the frequent assertions to that effect would seem to indicate. As will appear in the course of the discussion, the poetical form of a part of the prophecy, viz., xliv. 24-28, has a very important bearing upon both of the questions at issue. And it is to this feature, therefore, that we will devote the chief attention.

HEBREW METRICS AND THE QINA ARRANGEMENT OF IS. XLIV. 24 (23)-28 PROPOSED BY BUDDE AND CHEYNE

While the rare poetic beauty of many portions of the Old Testament not included in the so-called poetical books has always been more or less recognized—how could any appreciative and careful reader fail to recognize it in a book so markedly poetic as, for example, the Book of Consolation!—and while many attempts have been made to solve the problem of Hebrew Poetry, it is only within a comparatively short time, within, we may say, the thirty years which have elapsed since Julius Ley published his *Hebräische Metrik* that much has been accomplished in the way of opening up what, as Grimme remarks, is usually regarded as an especially " slippery " field.[9] These investigations have proved that Hebrew poetry was accentual and not quantitative, that the character of the verse was determined primarily by the number of accents which it contained and that the ratio between accented and unaccented syllables was not a matter of no consequence but had certain more or less clearly defined limits. The prominent role of the caesura has been recognized and various metrical forms have been distinguished. There is considerable difference of opinion, however, in regard to a number of important questions e. g. the limits of the foot, if we may use the word to desig-

altering the text on the basis of metrical considerations. Consequently it would be a very mistaken notion to suppose that the advocates of the Deut.-Isa. hypothesis are defenders of the integrity or unity of this group of prophecies.

[9] H. Grimme, *Grundzüge der heb. Akzent- und Vokallehre*, S. 58 " dieses als besonders schlüpfrig verschrieene Gebiet (d. h. der biblischen Metrik)".

nate an accented syllable together with the unaccented syllables which are connected with it,[10] accent elision, which occurs
especially frequently with monosyllabic words or stat. const.
complexes, double accent of polysyllabic words, the shifting of
the accent and the problem of the strophe—these are some of
the questions which have still to be more thoroughly investigated. Furthermore the question to what extent the metres
were uniform, to what extent irregular or mixed is unsettled.
Even more unsettled is the question as to the degree in which

[10] Sievers (*Metrische Studien*) finds the most usual feet x ⌣, x x ⌣ which
may be modified to x ᙦx and xx ᙦx, respectively. (N.B. x represents the unaccented syllable and ⌣ the accented, while ᙦx represents the simple accented syllable ⌣ replaced by an accented syllable ⌣ immediately followed
by an unaccented syllable belonging to the *same* foot.)   But he also
regards ⌣ and x x x ⌣ and their modifications, i. e., ᙦx and x⌣x ᙦx as ad-
missable though less frequent forms, i. e., the number of unaccented syllables may vary from none to four. (Cf. Sievers' *Metrische Studien*, p.
99, § 71, 3, Die normalste Form des heb. Versfusses ist dreisilbiges x x ⌣
bez. dessen Auflösung (§ 19) xx ᙦx ; doch können daneben infolge andrer
Phasierung auch einfaches ⌣ , ferner x ⌣ und x x x⌣ nebst deren Auflös-
ungen auftreten.)   Sievers has approached the subject primarily from
the standpoint of Phonetics and Metrics. Ley laid emphasis upon the
character of the Heb. syllable and the law of ascent (das Gesetz der
Ascendenz, Abstufung), according to which the character and position
of a syllable determines whether it is accented or unaccented. He recognized five syllable gradations, the highest being the syllable which regularly receives the main accent, the lowest the syllable with the half vowel
(vocal shewa). Since the law of accent as defined by him required that
within the foot, there be always progress upward, it is consequently clear
that, according to his view, a foot could not exceed five syllables in length.
(Were a syllable followed by another of a lower instead of a higher
grade, it must be accented.) It usually consisted of less than five and Ley
recognized that it might consist of a single accented syllable unaccom-
panied by unaccented syllables. He also recognized the legitimacy of the
frequently occurring unaccented syllable after the accent which he calls
" Tonfall ", and which appears, as we have seen, in Sievers ' modified
foot ', as well as the fact that the inseparable prepositions, the conjunction
waw and a number of short words, prepositions, etc., are used proclitically
and have no accent. And he also perceived that the character of a line,
light or sonorous, joyous or sad, is largely determined by the ratio of the
unaccented to the accented syllables. In view of these facts it is clearly
unjust when Sievers (*Metrische Studien*, p. 45, § 58), who in the main
shows great readiness to recognize the value of Ley's investigations, states
that, according to the view held by Ley and his followers, " the Hebrew

the prose literature of the Old Testament especially the " Latter Prophets " may be regarded as metrical. David Heinrich Müller[11] finds in them a very marked strophical but no metrical form. That there is an epic poetry in Hebrew in which, in contrast e. g. to the lyric, the rigid *parallelismus membrorum* need not be present was recognized by Ley, thus widening the conception of Hebrew poetry to include more than the preponderatingly lyric poetry of the " Poetical Books ", and is more fully appreciated to-day. But the extent of this epic poetry as well as of the lyric in these books is still very far from being definitely settled. A passage which one scholar would treat as poetry in the strict sense, another may regard as merely an example of lofty and what we may call poetic prose.

In view of these facts the according of an important place to metrical considerations in the treatment of questions involving Textual Criticism is ill-advised and unfortunate.[12]   The

verse consists of *a number of accented syllables* (Anzahl von Hebungen) which further can be surrounded fairly *ad libitum* with a varying number of unaccented syllables ". The limits of Ley's foot are practically the same as those of Sievers, as far as the number of admissible syllables is concerned and the data just given which are based on Ley's own statements show clearly that the arrangement of said syllables was fully as rigidly controlled in Ley's scheme as it is in Sievers'.

[11] *Die Propheten in ihrer ursprünglichen Form.* Wien, 1896.

[12] Grimme (cf. *Abriss der bib. heb. Metrik, ZDMG.* 50, 529) considers this the main purpose of metrical study, as compared with which the more perfect appreciation of the beauty of a poetical passage which naturally results from a thorough understanding of its metrical form is a secondary consideration. Marti feels " that the surprising help in healing and restoring the text which comes from giving heed to metre and strophe makes it impossible to doubt that in the accepting of both, we have to do with no fiction." He regards them indeed as not inferior to the witness of the ancient versions. But he says: " in detail it must be admitted that much which concerns metrics is still uncertain." Cheyne remarks, (cf. *The Book of Isaiah in Hebrew,* pg. 78 in the *Sacred Books of the Old Testament* series), " among the grounds of alterations those which have regard to metre and rhythm can no longer be neglected, especially in view of the present stage of cuneiform research." This latter statement is a little hard to understand. If Cheyne means by it that the prominence of metrical questions at present is due to the advance made in the Assyrian field, the statement is opposed by the facts. Ley and Sievers

"metricist" often attempts to alter the text to suit a certain metrical scheme, when the fact that it does not readily admit of such an arrangement should rather be taken as an indication that the metrical scheme is either itself at fault or at any rate not applicable to the passage to which he wishes to apply it.

attacked the problem entirely without reference to Assyrian; Ley from the standpoint of the "old Germanic accented poetry" and Sievers who is Professor of Phonetics in Leipzig, from the standpoint of metrics and rhythm and it was only after he had developed his system for Hebrew poetry that he applied it at the suggestion of Prof. Zimmern to Assyrian. Grimme has devoted especial attention to Syriac metrics but not to Assyrian and further claims to be primarily a disciple of Ley. Budde, the discoverer of the Qina-Verse, whose theory is described in Gesenius-Kautzsch (Gesenius, *Hebrew Grammar*, 26th ed. by Kautzsch, Engl. ed. by Collins and Cowley, § 2, r.) as "the only sound one" shows nowhere dependence on the Assyr. Bab. Instead he regarded the fact that the Qina verse early lost its distinctive character, being found in passages which are in no sense dirges (Qina), (according to Grimme, Budde has reversed matters, the Qina verse being but a special application of the more widely applicable pentameter line) an argument for the antiquity of the verse form and he considered it pre-Davidic. That the discovery of a similar accentual poetry in Assyr.-Bab., more especially the finding of several tablets in which the words of the poems are arranged in columns seemingly with reference to the metrical form (cf. Zimmern & Scheil), is a valuable confirmation of the results already independently obtained in the Old Testament field is clear. But it cannot be claimed that our knowledge of Hebrew Metrics is in any special sense the result of or dependent upon "cuneiform research". If, on the other hand, as is more probable, Cheyne means that the predominantly poetical form of the religious literature of the Babylonians necessitates the assumption that a large part if not all of the prophetic literature of the *OT*. must have originally partaken of the same poetical character, this is an assertion which must be proved. If the "Prophets" show the same or similar forms, well and good. This does not prove that they are Babylonian and not merely Semitic forms, and, even granted that they are originally Babylonian, this proves nothing with regard to the date of their appearance in Hebrew literature. (Zimmern tells us that the religious hymns of the Babylonians which show the Babylonian metres in their purest form remained for 3000 years practically the same. Consequently they could have been known to Abraham when he lived in Ur of the Chaldees.) If, on the other hand, they do not show the same metres, or if no metre is distinguishable, the attempt to force prose passages into Bab. metres can only proceed from and be justified by that "panbabylonianistic" tendency, which seeks to deny to the Jews all initiative and independence.

Such a procedure at once raises the question of the validity of textual emendation on the basis of purely metrical considerations,[13] whether the aim be to restore an original poem the mutilated remains of which are clearly discernible, so we are told, in the Massoretic Text, or to arrange a prose passage in the metrical form, which it must have had, they argue, because of the analogy of the religious literature of the Babylonians, or for some other reason of a similar character.

In 1892, Budde, the discoverer of the " Qina " [14] measure, defended his method, which involves textual emendation, against the objections raised by " a most distinguished " scholar, whose name he did not state, who objecting to Budde's method declared " least of all can I grant permission to undertake the altering of the text, on the basis of a presupposed Qina-verse theory ", as follows: " Under no circumstances do I start out with the intention of forcing any passage into the Qina-verse mould. On the contrary the study of the verse is always the first thing, and only when the data thus obtained preponderate for a certain compass," [i. e., when a majority of the lines have been shown to be Qina], " do I decide to lay hold of it. But then I can not relinquish the second prerogative which is gladly conceded in dealing with other passages;[15] viz. to undertake textual emendations, not on the basis of a presupposed Qina-verse theory, but on the basis of the evidence of an intended use of the verse, in order to restore to its rights as far as is possible that which was intended by the poet." A praiseworthy aim certainly! But we may ask does the presence of a preponderance of what may

[13] It is to be observed that we are not here discussing the Interpolation Hypothesis, which for reasons already indicated regards the allusion to Cyrus an interpolation, but a very different question, viz., whether purely metrical considerations can of themselves prove textual corruption or justify textual emendation.

[14] The Qina line is pentameter and has the caesura after the third foot so that the line falls apart into two members, the first, which is the longer having three accents, the second but two. The occurrence of this measure in a large portion of the Book of Lamentations has given rise to the name Qînā, i. e. lamentation (קִינָה) verse.

[15] The reference here seems to be to lyric passages, since the other objection of the " distinguished unknown " is to the application of a lyric measure to non-lyric passages.

be regarded as Qina lines in a given passage establish beyond peradventure the fact that a Qina poem is " what was intended by the poet "? Can Budde or anyone else be positive that in making alterations he will merely be restoring the poet to his rights and not rather giving him what he feels were or ought to have been his rights, and there is no small difference between the two.

We are prepared to test the validity of Budde's method in general, the permissability of textual emendation on the basis of purely metrical considerations by considering its applicability to the Cyrus Prophecy, xliv. 24-28. This we may do the more readily in view of the fact that it is one of fifteen passages of varying length in the second half of Isaiah which were cited by Budde in 1891 (*ZATW*. xii. II. 234 ff), as requiring the Qina verse form and his arrangement in a somewhat modified form is adopted by most critics at the present time. This arrangement will be found on the opposite page.

According to Budde's count this passage is composed of fourteen lines, only four of which are " damaged ", i. e. non-Qina lines, nearly three fourths of the poem being in and of itself Qina. Lines 5 and 6 consist of three half lines instead of two whole lines. Line 9 has a word too many and line 10 lacks a second member. In line 9 he proposed the reading " and his counsel (ועצתו)" as a substitute for the reading of the Massoretic Text " and the counsel of his messengers (ועצת מלאכיו)". But in line 10 he confined himself to calling attention to the fact that in the second reference to Jerusalem (line 14) the reference to the Temple supplies the second member while in the first reference (line 10) a second member is lacking.

According to Budde's method as explained by himself this poem must therefore have been originally a Qina poem since more than a majority of its lines are in his opinion Qina lines and therefore alterations with a view to " restoring the poet to his rights " are fully warranted. Other scholars (Cheyne, Duhm, Marti) have attempted a more thorough restoration than Budde, though along the same general lines. These scholars consider the first member of line 14, i. e. the second reference to Jerusalem, which has been already referred to, a

BUDDE'S QINA ARRANGEMENT OF ISAIAH XLIV. 23-28.

Sing, heavens, for-hath-done (-it) Jehovah	shout lower-parts of (-the) -earth[16]
Break-forth-into singing, mountains	forest and-every-tree-in-it
For-redeemed-hath Jehovah Jacob	and-glorified-himself in-Israel
Thus-saith Jehovah thy-redeemer	and-thy-fashioner from (-the)-womb
5 I-am Jehovah that-maketh all (-things)	that-stretcheth-forth heavens alone[17]
That-spreadeth-abroad the-earth who-was with-me	
That-frustrateth signs of-liars	and-diviners he-maketh-mad
That-turneth wise-men backward	and-their-knowledge he-maketh-foolish
That-confirmeth the-word of-his-servant	and-his-counsel he-performeth[18]
10 That-saith of-Jerusalem she-shall-be-inhabited	
And-of-the-cities of-Judah they-shall-be-built	and-her-waste-places I-will-raise-up
That-saith to-the-Deep: be dry!	and-thy-rivers I-will-make-dry
That-saith of-Cyrus my-shepherd (-is-he)	and-all-my-pleasure shall-he-perform
Even-to-say of-Jerusalem she-shall-be-built.	and-(of-the-) Temple: thy-foundation-shall-be-laid

[16] In this translation the hyphens indicate that words so joined together represent a single word or at least a single accent in the Hebrew, since it is impossible to make a literal translation (i. e., word for word in the exact sense of the phrase) which would be intelligible.

[17] Budde merely states that the second half of verse 24 consists of three verse members of equal length representing originally (?) two Qina lines, but does not say whether he prefers to read $\begin{cases} a - b \\ c - - - \end{cases}$ as above, or $\begin{cases} a - - \\ b - c \end{cases}$.

[18] In the original "and-the-counsel of-his-messengers".

corrupt repetition of the first member of line 10, and they feel that the second member of line 14 really belongs to line 10. Consequently by rejecting the first part of line 14 as spurious and restoring the second member to its original (?) position as the second member of line 10 the latter is " healed " and the poem *merely* loses half a line.[19] The reducing of the second member of line 9 from three to two words is accepted. And thus from line 7 on they obtain a perfect Qina poem. But they find it much more difficult to account for the three members of lines 5 and 6, which should be represented by two Qina lines. It is possible to treat them as 1½ Qina lines,[20] but difficult to get two full lines without making additions to the text. Cheyne thinks that in view of its extra length line6— he adopts the second arrangement given on pg. 590 (note 17) —may be regarded as making up for the shortness of the preceeding line, which in his arrangement seems clearly to need a second member. Duhm suggests the following arrangement:

I-am Jehovah that-maketh-all	that-stretcheth-forth heavens
Alone, spreading-out the-earth	who-was with-me[21]

[19] Marti thinks that the " he performeth " (ישׁלם) of line 9 (v. 26a) was taken over from line 13 and therefore, although rejecting it in line 9 as a corruption, reading with Duhm and Cheyne "and the counsel of his messengers" (ועצת מלאכיו) in preference to the emendation proposed by Budde, he feels justified in inserting after line 9, line 14, i. e. line 14b, since line 14a he regards as a corruption of 10a.

[20] " That-stretcheth-forth heavens " (נטה שׁמים) can probably be included under a single accent, although it would naturally require two. The same is true of "who (was) with me" (מי אתי) (if the Qrê "by-myself" were adopted, more than one accent would be impossible). The member scans well either way. *Rokâ' ha'áres mi' itti* = 4 accents ($\times \angle \times \angle \times \angle \times \angle$) a perfectly uniform measure, or *rokâ' ha'áres mi' itti* = 3 accents ($\dot{\times} \angle \times \angle \times \times$ $\mathcal{S}\dot{\times}$) the accent receding in pause and the " *mi* " losing its accent in view of the accented syllable which thus immediately follows.

[21]   נטה שׁמים   אנכי יהוה עשׂה כל
           מי אתי   לבדי רקע הארץ

Duhm also emends " and of the cities of Judah " (ולערי יהודה) v. 26 to read " and of the ruins of the land " (ולעיי אדמה) declaring, "in the third ' long verse '" [i. e., line 11 of Budde's poem, the third line of the second strophe according to Cheyne, Duhm and Marti] "the LXX has Ἰδουμαίας instead of Ἰουδαίας; the אדמה which lies back of it is better than the Judah which is derived from C 40, 9; since the suffix of חרבותיה clearly refers to it. Further the changing of ערי into עיי cannot be avoided, as

But, as Cheyne argues, the placing of the adverb at the beginning of the second line is inadmissable.   And at best the
arrangement is forced and awkward and would do little credit
to the poet although it technically fulfils the requirements of
a Qina line.   Cheyne, Duhm and Marti further find the beginning of the poem or strophe, not at verse 23 but at verse
24 and Cheyne considers verse 23 which consisted according
to Budde of three Qina lines, (the " long verse " of Duhm) to
be composed rather of six short or single member lines and
in either case it must be admitted that they are somewhat ir-

the latter harmonizes better with the second half of the line, especially with
the singular suffix, than does the עָרִי which draws upon itself the accent
which belongs to אמדה ".   An investigation of the usage of the LXX
makes it clear that in substituting אמדה for יהורה on the basis of the
LXX, Duhm has not only overstated the facts (Ιδουμαίας is only found in
Cod. B.) but has also drawn conclusions from them for which there is
very little warrant.   The facts are these: 1) A number of instances can be
cited where proper names are confused and interchanged in the versions.
In Hatch and Redpath's Concordance seven other instances are given where
in one or more of the Codices 'Ιδουμαία renders another proper name of
somewhat similar sound, in six instances it is as here הורה· in one Duma
Similarly four instances are given where 'Ιδουμαία in the Greek represents
another proper name in the Hebrew, showing that proper names are occasionally confused.   2) אדמה is, on the other hand, accurately rendered.
Only two cases are cited by Hatch & Redpath where it was confused with
other words.   In Neh. ix. 1 it is rendered " ashes ", evidently because the
preceeding word is " sackcloth ", which suggests the common phrase " sackcloth and ashes ".   In Isaiah xv. 9 it is rendered Ἀδαμα (Admah).   If
by this word אדם (Edom) is meant, we have here one instance in more
than one hundred where אדמה and אדם were confounded.   A confusion
is natural in this instance in view of the mention of Petra (Sela) in the
next verse.   In Isaiah xliv. 26 on the contrary an allusion to Edom is
most inappropriate and, had the original word been אדמה, there is every
reason to suppose that it would have been rendered " land ".   The natural
explanation of the occurrence of 'Ιδουμαία in B is " confusion of proper
names " and the best codices of the LXX as also the Syr., the Latin and
the Targum of Jonathan support the יהורה of the Hebrew text.   Retaining, therefore, as we have every reason for doing, the reading " Judah ",
we are entirely justified in retaining the reading " cities ", " cities of
Judah ", a phrase which is clearly parallel to the word " Jerusalem " in the
first member.   That the singular pronoun " her-waste-places " is an indication of corrupt text, cannot be argued, since this pronoun may find its
antecedent in " Judah " or even in " Jerusalem ".

regular, (the first line being 4-3, not 3-2). If the first three lines of Budde's poem are rejected as at least questionable, (and at any rate a new paragraph begins more naturally at verse 24 than at verse 23), and if the fourteenth line despite the fact that it is pentameter (Qina) is sacrificed for the purpose of restoring the incomplete tenth line a fairly good Qina poem (see next page[22]) of two strophes of five lines each is obtained, a poem reconstructed out of a mutilated poem of eleven lines, five lines of which were in need of alteration[29] and two lines of which remain imperfect if with Cheyne we reject Duhm's forced and awkward construction for lines 2 and 3. In other words of these eleven lines only six have been preserved in their original form and five need amending in order that the original form of the poem may be obtained. And he who will by this method " restore the poet to his rights " must argue that six out of eleven lines, a scant majority, prove that the Qina form was the one originally intended by the writer.

[22] This is primarily a translation of Cheyne's arrangement of the Hebrew Text as given in the *Book of Isaiah in Hebrew*. His translation in the " English Polychrome " has been consulted and followed fairly closely. But the translation has been modified at several points with a view to making the poetic structure as plain as possible in the English. His Hebrew Text is as follows (several pointings and diacritical marks are here omitted) :

ויצרך מבטן	כה אמר יהוה גֹאלך
	אנכי יהוה עשׂה כל
ר־קע הארץ מי אתי	נטה שמים לבדִּי
וקסמים יהולל	מֵפֵר אֹתות בַּדִּים
ודעתם יסכל	משיב חכמים אחור
ועצת מלאכיו	מקים דבד עבדו
[ו־ל־היכל תוסד]	האמר לירשלם תושב
וחרבותיה אקומם	ולערי יהודה תבנינה
ונהריתיך אוביש	האמר לצולה חרבי
וכל חֶפצי ישלים	האמר לכורש רֵעי

[29] Viz. lines 2 and 3, which, according to Budde, are three half lines where we would expect two whole lines, line 6b which has been reduced from a three accent to a two accent member, and line 7 which is made up of two imperfect lines, viz., 7a and what would otherwise be line 11b (Budde's line 14b).

CHEYNE'S ARRANGEMENT OF ISAIAH, xliv. 24-28.[22]

Thus-saith JHVH thy-redeemer,   and-thy-fashioner from-the-womb:

I-am JHVH, who-wrought-everything,

Who-stretched-forth the-heavens, alone,   who-spread-forth the-earth—who-was with-me?—[23]

Who-brings-to-naught the-omens of-the-imposters,   and-the-diviners he-makes-mad,

5   Who-turns the-wise backward,   and-their-knowledge he-makes-folly,

Who-ratifies the-word of-his-servants,[24]   and-the-prophecy of-his-messengers;[25]

Saying of-Jerusalem: Be-it-inhabited!   and (-of)-the-Temple: Be-thy-foundations-laid![25]

And-of-the-cities of-Judah: Let-them-be-built!   and-her-desolations I-will-raise-up;

Who-says to-the-flood: Be-dry!   and-thy-rivers will-I-parch-up;

10   Who-says of-Cyrus: My-friend[27](-is-he),   and-all-my-purpose will-he-accomplish.[28]

---

[22] Cheyne prefers the Kthibh. For his explanation of the extra length of this line cf. pg. 591.

[24] He prefers to read "his servants", a defectively written plural.

[25] Cf. p. 591.

[26] Cf. p. 589 bot.

[27] Reading עֵי instead of עֵי.

[28] Cf. p. 589 bot.

Notwithstanding the serious difficulties connected with its application, the view that the Qina arrangement of this poem is the true one seems to have been very favorably received in " critical circles ", cf., e. g., the recent commentaries of Box and Glazebrook. But we are justified none the less in raising the question whether the inference drawn from the presence of 6 Qina lines in a 10 line poem (if the seventh Qina line, line 14 of Budde's poem, be used to restore a mutilated line it must be itself treated as corrupt) or, according to Budde, of 10 Qina lines in a 14 line poem that the whole poem must originally have been Qina is so compelling as to warrant attempts at restoration? We have examined the alterations which have been proposed and find that except for one line the redacted poem (cf. Cheyne's arrangement) may be called a Qina poem. But it is well to remember that these textual alterations are made largely if not entirely independently of and without the support of the ancient versions. In so far then as they may claim warrant at all for these alterations it must be found in the evidence that the Qina form was intended. And despite the " majority of Qina lines " we are prepared to assert that the inference drawn from them that the poem was originally Qina is not warranted in view of the number of lines which can only with more or less difficulty be redacted into the Qina form.

The Numerico-Climactic Arrangement and the Argument of the Poem

Let us begin with verse twenty-four and analyze the paragraph for ourselves. The first line, " Thus saith Jehovah thy redeemer and thy fashioner from the womb " which has the Qina form is clearly introductory to the brief emphatic declaration " I am Jehovah " (אנכי יהוה). This declaration is followed by nine participial clauses of varying length, which, while all depending upon and qualifying it directly, at the same time form three distinct groups. The first group is composed of three single member lines each of which begins with a *qal* participle. The second group consists of three two member lines, the first members being introduced by *hiph'il* participles

and the second members being joined to the first by "and"
(*waw conj.*) and ending with finite verbs. The third group
consists of three lines which average three members each, the
first members in every case being introduced by the formula
"that saith of (or to)" (ל האמר), each subsequent member
being joined in the preceding by "and (or even)" (*waw
conj.*) and ending with a finite verb, as in the second group.
Furthermore the second group possesses the distinctive feature
that in it the "person" of the narrative abruptly changes,
Jehovah instead of being the speaker as in the first and last
groups is spoken of objectively and the third person appears
in the three finite verbs of the second members and with special
prominence in the "his servant" (עבדו) and "his messengers" (מלאכיו) of the third line. The reason for such a
change will appear later.

If we arrange the paragraph according to the scheme suggested by these outstanding features (cf. Plates I and II) it
is at once apparent that it has two very marked characteristics,
number and climax. The poem consists of three strophes of
three lines each, (numerical feature), while the element of
climax is obtained primarily through increasing the number of members in the lines of each successive strophe, the
first strophe having one-member lines, the second two-member,
while the third strophe averages three three-member lines,
although an extra climax is obtained by lengthening the last
line at the expense of the one which precedes it. In this way
the two elements, number and climax, are interwoven (the climax involving the number three) and the result is a numerical
climax. This will be the more apparent perhaps if we treat
for a moment the single members as units, thus obtaining the
following numerical scheme:

[30] Here as in the Qina arrangements words joined by hyphens are to
be treated as having but a single accent. An effort has been made to
make the translation exhibit as clearly as possible the metrical form of
the poem—This applies especially to the end-members of the second
strophe—But although in the main the approximation is fairly close, a
perfect reproduction is of course unattainable.

[31] Or "its foundation" if "Temple" is as some suppose construed
here as a feminine noun. [These two notes refer to Plate II].

```
                       I
Strophe  I             I
                       I

                       I         I
Strophe  II            I         I
                       I         I

                       I         I         I
Strophe  III           I         I
                       I         I         I         I
```

The progressive climax is very marked and is heightened by
the extra length of the last line of the third strophe.   This
additional climax seems at first sight considerably discounted
by the shortness of the second line of the same strophe, which
is correspondingly weaker than the normal first line, But it
is to be observed that if the last line is to be strengthened without marring the numerical symmetry of the strophe as a whole,
this is the best way in which it can be accomplished.[32]   That
from the standpoint of the strophe the symmetry is maintained
is clear when we cast up the totals as follows:

Strophe I	3	3
Strophe II	3 3	6
Strophe III	3 3 3[33]	9

Consequently this departure from an absolute uniformity
which we find in the third strophe has this in its favor at the
outset that it does not mar the numerical symmetry of the
whole.   And as we will now proceed to show, this seeming
irregularity is the result a second element of climax
·which, less perceptible in the first two strophes of the poem,
makes itself all the more noticeable in the third.

We have assumed for the purpose of clearly exhibiting the
structural form of the poem that the units of which it is made
up, the single members, are uniform and have so treated them

[32] That it would be better to weaken the second line than the first is clear,
since the first, as already remarked, gives the normal length of a 3rd
strophe line.

[33] It is certainly permissable to derive this 3 from the 2 + 1 of the first
arrangement and, in any case, the totals for the strophes show a uniform
increase.

in the numerical scheme. This is only partially correct. Eleven of the eighteen members which constitute the poem have three accents (three words)[34] each, all of the nine non-end-members[35] being three-accent members,[36] a further application as it would seem of the numerical (triple) principle. But there is a variation in the members of the first strophe and in the end-members of the second which is of great significance for the understanding of the variation in the position of the members in the third strophe. This variation is quite marked in the first strophe. The three members contain in all nine words (nine accents) an average of three to a member as in the first members of the other two strophes. But instead of a uniform triplet of three-accent lines we find a two-, a three-, and a four-accent line, i. e., speaking from the standpoint of uniformity the first member has been shortened and the third member lengthened to the extent of an accent, so that the numerical form of the strophe counting accents only is 2, 3, 4, and should we disregard the verb in the count since it is a constant factor, 1, 2, 3 which is the strophical climax in miniature. Furthermore the length of the last member is increased by the presence of the article " *the* earth " (הארץ).[37] All of

[34] We may use accent and word here interchangeably, since there are no cases of double accent or accent elision present in the passage.

[35] By this is meant of course members which do not stand at the end of the line.

[36] In strophe III, line 3, member 2, the maqqeph of the massoretic pointing should be removed, the correct reading being וְכֹל חֶפְצִי יַשְׁלִם instead of וְכָל־חֶפְצִי יַשְׁלִם, i. e., three accents, not two.

[37] It cannot be argued that usage favors this, since the concordance shows that the article occurs with "heaven" (שמים) if anything more frequently in proportion than with "earth" (ארץ). Nor can the presence of the article here be explained on the basis of metrical considerations. For although the insertion of the article before ארץ makes it possible for the preceding word to be accented on the ultima and avoids the necessity of the throwing back of its accent on to the penult, the same would apply to the first line. And since there the accent is thrown back, the line being made as it seems as short as possible, the inference seems warranted that the adding of the article in the third line is intended to produce the opposite effect namely to lengthen the line. Nor finally can it be argued that the purpose of the insertion of the article is to avoid the cacophony resulting from the coming together of an

which goes to show that there is a marked climax *within* the members of the first strophe and a decided heightening at the end.[38]

The same climactic heightening in a slightly modified form is characteristic of the end-members[39] of the second strophe. The first consists of two words (noun + verb, two accents), the second of two words (noun with pronominal suffix + verb, two accents), the third of three words (noun in stat. cstr.+ noun with pronominal suffix + verb, three accents). This heightening seems on the one hand closely parallel to that in the first strophe except that here the second step is only the addition of a pron. suffix, an addition which does not increase the number of accents in the member, while in the first strophe it is a noun which does. On the other hand, however, the second member of the second line is perceptibly shorter than the second member of the first line (not merely as written, unless both the vowels which are written fully in the former were written defectively, but also as spoken it is slightly shorter, and rhythmically lighter) while the third line is very considerably longer than either of the others, three quarters as long as both combined. Thus we notice a double climax in the second

Ayin and of an Aleph. For as Aleph and Hê are both gutturals it hardly seems as if the *Wohlklang* would be materially increased in this way.

[38] It might even be argued that it furnishes a clue to the construction of the poem as a whole, the lines of the first strophe losing the second

members and the lines of the third receiving them thus:
$$\begin{matrix} & 3 & 3 & & 3 \\ 3 & 3 & = & 3 & 3 \\ 3 & 3 & & 3 & 3 & 3 \end{matrix}$$

But this is perhaps too labored an explanation and it will be shown presently that this triple climax has its basis in the argument of the poem.

[39] The fact that there is no perceptible climax in the non-end-members of the second and third strophes—all have 3 accents and the slight variation in the length of the members, resulting from the difference in the length of the words has no significance—has its natural explanation in the fact that uniformity in these members gives an element of solidarity to the poem, which is necessary if the climactic feature appearing in the end-members is to be properly appreciated. It is this uniformity in the non-end-members which is calculated to call our attention to the heightening at work in the end-members, just as the figures in a bas-relief are all the more striking because of the solid background from which they emerge.

members of this strophe; in the one sense a progressive climax, similar to that in strophe I, even a heightened climax in
the last line, (for while, as has been indicated, the increase of
the second end-member over the first is only a pron. suffix
that of the third over the second is a whole word); in the
other sense, not merely a heightened climax in the third but
a slight weakening in the second. Consequently the second
strophe is clearly intermediate between the first and the third.
It shows elements of the uniform climax of strophe I and
at the same time prepares the way for the exceptional climax
of strophe III which as has already been pointed out is obtained through the weakening of the second line to allow for
the strengthening of the third. For what in the one takes
place in miniature, so to speak, within the limits of the end-
members, appears in the other, viz. in strophe III in a much
more pronounced form since the second line is weakened to
the extent of a whole member and the third strengthened to
the same extent, although the symmetry of the strophe viewed
as strophe, i. e. its numerical value, remains the same.

That this transposition of a whole member in strophe III
was intentional and not accidental is clear not only from the
facts just mentioned, namely that the symmetry is retained and
that this marked heightening in the last strophe is the result of
a heightening process at work in the whole poem which, at first
confined to the end-members, assumes larger proportions in
the last line of the last strophe, where if anywhere the greatest
climax might be expected, but also from the evident fact that
the end-members of strophe III were intended by the poet
to be end-members. For it is to be observed that the end-
members of this strophe are all two-accent members, while all
the others have three accents. Various explanations of this
fact may be given[40] but its meaning is evident. It tells

[40] Probably the simplest explanation is that the writer has made use of
the law of catalexis, for the purpose of clearly marking the ends of these
lines (Catalexis is by no means rare in Hebrew poetry. According to Ley
it is one of the most usual ways of indicating the end of the strophe.
Duhm seems to regard the Qina (pentameter) line as catalectic Hexameter, but whether this is actually or merely theoretically correct may be
questioned.) A catalexis in the end-members of this strophe is further

us that the second member of the second line is an end-member, i. e. finishes the line, but just as clearly that the third member of the third line does not complete that line. It is completed by the fourth member which is an end-member. In view of these facts it is impossible to assert that the second line is incomplete or that its end-member was lost or appended by mistake to the last line. The one has been intentionally shortened through the omission of a non-end member, the other intentionally lengthened through the insertion of the same non-end member[41] with a view to obtaining an increased climax the elements of which appear in the preceding strophes.

The Argument of the Poem

If we turn now from considering the form of the poem to an examination of its contents, it will be clear that the form (the numerico-climactic scheme, which we have been discussing) not merely in its more general features but even in its minute details is in harmony with, may even be considered but the outward expression of, the argument of the poem. First let us consider the relation between the theme and the numerical structure. The theme of the poem is the " Transcendence of Jehovah " (I am Jehovah) as exhibited in the catalogue of mighty deeds recorded in the nine participial clauses which immediately follow. These are arranged stro-

favored by the following considerations. The introductory formula is Pentameter, i. e., catalectic. The initial declaration " I am Jehovah " (אנכי יהוה) is two-accent, so is also, for reasons already given, the first member of the first strophe and the same feature appears in the first two end-members of the second. Consequently uniformity would seem to require that the first end-member of the third strophe should have but two accents and, as the heightening process has in this strophe clearly exceeded the confines of the end-members being produced by the transference of a whole member from the second line to the third and as uniformity in the end-members serves the important end just alluded to, i. e., of designating the end-members as end-members, the catalexis, is allowed to appear in all three end-members of this strophe.

[41] This applies, of course, merely to the *form* of the poem and not to the *argument*, since from the latter standpoint one line is as perfect as the other.

phically and topically in three groups. The first group
(strophe I) describes the work of Jehovah as creator. It
refers to events lying in the *past*. The second treats of the
attitude of Jehovah toward the longings, the efforts and
the pretentions of mankind to discern the future, to know
" the times or the seasons which the Father put in his own
power ". The answer is unequivocal—the future belongs to
God. He baffles every attempt to enter his domain and covers
the intruder with confusion. But just because it belongs to
him, he only can and does reveal its secrets and also bring to
pass all that he has revealed. As this is what may be called his
" fixed policy " it is true of the past and future as fully as of
the present. But the reference to " the servant " in the last line
together with the fact, which has been already mentioned,
that Jehovah is here referred to in the third person, suggests
at least that in it the speaker, who is as we shall see later
the prophet, refers to himself, and therefore that the reference is more especially to present time.[42]   And the position
of this strophe—between a clearly past and clearly future
strophe—shows beyond reasonable doubt that in the scheme
of the poem it is to be regarded as a *present* strophe. At
the same time the fact that it has what we may call a backward
and a forward reference, fits it admirably to be the connecting
link between past and future[43] and to show how closely and
intimately they are all bound together. The third declares
his purpose to deliver his people from captivity and to restore
them to their own land, and speaks exclusively of the *future*.
These data explain at once the meaning of the number three in
the metrical scheme. We have here no mysterious adumbra-
tion of the Trinity, no dependence on the " trilogy arrangement " of the Book of Consolation, advocated by Delitzsch.

[42] We must not, however, lay too much stress upon the fact that "servant " is singular, since it might be regarded as a " defectively written "
plural (cf. Cheyne's arrangement), although it is much more natural to
regard it a singular.

[43] The " forward reference " is especially marked, since " the word of
his servant " seems to find its echo in the thrice repeated " that saith "
of the third strophe and to call attention at the very outset to its being
a prophecy.

The number three is clearly the three of the ordinary categories of time—past, present, future[44]—and the prominence of this number in the scheme is due to the prominence of the chronological element in the poem and is intended to bring this feature with unmistakeable clearness before the mind and eye of the reader.

But not only does the recognition of the chronological element in the poem at once explain its numerical scheme it explains the climactic feature as well. The reason is not far to seek. It lies in the relative importance of these three categories in general and in the special prominence of the third category in this instance. Of the relative importance of these categories to us as individuals it is hardly necessary to speak since it is a fact of experience. The past is important. It is the foundation upon which the present rests. But it is past. We cannot recall it. We cannot re-live it. The best that we can do is to learn from it and apply its lessons to the present and the future. It is furthermore an historic past and though

[44] It is interesting to note that this chronological element is recognized to a considerable degree in the Peshito version. Thus the participles of the first strophe are all rendered by the finite verb in the past tense; the participles of the second strophe by participles, but the first two finite verbs by presents (i. e., by participles with appended enclitic pronoun); the participles of the third strophe by perfects, as if to indicate that the decree is of old, but the imperfect tenses with one exception by the imperfect (future). It is also interesting to observe in this connection that in Jer. xliv., D. H. Müller finds a poem in which there is a chronological, but not a climactic form. He divides the chapter into three parallel columns, A, B and C, i. e., verses 2-6, 7-10, 11-14. Each of these columns he arranges in strophes of the form $1 + 6 + 6$, the 1 being in each case represented by the introductory formula "Thus saith Jehovah of Hosts", etc., in its varying forms. Whether this strophical scheme can be accepted does not concern us particularly. It is sufficient to note that in the original the three paragraphs are of nearly equal length. The important fact is that he finds these three columns mutually parallel, while at the same time the chronological feature is prominent in each, the first treating of the past, the second of the present, (notice the prominence of the "and now" (ועתה) at the beginning of verse 7), the last of the future. This shows clearly that, as a chronological poem, the Cyrus prophecy is not without analogy. And even if Jer. xliv. be treated as simple prose (cf. Kittel's edition of the *Biblia Hebraica*), it is an example of the application of the chronological method to a carefully balanced discourse.

ofttimes we need guidance to read its lessons aright, it is in a sense an open book accessible to all. For none but beings incapable of reflection can be conscious of no past. The present is far more significant than the past for it is the time of action and of actuality. It is truly but as a narrow strip of land between two mighty oceans, but it is none the less " the accepted time ". The " living " of a man is made up of a fleeting succession of " nows " and they are in a very real sense ' all that he has to face eternity with '. The past is mighty but it is gone casting its mantle upon the shoulders of the present and this present is as much mightier than the past as " a living dog is mightier than a dead lion ". And yet the present is but the threshold of the future—a future which looms dim and mysterious, potent for weal or woe before life's pilgrim. We act in the present but for the future. Our planning, hoping, toiling is for the future. And why? Because we are bound thither by the inexorable law of destiny. Even the most thoughtless is sobered by the thought of this " Great Unknown ". For though we should strive to think of death as but a sleep, " yet in that sleep of death, what dreams may come when we have shuffled off this mortal coil, must give us pause ". The certainty of a future and the uncertainty of *the* future have tremendous significance for every thoughtful man. It is the goal of the race and of the individual. Is it any wonder then that in every age, the man who by wisdom or cunning, by fair means or foul could lift the curtain of the future has been held in high esteem? Is it any wonder that the office of the Hebrew prophet meant and means to many merely that of a " predictor "?

It is quite natural then that the writer of a chronological poem such as we have found this to be should introduce the element of climax to show the relative importance of these three classes of mighty deeds. What we may call the normal value or ratio of these three categories seems clearly given in the normal climax 3, 6, 9, in which the three strophes are composed of one-, two-, and three-member lines respectively. This is the normal climax of the poem and may therefore be said to represent the normal ratio between the categories of time, i. e. the ratio, when there is no especial emphasis on the events lying in the different categories, these being all of equal intrinsic importance, the emphasis being primarily on the category to which the events belong. Consequently we might expect that the extraordinary importance of an event or series of events lying in one of these categories might be indicated by, and consequently inferred from, an extraordinary emphasis upon it, or speaking from the standpoint of the metrical form, by an extraordinary climax at that point. In the metrical form, we have found an additional climax within the normal, a climactic process which reaches its height in the third (future) strophe. Does this as well as the normal find its explanation in the argument of the poem? Let us examine and see.

The first strophe has, as we have seen, three single-member lines so constructed as to produce a uniform climax of the form 2, 3, 4. The theme is the *creative* acts of Jehovah. In the first line it is stated briefly and generally, " that made all (things)" (עֹשֶׂה כֹל). In the " all " the monergism is described *in extenso*. In the second the sphere is limited " that stretched out heavens " (נֹטֶה שָׁמַיִם); and the monergism is explicitly expressed and emphasized by the addition of the word " alone " or " by myself " (לְבַדִּי) denying that he had a co-worker. While in the third line, which speaks with still greater definiteness of " *the* earth " (הָאָרֶץ) the monergism is declared in the form of an almost contemptuous challenge "who was with me?" (מִי אִתִּי) a challenge to man to deny that God alone created this earth in which he lives, to deny that God alone is great. In the increasing stress laid on the monergism of Jehovah the theme of the strophe shows a decided climax, together with, and the importance of this feature will appear more clearly later, an element of increasing definiteness (all, heavens, *the* earth).

The second strophe treats, with especial reference to the present, what we may call the " future problem ", i. e. it exposes the folly and futility of man's efforts or pretensions to discern the future as contrasted with the certainty of divine revelation. Three instances likewise are cited. The first line tells us that Jehovah "frustrateth the signs of liars and maketh diviners mad ", i. e. those who defy his moral government and try to discern the future by unlawful means are confused and confounded. Here the thought of open opposition is strong. In the second line it is less apparent and may even be said to disappear. "That turneth wise men backward and their knowledge he maketh foolish". "Those who in their wisdom know not God" their wisdom is deception and folly. There is not the same clearly marked opposition in case of the "wise men" (חכמים) as in that of the "liars" (בדים) and "diviners (קסמים) and they are less severely dealt with. So this second line seems weaker than the first. Yet in another sense there is a slight advance corresponding to the slight advance in metrical form. For while the "wicked" of the first line seem to recognize supernatural power and agencies although enemies of Jehovah, the "wise men" of the second line ignore him. Like the "fool", they have said in their heart, "there is no God": like the modern Positivist they have gotten beyond the religious stage, an attitude which in some respects at least is even more culpable than open opposition.[45] The third line "that confirmeth the word of his servant and performeth the counsel of his messengers" stands in contrast to the first two, the parallelism being antithetic. Jehovah overcomes opposition. True! But he also accomplishes his purposes. What he has declared or declares through his servant and his messengers, the prophets, shall surely be fulfilled. The climax of this line is clearly indicated by the antithesis and by the marked definiteness produced by the presence of the pronouns, "his servant", "his messengers", as contrasted with the indefiniteness of the first two lines. Thus the form and argument of this strophe are in entire harmony, there being in both a marked climax in the third line, and the second in the argument as well as in the metrical form being both stronger and weaker than the first.

The third strophe treats of the release and restoration. The first line is a general prophecy—Jerusalem shall be again inhabited, the cities of Judah rebuilt and their desolation come to an end. It is general and we may say corresponds more

[45] That "wise" and "knowledge" must have this significance is clear. For it is only a knowledge which leaves God out of acount which is condemned in Scripture. True wisdom is not only a priceless jewel, but it is also only to be obtained from God.

nearly to what we might *a priori* regard as the prophetic horizon of one who foresaw the exile as a certainty (xxxix. 5), the
fall of Babylon as well (xiii-xiv), and who like Paul was sure
that "God had not cast off his people" (cf. xxxv.)
than does the allusion to Cyrus in the last line. It speaks of
the future in general terms and in a general way. The
second line in what is probably its primary reference is even
less definite and distinctly figurative. The reference to the
" Deep " (צולה) seems to refer back to the Red Sea and to
the wonders of the Exodus and to declare that this deliverance
will be analogous to that other, which marked such an epoch in
the history of God's people.[46] It is possible, however, that this
figurative explanation of the word " Deep " does not exhaust
its meaning. While the view that it referred to the divert-
ing of the Euphrates from its natural channel by Cyrus in
order to make possible the capture of Babylon (Herodotus)
can hardly be regarded as tenable at any rate in its older
form in view of the cuneiform records which have come to
light and indicate that Babylon, i. e., the city proper, offered no
resistance to Cyrus's army, there are fairly clear indications
that Babylon is here referred to, the chief difficulty being to determine the degree of definiteness which is to be assigned to
the allusion.[47] The third and last line marks a decided advance

[46] Such an interpretation is favored by Jeremiah's words in xxiii. 7-
8. To the returning exiles, this restoration shall mean more than the
other. Thus interpreted, this line is less definite than the preceding.

[47] This reference may be of a two-fold character. It may refer primarily
(a) to the *geographical location* of Babylon. This is favored by Isaiah
xxi. 1 where the judgment upon Babylon is introduced by the words,
" Burden of a desert sea ". That Babylon is intended is clear from verse
9, and it is highly probable that we are justified (cf. Bredenkamp, Nägelsbach and Delitzsch) in connecting this enigmatical phrase with the name
of " Southern Babylonia " *mât tâmtim*, i. e. " land of the sea " (cf., e. g.,
the Bab. Chronicle Col. 11 line 8). Just how much of Babylonia could be
called " *mât tâmtim* ", at this time it would probably be impossible to say.
But that, as a general and more or less poetic designation it might well
have been applied to Babylonia as a whole or to the city of Babylon is by
no means improbable. The fact that Merodach Baladan, who, at the time
at which he sent an embassy to Hezekiah, was king of Babylon, was originally king of the sea-lands (*mât tâmtim*) and that the Chaldean dynasty,
to which Nebuchadnezzar, the conqueror of Jerusalem, belonged came from

over the first, probably also over the second, and this advance is
in respect of definiteness, for it connects the indefinite prophecy
of line one, together with its continuation in line two, with the
person of him who shall fulfil the same—Cyrus. Through the

Chaldea, i. e. from the sea-lands, makes such an allusion here and in xxi. 1,
very appropriate. Franz Delitzsch, furthermore, found " desert sea ", an
especially apt description of the location of the city itself. " The elevation
on which Babylon stands is a " Midhbar ", a great plain which loses itself
to the S. W. in Arabia Deserta and is cut up to such an extent by
the Euphrates as well as by swamps and lakes that it swims as if in a
sea." There may be further (b) an allusion to the fact that the Babylonians took advantage of these physical conditions to make their city, Babylon, secure from attack, much as centuries later did the Low Countries in
their struggle with Spain. Thus Nebuchadnezzar II, in the so-called " East
India House Inscription ", in recording the mighty fortifications which he
built tells us (Col. vi. 39-46) " that no desperate (*lâ bâbil panim,* " no
respector of persons ", Delitzsch) foe threaten the walls (sides) of Babylon, with mighty waters like the expanse of the sea, did I surround the
land, to cross which is like the crossing of the billowy sea, the great (?)
salt (? or bitter) sea (*ia-ar-ri ma-ar-ti*)". (Cf. Winckler's translation in
the *Keilschriftliche Bibliothek*). The exact meaning of the last two words
is uncertain. Friedrich Delitzsch seeks to explain "*Iarru*" through the
Hebrew יאר (river), which is applied to the Nile and thinks "*martu*"
may be for "*marratu*" (bitter), cf. *nâr marratu,* the name of the northern
end of the Persian Gulf. At any rate, it is clear that Nebuchadnezzar
aimed to render Babylon impregnable by means of an artificial lake or
something of the sort. We know also that more than a century earlier
Merodach Baladan sought ineffectually to defend Dur-Athara against
Sargon by piercing 'the dyke (?) of the river (canal?) Surappi' and
placing the surrounding district under water, cf. further, the account of the
defense of Bit Jakin by the same monarch (Winckler's Sargon). A reference to a recognized method of fortifying or defending cities in Babylonia would be very appropriate in a passage where the fall of Babylon and
the triumph of Jehovah's shepherd is predicted, and the sense of the passage would be that all the defenses of Babylon, whether natural or artificial, would be unable to check the victorious advance of the invader and
we have reason to believe that Babylon with the exception of the citadel
passed without bloodshed into the hands of the enemy.

If there were here a direct reference to Nebuchadnezzar's fortifications,
this second line would mark in definiteness a very decided advance upon
the preceding. It seems more probable, however, that the reference is
much more general, and it must be left an open question whether Babylon
is referred to at all, save in so far as Babylon was a second Egypt and
the restoration a second Exodus.

mention of his name as Jehovah's shepherd, the one who shall perform all his pleasure, the predicted restoration assumes definite shape. The element of climax is found in the first part of the line, in the mention of Cyrus, for the last two members of the line as a matter of fact only repeat in a slightly more definite form the prophecy of the first line. We have seen that Cheyne, Marti and others regard the third member of this line as a corrupt repetition of the first member of the first line and in a sense they are right. It is a repetition but not a corruption. The first line is a prophecy of the restoration without reference to the release, the second of the release without reference to the restoration. The third line discloses the name of him who shall both release and restore, who shall fulfil Jehovah's pleasure even to the extent of restoring his people to their land and sanctioning the rebuilding of the Temple. In form the last line is longer than the first, nearly as long indeed as both of the lines which precede it taken together (it has four members and the other two but five). In argument it repeats the first, involves the second, and introduces an element of definiteness which is probably only dimly and at any rate figuratively hinted at in the second. The reference to Cyrus is consequently the climactic element in this line. It is the mention of his name and the declaring that he is the deliverer which is significant and which forms the climax of the line, of the strophe and of the poem.

Jehovah and Cyrus. This is in a word the argument of the poem and its structure shows us clearly the estimate which we are to form regarding Cyrus and his mission. It makes clear to us at once his greatness and his littleness. Greatness: He is Jehovah's shepherd, Jehovah sends him to perform his will. Jehovah heralds his coming as the deliverer of his people and in xlv. 1 he gives to him that name which is to be borne by a greater than he, one of whom he is but a feeble type, who shall deliver Israel from a more grievous bondage than that of Babylon and shall fulfil Jehovah's pleasure not only for the chosen people but for the whole world. Cyrus, his name, marks the beginning of a new epoch in history. And the progressive climax of this poem exhibits admirably the significance of Cyrus and his mission. Littleness: This utterance and the eight which precede it, however important they may be in themselves, are primarily but illustrations and proofs of the transcendent greatness of Jehovah, of the supereminence of him who inhabiteth eternity and before whom the vast universe, past, present and future, is an open book, to whom "a day is as a thousand years and a thousand years as one day", to whom "the nations are as the small dust of the balance", and who "doeth according to his will in the army of heaven and among the inhabitants of the earth, and none can stay his hand or say unto him, what doest thou?". He is Jehovah and beside him there is none else and men and empires, Cyrus, Babylon and Israel are but his agents, his instruments, pensioners upon his bounty, creatures of his hand and he hath created them for his glory. Consequently the poem may better be called: "The Poem of the Transcendence of Jehovah" than the "Cyrus Poem" or the "Cyrus Prophecy". It contains, it is true, a part of the Cyrus prophecy, a great and glorious declaration of singular intrinsic importance, but the form of the poem makes it clear that this prophecy is recorded primarily only as a unique proof of the incomparable greatness of him who uttered it through his servant. And it is only as we keep the logical and poetical form of this declaration clearly in view that we are able to appreciate its beauty or fully comprehend its meaning.

As a result, therefore, of our examination of this passage we find not only a metrical scheme which shows exceptional evidences of design, but one which gives every indication of being but the metrical expression of the theme of the poem. For the poem despite the intricacy of its form cannot be considered artificial since it is not forced into the scheme, but as we have argued at length, is itself the basis of the scheme. A more perfect correspondence it were hard to find and this correspondence should be in itself a sufficiently conclusive proof that the arrangement proposed is the true one. For, be it remembered, the metrical structure has been explained and the correspondence between form and argument exhibited without the altering of a single consonant of the Hebrew Text. It would be hard to find stronger proof, that, to borrow the words of Budde, this arrangement is 'the one intended by the poet ' and that in arranging the poem according to this scheme me have merely ' restored it to its rights '. That, on the other hand, a Qina arrangement was not intended is clear from the fact that the " corruptions of the text ", the presence of which the advocates of this arrangement must recognize if they would account for the imperfections of their poem, not only occur exactly where we should expect *a priori* to find them were the attempt made to alter, or we may now venture to say " force " the poem into the Qina mould, but furthermore are most naturally explained, we may even say, can only be adequately explained, as having their origin in this " forcing " since these alterations are in the main neither based upon nor supported by the witness of the versions.

In proof of this statement let us look again for a moment at the scheme on Plates I. and II, and compare it with those of Budde and Cheyne. The introductory line is pentameter (Qina), as are also the first two lines of the second strophe. The same is true of the last two members of the first line of the third strophe, and of its second line, while the last line falls apart readily into two Qina lines.[48] But what is to be done with the initial declaration " I am Jehovah " (אנכי יהוה), with the three single-member lines of strophe I, with the extra accent in the second member of the third line of strophe II, and with the first member of strophe III line 1. Here is where according to our arrangement a *Qinaizing* of the poem would come to grief and here is exactly where the advocates of that arrangement find the original Qina poem mutilated. This residuum is relatively small. But it stubbornly refuses to be *Qinaized*. Could stronger proof be found in support of the statement made after discussing the Qina arrangement that the presence of a number of Qina lines can be recognized without the inference being necessary that the poem as a whole is Qina?

[48] וכל חפצי may, since the first word is monosyllabic, be readily included under a single accent the more readily since the first word is in the construct state. The maqqeph shows that the Massorites pronounced them as one. The general rule is, however, according to Sievers, that the nomen regens retains its accent and, although he regards the loss of the accent under these circumstances as perfectly proper, he seems to consider it the exception (cf. Sievers, *Hebräische Metrik*, § § 158, 2; 160.)

Such an inference is on the contrary opposed by the minority
of non-Qina lines and it is only when they have been " si-
lenced " that a unanimous verdict is possible. And furthermore, we have seen that the metrical form of the poem—its
numerico-climactic arrangement—is derived from the chrono-
logico-climactic form of the argument. And it needs but a
moment's reflection to convince the reader that such an utterance as this could not in the very nature of the case find expression in Qina-verse. The metrical form of any poem should be
in harmony with and should serve to exhibit and even to rein-
force the theme or argument. This requirement is fulfilled
in the case of our poem by the numerico-climactic arrangement to a remarkable degree. We have seen that the
theme of the poem is the " Transcendence of Jehovah " as
it is tersely expressed in the words " I am Jehovah " (אנכי יהוה)
and that all the rest significant as it may be in itself derives its
true significance from its immediate dependence upon these
potent words. In the Qina arrangement, on the other hand,
these words which should stand out conspicuously and instantly
attract our attention lose their commanding place and become
part of a line and a mutilated or at any rate imperfect line at
that (cf. Budde's arrangement, also that of Cheyne) and the
immediate dependence of the participles upon them is very seriously obscured. While, as far as the relation of the nine utterances one to another, which as has been shown is exceedingly
important, is concerned, this arrangement fails to indicate or
recognize that they are not of equal length, but constructed
with a view to a carefully planned climax and through the attempt to make them uniformly symmetrical the significance of
the closing declaration is greatly impaired. Indeed through the
attempt to arrange these verses in the Qina form the force of
the argument is nearly as seriously impaired as is the symmetry
of the poem.

Budde in the article already cited (page 588) disclaimed any
desire to force matters. He claimed that his method was objective based on the examination of the text and that he would
follow the method should it overthrow his whole theory.[49]

[49] Cornhill, in his *Introduction to the Old Testament* (English edition,

We do not wish to question his entire sincerity in affirming this but rather to call attention to the fact that his method, a method which has gained very wide acceptance, is neither so objective nor so certain as he believed. The reason is simply that he and others who follow the same method have shown themselves too ready to jump at conclusions, if we may be pardoned for using so blunt an expression. They have found here a passage which contains a number of pentameter lines and they have concluded that it must have been a Qina poem and that the non-Qina element therein contained is to be attributed to textual corruption. Had they however attached more significance to this minority of "irregular lines" they might have perceived that it is the seeming irregularities in this poem as Qina which show that it is not Qina. As long as the irregularities are allowed to stand, the possibility is always present that an arrangement may be found that will as we have seen explain them. As soon as the critic resorts to textual emendation, the irregularities are forced into conformity and the dissenting voice is hushed. These scholars aimed to "heal" a mutilated Qina poem. They have instead mutilated a perfect poem of another form. Why? Because they have failed to understand the two cardinal features of the poem, number and climax. In so far as number figures at all in their arrangement it is the number "five" involved in the $3 + 2 = 5$ of the Qina form, and in the dividing of the 10 lines of the "restored" poem (cf. Cheyne, Duhm and Marti) into two strophes of five lines each,[50] and not the num-

1907), in discussing Hebrew Metrics (p. 21) says: "The importance of Budde's work, *Das hebräische Klagelied* (*ZATW.* ii. 1 ff., 1882), lies in his application of strictly scientific method."

[50] While Isaiah xliv. 24,-xlv. 7 is frequently arranged in a series of five-line strophes, i. e. four five-line strophes and a four-line strophe (Marti thinks five-line strophes were originally intended), it does not appear that the number "five" has any such special significance in their eyes as the number "three" in our arrangement. D. H. Müller, who, as we have seen, refuses to recognize metrical arrangement not even the Qina measure, in the prophetic books, and lays the prime emphasis on the strophe and a strophe, in which number figures largely, regards the four-line strophe as the first of a descending series, which is in turn followed by two four-line strophes. His strophical scheme for xliv. 24-xlv. 13 is A

ber " three " which as we have seen is not only fundamental in the form but also has its origin in the chronological presentation of the theme. While furthermore the form of the Qina verse being characterized by balance and uniformity allows no place for a climactic development.

THE PURITY OF THE TEXT.

In view of the conjectures or claims of the " interpolationists " and " metricists " that this passage is more or less corrupt; the claim of the one group that at least the word Cyrus must be a later insertion, the claim of the other that although it is genuine there are other indications of corruption as shown by the irregularity of the Qina poem, we may well lay special emphasis upon the fact already alluded to that, in the arrangement we have proposed it is not necessary to alter a single consonant of the Hebrew Text in order to obtain a beautifully

$(5+5+5+5) +$ B $(4+3+2+1) +$ C $(4+4)$, (N. B., he omits the last half of verse 28 in his count) in which the letters indicate the columns, or, we may say, parallel paragraphs and the numbers the strophes with the number of lines contained in each. To discuss his method fully would take too much space. It is remarkable that he is able to develop such a symmetrical strophical arrangement along with an irregular and metreless line. Should his results gain acceptance, they would lead almost inevitably to the conclusion that a strophe based on the three elements, Responsio, Concatenatio and Inclusio, as he calls the forms of thought and word parallelism, which, in his opinion, determine the strophical arrangement and not a metrical line, as is claimed by Budde, Sievers and others, lies at the basis of the poetry of the prophets. That Müller's theory of the strophe is not without foundation in fact is shown by the prominence of strophical form—strophical parallelism—in such a passage as Amos i. 1-ii. 6, where the recurring words, " I will cast fire upon " and " thus saith Jehovah ", together with the parallelism in structure between the successive strophes, makes the recognition of strophical form unavoidable. That, on the other hand, the irregular length of his line which cannot be avoided, if the correspondence in form and length between strophe and strophe is to be maintained is a serious objection to his method cannot be denied. It is probable that there is a golden mean somewhere between the two positions and that the relative significance of metre and strophe is not fixed, but varies with poem and poet, and while an overemphasis on strophe leads Müller to mutilate lines and ignore metre, it is equally possible, as we have seen, to mutilate lines through a too great or mistaken emphasis on metrical form.

symmetrical poem and one which at every step shows unmistakeable evidence of design. We may go a step further and assert that it is practically impossible to alter this poem without
marring it and that when the true form of the poem is recognized it becomes at once a most conclusive argument not merely
for the integrity of the reference to Cyrus, which as we have
seen forms the climax of the poem and explains the carefully
inwrought double climax, but also for the integrity of the
passage as a whole. This proof of the integrity of the poem is
of especial importance not only in view of the repeated claims
that it is corrupt, but also in view of its testimony to the care
with which the sacred record was treasured and preserved by
the Jews.

When we consider the intricate structure of this poem and
the difficulties which confront the commentator or metricist,
who attempts to explain it unless he understands its metrical
form, when we observe the comparative ease with which some
of these difficulties could be removed and are as a matter of
fact removed by some critics, and finally when we recognize the
fact that the Versions indicate clearly that the structure of the
poem was forgotten (?) at a very early date,[51] it is significant
and noteworthy that this is the case. Thus when the strophical
arrangement is not recognized the *change of persons* which we
find in the second strophe is not readily explainable[52] and might

---

[51] The connecting in the LXX. of the words " who was with me "
(מִי אִתִּי), which stand at the end of the last line of the first strophe, with
the first word of the second strophe, as indicated by the rendering, " who
else will confound the signs of ventriloquists " (Τίς ἕτερος διασκεδάσει κ. τ. λ.)
together with several other data of varying importance shows clearly that
those who translated this passage into Greek were ignorant of the metrical form and we have no data on which to base the assertion that this
feature was ever clearly recognized by the Jewish church. The main
reason for supposing that it never was recognized is the fact that if once
clearly recognized it would not readily be forgotten cf. pg. 632.

[52] An abrupt change of person is not, of course, in itself of especial
significance, cf., e. g., Ps. lxxxi., lxxxix. and xci. But in a poem, which
is so clearly a logical unit as this one, and in which the development of the
argument is, in its main features at least, so simple and clear, this sudden
change is very difficult to understand, unless it is intended, as we have
argued, to emphasize the fact that this strophe is a *present* strophe. It is
interesting to observe in this connection, that change of person is of

easily be regarded as indicating a corrupt text. How easy it would be to substitute the first person for the third, as is done in the Peshito in its rendering of the first two lines of the strophe! Further the "even saying" (ולאמר) of the third member of strophe III, line 3; what student of Isaiah has not wrestled with it! How natural it would be to change it into "that saith" (האמר), following the analogy of the three "that saiths", which precede, a change which would be supported by both the LXX and the Vulgate, but one which would do more to mar the symmetry of the poem than any other change of like *simplicity,* which could be suggested. And finally it is to be noted that in the last line of the first strophe the reading of the Text (*Kthibh*) "who was with me" (מי אתי) is more correct than the reading preferred by the Massorites (*Qrê*) "by myself" (מאתי), (although the latter has the support of the Peshito version, and of the Targum) since, as has been shown, the structure of the poem requires here two words instead of one if the necessary total of nine accents is to be obtained. It would have been exceedingly easy for them to justify such a slight change as this,[53] a change which does not

frequent occurrence in Babylonian private letters, both of the early and late periods. Landersdorfer (Altbab. Privatbriefe, S. 19) has called attention to this phenomenon as a probable explanation of the changes which we find in the dialogue between Jacob and Esau (Gen. xxxiii. 5 ff.). He regards it, however, as a colloquialism and such is probably the true explanation. Consequently it can hardly be regarded as explaining the variation in a finished literary product like the poem under discussion.

[53] In view of the fact that there is no absolute rule governing the writing or the omission of the *w* and *y* when they are merely vowel-letters and consequently not an indispensable feature of the Mossoretic Text, it will not do for us to attach much significance to this fact. Still it is worthy of note that, in the *Kthibh,* the Massorites have preserved for us a reading, a *scriptio plena,* which supports the view that two words were intended instead of one, although they themselves preferred the *scriptio defectiva.* It may, however, be remarked in this connection, that the "defective writing", מאתי would not necessarily establish the correctness of the reading "alone" although it would undoubtedly favor it. For in Numb. xxiii. 10 the LXX. rendering makes it not improbable that מספר (read מִסְפַּר "number" by the Massorites) is merely a peculiar way of writing מִי סָפַר "who can count?", the מִי being written defectively and like the inseparable prepositions prefixed to the following word.

affect the consonantal text. But they preferred to keep it just as it was and merely indicated by means of the marginal reading (*Qrê*) their preference for the other reading. Such facts as these are in entire accord with the view that the text of the Old Testament was very carefully preserved and guarded by the Jews, to whom were committed the Oracles of God, but utterly opposed to the view of which we hear so much nowadays to the effect that it is very unreliable and has been so altered and revised and redacted as to make it often impossible to ascertain its original form with any degree of certainty.

Climax as a Feature of Hebrew Poetry

It was stated above that one of the reasons for the failure of the " metricists " to recognize the true form of this poem is to be found in their failure to appreciate the all-important climactic feature. It will be well for us at this point to devote a few paragraphs to the consideration and investigation of the rôle played by " climax " in Hebrew poetry. Such an investigation is important and even necessary because of the fact that climax is practically ignored by students of Hebrew metres. Inequality in verse length is often regarded as an indication of a corrupt text[54] and in the elaborate treatise of Prof. Sievers, which has been referred to, we have failed to find any reference to climax as a legitimate feature of Hebrew poetry. That it is rarely found we are prepared to admit. But if it can be shown as we believe it can that metrical climax despite its rarity is a recognized feature of Hebrew poetry, we will not only call attention to a feature, which is as beautiful as it is rare, but we will at the same time find confirmation of our claim that this rare feature is to be found and to be found in singular perfection in the passage we have been investigating. And finally as will appear later a thorough understanding

---

[54] We have seen that the extra length of the second member of the third line of strophe II is regarded by the advocates of the Qina form as an indication of corruption and they reduce the length of the line from three words to two for the sake of uniformity, failing to recognize the marked climax in the form and argument at this stage of the poem (cf. Rothstein, *Grundzüge des Hebr. Rhythmus,* S. 62 u 66.)

of this feature is of especial importance to us because of its bearing upon the problem of the date of the poem.

That the element of climax in Hebrew poetry is not prominent and receives little or no attention is not remarkable in view of the exceptional prominence of its opposite, balance or parallelism. Whether this parallelism has to do primarily with form, or with thought, whether it be a sound- (alliteration or rhythm), word-, member-, or line-parallelism or balance it is undeniable that this element is fundamental not merely in Hebrew poetry but in one form or another in poetry in general. Now it is at once apparent that in a rigid parallelismus membrorum, where there is a perfect balance of thought and metrical form, the element of climax, as a principle of progress or unbalance is excluded. Just in the proportion that the lines or members are unequal, is the parallelism or balance imperfect. As a matter of fact this parallelism is rarely so rigidly enforced as to exclude all climax or progress. It is generally recognized that the parallelism in thought may be " cumulative " (climactic) or antithetic as well as synonymous and instances could be easily cited. Examples of climax in form are hard to find. A fine specimen however is found in the Levitical Blessing (Numbers vi; 23b-25) for which Kittel gives the following metrical arrangement:

Jehovah bless-thee	and-keep-thee
Jehovah make-shine his-face	upon-thee and-favor-thee
Jehovah lift-up his-face upon-thee	and-establish for-thee peace.[55]

Form and argument do not correspond perfectly, it is true, since grammatically the " upon thee " (אליך) of line two belongs as much to the first member, as does the same word in line three. But allowing for this slight poetic license, the poem metrically considered shows a uniform numerical climax of the following form:

$$
\begin{array}{llllll}
\text{I} & \text{I} & & \text{I} & & 2+1=3 \\
\text{I} & \text{I} & \text{I} & \text{I} & \text{I} & \text{or} \quad 3+2=5 \\
\text{I} & \text{I} & \text{I} & \text{I} & \text{I} & \text{I} & \text{I} & 4+3=7
\end{array}
$$

an accent being added to each member of each line as the

[55]

וישמרך	יברכך יהוה
אליך ויחנך	יאר יהוה פניו
וישם לך שלום	ישא יהוה פניו אליך

poem progresses, while on the other hand the parallelism in form is sufficiently maintained to satisfy the poetical requirement and the " progressive " parallelism in thought is very marked. Another, though less clearly marked, example of climax in form is the Blessing of Noah, Gen. ix. 25-27 (cf. Kittel). The thought-parallelism is very carefully maintained. Each line begins with a curse, or a blessing (antithetic parallelism) and ends with a reference to Canaan as the " servant " (synonymous parallelism). There is also a play upon words in the " God of Shem " (שם אלהי) of the second line and the " in the tents of Shem " (באהלי שם) of the third. And in the metrical form a climax suggested by and involved in the theme seems clearly present, the three lines being a hexameter, octameter and decameter respectively, of the form:

$$2 + 2 + 2 = 6$$
$$4 + 4 \quad\quad = 8$$
$$3 + 3 + 4 = 10$$

Thus metrically considered the last line is equal to the first plus one half of the second.

A climax of this kind affects, mars we may say, the parallelism to a considerable extent and it is evident that the more marked the climax the weaker will be of necessity the parallelism. An element of climax may, however, be introduced in another way without marring this parallelism, viz. through the use of double parallelism or what may be called a parallelism of two dimensions (vertical and horizontal), the element of climax being confined to one dimension. Instances of double parallelism are easily found. Psalm xix. 7 is a good example :[56]

" The Law of Jehovah is perfect   converting the soul
  The Testimonies of Jehovah are sure   making wise the simple." [57]

Here the double parallelism is easily recognized. Not only is there a marked parallelism between the two lines as a whole

[56] Budde points out that the second half of this psalm is a poem in which the Qina form is most generally recognized.

[57] A similar double parallelism is found in the " Levitical Blessing ", but it was the prominence of the climactic feature which made it a suitable illustration of climax in metrical form at that point of the argument.

and between their respective members, a vertical parallelism, but there is also a parallelism, less complete it is true, since the second members have only two accents and are grammatically dependent upon and epexegetical of the first members, between the first and second members of each line, (what we call in contrast to the vertical a horizontal parallelism). This horizontal parallelism is less perfect as a rule than the vertical. The second member may be as in the instance just cited entirely dependent on the first and merely supplement it, or the two members may be clauses, one independent, the other dependent. E. g.

"Except Jehovah build the house   they labor in vain that build it
"Except Jehovah keep the city   the watchman waketh but in vain. "[58]

Or the second member may continue and be coördinate with the first or finally it may be entirely independent of and in as perfect parallelism with the first member as is the one line with the other, i. e. the horizontal parallelism may be as perfect as the vertical. Cf. Ps. xviii. 25-26 (= 2 Sam. xxii. 26-27.)

With the-merciful thou-wilt-   With-a-man of-uprightness
  show-thyself-merciful   thou-wilt-show-thyself-upright
With the-pure thou-wilt-show-   And-with the-froward thou-
  thyself-pure   wilt-show-thyself-froward.[59]

Here the two members of the first line are entirely coördinate and the parallelism is perfect while the members of the second line are merely joined by "and". As far as the form is concerned we might regard them as four trimeter lines (a single parallelism) and could arrange them in almost any order we might choose preferably as here in two hexameter lines (a double parallelism), since it is undoubtedly true as Grimme asserts that the shorter a line, the more likely is it to combine with another to form a "long line" e. g. two trimeters to form a hexameter, etc. But at the same time

[58] This poem Ley describes as distichal hexameter, i. e., a poem with two lines to the strophe, the lines consisting of two members with three accents each. Metrically the second members are equal to the first and grammatically the first members are dependent on the second.

[59] Ley calls it "tetrastichal hexameter", i. e., hexameter with four lines to the strophe.

Grimme recognizes trimeter as perfectly legitimate and it is interesting to recall in this connection that Cheyne prefers to treat the first three lines of Budde's Qina poem, i. e. Isaiah xliv. 23 as consisting of six short lines rather than of three long lines (pentameter) beginning the Qina poem at verse 24.

These examples suffice to make it clear that while double parallelism is not merely theoretically possible in Hebrew poetry but of very frequent occurrence the horizontal parallelism is easily and we may say usually subordinated to the vertical, examples of perfect double parallelism being rare. Now if the vertical parallelism is the more fundamental and significant and the horizontal less essential it is natural to suppose that the latter parallelism would lend itself more readily and fully to the exhibition of the climactic principle than the former. We have seen that as far as form is concerned the four parallel members of Psalm xviii. 25, 26 could be arranged in any order we might select. Were there for example six members and did the grammatical construction or the argument favor it we would be justified in arranging them in the following order:

I

I   I

I   I   I

i. e. a trimeter, a hexameter, and a nonameter or as Ley called the latter " a lengthened hexameter ", i. e. we could, provided there were a sufficient reason for so doing, arrange the units according to a climactic, as well as according to a uniform scheme such as three hexameter, or six trimeter lines would be. And in this way a horizontal climax in form would be obtained without affecting the vertical. For if all the members were equal and parallel as we assume them to be, the three first-members and the two second-members would stand in as perfect parallelism one with another as if the scheme were uniform. This is as we have seen the method by which the *normal* climax is obtained in our poem.

Thus it is clear that there are two distinct methods by which climax can be introduced into Hebrew poetry, the one accomplishes it through increasing the *length* of the verse mem-

bers, thus affecting the vertical parallelism, the parallelism of
the corresponding members in successive lines—what we call
vertical climax[60]—the other or horizonal climax through increasing their number without affecting their equality one
with another. Of the former we have cited an example in
the "Levitical Blessing" which while embodying a double
parallelism limits the climax to the vertical all the lines being
two-member lines. In discussing the latter we have called attention to the fact that a double parallelism such as we find in
Psalm xviii. 25-26 might readily admit of or even require a
climactic grouping instead of a uniform pairing of its members and that just such a grouping occurs in our poem and we
may add occurs in such a form as to make any other arrangement of these units than the climactic impossible.[61] This horizontal climax is as has been said the normal and fundamental
climax in the structure of the poem. But we have found also
an additional or extraordinary climax of a dual nature, a vertical climax which affects the members of the first strophe and
the end-members of the second and which prepares the way for
and passes over into a horizontal climax in the third line of the
third strophe, thus producing a double horizontal climax in the
last line of the poem. Hence it is clear that both of the forms of
climax which we have recognized as possible in Hebrew poetry
appear in this poem. Each is grounded in the argument of the
poem, the one in its chronological presentation, which gives
rise to the "triple" scheme and to the uniform (1, 2, 3)
climactic development, the other in the especial importance of
the declaration of the last line of the "future" strophe. The
great task in the constructing of this poem was the working

[60] The reader will doubtless observe that there is a slight inaptness in
speaking of this as a vertical climax. For in that it produces an increase
in the length of the line, it certainly looks like a horizontal climax. But in
view of the fact that it is a climax which is, as has been said, confined
within the limits of members standing in vertical parallelism to one another
and affects, we may say, weakens, this parallelism just in the measure
that it is itself prominent, the designation has its obvious advantages.

[61] The fact that the first member of each line is introduced by a participle,
directly dependent upon the declaration "I am Jehovah" and that the
succeeding members of each line are connected with the preceding by
"and (or even)", precludes, as we have seen, the possibility of any other
arrangement of the strophes.

out of this double climax, the superimposing of a second horizontal climax upon the first in the last line of the poem, in order to obtain at that point a maximum of climax. How to accomplish this without marring the symmetry was the most difficult problem in the technique of the poem. It was solved, as we have seen, by introducing the element of vertical climax into the first two strophes and thereby preparing the way for this additional horizontal climax in the third, and also by making the second member of the second line of the second strophe by reason of its peculiar intermediate character (we have shown that it is both stronger and weaker than the corresponding member of the preceding line) prepare for the marked weakening of the second line of the third strophe, which alone could make possible an extra climax of this kind in the third line. The more we study the poem the more are we impressed with the rare skill with which this problem has been solved. The maximum climax is obtained viz. a double climax in the last line of the third strophe. It is obtained without affecting the numerical symmetry. And indeed the symmetry of the poem as a whole is not only preserved in a remarkable way, but may even be said to be in a sense increased. For, although from the standpoint of an absolutely uniform climax, this second climax introduces an element of irregularity into the first, the two are at the same time so skilfully combined, the second climax so perfectly inwrought into the structure of the first that the beauty of the poem as a whole is very greatly increased, its very intricacy lending to it an added charm.

THE DATE

The Poem of the Transcendence of Jehovah God of Israel, as we have called these verses, may well, in view of its beautifully symmetrical form and of the elaborate care and skill with which a climax of an unusually pronounced character has been introduced into it, lay claim to a unique place in the poetical literature of the Old Testament, and did our investigation yield no further fruits than the recognition of the true form of the poem and the consequent proof of the unity and integrity of the passage it would not have been in vain. But

the recognition of the true form of the poem is also of importance because of the bearing which it has on the question
of its date and authorship. We have seen that there is a
double climax in the poem and that this climax in form has its
counterpart in the argument which reaches its climax in the
mention of Cyrus. The mention of Cyrus as the restorer is
the reason for this whole elaborate scheme. But this at once
raises the question: Why is this reference to Cyrus of so
exceptional significance that the writer feels it incumbent upon
him to use every possible means to throw it into bold relief?
The answer to this question is to be found either in the intrinsic importance of the utterance itself or in the exceptional
circumstances under which it was made or in both combined.
The first of these hardly needs to be discussed since, as has
been already remarked, the importance of the part played by
Cyrus in the history of the Jewish nation and in the history
of the world must be apparent to every one. And the mere
mention of Cyrus in a passage of this kind is in and of itself
of great significance and may therefore be regarded as a
climactic element *per se*. It is the second, therefore, with
which we are chiefly concerned, namely: Were the circumstances under which this utterance was made of significance,
and, if so, why?

There are, as we have seen, two principal views regarding
the date of the poem, viz. the Isaianic and the exilic.[62] Let
us see how well each is calculated to explain its unique features. According to the Deutero-Isaianic hypothesis, this passage was written during the exile and probably toward its
close, i. e. at a time when Cyrus had already appeared upon
the stage of history and had kindled the imagination of the
then world through his splendid record of unbroken victory
and conquest. Were he not already present and crowned with
success by Jehovah, " a great part of chapters 40-48 " would,
we are told, be " unintelligible ".[63] It was his glorious career

[62] The Interpolation hypothesis may be included in these two, since, according to its advocates, we may regard it as an interpolated Isaianic
poem, i. e., an exilic redaction of an Isaianic poem. The question is then,
is it essentially Isaianic or exilic? Which element predominates?

[63] Cf. statement to this effect by G. A. Smith which was quoted at the
beginning of this article.

which drew the attention of the prophet to him and led him to see in Cyrus the realization of Jehovah's promises, the fulfilment of past prophecies and the guarantee of the speedy fulfilment of the promise of restoration; i. e., Cyrus was a contemporary of the prophet, he was the realization of past promises and the Restoration though still future was imminent. According to the other view, the Exile and the Restoration both lie in a distant future, and Cyrus belongs to a generation yet unborn. Which of these views, we must now ask ourselves, is in accord with and favored by the form of the poem itself?

In our study of the poem it has been shown that the scheme is fundamentally chronological and climactic and that the argument and the metrical form are in as perfect agreement as possible, the whole arrangement being intended to produce an especial climax in the closing line of the third, or future, strophe. Three features which have been already alluded to will help us to answer the question with regard to the exact nature of and reason for this climax.

The first of these features is the abrupt change of person throughout the second strophe. We have argued that the position of this strophe between a clearly past and a clearly future strophe together with the present reference in the " his servant ", designates this strophe a present strophe. The change in person, shows further, that it is not merely a present strophe, as a literary product, but that it gives the actual historic present of the prophetic writer, and, therefore, within certain limits, the date of the poem. For it is significant that, while in the past and future strophes Jehovah himself speaks through the lips of his prophet, in the present strophe it is the prophet who speaks as Jehovah's representative and declares what he knows of the dealings of Jehovah with his creatures. Regarding a remote past and regarding the future, whether a distant future or one less remote, he cannot himself bear any personal testimony. He can only speak as Jehovah gives him utterance and can only declare Jehovah's words. But of the present he can speak and tell what he has himself experienced and knows to be true. The change in person can only mean a change of speaker and the speaker in the second strophe is clearly the prophet. That Jehovah speaks in the first and last strophes and the prophet only in the middle or present strophe, shows that the prophet is speaking of a period of which he is, as has been said, fully competent to speak and this is clearly the present. For past, or at any rate so remote a past, as is here referred to, and future belong to God. This is an adequate, perhaps the only adequate, explanation of the change in person. It is to be noted furthermore that in this strophe there is no allusion to the Exile or to Cyrus. This is reserved for the third and future strophe in which Jehovah speaks.

The second feature is the chronological perspective, as shown in the relation existing between this present strophe and the past and future strophes. The past strophe refers to a remote past, creation. This is significant when we consider how appropriate an allusion to a less remote past would have been. The Exodus would have furnished an admirable background for a prediction of this Second Exodus.[64] But the prophet does not avail himself of this attractive parallel. Similarly a far more recent event, an event which must have made an indelible impression on the minds of the contemporaries of Isaiah and their immediate descendents, the discomfiture of Sennacherib's army and the deliverance from the dread Assyrian, would have prepared the way admirably for a declaration that Jehovah would deliver his people from the thraldom of Babylon. Instead a remote past is cited, a past which marks the beginning of time, a past of which Jehovah alone is qualified to speak. It might be argued that this is accidental or unintentional. But such an explanation is hardly in accord with the indications of design which meet us everywhere in this remarkable passage. If it was intentional what does it indicate? It gives us clearly an insight into and a scale by which to measure the chronological perspective. We have the three periods in the three strophes. But one would naturally ask, what is the distance between them? The third strophe is future, but what future? Are the events described near or remote? By carefully regulating

[64] It has been pointed out that the thought of the Restoration as a second Exodus is present to the mind of the writer in the second line of the future strophe.

the interval between the past and the present strophes, it would be possible, in a poem as nicely constructed as this one to give the reader some idea at least of the interval which must be hypothecated between the present and the future strophes. That the measurement would have to be exact, need not be assumed. It would suffice if the interval between the past and the present served to call attention to that between the present and the future and furnished, at the same time, an analogy for the estimating of the latter. The past is a remote past, it is the most remote past, creation. The future is by inference a remote future. It does not lie at the threshold, it lies afar off and of it as of this distant past only Jehovah can speak. This view is further favored by the indefiniteness of the first two of the future utterances. It is only in the last line that the prophecy becomes markedly definite and the whole form of the poem, as has been pointed out is calculated to make it clear that this concluding declaration is very exceptional, very unusual, an utterance which must be made as striking as possible.

The third feature is the element of progressive definiteness which is present in the poem. It has been pointed out that in the first two strophes it is the increasing definiteness of the utterances fully as much as their increasing significance which constitutes the element of climax in these strophes. This climax in the argument has its counterpart in the vertical or intramembral climax in the metrical form of the poem, and since in the last strophe this vertical climax passes over into the horizontal with a view to obtaining a heightened climax, we are justified in supposing that since the element of definiteness is a characteristic of this climax in the first two strophes it will be increasingly prominent in the last strophe. And it is clear that, as has been already pointed out, the climax of the last line of the third strophe is essentially a climax of definiteness, the indefinite utterances of the first two lines being in the last line connected with the name of Cyrus and thereby given definite shape. Consequently since this extra climax in the metrical form shows that this declaration is of extraordinary significance and since the form of the argument shows that this climax is essentially a climax of definiteness and finally since the definiteness of the utterance would, as all must admit, be unique and remarkable in proportion to its antiquity, to the depth of its prophetic perspective, we are justified in asserting that this feature of the poem favors its early date.

Thus we conclude that the most striking and significant features of the poem favor the view that while this utterance was significant in and of itself, it was chiefly significant in view of the exceptional circumstance under which it was spoken, i. e. in view of its *early date*. The chronological arrangement of the poem assigns the Restoration and Cyrus to the future. The perspective of the poem, together with the abrupt change of person in the second strophe argues that this future is a *remote* future. And finally the carefully constructed double climax attaches a significance to the definiteness of the utterance which is most easily accounted for if this future was so remote that a definite disclosure concerning it would be of extraordinary importance.

On the supposition that the poem is exilic we should, on the other hand, expect Cyrus to appear in the second, the present strophe, since according to this view he was "already embarked upon his career of conquest", while the third strophe should connect his name with the destiny of the chosen people since the prophet saw in him the promised champion of his oppressed nation. And if, as we are told, the overthrow of Babylon was imminent and was so conceived of by the prophet, the long interval between the past and present strophes in a poem where the chronological element is so pronounced is as poorly calculated as possible to call attention to this fact. As we have seen, the form of the poem is intended to throw into bold relief the unique features of the prophecy. If the prophecy is not unique, if the future is not a remote future and if the definite allusion to Cyrus is not especially remarkable, we are at a loss to explain the fact that the utterance is cast in so striking a metrical form. In an exilic poem such a carefully wrought out *chronological* climax is an anomaly. But if we have here a prophecy which in its perspective and in its definiteness is singularly unique, the unique features of the poem, upon which we have laid so much stress, are at once explained. They have their origin in the uniqueness of the prophecy and are intended to exhibit and emphasize this uniqueness. The numerico-chronological scheme, the normal and the exception climax, all the peculiarities of this poem, are readily understood as the appropriate setting of a strikingly unique prophecy. If the utterance is not particularly unique and if there is no special emphasis upon a distant future, how are we to explain this strikingly unique arrangement? We have seen that it is impossible, if justice is done to the plain declarations of Scripture, to limit the prophetic horizon of the prophet Isaiah to the preëxilic period and that consequently the most important argument in favor of late date is the claim that the utterance itself shows unmistakable indications of ex- ilic authorship, and we argue that when the form of the poem is recognized, there is every reason to assign it to a pre- exilic prophet, to Isaiah, since the form of the poem is ad- mirably calculated to emphasize the fact that Cyrus and the Restoration belong to a *distant* future and to make it clear that it is just because of this fact that the definiteness of the prophecy, the mention of Cyrus by name, is so remarkable and of such unique significance.

The statement is frequently made that the religious value of the second part of Isaiah is unaffected by the question of its date and authorship.[65] This depends entirely upon what is understood by the words " religious value ". If, for example, the religious value of our poem is to be determined in whole or in part by the revelation which it makes concerning the wondrous attributes of the God of Israel (the theme is as we have seen " The Transcendence of Jehovah ", a religious theme par excellence) and if the attribute of foreknowledge is a distinctively divine attribute—this attribute is, be it ob- served, frequently alluded to by the prophet, who considers the ability of Jehovah to predict and fulfil a conclusive proof that he is God, and the inability of the idols to do either, the one or the other an equally conclusive proof that they are things of naught[66]—it would seem to be self-evident that,

[65] This is the contention of G. A. Smith in his *Commentary on Isaiah* in the " Expositor " series.

[66] Bredenkamp speaks of this argument as a "seven-fold repeated syllog- ism " in view of its frequent occurrence.

other things being equal, the religious value of this passage
will depend on the degree in which it exhibited this glorious
attribute. To argue that it is a matter of no consequence
whether these words were uttered by Isaiah a hundred years
before the birth of Cyrus, in which case we must appreciate,
as he is said by Josephus to have done, the " unique divinity "[67]
exhibited by them, for it is clear that no uninspired man could
perform such a feat, or whether they were spoken by an unknown prophet of the exilic period, who was acquainted with
Jeremiah's prophecy of the seventy years, perhaps even with a
more definite utterance of the same prophet which has not
been preserved[68] and who saw in Cyrus the destined deliverer
—a view, which, while it lays more or less emphasis on the fulfilment of former prophecy, reduces the distinctively predictive
element in this passage to a vanishing minimum[69]—is equivalent to saying that prophecy *per se* has no religious value.
And yet the Bible teaches us to see in miracle and prophecy an
indication that God has drawn nigh unto man and that the
ground ' whereon he stand is holy ground '. Anyone can
predict the tempest when " the heavens are black with clouds
and wind ". But only the prophet of God can foresee its
coming when the heavens are as brass and when the uninspired servant must needs go and scan the western horizon
seven times in vain before he discovers even " the little cloud
like a man's hand " which is its harbinger. As an Isaianic
utterance, our prophecy possesses a " unique divinity " which
shows it to be beyond all peradventure the very Word of

[67] Josephus tells us that Cyrus was impressed by the " unique divinity "
of the ancient Isaianic prophecy and consequently resolved to fulfil it.

[68] The existence of such a prophecy can, however, hardly be inferred from
Ezra i. 1, since there the reference seems to be, as in Daniel ix. 2, to the
prophecy of seventy years, the first year of Cyrus marking the end of the
seventy years.

[69] At the time to which this utterance is assigned (i. e., shortly before
the fall of Babylon) it would have required no prophetic vision to foresee
that degenerate Babylon with its " monk-king ", Nabonidus, would fall
an easy prey to the warrior of the North, and, while the captive exiles
could not have been sure that Cyrus would liberate them, they must certainly have hoped it and *might* have *guessed* it. That is, the predictive
element *can* on this view be reduced to " premonition or conjecture ".

God. As an exilic utterance, it is so markedly less unique that it might be regarded as but a " man's word " were it not expressly declared to be the word of Jehovah. And as a matter of fact many who assign it to this late date consider it merely a man's word. Can it be denied then that the significance of this utterance, its religious value, is very much less on the one view than on the other?

This does not in itself prove in any sense of course that this prophecy is or is not Isaianic. To argue that it must be Isaianic for no other reason than because as Isaianic its religious value would be greater than if it were of exilic authorship would be but the weakest kind of an argument, if indeed it were worthy to be called an argument at all. Our contention is a very different one. We argue merely that the religious value not being the same, it is an important, we may say, a vital question, which is the correct view and by no means a matter of indifference. And we argue further that the fact that the unique structure of the poem finds an adequate—in our opinion, its only adequate—explanation in the acceptance of the early date of the prophecy, since under these circumstances and under these only would the definiteness of the prophecy be of sufficient significance to account for the exceeding care with which as we have seen attention is directed to it, is, in view of the difference in the religious values, a very remarkable indication that the prophecy should properly be assigned on the basis of " internal evidence " to the time of Isaiah and even to the great " evangelical prophet " himself. That Isaiah, had he written, as we believe that he did, so unique a prophecy, would have done well to cast it in such a mould as would indicate and emphasize this uniqueness, that, could he have foreseen the future of this " his " prophecy, it would not have been to him a matter of indifference whether it were attributed to him or to the " Great Unknown " of the exilic period, can hardly be questioned. Just in how far he did realize this or whether he realized it at all is, of course, another question and one which we cannot answer with certainty. To him, living as he did so long before the events took place whose coming he foresaw, the first consideration would naturally be " to search out what or what manner of time the Spirit of Christ, which was in him did signifty to be the time of their coming ". And the chronological climax of the poem would be intended primarily to make it evident to his contemporaries and to all who lived before the time of fulfilment, that, viewed from the standpoint of the time of the utterance of the prophecy, this lay in a far distant future, and to teach the lesson of patience and hope: " though it tarry, wait for it ". He may have recognized also that a poetical arrangement which would make this clear to his contemporaries, would, or at least should, establish for all time the early date and consequent uniqueness of the prophecy. Whether he did or did not realize this we cannot say. We cannot even say to what extent he himself understood either the form of the poem or the purpose which it subserved, despite the indications of design which meet us at every point in its construction. For no one will deny that the prophets ofttimes failed to realize the full meaning of their inspired utterances, that they builded wiser than they knew. If both thoughts were present in the mind of Isaiah, we would see a double reason for this intricate arrangement, which, as we have argued, shows everywhere indication of design. But as the former and,—as we try to think ourselves into the inner consciousness of the prophet,—more natural reason gives an adequate explanation it is not necessary to assume that he was conscious of the latter, although to us, who live centuries after the fulfilment of the prophecy, it is the latter naturally which is of especial importance. In any event the form of the poem may be readily accounted for if it is Isaianic, for it is then the singularly appropriate garb of a very remarkable prophecy. But as an exilic production we fail to find any satisfactory explanation of the remarkable features of the poem.

The writer is fully aware that in arguing for the Isaianic authorship of this prophetic poem he is opposing a view which, according to so able a scholar as Dillmann, " could long ago be regarded as one of the most certain conclusions of more recent literary criticism ". But he would call attention to the fact that he has rested his contention almost entirely upon the form and argument of the poem, upon those purely literary considerations, which, according to Prof. Cheyne, should prevent one from even " dreaming " of assigning it to Isaiah. Cheyne tells us: " There might have been a case for the Isaianic origin of ' Thus saith Yahwe to Cyrus ' (xlv. 1) if the passage had been introduced by ' Behold I will raise up a King, Cyrus by name '." But it is clear that the Cyrus prophecy of xlv. 1-7 is merely the continuation of the poem of xliv. 24-28 and, had Prof. Cheyne recognized the chronological climax of this poem instead of trying to force it into a uniform Qina measure, he might have seen that the whole plan of the poem aims to say just this, namely, that Cyrus and the Restoration belong to a distant future.

Concluding Remarks

It remains for us to say but a word in closing with regard to the bearing of our investigation upon the problem of the " Book of Consolation " as a whole. A full discussion of this question would add too materially to the length of this already lengthy article and we must confine ourselves to a couple of the most obvious inferences. It has just been pointed out that the " Poem of the Transcendence of Jehovah ", although it contains a Cyrus prophecy, is in a sense only introductory to the more extended Cyrus prophecy of xlv. 1-13 and that it must therefore be regarded as giving to the latter its true historical perspective as a prophecy relating to a distant future. We may venture a step further and assert that the admission of the Isaianic authorship of this poem leads to the admission of the Isaianic authorship of at least xl.-xlviii., i. e., the chapters to which the Deutero-Isaiah is frequently limited in the more recent form of this hypothesis, for the simple reason that this brief poem is the epitome, or condensed summary, of the argument of these chapters.[70] Its main thoughts are: the incomparable greatness of Jehovah as shown in creation, providence and redemption; the utter folly of heathen practices; and the certainty of release and restoration through Cyrus. And these are central thoughts in these chapters. Cyrus is alluded to in other passages of the group

[70] Nägelsbach, for example, declares that these verses only repeat the main thoughts of chapters xl.-xliv.

but here, where he is called by name, it is made clear that he belongs to a distant future.[71]   And finally, the fact that the mention of Cyrus by name has long been regarded as the argument par excellence for the non-Isaianic authorship of the second half of that wonderful book which has been for so many centuries inseparably connected with the name of the great contemporary of Hezekiah, makes it, as soon as its early date is recognized, an argument par excellence for the early date of the very book, whose late date it was supposed to establish.   For it is clear that if this prophecy is by Isaiah there is no other in the whole Book of Consolation which could not have been uttered by his lips.

[71] In like manner the placing of this group of chapters with their burden of hope in such close connection with the prophecy of judgment in chapter xxxix. makes it clear at the very start that the prophet is speaking prophetically and proleptically of a time in the future when the woe just uttered shall have been accomplished.

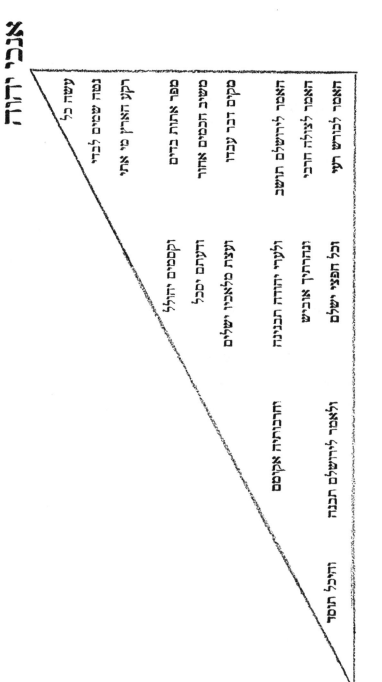

ISAIAH XLIV : 24-28
The numerico-climactic
structure of the poem

PLATE I.

Thus-saith Jehovah thy-redeemer   and-thy-fashioner from(-the)-womb

I-am Jehovah

that-made all(-things)

that-stretched-out heavens alone

that-spread-out the-earth: who was-with-me

that-confoundeth (the-)signs of-liars   and-vaticinators he-maketh-frenzied

that-turneth wise-men backward   and-their-wisdom he-maketh-folly

that-confirmeth the-word of-his-servant   and-the-counsel of-his-messengers he-perfor

that-saith of-Jerusalem she-shall-be-inhabited   and-of-the-cities of-Judah they-shall-be-buil

that-saith to-(the-)Deep: dry-up   and-thy-rivers I-will-dry-up

that-saith of-Cyrus: my-shepherd(-is-he)   and-all my-pleasure shall-he-perform

ISAIAH XLIV 24-28

The numerico-climactic
arrangement of the poem.[30]

-their-waste-places I-will-build-up

ı-to-say of-Jerusalem she-shall-be-built

and(-of)-the-temple: thy-foundation-shall-be-laid-[31]

PLATE II.

Other Related Titles

History of Princeton Seminary: Volume One
Faith & Learning 1812-1868
by David B. Calhoun

From its very inception in 1812, Princeton Seminary became a notable center for academic excellence and Presbyterian orthodoxy. Combining a commitment to serious scholarship and deep spirituality, it maintained a unique position of leadership in American evangelicalism throughout the nineteenth century. In this first of two volumes, Calhoun traces the history of this Princeton Seminary up to 1868. He provides insightful accounts of the labors of such men as Archibald Alexander, Samuel Miller, and Charles Hodge. Thus, he supplies a readable introduction to an institution which left a permanent mark upon several succeeding generations.

Banner of Truth, hardcover, 528 pages

History of Princeton Seminary: Volume Two
The Majestic Testimony 1869-1929
by David B. Calhoun

In the second and final volume, spanning the period from 1869 to 1929, we are privileged to see the blessing of God upon the labors of men like the Hodges, Warfield, and Vos, but we also see the controversy, declension, and abandonment of first principles which marked Princeton's end as a voice for Reformed truth.

This is indeed a "majestic testimony" and it leaves upon us the same conviction that Archibald Alexander's grandson expressed at the Seminary's centenary in 1912: "If the sort of theology which is taught here should die, and its enemies should grant it a decent burial, like the Lord of life Himself, it will have a triumphant resurrection. For the Gospel which it teaches is an unconquerable force."

Banner of Truth, hardcover, 560 pages

Purchase these volumes from Solid Ground Christian Books by calling us at 205-443-0311, or visiting our web site at solid-ground-books.com

Other SGCB Classic Reprints

A History of Preaching by Edwin Charles Dargan is a two volume hardcover set that is the standard work of its kind in the field of Homiletics. Every pastor, student and teacher of religion should own it.

Homiletics and Pastoral Theology by W.G.T. Shedd expounds almost every aspect of preaching, analyzing its nature, outlining the main features which should characterize powerful preaching. The second part is devoted to the vital subject of Pastoral Theology. Briefer but equally valuable.

The Power of God unto Salvation by B.B. Warfield is the hundredth anniversary edition of Warfield's first volume of sermons. This volume includes a warmly written Preface by *Sinclair Ferguson,* and an Appendix of Four Hymns and Eleven Religious Poems written by Warfield.

Christ in Song: Hymns of Immanuel from all ages compiled by Philip Schaff drew forth the following high praise from Charles Hodge, *"After all, apart from the Bible, the best antidote to all these false theories of the person and work of Christ, is such a book as Dr. Schaff's 'Christ in Song.'"*

The Shorter Catechism Illustrated, from Christian Biography & History by John Whitercoss first appeared in 1828 and passed through many editions. It last appeared in the 1968 edition done by Banner of Truth.

The Lord of Glory by B.B. Warfield is considered one of the most thorough defenses of the Deity of Christ ever written. Over 320 pages of exposition of the designations used of our Lord throughout the New Testament.

The Preacher and His Models by James Stalker is the substance of the Yale Lectures of Preaching from 1891. This gifted Scots preacher uses both the Prophets and Apostles to stimulate modern preachers of the Gospel.

Imago Christi: The Example of Jesus Christ by James Stalker was called by C.H. Spurgeon *"an immortal book."* Our Lord is presented as a model for every aspect of life in this world of sin and misery. Thoroughly evangelical!

The Church Member's Guide by John Angell James was once the most popular book in both the UK and the USA for instructing Christian's in their privileges and responsibilities as members of the body of Christ.

Young Lady's Guide: to the Harmonious Development of Christian Character by Harvey Newcomb sets forth the biblical foundation needed for a young lady to grow to Christian womanhood. A manual for Christian maturity.

Call us toll free **1-877-666-9469**
E-mail us at **sgcb@charter.net**
Visit us on the web at **solid-ground-books.com**

Printed in the USA
CPSIA information can be obtained
at www.ICGtesting.com
LVHW050845290124
770076LV00004B/476/J